Stroheim

Stroheim

Arthur Lennig

THE UNIVERSITY PRESS OF KENTUCKY

Published by The University Press of Kentucky
Scholarly publisher for the Commonwealth,
serving Bellarmine College, Berea College, Centre
College of Kentucky, Eastern Kentucky University,
The Filson Club Historical Society, Georgetown College,
Kentucky Historical Society, Kentucky State University,
Morehead State University, Murray State University,
Northern Kentucky University, Transylvania University,
University of Kentucky, University of Louisville,
and Western Kentucky University.
All rights reserved.

Editorial and Sales Offices: The University Press of Kentucky
663 South Limestone Street, Lexington, Kentucky 40508–4008

04 03 02 01 00   5 4 3 2 1

Library of Congress Cataloging-in-Publication Data

Lennig, Arthur.
    Stroheim / Arthur Lennig.
        p.   cm.
    Filmography: p.
    Includes bibliographical references and index.
    ISBN 0-8131-2138-8 (alk. paper)
    1. Von Stroheim, Erich, 1885–1957. 2 Motion picture producers
and directors—United States Biography. I. Title.
PN1998.3.V67L46 1999
791.43'0233'092-dc21   99-27365
[B]

This book is printed on acid-free recycled paper
meeting the requirements of the American National Standard
for Permanence of Paper for Printed Library Materials.

Manufactured in the United States of America

Contents

Photos follow pages 142, 238, and 334

Fade-in

This book deals with a complex man, a great man, and certainly a tragic man. It deals with someone who held his artistic mission higher than worldly success, who felt that the integrity of his vision and his undoubted sincerity and even genius would somehow triumph over the money-grubbers of Hollywood and the beclouded millions who filled the theaters.

He was wrong. His mighty film, his full evening's offering, would not be. Never would he share that vision. What had been so painstakingly wrought would be shattered again and again, as if by some malicious demon. Not only would his visions be smashed. That urge to direct, to put upon the screen what this meticulous and unwavering man saw, would be thwarted. The last years of his life would be spent in creative impotence, acting in films directed by men without one shred of his talent and often doomed to portraying little more than caricatures of himself.

Does greatness breed tragedy? Can only the mediocre succeed? Certainly in the history of film its most gifted artists have suffered. Griffith, Stroheim, Eisenstein, Gance, Dreyer, von Sternberg, Pudovkin, and Welles were all curbed or stopped when they yet had a great deal to offer. Movies demand money, and without it even the greatest talent can do nothing. The moral to this is not an encouraging one.

But we are not dealing with morals. Ostensibly, there was no greater realist than Erich von Stroheim, yet how unrealistic he was! He was a cynic, they say, a depicter of man's worst motives and often the perverse symbol of them in his own screen persona. Yet we have here, in his own strange way, an idealist beyond all belief, a man who when he got near cameras could not let go until he told all, got every detail precisely right. And he was correct. Time has vindicated him: now we read about this man, and film companies rent out his works, while other talents and films of his period—once so highly regarded by executives, exhibitors, and audiences—lie moldering in neglect.

But time erodes all. Except for students of film, Stroheim has faded into the past. Perhaps a few remember a commandant in *La Grande Illusion* or a sour-faced old man with an accent in *Sunset Boulevard*.

Stroheim speaks in *La Grande Illusion* about "the sole flower in the fortress." He is not the sole flower in the barren prison of the American cinema, but he is in a select garden. He is not the rose unfurling and dropping its petals, which perhaps would represent Griffith, but the cactus that from its spiny case emits a flower of intricate design and incomprehensible radiance.

Preface

This examination of the life and career of Erich von Stroheim stems from a number of personal factors. During my grade school days, I was drawn to the work of two actors, John Barrymore and Bela Lugosi. Soon, they were joined by Erich von Stroheim, whom I first encountered in *The Lady and the Monster* and, shortly after, in *The Great Flamarion.* Each of these three men had an overwhelming screen presence that radiated intelligence, personality, and panache—they were flamboyant characters with ironic twists. To me, as a young boy, they were extraordinarily fascinating.

In those days, I also became intrigued by silent films, Chaplin's reissue of *The Gold Rush* probably being the impetus, followed soon by C.B. DeMille's *King of Kings.* Their silence was intriguing. I never missed the rare occasions when such "golden oldies" were shown. In them I found beauty and charm. For reasons I cannot quite explain, I became nostalgic about a time long before I was born. This looking backward was reinforced by my intense interest in pre-1925 recordings, which led me to Enrico Caruso and eventually to opera.

By the time I reached the eighth grade, I was attending the Metropolitan Opera, corresponding with Bela Lugosi—he later visited me at my home—and trying to learn as much as I could about the art of the cinema, which, in those days, was considered almost a joke. I was most impressed by Lewis Jacobs's *The Rise of the American Film,* Paul Rotha's *The Film till Now,* and, a few years afterward, Peter Noble's *Hollywood Scapegoat,* the first biography of Stroheim. Later, I was entranced by *Sunset Boulevard,* for it combined silent film, nostalgia, and Stroheim all in one bravura production. When Gloria Swanson appeared in the play *Twentieth Century* on Broadway, I went backstage and interviewed her for well over an hour. As a teenager, I got in.

Twenty years later, as a professor, I was refused an audience by her assistant!

I also began shooting 16 mm films, which made me more aware of lenses, composition, camera placement, and, of course, editing. Hollywood, however, seemed an impossibility in those days to an idealistic youth devoted to The Cinema. So when I went to college I majored in English. I consoled myself as an undergraduate by running a film society, which showed mostly silent films, and writing program notes.

In the late 1950s, while working on a doctorate in English and American literature at the University of Wisconsin at Madison, I joined the Wisconsin Film Society, which showed classics and provided informative notes for its members. My main interest then was in the German and Soviet silent cinema. At the time, film was seen as a foolish preoccupation, looked down upon by my fellow doctoral candidates and most of my professors. Writing about film was even worse. Despite such derision, I became the film society's president and persuaded fellow students to write articles, which were printed in 1960 in a book called *Film Notes.*

The society indulged my curiosity about Stroheim by booking the only films then available on 16 mm, *Blind Husbands, Foolish Wives,* and *Greed.* In my program notes, I discussed the Stroheim persona and identified at least some of his obsessions. These notes were later reworked and published in *Classics of the Film* (1965), a volume that also included the first serious examination of Bela Lugosi's career.

After receiving my Ph.D. in 1961 (my thesis was on Ezra Pound's *Cantos*), I traveled in Europe for a year, visiting film archives and attending many screenings at the Cinémathèque Française. There I met Lotte Eisner, Jean Renoir, and Henri Langlois. I also screened films in Rome and visited the UFA studios near Berlin.

On my return to America, I became a professor in the English Department at Russell Sage College, where I started another film society. This led, in 1966, to my being asked to become a professor of cinema in the once-adventurous Art Department at the State University of New York at Albany. There I completed *The Silent Voice* (1966), which included essays on Stroheim and his films. Among the several courses I created, one dealt exclusively with the works of Griffith and Stroheim. For it I issued for my students "booklets" of several hundred pages on each director. During the ensuing years, the Stroheim volume—a compendium of articles, reviews, studio documents, script excerpts, and my own writings—continued to grow. Some of its material proved useful to Richard Koszarski when he prepared his doctoral thesis on Stroheim at New York University. (William K. Everson, Andrew Sarris, and I served on his doctoral committee.) Koszarski's thesis would later be revised and published as *The Man You Loved to Hate,* a well-researched book containing valuable information.

In 1972, I reconstructed *Foolish Wives* from two entirely different 16 mm prints for my cinema classes. Later, the American Film Institute asked me to make an official reconstruction from 35 mm material; thus I became the only Stroheim editor ever to *add* footage. That version seems to have become the standard print.

During this period I not only expanded and revised my book on the silent film but also continued adding to the Stroheim and Griffith booklets. I stopped work on those projects to complete another labor of love, a book on Bela Lugosi, *The Count,* published by Putnam in 1974. I spent further years preparing booklets for my other university classes, as well as a variorum edition of *Intolerance,* which publishers liked but felt was commercially impossible.

Sensing that time's winged chariot was fast approaching, I decided finally to complete this work on Stroheim and then to begin finishing the one on Griffith. Although a few insights and unique material, which derive from articles written decades ago, may now have slipped into common knowledge, most of this volume should still appear quite new.

During my research, it became clear that Stroheim's life in Austria and his years in America before he made his first film have been seriously misrepresented. The most reliable information about the cinema's past cannot be found in books written by so-called historians or by recollections of people in the industry. Many early film figures—such as Billy Bitzer, Lillian Gish, Karl Brown, and Miriam Cooper—refreshed their failing memories by consulting books containing erroneous information, which they then incorporated into their own recollections. And one must always be wary of the oral histories of aging raconteurs who spin great tales that are then accepted as gospel.

I have spent countless hours trying to establish the facts. The most reliable ones derive from contemporary sources. Mundane nuggets—telling when sets were being built, who fell off a platform, or who went to New York—are far more accurate than fifty-year-old memories. I have therefore depended on trade journals (such as *Moving Picture World*, *Motion Picture News*, the *New York Dramatic Mirror*) as well as movie fan magazines (*Motion Picture Classic*, *Photoplay*), studio newspapers, interoffice memos, readers' reports, scrapbooks, clipping files, press books, stills, and other memorabilia. Particularly useful was the Theatre Collection at the New York Public Library, the Library of Congress's copyright registrations, a number of interviews I conducted in Hollywood, oral histories, and information from libraries at the University of Southern California, the University of California at Los Angeles, and the Academy of Motion Picture Arts and Sciences.

In this book I mention specifically some of the grossest errors published, but otherwise I proceed with my own account without always stopping to refute misinformation. One cannot necessarily blame previous writers for some of the errors, because Stroheim himself—a notorious fabricator—was a source of many of those "facts." Nonetheless, a number of respectable writers—I shall charitably not list the names of these miscreants—have embroidered on these so-called facts by not only describing nonevents but also sometimes inventing dialogue. Thus, we can read how Stroheim, incorrectly believed to be Griffith's assistant director on *The Birth of a Nation,* strode around the studio lot barking out orders when, in fact, he was never even present. Other stories that are actually legends are less harmful to film history and make good reading. For example, Stroheim's insistence that his aristocratic hero should wear a pair of monogrammed pajamas was transformed into the fiction that he demanded hundreds of extras don a particular kind of underwear. This book will omit many of the famous anecdotes—not because I do not know them but because they are simply not true.

Some of my research in Hollywood was conducted in the late 1960s and mid-1970s. My examination of Stroheim's early years in Austria was made in April 1980. Two months later, after checking prints in archives, I traveled to Paris, where I spoke with Stroheim's companion, Denise Vernac, and had lunch with the charming Thomas Quinn Curtiss (Stroheim's biographer), who assured me that any evidence about Stroheim's Austrian background had been destroyed in the war. I did not have the heart to tell him that I had just left Austria, where I had found all kinds of information about Stroheim's family, schooling, and military service, which proved Curtiss's account almost entirely wrong, although it is highly readable.

No one, as far as I know, has examined Stroheim's later career at all. I originally planned to cover this period, spanning over twenty years, in a brief chapter, but I soon realized that although Stroheim's creative genius had been curtailed during that time, it had not been halted. I wisely canceled a publishing contract for this work in 1980 because the space limits were too confining. During the past five years, I have spent all of my free time revising and rewriting and rethinking my early material and adding to it. Besides wrinkles, age sometimes provides further insights.

It has been said that, in politics, the last refuge of a scoundrel is patriotism. In film, the last refuge is in summarizing plots. The reader will observe that in this book I do just that at times, for the simple reason that such information has hitherto been entirely unavailable (except for *Greed*). Because Stroheim wrote his own scenarios and his films have been so ruthlessly cut, this story material is vital to any understanding of his work.

I am grateful to the American Film Institute for allowing me to read the scripts of *Blind Husbands,* to Richard Koszarski for providing me with the scenario for *Merry-Go-Round* and the cutting continuity for *The Wedding March,* and to the late Herman G. Weinberg for allowing me to copy his treasured shooting script of *The Wedding March.*

I am also indebted to the State Historical Society of Wisconsin—my old stamping grounds—for making the financial books of the Mutual-Reliance Companies available back in 1973; to the New York Public Library's Theatre Collection; to the staff of the Library of Congress, for providing a congenial place to work, where I spent many a spring break; to the British Film Institute, where I did some research in 1980; to the UCLA archive; and to the Museum of Modern Art Film Library for providing rental prints to those of us running film societies in the 1950s.

In terms of interviews, I am particularly grateful to Joseph Henabery for his great kindness, as well as to Karl Brown, Margery Wilson, Rouben Mamoulian, Gloria Swanson, Miriam Cooper, and Lillian Gish, all of whom, alas, are now deceased.

A special thanks is due to Herman G. Weinberg, who during his life almost single-handedly kept the Stroheim banner waving and who provided the world with books containing many of the stills of Stroheim's films. Our conversations and correspondence over a twenty-year period were fun, even though he was reluctant to acknowledge the recurrent patterns that I perceived in Stroheim's work.

Although Peter Noble's pioneer book on Stroheim, *Hollywood Scapegoat,* was an appreciative but unreliable labor of love, it prompted Stroheim to type over sixty single-spaced pages about his films. Copies of those letters, now in the Museum of Modern Art's library, have proved a valuable resource.

Years of running various film societies and thirty-one years of teaching filmmaking and the history and art of the cinema have given me great satisfaction. In fact, it was kind of a holy mission! Convincing students so used to wide-screen, color, and sound that there was beauty and art in the cinema's past was a distinct pleasure. Whereas in the past few decades, film has become an important presence in the academic world, alas, my own department at the university perversely grew less appreciative of cinema, although it was not averse to the hundreds who enrolled in the subject each year. Having retired in 1998, I miss the genuinely interested students but less so some administrators and colleagues. On the screen, during the years of the old censorship code, the good guys were always rewarded and the bad guys punished. Real life is not so morally neat. Such justice does not always prevail in academia (where the stakes are low), or in Hollywood (where the stakes are high).

Fortunately, however, there are people genuinely committed to film and to education rather than to mere careerism. Preeminent among them was my close friend, the late Professor William K. Everson, who often shared his film collection and special knowledge with others, and certainly with me, for over forty years. I miss him sorely. I am also most grateful to Kevin Brownlow (who has done so much for cinema history through his praiseworthy books, film restorations, and television work) for generously providing copies of Stroheim's personal letters, as well as a gift of one of the originals. I should also like to thank Eric and Larry Chadbourne and Eric Rebillard, who made available several rare films from Stroheim's French period; thanks are due to countless others, such as Tony Slide and David Shepard, who helped me, years ago, to meet some of the people involved in Stroheim's career. Also helpful were Edward Cowley, Robert Gitt, Thomas Hoey, Michael Mascelli, Thomas Nader, and Jean Wiley.

With regard to the manuscript, I am profoundly indebted to Professor Paul Jensen, who, in the midst of his research for his own excellent books, provided many useful items. Above all, he carefully read this manuscript innumerable times and made brilliant suggestions (some of which have set me back years!). A great organizational conscience, he has kept me from wandering off—like the great Stroheim himself—into interesting but not germane byways. If Stroheim had had a Jensen at his side, his career would have been even more rewarding.

Unbounded thanks go to my wife, Cheryl, who, in her saintly fashion, has been with "The Man You Love to Hate" for more than twenty years. Her advice and encouragement, as well as her skills at the computer when I pressed the wrong key, have made this long manuscript a reality. I hope, also, that my three sons, Kurt, Erich, and Tristan, will forgive me for spending so much time on The Book.

When Stroheim was invited to the British Film Institute in 1954, his admirers gathered around and gave him a laudatory toast. Stroheim acknowledged the praise, stood up from the table, raised his glass, and replied:

Now to you, please.
Gravediggers, buzzards, scavengers!
That's what you are!
Dealing with dead and old stuff.
Here's to you. All of you.

1

Beginnings

Erich von Stroheim was no mere mortal. To speak of his birthdate, family, schooling, or personal life is to succumb to facts. What is extraordinary about this man is the fiction, a fiction more real than reality. After he left Vienna at age twenty-four to come to America, he foundered for years in poverty and failure, one disappointment following another. His sense of destiny, however, gave him the strength to persevere, for when happenstance and hunger brought him to the fledgling movie industry, he not only found his métier, but soon grew to master it. Where else but in the fantasyland of Hollywood could he have realized his dreams? Those visions that surged within him took form and, through the authority of his aristocratic stance, he was able to convince Hollywood, at least for a while, to come to his terms. Such an incredible presence was not fathered by a press agent; he gave birth to himself.

Even as a penniless immigrant, he had a sense of that self. When he arrived at Ellis Island in 1909, he might have mumbled out "Erich Stroheim" or meekly stood by while an immigration officer simplified his proffered name. But, with the supreme confidence of a man who knew he would ascend the heights of his own invention, he grandly declared that he was Erich Oswald Hans Carl Maria von Stroheim. Like the soul of Walt Whitman that contained multitudes, he would be equal to that long list of names.

Later, in Hollywood, Stroheim became an officer and an aristocrat and an unforgettable rogue. As an actor, he won fame first as a villain-ous Hun and shortly afterward as "the man you love to hate," but he soon began writing, directing, and often starring in his own films. Always at the center of a maelstrom of activity and contention, he provided good columns for the press: Stroheim became not only an uncompromising stickler for authenticity who raged about details that no audience would ever notice—real champagne, not soda water; caviar, not blackberry jam; Death Valley, not a sand dune—but also an incor-rigible martinet barking out orders from morning to the next dawn to shoot eight-hour movies that would never be seen. His scarred face was notorious, as were his hairstyle, his military bearing, his monocle, and even his heel. It was a heel that was always being spun upon. Two examples will suffice: when Irving Thalberg, the newly installed pro-duction chief at Universal, called a halt to the shooting of *Foolish Wives,* "Von Stroheim stood glaring at the young studio boss, then turned on his heel and stalked off."[1] A year later, when Thalberg fired him from *Merry-Go-Round,* Stroheim again glared and, "turning on his heel, walked out."[2]

When almost every major studio had experienced that spinning heel, Stroheim was finally banished and relegated once more to acting for others. He played a mad ventriloquist, a mad vaudevillian, a mad scientist, a mad director—always a mad something. To the world, and even to the professionals in Hollywood, he was indeed mad, a genius who did not know where or when or how to stop and so could never be allowed to direct again.

The living, breathing Erich von Stroheim was so outrageous that only a gifted scenario writer could have invented him, as indeed was the case. The man was a host of contradictions: he played at being a nobleman yet gave us great insights into the lower classes. He appeared cynical yet showed he was the most dedicated of men. He provided glossy fiction yet depicted a gritty truth. Although he came from the mercantile class, he became the least commercial of directors. Always fascinated by the wheels of fate, he eventually found himself ground up by them. In his films, he fused art and reality, myth and naturalistic detail, love and lust, idealism and cynicism, discipline and unbelievable excess. In the process, he became the legend that he had created: Erich von Stroheim.

Stroheim spent so many years creating a mythic past for himself that uncovering the truth is perhaps a desecration. After all, the fairy coach is lovelier than the lowly pumpkin, well-groomed horses nobler than mice, and gloriously garbed coachmen more elegant than rats. Fortunately, the truth never came out in Stroheim's lifetime, for it might have crushed what dignity he still had. His friend Thomas Quinn Curtiss acknowledged that Stroheim "had a morbid fear of being mocked"[3]—but in the perspective of time, the facts now make his achievements even more extraordinary.

Despite his artistic sincerity, Stroheim was a fibber incarnate. His autobiography, as reported in interviews and told to biographers, reveals that this supreme realist of the screen was personally unencumbered by facts. Truth rarely interfered with many of his recollections, even in his last years, when it no longer mattered—or perhaps mattered even more.

Throughout his career, Stroheim offered several versions of his past. In 1919, he told an interviewer,

> "My father was a count, and my mother, before she married him, was a baroness and lady-in-waiting to the late Empress Elizabeth."
>
> "Then you are a count?" [asked the interviewer.]
>
> "A 'no-count' is more like it," he replied modestly. "Titles are not worth a *pfennig* in Austria. In any case," he added, "I've been an American citizen too long to care for such baubles."[4]

He repeated this thought in another interview a few months later: "Titles mean nothing. I gave up mine for I am an American citizen."[5] (Actually, he did not become an American citizen until 1926.)

This explanation of his background was a bit more fanciful than later ones. After a while, he dropped the count business and transformed his father into a colonel in the Sixth Regiment of the Dragoons; his mother, however, remained a lady-in-waiting to Elizabeth. In another, more modest, recollection, he averred that his father was Hans Stroheim, a civil servant. In still another, his father was a commanding officer. Although the rank of the father and the status of the mother varied—she was not always a lady-in-waiting—the Stroheim family was always highly connected.

This aristocratic background was an important part of Stroheim's persona. Sam Goldwyn's ghost-written book *Behind the Screen,* published in 1923, quoted Stroheim's distinct recollections of his upper-class past:

> When I was a young man at home I remember that one day at the dinner-table I unhooked the high collar of my uniform—just the top hook, you understand—because the day was so warm and the collar so tight. My stern old father glared at me across the table and then he sent me away from the room. "Low-born," "vulgarian"—these were some of the words he hurled at me as I went out. And, now, behold! I sit here without any collar and in my shirt-sleeves, and when I go home tonight I shall sit down to dinner without putting on either collar or coat. My wife doesn't mind—neither do I. There you are.[6]

Thus the public image of a now-democratized Austrian nobleman!

What was Stroheim's past before the magic wand of imagination transformed it? The mystery began to unravel in the winter 1961–62 issue of *Sight and Sound,* when Denis Marion printed a copy of Stroheim's birth records. In 1971, Thomas Quinn Curtiss, a newspaper reporter who was a close friend of Stroheim, issued a biography and chose to ignore these facts, although he parenthetically mentions "an alleged Austrian birth certificate." Curtiss, for years, had listened by the hour to tales told by this "splendid raconteur" and felt there was "a consistency" to Stroheim's recollections that he found entirely convincing.[7]

What was the truth? I went to Austria to see for myself. As a result of that detective work, plus a thorough examination of Stroheim's early years in America, the so-called facts have eroded considerably. Curtiss's rendition of this period reads entertainingly, but it is almost entirely fiction.[8] Therefore, the information in the following pages will differ markedly from what has hitherto seen print. For the most part, I shall not quibble with what others have written—the errors are legion—but where certain important matters have been considered immutable fact, I shall explore the issues more fully. Clearly, I differ with the adage "print the legend."

Erich Oswald Stroheim was born on September 22, 1885, the son of Benno Stroheim, who was born in Gleiwitz, in Prussian Silesia, and

Johanna Bondy, born in Prague, where the two were married on August 3, 1884. Both parents were Jewish. After the marriage, the couple moved to Vienna, where Benno had lived since the early 1880s. The father was a *Kaufmann* [merchant] and had a hat store. According to the Vienna city directories, the couple lived in the Seventh District, Lindengasse 17A, from 1884 through 1886. Erich Oswald was born at their home, the delivery assisted by a midwife. According to the birth certificate, his father was in the business of manufacturing and selling straw hats. The term *manufacturing* might be misleading. The general procedure of the time would be to take a circle of straw and add to it feathers, pieces of fur, and other decorations to make an original creation, an operation that could easily be done in the back of the store.

The firm, Baeger and Stroheim, was located at 26 Kirchengasse 7. In 1891, the business moved to 8 Lindengasse 7, and by 1896 it became known as Stroheim and Company. By 1907, it produced not only straw hats but those made of felt as well and also handled imported hats and fashions. It was in this reasonably successful milieu that Erich was reared. The family adhered at least superficially to its Jewish heritage, for Erich was circumcised on September 29, 1885, according to the Israelitische Kultusgemiende in Vienna. A brother, Bruno, was born on February 18, 1889.

Emil Feldmar, Stroheim's cousin, in an interview in the early 1960s,[9] mentioned that Stroheim's mother was a docile lady of great charm, whereas Stroheim told Curtiss that she was a nervous woman often on the verge of hysterics. The father, said Feldmar, was a self-made type and somewhat of a tyrant. Stroheim seems to have been an uneasy mixture of his parents' character traits—a charmer and a tyrant. Both Curtiss and Feldmar agreed that after the birth of Bruno the couple grew less happy and that there was a good deal of squabbling caused, apparently, by the father's profligate ways and infidelities. This unhappy marriage may have found echo in Stroheim's film scenarios.

The mother and the children often went to the Tyrol to enjoy the summers and, Feldmar implies, to escape the tense atmosphere at home. The family may not have been rich, but they were comparatively well off. One day, when Stroheim's younger brother was about eleven or twelve years old, Bruno accidentally killed a childhood companion while hunting. This event, mentioned by both Curtiss and Feldmar,[10] could have ended with attorneys' fees and perhaps a cash settlement to prevent the boy from being brought up on manslaughter charges. Bruno's police file mentions nothing of this, however, and certainly there was no personal pardon by Emperor Franz Josef on Christmas Eve 1902, as Curtiss claims. Stroheim hinted to Curtiss that the costs of settling Bruno's accident helped put the family in dire financial straits;[11] more likely, the family business failed because of mismanagement and the father's spendthrift habits.

Stroheim's youth in Vienna acquainted him with various realities. Besides witnessing his warring parents, he saw the high and somewhat decadent lifestyle of the aristocrats and the seething underbody of the city—its business deals, hypocritical postures, mistresses, and prostitutes—a teeming environment in which Hungarians and Poles and Croats, Jews and gentiles contended for survival and even mastery.

The Austro-Hungarian Empire was always in turmoil, but despite the uneasy political climate, the capital city of Vienna was experiencing its golden age. Music, theater, military bands, and the cavortings of the aristocracy gave color to the city's life. In 1898, at the age of thirteen, Stroheim may have seen Emperor Franz Josef (on the fiftieth anniversary of the emperor's ascension to the throne) riding in the gold Hapsburg coronation coach from the Hoffberg Palace to St. Stephen's Cathedral to celebrate Corpus Christi Day. With only slightly less pomp, the emperor would continue to make an annual appearance on this holy day, an event that would be faithfully reenacted in Stroheim's film *The Wedding March*.

Stroheim undoubtedly attended concerts, operas, and plays. In his scripts, he makes reference to Gustav Mahler, who was the director of the Vienna State Opera from 1897 to 1907, and to Richard Strauss, who contributed to twentieth-century "modernism." Stroheim was familiar with the cultural milieu in which playwrights such as Artur Schnitzler cynically but wittily observed contemporary mores. As one of the playwright's biographers put it, Schnitzler sang "the swan song of old Vienna" and "caught in his gentle hand the last golden glow of its setting glory and converted it into art."[12]

Although Schnitzler reflected the brittle life around him, as in *The Affairs of Anatol*, he also showed how sophisticated men of the world could be entranced by "the sweet little girl," whom Anatol defines: "She's not fascinatingly beautiful—she hasn't a particle of style—and she certainly is not brilliant." But, he adds, she "has the soft charm of a spring evening—the grace of an enchanted princess—and the soul of a girl who knows how to love." Such a girl would appear in several of Stroheim's films.

Besides Schnitzler, Stroheim also remembered the charm and sentimentality of the Volksoper, with its offerings of old and new operettas. But nestled also in Vienna was Freud, whose case histories reveal a dark vein running through the city: solid citizens beset with neurotic dreams, foot fetishes, molestations by relatives, and a host of paranoid fears and aberrant desires.

If Vienna was divided into intellectual, aristocratic, and common work-a-day levels, the great melting pot was the Prater, the Coney Island of the city. An immense Ferris wheel, a carousel, freak shows, games of skill, and shooting galleries allowed all the classes to mix. This type of amusement park appears in *Merry-Go-Round,* the cut portions of *Greed,* and *Walking down Broadway.* Other mixing grounds were the wine gardens in the city's suburbs, the kind of place where the heroine works in *The Wedding March.* There is still another area of commonality: the brothels. Although the lower classes of Vienna could hardly afford them, the aristocrats and the mercantile classes could.

In all these places where social classes mingled, a young man could observe the military, the aristocrats, and the middle and lower classes unencumbered by the rigid rules of society. Their common denominator was sex—the great leveler. Thus, in Stroheim's work, we have fanciful images of an aristocratic world undercut by the realities of a less noble one, a proletarian world with which he became painfully familiar during his early years in America.

The Viennese world was not the invention of a soured writer. As one commentator put it:

> Taken as a whole, Austrian upper society, while charming and pleasant, was gripped by moral indolence and without much initiative or sense of public responsibility. It was, in fact, an anachronism, out of place in an age of capitalistic industry and bustling commerce. The class was astonishingly ignorant and narrow-minded; shallow, pompous, futile; there was much marital infidelity and unconventional licentiousness. Bourgeois morality represented a code of personal conduct beneath the

notice of the aristocracy. One writer characterized the patrician order in general as "irresponsibly frivolous, irresistibly gay, fundamentally ignorant, devotees of sport and fashion, hopelessly gregarious, and class conscious."[13]

Although Stroheim left his homeland as a young man, he could never forget its vivid impressions and continually recreated its settings (and his boyhood fantasies) with extraordinary accuracy. He had almost total recall of myriad details, from candy boxes to streetcars. Stroheim's genius lay in making his fantasy seem real rather than in reproducing actual happenings. But intermixed with his nostalgia was a clear and unswerving vision of life as it really was. In 1968, Josef von Sternberg stated that it was Stroheim's

> capacity to recreate the tapestry of old Vienna, its glitter, its tinsel, its uniforms and pageantry that made him formidable. Drawing upon his Viennese background, no flaw escaped him. His attention to every blossom on every tree that confronted his camera, to every button on each uniform, to every prop used, to the authenticity of each scene, was unequaled. How he acquired the ability to transfer imponderables to the screen is not known. He was about twenty years old when he left Vienna [actually twenty-four]. His experiences there were hardly enough to make him an authority. His talents came from a secret desire to master other human beings and to create their environment.[14]

Stroheim spent his grade school years in Vienna. The boy must have observed his father's customers. Young girls and their mothers, single women, reluctant husbands, and men with their mistresses would have frequented the shop. Hats, scarves, and lace were taken from boxes or from the glass counters and studied before a mirror. Perhaps as a result, Stroheim became acutely aware of what people wore. The lesson for him was not "all is vanity" but how clothing defined a person and revealed the character beneath. Unlike D.W. Griffith, who often left clothing details to his actors and actresses, Stroheim, for his films, always carefully selected every item and frequently drew sketches for the wardrobe department. Even much later in his life, in two BBC

broadcasts about fellow directors Griffith and Robert Flaherty, he minutely described their apparel.

But what most interested Stroheim as a young boy, and what continued to interest the man, was soldiers. Only a few blocks from his
residence were the Hapsburg palace and the imposing government
buildings, with the military personnel standing guard and marching in
parades. He longed to be not only one of these men, but an officer.
Such a career often required family connections, education, and of
course money, for officers had to live up to their rank in their dress,
their means of transportation, their restaurants, and perhaps even their
mistresses. Later, Stroheim's films would satisfy these longings, for he
invariably cast himself in officer roles.

Stroheim endured much pain as a youth. Undersized, not terribly
attractive, and hampered by a Jewish ancestry in a Catholic society, he
longed to be something else: an aristocrat, an officer, a hero, a Don
Juan, a heavy drinker, and an apparent practicing Catholic.

What his religious beliefs were, we of course cannot know. The
young Stroheim probably had little religious faith, considering his taste
in plays, his interest in Freud, and his essentially rebellious nature. Having been born Jewish, claiming in his teenage years to be Protestant,
and later assuming the mantle of a Roman Catholic, he undoubtedly
was a skeptic, like many bright young men in Vienna. However, from
at least 1915 on in America, Stroheim often attended Mass in California.[15] Needless to say, practice did not make perfect, for his Catholicism hardly interfered with his lifestyle. However, when he married
his third wife, Valerie, on October 16, 1920, the wedding took place in
a Catholic church.

The frequent Catholic references in Stroheim's films could have
been included for their visual appeal and for their aid in characterization rather than from any deep-seated beliefs. In short, they could have
been employed as a kind of theological costuming. But some of the
letters that this seemingly skeptical, worldly, and cynical man sent his
wife Valerie and his son Josef in the early 1940s—a time when he was
living with his mistress—are studded with phrases such as "May God
grant . . ." and "My prayers" and "I am praying everyday for you and
your welfare."[16] However, his religious views were so intertwined with
superstition, with a belief in fate and the wisdom of fortune-tellers,
that they would hardly pass muster at a seminary. In short, his religious

beliefs were a host of contradictions, as simple and complex as the man himself.

According to Curtiss, in 1897, at age twelve, Erich "was physically robust" and was "dispatched to a preparatory boarding school for cadets,"[17] from which he was graduated as a second lieutenant, a rank that he held from 1902 until 1909. The young man experienced machine-gun fire in a minor skirmish on the Bosnian border, sneaked off to a gypsy camp one night for some illicit love amid throbbing violins, and returned to Vienna, where financial reversals in his family made it difficult for him to maintain an officer's expensive lifestyle.[18] In interviews in America, Stroheim discussed his military past. "I became an officer in the army, and I saw service in the Bosnian campaign and in Mexico." He explained that his facial scar came from the Bosnian battle.[19] In another account, the Bosnian campaign became even more bloody. He said that he crossed the lines into Bosnia on horseback and came out in an ambulance with sixteen inches of cold Bosnian steel through him. A group of Viennese surgeons repaired the damage. Then, he said, something went wrong, and he was banished for five years. "It comes under the head of private troubles," was the laconic description by the banished.[20] It is a heroic tale, a romantic tale, a plausible tale, but unfortunately a completely fanciful one.

Reality was much more prosaic. Stroheim's parents planned for young Erich to go into the family business to manufacture and sell hats. As a result, in 1901 he was sent to the city of Graz, where he attended Die Grazer Handelsakademie, a business high school and by no means a *Gymnasium* (where higher and more intellectual studies were offered). This school still exists, and its director and his staff were astonished to hear, when I arrived in Graz in 1980, that they had had such a famous student. After I gave them certain dates, they went into their archives and found Stroheim's school records. With a look of chagrin (Stroheim was hardly a prize scholar), the school officials handed me the documents and kindly provided photocopies.

Although Stroheim's German language skills were "satisfactory," his studies of French and English were not. His grades in bookkeeping and economics and other business skills were poor, a judgment with which his employers in Hollywood surely would have concurred. His written assignments also received "the least possible recommendation." He was, however, outstanding in one area: he was an extraordinary class-cutter. Of the 225 hours of absences listed on his record—a truly impressive number to begin with—62 did not even have the faintest excuse, and he was listed as "truant." In the future, Stroheim would be known as a great authoritarian, yet, ironically, the man had a long and consistent history of ignoring or subverting authority.

In Austria, citizens had to register where they lived. The records in Graz reveal that Stroheim boarded in a private student dormitory housing six students, located in an apartment house at 26 Wielandgasse—a building that still stands. It is a respectable edifice in a good part of town and shows that he was reasonably well-off at the time. The teenager stayed there from September 17, 1901, until September 21, 1903.

When Stroheim moved to Graz in September 1901, he was already trying to mask his background. The school's records list him as Jewish—he could not avoid the written documents—but when he reported to the police to establish his residence, he stated that he was Protestant. These records also show that he spent some time in the summer of 1903 in Innchen in Tyrol, the mountain area of Southern Austria, near the setting of his first film, *Blind Husbands*. On September 24, 1903, he moved to other rooms in Graz—apparently cheaper ones—and on April 30, 1904, he changed residence once more. Even after graduation, he continued to live in Graz.

A terrible student, and probably a spoiled brat as well (mothers who hate their husbands tend to love their sons fervently), this bright but incorrigible boy tried his best to escape his mercantile background. A lad with poetic leanings does not want to help out in a hat store, not when others are engaged in a fantastic life of coaches, balls, ostentatious wardrobes, and elaborate public ceremonies—the life of the "rich and famous." Also, Stroheim was a loner. In a 1941 letter, he would advise his son Josef "to be a good mixer. That was one of my many shortcomings. I couldn't mix to make friends."[21]

A significant aspect of Stroheim's life was that he was always in some way the outsider. In Catholic Vienna, he was a Jew; in melting pot America, he was the aristocratic European; and in France, in his later life, he was a curious mixture of Austrian and American. Thus, he was always the Auslander.

Two world wars, a cold war, and various international skirmishes have eradicated much of the glow of a military career. But in the days of Stroheim's youth, the army seemed like a colorful and exciting—

and not very dangerous—way of spending a life. In Austria, according to one commentator, the army was a "State within a State."

> It was in the army and the army alone (for not even the Church was all embracing) that the concept of the Empire with the Emperor at its head was translated into reality. All races served in it. Hungarians too. All who served in it, their families in civilian life divided from each other by religion, national hatreds, conflicts of political and economic interest, political ideas, found in their military duties a common tongue, a common ideal, a common loyalty.... In the simple, hierarchical organization of this great closed society with its career officers, its unceasing flow of conscripts from half the lands of Europe, there was indeed something splendid and unearthly, a glimpse of the true supra-national society. In membership of this unique institution, which transcended all civilian bitterness and lifted them up and set them apart from the welter of nationalist and party strife, individuals of all kinds found fulfillment in service. For many short-term soldiers the brief time of army service was a return to a golden age when all problems were solved by simple obedience in a mood of universal brotherhood to a remote and ineffable father-figure, Franz Josef.[22]

As far as we know, Stroheim's first contact with the military occurred while he was still living in Graz on April 19, 1906, when he was given a conscription examination. The military records kept at the Kriegsarchiv in Vienna reveal that Stroheim was a graduate of a *Handelschule,* that he was 168 cm tall (five feet, six inches), and that he was proficient at playing the violin. He was classified as "derzeit, untauglich, Schwach, Zuruckstellen" [currently unfit, weak, (and) to return to the rank of civilian].[23]

These results must have been devastating to this proud young man with his martial dreams. The army could have been a way for him to escape the commercial world for which he seemingly had little interest. But the young Stroheim did not give up. A short time later, he reapplied and prevailed upon the military authorities to accept him in the Royal and Imperial Training Regiment 1, which was stationed in Vienna, "auf eigene Kosten" [at his own expense]. He would pay for his own uniforms and his own horse, if he had one. He entered the supply and transport division, where he undoubtedly became familiar with horses, then the main military means of transportation. It was probably at this time that the photo of the young Erich that appears in Curtiss's book was taken. Shortly after, Stroheim received the pronounced scar on his forehead. One interviewer, in France in the 1950s, suggested that maybe it had come from a duel. Stroheim answered that he was not the Prussian type who dueled, adding that he had been injured by a horse. "J'ai reçu un coup de pied de cheval en Autriche, quand j'étais officier" [I was kicked by a horse in Austria, when I was an officer].[24] The young Erich proved himself somewhat capable and was commissioned on December 23, 1906, as a "one-year voluntary soldier-in-training with the title Corporal."[25]

In late 1922 Stroheim lent his *Merry-Go-Round* scenario to another writer to be transformed into a novel. In it there is a passage about soldier life in Austria that mentions "a little lieutenant" who shows up at a fancy party. He is sneeringly looked upon by a count as a "Mosesdragooner." A footnote in the novel explains that this term was a "slurring way of referring to men of the train and transport service, because so many Jews served under this branch unable to be admitted to the cavalry."[26] This passage has an autobiographical ring and surely is as close to the humiliating truth as Stroheim ever came.

There is another section in that novel that might be all fiction but could possibly be true. The count recalls that one day, when he returned home from school, he found his mother in "a very sheer negligee" with another man. This is followed by a passage about the father, who would go away for days and come back from his escapades "fatigued."[27] Although Stroheim might have invented this, there was no doubt that his films often had philandering fathers and unhappy marriages.

Now that Stroheim had joined the army, the usual Hollywood script would have him rapidly rise in the ranks, thanks to his intellectual and literary gifts, his extraordinary feeling for detail, and his intense energy and ambition. Reality, however, was different. After only four months, on April 20, 1907, Stroheim's conduct, skills, and performance were examined and he was classified as "invalid [that is, what we would call 4-F], incapable of bearing arms, to be discharged from the service, but capable of work as a civilian." As a result of these findings, Stroheim was given leave on April 23, 1907, and was discharged from the Royal-Imperial Army on May 29, 1907. His entire military career had lasted five months. This is quite a contrast to Stroheim's obituary in the *New York Times,* which stated that he "was an officer in the Austrian cavalry at seventeen and served in the Army for seven years."[28]

One year later, in 1908, Stroheim again tried to enter army life, but on June 25, he was once again classified as "unsuitable for military service, unable to bear arms." Whatever dreams he had for a military career were now completely shattered. When the Bosnian crisis occurred in October 1908, Stroheim remained a civilian in Vienna at the family store and certainly was far from the machine-gun fire, the flashing swords, and the nearby passionate gypsies. Having given up any hope for a military career and after perhaps going through a session of soul-searching, on November 17, 1908, he officially left the Jewish faith.

Stroheim's brother, Bruno, was no more successful with the army. In 1910, 1911, and 1912, the military archives mention that he was a graduate of a *Gymnasium* and that he was employed as a bookkeeper. The army noted that he also was too weak and narrow-chested for military duty. On December 8, 1913, Bruno also left the Jewish religion. Although Jews were quite successful in Austria, there is a possibility that the weaknesses ascribed to both Stroheim boys might have stemmed from the military's religious prejudice. However, a five-foot-six-inch fellow like Erich would be at a disadvantage with a six-foot enemy. Incidentally, not long after, on February 5, 1914, Adolf Hitler was rejected by the Austrian military as being also "too weak" and thus "unable to bear arms."[29] Six months later, when the First World War broke out, Hitler volunteered his services to the German army and was accepted. World history and film history would be far different if the Austrian standards had not been so stringent.

Stroheim's lifelong passion for uniforms shows that he had watched the various ranks of the military avidly and longed to be one of those smartly dressed soldiers. When his numerous attempts to join the army—a quick way to vault from his class into another—failed, his despair at having lost a military career gave him an enduring wound, one that he could never quite overcome. In his fantasies, he provided the life he should have had. In all of the biographical information that he later

offered, he *always* included a military background: an Austrian lieutenant, a dissolute officer, a member of the National Guard, a trainer of
troops at Plattsburgh (in upstate New York during the First World
War), an officer in the Mexican army, and sometimes a member of the
U.S. army as well.

After being rejected from the Austrian military, according to his
cousin, Emil Feldmar, Stroheim worked in the family store. The cousin
recalled that he and Stroheim spent much of their time flirting with
the pretty milliners of the neighborhood. Stroheim, with the personal
charm he inherited from his mother, apparently could be quite winning in his ways.[30]

The family hat concern was faltering. The father probably had
made bad business decisions or was frittering away his money. Although the store in 1908 had a listed capital of forty-five thousand
kronen, it quickly came onto hard times, then went into bankruptcy,
and was liquidated in April 1909. Meanwhile, the father entered a
kind of partnership, called Ludwig Macho and Company. He must
have proven himself a rather irresponsible businessman, because the
new firm's incorporation papers had a clause stating that accounts had
to be cosigned by Macho and Johanna Stroheim and not by Benno,
her husband. The new firm was capitalized at thirty thousand kronen
in 1910 and 1911 and then advanced to fifty thousand by 1912. By
1913, however, it also went into liquidation. On December 22, 1913,
Stroheim's father died at age fifty-six, his troubles finally over. A few
months later, in 1914, Macho was listed as liquidator of the firm.
Stroheim's cousin said that the father had divorced shortly before his
death, but I could find no record of that. The father was living at a
different address at that time; perhaps the couple had just separated.

After her husband's death, Johanna moved in with her sister-in-
law, Ernestine Stroheim, in an apartment house at 22 Esterhazy 6. Also
living there was her brother, Emil Bondy, not an "Imperial Counse-
lor" but a "chemiser" in an optician shop, who died on July 31, 1917.
Johanna was first listed as living with Ernestine in the 1915 directory.
By 1921–22, her son, Bruno, then cited as a "civil servant," was also in
residence. Ernestine died in 1923 at age eighty, but Johanna continued
to live in the building with Bruno until 1941, when she died at sev-
enty-eight years of age of arteriosclerosis, a rather broad term that
included heart attacks and strokes. She was buried in the Jewish sec-

tion of the Vienna cemetery. Bruno spent the last two years of his life "incurably insane" in an asylum and died on December 29, 1958.

In 1908, when Stroheim made his last attempt to get into the army, the family firm was experiencing its first bankruptcy. There was now no way that Stroheim could be supported; he would have to earn a living on his own. Echoes of this situation would certainly appear in *The Wedding March:* the unhappy battling parents and the family beset by bills. If Stroheim would not "blow out his brains," as a title from that film stated, he could "marry money." However, there was no money that wanted the penniless and unaristocratic Stroheim.

In his later years, Stroheim mentioned to Curtiss that he had resorted to the blandishments of a moneylender and had become embroiled in a serious debt. Whether the headstrong youth had actually done this or whether it was pure invention to cover the embarrassment of the family's bankruptcy, no one knows, but Stroheim had referred to a similar financial difficulty in a semiautobiographical play that he had written after arriving in America. His cousin, Feldmar, felt that there was some secret cause for Stroheim's sudden departure "in a couple of hours," which otherwise appeared "a perfect enigma." In any case, there was America—the one hope for this desperate young man.

The year 1909 must have been full of frustration and dissatisfaction for the twenty-three-year old. He wanted to do something—but he could not get a foothold. Money was not a prime object. His Hollywood career showed that; he was paid by the picture, not by the week, but he would never rush production or issue anything short of perfection.

Stroheim must have taken stock of himself. Coming from the middle class, educationally deprived (a *Handelschule* was no recommendation for a position entailing "brains"), and born Jewish, he desperately wanted to belong to a culture that did not want him. Perhaps as a writer or a journalist he might have succeeded, but his limited scholastic background would hardly have helped him in that field. His accent, too, was not that of the elite. In Europe, furthermore, a man's past could never be entirely forgotten or ignored. The documents remained. But across the sea lay America, so Stroheim made his decision. He bade farewell to his family, traveled to Bremen, took ship on November 15, 1909, and arrived in New York on November 26.

In America, he could be reborn. He would be an aristocrat, a high-ranking army officer, and a Catholic. The entry book at Ellis Island was his baptismal certificate. He crowned himself "von," and he would live up to it with a vengeance.[31]

But when the penniless twenty-four-year-old ex-Jewish trades-man stepped off the boat on that November day, he realized that a newborn Christian aristocrat could also be hungry. Christmas was approaching, and he obtained a job gift-wrapping packages. What must his feelings have been on that first Christmas Eve in America—his temporary job now ended—as he sat alone, far from his family and his homeland, with only a few dollars in his pocket? That lonely and hungry Christmas may have made a permanent imprint on his mind (perhaps coupled with the fact that his father died a few years later on December 22), for throughout his films and scripts, the Christmas season is when the worst events invariably occur.

If Stroheim hoped for success in the new year, it did not come. What menial jobs he held, we do not know. Around December 1910, he witnessed the fall of a horse on a Brooklyn street and helped the animal to its feet. A member of the National Guard, Captain McLeer Jr. (Stroheim remembered the name as McLean), introduced himself and, after some conversation, suggested that Stroheim join the regiment. He did, but although promised the rank of sergeant, according to Curtiss, he was made a private. Curtiss also states that Stroheim enlisted in the U.S. Army for two years, and the *New York Times* obituary[32] mentions that he served two years in the U.S. Cavalry.

In an American interview in 1919, after he became famous, Stroheim said that, while a member of Squad C of the first Cavalry of the National Guard of New York, he worked at a military camp in Plattsburgh, New York, as an expeditionary officer training men for World War I.[33] In another interview at that time, he added the following to his military background: "About six weeks before the armistice was signed I was offered a commission in the Intelligence Department of the United States Government. I had served four years in the U.S. Army when I first came over ten years ago."[34] In 1954, Stroheim claimed that he had "served in the American army for three years."[35] He referred to his military service also in a letter to Peter Noble that mentioned "Squadron C First Cavalry in New York, the outfit in which I served as private from 1909 to 1912." I cite these examples just to prove that this was his story, not a misquotation by a newspaper reporter. Official records show, however, that Stroheim (there was no "von" mentioned) enlisted in the New York National Guard (Troop 8, Squadron C) on January 30, 1911, and was "dropped" two months later on March 27, 1911.[36] So much for his American military career.

We must rely on Stroheim's memories, as repeated by Curtiss, to discover the events of the next few years. In 1911, we are informed, he began work for a fashion house in New York—drawing upon his previous experience in the family business—and in 1912, he arrived in San Francisco as a traveling salesman for the firm. Clashes of personality within the main office resulted in his being discharged. He stayed in the San Francisco area and, he claimed, took jobs as a flypaper salesman, a telephone company repairman, and a travel agency clerk. In short, his early years in America, like his dreams of a military career, were a series of failures. Like many bright men, he felt himself too superior to be a mere clerk or a businessman. His brother, Bruno, back in Austria, also tried to become something else. He, too, attempted to join the gentile establishment, and strove to become a writer.

Bruno would later contact the Hubertus publishing firm in Austria, which specialized in hunters' novels, poems, and novellas. Shortly after, Bruno's twenty-two short stories were printed in a volume titled *Im Schilf* [In the reeds]. They are sensitive, though sentimental, tales of lonely hunters up in the wooded hills, of poachers, and of nymphlike girls bathing in mountain lakes. They deal mostly with the joys and guilt of shooting animals. (A curious subject matter, considering the childhood accidental murder.) One, the title story, concerns the legend of Pan. In another tale, "Der Sprung" [The leap], a policeman and a hunter are lying in wait to capture a poacher who kills for sport and leaves the bodies to rot. When they catch the young man, he leaps to his death. His dying cry haunts the hunter, who says an Our Father for the man's soul. At that spot, now, says the narrator, can be found a wayside cross proclaiming for all to see that here, in 1920, a man met his death. The sign advises the passing wanderer to pray for the man's soul. Another story, "Verwehtes Lied" [A song fading away in the wind], is about a poacher who fires at a ranger who, in turn, shoots back and kills him. A church bell tolls, calling the faithful to early Mass, and the tones are carried on the wind over the fields and meadows, where the sounds fade away like a song.

Bruno's stories seem to indicate that certain thoughts and attitudes and settings were common to the two brothers: the wayside cross with its admonitory message, the church bells sounding over the valleys, the hunting lodges, the references to Pan, and women giving themselves to lovers in almost mystical unions. Similar content can be found in the first film that Stroheim directed, *Blind Husbands.*

Stroheim, living in the San Francisco area, was far from the mountains of Austria, although he still longed for them. On one of the days Stroheim was unemployed—of which there were many—he explored the countryside a few miles north of Oakland and climbed the 2,608-foot Mount Tamalpais, an adventure that recalled his previous experience in the Dolomites. While hiking and enjoying the stunning vistas, he encountered the proprietor of the West Point Inn, an Austrian known as Captain Henry Masjon, whose continental manner and Franz Josef whiskers made him locally famous. According to Curtiss, Stroheim became a handyman at the inn. There he met Margaret Knox. She was not a "practicing physician" as Curtiss avers,[37] but her mother, Dr. Myra Knox, did have a medical practice in Oakland. Margaret was one of the smart set but unmarried and lonely, and the sunsets over the bay must have been romantic. Stroheim probably turned her head with tales of his wonderful youth in Austria. This encounter with Margaret at a mountain hotel undoubtedly inspired his story "The Pinnacle," which would become *Blind Husbands.* Whether this was a real love match or an affair of convenience cannot be ascertained, but the two began to live together in Mill Valley at the foot of the mountain.

Meanwhile, Stroheim decided to become a writer, and on November 16, 1912, an "E.O.H. von Stroheim" (using Dr. Knox's address in Oakland as the return address) copyrighted a short play called *In the Morning.* This is probably a variant title for *Brothers,* which was printed in 1988 in the magazine *Film History.*[38] Although the play is somewhat reminiscent of Artur Schnitzler's work, it lacks his theatrical wisdom of short speeches and deft character interaction. Stroheim's people are often given to extended observations that would prove deadly on a stage.

As the play opens, we find that Nicki (short for Nicholaus Maria Erwin Count von Berchtholdsburg), a young Austrian dissolute, is deeply in debt to Eppsteiner, a Jewish moneylender, who visits him and suggests that his one hope is to marry money.

Eppsteiner: There are always a few rich, very rich girls, who would like to marry a man like you. Of course, you will have to overlook the religion—

Nicki: And more or less bent noses—No, Eppsteiner, if I could buy my life that way—in marrying a Miss Kohn, or Rosebluh—Better die. Not that I have anything against the religion—No, no—It's—I don't know what it is. Maybe it's the blood—I could not do it to save my life.

After the moneylender exits, the doorbell rings, and Mitzi, his girl-friend from the theater, visits, bringing some bills for him to pay. However, when he informs her he is both penniless and deeply in debt, she does not leave him (as would happen in most melodramas) but passionately kisses him and says, "I love you Nicki, you the man, not the uniform—not the title—you—you all alone."

After Mitzi leaves for the theater, Nicki writes some farewell letters and prepares to commit suicide. A stranger, having just escaped from the police, enters and explains that he is a robber. Nicki asks him why he does not work. The stranger accuses him of being "a child—an infant." The outside world is "no place for men like you—for men with manicured nails and monocles. You couldn't stand the smell of horsemeat and poverty." When Nicki offers him a champagne cup, the stranger tells him his own recipe: Moselle (Berncastler, specifically), some Cliquot (brut), a pressed orange, two glasses of curacao, a lemon, powdered sugar, pineapple. Thus, the play abruptly stops while Stroheim gives us details of a fruit punch! (Should we be surprised that twenty-five years later, in *La Grande Illusion,* a punch with some of the same ingredients appears?)

The stranger hints that he is as wellborn as the count and then discusses how wine, women, and song have contributed to his downfall. "It's rather interesting, let me tell you, to observe yourself—at first slowly, then rapidly progressing downward, and to realize how close to the surface the old, old savage lies. With every tie broken, the veneer goes quickly and the primitive—the predatory, comes through. It's very interesting—a study worthwhile—Naturally it's rather hard, to take the first steps down—But those once accomplished, it's astonishing how very easy the others come." What is remarkable about this speech is how it echoes Joseph Conrad's *Heart of Darkness* and how it uncannily prefigures the main theme of *McTeague,* a book that Stroheim probably had not yet read. Furthermore, it seems to reflect Stroheim's own descent from a somewhat well-off Viennese into a poverty-stricken immigrant in Oakland.

The stranger takes away the suicide implements, binds Nicki, and leaves. In a brief scene the next morning, Nicki's servant unties him, and a letter reveals that his aunt has died. He will now have money.

This short play, although fascinating in what it reveals about Stroheim's thoughts at this early date, has too heavy a subject to be handled in about twenty minutes. It also contains some improbabilities, such as the stranger's arrival and the binding of the hero. Actually, the stranger is more a messenger of fate, a kind of good angel, as well as a *doppelganger,* and not perhaps a credible human being. Unfortunately, except for a moment or two, the play is a poor piece of theater.

Stroheim later said that he had mailed a copy of this play to Bronco Billy Anderson, the western star, at Essanay studios. What a weird choice, because the play had very little plot and was all dialogue, and slow-moving dialogue at that. By no means could it have been converted into a western or, in fact, into any kind of film.

One can readily see that Stroheim's play contains striking parallels to his later scenarios *Merry-Go-Round* and *The Wedding March*—he constantly reworked his ideas—but whether it gives us any insight into his former life in Vienna is another matter. The family firm had gone bankrupt and there was no longer any money to support the young man. Was this the reason that he left Austria? Did Stroheim imprudently become indebted to a Jewish moneylender, as he hinted? Was he urged to marry a well-off Jewish girl? Or did he invent these dramatic events? In any case, there is no doubt that in America he saw himself as an impoverished count who, being too educated, sensitive, and genteel to fit into a crass world, had sunk low in society.

During the time Stroheim was writing this play, his real-life affair with Margaret progressed. Curtiss mentions that she introduced him to such books as Stephen Crane's *Red Badge of Courage* and Edgar Lee Masters's *Spoon River Anthology.* (Masters's book, however, was not published until April 1915.) Stroheim implies, via Curtiss, that he charmed Margaret's upper-class mother in the family mansion at 958 Fourteenth Street. He may have temporarily ingratiated himself with the mother, who had some respectable social connections, but she was not rich, nor was the house a mansion. In fact, the neighborhood was not especially affluent. The 1913 Oakland directories list the occupations of the residents in the area as messenger, worker, barber, clerk, corset-maker, and tailor. No doubt, Dr. Knox had her office in the family home. (This whole side of the street was torn down years ago.)

On February 19, 1913, Stroheim and Margaret Knox were married. The *Oakland Tribune* of that date printed his age as twenty-one and hers as eighteen. The license shows that the twenty-seven-year-old Erich listed himself as the son of the Baroness Bondy and Benno von Stroheim. The *Oakland Tribune* of February 21, 1913, described the wedding: "Dr. Myra Knox is making the announcement of the marriage of her daughter, Miss Margaret Knox and Erich O. von Stroheim of San Francisco, which was a quiet home ceremony at the family home on Wednesday afternoon. Rev. William Day Simmons officiated at the service in the presence of a few relatives. The couple will make their home in Mill Valley, where they went immediately after the ceremony. The bride is an attractive girl with musical tastes and has been popular among the younger set here. Von Stroheim is connected with a large importing firm across the bay." The only thing that Stroheim was importing, however, was fantasy.

Curtiss weaves an imaginative account of this period. He says that, shortly after the wedding, Erich received an appointment as a captain in the Mexican army and arrived in Mexico on the day that President Madero was assassinated. As a result, he was advised by the American consul that such military appointments would not be honored and that he should return. The fact that Madero was killed on February 22, just three days after the wedding, is ample proof that this is fiction.[39] Later, in *Picture Play Magazine,* Stroheim claimed that he had served as an officer "in the Bosnian campaign and in Mexico."[40]

Within two months, the marriage began to erode. The "scion of the Austrian nobility" still could not find an adequate job, and he began drinking. The more humiliated he felt because of his poverty, the more angry and abusive he became. There were fights—Margaret claimed that he blackened her eye and punched her on the side of her head—and she rushed back to her mother in Oakland. There was a tearful reconciliation, and they found quarters a few blocks away. When the frustrated Stroheim still could not find a position appropriate to his talents, the fights began anew and again Margaret moved back to her mother's house. Angry at himself, at society, and at Margaret, Stroheim grew absolutely furious and telephoned his wife one day in the early part of May 1914 and threatened to punch her in the face. That was enough for Margaret, and at the urging of her mother (who saw Stroheim as an eternal loser), she filed for divorce on May 28. When Stroheim failed to appear, the divorce was granted.[41]

Not only had the young Stroheim failed at marriage; he had also failed at life. In the six years since his rebirth in America, he had accomplished nothing—not happiness, not vocational success, and not monetary security. His experience in America consisted of boarding houses, occasional daily wages, and grinding penury—a world captured faithfully in *Greed* and in the original version of *Walking down Broadway*. At this period of his life, he would have understood Ambrose Bierce's definition of a year: 365 disappointments.

2

The Ascent

The year 1914 proved no better for the hopeful Erich von Stroheim than the previous ones in America, but soon his fate would change. Stroheim claimed as early as 1919 that he became a lifeguard at Lake Tahoe during the summer of 1914. Even this was probably an exaggeration. More likely, his function was rowing tourists around the lake. One day, he met an affluent woman to whom he confided his theatrical ambitions. Impressed by his enthusiasm and intelligence, she promised to help him. "When the summer season ended," according to Curtiss, "Stroheim was told to take the 24 horses at the riding stable to their winter quarters in Pasadena. Stroheim did not find himself escorting lovely ladies, as was promised in the job description, but cleaning stalls, sleeping on a cot, and eating in a corner café."[1]

With some backing from the woman he had impressed at the lake, according to Curtiss, Stroheim put on his play, which was hooted.[2] Many years later, in a 1947 letter, Stroheim recalled its solitary public performance. Playing the count himself, he produced it in Oakland in 1914, at a charity affair for the "Woodmen of the World." He explained that "unfortunately the people laughed when they were supposed to cry and vice-versa."[3] Curtiss writes of this premiere and, unusual for him, provides several details (the names of two of the actors, street addresses, and the specific theater), but he claims that the playlet appeared on amateur night in Los Angeles and that the actors were pelted with vegetables. Obviously there are discrepancies here.

Stroheim had no reason to lie about the play being performed in Oakland, and yet Curtiss probably received most of his information from Stroheim. In any case, Stroheim's career as a playwright ended. But soon a new one beckoned.

What happened next has been garbled by Stroheim and his commentators. Somehow (through the play?) Stroheim evidently met a few actors working as movie extras who convinced him to seek work in the growing film industry. Legend has it that he was almost immediately engaged on *The Birth of a Nation* and quickly rose from lowly extra to the rank of assistant director.

Decades later, in 1947, Stroheim recalled that he was at first rebuffed at the studio but then eventually obtained a few days' work playing soldiers and blacks in *The Birth of a Nation*. He also claimed that he convinced Griffith that he was a good stunt man and, as a result, portrayed the soldier who falls off the roof during the guerrilla raid. Stroheim noted that he broke two ribs in the fall.[4] The camera, however, is not close enough for a viewer to discern any facial features. Curtiss also mentions that Stroheim donned blackface and put on a Confederate uniform, certainly an oddity in the Southern army!

In fact, Griffith shot *The Birth of a Nation* between early July and late September 1914 and did a few pickup shots perhaps in the first week of October. There would simply not have been enough time for Stroheim to have closed the season at the lake, brought down the horses, rehearsed his play, failed, and still have appeared in Griffith's Civil War epic. Furthermore, had he really appeared in *The Birth of Nation* and played such a stunt part, would he have done absolutely no other film work for the next six months? In 1916, after the release of *Intolerance,* Griffith in an interview spoke of the scene of the man falling from the roof. "Many think the fall is made by a dummy. A real man does it and practiced it in a fire net until he got his fall just right, timed exactly as it has to be done to fit in with the scene."[5] Wouldn't this have been a good time for Griffith to mention that, from this humble beginning, the stunt man later became an actor appearing with Douglas Fairbanks and an assistant director on *Macbeth* and *Intolerance*? Certainly, Griffith by now knew Stroheim and was sufficiently aware of the name to include it in the credits for *Intolerance*. And wouldn't the assertive Stroheim have reminded Griffith, in case the great man had forgotten, that he was the fellow who fell from the roof, ribs and all?

Stroheim himself, in interviews from the 1920s, never claimed that he was involved with *The Birth of a Nation* at all; he never said that he even worked for Griffith at this time. He knew better. In his tribute to Griffith, broadcast on the BBC in 1948, Stroheim said that, after sweeping Griffith's stages, "in short order I became extra man . . . , played bits, worked myself to small parts, and the eyes of D.W. fell upon me. I was engaged as assistant director to John Emerson."[6] Note, he did not say "an assistant to Griffith." John Emerson was then working at the Majestic Studios, where Griffith was the leading director.

However, Billy Bitzer and Karl Brown in their respective books—written decades later—state that Stroheim was an assistant director on *The Birth of a Nation,* an assertion that should at least give us pause. Most likely these pioneers, in refreshing their memories, looked up previous statements and based their accounts on them. Although Brown says that Stroheim was an assistant director on *Birth,* he also frequently confuses *Birth* with *Hearts of the World.* And Bitzer's manuscript was not only written many years after the fact but also was "added to" by various hands who quite carelessly altered the original.[7] Lillian Gish also refers to Stroheim as an assistant director in her 1969 autobiography, but by that time she remembered very little, so she and her cowriter had to rely on other sources.[8]

On March 27, 1975, I interviewed Joseph Henabery, who had worked on *The Birth of a Nation,* at his home in Tarzana, California, for six and one-half hours. Henabery was not only a delightful gentleman but also a man of intelligence and extraordinary memory. He had read many books on the period, particularly on Griffith, and was annoyed that they were "so damn full of lies." He said, "I hoped, I honestly hoped that when I read Gish's book and Brown's book there would be some good solid information, and here they both turned up with a lot of tripe. They made me sore." He was amused that he had been listed as assistant director on *Birth.* He was not, he assured me, and certainly Stroheim was not, either. As for the story that Stroheim jumped off the roof, he laughed. Why would a director use a "green" man to make such a fall, especially when most of the stunts were done by "a half-drunk, half-Indian, half-Mexican guy whom we called 'Eagle Eye'?"[9]

Eagle Eye was a member of Griffith's Biograph troupe in California as early as 1912 and was considered important enough to be taken to New York, in July 1913, to do stunts and help out. When Griffith left Biograph and returned to California, he took Eagle Eye back with him. The stunt man remained with Griffith during production of *The Birth of a Nation* in the summer of 1914 and at least up through the completion of *Intolerance* in 1916, in which he played the barbarian chieftain in the Babylonian section[10] and received billing as "Chas. Eagle Eye." He also doubled for Miriam Cooper in the modern story of *Intolerance*.[11]

Henabery allowed me to look at the typescript of his autobiography, and while he was talking, I rapidly flipped through the pages to find additional information on Griffith and Stroheim. When I ran across some relevant item, I would ask him to explain it more fully. Eventually, his autobiography was published in 1997, long after I had written these chapters, and what it contains only confirms my conclusions.

Henabery recalled in his memoirs that *after* the New York showing of *The Birth of a Nation* (this would be in March 1915), while he was at the Los Angeles studio, he noticed an expensive black town car drive up to the curb. When the chauffeur opened the door, out stepped "a rather short man, wearing a close-fitting black overcoat so long that it just missed touching the ground. He wore a monocle. He reached into his pocket, took out money, and paid the chauffeur, who then drove off. The man came on the lot and sat down on a bench, without any evident purpose. His name was Erich von Stroheim."[12]

Was Stroheim here just a "show-off"? "No," writes Henabery, "I believe it was showmanship. I'm sure he had a reason for attracting attention, and he did just that. You can bet that anyone who arrived at a movie lot in such style, spending dollars for fancy transportation, would be noticed and talked about by everyone."[13] This is a wonderful story, but Henabery, almost sixty years after the event, was slightly confused about what happened. His observations are quite accurate about the car and the outfit, but what he describes actually occurred later, a few weeks after Stroheim had arrived at the studio. The young actor had talked himself into a small role in *Old Heidelberg*. During some scenes in the film, he rode around in a fancy car, wore a long black overcoat, and was adorned with a top hat and a monocle. Stroheim may well, for a lark, have driven up to the main gate where the indelible impression was made. At the New York Public Library I discovered a photograph of Stroheim in this expensive car and wearing the very outfit that Henabery so accurately recalled. Certainly, Stroheim made a significant impression on Henabery, who perceptively discussed in his autobiography Stroheim's famed arrogance and concluded that it was mostly "put on." "I could never see him as the contemptuous personality that became his reputation. I talked with him several times after he was highly acclaimed, and our conversations were on exactly the same level as when I first met him—quiet and pleasant. He gave no sign of a 'swell-head.' It is my guess that von Stroheim was by nature a far more considerate man than he has been pictured."[14]

Henabery's recollection of Stroheim's appearance so many years after the event is far more accurate than Stroheim's accounts. Like most people who embroider the truth, Stroheim had difficulty making the facts fit his fantasies. In his reminiscences, he recalled that he was hired to ride a horse in a film titled *Captain McClean,* which he said was made in 1914. However, Stroheim moved the date a year earlier in order for his story to be consistent. In actuality, the film was *Captain Macklin,* and it was shot during March 1915, at the Majestic studio and on location in Los Angeles and San Diego.[15] He recalled leading a troupe of cavalrymen in Griffith Park "when the staff of my standard hit one of the [overhead] branches. I, naturally, was thrown and the whole crowd of rough riders went over me. I surely thought my last moment had come, but I had not been scratched. For quite some time after I had to stand the more or less rough kidding about my ability to ride, and they did not think very much of the Austrian cavalry."[16] (When the picture came out, the whole sequence had been cut.)

In another film, directed by Fred Kelsey, whose title Stroheim forgot, he recalled that he was to jump with his horse into the ocean. "I wanted to, but the mount did not." When one of the cowboys blew pepper in its eyes, the horse and the rider dashed into the water. Stroheim claimed that a member of the society against cruelty to animals had him arrested and that after a night at a police station he was released.[17] This film was most likely the two-reel *A Bold Impersonation,* released months later in August 1915. A review mentioned that the heroine does "a graceful dive off a dock."[18]

That Stroheim vividly remembered these two incidents of March 1915 but could not recall any events prior to this date makes his claim of doing stunt work and playing other parts in *Birth* during the summer of 1914 most dubious. If he had been in the film, would he then have done absolutely nothing for over half a year? Most likely he did not arrive at Majestic until late February 1915, when his initial employment would have made indelible impressions.

While squads of soldiers in military uniforms were drilling on the studio lot for the West Point scenes of *Captain Macklin,* Broadway actor-director John Emerson arrived in Hollywood in the middle of March 1915.[19] He had been hired to portray Oswald in a film version of Ibsen's famous play *Ghosts,* to be directed by George Nichols.[20] Several years later, in 1919, Stroheim remembered that after appearing in *Captain Macklin* he languished on the extra's bench "every day for two months"[21] (actually, it was only for a few days), until he observed Emerson crossing the studio lot on the way to a costume test for *Ghosts.* Stroheim noticed that Emerson was wearing an honorary ribbon and hurriedly left the casting bench. "For the first time in my life I was nervy," said Stroheim modestly and quite inaccurately—he certainly was often nervy. "I stepped up, told him my name and asked if he was playing comedy or drama. When he said drama and that the ribbon was a badge or decoration of a chamberlain, I told him that it was not correct. 'What do you know about it?' he asked. I replied that it was too long a story to tell him, but that I did know, for I had worn such a ribbon myself. 'Alright,' he said, 'go ahead and get me the real thing.'" Stroheim would recall this incident—which really began his career— many times during interviews. He clearly remembered it as his first big break.

Stroheim's success came not only from noticing things but also from being noticed. He shrewdly realized that if he tried to look and act like American actors, he would fail. After all, he was hardly tall, dark, or handsome. But if he had a unique appearance, he would stand out. Imagine the effect on a casting director used to numerous ne'er-do-wells looking for a day's work when a fellow marches in with white gloves, shaved head, and monocle, accompanied by heel clicking, hand kissing, and European accent, and takes his seat on the extras bench. Certainly he would get at least a second look. "Hey, you, Prince," he might have been addressed, and he could easily have given the modest rejoinder, "I am not a prince, but I am a count."

Stroheim claimed later that in order to purchase the right ribbon he had to borrow money from his landlady.[22] Meanwhile, Emerson, the sophisticated New Yorker, scrutinized the script for *Ghosts* and backed away, fearful that the studio's transformation of Ibsen's classic play about hereditary syphilis into one dealing with alcoholism would make him a laughingstock among his theatrical friends. An article dated April 4, 1915, announced that the studio had changed its plans and that Henry B. Walthall, rather than Emerson, would star in *Ghosts*.[23] Stroheim's services to Emerson were quickly transferred to Nichols, the film's director, and he was soon advising on certain aspects of *Ghosts*. The nonnervy beginner even wangled the small part of a gray-haired school clerk. The one shot in which he appears lasts forty seconds. *Ghosts* was finished prior to April 25[24] and released on May 29, 1915.

Stroheim's love of detail and his skill at set decoration were already evident in *Ghosts*: according to one contemporary review, "A high compliment must be paid also to the settings. . . . They are admirably chosen in exteriors and are the result of fine taste, together with infinite pains, where interiors are shown."[25] *Variety* also took note of the settings: "The staging is splendid, the house party interiors as well as the wedding scene . . . being most effectively set." However, the review concluded that the film had "a very morbid, gruesome subject."[26]

At about this time, probably late March, Christy Cabanne directed a film called *The Failure* (released in May 1915), starring John Emerson. The film is now lost, but again Stroheim had a bit part.

By April 19, Emerson had left acting and was now slated to begin his first directorial project,[27] *Old Heidelberg*. According to the Majestic Company books, costs began on April 21, 1915, and shooting, said *Motion Picture News,* started on May 24 and was completed in July. *Old Heidelberg* told the story of a prince who, while at the university, falls in love with a commoner. Stroheim, calling himself Count von Stroheim, claimed that he had seen the play in Vienna a number of times and that, as a former military and university man, he would be of great help making the film look authentic. Impressed by Stroheim's attention to details in *Ghosts* and *The Failure,* Emerson engaged him as his helper. Stroheim also talked Emerson into letting him play the valet Lutz, a rather stiff-necked, strict, and slightly absurd overseer of the young prince. Besides acting, Stroheim assisted with the costumes, selected extras from the bench where he had formerly sat, and advised on student life. His efforts were not unnoticed when the film was reviewed. "Whoever is directly responsible for the casting of the other members of the organization is a positive genius for selecting 'types'"[28]

The film tells the story of Prince Karl, who from his youngest years is constrained by his tutor, his valet, and his strict family to the lonely life of an heir apparent. The lad is allowed to play with toy soldiers but not with other children. Occasionally he encounters a little girl, Katie, but his valet (played by "Erick von Stroheim," as stated in an intertitle) watches over him and prevents the boy from ever having a good time. Katie's father had gone off to a previous war and come back with his right arm missing. (Because of Stroheim's persistent fascination with the physically maimed, this was probably his addition to the script.) The father now earns his living cranking a hand organ. A shot of the man is crosscut with a scene of the high-ranking officers at the court, a Griffith-like juxtaposition that points out the cause of his misfortune.

When Prince Karl (Wallace Reid) grows up, he becomes a student at Heidelberg, and there he meets Katie (Dorothy Gish), who has become a servant in the quarters where he lives. Although the two grow to love each other, his family has him betrothed to a Princess Draga. The prince stands in front of a vast array of white crosses in a military cemetery while the one-armed hand-organist speaks about the horror of war. Later, some veterans explain to the prince that war is "hell." In a flashback, we see some battles and lots of wounded and dead men. If the young prince follows his heart by marrying Katie, he will lose his power and thus be unable to prevent the war that is now threatening. Sadly, he goes back to Heidelberg, bids farewell to Katie, and returns to do his duty for his country. And so the film ends.

Although Stroheim's small role did not give him much opportunity to demonstrate his talent, he does succeed, in his frequent bowing and general demeanor, in making his character somewhat pompous and unsympathetic. Stroheim adds one unique touch. As he strides down a path, two children are playing. Although the image is not clear (in my print), he seems to kick something on the path away from him and then grabs and shoves the two boys to the side. Not too many actors at this sentimental time would have gone out of their way to be unkind to children. In another scene, Lutz, elegantly dressed in formal clothes and a top hat, arrives in an expensive automobile to see the prince at Heidelberg. This image is the first instance of Stroheim's upper-class, monocled persona, the beginning of his screen fantasy life. If he looks pleased, he had a right to be pleased. After only a few weeks in the movie business, he had already done quite well. He was on his way.

At this time, Stroheim's abilities as an actor were hardly impressive—although he was already stealing what scenes he could—but his skills as an art director were. "Somewhere in my subconscious mind I have a sort of photographic plate," he said years later. "I did not know this until I had worked on pictorial productions, but since then I have discovered that I see everything in the form of a scene for a picture. Something strikes me as a scene for a film and I will never forget it."[29] (Several producers wished that he had.) The Mutual Studio paper for May 22, 1915, contains a photo of Emerson and Stroheim, proof that Stroheim had risen from obscurity in just a few weeks. What Stroheim did immediately after *Old Heidelberg* cannot be clearly ascertained. Tales that he became Griffith's assistant are fanciful. Certainly up to this time he could not have had much—if any—contact with Griffith, for the great director had left Hollywood for the East Coast in early January 1915, after completing *The Mother and the Law*, which he had begun shooting October 17, 1914. Griffith had gone to oversee the various showings of *The Birth of a Nation* in Washington, New York, Boston, and other cities, where he was handling exploitation, doing additional editing, polishing the musical accompaniment, and battling the efforts to censor his film.

When Griffith returned to Hollywood in May 1915, overwhelmed with the artistic and financial success of *The Birth of a Nation,* he soon plunged into what he hoped would be the greatest film ever made. Having decided that the modest feature *The Mother and the Law,* which he had completed in January 1915, would be an unworthy follow-up, he planned to expand and improve the film and then intercut it with three other stories to form the grandiose *Intolerance*.

Although it is tempting to credit Stroheim with work on the modern story of *Intolerance,* as some film historians have done, his influence—and even his presence on the sets—could only have been minuscule. He had been Emerson's assistant up until the completion of *Old Heidelberg*. At best, he could only have been available during late July, August, and early September. Certainly, he never mentioned helping Griffith.

Costs for *Intolerance* resumed on the company books on June 14, and on June 26 salaries for actors began again. During the summer,

Griffith began reshooting scenes from *The Mother and the Law* that no longer pleased him, which he continued doing until *Intolerance* was released in September 1916. Every time Griffith decided on a change, sets had to be rebuilt, and many—including the girl's room, the musketeer's apartment, and the hallway—were reassembled three or four times in 1914, 1915, and 1916. The statue of the Virgin Mary, a religious print on the wall, and the hopeful geranium in the girl's room, as well as the erotic statuary, the pictures, and the pornographic book in the musketeer's apartment, are quite reminiscent of Stroheim's later work and suggest that Stroheim dressed these sets. However, internal evidence shows that the initial set design stems from 1914, long before Stroheim could have been involved. Probably these sets influenced *him!* Only the erotic book, *The Loves of Lucille,* may have been a late addition and possibly a Stroheim suggestion. It could have been a sardonic reference to the Universal serial *Lucille Love, the Girl of Mystery,* the first chapter of which was released on April 14, 1914, or an in-joke that referred to Lucille Young, a comely lady who costarred with Stroheim in *Farewell to Thee,* a one-reel melodrama (released in August 1915) now lost; in it, Stroheim played a monocled villain who, along with his companion, tries to swindle a husband out of his inheritance. If some of Griffith's sets were dressed by Stroheim, at all, they were most likely not done until the early part of 1916.

When production ended on *Old Heidelberg,* Stroheim was presumably out of a job and took an acting role in *Farewell to Thee.* At best, he could only have watched Griffith at work during the early part of the summer of 1915, for Emerson abruptly decided to make his next film, *His Picture in the Papers,* on the East Coast. In a 1919 interview, Stroheim recalled that "then, one day he asked me how long it would take for me to get ready to go to New York with him. Thinking of my limited wardrobe of a couple pair extra hose, a shirt or two and a few stray collars, I replied that about seven minutes would do. Then, like a flash I remembered the many debts I owed—who would pay them? I told Mr. Emerson about them and jumping into a car he drove around with me and paid them all. Great, wasn't it?"[30] Another interview filled in the details of the exodus and described how "the young actor went to his little hall room and wrapped up both his shirts and his extra collar in a newspaper and reported at the train for the trip to the foot of the rainbow."[31]

According to an entry in the Majestic Company's books for September 16, 1915, Stroheim was given train fare to accompany the director to New York, where they would make a film with Douglas Fairbanks. Stroheim and Emerson probably spent some of the train journey discussing the picture's locations, costumes, and props.

Soon after Emerson and Stroheim arrived in New York on September 20, 1915, they spent about two weeks preparing for *His Picture in the Papers.* Fairbanks arrived in New York on October 2 and reported two days later at the Triangle Studios in Riverdale, where production began.[32] Meanwhile, Stroheim encountered Mae Jones, whom he may have known during his earlier years in the city. Curtiss states that she was the daughter of his landlady, although he misidentifies the year as 1918.[33] (A close examination of New York City directories, telephone books, and census records regarding Stroheim or the Jones family proved unrewarding.) In any case, a relationship began and Mae became pregnant. Stroheim's final decree of divorce from Margaret Knox had been granted on November 10, 1915, almost simultaneously with the baby's conception. Soon the parents-to-be were wed, but this second marriage proved no happier than the first. When Stroheim returned to Hollywood in January 1916, Mae accompanied him and found work as a seamstress at the Griffith studio, where her husband was working. A son, Erich von Stroheim Jr., was born on August 25, 1916.[34] The couple grew incompatible and, by July 1919, there was another divorce. (The Los Angeles County Hall of Records has no mention either of the marriage or its dissolution.) This relationship was not as easy to forget as the first, because support payments for the son would continue to be an issue until Erich Junior came of age.[35]

Working on *His Picture in the Papers,* in New York, Stroheim functioned as assistant director and was in charge of dressing the sets. In addition, he wangled an acting role as the film's villain, and for the first time he had a chance to develop a character. Stroheim seems to have been familiar with Griffith's 1914 films, and he probably had seen *The Avenging Conscience,* partially based on Edgar Allan Poe's "The Tell-Tale Heart." In it, one of the main characters sported a black eye patch, a detail that gave him a repellent and evil appearance. Stroheim may have recalled this image when he created his characterization. Years later, he explained that to "make this bit outstanding, I wore a black patch over my right eye and a black glove on the hand of my supposed paralyzed right arm,"[36] an early instance of his lifelong obsession with people crippled by nature or happenstance. In this way, Stroheim transformed what could have been a conventional villain into a memorable grotesque. Although it was a good, if minor part, *Variety* did not include him among the eight actors it listed when reviewing the film.[37]

Stroheim said in 1919 that he had envisioned a different career for himself in the "movie game." He stated, "I thought I was going to be another Fairbanks or Kerrigan. I imagined myself rescuing fair damsels in distress and running bad men to their sinful lairs. I thought I was to be a romantic hero. Instead, I've committed every crime in the calendar from murder to arson, I've thrown babies out of windows, shot old men in the back."[38] That Stroheim really believed he could have been such a hero might seem ridiculous, yet he did cast himself in leading roles and certainly played the "hero" in *The Wedding March*. However, he neglected to mention that the unheroic roles he otherwise took, and the odious deeds that he performed, were of his own invention. He probably thought that if people considered him ugly—in some ways he thought he was—he might as well commit ugly deeds. In short, he would rather be a famous monster than an obscure actor. Like Lucifer in Milton's *Paradise Lost,* he deemed it better to reign in hell than serve in heaven.

His Picture in the Papers certainly reveals that it was shot on location in New York City and the vicinity. In mid-October, they shot in Yonkers;[39] and during the last week of November, the prizefight scenes were filmed in the famous boxing club, Sharkey's.[40] Some episodes took place in Atlantic City. Despite the location work, the film was handled efficiently and cost only $42,599.94.[41]

Stroheim, from the very beginning of his career, believed that realistic details contribute to verisimilitude and to the creation of character. Some of the interiors of *His Picture in the Papers* appear to be actual locales because they do not have the bare look of many sets of the period, which often were hastily built and sparsely furnished. However, such realistic interiors were actually built in a studio, under Stroheim's supervision. In a number of stills from the film (preserved in the Theatre Collection of the New York Public Library), the photographer stood far enough back that we can see the whole shooting stage. Fairbanks's bedroom has college posters and many photos and doodads on the walls. In a restaurant set, one wall contains a number of mirrors, many beer steins, mounted animals (a fish, a moose, and a turtle) and animal horns, pictures (including one of the Colosseum), and other such "masculine" decorations that denote a genuine steak restaurant. Here, the hero (Fairbanks) could have a decent meal, not the vegetarian goop he was offered in an earlier scene. One photo shows the restaurant set roped off and a hand-lettered sign reading "Keep off the set." The printing of the f's in "off" reveals Stroheim's European calligraphy. The sign indicates how adamant he was that no one should touch anything.

Another example of Stroheim's methods is revealed in a photo of a jail cell. Only a portion of the photo survives, but what a portion! Even here, in the fall of 1915, with Stroheim not yet six months into filmmaking, we can see his fascination with realism. On the wall facing the camera are graffiti of hands, faces, a heart crossed with an arrow, and various writings, including: "Women, wine, and song," "Dreckiger sauhund" ("dirty pigdog," literally, but "dirty bastard" in spirit), "Défense de fumé" and "Rauchen Verboten" ("no smoking" in French and German), and "Si pregar di non sputare" ("please don't spit" in Italian). Obviously Stroheim wanted to have an international clientele in this jail cell but knew few foreign expressions other than what he had heard or read on signs. On the side wall, barely visible to the motion picture camera, but clear in the still photo, is the statement "Thank John Emerson only fools write this nonsense." In the film, almost none of this would be in the frame, but Stroheim included it all.

In one scene, the hero needs a disguise and, finding a goat, cuts off its beard—a curious incident, at best. A still photo shows Fairbanks holding the goat while Stroheim, dressed in a suit and hat, holds its leash. Not many years later, in Stroheim's *Foolish Wives,* a goat would make another appearance. Goats, like pigs, seem to represent the ugly side of life to Stroheim.

When he first became a set decorator and then assistant director, Stroheim certainly demonstrated his skills. They were not just the contributions of a bright young man, but something more. He brought to these sets a personality fraught with private obsessions. In *His Picture in the Papers,* for example, we have, besides the goat, a maimed person and an extremely odd interest in the number three—all of this in a light-hearted, frivolous Douglas Fairbanks comedy. Throughout Stroheim's work, whenever a number is used, he will employ a three or a thirteen or a variant. When Fairbanks goes to an actual brownstone in New York, its number is 303, and in another scene the date on the calendar (evident in a still) is thirteen.

Shooting on *His Picture in the Papers* concluded sometime in December 1915. Emerson was pleased with Stroheim's contributions and invited him back to Hollywood to work on *The Flying Torpedo,* a film now lost. In this picture Emerson acted the part of a novelist-detective and left the general direction to John B. O'Brien and the battle scenes to Christy Cabanne. It was one of the few films of the period that took place in the future—1921—and dealt "with an invasion of the United States by yellow men and their defeat by the ingenious invention" of missiles.[42] Stroheim played one of the international criminals who murder the inventor of these "flying torpedoes." By the first week of January 1916, the film was shipped to New York, and it was released in March 1916.

Earlier, in the late summer of 1915, Harry Aitken, the president of Triangle Film Corporation, persisted in the ill-founded notion that hiring famous theatrical personages was good business. (His sole success in this endeavor was Doug Fairbanks.) Aitken remembered that Sarah Bernhardt had been a great draw at the box office a few years before and thought that the renowned Shakespearean actor Sir Herbert Beerbohm Tree would do equally well. Tree's presentations of the Bard were not doing well in England because of the war, so he agreed, against his better judgment, to appear in two silent films based on Shakespeare's plays. The offer of fifty thousand dollars for each film did not hurt, of course. On November 24, 1915, Tree arrived in New York. Slightly bemused by the idea of a silent version of Shakespeare, he laughingly stated that "no epigram will dispose" of the fact that people do go to the movies. Tree did not know exactly what play he would act in, he said, but hoped it would be a comedy or perhaps *King Lear.* Griffith, who was supervising all Triangle projects, at first leaned toward *The Tempest* but, after conferring with others, decided on the less complicated but more familiar *Macbeth.*

Although Tree sought to salve his conscience by thinking of the presentation as "Tales of Shakespeare," he was constantly annoyed at the interruption of his acting to set up new shots. He would do much better, he declared, if that damn black box was absent. He said in an interview, "To my limited experience it has seemed that the constant flashing change of scene that is characteristic of so many American productions is disturbing, disquieting." He preferred the British style of just recording an entire scene in one shot. He felt that the "flash" was "obviously nothing but a nuisance."[43]

Tree consoled himself with the thought that his performance would be preserved on film. "The actor leaves nothing to posterity but the rosy-tinted obituaries by you fellows," he said to reporters. "The film is a Godsend in that way."[44] He could not know that his effort would come to naught, for the film is now lost and only a few imperfect stills remain.

John Emerson directed this opus, and R. Ellis Wales, the studio librarian and artistic advisor (who was also assisting on *Intolerance*), was given the task of making the film historically accurate. Years later, Stroheim claimed that this was the first time he received a screen credit as assistant director and art director, but there is no mention of this in surviving documents; a Los Angeles newspaper, however, did state that a "constant check" is kept on all the details of the film by "Director John Emerson and his assistant, Von Stroheim."[45]

The studio tried its best to capture the spirit of the play. Stroheim busied himself dressing the sets with pots, utensils, robes, and furniture and seeing that the costumed actors handled their swords, helmets, and shields correctly. At one point, Stroheim devised an electrical apparatus intended to cause the witches to emit sparks, but besides shocking the actors, the experiment did not work. His later comment that this scene cost ten thousand dollars is, of course, fabrication. High-voltage spark coils could be rigged for a few dollars.

Harry Aitken, the president of Triangle, bragged that in *Macbeth* "no expense was spared to obtain the appropriate backgrounds and costumes,"[46] a statement that could well apply to all of Stroheim's future work. A review said that the film was "marked by artistic lighting."[47] *Variety* observed, "Scenically the production is truly marvelous."[48]

Emerson finished directing *Macbeth* by the third week of March 1916.[49] Perhaps affected by Stroheim's constant energetic attention to detail, Sir Herbert wearily averred, at the end of the eight weeks of shooting, that "ordinary activity would be a pleasure." He added, "I never worked so hard in my busy life."[50] As he explained, "Frequently

I worked eighteen hours a day, far into the night and sometimes after midnight. But we had to do it."[51] This description anticipates Stroheim's own demanding work habits not many years in the future.

When *Macbeth,* in eight reels and divided into two parts with an organ interlude,[52] opened in June at New York City's Rialto, the theater lost thirty-five hundred dollars for the week because of the film's "small drawing power."[53] If cosmopolitan New Yorkers failed to attend, one can imagine the box-office disaster it became in the rest of the country. More moviegoers were fans of William S. Hart than William Shakespeare, it seemed. Any thought of using the great actor in another of the Bard's plays vanished, and Sir Herbert, in the summer, fulfilled his contract by playing a U.S. senator in *The Old Folks at Home.* "Sir Herbert left the company flat on the lot after the picture was completed," noted *Variety.*[54] The film was another commercial failure and, humbled but richer, its star returned to the legitimate theater on Broadway. After performing there for almost a year, he returned to London, where he died a few weeks later on July 2, 1917.

In March 1916, just as Stroheim was completing his work on *Macbeth,* Griffith began shooting the giant battles for the Babylonian scenes of *Intolerance.*[55] (Stroheim recalled that the first day of shooting these scenes coincided with Brigadier General Pershing's entry into Mexico. This would have been March 15, and for a change Stroheim is about right.) It is not unlikely that the personnel of the entire studio were borrowed for the big event, and it was reported that Tree, Fairbanks, and other notables visited the set. Supposedly, they donned costumes for a few shots, but this may be more legend than fact.

About two weeks later, in April, Griffith filmed the Feast of Babylon—one of the most famous scenes in the history of silent films. Many hundreds of extras had to be costumed, fed, grouped, and directed. Griffith's major aides—George Siegmann and Joseph Henabery, assisted by Raoul Walsh, Christy Cabanne, and Tod Browning—clad in costumes in case the cameras picked them up,[56] joined in this giant undertaking. Stroheim was probably pressed into service to handle some groups of extras, but he was by no means a major contributor.

Stroheim has sometimes been identified in an often-reproduced still of Christ and the pharisees,[57] but when I examined this photo with Joseph Henabery, he pointed out William Courtright as one of Jesus' followers, Baron Erik von Ritzau as the shorter pharisee,[58] and himself ("You can see my long horse face") as the taller Pharisee—but not Stroheim. I had brought a vast number of frame blow-ups in the hopes that Henabery could identify Stroheim in them, but he fairly shouted at me, after persistent questioning, that Stroheim was not in the film. "Point him out," he said. I could not, and neither can anyone else, either.

If this be the case, then how did Stroheim get included in the credits? A photo of the pharisees, as early as the November 1916 issue of *Motion Picture Classic,* is captioned "Baron von Ritzau and Count von Stroheim," and the cast list in *Variety*'s review also mentions him.[59] Why include Stroheim's name if he did not play a role? Griffith had first filmed Henabery as one of the pharisees and later decided to use him as Admiral Coligny in the French sequence. Such a dual appearance would seem cheap for a lavish film and had the potential of being embarrassing, so Griffith chose another name for the pharisee. He saw a certain consistency in having both of these hated hypocrites played by men with aristocratic and Teutonic names. Whether Griffith chose Stroheim's name—he was fascinated by it and later wanted to use it for the villain in *Hearts of the World*—or whether Stroheim, eager for any kind of notoriety, offered it, cannot be ascertained. Although Stroheim never disagreed with this "fact" that he was in the film, he never claimed that he was in the released *Intolerance* either.

Although Stroheim did not appear as a pharisee, he did contribute to the scenes Griffith filmed of Christ's passage on the Via Dolorosa on the way to the Crucifixion. According to an article in *Variety,* datelined April 2, Griffith sent someone to "the local Ghetto and hired all the orthodox Hebrews with long whiskers he could secure." This someone was probably Stroheim, who clearly recalled going to the Jewish quarter and enlisting men with beards.[60] Stroheim may have been able, by means of his German—or Yiddish—to talk to them. After they appeared in the Crucifixion scene and were paid, they complained to their brethren about Griffith's handling of the event. Soon, Griffith was embroiled in a controversial issue. Who killed Christ? The New Testament clearly states that "the chief priests and scribes" clamored for his death. As a result of their attitude, Christ was condemned, although the Crucifixion itself was carried out by the Romans. *Variety* noted that Griffith was forced by B'nai B'rith and other "prominent Hebrews" to omit the big Crucifixion scenes from his film: "They

supplemented their 'proofs' [that the Jews did not crucify Christ] with
a 48-hour ultimatum to destroy that portion of the 'masterpiece' negative on penalty of a concerted campaign of blacklisting and other pressure which powerful financial and industrial interests might bring to
bear, which included the assertion that censors, governors of states and
even the President would do all in their power to prevent the showing
of the picture with the objectionable scene."[61] The episode was then
retaken, showing "Roman soldiers nailing Christ to the cross."[62]

Stroheim told Curtiss that he was one of the men doing the nailing. This is perhaps the only time that Stroheim could have appeared
in the Judean section, for most of it had been shot the previous fall,
while Stroheim was on the East Coast. Ultimately, Griffith chose not
to show any details of the Crucifixion and included only some long
shots of Calvary, perhaps because closer shots of the event slowed the
pace. As a result, Stroheim's brief appearance, if he was in the film at all,
fell onto the cutting-room floor.

Although Stroheim has often been connected to *Intolerance* by later
writers, his input into the film was minimal. How could he have been
an "assistant director"? There was no time for him to have performed
any vital duties. Perhaps proof can come from Stroheim's own words.
In his 1948 broadcast for the BBC, he said that Griffith, for *Hearts of
the World,* "selected me as his personal first assistant. . . . In that capacity
of Griffith's assistant and actor I had the opportunity to become personally acquainted with the man."[63] Had he been Griffith's assistant earlier,
would the two not already have become "personally acquainted"?

Although Stroheim was not Griffith's assistant at this time, he remained Emerson's efficient and eager helper. Stroheim was a familiar
presence on the studio lot. Margery Wilson (Brown Eyes in *Intolerance*)
told me in 1969, at an interview at her home, that one day Stroheim
asked her out for a date. She conveyed this information to her fellow
girls, and they all feared for her virtue. The man with the short hair
and the military bearing met her after work, gallantly bowed, and took
her out for an ice cream soda!

In May 1916, Norma Talmadge, Emerson, and Stroheim entrained
for New York and arrived on May 30 to begin shooting *The Social
Secretary.*[64] During the trip east, the enthusiastic Stroheim must have
waxed eloquent about the importance of set decoration and realistic
detail. The evidence can be seen in an interview given by Miss Talmadge

a few days after her New York arrival. This restrained and unintellectual woman usually had little to say about her career or indeed any other matter. Desperate, however, to mention something, she started to speak about the importance of accurate sets.[65] Later, the company's little newspaper, *The Triangle,* described the film as having settings that were lavish and of "astounding" cost.[66] There were no spectacular scenes, by any means, but rooms were appropriately dressed and the walls were adorned with countless details: paintings, hangings, and trophies. The furniture, too, had been carefully chosen and not just grabbed willy-nilly from the prop room.

In *The Social Secretary,* Stroheim played, in his own words, the part of a "Yellow Journal-snooper." In the credits, an "Eric von Stroheim" was listed sixth and last as "The Buzzard," who was described as "a villainous reporter."[67] The picture was released on September 8, 1916, three days after the premiere of *Intolerance.*

The Social Secretary deals with the unexpectedly modern issue of sexual harassment. Talmadge plays a secretary who has lost previous jobs because of lecherous employers. As the film opens, she arrives at the offices of the New York Purity League. The gray-bearded boss is first seen looking at (presumably) dirty pictures and quickly hides them when the attractive applicant enters. As she takes dictation, he stares at her legs. She then gives him a disapproving look and pulls down her skirt. When he makes a more overt pass, she leaves and later comments to her friends, "A girl's got to look like a black Saturday fright to keep some men in their place." The secretary tries another position with Portuguese Count Limonittiez, whose office is room 131 (an early instance of Stroheim's entrancement with permutations of the number thirteen).

Meanwhile, at the mansion of the Peabody–de Puyster family, the social secretary of the formidable lady of the house announces that she is quitting to get married. The son, Jimmie, who has been up all night partying and now, in the morning, is taking another little drink, joins his mother downstairs. She is writing an advertisement for a new secretary, and he adds that the applicant must be "extremely unattractive to men." The out-of-work former secretary sees the ad, pulls her hair back, puts on glasses, and dresses in a severe, matronly fashion. When she arrives for the interview, the son gives her one quick glance and whispers to his mother, "You'll never lose her by matrimony."

One night soon after, the son comes home drunk. The new secretary, in a nightdress and with her hair down, mistakes him for a burglar and hits him over the head. When he sees that the drab woman is really a natural beauty, he becomes smitten. Soon they are seeing each other on the sly. It is at this point that Stroheim, playing a sleazy reporter (but one wearing pince-nez held on with a ribbon!), spies the loving couple. "No clandestine affair is ever safe from prying eyes,—in this case Adam Buzzard, social scavenger, who has been trying to get his carrion copy used by a society sheet." In Central Park, Buzzard (Stroheim) stands by a garbage can, reacts slightly to its smell, and thus emphasizes the concept that he is a buzzard looking for carrion.

Soon after, the Portuguese count, "whose lime business has been squeezed by the war," is now without money and begins to woo the daughter of the rich employer. Their planned elopement is foiled by the secretary, who hurries to the count's quarters and extracts the daughter from what would have been a scandal. In the apartment can be seen a seminude painting of a woman, one of the first instances of Stroheim's attention to libidinous art works. Of course, the film ends happily, with the secretary and Jimmie to be married. The snooper, however, does not suffer any serious retribution. As with most of Anita Loos's other scripts, the film as a whole is urbane and somewhat witty.[68]

Stroheim does not have much to do in *The Social Secretary,* but what he does is more restrained than usual. In his earlier films, he was so anxious to be noticed that he sometimes overacted, or to put it unkindly, tried to steal scenes. Director Emerson, too, showed that he had progressed. The film is crisply handled, with the camera placements varied but without the choppy transitions from shot to shot so evident in *His Picture in the Papers* (made less than a year before). Griffith's influence is apparent here, but not in Emerson's direction of Talmadge's acting. There are no cutesy gestures, no timorous glances, no heartfelt moments, and none of the mannerisms that sometimes cruelly date Griffith's heroines. Talmadge comes off as an attractive, pleasant, and mature woman without even one overwrought gesture, a restraint that Loos, years later, unjustly ascribed to Talmadge's "poker face."[69]

Stroheim remained Emerson's assistant director on Mary Pickford's *Less Than the Dust,* which was shot in August and September 1916, on Long Island and in New Jersey. Stroheim must have had quite a time creating villages in India and settings in England, and even arranging for camels. It was while making this film that Stroheim met Cesare Gravina, an Italian actor whom he would later use in *Foolish Wives, Greed, Merry-Go-Round,* and *The Wedding March.* The plodding *Less Than the Dust* (a viewer referred to it as "Cheaper Than Dirt") became one of Pickford's few failures.

A few years later, in an 1920 interview, Stroheim spoke his mind about *Less Than the Dust:* "I know of a picture in which a star of international reputation appeared," he said. "The picture had a strong coherent story, and when it was finished, it was a work of art. But it had to pass through the star's hands before it would be released, and when she finished cutting out scenes in which she did not appear, the picture was just mediocre stuff. The scenes which she did not consider important because she was not in them were absolutely essential to the continuity and logic of the story."[70] Stroheim's opinion seems to be corroborated by the fact that a year later Pickford was chosen to appear in a C.B. DeMille film only if she promised not to "interfere."[71] Stroheim had seen enough of Pickford's self-centeredness to grow wary of "stars," and so, when he became a director, he chose to work with virtual unknowns.

Emerson, wearied by Pickford's demands, left for the West Coast around October 20, 1916,[72] to direct *The Americano,* starring Fairbanks. Meanwhile, *The Social Secretary* proved to be an outstanding success. Norma Talmadge was so pleased with Stroheim's work that she recommended that he be an assistant director for her next feature, *Panthea.* As a result, Stroheim quit Emerson and stayed east to work with director Allan Dwan, who rapidly realized that Stroheim's military bearing and authoritative manner, which often proved offensive to his coworkers, would be just right for the part of an arrogant Russian officer. This was Stroheim's first "Hun" role. Dwan recalled in 1969 that Stroheim was very commanding as the officer and enthusiastically cracked his whip at his troops. "He made the mistake of socking them with it a couple of times and finally they started to beat hell out of him," Dwan declared. "I had to pull him out from under a lot of Cossacks, and I didn't dare put him back in again, so after that, he was just my assistant. And he was very, very good, particularly in this instance because I asked him to dig up a lot of authentic Russian information for me and he did."[73]

When *Panthea* was released in January 1917, a "Count E. von

Stroheim" was listed playing a "Lieutenant of Police."[74] A review in *Photoplay* reflected the public's opinion: "The lieutenant who comes to arrest Panthea in the early episodes is the perfect picture of the 'well, it's all in the day's work' type of blasé young militarist. Wonderful is the revelatory close-up when the Baron attends Panthea's recital: all the other old men, we infer, are watching her hands, for there is a great keyboard close-up; but when it is the Baron's turn we get a close-up of Panthea's shapely foot and promising ankle, upon the pedal."[75]

Although there is no proof, the scene is so typical of Stroheim that one can suppose that he had suggested it to Dwan. Later, Stroheim would repeat this kind of editing in *The Merry Widow*, when a foot fetishist looks at the heroine's feet, the lecherous villain evaluates her middle region, and the hero observes her face.

After the completion of *Panthea*, the "count" languished in New York and waited for employment. Meanwhile, the ever shrewd Fairbanks had formed his own corporation and, for his first independent film, engaged Emerson as his director, with Stroheim assisting. In this film, *In Again, Out Again* (released in May 1917), Fairbanks's character is arrested for drinking too much and put in jail, where he falls in love with the jailer's daughter. The jailer, not wanting his daughter to get involved, frees him, and the young man spends the rest of the film trying to get arrested again. At one point, he impersonates an arch criminal who blows up munitions factories. When Stroheim went out on location to find these factories, understandably he created a good deal of suspicion, for this was a time when there actually were saboteurs. "In the middle of the picture," Stroheim recalled, "I was discharged on account of Doug's apprehension about having a man with a German name in his employ when even German-fried-potatoes had to be rebaptized 'Liberty' potatoes."[76]

Stroheim was not fired immediately but performed some minor functions for the New York scenes of Fairbanks's next film, *Wild and Woolly* (June 1917). Most of the picture was shot out west, while Stroheim remained in New York. Emerson's next Fairbanks film, *Reaching for the Moon* (November 1917), contains a considerable number of New York City location shots. In one sequence, a car pulls up in front of a row of elegant townhouses, and out step some representatives of the Kingdom of Vulgaria. Among them (shot mostly from the back) appears a smartly uniformed man wearing a white jacket, dark pants, and an officer's cap. It is Stroheim, and this is his only appearance in the film.[77]

With his employment by Emerson and Fairbanks ended, Stroheim, still on the East Coast, convinced director George Fitzmaurice to engage him as assistant director and actor in *Sylvia of the Secret Service,* also known as *Carroll of the Secret Service* (completed in June and released in November 1917). A photograph of Stroheim as the villain can be seen in *Moving Picture World,* May 26, 1917. Arthur C. Miller, the cinematographer, recalled that Stroheim

> was a sort of technical director for this picture. Von had considerable knowledge of German militarism, or at least everyone thought he had. The plot of *Sylvia of the Secret Service* had something to do with the Germans blowing up an ammunition dump, and Von went to New York to research the names of the different explosives to be painted on cases stored at such a place. I don't believe that anyone ever saw Von Stroheim when he was not dressed other than as a dapper gentleman, with rather short clipped haircut, Prussian style. These were the war years, and between his appearance and the sort of questions he was asking, it was no time at all before he was in the clink. The studio, of course, immediately went to his rescue and he was released. I am convinced, though, that the clever Von Stroheim pulled the whole thing off for its publicity value.[78]

Stroheim's difficulties with suspicious authorities sound quite similar to the problems he had on Fairbanks's *In Again, Out Again.* One might think that the two events have been misremembered, but Miller clearly recalled that this occurred on *his* movie.

As the First World War continued to inspire propaganda pictures and as patriotic feelings grew more virulent, Stroheim found himself typecast as a Prussian officer, and his familiarity with military details proved useful. He appeared as the evil Hun in *For France* (September 1917), "handling his role of heavy with an efficiency equaled only in reality." Perhaps as a result of Stroheim's assistance on the film, the photography and lighting effects elicited praise, as did the "general detail of the production."[79] Anita Loos recalled that during the shooting of *For France*

Von used to leave the studio to prowl Fifth Avenue in full make-up, flashing his monocle at every pretty woman who crossed his path. Such behavior mystified passersby, who wondered how a German officer had been allowed to invade the USA in the midst of war.

Peg [one of the Talmadge girls] used to warn Von not to wear that uniform on the street. "You're making yourself a target for rocks!" she'd say. Von would agree, with an enigmatic smile, but he went right on courting disaster.

It seemed obvious that Von harbored the "Prussian" trait of loving to be hated. Yet, on the other hand, we knew him to be as sensitive as a kitten.[80]

Stroheim was also a "military advisor" on *Draft 258,* which was shot in the early fall of 1917 and released in February 1918. Although he is not among the eleven cast members listed in the copyright registration of November 10, 1917, he apparently did have a small part. He received a larger one in Edison's *The Unbeliever* (released in February 1918), although he was listed in the credits as "Karl Stroheim." In the role of Lieutenant Kurt Von Schnieditz, Stroheim suspects a Belgian family of signaling the Allies with windmill vanes, so he shoots a mother and her little son but spares the heroine, who gasps, "You foul fiend!" Later, Von Schnieditz shoots an old lady, then is himself shot by one of the good Germans, as his troops rise in revolt with cries of "Long Live Democracy!"[81] (Such evildoings in the First World War by the military occurred only in isolated cases, but as the war continued, Germans began to receive a bad press almost continually in American newspapers. Ironically, the kinds of atrocities that had been perpetrated by the Belgians on the blacks in the Congo were now attributed to the Germans occupying Belgium.) *Variety's* review of *The Unbeliever* took careful note of Stroheim's character: "German cruelty is driven home forcibly by Karl von Stroheim in the role of a lieutenant of the Prussians. It is true to life in its military bearing. He is the German officer to perfection. So much so that there was a groan and a hiss from the audience at the Rivoli Monday when he committed several heart-wringing atrocities."[82]

Stroheim's influence on the production must have been strong. *Variety* noted that the trench scenes look "like the real thing" and also praised the other sets.[83] The film was made in cooperation with the U.S. Marines, which allowed Stroheim to become acquainted with the American military. Later, in some of his scenarios, he would sometimes have our marines come to the rescue.

One wonders about Stroheim's feelings at this time. He was playing the officer that he had always wanted to be, but he is completely hateful, providing a despicable image of his fellow Teutons. Did some of his self-hatred become objectified in these roles? Or did his resentment about his past find some grim satisfaction by settling old scores? Or was he, in a less Freudian fashion, merely trying to earn a living any way he could? Yet he must have been torn—after all, he was maligning his own Germanic people—for deep within him he also harbored a nostalgia for his childhood world, as his later recreations of Viennese life would demonstrate.

In any case, Stroheim had come a long way in just two years. He had assisted John Emerson and Allan Dwan, had worked with three major stars—Fairbanks, Norma Talmadge, and Mary Pickford—and had established that he could play a convincing Hun. However, for a man who wanted to write—he was already working on some screenplays—and who, we assume, also wished to direct, 1917 was not proving a success. He had not risen from the rank of assistant director; he had only added the profession of actor.

In October 1917, D.W. Griffith returned from Europe, where he had shot miles of film that would appear in *Hearts of the World* and his subsequent war pictures. Stroheim, then living at 152 W. Forty-ninth Street, had finished work in *The Unbeliever* and was presently unemployed. When he heard that Griffith was temporarily in New York, he visited the great man and asked for a job. He no doubt knew that Griffith was working on a big World War picture and offered his services as military advisor and actor. Griffith realized that Stroheim could be of help and, in his casual way, asked him to come to California. Griffith apparently forgot about the engagement, for Stroheim telegraphed him on November 2, 1917: "I have ascertained exact number of costumes on hand of costumer here anxiously awaiting your order to leave." A penciled note on the telegram (now in the Griffith files at the Museum of Modern Art) said that Stroheim should "come at once" and then would go on salary.

Griffith had formulated at least a rough idea of a story while in Europe and had shot scenes in England and a few in France. He now had sets built in Hollywood. He envisioned a German soldier attacking Lillian Gish and, although he rehearsed Stroheim for the villainous part, he finally chose George Siegmann. The decision was based primarily on experience and size. Siegmann, big and burly, was a far more threatening rapist. (In *Blind Husbands,* Stroheim has to stand on his toes to kiss the heroine, a rather ludicrous image.) Lillian Gish recounts that Stroheim cried when he got the bad news—it was the first time she had seen a grown man so moved—and that Griffith put his arms around him and comforted him.[84] Griffith wanted to name the villain "Von Stroheim," but the prototype objected, so the character was instead called "Von Strohm."

Many so-called critics have discussed Stroheim's brilliant portrayal of this main role, thus betraying the awkward fact that they never saw the film. Stroheim appeared only in a minor part, one that is even smaller in most surviving prints because several of his scenes have been cut. Curtiss, who did know which part Stroheim played, claimed that "the superiority and histrionic cunning of von Stroheim's performance outshone the routine work of Siegmann."[85] In fact, Stroheim's is not a totally satisfactory performance. Conscious that he has only a few minutes of screen time, he overacts by including as much heel clicking, leering, and leching as he can. He salutes often, cruelly selects young women to be taken to the front lines, ravishes a girl in a barracks bunk, and smirks lasciviously. Certainly it was Stroheim's imagination that created the orgies in the German barracks, for such events did not occur in the war and were unlike Griffith's usual work. (In script conferences on *La Grande Illusion* in 1937, Stroheim tried to talk Jean Renoir into including such wild parties, but Renoir, who had actually been in the war, dismissed Stroheim's fantasies as ridiculous.)

Stroheim did more than carry out Griffith's orders; he also made creative suggestions. As a result, *Hearts of the World* has a stronger sense of sexuality than Griffith's previous works. In one scene, Von Strohm looks into a garden and leers at the ankle of the seated heroine Lillian Gish. Indignantly, she closes the rustic wooden door. Strohm then places a flower in a knothole in one of the boards and pushes it through with his walking stick—a Freudian touch that seems foreign to Griffith's imagination. In another detail clearly influenced by Stroheim, as the distraught heroine wanders over the battleground, she passes a road-side cross.

Hearts of the World, released in the spring of 1918, was an outstanding success, but it did not help to make Stroheim's name widely known. *Variety's* review of the film listed a cast of thirty people, but not Stroheim. This was no journalistic oversight, for in programs subsequently supplied for the film, the cast list is the same: no Stroheim. This omission did not necessarily mean that Griffith and Stroheim had had a falling out, but rather that his name was too close to that of the main character, Von Strohm, and so would confuse audiences. There is a certain irony here: Stroheim was given credit in *Intolerance,* in which he did not appear, and was omitted from *Hearts of the World,* in which he did play a recognizable part.

Griffith may have appreciated Stroheim's skills on the set, but he made no effort to give him a directorial job, although he did so for some of his other assistants. This may have been at least partly because of the considerable difference in the men's temperaments. Karl Brown, Griffith's assistant cameraman, told me that Griffith "hated his guts, he really hated him. When we were doing the battle scene, the camera was upon about a twenty-foot platform and Stroheim, who was in the picture, came up to the foot of it and had to crawl up the twenty feet to Griffith and he told him a story, a filthy story in which he was the hero and so filthy I won't even hint at the subject, and it so disgusted Griffith with him telling this in public in the presence of several hundred people, that he had very little use for him."[86] It is possible that Brown, a rather unsophisticated teenager brought up on Victorian values, may have reacted to this event more strongly than Griffith. In any case, Stroheim continued to work at the studio.

In the early part of February, while Griffith was still finishing *Hearts of the World,* he engaged a young director, Chester Withey, to make another war picture that would employ more of the European footage that he had shot.[87] Called *The Hun Within* and starring Dorothy Gish, it was not released until months later, in September 1918. This film dealt with "the influences of German propaganda and the effect of enemy work within our own borders."[88] Stroheim, cast again as a Hun, Von Bickel, played only a minor role—he was not mentioned in reviews and was listed ninth in the credits.[89]

In the fall of 1918, Stroheim began working on a script called *The*

Furnace, which he wrote with Roberta Lawson. It told of the twin daughters of an American father and Belgian mother. One girl is executed on the evidence of a German surgeon; the other later marries the surgeon. A reader's report (dated January 11, 1919) observed that even though the surgeon is supposed to be a "good" German and not in sympathy with the war, "this is rather too much to ask an American public to accept. If the author of the story thinks that, in its present form, it would be tolerated by the American public, he has the same colossal and, to them, very regrettable misunderstanding that the Germans had of the American people before the war. The idea . . . is too appalling for words." Stroheim got the message. His next scripts would not be favorable to Prussian types, who would always die in the end. (The public's aversion to its former enemy was such that Stroheim made the lead in *Foolish Wives* a Russian, even though he is distinctly Teutonic.)

Stroheim was never one to give up on his story ideas, and seven years after the end of the war, he reworked *The Furnace* and retitled it *The Crucible.* In the spring of 1925, he submitted a twenty-two-page summary to MGM. An American marries a Belgian woman and settles in that country, where he has three children. The son, Raoul, is a successful artist with a mistress named Mimi. There are also twin daughters. One, Lucienne, becomes a doctor and is engaged to Dr. Kraft, a German physician. The other twin, Angela, gives music lessons. When the World War begins, Kraft becomes a medical officer stationed in Belgium at a hospital housed in a convent, where the twin girls tend to the wounded soldiers. Mimi, resenting Lucienne, substitutes water for medicine and, as a result, many of the German patients die. Lucienne is blamed and sentenced to death. The execution is to be carried out by von Below. Dr. Kraft, however, knows that von Below had brutally killed someone years before and threatens to expose him unless he agrees to a fake execution in order to spare Lucienne. Kraft explains to the nuns that the rifles of the firing squad will be loaded with blanks and that she will fall down and pretend to be dead. However, that night von Below loses at cards, signs IOUs he cannot honor, and decides to commit suicide. But before killing himself the ne'er-do-well attempts to rape a girl at the house where he is lodged and is shot in the head. Kraft is immediately called to operate on von Below and saves his life, but Kraft arrives at the place of execution only to discover that the sentence has been carried out with real bullets. Later, he brings flowers to the new grave, where he meets the dead girl's twin, who scorns him and throws away his bouquet.

When the Germans retreat, Kraft stays with his patients and staff, as the victorious Americans take over the town. Meantime, Mimi tells Kraft that shortly before the execution, Angela drugged Lucienne and took her place before the firing squad and that his fiancée still lives. Kraft learns that von Below, one of the last Germans to leave town, has abducted Lucienne, who had nursed him at the hospital. Kraft, with a pistol and a staff car, and accompanied by some American marines, arrives just in time to prevent the rape. Lucienne still scorns Kraft, regarding him as the cruel enemy and a murderer, but Mimi proves to Lucienne that Kraft tried to save the girl's life. At the end of the film, the couple will marry and live in America, where they will work at a children's hospital.

A comment by one of the readers at MGM on May 11, 1925, was more positive than the original reaction to *The Furnace*. "The theme and symbolism which the author includes as a foreword . . . are excellent, but I do not find them carried out in the story itself. The story is certainly well knit, and the characterizations are convincing, and yet the idea is strong in my mind that it is a director's story. I mean that it is one which would yield well to the weaving of intricate patterns of plot, rather than to beautiful or interesting patterns from an audience viewpoint. . . . For my own part I do not find myself interested in the story."[90] Neither was any other studio, when Stroheim continued to submit his scenario.

Although his writing career was going nowhere, in 1918 Stroheim's portrayal of villainous Huns in *Hearts of the World* and *The Hun Within* brought him some notoriety, although he was still a relatively obscure actor. When Universal decided to make a war film, called *The Heart of Humanity,* Stroheim finally won a leading role. Although the on-screen image he was building for himself was often repellent, he obviously took some grim pleasure in it. He recalled, many years later, the time in 1918 when he was "going with a girl [Valerie] who now is Mrs. Von Stroheim. She wanted to see my picture *Unconquered*. [He meant *The Unbeliever.*] I put on my cap and pulled it down over my eyes and took her to the picture. After the show, she took one look at me and ran away. I finally caught up with her, and she said, 'I don't think I want to go home with you.'"[91]

Stroheim told Peter Noble that there was "a long argument" before he convinced Valerie "that in real life I am not exactly like in reel life." Eventually, his wife-to-be grew used to the fact that, in restaurants, people would throw rolls at him and that he often would be hooted. In a 1919 interview, Stroheim said: "Probably I could never have given such a villainous characterization in . . . [*The Heart of Humanity*] had I not been conscious of the hatred which every member of the cast felt for me. I sensed their antipathy so distinctly that it was reflected in my acting and I put into the role just what they were thinking of me."[92]

The Heart of Humanity, directed by Allen Holubar, shamelessly borrowed plot elements, actors, characterizations, and even the phrasing of intertitles, from *Hearts of the World.* In that sense, it was almost a remake of Griffith's film, and it must have given Stroheim some pleasure to show what he could have done with George Siegmann's part. Siegmann was brute strength, Stroheim more intellectually lecherous and evil.

Although *The Heart of Humanity* was not directed by Stroheim, its content, characterizations, and incidents indicate that it is, in many ways, a Stroheim film. Indeed, the film provides a storehouse of images and scenes that reappear throughout Stroheim's career.

The Heart of Humanity opens in an idyllic village far in the Canadian forest. A more devout place could not be imagined. When the bell for the angelus rings in the church tower, pigeons fly out and the Catholics pray. The emphasis here is on one family, a mother with five sons in their teens and twenties. The older boys are smitten with the heroine, Nanette, the niece of Father Michael, but she likes only one of them. To this humble place in the country comes a German lieutenant (Stroheim), dressed as a civilian with his golf cap and cane. What he is doing there in the north woods we never learn. The heroine goes out in the forest and, holding a flower to her bosom, talks to a cute squirrel up in a tree, which evokes Flora in *The Birth of a Nation.*

Shortly after, a title informs us: "To the little shrine at the full of each moon—Nanette comes to pray." Garbed all in white, she is saying her rosary when the lieutenant approaches and glances at the shrine, then back at her. "What a beautiful picture you make—you almost convert me to your weakness," he says. To her reply, "Weakness? My religion is my *strength,*" he responds, "Strength needs no religion—it is a religion unto itself." He adds, "Might is right, there is no place in this world for weakness." He somewhat familiarly wraps her shawl around her upper body and thus reinforces her similarity to a statue of the Virgin Mary in an adjoining outdoor shrine. As a large spider crosses along a thread and climbs on the statue's face, the lieutenant presses closer to the frightened girl and grabs her hands. His attack is thwarted by the arrival of her boyfriend. The stranger politely offers his rival a cigarette, then lights his own and puffs on it as the couple leaves.

Not long after, the hero and the heroine are married by Father Michael. At an outdoor party, the family members rather animalistically gobble up the wedding cake (not dissimilar to the feast in *Greed,* a curious departure from politeness for such an idyllic family). The wedding reception is crosscut with impressionistic shots of a horseman riding from a distance through a heavy mist into the foreground. He is like one of the Four Horseman of the Apocalypse, suggesting fate or destiny. His message is war. A shot of the saddened Father Michael is followed by a close-up of the lieutenant, now wearing a monocle and flicking ash from his cigarette: a contrast between a gentle soul and a martial one. "You should use your influence," he says to the priest, "to keep your peaceful people from fighting the battles of a distant France or Belgium." The priest replies, "It is God who calls my sons—to save humanity." The lieutenant reacts to this naive statement by flicking away his cigarette and bowing sarcastically.

Although the hero and his brothers leave a month later for the war, the groom has had time to get his wife pregnant. The child is born while the father is fighting in Belgium. Feeling that she is needed more in Europe than at home, Nanette leaves the baby with grandma (an odd decision for a young mother in those conventional, prefeminist days) and becomes a Red Cross nurse.

The film now shifts to Europe. "Shorn of his incognito Lieutenant Eric von Eberhard, scion of the Prussian military autocracy, came into his own." Now in uniform, he is shown lighting his cigarette. When starving Belgian children cry out for food, a load of American milk cans arrives and the lieutenant gleefully empties the containers into the mud, as the children wail. The propaganda does not end here. When our heroine goes out in the field to help a wounded German soldier, the randy fellow cannot contain his lustful nature and, despite his injuries, tries to rape her. Fortunately, she is accompanied by a Red Cross dog, which attacks and kills him. At another point, a German soldier who is firing a machine gun in a trench jumps back and cowers. Seeing this as weakness, the lieutenant kicks, slaps, and then punches him. On another occasion, the lieutenant attacks the Canadian trench, shoots one of the brothers, and then gives the dying man a good stomping.

Not only did Stroheim outdo himself in being hateful, but he also added certain visual details. From the very beginning of his career, Stroheim paid close attention to costuming. In this film, we see him with goggles perched on top of his helmet. (Much later, as an actor, he would often wear a pair of spectacles on his forehead.) Here he also here sports a monocle as well as a mourning band on his arm.

At the conclusion of *The Heart of Humanity,* the Germans overrun a town. Our heroine, who is taking care of children, finds herself in a bombardment and tries to rescue a small child. When the lieutenant sees her running down the street, he removes his monocle, smirks, and then pursues her into a Red Cross building. He tears down the sign and races up to the second floor with his troops, where they break down her locked door and discover her clutching the child. She looks quite appealing, so Stroheim inserts his monocle, adjusts his collar, and enters with a salute. As his soldiers leave, he pretends to join them, but suddenly wheels about and slams the door. Ah, the sex drive of those Huns! He takes off his overcoat, pats down his hair, and begins his merry pursuit. He takes away the baby and rips off the heroine's Red Cross hat and then, grinning, starts to remove her clothes; eventually—in growing exasperation—he resorts to tearing off her blouse with his teeth. The struggling woman and the screaming child compound his frustration. He temporarily halts his attack, picks up the wailing babe, and tosses the child out the window! Seeing this, the woman goes berserk and locks herself in the next room. But of what effect is her hysteria, when his lust is up? For the next few minutes, he repeatedly hammers at the heavy door and finally ends up firing his pistol again and again to shoot off the hinges. Meanwhile, Nanette reacts with maniacal expressions, eye rolling, and wild gestures. If the director was trying to achieve Griffith's suspense, he does not wholly succeed.

At long last, the distraught woman decides to stab herself rather than experience the Fate Worse Than Death. Meantime, her husband, rushing to the rescue, comes running down the street and enters the house. Spotting the lieutenant, he shoots the miscreant and starts banging at the door. Believing the lascivious lieutenant is about to enter, Nanette wields a knife above her bosom several times and, as the door breaks open, stabs herself. No, she does not die; she recovers and later, accompanied by homeless Belgian waifs, returns to Canada and to her own child. What matter that the brothers were all killed, save one? The adopted kids will be good substitutes.

The film reflects many of Stroheim's personal concerns. The ringing bells, the Catholic milieu, the Virgin Mary and the spider, the crosses (red and otherwise), the uniforms, the mourning bands, the abject cruelty—they are all his. Obviously, director Allen Holubar listened carefully to Stroheim's suggestions, and it is these contributions that give the film texture as well as impact. Otherwise it is almost devoid of characterization and, except for the opening and the closing, there is not much of a story. It is just events—bombardments, machine gunnings, explosions—but little to make one care except for Stroheim's repellent actions. Certainly, he would never be less charming. When the film was released in January 1919, its great success thoroughly established Stroheim's reputation as "the man you love to hate." Even so, *Variety* listed him only ninth in the cast.[93]

In a 1943 interview, Stroheim recalled the notorious scene of the baby being thrown out the window. He said that it was a genuine, live baby and that the assistant director was on a mattress out of camera range to catch it: "I felt badly about that. That child screamed madly after the fourth take and went into hysterics on the sight of my gray uniform. I was the villain in the picture, but the real villain was the mother who would let her child suffer like that."[94] In the same vein, the reviewer for the *New York Times,* when the film was released, offered this rather laconic and delicately phrased observation: "One receives the impression, however, that the making of a few of the scenes in which the children appear was not very good for the children."[95]

Stroheim's gift for dramatizing himself was encouraged by Universal's publicity department. An article in the *Ohio State Journal* shows just how famous a movie star he had become: "Erich Oswald Hans Maria von Stroheim, in Archduke Karl's Austrian regiment, member of the late Emperor Franz Josef's lifeguards, makes his most recent appearance on the screen in the cast of *The Heart of Humanity.* This 'reformed' Austrian 'soldat,' famed for his superb representations of

Teutonic kulture on the screen, has the most graphic role of his histrionic career. . . . He was persuaded against his will once again . . . to
typify the exponent of frightfulness by the argument that he was performing, in effect, a patriotic service in delineating the cruel product
of an aristocratic system."[96] Needless to say, Stroheim had not needed
persuasion but rather, in fact, relished his role. After all, the repellent
acts were his idea in the first place.

   Although Stroheim was now identified in the public imagination
as an aristocrat who played the definitive Hun, the war had ended, and
his type of role suddenly became outmoded. What was he to do now?
The success of Universal's *The Heart of Humanity* and his own new
stardom gave Stroheim enough courage to speak to Carl Laemmle, the
head of the studio. There are various accounts of that meeting. In one,
Stroheim, in a new suit of clothes, waits in Laemmle's outer office for
two weeks;[97] in another, he pursues Laemmle as he walks around the
lot; in a third, he "literally" breaks into Laemmle's room in a hotel;[98] in
a fourth, John Drinkwater's authorized biography of Carl Laemmle,
the story differs yet again:

> at the end of the war von Stroheim, an Austrian, was drifting
> about Hollywood with a scenario in his pocket which no-
> body would read. [At] Universal City . . . he was refused a
> hearing, and in final desperation he went to Laemmle's house.
> It was evening, and the family was at dinner. The servant, not
> caring for the stranger's appearance, refused him admission.
> Von Stroheim protested loudly. "I only want to see him for
> ten minutes." It was overheard by Laemmle, who left the table
> and went to the door. "Who wants to see me for ten min-
> utes?" Von Stroheim on the doorstep made frantic efforts to
> explain in one, before he should be shut out, what his business
> was. Laemmle had a theater engagement, but would give him
> ten minutes exactly.
>
> They went in, and talked till midnight, the family being
> sent off to the theater alone. The result of the interview was
> the production of *Blind Husbands*.[99]

This account, printed in 1931, is probably the best version, but in
May 1920, only about a year after the event, Stroheim gave a speech to

the Associated Motion Picture Advertisers, who seemed to have been fascinated by Stroheim's account of his years of privation in America. A reporter summed up Stroheim's speech: "His message to would-be writers for the screen was 'faith'—faith in something, in an ideal, in themselves. It was this quality, said Mr. Stroheim, that with a tinge of romance had pulled him through when he was *vis à vis de rien*—up against it, and had led to his writing and directing his first success 'which,' said Mr. Stroheim, 'I waited two and a half days hanging round the producer's office to land.'"[100] This version is probably closest to the truth, although less dramatic than the others.

What was this discussion with Laemmle like? Stroheim probably slipped into his native language to appeal to the German-born mogul and told him he had a great story called "The Pinnacle" and began to act it out for him. Laemmle may have agreed it had possibilities, but Stroheim did not want to sell the property for someone else to direct. He no doubt told Laemmle that he had helped Emerson, had learned to direct from watching Griffith, had been a vital factor in the success of *Hearts of the World,* and had partially directed *The Heart of Humanity*'s most memorable portions. In short, all of the best bits were his! He surely added that the last film had been an extraordinary success for Laemmle's studio. Drawing on his personal charm and his youthful enthusiasm and confidence, Stroheim brazenly dangled a bargain before the canny Uncle Carl. He would provide him with the story, the star, and the director—and all, he stressed, for almost nothing. Persuaded by Stroheim's eloquence and passion and, as usual, unable to resist "a deal," Laemmle took the gamble, and thus the stormiest career of any director in the whole history of the movies was launched.

3

The Artist

Stroheim was hardly a youth when he embarked on his directorial career in 1919. At the age of thirty-three, he not only knew the lifestyles of two countries but also had been through two marriages, fatherhood, and four years at the heart of the film industry. He also harbored in his psyche a number of ideas—obsessions may be the better word—that would be part of all of his subsequent works.

All major directors (perhaps minor ones, too, if we cared to notice) bring to their films a degree of individuality. The auteur theory is no fantasy. In Stroheim's works, in particular, the man's personality predominates. Certain ideas, techniques, and details run throughout the films he directed, the scripts he wrote, and even the films in which he merely acted. Jean Renoir's *La Grande Illusion* and Billy Wilder's *Sunset Boulevard,* the two pictures in the sound period for which Stroheim is best remembered, are not just films that he acted in but works that he substantially influenced. If Stroheim managed to affect these two great directors, one can imagine the impact of his suggestions and contributions on lesser men. There is no film, however awful or cheap, that his strong personality did not alter—and, seemingly, always for the better.

Despite his austere appearance on screen, Stroheim had a powerful allure, which he employed not only with women but also with men. Under the facade of the exiled aristocrat, he was capable of convincing many people, some of them shrewd and cynical, to provide him with power and money. During his early days in the movies, his fellow extras probably thought him amusing, if not actually absurd. After he proved himself a capable assistant director, and then an effective actor, he seemed to take a perverse pleasure in being disliked. As has been noted, he would stride around in public with his monocle, white gloves, and irritating hauteur—a procedure not terribly wise during the patriotic fervor of the First World War.

Many of the people who worked with Stroheim, even some who acknowledged his genius, did not like him. Generally speaking, the more conventional the person, the less he or she appreciated Stroheim. Lillian Gish remarked to me that he was an "awful" individual, and Miriam Cooper told me the same. In her book, Cooper remembered him as "a foul-mouthed terrible man."[1] However, more worldly people saw behind the mask. Anita Loos, a sophisticated woman and a lifelong friend, felt that Stroheim's behavior was "too phony to be really sadistic. At heart Von was as good as gold."[2] Others also perceived this side of him.

Feminine interviewers (many of them seasoned professionals) often ignored his evil screen image of lecher, rapist, and sadist and found Stroheim a wonderful, sensitive, and sincere man. Nor were they wrong. Even hard-bitten male journalists—those who did not pontificate about morals—were drawn to Stroheim. Richard Watts Jr., one of the few perceptive movie critics of the 1920s, later in life became personally acquainted with Stroheim. His comments after Stroheim's death capture the man astutely:

> It is certainly not my intention to suggest that the outrageousness was a mask and the sensitivity the true von Stroheim. That would be a ridiculous oversimplification of an extremely complex man. The outrageousness was very real but so was the sensitivity. A conflicting dual pattern ran through his life. The scoffer, the cynical and sophisticated mocker of conventional morals and morality, was also a mystic and a deeply religious man, whose Catholicism was no less sincere because it was mixed with a kind of perversely sadistic diabolism. Certainly there was no hypocrisy in the intermingling of faith and cynicism. He was far too brutally frank for any such weakness.[3]

Stroheim may have been cynical about life, but he was passionately dedicated to his creative work. Even as a first-time director, he fought film exhibitors and his boss at Universal when they changed his film's title to *Blind Husbands*. Already he was nibbling, if not biting, the hand that fed him. In the spring of 1919, he had been a penniless actor begging for a job; by December of that year, he was taking out ads complaining about the money-grubbing studio and its gross insensitivity.

Stroheim seemed to go out of his way to be impossible. There was no doubt that he was a gifted scenarist and a fine director with a great eye for composition, lighting, detail, and psychological truth. He could portray great beauty (not just in prettiness, but in characterization) and transmit his perceptions with passion, sensitivity, and perfect detail—and then he would mar his efforts by being so intransigent that the work was ruined. In short, he harbored a self-destructive urge, as if he wanted to spite the world. His films' inordinate length made him as hateful in producers' eyes as his Hun portrayals had seemed in the eyes of the public.

As an actor, Stroheim liked to offend most decent people. Who else would liken his screen self to a spider and present himself stomping on dying men, throwing a small child out a window, and ravishing young girls? Yet he would also impose retribution on his screen self. The lizard that he portrayed in *Blind Husbands* plunges from a mountaintop, and in the later *Foolish Wives,* his character's corpse is stuffed into a sewer.

Eager to appear hateful, and then to be resentful at being hated—this is the essence of the man and the key to his work and his life, a life that was noble and tragic and exasperating. He even makes those who love his films hate him for providing so few of them.

In a revealing and self-perceptive 1935 interview, Stroheim said:

I recognize that, in those days, as now, I had my faults, and made my mistakes. Everybody does. Among my weaknesses from the studio's point of view you might have reckoned my enthusiasm, my sincerity and my thoroughness. I could not take up any subject with which I was not completely enthused, and when I did start on a job I became utterly absorbed in it until I had finished it my own way. My sincerity demanded that I follow my own line of inspiration in whatever I might undertake. Call it pig-headedness if you like—others have done so—but I maintain that it was personal sincerity and a determination that, unless I could put my very best into any particular film, I wouldn't touch it at any price. I never worked for salary and salary alone. I should have enjoyed working equally hard without being paid—if it had been possible for me to live in that way.[4]

Like most human beings, Stroheim was a mixture of the mature and the immature. But unlike most human beings, he was an extreme in both aspects. No director saw life quite as grimly as Stroheim; at the same time, none saw it filtered through a more naive mind. Jean Renoir provides a telling insight into the man: "The ideal he sought to live up to might have been the invention of a twelve-year-old boy; it was an impressive reincarnation of the Musketeer, but this would not have satisfied him. He wanted to resemble the Marquis de Sade. He had dreams of boundless luxury, perverse women, flagellation, sexual exploits, bacchanalia and drinking bouts."[5] In his easy French manner, Renoir here caught more of the essence of Stroheim than many more pedestrian commentators. Renoir saw it all, then gently backed away.

Stroheim's strong personality and peculiar attitudes influenced the films that he acted in for other directors, both early in his career and much later, and he certainly authored all the films he himself directed. True, some of them were based on existing material, but they were so altered that the original stories, at best, provided only a framework. (The only exception was Frank Norris's *Greed,* and even that was expanded considerably by Stroheim.)

Stroheim's first directorial work, *Blind Husbands,* was essentially autobiographical. His other films, which also had deep personal overtones, can be divided into two main subjects: aristocratic life *(Merry-Go-Round, The Merry Widow, The Wedding March,* and the first half of *Queen Kelly)* and proletarian life (*Greed,* the last half of *Queen Kelly,* and *Walking down Broadway*). However, even the "imperial" films include some aspects of proletarian life, and *Foolish Wives* is an odd mixture of both (as is, perhaps, the now lost *The Devil's Pass Key*).

Stroheim's films offer an often unflattering but accurate vision of the human condition, a vision that would irritate many American moralists. Yet an undercurrent of compassion accompanies his supposedly cynical views. He felt sorry for the poor souls (royal and not-so-royal) caught in the net of fate: humans predestined to failure by heredity and environment. However, sympathy never led to sentimentality; Stroheim invariably "told it like it was."

The story of a person of royal blood falling in love with a commoner furnished the main action of *Old Heidelberg,* with which Stroheim had been associated in 1915. This situation undoubtedly prompted his "imperial" films. It first appears in the aborted *Merry-Go-Round,* then in *The Merry Widow,* and returns with a vengeance in *The Wedding March* and *Queen Kelly.* Much of the richness of this material, however, stems not just from the hoary tale of *Old Heidelberg* (novel, play, and operetta), but also from the news headlines from Stroheim's youth.

The tragic story of Crown Prince Rudolph—the most famous scandal of the era—loomed in Stroheim's mind, because he could in some way identify with the protagonist. Rudolph was a freethinking, rebellious, and anticlerical fellow constantly at odds with his conservative father, Emperor Franz Josef. Rudolph married, but after a few years he found conjugal pleasures elsewhere and eventually was ordered to stop his liaison with his new seventeen-year-old mistress. In despair about his future (his father rejected the son's forward-looking political ideas), Rudolph and his girlfriend committed suicide on January 30, 1889, in his hunting lodge at Mayerling, a few miles outside Vienna. (Appropriately, Stroheim plays the character Max von Mayerling in *Sunset Boulevard.*) The death of the heir to the throne was, of course, an immense catastrophe for the royal house. It caused Archduke Ferdinand, the Emperor's nephew, to become the heir presumptive. As a consequence, Ferdinand's own romantic urges and marital choices became open to severe scrutiny. The Austrian court had strict protocol and decreed that only a few highborn women would be acceptable as Ferdinand's mate.

In 1894, the archduchess Isabella had a fifteen-year-old daughter who would in a few years be prime marriage material for the thirty-one-year-old Ferdinand. The ambitious archduchess frequently contrived to bring the two together. The girl did not appeal to Ferdinand, but Isabella's lady-in-waiting, Sophie (a countess in her own right), did. In the summer of 1899, after a tennis party, Ferdinand forgot his gold watch and some trinkets attached to it. The nosy Isabella opened the locket and was shocked to see a photo, not of her now marriage-able daughter (age twenty) but of Sophie (thirty-one). The enraged archduchess ordered Sophie to leave the royal court. Popular legend at the time was that Sophie was sent to a nunnery. (In the second part of *The Wedding March,* the script has Mitzi retreat to a nunnery.)

At first, Ferdinand's affection for Sophie was considered a mere peccadillo. Franz Josef and the rest of the court could not believe that the future emperor would be so imprudent as to marry beneath his status. Everyone thought that he would sacrifice love for duty. (This dilemma is central to all of Stroheim's imperial films.) But Ferdinand was not so dutiful. Secret letters, as well as coded telegrams and post-cards, passed between the two lovers. Franz Josef and his royal family were furious, but Ferdinand remained adamant. What was the aged emperor to do? He had already suffered the despairing Rudolph's sui-cide and was afraid that the distraught Ferdinand might do the same. Reluctantly, Franz Josef agreed to the marriage, a marriage, however, that would be morganatic; that is, the wife would not be treated as royalty and the children would not have the right to succession, a catastrophic situation for the already-beleaguered monarchy. In June 1900, the wedding took place. It rained. The emperor did not attend, nor did most of the court.

Stroheim was almost fifteen when the ceremony occurred, and he, like most Austrians, would have been aware of the conflicts between the archduke and Uncle Franz Josef. This romantic story, with its ele-ments of true love and its political and familial complications, later would be transformed and enhanced by Stroheim. The story had be-come even more poignant and fateful by the time he wrote his scripts, for in the interim there had been the assassination of Archduke Ferdinand, a world war, the collapse of the economy, the downfall of the monarchy, and the dissolution of the Austro-Hungarian Empire—the end of an era.

Stroheim drew on these events and blended them with the *Old Heidelberg* plot when he wrote the script for *Merry-Go-Round.* The lead character would not be Rudolph or the Archduke Ferdinand, but a count (a part that Stroheim intended to play) who was supposed to marry a countess but does not because he falls in love with a com-moner. This situation would later reappear in Stroheim's script for *The Wedding March,* in which the aristocrat would be a prince (played by

Stroheim). The girl would not be a thirtyish lady-in-waiting but a young commoner, and the prince would be practical enough not to marry for love, unlike his brave or foolhardy counterpart in real life. Although the story was changed (money, not the succession, would be the issue, as it had been for Stroheim himself), other elements remain: the intrigue, the family fights, the hunting lodge (in the second part of *The Wedding March*), and even the rain. Stroheim may have seemed like a hardened realist, but he had a sentimental side that found release in these sad and seemingly doomed dilemmas in which practicality conflicts with romance.

A journalist from the *New York Times* interviewed Stroheim in 1920 and asked why he used continental settings. Stroheim explained that he knew "European life, its intrigues and its atmosphere" better than he knew any other subject, and he believed that a director should confine himself to "pictures portraying life and customs with which he is familiar."[6] Eight years later, when Stroheim was interviewed about his forthcoming *The Wedding March,* he said that he got the idea for the film

one day when I was so homesick I felt physically ill. It is not because I do not love my adopted land—it is the natural feeling of one far from home, who remembers those carefree, happy days when life flowed at full tide, without responsibility, flashing past one like the drama in a fascinating story of adventure and romance. . . .

How beautiful were the Viennese women—like magnolia blossom—and the flowers and music and perfume, and uniforms covered with gold braid! I can see it all just by closing my eyes—a panorama of life lived each day at its highest tempo; each morning bursting with all the freshness of a new appleblossom; each night a dream of waltzes, music and joyousness; a Paradise on earth destined to perish like a butterfly at sunset.[7]

In his scripts, Stroheim may have viewed the past in Austria with nostalgia, but he certainly did not gloss over the grim facts of his own youth and his more recent memories of America. The five years from his arrival in New York to his employment in the movies in 1915 were full of humiliation, pain, and poverty: the cheap saloons, the boarding houses with the shared bathrooms, the dirty streets, and the camaraderie of the working and nonworking poor. The "imperial" films may have been partly fantasy for Stroheim, but aspects of those films—as well as of *Greed* and, later, *Walking down Broadway*—also drew directly upon Stroheim's own experience. He learned all too well the life of the lower classes, a life he may have had a taste of in Austria, and presented it with grim realism. Stroheim never forgot a pain to his psyche; he could recollect it with unrelenting clarity.

Some so-called purists argued in 1928 that Stroheim abandoned realism for fantasy in *The Wedding March,* but they were answered quite astutely by Richard Watts Jr.:

> A number of observers, pondering *The Wedding March,* have considered the pageantry, the plethora of uniforms, the romantic gestures, the colorful background and the general air of sentimental decadence in the work and have thereupon indulged in a bit of sneering. What, they say, do you fellows mean by calling Von Stroheim a realist? Why, he is just a devisor of romantic fables for sentimental servant girls. . . . The point of view seems to be that if a narrative is set outside of an urban slum or a drab Middle Western town, and if the characters wear any clothes that might be vaguely described as decorative, you can't accept the story as realistic....Von Stroheim, for all his preoccupation with the trappings of romanticism, is essentially, if half unwittingly, the most complete debunker of the cinema's costumed sentimentalities extant. He may give way a bit exasperatingly to the exhibitionism of florid histrionism and his interests may not be devoid of a certain concern with uniforms and pageantry, but such minor pictorial interests cannot hide a ferociously unsentimental point of view.[8]

Throughout Stroheim's films, he also offered a rather sophisticated view of sex, which stemmed not only from his European background but also from his own libido. Prompted by Schnitzler, and at least superficially aware of Freud, he knew about the sexual dalliances of turn-of-the-century Vienna and about some of the offbeat methods that its solid citizens employed to achieve satisfaction.

Stroheim viewed women with an eye more continental than Ameri-can, an attitude that was radical for its day. Unlike Griffith, his mentor and contemporary, Stroheim understood mature sexual desire within the context of romance and had no compunction about depicting it with great honesty. Griffith, steeped in Victorianism and the sentimen-tal attitudes of his small-town past, was reluctant to deal with some human emotions. Fragile and vulnerable girls appeared in one Griffith film after another, almost none capable of sexual desire. These girls, though "in love," seem wholly unaware of the mechanics and joys of sex. In short, Griffith could depict innocence, but he found it difficult even to acknowledge the concept of a mature, responsive woman.

Cosmopolitan Vienna certainly exerted a different influence than an uptight Kentucky village. Griffith saw sex as rape, Stroheim as se-duction. Griffith's lovers were high-minded; Stroheim's were driven by desire. In short, Stroheim was a realist, not merely in terms of set-tings but also in his awareness of sexual needs, whereas Griffith simply found reconciling romance with physical love almost impossible. But if Griffith repressed such matters, Stroheim bravely exhibited them. In fact, he gloried in them.

In 1923, Stroheim said: "When stories were first visualized through the camera, plot was paramount, and the people were rubber-stamp persons. All heroes had curly hair, heroic noses, arched eyebrows, and dimpled chins. All heroines were sweet and girlish, having a pet kitten or a canary with which to play. . . . Little realism has been seen on the screen, and it is my humble ambition to furnish some of it."[9]

Indeed, in most American films of the time, heroines were inno-cents, passive and unaware of sex—romantic objects with no hint of carnal desire, no urge more compelling than to serve and please. Their opposites were either scheming tramps or exotic femmes fatales—demonic, exaggerated fleshpots fornicating their lovers to abject weak-ness (for example, Theda Bara in *A Fool There Was,* 1915).

In contrast, Stroheim was one of the first directors to create a believable, non-Victorian woman, one who was good but also had physical desires. The heroine in his initial film, *Blind Husbands,* frus-trated by her husband's neglect, is drawn to a dashing lieutenant. She remains virtuous, but even to contemplate breaking her marriage vows makes her a remarkably modern woman, especially in 1919. Later, in *Foolish Wives,* another wife, also somewhat ignored by her husband, is captivated by a count's impeccable manners. The wife in *Greed,* though anxious about the honeymoon night, is not unresponsive to her husband, as both the author of the novel and the director clearly indicate. In fact, she rises on her toes as they kiss and (in cut scenes) remains desirous of her lumbering husband during their first years of marriage.

In Stroheim's later films, he no longer concerns himself with wives—foolish or not—but rather with sweet and virginal women who ultimately sleep with their lovers without the benefit of wedlock. Stroheim audaciously does not condemn them for having "fallen"; they remain "good," even after succumbing to their lovers' desires—and their own. Stroheim's works are sophisticated in their acknowledgment that *both* men and women are sexual beings, an attitude far in advance of the mores of the period. To Stroheim, there is no sin, if there is love.

Curiously, Stroheim often gave his secondary women characters some masculine habits—such as smoking cigars—but never gave any of the men feminine characteristics or ever suggested any kind of male homosexuality (except for a gay tailor in a cut scene from *The Honeymoon*). Chaplin hinted at this many times in his comedies, but Stroheim, the great realist and observer of an imperfect universe, avoided this subject in his catalog of sexual aberrations. If he himself had any such tendency, not unlikely considering the narcissistic and vainglorious heroes he portrayed, it was entirely repressed.

In most of Stroheim's scripts, there is a concentration on a particular woman confronted with two men who, to some extent, echo the conflicting sides of Stroheim's own nature. This polarity would first be seen in *Blind Husbands,* which contrasts a lecherous lieutenant to a decent but inattentive husband. What gives the film interest is Stroheim's shading of this goodness-badness contrast. However self-serving the lieutenant's motives might be, he does pay attention to the neglected American wife by giving her flowers and a jewelry box and caring whether she is comfortable or chilly. Although the husband's preoccupations are with healing others, climbing mountains, and reading himself to sleep, he is not misunderstood by the wife; in fact, he is well understood. Even so, she loves him, despite being taken for granted—and being sexually unfulfilled. *Foolish Wives* offers a similar pair of men: the superficially attentive continental officer with his elegant uniforms and manners and a provincial American husband with few manners (at least of the showy type) who also neglects his wife.

In *Merry-Go-Round*, the conflict is between a count and his plebeian rival who merely lusts after the heroine; the count, at first, also lusts, but then grows to care. In *Greed*, which was based on a novel, the two male leads also fit this pattern: Mac is a good, lumbering oaf, whereas Marcus is mean and vindictive. In *The Merry Widow*, there is a good guy (though passionate) and a nasty, sneaky fellow capable only of lust and greed. *The Wedding March*, in some ways a reworking of *Merry-Go-Round*, again presents the two contrasting males. In *Queen Kelly*, however, the opposites—the royal, young, handsome male and the old, repulsive planter—barely meet. The polarity therefore is muted, perhaps existing only in the dramatic opposition of the women—a mad, jealous queen and an innocent convent girl. Here the conflict is more general: an orderly but hypocritical Europe contrasted to an outpost of civilization in Africa where lust runs rampant, the institution of the convent supplanted by the brothel.

Stroheim's final film as a director, *Walking down Broadway*, returns to opposing males, one a sincere lover, the other a conniving would-be rapist. This contrast also appears in Stroheim's later scripts, such as *General Hospital*, which includes a lecherous, bad doctor and a dedicated doctor capable of true love.

The first two films that Stroheim directed and starred in present a "man you love to hate," similar to his Hun persona. Although the character no longer commits atrocities, he remains morally repellent. Aware of his darker side, Stroheim portrays his screen self as an insincere lecher who clearly is selling women a bill of goods in order to sleep with them. These films reveal that a man can carry on affairs with a number of women at the same time yet have no love for any of them. They are merely bodies to use. In *Foolish Wives*, this character is even capable of rape.

In Stroheim's later work, the contrast between the two male characters is complicated by an additional conflict within the protagonist's screen self. In *Merry-Go-Round*, *The Merry Widow*, *The Wedding March*, and *Queen Kelly*, the not-so-pure heroes enjoy dirty postcards, go to brothels, and seduce women, and yet these flawed but likable rakes, at first only seeking sex, eventually fall in love, almost in spite of themselves. Their ultimate seduction of the heroines is not seen as "evil" because their sincere emotion redeems the act. Furthermore, the women themselves are not distraught that the deed was done.

Stroheim's recognition of his own complex desires enriches the characterizations of his male leads, although his sweet and loving heroines are more figments of Stroheim's romantic dreams than real people. Through these characters, Stroheim seems more aware of his own manipulative charms than of women's. In a sense, he "accuses" himself of being phony, but his egotism does not allow him to see the opposite sex capable of being potentially as selfish and predatory as men, that some of their naïveté and innocence might be disingenuous. There are no female vamps in Stroheim's films. *He* is the vamp.

Other than Frank Norris's *McTeague,* we have no idea of what Stroheim may have read during his youth or his early years in America. In fact, except for *Greed,* which, of course, was based on *McTeague,* his films seem to show few literary influences, apart from Schnitzler's works (some written after Stroheim left Austria). Yet he must have done considerable reading, for he was well aware of the various social and financial and moral aspects of the Austrian-Hungarian Empire's collapse.

Once Stroheim entered the movies, he did not have much free time for reading. He was influenced less by literature than by the films on which he worked. In them, he encountered ideas and situations that he would later develop or improve upon in his own films. For example, the content of *Old Heidelberg* frequently returned in Stroheim's own works.

Other influences from films can be seen in the script of *Merry-Go-Round.* The main source for this, his first (though aborted) epic, was *The Birth of a Nation.* Both works start out in a basically golden age. Then war comes, the idealized world collapses, social chaos ensues, and personal tragedies abound. Each film has a grandiloquent ending in which the god of war (Mars) appears. Griffith shows Mars being overcome by Christ, the Prince of Peace, whereas Stroheim shows a mythological figure looking down on humanity and laughing, an interesting illustration of his belief in fate. Another embodiment of fate appears in *The Wedding March,* with the "Iron Man" perched on top of the Vienna Town Hall, observing the petty drama of mankind. In *Greed,* Mac and Trina are seen crushed in a giant hand of destiny. Such symbolic figures also appear in Griffith's *The Avenging Conscience* (1914), and similar ones occurred in an episode (now cut) in *Blind Husbands,* where satyrs and Pan dance about in a vision.

Not only films, but also the magisterial presence of D. W. Griffith at the studio—with his bold projects, innovative methods, and often quoted opinions—influenced Stroheim. Griffith's desire to be "serious," his concern for having details correct, his use of allegory, his desire to make a long film—all these became an essential part of Stroheim's artistic creed.

Although most cinema books intimate that Stroheim somehow invented realism, this is hardly true. Many films of the teens dealt with romance, but others did not shy away from the so-called grim facts of life. One of the most audacious was Griffith's 1914 production *The Escape,* which hinted at naturalism in its emphasis on heredity and environment. In Stroheim's 1948 BBC reminiscence about Griffith, he recalled the film, which, unfortunately, no longer exists.

The Escape contains a prologue showing the reproductive process of microbes, then observes the careful breeding of farm animals. With humans, however, there is random selection, illustrated by a reckless dance party where mating results from impulse. The effects of such unwise selection are illustrated by the Joyce family. The brutal father turns his gentle dreamer son, Larry, into a deceitful sadist who wrings a kitten's neck. While treating Larry for venereal disease, a doctor advises Larry's sister, May, to leave home. The young lady does, but, unable to find work, she becomes the mistress of a wealthy man. Meanwhile, May's consumptive sister, Jennie, marries Bull McGee, May's loutish former suitor. Jennie gives birth to a sickly child who is crushed to death by the drunken father when he trips over the baby's crib. Jennie becomes deranged and subsequently carries around a wax doll as a replacement. (This detail may have influenced Stroheim, for the mentally ill girl in *Foolish Wives* also carries around a doll.) McGee then sells Jennie to a gang of pimps. Although she is rescued from a life of prostitution, the girl dies shortly after. In the end, an operation restores Larry's gentle nature, and May, having left her wealthy lover, accepts the doctor's proposal of marriage.

The Escape was too grim for its audience. Perhaps Griffith intended to equal the success of various vice pictures then current, but it lacked the glow of "sin" to make it popular and was mostly just depressing. *Variety* summed up its theme: "All-wrongness runs from the father down to the dog, if there is one." The review added, "Why, oh why push so much misery on the screen when no one is looking for it?"[10] Other reviews praised Griffith for his audacity and honesty: "Every character is an expression of an unfortunate heredity, in turn the outcome of environment."[11] The film echoed some of the gritty subject matter of some of Griffith's early work, but it contains almost none of the romanticism or sense of beauty for which he became famous; it showed there was a serious, even deep, side to this Victorian showman. However, he would never touch such a subject again (the overwhelming success of *The Birth of a Nation* in a sense corrupted him and turned his attention to big box office). Stroheim, though, was intrigued by the consequences of poor environment, family weakness, hereditary diseases—in other words, by a world peopled with misshapen bodies and minds.

The Escape (despite its upbeat ending) helped show Stroheim that such aspects of life could be recorded on film and probably encouraged his realistic, naturalistic side. Thus, although no one knows when Stroheim first ran across Norris's *McTeague,* this novel's subject appealed to him, and by 1919 he was already thinking about filming it. Later, when he made *Greed,* there would be no happy ending but instead one of the most uncompromising and depressing conclusions ever shown on the screen.

Stroheim's philosophy of film in some ways stemmed directly from Griffith. Even if Griffith did not always follow his own advice, as offered in many of his statements to the press, Stroheim fervently agreed with the famous director's idea that "motion Pictures must be true to life. The truer they are the greater they are."[12]

After the failure of *Intolerance,* Griffith forswore his crusading spirit, sourly acknowledging in 1920 that the "nine year old mind" of the public wanted "primitive emotions." Still, he felt obligated not to lie to his audience, because "untruth is the most immoral thing in the world." "As long as we go on producing stories which show life to be the definite and invariable triumph of good and the sure defeat of evil, to instill the theory that people either are all good or all bad, to go on filling up people with a completely false theory of existence as it is, we are actually harming humanity. We often hear of the word immoral applied to something salacious, but the real menace of immorality is in an entirely different quarter."[13] Stroheim shared this view and, throughout his work, would try to avoid any "false theory of existence."

Stroheim was not just a glorious but obsessive nut who would go to any lengths for accuracy. Indeed, he did not just reproduce reality; he recreated it and improved on it—in many instances stylizing it. He sought not mere authenticity but truth, possibly through camera angle or through the adjustment of the background or the lighting. When he could use the real thing, he would, but he was quite willing to enhance reality.

In short, Stroheim modified reality to fit his overall plan. In reproducing Cortina d'Ampezzo for *Blind Husbands,* he kept the village primitive by omitting any instance of modernity, such as automobiles. He wanted to create an innocent world that the main character, like the serpent in Eden, would attempt to violate. For *The Wedding March,* Stroheim authentically reconstructed the exterior of St. Stephen's Cathedral, but he transformed its actual dark, Gothic interior into a wholly stylized area of glistening white. Later, that film provides an apple orchard with a barking dog, a sow and its litter, and a slaughterhouse— all quite true to life—yet this orchard also contains such symbolic items as a large crucifix and a fairy coach with cobwebs. Stroheim included enough realistic details to keep his imagined world from looking like a studio set, but he altered reality to maintain the purity of his artistic intentions.

Stroheim may have been a grim observer of life, yet he also had an extremely good, if sardonic, sense of humor. Unlike Griffith, to whom laughter was somewhat foreign, Stroheim could poke fun at his characters and even at his screen self. This was not a sense of humor like Mack Sennett's slapstick farce, but bitter or ironic or sarcastic. Almost always it exists to reveal character, as when, in *Blind Husbands,* the jealous hotel maid sees the lieutenant talking to the heroine and sweeps dust all over them. Sometimes, Stroheim's humor serves to undercut a sentimental moment: in the same film, when the doctor picks up a baby (showing that he loves children and would like one of his own), it wets on his arm. At other times, the humor comes from the fact that the audience knows more than some of the characters: the lecherous lieutenant's full-blown line that a woman is "made for love" only becomes laughable when he repeats it word-for-word to a second woman.

In *Foolish Wives,* as the phony count marches down the street, children mock his military walk behind his back. Later, when he sneaks a look at a disrobing woman, a goat backs its smelly rear end into his face. At another point in the film, when the count bamboozles his maid into giving him her pitiful savings, he pretends to weep by dropping water from his fingers. Even *Greed* has some funny moments: the German father—played by Sennett comedian Chester Conklin—pompously marching his family on an outing, and the miscues during the marriage ceremony.

There are many moments in Stroheim's films in which pretension is undercut by humor. In *The Merry Widow,* the irate king slams his fist on the window sill, then howls in pain as he gets a splinter. The film also has flypaper that sticks to the back of the villain's head and a bowl of soup spilled in the heroine's lap. *The Wedding March* also has considerable humor: squabbling parents throwing pillows at each other, the rear of a horse in Schani's face, a nail that Nicki sits on during the love scene, and the luring of a watch dog with a string of frankfurters.

In *Queen Kelly,* the heroine's drawers slip down around her legs, and there are several humorous moments at a midnight repast. In *Walking down Broadway,* a frustrated old maid falls into an open sewer trench and avers at another point that she is just wild about big dill pickles. There is a rough-and-tumble slam-bang fight on a stairway that appears intentionally both serious and farcical. In a concluding scene, a couple is seen pushing a baby carriage, but the carriage turns out to be full of bootleg booze. In short, all of Stroheim's films contained humor, not just for comic relief to amuse the groundlings, but also for the enrichment of the characterizations. Life is a mixture of comedy and tragedy, often with the difference depending only on one's point of view.

To beginning film students, Stroheim's works might seem disappointing. If they are looking for Griffith-like rhythms, Eisenstein's ideological montage, or expressionistic sets and lighting, they will be dissatisfied. There is nothing flashy or exciting; Stroheim lacks this kind of grandiose dramatic flair. Although he is indifferent to showy techniques, he is no mere recorder of detail, despite what so-called critics have said. Instead, he uses the language of the cinema to tell a story clearly, subtly, and with sensitivity. His later films, in particular, are intricately edited, but the cuts are essentially "invisible." That is, he varies his camera placements so gently that he never distracts the viewer with self-indulgent technique. Everything is subservient to the artistic whole: characterization, milieu, and theme.

To read some critics, one would think that Stroheim merely set up a scene, got all the details right (furniture, costumes, lighting, and movement), and then started the camera running. This view probably stems from Lewis Jacobs's pioneer work, *The Rise of the American Film* (1939), which says that Stroheim's films "are not based on the editing principle but on the piling up of detail within the scenes." Jacobs concludes, "Details, action, and comment were selected and brought into the camera's scope without any changing of the shot."[14] Joel Finler, in his book on Stroheim, quotes this passage and unwisely agrees with it, putting Stroheim in opposition to the montage method and identifying him as a mise-en-scène filmmaker. André Bazin says, "Theoretically one could imagine a von Stroheim film composed of a single shot"[15] (only the French can carry an idea so far). Bazin may have loved his deep-focus, long-take concept of what cinema ought to be, but he is simply wrong about Stroheim.

Critics often seem to read each other instead of looking at the films, which reveal that Stroheim is by no means a director who merely sets up the camera and shoots. He knew quite well how to break a master shot into component units and, in fact, does this far more than most directors of the period. Indeed, he has an excellent eye and, except in *Blind Husbands,* does a considerable amount of cutting. He might establish the setting in a long shot, but thereafter the camera shoots many isolated details, adding up to something that is visually interesting and psychologically intense, although not rhythmic or didactic. He probes space to give us truth.

A very discerning (but anonymous) observer already noted this fact in 1920, regarding *The Devil's Pass Key.* "When Mr. Von Stroheim uses a close-up, for example, it is because at that particular moment spectators are naturally straining to see some character or detail of action more closely, and when he suspends the story's action to introduce what is known as 'atmosphere,' it is because at the particular moment there is dramatic significance between the relation of the action and its environment."[16]

In *Greed,* the cutting may not be rapid as in the Soviet school—nor should it be—but Stroheim constantly breaks scenes into small but telling close shots and, when useful, he even employs metaphorical cutting (as when he parallels Marcus to a cat stalking a bird). The only time Stroheim eschews cutting in the existing print of *Greed* is for a specific purpose: to show Marcus's annoyance with Mac in the saloon when he plays with a coin in the foreground while McTeague remains in view in the background. This shot lasts for a long time to show Marcus's drunken anger growing. The use of close-ups here would have disrupted the psychological intensity. But in other scenes, Stroheim does use close-ups—and many of them.

To illustrate this point, the much-truncated print of *The Wedding March* is composed of 1,560 shots plus 238 titles, almost as many as the 1,716 shots in the much longer *Intolerance*. The cutting for *The Wedding March* might seem invisible because it follows action, but the film is actually one of the finest examples of effective editing from the whole period. In the titleless scene where Cecelia contemplates her marriage to the prince, there are nineteen shots: she looks at her face in a mirror (followed by a tight close-up of her), then glances at her wedding gown, at her engagement ring (which she rotates on her finger to look like a wedding band), at her crippled foot, and at her princess's crown. Here, Stroheim communicates much about Cecelia's thoughts and feelings through the fluid use of editing. This sequence is certainly montage, not eye-piercing but heart-piercing; it truly exhibits the art of the motion picture.

In addition to editing, Stroheim makes sophisticated use of light and shadow to enhance his stories. Reflections fascinated Stroheim. He liked the effect of light bouncing off a sword or a shiny hat, an effect that cameramen and other directors at the time would have considered a blemish. He often makes use of light for psychological purposes. In *Foolish Wives,* an afflicted young girl sleeps in a room illuminated by sunlight filtered through slatted shutters, a visual echo of her dimmed mental state. In the shadowed tower room of that film, the light comes mostly from candles. Even in Stroheim's most "realistic" film, *Greed,* he used pools of brightness and areas of darkness to strengthen the narrative. When McTeague stands outside Trina's window to ask for money, he glows in the moonlight, and when he kills her, light streams in through the doorway and the murder occurs in darkness pierced by dramatic shafts of light.

Stroheim may have enhanced his images and gone beyond reality into a kind of stylization, but he still wanted the impression of reality.

As cinematographer William Daniels noted in discussing *Foolish Wives* and *Greed,* Stroheim was well ahead of his time in many technical respects. "He was one of the first to insist on no make-up for men, on real paint on walls which were shiny, real glass in windows, pure white on sets and in costumes. . . . Everything up to then had been painted a dull brown."[17] Of course, there was a reason for the dull brown; it tended to hide the scratches, which became more visible on light backgrounds in worn release prints. Obviously, Stroheim did not care about such practical matters.

Stroheim also was quite keen on having visual activity, not only in the background but also in the foreground of his shots. There is much of this in the street scenes of *Foolish Wives,* as people not only walk by in the distance but also pass in front of the camera, a procedure rare for its day. This method was explored further in *Greed* when a funeral procession is seen through a window during the wedding. In short, Stroheim's characters are placed in their milieu, not isolated against blank backgrounds. Even in highly personal moments, life goes on.

Sometimes Stroheim also makes use of moving backgrounds. His introduction to the main characters of *Blind Husbands* in a horse-drawn carriage shows the countryside moving by in the background, an almost unprecedented approach for the period. At other times, but only at very significant moments, Stroheim makes use of the dolly shot. The camera moves from a long shot into a close-up of the maid in *Foolish Wives* for the decisive moment when she decides to set fire to the house before her suicide. There is also camera movement in *The Merry Widow,* as well as in his later work. Generally, though, Stroheim's camera was stationary (as in most American films up until the late 1920s), nor did he frequently vary the camera's angle by shooting up or down on someone unless it was a point of view shot. The fancy work of Abel Gance or F.W. Murnau was not part of Stroheim's artistic vision. Instead, he obtained a kind of dynamic intimacy by cutting back and forth, often between close-ups. It was this intense observation and interplay that revealed character.

A significant aspect of Stroheim the artist was his need to make long films. Like his contemporary, the playwright Eugene O'Neill, he wanted to tell a more complete story than was commercially acceptable. Stroheim's scripts were basically novels, not short stories, and they were long because he had an extensive tale to relate. Perhaps he accepted Griffith's prediction (made in May 1915) that "the day will come when, outside of the real gems among the shorter pieces, the long picture, so long that it cannot be shown in a day, will be regarded as the master-piece, and people will see it in installments, just as they read a book a chapter at a time." Griffith envisioned a time when a "man will drop in early in the afternoon and stay until the theater closes at night, and then come back the next day to see the rest of it." He obviously did not concern himself with people who would have to take off from work to see such a film, nor did he worry about the theater owner who could have only one show every two days. These words, idealistic but impractical, must have burned into Stroheim's brain, for a few years later this mad dream would become Stroheim's fatal attraction. And Griffith's other major statement, made at the same time, also would stay with Stroheim: "Motion pictures must be true to life, the truer they are the greater they are."[18] When *Intolerance* proved a financial failure, the somewhat practical Griffith chose to abandon his idealistic and youthful dreams. Stroheim, however, persisted in this noble quest.

One is not sure what Griffith wanted to do with such a long movie, but there is no doubt of Stroheim's intentions. He wanted to explore character, and there was no way that the complexity of the human condition could be demonstrated unless hours of screen time were devoted to in-depth observation. Stroheim was not interested in vast epics, but rather devoted his time to a close examination of personalities and how they interacted with each other and with the environment.

This examination was the result of considerable advance thought and extensive planning by Stroheim, who prepared lengthy and me-ticulously detailed shooting scripts. In this he differed from Griffith, who rarely worked from a detailed script and frequently worked from no script at all. Less interested in the content of his stories than in how he filmed them, Griffith was vitally concerned with multithreaded stories that gave him the opportunity for crosscutting and rhythm. He would time his shots with a stopwatch, then try to shorten them slightly, and redo them. He was more interested in the cascade of images on the screen than in the careful and orderly breakdown of scenes into long shots, medium shots, and close-ups. A Griffith film was a kind of controlled chaos: it had vitality but was at times an arbitrary assem-blage of mismatched shots and jumpy continuity.

Stroheim may have followed the master in terms of trying to tell the truth and in devising long films, but his directorial methods were entirely different. Griffith was essentially an improviser who would figure out during rehearsals what he wanted to do. Often production was halted as he considered a different costume or a new prop or another set. Then days or months after filming ended, he would realize he had forgotten to shoot a linking shot or would decide in the screening room that he did not like the scene and would then reassemble the set and the cast and do it over again. His off-the-cuff method proved costly. Stroheim's method was also costly, but in a different way.

Stroheim was not an improviser, nor was he indecisive. He knew precisely what he wanted. He spent his time trying to achieve what he had envisioned. His scripts were full of closely observed action and details, so that scenes a more commercial director would have given five minutes of screen time ended up taking twenty minutes. Stroheim was not concerned with rapid pace, but with the slow and inevitable accretion of detail.

Stroheim's precise but lengthy scripts included shot descriptions (such as whether the camera was on a perambulator or stationary, whether the camera was close or far away), complete dialogue, and indications as to the use of color or tinting. His scripts for *Merry-Go-Round, Greed* (which has been published), *The Wedding March,* and other films show this clearly.

In an interview toward the end of his life, Stroheim described his scenarios.

I wrote down when they blinked with their eyes. In fact I was . . . made fun of by every producer and everybody that ever had seen the script of mine. . . . They compared it with the New York telephone book. But, which was a great honor to me because other scripts were about, oh, between 60-75 pages and didn't have anything except the master scene as we call it. But I had written my own scenario, I'm the director, and I'm the cameraman. I mean my cameramen don't say 'Now we're going to shoot here.' It's me that says 'You're going to put the camera there, now.' And shoot up or down, whatever it was. So I had a complete shooting script. That is, not a master scene—

thank you—but Mr. N.N. enters there on the right. He makes one step into the room. He stops and sees Miss Vernac at window foreground. Calls out 'Miss Vernac.' She, looking at book, looking up, seeing Mr. N.N. and entering. Back to medium-long shot. Mr. N.N. makes 5 steps forward, back to Miss Vernac. Rises. Medium-long shot. Miss Vernac walks toward Mr. N.N. Medium shot. They meet in center. They shake hands, etc. etc. Worked out with a Swiss watchmaker's precision. That's all it is. It's a watch being made. The mechanism of a watch. If . . . it ticks, it's all right. If it doesn't, well you know.[19]

Unfortunately, Stroheim may have intended to make a wristwatch but he invariably ended up with a grandfather clock.

Such detailed filming obviously took time, and Stroheim devoted not only many days to making a film but many nights as well. He was essentially an evening person, so whenever he could, he would start late and work into the wee hours of the morning. He could not, of course, do this for daylight exteriors, but interiors would almost always be filmed at night, much to the irritation of the crew. His cameraman, William Daniels, recalled that, during *Foolish Wives*, "We would never stop for meals at the proper hour. We'd stop for lunch at three and have an evening meal maybe at ten, and then go back to work. We had very little sleep, and no overtime, of course."[20] The story was no different for *The Merry Widow*, with "the same hectic twenty-hour schedules as before. We had to bring in two crews; electricians and everyone."[21] The same night-owl habits applied to all of Stroheim's films, even his last one, *Walking down Broadway*. In fact, if Stroheim had not had these long working days and nights, he would have fallen even further behind in his schedules.

Griffith had also been cavalier about time, but he did not wear out his coworkers in this manner. Most of Griffith's actors loved the man, his kindness, his gentle talking behind a scene to help create the proper emotional mood. Love, though, is not quite the word describing how actors felt about Stroheim. Some of them suffered much torment as he begged, yelled, and cajoled performances out of them. A spoiled and self-indulgent star like Mae Murray absolutely hated him, but others saw what he was trying to do and shared his enthusiasm and his sensibility.

In a 1988 interview, Fay Wray recalled her first scenes with Stroheim, which ran late into the night.

> Towards the morning when the sun was rising, we rushed to finish because the light was spoiling the night effect. Of course we had the dialogue that von Stroheim had written, and even though it was a silent film the dialogue had to be just right and letter perfect. He forgot his lines and I was able, because I felt so much in the scene and was relating to him, to throw him cues that didn't spoil the scene, we kept going. Well, he was astonished, he was just so astonished that I could do that, and then excited, very excited, so there was a rapport between us that was wonderful.
>
> Sometimes he'd get a little unreasonable and want me to cry, even in rehearsal. I thought that was unfair. I learned how to cry on that film, I think. But there were a lot of lovely moments, and they all seemed so real, everything was so real. I never felt there was any acting going on. When I took the string off the box of candy, von Stroheim said, "When you do that, put it around your neck like you're saving it" and I thought that was a brilliant little thing to do, because if she's a peasant girl she would think of that, and would save the string, every bit of it would be important to her. That was a sweet scene.[22]

Unfortunately, subtle details like this would add to the already gigantic length of the scenarios. Fay Wray perceived Stroheim's greatness even at the time and regretted that she did not work with him in more films. "None of the quality I had in *The Wedding March* and none of the freedoms that were allowed me . . . ever came my way again."[23]

Although Stroheim stressed realism in terms of dialogue being rendered correctly, he also had music played on his sets. The music was intended not merely to overcome background noise on the set but also to create a proper mood for the actors. What an odd idea to find in the middle of the grim Death Valley settings in *Greed* a harmonium and a violin off to the side to lend music to the scene! This was one aid that Stroheim's mentor Griffith seldom used, although many other directors did.

Stroheim was mainly concerned with making characterizations

convincing and natural. He eschewed the wildly dramatic moments and emotional states to which Griffith was partial and allowed no so-called "silent" acting. Occasionally, he may have overstressed a point—such as Schani's repeated spitting in *The Wedding March*—but there was little, if any, overplaying.

Stroheim believed that action is character and character action. For this reason, he seemed unable to present an event without revealing it in full detail. If you saw how a man woke up in the morning, how he yawned, how he had left his clothes the night before, how he shaved, how he bathed, how he brushed his hair, how he had his breakfast, how he dressed, how he had decorated his room—if you saw all these things, you would know him better than if he just appeared in a scene. These details are exactly what Stroheim intended to depict, for example, when Prince Nicki wakes up in *The Wedding March*. They were all in the script, and some stills show that they were shot, but most were eliminated. Although they were expendable, they would have contributed to the film by making unique what could have been merely routine or a cliché. Certainly, we would have known Nicki's personality and attitudes more thoroughly. In short, Stroheim felt compelled to dot every *i* and cross every *t* in his already quite extensive scripts. Then, while shooting, Stroheim would often add even further detail. From this procedure came the extraordinary lengths that transformed his initially long scripts into many-houred splendors that no one but Stroheim and some friends would ever see.

A reporter who visited during the shooting of *The Devil's Pass Key* described Stroheim's working methods. With an orchestra playing the "Je T'Aime Waltz," "Mr. Von," as the director was "affectionately addressed by his company," began staging an episode. "He acted out the entire scene in detail for each one, rehearsing several times until it was satisfactory. He knew exactly what he wanted portrayed—subtle touches, mere suggestions—which carry such weight in the psychology of a picture." He explained that "I try to have the scenes taken consecutively, whenever possible, and the big, crashing final scene will be made last of all, for by that time the actors will fully grasp the undercurrents and depths of the preceding situations. Taken now, they would not feel the true values."[24]

William Daniels, the cinematographer, recalled that Stroheim "was terribly, terribly slow; there would be constant rehearsal; he would select 'types,' too, for parts, rather than accomplished actors or actresses. It was his job (he was proud of that) to be more or less a Svengali, to turn the 'types' into 'great performers.' That took a terrible lot of time, endless time."[25]

Stroheim's methods, when he himself acted, were not much different. A writer for *Motion Picture Classic* (December 1927) observed Stroheim's direction during the shooting of *The Wedding March:* "He stood behind the camera and directed the lighting, had some one take his place . . . while he looked through the lens to get the right angle for shooting—and then stepped in front of it to play his part. He uses no substitute directors."

Stroheim was described as using "Prussian methods in his directing. He is dictatorial—arrogant. A dangerous man to cross!" He frequently lost his temper, particularly at technical problems, such as lights blowing out, but then he would calm down and have "the patience of Job." Sometimes Stroheim would go into an absolute rage about some detail. At this point, his wife Valerie, "always with him on the sets as a sort of steadying wheel for his moods," would try to soothe his ruffled nerves. "He will never work without her." The two would talk about the problem, after which he would then return, the storm over. Although he often slashed into his stars "for failing to get over a bit of action the first time it was rehearsed," he would kindly explain a piece of action to "a bewildered old man among the extras who could not remember what he was supposed to do."[26]

On the hunting-lodge set for the second half of *The Wedding March,* Stroheim was rehearsing a group of Alpine mountaineers when he sensed a flippant attitude. "He swore at them in every known language, and some unknown, until he was hoarse. And then, when they all looked scared to death and expected to lose their jobs, he suddenly turned his back on them and burst out laughing. 'I can't get any madder—they are so funny!' was his explanation to some one near him."[27]

As the years passed, Stroheim became even more meticulous, but in 1927 he defended his methods: "A capable director is not necessarily content with a scene after it has been shot five or six times, or after he has spent the scheduled four days on it. Perhaps one more shot, or another day would give him the desired result; does that not justify his delay? After all, no director enjoys retakes any more than the producer does the additional expense, but if he feels that he has not achieved the desired result, that in itself is assurance something better is possible, and that he can give it. What we want is better pictures, but restraint will never produce them."[28]

Stroheim complained, around 1927, about the problems of subtlety: "'The average audience,' he says, 'is not prepared to exert itself, and remains stubbornly conservative until jerked out of its groove by some startling picture. We are wasting our time if we attempt a call upon the imagination. We have adopted, therefore, this course if we want to stress some subtle meaning. We play the scene in such a way that it shall not offend the mass of the public. But for the benefit of those who bother to use their brains we provide one or two pointers which suggest an additional attraction is there. The idea involves,' he added, 'much careful planning, but it is worth trying. If only the public would make an effort and ask for something more intelligent, we should all have a chance of advancing.'"[29]

Stroheim's statements are not fanciful ones. Perhaps more than any other director, he gave his scenes a density by means of background authenticity and symbols that are occasionally direct and sometimes almost too subtle to find. Perhaps the most remarkable thing is that even his first film reveals this kind of close attention. Who but Stroheim would include at the bottom of the frame (and, in a brief shot at that), the tombstone of Franz Huber, a detail that almost no one could notice—and then hope that viewers would recall the name when, later in the film, they encountered his commemorative marker on the mountaintop? Stroheim has buried nuggets in his films that can be found. And, remarkably enough, they prove to be not dross but real gold. Producers, however, could not have cared less about such nuggets; they were more interested in fool's gold, the glitter that attracted the public.

Producers may have been venal, but they also could be persuaded by Stroheim's imaginative scripts. These men, he noted in an interview conducted at the British Film Institute in 1954, were either Jewish or Irish. Stroheim jokingly said that being Irish "is the nearest thing to Jews, commercially speaking. [*laughter*] Well, I mean it's no reflection on the Jews."[30] Stroheim did have an affinity for these two groups, perhaps because they were feisty and willing to take chances. After dealing with Carl Laemmle, the Goldwyn Company, and Irving Thalberg, he switched to the Irish with Pat Powers, Joseph Kennedy, and finally Winfield Sheehan at Fox. To each of them he promised a great bill of goods, but each time his compulsive nature caused him to ruin the relationship.

Even if his producers were somewhat sympathetic to the long films that Stroheim gave them, they were hamstrung by exhibitors whose main concern was the sale of tickets. The influence of these theater owners was voiced succinctly by Joseph L. Mankiewicz many years later: "Isn't it true that a real-estate operator whose chief concern should be taking gum off carpets and checking adolescent lovemaking in the balcony—isn't it true that this man is in control?" Why should such a person, just because "he owns an enormous barnlike structure with seats in it" have such power and take so much of the profit?[31]

Stroheim may have been difficult with his producers and a hard taskmaster with his actors, but he managed to force or cajole brilliant performances from all of his players. Some of them he had met while working on films (George Fawcett, Sam de Grasse, George Nichols, Gibson Gowland), so he was familiar with their proven abilities. Others he chose for their faces or personalities and attempted to mold them into expressive performers.

In the case of players such as Mary Philbin and Fay Wray, Stroheim was entranced by their innocence, their good looks, and their lack of experience, which meant, in his opinion, a lack of bad acting habits. He would cajole, whisper, scream, and bully them—but to good effect. When he was directing, they were excellent. When he was not in charge, they were less effective. Indeed, Mary Philbin's performance in the scenes of *Merry-Go-Round* that he did not direct is not always very good, and in *The Phantom of the Opera* (1925) she is simply awful, demonstrating every hackneyed mannerism known to the silent screen actress.

Fay Wray, a minor player at Universal, heard about Stroheim's new film and applied for a role. Ushered into his office, she confronted a man "wearing a beautiful white linen shirt, with a very cut-down neck, and no sleeves at all, but he looked elegant at the same time." He asked her to sit down and began telling the story, occasionally glancing at her out of the corner of his eye: "He paced up and down, too, and he would stop in front of me and look at me. Suddenly he offered his hand to me. I stood up and he said, 'Good-bye Mitzi,' and that was it. . . .

I was very much affected and I burst into tears. He found that very exciting, I think, and he said to the agent, 'Oh, I can work with her. I can work with her.'"[32]

Another of Stroheim's inspired choices for a heroine was Boots Mallory in *Walking down Broadway*. This lovely girl, exuding warmth and radiating innocence in her role, might have gone on—with proper direction—to a notable career, if the film had not been ruined.

Probably Stroheim's most notable discovery was Zasu Pitts, a woman most people thought was too peculiar and fluttery to be anything but a comic. Shortly after the completion of *Blind Husbands,* but before it was released, an article on Stroheim appeared in the November 1919 issue of *Picture Play,* which the relatively unknown man must have relished. That same issue had a piece on Zasu Pitts, including some photographs in which she quite closely resembles Lillian Gish. It was this plaintive, yet spiritual, quality in her face that appealed to Stroheim, and he would state many times that Zasu reminded him of Gish. Because he could not use Gish (she disliked him, and besides, she was under contract to Griffith), he chose Zasu and gave her the only truly serious parts she ever had in the movies; in *Greed* and *The Wedding March,* he cleansed her of her nervous quirks and brought out the fine and sensitive actress she could be.

Years later, Zasu was cast as the mother in *All Quiet on the Western Front* (1930), but preview audiences laughed at her presence, and the scenes were retaken with Beryl Mercer. Not long after, Stroheim cast her as a frustrated old maid in *Walking down Broadway* and wanted her to be both pathetic and funny. But by this time she was seen only as a ditzy comedienne, and some of her serious scenes, if we are to believe preview reports, elicited unwanted laughter. By the time she appeared with Will Rogers in *Mr. Skitch* (1933), she was daffy and vague to such an extent that one of the other characters in the film imitated her.

Another find for Stroheim was Gibson Gowland. Stroheim first met him as an actor in *Macbeth* and saw him as a big, lumbering, simple creature. He played the faithful Sepp in *Blind Husbands,* and as McTeague in *Greed* he created one of the greatest performances in the whole history of film. Gowland's career was not a very successful one, less because of his talent than because of his appearance.

For supporting roles, Stroheim created what could be called his stock company, a number of players whom he used to build his peculiar universe. When writing his scripts, he would often have these actors in mind (sometimes their names were even mentioned).

Tully Marshall had won fame in the theater by playing a "morphinist" in the "gruesome" play *The City*, noted a movie magazine in 1917. "His best work seems to be in his picturizations of some weird conception of human nature or distorted characterizations."[33] At times, he played fairly normal people in film—for example, a wizened old fellow in *The Covered Wagon* (1923)—but Stroheim felt him redolent of ugliness and evil, so Marshall played the crippled baron with a foot fetish hobbling around on crutches and afflicted with syphilis in *The Merry Widow* and the crippled, tobacco-chewing, and lecherous planter in *Queen Kelly*.

Cesare Gravina, an Italian comedian and a friend of Enrico Caruso, had a strange, rather ugly face and a predilection for overacting, but in *Foolish Wives* and *The Wedding March* he gives restrained performances. He also had a major role in *Greed* but was cut from the film. He can be seen in *The Phantom of the Opera*, where, without Stroheim to hold him down, he returns to mugging.

Dale Fuller, a not-too-attractive woman whom Stroheim often made uglier by darkening her nostrils, was versatile enough to play the various but thankless roles that Stroheim assigned her: the betrayed maid in *Foolish Wives*, the villain's beleaguered wife in *Merry-Go-Round*, the crazed Maria in *Greed*, the heroine's maid in *The Merry Widow*, and Mitzi's nasty mother in *The Wedding March*.

Maude George was another Stroheim type, one whom he felt embodied corrupt sophistication. She was cast as a scheming modiste in *The Devil's Pass Key*, the "cousin" in *Foolish Wives*, a kind of madam in *Merry-Go-Round*, and a cynical, soured, cigar-smoking mother in *The Wedding March*. In his scripts, he would often refer to a "Maude George" kind of nasty smile.

Stroheim employed an old crone to play the witchlike woman in *Foolish Wives*. This bit player had previously appeared in *Hearts of the World* (1918)—probably selected by Stroheim, who was assistant director—and had a long career as a nameless extra. She can be seen, years later, standing in a soup line in the beginning of *King Kong* (1933) and in the opening moments of *Mark of the Vampire* (1935).

Stroheim, like Federico Fellini many years later, was drawn to odd-looking types and used such grotesques as extremely fat people, midgets, and hunchbacks. More, perhaps, than any other director, Stroheim created a universe in which an arbitrary fate has afflicted its inhabitants. In this imperfect world, people are maimed, misshapen, crippled, and paralyzed. He was preoccupied with showing handicapped people suffering from congenital or acquired diseases of the body, and sometimes of the mind. He was also fascinated by such peculiar subjects as amputations, sexual aberrations, and the consequences of syphilis. The origin of these interests is possibly psychological. It might have stemmed from personal wounds, such as his rejection from the army because he was "weak" and "invalid," or because of his own appearance (of which he was quite critical), or perhaps more broadly because he thought of his less-than-aristocratic birth as a handicap. Maybe, in a less Freudian way, he merely wanted to convey that we dwell in a blemished cosmos where God (or Destiny) helps some people and hampers others.

These afflicted people are not used for sentimental or clearly symbolic purposes but appear peripherally, in the background, to suggest a less than benign universe. In *Old Heidelberg* (1915), the first film in which Stroheim could have had creative input, the father of the girl has lost his arm in a previous war. A year later, Stroheim gives his first clearly defined character (in *His Picture in the Papers*) a paralyzed arm and an eye patch. In *Foolish Wives,* he plays a physically fine but morally depraved count who circulates among people physically or mentally maimed: an armless marine, a hunchback, a witchlike cripple, numerous soldiers on crutches or in wheelchairs, and a simpleminded girl. In *Merry-Go-Round,* Stroheim includes a hunchback, a legless lady, a fat woman, a heroine who (in the script) works in a factory manufacturing prosthetic devices for the war-wounded, and a hero who (also in the script) loses a leg in the war. In *Greed,* we have a man with an adhesive plaster on his face to cover a boil and a boy on a crutch following a funeral. A sign in the saloon-brothel where Mac's father drinks himself to death mentions "Misfit Minstrels" (a scene cut from the film). There are also numerous grotesques who, in the release print, are seen only at the wedding: a fat man and his midget wife, a hunchback, and a woman with severe buck teeth. In *The Merry Widow,* we have the baron's syphilitic sores and *locomotor ataxia* (necessitating the use of crutches) and a one-eyed doorkeeper, also on crutches. We see in *The Wedding March* a leg-wounded heroine and a permanently lame heiress; in the film's second part, a hunchback attacks Mitzi, and Cecelia becomes paralyzed from a spinal wound. In *Walking down Broadway*, a dog has an injured leg and countless cripples hobble about the street. In Stroheim's script for *The Devil Doll*, a witchlike woman uses a crutch, and his script for *General Hospital* contains many morbid references to amputations.

During the latter part of his life, when he acted in other directors' films, Stroheim created for himself a whole raft of ailments. His most famous physical problem was the injured spine necessitating a neck brace in *La Grande Illusion*, but there are many other afflictions. In *Three Faces East*, he first appears hobbling on two crutches. He has paralyzed legs in *Ultimatum*, an infected ear in *Les Disparus de Saint-Agil*, a severely disfigured face in both *Menaces* and *La Foire aux chimères*, and a bad leg in *The Lady and the Monster*. In *Sunset Boulevard*, he tried unsuccessfully to convince Billy Wilder to allow him to have a limp.

Besides the problems of the body are problems of the mind. There is the retarded boy at the Alpine hut in *Blind Husbands*, the counterfeiter's simpleminded daughter in *Foolish Wives*, the slightly "touched" Maria in *Greed*, and the dim-witted yet lustful guide who leads Mitzi up the mountain in *The Honeymoon*. In *Queen Kelly*, the queen is mad as well as oversexed; in *Walking down Broadway* we have a pathologically jealous, frustrated, and perhaps lesbian character played by Zasu Pitts.

Stroheim himself seems to exhibit a rather perverse interest in feet. Steuben eyes Mrs. Armstrong's ankles in *Blind Husbands;* in *Foolish Wives,* the American wife sprains her ankle, which Karamzin bandages; in *Merry-Go-Round,* the villain steps on the heroine's foot and Franz Josef (in a cut scene) washes the feet of beggars on Holy Thursday; in *Greed* (in a cut scene), Poppa Sieppe soaks his feet in a pan of hot water and a poster mentions "Werner's Notacorn." In *The Merry Widow,* we have a rather strong concentration on Mae Murray's feet, the baron's pronounced foot fetish, and a cut scene of the king attending to his corns; in *The Wedding March,* Cecelia has a lame foot, her father is a manufacturer of corn plasters, and the heroine uses a crutch after hurting her foot.

Stroheim also pays close attention to women's lingerie. In *The Merry Widow,* the hero plays with the heroine's undergarments in a scene in her dressing room (now cut). We see drawers hanging on a washline in *The Wedding March,* and a convent girl loses her underpants in *Queen Kelly.* In *Walking down Broadway,* the jealous Zasu accidentally burns a hole in her slip. In *Three Faces East*, Stroheim handles the garments he takes from the heroine's suitcase, in *Macao* he dangles a woman's intimate clothing, and for *Sunset Boulevard* he suggested washing out Norma Desmond's underclothing, an idea rejected by Billy Wilder.

Stroheim's emphasis on such details could have been just a director-actor's means of enriching characterization. To Billy Wilder, however, Stroheim seemed to be quite serious: "This obsession with foot fetishism, underwear fetishism, other sexual perversions which his pictures are filled with, was the *real* Stroheim. He loved to go into details about his own fetishes and how he had satisfied them. The movie he should have made was an adaptation of Krafft-Ebing's *Psychopathia Sexualis.*"[34] Was the worldly-wise and skeptical Billy Wilder conned by these confessions? Or did Stroheim really have such obsessions in his life? It is hard here to discern the truth. Perhaps Stroheim pretended to have them in the same way he created his aristocratic and military background—in this case, to make his persona more intriguing to his impressionable younger colleague? Certainly, he never let a fact interfere with his legend.

Another of Stroheim's major interests, as revealed in his films, was religion. Throughout his work runs a strong vein of Roman Catholic references, with which he counterpoints man's lowly actions to a pure and ideal universe.

In the imperfect world that Stroheim depicts, a world of disappointments, betrayals, and quirks of fate, religious holidays add a sardonic contrast. In *Blind Husbands,* the main characters arrive in the village on the Feast of the Transfiguration. In the script of *Merry-Go-Round,* the emperor performs the ritual of the washing of the feet of the poor on Holy Thursday. In *Greed,* Trina first shows her miserliness as she purchases lilies on Easter Sunday; and in *The Wedding March,* the romance begins during a Corpus Christi procession.

Christmas, in particular, fascinated Stroheim. Whenever he could, he had the most depressing events occur during this season. In *Greed,* Trina is murdered on Christmas eve (it occurred a few days later in the book), in *The Merry Widow,* the heroine (in the script) spends the holidays with her semicomatose husband, and in *Walking down Broadway* as well as in the script for *General Hospital,* dispiriting events provide an ironic contrast to the merriest of seasons. (Christmas even enters into *La Grande Illusion* but, for a change, not ironically.)

Besides these Christian holidays, Stroheim was fascinated by religious imagery. There is a question about whether this imagery has true spiritual meaning for him, or whether he uses it mainly for visual interest. Whatever the reason, it certainly is pervasive. An evil deed is merely an evil deed in most films, but Stroheim contrasts such an act with something that is good, therefore adding a piquancy to the action. In short, Stroheim was fascinated by the contrast of the sacred and the profane. In *The Heart of Humanity,* Stroheim's character tries to seduce the heroine near a statue of the Virgin Mary, which provides ironic reverberations. Another attempted seduction, in *Blind Husbands,* takes place literally at the foot of a cross; there are also crucifixes in the rooms at the inn and the mountain hut, along with religious posters. In *Foolish Wives,* a cross hangs over the retarded girl's bed, and a large crucifix is affixed to the wall outside her bedroom. In *Merry-Go-Round,* religious images hang on the wall in the dying mother's room. The script of *Greed* has Marcus place two pins on the railroad tracks to make a tiny cross, over which the children later squabble. In *The Merry Widow,* the private chamber in the house of assignation is replete with religious artifacts and, at significant moments, large crosses can be seen in the background. *The Wedding March* contains a statue of Christ that hovers over the garden. The girl's room in *Walking down Broadway* contains a cross and a reproduction of Raphael's *Madonna and Child;* later, the doctor's office contains a copy of DaVinci's *The Last Supper.*

Churches figure strongly in Stroheim's films. Their first use occurs in *The Heart of Humanity,* in which a village church and its bells establish the idyllic background. The setting is used more ironically in *Blind Husbands,* where (in a scene now cut but in the original release) Steuben kisses the wife in a church tower. In *Foolish Wives,* the villa, with its braziers, paintings, and crosses, so resembles a church that the simpleminded girl crosses herself when she enters. Trina first reveals her miserliness, in *Greed,* in front of a church. The script of *Merry-Go-Round* contained a confession scene that reappeared in *The Wedding March.* Also in that film, the parents' mercenary choice of Cecelia as mate for Nicki is made even more horrendous because it occurs in a church. *The Merry Widow,* too, contains a number of church scenes. In *Queen Kelly,* the girl prays to the Virgin Mary in a chapel and later is abducted from this religious setting. Incidentally, in *La Grande Illusion,* Stroheim convinced Renoir to place Rauffenstein's quarters in the fortress's chapel.

In almost all of Stroheim's films, there are shots of ringing church bells (*Blind Husbands, Greed, The Merry Widow, The Wedding March*). In one of *Greed*'s cut scenes, the church bell of St. Patrick's peals out on Christmas morning, right after the murder of Trina.

Stroheim was also fascinated with nuns, or with making his heroines resemble them. When McTeague puts a white cloth over Trina's head in the dental chair, she appears nunlike, which makes McTeague's act of kissing the anesthetized girl even more profane. Even in *The Merry Widow*, there is a shot of Mae Murray comforting the wounded Danilo, with a white covering on her head and a scarf around her chin that resemble a nun's habit. Mitzi looks angelic in many of her scenes in *The Wedding March*, and later Cecelia is dressed in white (suggesting a nunlike purity), an appearance reinforced by her rather churchlike bedroom. Cecelia's wedding habit (a white headdress, gown, and band across her forehead), provides a further religious overtone. In *Queen Kelly*, the girl's school is presided over by nuns. In *Walking down Broadway*, the Zasu Pitts character originally was filmed in a hospital attended by nuns and a priest. The nunlike nurse who attends Boeldieu's death in *La Grande Illusion* quite possibly stemmed from Stroheim's suggestion.

There are also numerous men of the cloth. The priest in *The Heart of Humanity*, who has a more central role than usual for a war film, may have been a Stroheim contribution. A monk interferes with the seduction in the witch's hut in *Foolish Wives*, and in *Greed* Marcus and McTeague sit at the Cliff House in front of a picture of a jolly monk. A priest hears confession in *Merry-Go-Round* (and in its virtual remake, *The Wedding March*), a priest in *The Honeymoon* gives the last rites to Cecelia, a black priest officiates at the interrupted wedding in the African section of *Queen Kelly*, and a priest gives the last rites to the dying Zasu Pitts in *Walking down Broadway*. Later, in films made in France, Stroheim several times appeared in monklike outfits.

Stroheim, in all his films, presents a curious mixture of religion and superstition. He seemed to adhere to Catholicism, but perhaps it was only the trappings: the ritual, the music, the incense. He did have some belief, for in letters to his wife Valerie and his son Josef during the 1940s, Stroheim made frequent reference to God and said that he would pray for them. When he sent a Christmas present of a gold brooch and a "lapel-hanger" to Valerie in 1942, each of which contained a pin, he revealed a belief in the old superstition that if you give something sharp to someone, you must receive coins in exchange. "Please," he wrote, "send me *at once* 2 cents in pennies for the 2 pins."[35]

In his films, however, Stroheim's use of religion is perhaps more an example of superstition than genuine faith. Certainly, there is no doubt that he was superstitious. Throughout his life, he was a strong believer in fate and, perhaps as a consequence, also believed in fortune-tellers. He regularly went to "psychists" and made major career moves according to their advice. In his letters, he often cited their predictions and their accuracy. He strongly believed that there is some kind of destiny that shapes our lives, a belief that runs throughout his scripts. He felt that somehow man was predestined, squirm and twist as we humans may.

Stroheim's palm print appeared in an odd book called *Cheiro's Complete Palmistry*, along with those of many notable people, among them Mary Pickford, Lillian Gish, and Sergei Eisenstein. The author's analysis (made in the early 1930s) showed that Stroheim had "a strong and independent nature that could stand little or no control by others." This insight could have come from reading the newspapers. However, the next prediction seemed remarkably correct.

> It will be noticed that the line of fate or Destiny appears to be stopped or arrested by the head line at a little past the center of the career.
>
> Shortly after the change shown in the centre of the hand it will be noticed that a new line of fate appears, and with the excellent line of Sun continuing to the base of the third finger, there is no doubt whatever that Erich von Stroheim's remarkable talents will gain for him renewed recognition and success in the world of pictures.[36]

Stroheim was entranced by the number thirteen or permutations of it. Even in an early interview, at the time of *Blind Husbands*, he mentioned that as a lifeguard at Lake Tahoe he had the unlucky number 313.[37] That there were enough lifeguards to warrant that number seems unlikely; Stroheim was already enhancing reality. Whenever a number was used in a film, Stroheim would employ three or thirteen if he could. In *His Picture in the Papers* and *The Social Secretary*, certain rooms and addresses contain these numbers. In *Blind Husbands*, the character played by Stroheim stays in room thirteen at the inn and in room three at the Alpine hut. He dies on the thirteenth. In *Foolish Wives*, a page from a book by "Erich von Stroheim" is number 130 and the night in the witch's hut is the thirteenth. In the uncut *Greed*, when McTeague learns (from a letter written on Christmas Eve) that his mother died on December 23, Stroheim's script notes that McTeague glances at a calendar and sees that it is the twelfth. The next day—the thirteenth—he starts on his new life and meets the man who will destroy him.[38] On other thirteenths, Mac encounters Trina and, much later, learns of the end of his dental practice. Even the street numbers in *Greed* have threes in them. In *The Merry Widow*, the wedding (in the script) is to take place at 3:30. This fascination with three or thirteen also appears in films Stroheim acted in. In *Crimson Romance*, for example, he shoots down thirteen planes.

Stroheim also includes many other aspects of superstition. In *Foolish Wives*, at the gaming tables, he rubs the hump of a hunchback for luck. In *Greed*, as the wedding ceremony begins, McTeague trips on the threshold, a bad sign. In the second part of *The Wedding March*, a carriage wheel falls off the honeymoon coach, which to Stroheim is an ill omen, as is Cecelia's tripping on the threshold. After *Queen Kelly*'s hero spills salt, he throws some over his shoulder; years later, in Billy Wilder's *Five Graves to Cairo*, Stroheim, as Rommel, does the same. In James Cruze's *The Great Gabbo*, Stroheim includes such harbingers of bad luck as hats on the bed and walking under ladders.

Besides superstition, Stroheim used animals to enrich characterizations and, sometimes, for symbolic purposes. In this sense he again followed in the footsteps of Griffith, who employed animals as a kind of visual shorthand to reveal personality. In *Blind Husbands*, Mrs. Armstrong fondles a dove (as Lillian Gish had in *The Birth of a Nation*), and the faithful Sepp is linked with his equally faithful dog. A frog lends a touch of the bizarre to the witch's hut in *Foolish Wives*, and a goat provides an appropriate odor, as well as pagan overtones. In a display of marksmanship, the "count" shoots live pigeons, and when a black cat crosses his path, he kills it with his cane. Later, his body and the cat's are both thrown into a sewer. In *Greed*, a black cat is associated with McTeague's murder of Trina. In the opening of the film, Stroheim shows Mac tending a wounded bird, an indication of Mac's kind nature, an act that enriches his later affection for his canary. In the uncut version, Marcus kills puppies, dumping their bodies in a garbage can, and torments seagulls by tying two pieces of bread to one string so that they end up fighting each other.[39] Notice, too, the presence of a Gila monster and a rattlesnake in the Death Valley scene. In *The Merry Widow,* in a cut scene, Mirko puts hot pepper on a bone, which he gives to a hungry dog. In *Walking down Broadway,* a lonely and frustrated woman has a pet turtle, a creature as hopeless as she, and Jimmy's rescue of a wounded dog shows his kindness and sensitivity.

Animals may be useful in establishing character, but Stroheim was not interested only in people but also in the society in which they lived. If there is an underside to humans, there is also an underside to the world they inhabit. If there are beautiful vistas, there are also swamps. Civilization has its elegant moments and seems orderly, but there is also a necessity for sewers, for the cleaning of streets, for ambulances, for hospitals, and for prosthetic devices.

In a world balanced between good and evil, between love and hate, and between beauty and ugliness, Stroheim certainly does not avoid the unpleasant details. In fact, he relishes such ugliness and includes it whenever he can. In *The Social Secretary,* his character stands by a smelly garbage can. *Foolish Wives* contains a swamp and a filthy hut, and at one point Karamzin brings his handkerchief to his nose because of the odor coming from a sewer being cleaned. At the end of the film, his corpse is thrown into the same sewer and, in scenes at least planned, it floats into the harbor, where, amid the garbage, it is devoured by a giant octopus. In *Greed,* Mac courts Trina near a sewer, with a dead rat in attendance. *The Merry Widow* includes a mud puddle and some wallowing pigs, and at the end of the film, Mirko falls into a puddle in the street and dies. In *The Wedding March,* there are more pigs and an attempted rape in an abattoir. Even in *Walking down Broadway,* the Zasu Pitts character falls into a sewer trench.

Stroheim also uses garbage trucks and street-cleaning devices. In cut scenes from *Greed,* a garbage truck passes by in the midst of a gentle love scene. In *The Merry Widow,* a street-cleaning truck removes the offal thrown from the windows during a long night's orgy, and in the original opening of *The Wedding March,* a garbage truck picks up empty champagne bottles and other refuse from Prince Nicki's residence. In such scenes there is sometimes humor, but always they demonstrate that life has its ugly side.

Stroheim's world is full of actual or impending disaster. For such a universe, society has created emergency services, in which Stroheim showed an unusual interest. As early as *Blind Husbands*, army troops serve as a rescue team. In his subsequent works, Stroheim seems to relish fire trucks and ambulances, as well as the means by which they are summoned. *Foolish Wives* includes a call box and also shows in some detail how the firemen scramble down the pole, hurry into the trucks, and set up emergency nets. In the script of *Merry-Go-Round*, a character walks past the fire department.[40] Later, also in cut shots,[41] there is a police call box, an ambulance going down the street, stretcher bearers carrying a body, and then the vehicle driving away. The death of Maria in *Greed* prompts several shots (now cut) of an ambulance, as well as of the doctor and an orderly. In *The Wedding March,* when a horse hurts the heroine, a police call box is used and an ambulance arrives to take her away. In *Queen Kelly,* the hero sets a fire and calls in an alarm so that he can abduct the heroine, and the original finale of *Walking down Broadway* featured an explosion, fire trucks, a raging conflagration, and an ambulance that takes an injured woman to the hospital.

Even films that Stroheim only acted in include his obsessions. In *The Lost Squadron,* we have a fire truck and an ambulance. There is a longish scene with an ambulance in *Crimson Romance,* another one in *Fugitive Road,* and even the first shot of *The Crime of Dr. Crespi* occurs in an ambulance. One can imagine Stroheim sitting next to the director, trying to convince him to add an ambulance or a fire truck. Even at the end of Stroheim's sequence in *Pièges,* there is a scene that includes a fire alarm box.

Stroheim also had a peculiar interest in that lowly plant the geranium, which seems to have no profound symbolic meaning but merely to represent a bit of affordable beauty in a drab universe. In *Intolerance,* Griffith had a brief scene of Mae Marsh caring for what is termed her "hopeful geranium." Whether this was Griffith's idea or Stroheim's cannot be ascertained, but the plant reappeared in many of Stroheim's own films. In *Foolish Wives,* a geranium is on the simple-minded girl's window sill. Several of these plants appear in the cut portions of *Greed:* Miss Baker is first seen with one, and later, when Maria and Zerkow's child dies, Maria uses a geranium plant for a funereal flower. Others can be seen in the jail cell in *Queen Kelly,* in a love scene in *Walking down Broadway,* and most notably in two important scenes in *La Grande Illusion*. Stroheim also added this flower to several of his scripts (one is in the blind mother's apartment in *The Devil Doll*) and to films he acted in. (There is a verbal reference to one in *Sunset Boulevard*.)

Stroheim, the meticulous observer of detail, also concerned himself with food and drink, for to him, what was consumed and how it was eaten revealed character, rank, and attitude. His very first written work, *In the Morning,* includes an elaborate recipe for a punch. In *Foolish Wives,* the superficially polite Count Karamzin crudely dumps food on his plate; during *Greed's* wedding feast, the characters eat like pigs, except for the dainty minister. In *The Merry Widow,* an elegant feast contrasts ironically to the hero's lustful behavior. The heroine of *The Wedding March* receives a fancy box of chocolates, whereas Schani eats a piece of raw meat before attempting to rape her. *Queen Kelly* contains both a big banquet and an intimate, yet elaborate, seduction repast. In *Walking down Broadway,* the characters eat in a Chinese restaurant and later send out for sandwiches. When Stroheim had to return to acting, he embellished his roles with details about both how people eat and what food they order. In *The Great Gabbo,* he telephones a restaurant for an elaborate meal, and in *La Grande Illusion,* he orders a complicated fruit punch.

One of Stroheim's more specific concerns was coffee and its quality and temperature. He complains about coffee in his first talking film, *The Great Gabbo,* and from then on he comments on it whenever he can. For example, in *La Grande Illusion,* he says that it tastes like "liquid manure" or "slop." Coffee is also referred to in *Five Graves to Cairo, The Lady and the Monster,* and other films. Stroheim was equally concerned with champagne, which appeared in his imperial films and in several pictures that he only acted in, including *The Great Gabbo, Friends and Lovers,* and *As You Desire Me.*

Stroheim always sought to give himself screen "business," and for that there was probably no better prop than the cigarette. In his own films and those directed by others, he is almost always handling a cigarette—lighting it, puffing it, flicking the ashes from it, or otherwise fussing with it. These actions enhanced his characterization, while allowing him to stay on the screen longer and perhaps to steal the scene;

they also gave the otherwise self-conscious actor something physical to do.

Stroheim, even when he played a villain, often wore a black mourning band to indicate that there was perhaps another side to him and that even such a person could feel sorrow. We see it in some of his Hun roles, specifically *The Heart of Humanity,* and it appears frequently in such subsequent works as *Foolish Wives, Three Faces East, Crimson Romance, La Grande Illusion, Mademoiselle Docteur,* and *So Ends Our Night.*

Along with the mourning bands, Stroheim often wore white gloves. *Foolish Wives* shows them to advantage by contrasting Karamzin's easy grace with the awkwardness of the American husband, who has trouble even pulling off his gloves. White gloves never seem to leave Stroheim; they are featured in *La Grande Illusion,* where both Boeldieu and Rauffenstein wear them, and at one point there is a mention that the white glove supply is dwindling. In *Macao,* Stroheim complains that his servant does not wear them. In *Sunset Boulevard,* Stroheim wears them—even while playing the organ!

Stroheim's gloves were usually accompanied by a cane, and part of his "acting clothes" was his monocle. Stroheim seemed to have been born with it; he certainly was the most famous user of that ocular device. In fact, he and his monocle were almost synonymous. There was no one in all Hollywood who could equal this master of the monocle or could wear it with such aloof confidence.

His unique appearance on screen was not just a trick necessary for his profession. When, in 1909, the young immigrant baptized himself von Stroheim, he began a lifelong career, both off screen and on, of playacting. An essential part of this new role demanded a facade that he maintained throughout his life. This image hid a man who was well aware that he was not tall and handsome, not a Christian, and, at least in his accent, not an aristocrat with cultured speech. But he could overcome these drawbacks by his "acting clothes" and his somewhat assumed manners. One can understand how difficult it was for him to appear in the early 1940s on stage in *Arsenic and Old Lace,* for which he had to forswear all his classy allure and wear a shabby suit. This role was too close to what he could have been, were it not for his lucky arrival in the movies.

All of the obsessions, mannerisms, and motifs that run through Stroheim's work might seem repetitive or excessive or even ridiculous, but they enrich both his films and those of other directors, giving them a density that makes them more meaningful. Indeed, it might well be that his long career as an actor was sustained because of his concern with such details. Audiences may not have known specifically what he was doing, but the subliminal effect gave his roles vitality. He was not a character actor, one who could lose himself in a role, but he was a character! And that made all the difference.

An unsympathetic viewer of Stroheim's directorial work could say that much of it was repetitive. He was not the only Hollywood artist to be so accused. In 1965, Orson Welles, another doomed genius of the cinema, responded to a claim that he repeated himself in his film *The Trial:*

> Exactly, I repeated myself. I believe we do it all the time. We always take up certain elements again. How can it be avoided? An actor's voice always has the same timbre and, consequently, he repeats himself. It is the same for a singer, a painter ... There are always certain things that come back, for they are part of one's personality, of one's style. If these things didn't come into play, a personality would be so complex that it would become impossible to identify it.
>
> It is not my intention to repeat myself but in my work there should certainly be references to what I have done in the past.[42]

In much the same way, Stroheim's films, diverse as they may be, have their similarities. And Stroheim's personality is identifiable. Yet sometimes, the more we know, the less we know. Who was the real man beyond these glorious but mutilated works, this rich texture of details and obsessions?

Josef von Sternberg, another complex man, was, by his arrogance, his love for visual beauty, and his intransigence, also doomed by the Hollywood system. He had conferred with Stroheim in 1927 when Paramount gave him the thankless task of trimming *The Wedding March* to manageable size. In 1968, Sternberg wrote about his impressions of his fellow "von" and noted "his proud bearing, his aloof composure, his hands always in clean gloves. . . . But this is not the man I got to know. Alone with me, his voice was lachrymose, his eyes wet with an occasional tear, and his bearing downcast and hopeless. He spoke German with me, his mother tongue, and it was the voice of a Viennese cabdriver. But this explains nothing. It certainly fails to give a clue to his work."[43]

But it *does* give a clue to his work. Stroheim, beneath all his bluster and arrogance and playacting, was at heart a sensitive, sincere, and wholly dedicated man. Torn by the conflicting sides of his personality, he was bedeviled by fears and anxieties, a man who tried to make something lasting in an ugly, ephemeral world. To some he was a dirty-minded, mean, and arrogant creature, happy to rain on everyone's parade. To others he was a softie, a sentimental, hardworking artist whose only desire was to create out of reality a kind of beauty beyond mere prettiness. In this blighted universe, the only beautiful thing was love, a euphoric state complicated and beset by lust and selfishness. Stroheim could imagine a paradise—a world before the fall of man, an Eden—which he hinted at in the garden scenes of *The Wedding March*. He could envision a perfect love, even though he himself, as well as mankind, could never hope to attain it fully. Perhaps art, the creation of beauty out of truth, is man's only redeeming feature. A line from *King Lear* that Stroheim used in the aborted *Merry-Go-Round* and later revived in *The Wedding March*—and finally omitted from both—could well sum up his own dedication to the art of the film: "Upon such sacrifice . . . the gods themselves throw incense."

4

Blind Husbands

After Carl Laemmle said "I do" to Stroheim's proposal for *Blind Husbands*, the fledgling director devoted all his time to smoothing out his shooting script and consulting with the set department. He had innumerable suggestions as to how the "village" ought to look. Although the exterior set was rather modest, it was a permanent one that would remain on the Universal lot for a number of years. Stroheim tried to make the interiors authentic by paying close attention to details: carved chairs, tablecloths, menu holders, posters on the walls, other furniture, and even the way the electric wiring was attached to the wall.

Stroheim assembled his cast, choosing Sam de Grasse, who had played the grim and cold industrial overlord in the modern story of *Intolerance,* for Dr. Armstrong, the husband. He was the perfect embodiment of a WASP's rectitude and restraint. Francelia Billington, who took the part of Margaret, Dr. Armstrong's wife, had worked on the Reliance-Mutual lot during the making of *Old Heidelberg;* although she had appeared in a number of films, she was by no means a "star." For the Alpine guide, Sepp Innerkofler, Stroheim chose Gibson Gowland, who would later win permanent fame as McTeague in *Greed.* Stroheim's girlfriend and future wife, Valerie Germonprez, was picked to play one-half of the hot-blooded honeymoon couple. And of course, Stroheim cast himself as the vacationing lecher, Lieutenant von Steuben.

The contract selling the rights of the screenplay to Universal for four hundred dollars was signed on April 14, 1919, merely as a matter of formality, for filming had begun on April 3. The *Dramatic Mirror* of April 29 mentioned that Stroheim, "who acted the hated Hun in *Hearts of the World* and *The Heart of Humanity* has turned director. He has written a story bearing the tentative title of *The Pinnacle.*"[1] Location scenes were shot in California, at Big Bear Lake, where Griffith had shot some scenes for *The Birth of a Nation,* and at Idlewild, for the mountain.[2]

Now that Stroheim was a director, he not only took special care that everything should look authentic, but he also involved himself with every aspect of the film: acting, camerawork, and lighting. If there were temper tantrums, as yet they were not newsworthy. Production began on April 3, and after a relatively long shooting period for a Universal production of this era, the picture was completed on June 12. It cost about $125,000,[3] a sum larger than the studio usually spent, but not an unreasonable amount.

Between the end of shooting in June and the first part of August, the film was edited and titles inserted. A continuity—that is, a description of each shot, including a subtitle list—was made in early August by Stroheim and someone else. The film had ninety-eight titles, a relatively small number for a dramatic picture.

Because several writers have supposedly examined Stroheim's visual style and come to the erroneous conclusion that he was more interested in *what* he filmed than *how* he filmed it, the continuity's footage and shot count might prove informative:

Reel	Feet	Shots
1	1,029	130
2	1,102	137
3	967	105
4	994	105
5	1,027	118
6	998	101
7	928	94
8	666	102

There are some penciled changes on the original continuity, and a few other shots were later omitted. Ultimately, the picture contained 792 shots in a total of 7,702 feet.[4] Unlike many pictures of the late teens, which were still made mostly in long shots, Stroheim obviously adopted Griffith's procedure of breaking space into medium and close shots.

The film was shipped to New York on August 28, 1919, and had its official premiere in New York's Capitol Theater on December 8. A week before the opening, the theater advertised the film in its program:

Coming Soon to the Capitol Theatre:

The Most Enthralling Picture Drama
that the Art has ever produced

Stroheim's Wonder-Play

Directed by Stroheim himself

BLIND HUSBANDS

A Love-Story as appealing as the most beautiful romance in your memory—an adventure picture as thrilling as any Serial Thriller—a scenic marvel as wondrous as the most inspiring travel picture you've ever known. But most of all, a human drama whose people are real flesh and blood—whose story holds your heart a helpless prisoner till the last tremendous moment comes and brings the glorious surprise that sends you away in a glow of happiness. Wait for it—watch for it— here at the Capitol—the picture you'll never forget.

During the making of the film, there was much discussion at Universal about its title. Legend has it that Laemmle, not knowing what "pinnacle" meant, was afraid viewers would not pay to see a film about a card game (pinochle). When some exhibitors were asked their opinions, the decision was that a better title was needed.

Although Stroheim opposed any alteration, he was aware that the title might be changed. After the film was finished, he told an interviewer that it was called *The Pinnacle*. "At least," he added, "that's the working title."[5] In the November 1919 *Photoplay*, it was still *The Pinnacle* (usually magazine articles were written a month or two before the issue date). When the picture was released as *Blind Husbands,*

Stroheim was furious at the change. The multiple meanings of "The Pinnacle"—mountain, ecstasy, fulfillment, goal, the height of love— were, he felt, reduced to the vulgarity of "Blind Husbands." He was reported widely in the press for having said to Laemmle, "It is my masterpiece and I will not let anyone spoil it."[6] This would be his refrain for the next decade.

Stroheim, self-assured and angry, soon took out a full-page ad in *Motion Picture News*. In it he explained that the film "was the child of my brain—and heart. I had created it—I loved it." He claimed that "the *title* was just as much a part of the picture as any scene in it." Waxing eloquent, he complained about Universal's change: "A beautiful title, a meaningful title, a title that meant everything to the man who created it, a title that represented months and years of creative effort in producing this picture—all tossed away in a moment for a name which is the *absolute essence of commercialism*. A name in which there is no beauty—no sense of the artistic. A name which I would have rejected in disgust had it been submitted to me. I would, in fact, have been ashamed of myself had I even thought of it."[7]

Not bad, from a fellow who, a few months before, had been penniless. There is no doubt here of Stroheim's sincerity. However, the seeds of his destruction are already apparent: his disdain of commercialism, his commitment to artistic "rights," and his unwillingness to concede that someone else might have a valid idea. To the exhibitors and, by extension, the public, *The Pinnacle* did not suggest anything, but *Blind Husbands* is pithy and provocative, implying deception, intrigue, and, of course, sex.

In an interview conducted a few days after *Blind Husbands* opened in New York, Stroheim expanded on the theme of his film: "You will find the most selfish husbands in the world right in New York City. . . . Not deliberately selfish. No; never blindly selfish. They expend tons of energy making enough money to buy the wife . . . [costly things.] Irony of fate. Perhaps the wife would trade every gem in her possession for the candid companionship of her husband."[8]

The fact that the original advertisements omitted the "von" from Stroheim's name was a sop to the anti-Teutonic feeling still quite prevalent, not the result of any false modesty on Stroheim's part. In existing prints, his opening directorial credit does not have the "von," but the list of players includes it. Shortly after the release of the film, Universal decided to emphasize the main character's memorable unpleasantness by resurrecting the "Hun" image. As a result, the "von" began appearing in advertisements.

At the film's original presentation in New York, the *Dramatic Mirror* noted some instances of the background music. It opened with Grieg's "Daybreak" from *Peer Gynt*. An organ came in at the point where Margaret goes upstairs to the piano, followed by the "Kreutzer Sonata."[9]

The film received excellent reviews, and, even more vital, it did extremely well at the box office. The *Dramatic Mirror* summed it up as "a money-maker."[10] As a result, Stroheim immediately became a significant personage in Hollywood, not for his directorial style, but for the popular appeal of his subject matter.

Blind Husbands deals with the stock triangle: A lecherous other man enters the lives of an affection-starved young wife and her inattentive husband. Dr. Armstrong is an American surgeon who, years before, had climbed in the Alps. He returns to the Tyrolean resort village of Cortina d'Ampezzo with his younger wife, where they encounter Lieutenant Erich von Steuben. Beneath the vast peaks, which stand out against the horizon like mute and impassive gods, the destiny of these human beings will be resolved.

Stroheim is noted for his emphasis on real-life details, so it is not surprising that the setting for *Blind Husbands* (made in the United States) resembles the actual one in Europe. When Stroheim had visited this area of the Tyrol as a youth, he no doubt walked the hilly terrain and perhaps did some mountain climbing. The records of his visit do not show where he stayed, but for the purposes of his film (and his obsessions) he has his characters stay at the Croce Bianca [White Cross] Hotel. A glance at a pre–World War I *Baedeker* guide book indicates that in Cortina d'Ampezzo there actually was such a hotel. A few miles up from the village can be found Passo Tre Croci [the Pass of Three Crosses], where Steuben makes one of his attempts at seduction. I visited the pass, and indeed there are three crosses, and also a small chapel (which may have been added later). It is a long hike, but it entails no arduous climbing, and today the pass can be reached by road.

In the film, Stroheim draws not only on his geographical memories of Europe but also on his personal life. He uses the name of his wife, Margaret, but transforms her mother, who was a doctor, into Margaret's husband, Dr. Armstrong. Stroheim may also have realized that his mother-in-law did not approve of him and that he had become an intruder in the mother-daughter relationship. In any case, in the film he cast himself as the interloper.

Essentially, Stroheim explores the thesis that he presents in the opening title (with the original punctuation):

> One of the most frequent reasons for divorce is "alienation of affection" . . . and the reason within the reason is the fact that "the other man" steps in with his sincere (or insincere) attentions just when the husband in his self-complacency forgets the wooing wiles of his pre-nuptial days. . . . Guilty! says the world condemning "the other man.". . . But what of the husband?

Such an idea, that the husband could also be guilty, that his neglect rather than his wife's basic depravity or the other man's ruthlessness might cause this alienation of affection, was shocking for 1919. What was even more shocking was the intimation that a wife also has her emotional and sexual needs. Admittedly, the First World War had undermined many conventions of morality, but it was still felt that no respectable married woman should ever be attracted to anyone else, however much she might be neglected. Stroheim helped change this attitude by depicting quite boldly that a frustrated wife (who was sweet and good) might have just cause to consider—if not exactly accept—the attentions of another.

Stroheim plays the Austrian Lieutenant Erich von Steuben, the embodiment of "the man you love to hate." Besides gaining some perverse pleasure from the similarity of the names, Stroheim exploited the vast reservoir of antimilitarist, anti-Teutonic prejudice that permeated the hate-filled days of the First World War and the period immediately after, when a Germanic name often provoked hisses from audiences. (Even as late as December 1924, D. W. Griffith found it expedient, after the premiere of *Isn't Life Wonderful?* to transform Germans into Poles and to change the leading character's Germanic name to Paul.) Stroheim taps into this prejudice in his unsympathetic depiction of von Steuben. Certainly audiences of the time must have delighted to see a supposedly brave lieutenant, so steeped in arrogance, vanity, sin, and corruption, prove himself to be a coward and a weakling at the end of the film.

Modern viewers, removed from this anti-Teutonic atmosphere, sometimes mistakenly inflate von Steuben into a continental rogue, a kind of monocled Don Juan; for this reason, they are disappointed at his ultimate ineffectuality and abject cowardice. Steuben, however, is by no means a heroic figure but rather a puffed-up dandy, a petty lecher, a strategist of backstairs intrigue, pursuing waitresses, wives, and anyone else who happens to be around.

At the time of the film's premiere in New York, Stroheim described the lieutenant as a

> swanking, swaggering scion of militarism, an officer in the Austrian army with all the absurd vanities, the ugly hypocrisies, the silly affectations of the kulturist. He is so obvious it seems a child could read him, yet he succeeds in entangling a high bred wife who loves her husband.
>
> I have tried to make the Austrian interloper just as hateful as possible.... I have played this role myself to be sure it would draw out the maximum amount of hate.[11]

Another newspaper quoted Stroheim as saying, "I want the audience to see red when I appear."[12] Mae Tinee, in the *Chicago Tribune,* wrote, "He knows how to be a devil, does Count Eric Oswald Hans Carl Maria Stroheim von Nordenwall." (She added, in a caption: "Er Macht It der Fillum All bei Himselfum.")[13]

That Stroheim intended his character to be unsympathetic was understood by reviewers of the time: "His appearance is repulsive and his morals are appalling. But his technique with women is perfect."[14] Another magazine stated, "You do not look upon him as a moral leper or a despoiler of feminine virtue; you only see the weakling, the youth irresponsible for his actions."[15]

The studio's synopsis of the original script is revealing: "The Lieutenant's gold braid might well have been a yellow streak, but it had the dazzle of battle and the form of a man which concealed the foul plumage of a love-vulture." This thematic statement perhaps clarifies the ending of the film, when this vulture of love is pursued by a real vulture.

Through the character of Steuben, Stroheim is starting to say something about the decadence of the military and aristocratic circles of Europe, however muffled and inarticulate this first expression of his subject might be. The aristocratic society that he would so often explore in his films is barely perceptible here; instead, we have a single lecherous military man. Essentially a moralist, and perhaps amazed at the quaint fact that he is one, Stroheim depicts the sins of the world with scientific, dispassionate, and—contradictorily—prurient interest.

Stroheim considered himself a person of keen sexual appetites, and he projects this image on Steuben. However, Steuben is not Stroheim but rather an extension—and sometimes an amusing one—of some aspects of the man's inner self, a portrait brilliantly sketched, wittily presented, and minutely observed. He depicts the Mr. Hyde side of his own psyche with the fidelity and skill of a man who knows its nature all too well. His portrayal is a kind of aesthetic confession, which exorcises something within himself. At the time it was released, *Blind Husbands* showed a maturity and command far beyond other films in terms of psychological probing. It is, however, primitive and crude in comparison to Stroheim's later *The Wedding March,* which would pick up some aspects of this theme and explore them further.

The version of this film that can now be seen provides a somewhat different visual effect than that created by the original. Although the negative of the 1919 film was, of course, in black and white, prints of the silent period were often tinted, and *Blind Husbands* was no exception. Scenes of the Festival of the Transfiguration were tinted in amber, and shots of the moon were "amber-blue." Other amber-tinted shots included those in the Alpine hut toward the end of the film.

When the picture was rereleased in July 1924, Universal trimmed it by 1,345 feet, and this is the version that survives. (Stroheim was no longer at the studio and therefore could not argue against this unauthorized shortening.) Fortunately, Universal preserved the original synopsis, script, and final continuity, from which we can tell what Stroheim initially had in mind, what he probably shot, and what was included in the original release version.

One cannot be sure when Stroheim wrote *The Pinnacle*—it was probably worked on in 1918 and early 1919. He was well aware of

America's angry feelings toward Teutonic types and aware that Americans traveling to the land of the enemy and mixing with an Austrian officer might appear unpatriotic. To save himself this political problem, Stroheim said during production that the story would take place in the future, "four years after the war."[16] This time shift was ultimately omitted.

As the film begins, the credits inform us that the story is based on a novel, *The Pinnacle* (which, of course, never existed). There is an opening shot of the main square of Cortina d'Ampezzo, then a title saying that it is the seventh day, followed by a shot of church bells ringing with pigeons hovering around. Here, the content and tone are quite reminiscent of the beginning of *The Heart of Humanity,* made the previous year. The villagers, "a simple and faithful people," are shown at their worship, establishing a kind of moral norm that Steuben, the vulture, will violate. One of these shots shows worshipers passing by a graveyard. Barely seen—no close-up of it is used—is the gravestone of Franz Huber, a villager who, we find out later, had had a liaison with someone's wife and had been thrown to his death from the mountain. (The facts of his demise are cited on a roadside "shrine" that is encountered later in the film. A small painting on the sign shows the man being hurled into the pit of hell.)

We then shift to the mountain road and a horse-drawn conveyance carrying the three main characters to the village. Dr. Armstrong busies himself reading a book as his wife sits passively at his side. He has been to this mountain area before but does not attempt to share the view with Margaret. Steuben sits opposite her and stares, through his monocle, at her legs. When she asks what time it is, the husband ignores her, but the ever alert lieutenant glances at his wristwatch and tells her. Steuben's interest has no hint of the romantic. He does not look admiringly at her face but lustfully at her limbs. In the original release, Steuben was introduced with this title:

Lieutenant von Steuben, an Austrian cavalry officer, with a keen appreciation of three things: wine, WOMEN, song.

NOTE: Shell shock, trench fever, and mustard gas necessitated his sick leave (so von Steuben said).

This habit of adding a "note" to a title card stemmed from Griffith, who used the device in *The Birth of a Nation, Intolerance,* and many other films. Present prints omit the note.

When the threesome alight from the horse-drawn conveyance, the mountain guide, Sepp Innerkofler, greets his old friend Dr. Armstrong (who has previously saved Sepp's life) and the doctor's new bride. Steuben looks at Sepp as the camera (in a point of view shot) tilts upward from Sepp's feet to his face. Sepp scowls contemptuously at the puny and self-important officer, as the camera cuts to Steuben's face and tilts down to his boots. In contrast to the short, frail dandy, Sepp is big, strong, humble, and basic. That the guide is a decent and reliable man is reinforced by Stroheim's use of animal symbolism, for Sepp is almost always accompanied by his faithful, loving dog.

Sepp, the mountain guide (to whom the film is dedicated), is not an entirely fictional character. A book by S.H. Hamer called *The Dolomites* (published in 1910) describes the mountain-climbing exploits of the Innerkofler family. One peak was first climbed by Franz Innerkofler in 1869. Later, one of the mountains, the Innerkoflerthurm (10,073 feet), was named after Michel Innerkofler, who, in 1880, was the first man to ascend it. The peak was about three and one-half hours from the Langkofel Hut. The book also mentions an ascent by Michel and a Dr. Minnigerode in 1877. Michel, the most famous of all the guides in the area, was killed in 1888 at the age of forty when a snow bridge collapsed under him. In 1899, the face of one peak was climbed by a Dr. T.K. Rose, C. Moss, Sepp Innerkofler, and another family member. Perhaps the most difficult of all the ascents occurred in 1906, when Sepp and two others climbed the Innerkoflerthurm. This was accomplished at about the same time that the young Stroheim visited the area, and some of these facts, and of course the name of Sepp, had stayed in his memory. Incidentally, the descendants of the Innerkoflers can be found today listed in the village telephone book.

Although the film takes place after the First World War, Stroheim remembered Cortina as he had seen it earlier. For example, framed photographs of the village (taken during the teens and in 1980 on view in some of the public buildings of Cortina D'Ampezzo) show numerous automobiles in the village, whereas Stroheim, drawing upon his memories, depicts an earlier time of horses and carriages that reinforces the image of these good, but simple, people.

On the morning after Steuben arrives at the hotel, he leaves his room—significantly number thirteen—to go down to breakfast. At the end of the hallway, a dark cross stands out vividly in front of a sunlit window. As the Armstrongs descend the stairs, Margaret feels chilly and tells her husband she has forgotten her sweater. He informs her that he saw it on the bed and continues down. Steuben, overhearing the conversation, retrieves the sweater from her room and hands it to her. She accepts it somewhat angrily and joins her husband for breakfast, who again ignores her. Irritated, she goes outdoors. Steuben observes this minor contretemps. Then, after finishing his coffee, Steuben flirts with the waitress and gives her a quick kiss. Meanwhile, Margaret sits in front of the hotel as villagers pass by in the foreground. She plays with a pigeon, much as Lillian Gish does in *The Birth of a Nation;* in both cases the animal imagery reinforces the woman's sweet nature.

Steuben goes outside, perceives that Mrs. Armstrong is not entirely comfortable, and gets a pillow, a footstool, and a blanket for her. She is pleased at his attention, and he joins her at the outdoor table. The jealous waitress sees this and purposely sweeps the front steps with enough vigor to raise dust on the two. This moment is typical of Stroheim's use of comedy, for it arises from his close observation of human nature.

That night, the village celebrates the Festival of the Transfiguration. This church holiday, taking place on August 6, commemorates Christ's ascent of Mount Tabor with Peter, James, and John, where he was transfigured before them (Matt. 17:2). Christ ascends the mountain to become closer to God, and that spiritual joining is revealed through his transfiguration. Steuben, in a somewhat sacrilegious analog, climbs a mountain for a very different reason, not to commune with God but to cohabit with woman. His purpose is to *conquer* the mountain, not to make a spiritual journey and to become one with the universe. Steuben, too, will be transfigured—not by the radiance of God, but by cowardice.

Later that night, at a lovers' lane close by the cemetery, Steuben offers his standard line to a village woman. This "wonderful night is ours—yours and mine," he tells her and smoothly adds, "Even the good old moon seems to give us her blessing." He concludes his litany with "I love you." As the couple pass through the graveyard, the top of

Huber's gravestone again appears in a portion of the frame, although the name cannot readily be seen.

Outside the hotel, at a kind of street café, Armstrong, totally ignoring his wife, is busy speaking to three Americans who plan to climb the mountains. As the men continue to talk, Stroheim introduces a honeymoon couple, also guests at the hotel. The new bride momentarily takes her eyes off her husband and observes the lonely Margaret. She asks her attentive and ardent husband, "You will never neglect me like that?" This not only provides a telling contrast but also indicates the different stages of marriage, from initial intensity to dulled familiarity.

The original scenario had followed the love scene in the cemetery (where Steuben delivered his usual line) with one in which Steuben dances with Margaret, then lures her to the cemetery, where he repeats his line and kisses her. Stroheim changed this sequence during shooting, apparently feeling the episode was too abrupt. Instead, he has the neglected Margaret leave the outdoor party and enter the hotel. Lonely, she sits down at a piano to play. Steuben sees her departure, enters the room, picks up a violin, and accompanies her. Of course, he would like to make "beautiful music" with her in another way, too. Steuben inadvertently knocks some sheet music off the piano, but, rather than reshoot the episode, Stroheim let the apparent mistake remain, something he would not tolerate even a few years later. Here, Steuben repeats his lines about love and the moon. The repetition, of course, is funny, and audiences still laugh at it, which was Stroheim's intention. When he says, "You were created for nothing else but love—its ecstasies," he means physical love rather than affection. In the original script, Margaret was more attracted to the lieutenant than in the actual film. Perhaps Stroheim tempered her interest a bit to keep the audience's sympathy for her.

Afterward, Steuben goes outside and joins a discussion with Armstrong and some other men about mountain climbing. The lieutenant says that the ascent of a mountain is not a spiritual experience, a cleansing of the soul, or a drawing closer to the feet of God. He sees no mystique in it at all, stating that mountains are only "lifeless rocks." "My pleasure," he says, "is to master them." For *rocks* read *women,* and you have Steuben's attitude toward love, an attitude that shocked, offended, and titillated America. "You want sex," he seems to say, "and I want to give it to you, so stop being so hypocritical." At the same time, his attitude reveals his disinterest in his partner—his concern is only with his own satisfaction.

In opposition to Steuben's lust, Stroheim does not offer the sentimentalized image of innocent love to which Griffith was so partial. Even the honeymoon couple, whom Stroheim includes for contrast, do not simply represent pure romance. There is sensuality as well. The newlyweds are shown hurrying from the outdoor café back to their room, and, in one extraordinary shot later in the film, the young husband pulls the edge of his jacket over his lap as he brings his wife's hand onto his inner thigh. Imagine Bobby Harron doing this with Lillian Gish in a Griffith picture! In the history of the American film, Stroheim was the first to depict mutual desire and passion in a positive, noncritical way. (This amorous bride is played by Valerie Germonprez, Stroheim's fiancée, who a year later would become his wife.) After everyone else enters the hotel, Steuben stays outside, where the village woman he was with in the cemetery berates him. After a short explanation, he puts an arm around her and they leave together.

Later that night, Margaret looks at her face in her bedroom mirror. Behind her, the reflection of her husband reading in bed dissolves to the happy honeymoon couple, then back to the husband. Soon he is asleep, and his wife begins another unfulfilled night. Here, Stroheim demonstrates his early mastery at conveying psychological states visually, without resorting to explanatory titles.

The next day Margaret, the doctor, and Steuben stroll along a village street and stop at a stand selling curios, where Margaret admires a small antique box. The husband, paying no attention to her enthusiasm, picks up a child and holds it affectionately. This moment is saved from sentimentality when the child wets his arm. Here, Stroheim shows that the husband is a good man, but his inattentiveness hardly makes parenthood a likely possibility for him. The village doctor then comes by and asks the husband to assist him on a case, leaving Margaret with Steuben. The lieutenant takes her up to the Pass of Three Crosses, where, at the base of one of them, he again starts to romance her. Standing in front of the seated woman, he places one foot on a higher rock, in a rather obvious sexual stance. Then, embracing her, he puts his hand on her breast. Seduction at the foot of a cross is a perfect example of Stroheim's fascination with juxtaposing the sacred and the profane. Meanwhile, Sepp watches from behind a tree and reacts to Steuben's actions by spitting. Sepp then interrupts the scene and, much to the lieutenant's annoyance, accompanies them down the mountain.

Originally, this scene by the Three Crosses was more complex. Stroheim cut to a shepherd boy nearby playing a flute. There was a dissolve to Steuben in faun costume playing the flute into the ear of Margaret, who is depicted as a cowherd nymph. This kind of heavy symbolism stemmed directly from Griffith, particularly from *The Avenging Conscience* (1914), which included Pan and nymphs and satyrs. The scene seems to have worked, for there is no criticism—or even mention—of it in contemporary reviews, but it seems a bit too literary and heavy to fit in with the rest of the film. Although one is grateful that this episode in *Blind Husbands* was removed when the film was reissued, it is not untypical of Stroheim's work, which often leaned to the allegorical.

The three reckless Americans, who unwisely dared the mountain by climbing on a difficult side, have met with an accident, so Dr. Armstrong joins the rescue party. In a scene cut from surviving prints, Steuben escorts Margaret to the village church. A hunchback opens the door to the bell tower, and Steuben bribes him to stay away. He climbs with her to the top, where they can see the minute dots that are Armstrong and the rescue party. Steuben kisses her, saying that he would not neglect her if she were his loved one. "A husband that leaves a woman like you, to ramble around in the mountains, deserves to be betrayed. . . . I love you." Fade out.[17]

In other scenes cut after the initial release, Steuben and Margaret have lunch in the hotel dining room. While he discusses the meal with the innkeeper, Margaret leaves. She has decided that the relationship is growing dangerous. In her room, she asks the maid to tell Steuben that she will not be down later for dinner. Back in the dining room, a girl with a basket of flowers enters. Steuben buys a bouquet and then grabs her hand. A title reads, "A blossom bloomed and was broken," evoking Griffith's *Broken Blossoms,* released at about the same time that Stroheim was shooting *Blind Husbands.* When the maid tells Steuben that Margaret will not be down, he goes upstairs and knocks on her door. She looks sad, then smiles, but she does not let him in. He considers forcing his way in but thinks better of it. As soon as he goes downstairs, he sees the maid and they kiss.

These omitted episodes help to establish Steuben's character, showing him to be quite unprincipled as he works to seduce the flower girl, the village maiden, the hotel servant, and Margaret simultaneously. After these missing scenes, the current version picks up the narrative as Steuben, during the siesta time, buys the wooden box for Mrs. Armstrong. As he marches down the street, the village children mock his precise way of walking. Stroheim is not above laughing at his own character and may have drawn upon some memories of American children imitating him. It is less likely that European children, used to such military manners, would have bothered.

Returning to the hotel, Steuben inveigles himself into Margaret's room and presents her with the little box, but she puts off his sensual attentions by promising to meet him later.

The church bell rings, and Stroheim personifies it with the title "I call the living—I mourn the dead." The rescue party returns with an injured American climber. When Margaret's husband fails to appear, she fears the worst and faints. Carried back to her room, she has a nightmare in which the camera dollies in on Steuben with a cigarette clenched in his mouth, his lips curved in an evil smile. We then see his rather phallic index finger point to the camera. This gesture clearly has Freudian overtones for the wife, but it also functions as the author's admonition to husbands in the audience.

Armstrong, who returns shortly after, plans the next day to climb the mountain with Steuben; his wife pleads to go along, at least as far as the halfway hut. During their climb, they pass a roadside shrine erected to Franz Huber, which says, "Passersby, pray for the condemned soul of the poor sinner." Steuben and Margaret exchange looks. The scene is shot in fog, and Armstrong, with his cape and broad hat, looks like a figure out of a nineteenth-century romantic painting. These shots, in fact, have a kind of *stimmung,* a foggy and misty atmosphere, which seems extremely Germanic, even though such a style would not appear in German cinema for another year or two. Here, at least, Stroheim anticipates Germanic visual techniques.

In the original script, the three climbers pause on a plateau and look down at the Pass of Three Crosses, where Steuben and Margaret again exchange looks.

At the halfway hut that evening, a number of guests sit around relaxing. The room is full of posters that provide an authentic atmosphere. On one wall, a calendar reads August 12, implying, of course, that the next day will be a fateful thirteenth. The honeymoon couple, after some mutual fondling, hasten off to their room. A hunchbacked idiot on crutches, instinctively perceiving a relationship between Steuben and Margaret, points his finger at them and laughs.

Stroheim includes a remarkable shot of Margaret sitting in a high-backed wooden chair, her head resting on the sunburst pattern of the netting. This circle, in turn is supported by outward rays of twine. She seems to be haloed by the pattern. In suggestive ways, she is both a madonna and a St. Sebastian pierced by arrows of light rope. Margaret states that she is tired, and Sepp escorts her, not to room number 3, where she was first to go, but to another one. She and Dr. Armstrong are staying in separate rooms because he has to get up early and does not want to disturb her. In her new room, she writes a letter (in a still photo of that action, the name reads not "Erich von Steuben" but "Erich von Stroheim"!), which she slides under Steuben's door. Meanwhile, the eager lieutenant prepares for his assignation—he intends to slip into her room—and smiles at the motto on his wall, "There is no sin in the Alps." He puts on some cologne, brushes his hair carefully (using mirrors so he can see the back of his head), and dons an attractive, silken robe. At this point, he spies the letter near the door and reads it with an odd smile. Then he leaves his room and enters the hallway. Over each door is a set of animal horns, suggesting, no doubt, the cuckoldry that Steuben intends. He opens her door only to encounter Sepp smoking his pipe! Steuben pretends he has made a mistake, but the all-wise and protective Sepp escorts the frustrated man back to his room, then stations his dog before Margaret's door as a sentinel. There will be no liaison that night.

The next morning, Armstrong and Steuben start off for the mountain peak, but when the husband notices that Steuben has a letter from his wife, he demands to know its contents. When Steuben resists, the two men struggle and the letter plummets down the mountainside. Armstrong grabs Steuben's throat and threatens to kill him unless he tells the truth. Steuben's reply in the original script was that an affair had occurred; the existing version contains the tamer statement that she had promised to go away with him. This confrontation is crosscut with Austrian troops on maneuvers. The wife—sensing trouble—convinces the troops and Sepp to go up the mountain after her husband.

Armstrong, heartbroken at Steuben's statement, sits stunned. Steuben removes a knife from his pocket and looks as if he is about to plunge it into his adversary's back. Armstrong senses this, takes the knife, and grasps the rope around Steuben's waist that links them. He cuts it at a point a few inches from Steuben's crotch! Armstrong declares that no law of God or man can force him to aid Steuben in descending the mountain. Steuben cries out in panic that he lied about Margaret's intentions because he feared Armstrong would not believe him, but Armstrong ignores his craven pleas and starts down alone. On the way he finds the letter and reads that his wife is innocent. Deciding to return for Steuben, he slips and falls. Steuben, alone, grows more afraid on the mountain peak and, as the shadow of a vulture comes near, falls to his death, paralleling Franz Huber's fate. The original script had the troops cross themselves as they see the body plummet. The troops and Sepp then bring down the injured husband.

A few days later, the bandaged Armstrong and his wife leave the village. Sepp says tearfully, "Be good to her," and declares that he knows little of the world, but there is one beautiful aspect of it—love. As the carriage pulls away, Armstrong holds his wife's hand, and the film ends.

The final dramatic moments on top of the mountain prove somewhat disappointing. When Stroheim tries to evoke suspense by intercutting the nervous wife, the troops, and the struggle between Steuben and Armstrong, he fails. This sequence is mostly photographed in long shots, so there can be no cascade of intense close-ups of the angry Armstrong, the fearful Steuben, the worried wife, and the commander of the troops to heighten the dramatic action. Stroheim's main concern was not Griffith's ride-to-the-rescue style of melodrama.

Stroheim presents mature people and does not choose to exaggerate their movements and gestures. The acting of the principals is restrained, without any of the extravagance or mugging seen in some other films of the period. However, his characters are not sufficiently appealing for us to care emotionally about them. There is no beleaguered heroine, no dashing husband, no rapist. Instead, the wife is a dull creature, the husband even duller, and Steuben a cowardly runt. However, Stroheim did learn a valuable lesson from this film's climax, for his later work generally eschews any possibility for Griffith-like suspense and, instead, concentrates on minute observation of character and milieu—the very lifeblood of his talent.

Stroheim's skill at creating believable but somewhat drab characters, his evocation of the Alpine atmosphere, and his portrayal of a corrupt and calculating rake are what distinguish *Blind Husbands*. His own portrayal of the lieutenant as a rogue is believable and falters only when the script puts him in an impossible situation by making him consider stabbing Armstrong and panic at the vulture flying overhead. Even Stroheim's acting cannot quite make these events convincing, and the camera, which should have cut closer, stays at an unengaging distance. Although Stroheim's screen self will also reveal cowardice in *Foolish Wives* (when he leaps into the fire net before the woman), his behavior there is more credible because it is less extreme. Stroheim made Steuben more craven and villainous than he needed, perhaps as a sop to American audiences, who were delighted to see the swaggering lieutenant prove himself a coward and die. This reaction did not occur, however, when the film played in England in 1920. An article in *The Bioscope* noted, "Dr. Armstrong . . . hardly elicits more sympathy than Von Steuben, a little monkified fop whose conduct rather merited an undignified castigation than a tragic and violent death." Postwar sentiments in England, however, were sufficiently anti-Teutonic to warrant changing the director's name to a more neutral "Eric Strome," although the character remained "Eric von Steuben."[18]

Stroheim was only beginning to learn his craft while making *Blind Husbands* and so occasionally errs by failing to break up space into smaller units. When Steuben plays the violin while Margaret plays the piano, or when she inspects the jewelry box with Steuben (while the husband merely stands by), the camera does not make use of its potential. When Stroheim does use close-ups, they are sometimes choppily inserted, not unlike the casual procedures of Griffith and Emerson. At other times, however, Stroheim's technique is inventive and equal to the content. The early scene in the horse-drawn conveyance has varied shots of faces and Margaret's ankles that reveal clearly the personalities of the passengers. Later, when Margaret envisions the honeymoon couple in the mirror and a shot of her husband reading is followed soon by one of him sleeping, her frustration is clearly and fully dramatized.

Most of Stroheim's visual compositions are without much interest, and except for the foggy scene halfway up the mountain and the wife's dream, the lighting is generally flat. Nor does Stroheim make much use of landscape, despite the presence of the mountain terrain.

In terms of other films of the time, such as Marshall Neilan's *M'Liss* (1918), Stroheim's style here is quite advanced, but it is by no means up to the skills he would soon demonstrate. *Blind Husbands* remains interesting more for its content than for its cinematic treatment. This would not be the case in Stroheim's subsequent work.

Stroheim's first film clearly has an autobiographical resonance. In some manner, he drew on his experiences with his first wife on the mountain near Oakland and with other women later at Lake Tahoe. He knew that people on vacation, unhampered by friends and neighbors, were more open to sexual adventures. Stroheim, no doubt, played in real life the dandy officer—although without uniform—with his continental manners of hand kissing, heel clicking, and polite modes of address. Stroheim probably added to this elegant impression by making vague references to his sad and mysterious past in Austria and plaintively remarking that he was now a fallen aristocrat having to live and work in America—a sensitive and gifted soul thrown into a maelstrom of crassness. This was a good recipe for a young man with a strong sex drive who wanted it satisfied. Despite Stroheim's unattractive looks and unimpressive body, his charm worked. When he became famous, many women were entranced by his public self.

In some ways, Stroheim presented a complex persona. Years later, he explained that he was typed as a villain in his films—"or perhaps better said, I have typed myself"—but he explained that his portrayals "in reality are just men not much out of the ordinary, only appearing to be so to motion picture audiences, because to follow one's sex instinct was taboo up to that time."[19]

Stroheim was quite aware of his lecherous side and, indeed, took pride in it, but there was also another side, one that was sensitive, poetic, and sincere. He could not reconcile these aspects—most humans cannot—and so in his art he tried, at times, to separate them. He knew that in some ways he *was* von Steuben, that he was a rotter. But he also felt guilty about this "bad" side, and so would kill off his persona in *Blind Husbands* and, later, *Foolish Wives*. Perhaps, his wooing of Margaret Knox in the mountains and the ugly collapse of their marriage haunted his imagination and caused him to write this scenario. His guilt—Catholic? Jewish?—necessitated that he be strongly punished. One wonders whether his need to make films of inordinate length was also a peculiar fusing of sincerity, high-mindedness, and an unconscious desire to be punished by having his creations ruined by commercial necessity. In any case, Stroheim would forget nothing, not the mountains at Cortina, not the Three Crosses, not the Innerkoflers, and certainly not Margaret Knox and the man who wooed, wed, and then disillusioned her.

In some ways, *Blind Husbands* is Stroheim's most complete film, in that it has a clear structure, a confident working out of the characters. It also is unencumbered by the numerous incidental plot details that, in the future, would so complicate each film: *Blind Husbands* may subsequently have been cut by a few minutes, but it did not lose major chunks, which would have spoiled the overall effect. Critics and audiences admired the film; it was a glorious beginning to a tempestuous career, and it remains a significant achievement.

5

The Devil's Pass Key

As soon as Blind Husbands was finished, Universal knew that it had a good picture, possibly a great one, and sensed that the film would do well at the box office. As a consequence, the studio encouraged Stroheim to begin on another. He had no screenplay at hand—his success had been that sudden—so he chose an unpublished story, "Clothes and Treachery," by Mahra de Meyer, a woman of international connections who had managed to become a baroness.[1] This he transformed into *The Devil's Pass Key*,[2] a film now totally lost.

Even before Universal bought the story's rights in August 1919, Stroheim had begun on a screenplay that he completed by October, an extraordinarily brief period for a man who usually wrote scenarios running hundreds of pages. Shooting began that same month and ended by December 4, 1919.

In casting *The Devil's Pass Key*, Stroheim drew again on Sam de Grasse (the husband in *Blind Husbands*) and came upon two actresses whom he would use again in *Foolish Wives*, Mae Bush and Maude George. Radiating sophisticated corruption, George would also have roles in *Merry-Go-Round* and *The Wedding March*.

During production, Stroheim became more confident (not that he was ever a shrinking violet) and began striving for perfection, a goal that demanded countless retakes. Furthermore, he wanted to give his major characters more psychological dimension than the American cinema was used to, so the original short story became a longer one on film. After shooting was finished, Stroheim faced the problem of putting together the miles of footage. Multiple takes, especially when there are only minute differences between them, make the task of picking the best shot a time-consuming process. After about three months spent in the editing room, he had assembled a print.

There is little doubt that Stroheim was already embarking on a fatal obsession: to make films longer than exhibitors needed to fill their programs. Theaters tended to have seven and nine o'clock showings, so the entire program, including a newsreel and a short, could not last more than two hours. Features ran from five to seven thousand feet. Despite this commercial reality, Stroheim gave the studio a film that was too long. The original cut of the complicated plot may have run about twelve thousand feet.[3] Although Richard Koszarksi believes that this estimate has "no basis in fact," I believe it does. After all, if *Blind Husbands*'s simple story ran the full length of a standard feature, how could this multifaceted plot not have required considerably more footage? It may not have been twelve thousand feet, but it was probably much longer than the almost nine thousand feet he edited it down to, at the urging of Universal, by March 1920. That version was still about twenty minutes too long. After a California preview, *Variety* noted the troubles with *The Devil's Pass Key:* "'He's a one picture man,' was the verdict. The thing skidded for the shelf and the director hit the trail east. The final settlement was an agreement on von Stroheim's part to recut and retitle his picture. This he has done, and it is now announced for release, while the trade is anxiously waiting to see if this director is a flash in the pan or the real thing."[4]

When Stroheim arrived in New York on April 6 to oversee the film's initial presentation,[5] it had been trimmed to seventy-five hundred feet. Universal remained silent on this issue, leery of letting the press know about the severe cutting that would have encouraged critics to scrutinize its continuity. In fact, the studio seemed optimistic. It even took out a two-page ad in *Moving Picture World:* one page publicized *Blind Husbands,* "the marvelous picture that made an Unknown into a world-famous Author, Director and Leading Man overnight," and the other offered *The Devil's Pass Key,* "A picture of Paris the wicked and Paris the wonderful—painted on the screen by a Master Artist."[6] Stroheim did not put up a fight about the major cutting of *The Devil's Pass Key* in April, nor did he complain about the changes to the press, because he was already deeply engrossed in his new project, *Foolish Wives*. Set construction began that month, while he was still feverishly working on his screenplay. When *The Devil's Pass Key* finally opened in New York, he was already in the second month of shooting *Foolish Wives* and was not inclined to return east for additional promotion. He was not looking backward to agonize about a film that no longer concerned him. Despite his absence, the film received a good deal of attention and garnered appreciative, but not overwhelming, reviews. As contemporary remarks indicate, the film appeared disjointed, probably because of its severe cutting. After a considerable amount of publicity during the spring of 1920, Universal decided to postpone the release until August, mainly because it did not want to have two Stroheim pictures in distribution at the same time.

Although the film would become a modest success, it was by no means as popular or impressive as *Blind Husbands*. Its released length was normal, its costs modest, and its subject matter relatively mild. Certainly it was no cause célèbre and, in fact, is the only Stroheim work that did not leave some kind of brouhaha in its aftermath. It came, it was seen, and it vanished. Now it is a completely lost film, but basically it has been lost since 1921, having never been given a revival. Furthermore, it was a lost film to Stroheim himself. After it came out, he rarely referred to it. In fact, when he wrote an account of his career in 1947–48, he had many things to say about films on which he was the art director or in which he had played minute parts, but he had absolutely *nothing* to say about *The Devil's Pass Key*. To him, apparently, it had never existed.

What can one comment about a film that Stroheim chose to forget and for which there is not even a surviving scenario? Not much. There are few contemporary accounts of the project, no interesting anecdotes, and a paucity of stills. All that remains are reviews in film magazines and newspapers. The best one can do is recount its plot and identify some elements that would later appear in Stroheim's more mature works.

Warren Goodright (Sam de Grasse) is an American dramatist residing in Paris with Grace, his attractive bride. Madame Mallot, a modiste who designs dresses for only the most exclusive people, encourages Grace to wear expensive clothing to make herself appear more beautiful to her husband. Unfortunately, the husband's plays have failed, and the couple have run up a multitude of bills. In addition, but unknown to Goodright, his naive wife's desire for expensive clothes has placed her deeply in debt to Madame Mallot, who is now demanding payment. In a subtle kind of blackmail, the worldly modiste suggests that the wife need not worry because there are men who like to make the intimate acquaintance of attractive women and could, perhaps, be financially generous. Among these attentive men is the handsome Rex Strong, a well-off American officer, who has chosen to remain in Paris as an attaché after the end of his service in the First World War. In *Variety*'s words, he is "a plain blackguard, and a client of the dressmaker in her capacity of procuress."[7] The term "blackguard" seems a bit harsh; he, like many of Stroheim's other male characters, is probably just a sensual man looking for a good time and willing to pay for it.

After introducing Grace to Rex, Madame Mallot provides a private, sumptuously appointed apartment where the two can enjoy each other's company discreetly. In the background is a bed that, the film hints, will be part of the bargain. This military officer would not mind negotiating a "loan" to the beautiful woman, if she would be cooperative. The sexually keen Rex embraces and tries to kiss the heroine, who is shocked at his behavior. She starts to cry, an act that touches his conscience, so he stifles his desire. This situation of a roguish hero confronted with innocence and having enough qualms not to take advantage of the moment will reappear in many Stroheim films, most tellingly in *Merry-Go-Round* and *The Merry Widow*. Although the woman in *The Devil's Pass Key* is hardly sexually naive (after all, she is married), her sweet vulnerability strikes a sympathetic chord in Rex.

In the meantime, much of Paris has heard of the wife entering a house noted for its immoral reputation and draws the inevitable conclusion. A scandalmongering newspaper prints the juicy details of this seemingly nasty liaison (shades of *The Social Secretary*), but without naming names. The oblivious husband reads this tidbit and decides that the situation could make an effective drama. Shortly after, the play is produced in Paris and becomes a great success. Many in the first-night audience, who know the true story, snicker at the author's naïveté and jeer at what they think is his cuckoldry. As the gossip grows more intense, the husband ultimately learns all the facts and, although embarrassed at the "horse-laugh,"[8] overcomes his fury and finally embraces his slightly erring, but technically pure, wife.

When *The Devil's Pass Key* had its release in August 1920, the unusually perceptive anonymous reviewer for the *New York Times* appreciated the film's artistry. He felt that Stroheim, in some ways, had "gone beyond his achievements" in *Blind Husbands* and that he showed even "more promise of future success." Although Stroheim's pictures "resemble the usual film offerings" in many ways, his work "is different and new . . . for he has realized that the substance of the photoplay is the dramatic motion picture; not the subtitle nor the spectacular scene, nor the beauty or the tricks of any star, nor the sentiment or surprises of any story, but moving pictures that have meaning . . . [and that present characters who] are definite and comprehensible individuals." The reviewer then described Stroheim's directorial style and noted that the camera was brought closer to the actors to reveal character and to show specific details. He observed Stroheim's astute creation of atmosphere, that the dramatic situations were enhanced by the settings.

> The scene of *The Devil's Pass Key* is Paris, and views of the city and its life are shown throughout the photoplay as they heighten its successive crises. Furthermore, in the pantomime of his players, Mr. von Stroheim's direction is evident. Of course, ability on the part of the actors is necessary, but many of the eloquent little things they do, and things they effectively refrain from doing, seem the result of his skillful guidance. Altogether, *The Devil's Pass Key* is a photoplay which is chiefly, and most importantly, a work in moving pictures—and this is its distinction.[9]

One regrets that the astute reviewer did not cite some examples, for he certainly understood Stroheim's artistry. He also perceived that the director's honest rendering of humanity had been compromised by the film's obligatory and reassuring conclusion. "It deals ironically with two American innocents abroad in the sophisticated, cynical and altogether physical life of a Parisian group. The irony is almost, and should be completely, tragic, but at the last moment a happy ending is contrived, which weakens, but does not destroy, the force of the story. One imagines that this ending is simply a concession on the part of Mr. von Stroheim." *Variety,* too, took exception to the "unconvincing" finale. "By some miracle, known only to Von Stroheim and the scenario writer, [the husband] . . . embraces the wife."[10]

This review, hardly as enthusiastic as the one in the *Times,* pointed out various flaws, the same flaws that soon would be seen in *Foolish Wives.* According to *Variety, The Devil's Pass Key*

has many points of interest, but before the end it becomes wearisome. The interior settings are rich and must have been costly. It would seem that Universal piled up footage on the principle that having spent so much for studio sets they might as well use them as long as possible.

The story is jerky and jumpy, its multiplicity of characters is confusing, and it is made up of jumbled material enough for a Pathe serial. There are no less than three plays incorporated into this one. From the beginning to the scene in the Parisian modiste's "chambre particulaire" would make a complete unit. The struggle for fame of the dramatist would make another and the material from the production of his play to his reconciliation with his wife has material for the third. Any one of them could have made a picture. When the trio were jammed into one story, the result was distraction.

It is probably due to this circumstance that the play seems interminable. Impatience is always engendered when a story completes an episode and then begins anew, instead of having each scene built upon the preceding one into a cumulative climax.[11]

Perhaps the uncut version of the film would have alleviated these problems.

The *Variety* reviewer noted that "the scenes in the modiste's establishment are gorgeous" and that the "apartment's most prominent feature" is a four-post bed, which had "the plain intent" of suggesting something gross. He concluded by saying that "Mr. Von Stroheim's 'master picture,' as the program has it, leaves a bad taste."[12]

One can surmise from the plot outline and the various reviews that Stroheim here touched upon material that he would expand in his later work. The house of assignation—with its lavish apartment, suggestive of erotic endeavors—reappears in *Merry-Go-Round* and *The Merry Widow.* Other reviews noted how authentic some exterior Parisian settings appeared and how each interior was richly detailed, characteristics that would persist in all of Stroheim's films. One of the minor characters in this film is Count De Trouvero, "a decrepit old roué," a part that Stroheim once planned for himself. Comparable lechers appear in *Merry-Go-Round,* *The Merry Widow,* and *Queen Kelly,* portrayed by the inimitable Tully Marshall in the latter two films.

Stroheim included several scenes involving two of his favorite obsessions: physical deformity and feet. There exists a still of an outdoor party held for the war wounded that contains a number of men using canes or crutches. No doubt, Stroheim provided further foot references, but the only other known instances occur when an exotic dancer's feet are repeatedly shown in close-ups and, later, in her bathroom, when she receives a pedicure.

The Devil's Pass Key repeated certain elements from *Blind Husbands,* including a woman who is wooed by a lustful sexual predator and who is married to a man more concerned with his career than his wife. In *Blind Husbands,* the retarded fellow at the mountain hut perceives the von Steuben–Margaret relationship and laughs, whereas in *The Devil's Pass Key* all of Paris jeers at the husband. Furthermore, the theme of innocent Americans thrust into a sophisticated, cynical and, indeed, corrupt Europe would soon return in *Foolish Wives.*

The plot premise of someone getting deeply into debt was an essential part of the original "Clothes and Treachery" story, but it had also appeared in Stroheim's youthful play, *In the Morning.* Whether or not the young Erich had been in debt to an unscrupulous moneylender in Vienna, the subject of indebtedness certainly meant more to Stroheim than a mere convenient plot device.

Although there may be a few autobiographical elements in this film, they are hardly important ones. Stroheim's other pictures contain many strong personal overtones, whether understood by the public or not. He either appeared in his films (*Blind Husbands, Foolish Wives,* and *The Wedding March*), thereby revealing parts of himself, or had surrogates (as in *Merry-Go-Round, The Merry Widow,* and *Queen Kelly*). Perhaps in this film he felt some kinship with Rex, the "other man," who was a rogue to some extent, but the attaché is essentially too kind and decent and the husband too wimpy and ineffectual for either of them to win empathy from the director-author. Their names certainly lack subtlety in their symbolic implications: Rex Strong, Goodright, and Grace.

The story of *The Devil's Pass Key,* in terms of today's values, has little to recommend it: it seems heavy-handed, "moral," and ponderous. At best, it has a semitragic plot—a tedious working out of a complicated story that leads up to one vital point and, as such, is really like a one-joke comedy, however mean-spirited it might be. The film's saving grace must have been in its characterizations, the very area that a plot outline cannot communicate. Of course, the disappearance of this film is a loss, but it is one that by no means equals the tragedy of the loss of major portions of *Greed* or *The Wedding March.* Stroheim survived the disappearance of *The Devil's Pass Key* with no trouble, and we no doubt can do the same.

If Stroheim, at least on some level, felt himself in a kind of competition with Griffith, he had to be chagrined when he compared *Variety's* tepid opinion of his new film with the absolutely glowing reviews and extraordinary box-office success of Griffith's *Way Down East,* which opened one month later. However, he surely perceived *The Devil's Pass Key* as a mere stepping-stone, more an assignment than a fully realized personal project.

Conscious of himself as a sincere film artist and confident of his skills, Stroheim must have hoped that, if given a free hand with his own script, a healthy budget, and unlimited time, he could create a profound psychological study that would surpass his own work as well as Griffith's. His dream was not to rival *Intolerance's* epic grandeur but to impress audiences with an encompassing, mature theme, a theme dealing with the turmoil (moral, social, and financial) following the World War. Stroheim would take over Griffith's mantle, if he could, not with Victorian melodrama—a chase over the ice floes—but with the deep probing of the human spirit.

Stroheim was more than just a meticulous assembler of detail and a critical observer of human nature. *The Devil's Pass Key* moves beyond just a few individuals and starts to examine the various layers of society and the social milieu. Soon, he would try to encompass a much more extensive political/social/cultural perspective, interlarded with drives for money and sex and position. Starting here in *The Devil's Pass Key,* he attempts more in *Foolish Wives* and creates perhaps the widest view in *Merry-Go-Round*. This compulsion to tell all, to show all, and to interpret all, as much as any other, was his undoing because it required more and more length to create the social structure in front of which he could explore character.

6

Foolish Wives

After the critical and financial success of *Blind Husbands* and the satisfactory completion of *The Devil's Pass Key,* Stroheim became the close-cropped but fair-haired boy at Universal. The studio announced in January 1920 that Stroheim's next project would be *McTeague,* starring Gibson Gowland, but this plan must have seemed of questionable practicality, for Frank Norris's novel had never been a best seller and was, in fact, one of the most depressing books ever written.

Temporarily putting aside his dream of showing the underbelly of American life, with which fate had made him well acquainted, Stroheim decided to continue depicting Europe with an original story that eventually became *Foolish Wives.* The now famous director talked Carl Laemmle into a big production, one far bigger than either gentleman ever dreamed. Although Laemmle was leery of the giant sets Stroheim was planning—after all, he had made Universal a success by producing inexpensive films—he feared his ace director would be hired by some other studio. A gambler, like all the early moguls, Laemmle was reluctant to break his winning streak and so gave Stroheim the go-ahead. The film was intended to cost about $250,000. Eventually, when expenses approached $1 million, it would cause financial headaches for Laemmle and artistic heartaches for its creator. One reviewer, after the film's release, said: "If Carl Laemmle were of a homicidal turn he might either shoot von Stroheim at sunrise or step on him and squash him."[1]

Stroheim had recreated only a small village street and a few buildings for *Blind Husbands* and some Parisian settings for *The Devil's Pass Key,* but now he virtually rebuilt the entire central plaza of Monte Carlo. This independent European principality, presided over by Prince Albert I, had been a rest and recreation spot during the war. After the armistice, it drew to its warm climate and gambling casinos an international crowd of soldiers, adventurers, rogues, and vacationers. It was an appropriate place for Stroheim to comment on the postwar world. In his own mind, it might also have been a symbol for Hollywood.

Not only was the Monte Carlo set faithful architecturally, but the film itself perceptively depicts the interaction of a number of nationalities, lifestyles, classes, and personalities. Its theme contrasts the counterfeit with the genuine. It provides us with a phony count, phony cousins, phony roulette wheels, phony manners, and phony banknotes. There is lust by the count for every woman, and lust by him and several others for money—in short, greed. It again deals with a neglected American wife bedazzled by a suave European and shows Americans to be without class, polish, or style. But underneath—too late to pacify many of his viewers—Stroheim shows that Americans are basically good people. There is also love: the counterfeiter for his daughter, the maid for the count, and even—though much hidden—the American husband for his wife.

Stroheim's vision was a broad one—so broad, in fact, that he could not narrow it to an acceptable length. The film would be the first of many truncated efforts issuing from a master who felt, like the naturalist novelists whom he so admired, that reality—and, indeed, art—was the accumulation of detail. The more detail, the greater the accuracy; the greater the accuracy, the greater the art.

Stroheim had created his acting career out of being "the man you love to hate," and the advertisements for this film would also use this line. Writing himself a major role in *Foolish Wives,* he would continue to indulge in villainy. In the film, he plays a lecher, a crook, a coward, and a rapist. He also enjoyed mixing his screen image with that of the real Stroheim. All art may be exorcism, and certainly Stroheim revealed his inner psyche, giving it fair (and often unfair) treatment on the screen. The lengths to which he went, of course, were not entirely known to the public. The Russian "count" of *Foolish Wives* was no more a real member of the nobility than Stroheim himself, with his tales of the military and aristocratic circles of Vienna. Stroheim must have enjoyed his daring private joke: here was a phony count playing a phony count for an audience that believed he was a real count! Stroheim's well-developed sense of irony must have reveled in this risky masquerade, but no one was shrewd enough to figure it out. Indeed, unlike the count in *Foolish Wives,* Stroheim would never be unmasked during his lifetime.

After Carl Laemmle agreed to Stroheim's new film in the spring of 1920, the director ordered the construction of immense exterior sets (including even an artificial lake) and vast interior ones. The *Dramatic Mirror* in June mentioned that "the terrible Eric von Stroheim has announced that he is going to build a replica of Monte Carlo. . . . Eric says he ought to know what Monte Carlo looks like for he was 'busted' there twice."[2] Stroheim, with his penchant for authenticity, also had a man engrave French money; unfortunately, the bills were so realistic that Stroheim was arrested for counterfeiting and appeared in a U.S. court on July 14, 1920.[3] He protested "that the money was for use in pictures only"[4] and was eventually released. Although this event seems suspiciously like a publicity stunt, it was not.

Stroheim started shooting in July 1920, and he continued to shoot for almost an entire year, until the cameras were taken from him in June 1921! As expenses mounted, Universal tried to capitalize on its depletion of money by erecting an electric sign on Broadway that announced each week how much more money the picture had cost. Partially because of this sign, Stroheim achieved a reputation as a spendthrift, not that he needed additional publicity for his extravagance. This dubious fame never left him, nor did he ever give his subsequent backers any reason to believe otherwise.

In the fancy program printed for the premiere of *Foolish Wives,* a note by Laemmle reminded the audience how much footage Stroheim had shot and that $421,000 had been spent on the settings alone. It stated that the complete cost was $1,103,736.38. Stroheim, years later, claimed that the total was only $730,000.[5]

Although the advertisements consistently mentioned that the film was made by "the man you love to hate," Laemmle was afraid that it might be considered a foreign production, or even worse, a German one. Thus, he was careful in the program to mention that the entire film, except for the oceanfront scenes, was shot on Universal's back lot and that nearly all the artisans and actors were of American origin.

Even before the film was shown to the public, it had gained a dubious reputation. Certainly, the tone of an early article in *Photoplay* was already quite snide:

We are given to understand that Erich von Stroheim's master-piece, *Blind Wives* [*sic*] is completed.

We hesitate to believe such news. We had decided that *Blind Wives* was one of those things like the babbling brook—that go on and on forever.

It is rumored that Mr. von Stroheim has purchased his ticket for Germany, where he will continue to make pictures.

He will sail before *Blind Wives* is released, such of it, that can get by the censors.

The picture is said to be magnificent in scenery, daring, nerve, and several other things.

It certainly cost enough—somewhere very close to the million mark; and took long enough—a little over a year—to produce great results.[6]

The article discusses how Stroheim's habit of showing up on the set late was "in some measure responsible for the length of time" of production, although it did not mention that he frequently worked far into the night. Then it claims how, apparently, he had cussed at some union workers with such vehemence that they threatened to quit. Stroheim, the article notes gleefully, had to apologize. Whether Stroheim's carryings on had alienated the press or whether the content of the film had already ruffled various feathers, one cannot be sure.

Foolish Wives, at least as it now remains after more than half of its footage was cut, opens at the Villa Amorosa on the shore of the Mediterranean at Monte Carlo. There, Karamzin (Stroheim), pretending to be a Russian count, lives with two women confederates, who masquerade as his cousins. He is sleeping with one, if not both, of them. He also has slept with the unattractive maid, whom he has promised to marry. He seems to have his hands full—or beds full—with them, and it is no wonder that he drinks ox blood for breakfast! Karamzin is an excellent marksman, and in the beginning of the film he is seen target shooting.

He ascends the stairs and has breakfast on the terrace. A counterfeiter, accompanied by his simpleminded daughter, arrives to deliver some recently printed money. The count eyes the young girl and finds her innocence attractive.

The count learns from the newspaper that a new American envoy (in the original program he was referred to as an ambassador, but the credits call him an envoy) is coming to Monte Carlo, so he and his cousins decide that he should meet the envoy's wife. Being inexperienced, she might believe his aristocracy and, if he can charm her into a relationship, this might provide some leverage in case they are caught passing their bad money. Furthermore, such an acquaintance would possibly draw other rich people to patronize their crooked roulette wheel.

Mr. Hughes, the envoy, is basically a decent man, but one without class, polish, or attentiveness. As one review put it, he is a "good-natured boob."[7] He struggles to take off his gloves while being formally introduced to the prince at a royal reception. In contrast, Karamzin deftly removes his gloves in his contrived meeting with Mrs. Hughes on the hotel terrace. At first, she is offended by his obvious staring at her legs, and she straightens her skirt. When he tips a bellboy to call for "Count Karamzin," she looks around to see who that personage would be and realizes that the elegantly dressed man opposite her is the count. Flattered by his attentions, she becomes fascinated with this dashing man with such elegant manners. At several points during the film, when Mrs. Hughes drops an object, a nearby American marine neglects to help her. This boorish behavior is contrasted to Karamzin's quick offering of aid. Only later do we find out that the supposedly impolite marine has lost his arms in the war: He is a real hero, not a phony with manners. In another scene, Mrs. Hughes and her husband witness a pigeon shoot where the count proves himself an excellent shot. She is enthralled, but her husband is not impressed, particularly by the slaughter of the innocent birds.

When the count invites Mrs. Hughes to join him and one of his cousins for a walk in the countryside, he succeeds in getting the wife and himself hopelessly lost in a storm. They seek shelter in the hut of a crippled, witchlike hag, where they have to spend the night. Thoroughly drenched, the American wife reluctantly agrees to change into some dry clothes while modestly refusing Karamzin's help. Although he sits across the room, he slyly observes her with a little pocket mirror. At this point, the rear end of a goat appears in the frame; Karamzin, noticing a nasty smell, elbows the animal away. Soon after, just as he is about to seduce or attack Mrs. Hughes, a monk comes in out of the storm and interrupts his plans. After trying to slip the woman's hand into his lap, Karamzin finally leaves her alone.

The next morning, Karamzin and Mrs. Hughes return to Monte Carlo. The cousin asks, "And did Sergius behave himself?" This title was changed by the New York censorship board into "And did Sergius take good care of you?" The wife slips back into her room, the husband unaware that she was out all night.

Later, the Hughes couple, the cousins, and the count go gambling at the casino. Karamzin has borrowed the pitiful life-savings of his maid, after feigning tears and assuring the drudge, whom he has seduced, that he will marry her. He loses money at roulette, while Mrs. Hughes wins heavily. The count slips a note to Mrs. Hughes and inveigles her into coming to the villa, then to an isolated tower room, where he explains that he desperately needs money and asks her to lend it to him. The maid, jealous at this assignation, sets the building on fire and, after freeing her canary, jumps off a cliff. As the flames leap up, Karamzin and Mrs. Hughes rush out onto the balcony, and when she is hesitant to jump into the fireman's net, the panicked count abandons her and leaps to safety. She finally jumps, as Mr. Hughes arrives. Karamzin, having proved himself a coward, is punched by Mr. Hughes. (Missing from surviving prints is an arrangement for a duel to take place the next morning and a scene that includes the cousins, angry that he has allowed his sex drive to overcome his money drive, kicking the count out of the villa.) Standing on a street corner, Karamzin puffs a cigarette and decides on a little sexual adventure—to seduce the counterfeiter's daughter. He slips into her room but knocks over a pot of geraniums, which awakens the father, who kills Karamzin and stuffs his corpse into a sewer.

In its original version, *Foolish Wives* must have been a shocking revelation of postwar life, as well as a long and rambling one. Every shot was taken innumerable times, as Stroheim experimented with content, acting, and style. As a result, he ended up with 320 reels of negative, a staggering amount when one remembers that Universal films seldom ran more than 5 or 6 reels and that even Griffith never released a feature longer than 12 or 13 reels.

Toward the end of the filming, Rudolph Christians, who played Hughes, died. When Universal informed Stroheim that he would not be allowed to retake all the husband's scenes with another actor, he had to settle for a double, Robert Edeson. That someone as meticulous as Stroheim ignored the fact that Christians had black hair and Edeson gray hair has always been a puzzle. Stroheim did not seem to care about the scenes necessary to complete the picture. Instead he merely placed the camera behind Edeson's head with its gray hair. By carefully blocking his actors, Stroheim could have taken the innumerable close-ups of Christians (shot for earlier scenes) and inserted them at crucial moments to clarify the new scenes. Here is a case where Stroheim was clearly incapable of "faking it." Certain scenes at the end, such as the envoy's discovery that the gambling wheel at the count's villa is fixed, were eventually eliminated by the studio because the matching of the double was so unskillful. The story was then modified so that in the surviving versions the husband is unaware of the crooked roulette wheel. Another scene, in which the principal characters go for a boat ride, still remains but makes little sense, for it is not clear that the husband has been put in a boat with the cousins to allow Karamzin to flirt with the wife. In fact, these boat scenes were the last ones shot before Universal finally halted production.

Stroheim now faced the awesome task of trying to put the film together. He went to his editing rooms and, for the next six months, from June to December 1921, pieced his picture together. He ended up with what he claimed was "a perfect story." Unfortunately, it ran thirty-two reels (close to eight hours). Asked how it would be possible to present thirty-two reels for an evening's entertainment, he is alleged to have said, "That is a detail I hadn't time to bother about."[8] (Stroheim always made good copy!) *Photoplay*, reacting to news of Stroheim's lengthy final cut, suggested that it should be retitled "Foolish Directors" and be released as a serial.[9] Finally, the task was taken from him, because Universal had to start earning back some of the money its resident genius and madman had spent.

It was reported at the time that Stroheim then cut the film to thirty reels (the numbers vary), after which it was trimmed by editor A.D. Ripley to eighteen reels, a version that was previewed at Universal City in late December 1921.[10] This four-to-five-hour rending of the spirit and humbling of the flesh was obviously still too long.

Wishful thinking at Universal had set the New York premiere for the second week in January, and the now frantic studio had to meet that date. A special railroad car was added to the train headed for New York, and in it editors furiously tried to trim the film down to acceptable limits. This transcontinental editing, although a reality, was also a great publicity stunt. By the time the train reached New York, *Foolish Wives* had shrunk to fifteen reels.[11] There might be some exaggeration to this account, but there is no doubt that everyone was hurrying to get the film into presentable shape. Finally, another reel was removed, some new titles were probably added to bridge the gaps, a score by Sigmund Romberg (now, unfortunately, lost) was concocted, and the film, at fourteen reels, was shown on January 11, 1922, at the Central Theater on Broadway at Forty-seventh Street. The first-night audience saw a picture that, after a few days, no one would ever see again. That rare experience took about three and one-half hours, plus a five-minute intermission to satisfy the call of nature.[12] Stroheim loathed the fourteen-reel version shown at the premiere because it was so brutally cut; he complained that all that was left of his masterpiece was "the bones."[13]

Years later, Stroheim defended his original version's extreme length by claiming that his intention was to have a two-part film, which would have allowed the audience to go out for dinner and then come back to see the concluding half. Here, Stroheim chose to misremember certain awkward facts and to disregard mathematics. Each section, he said, would have run only one and one-half hours,[14] thus making a total of 180 minutes. Yet, in 1922, he had complained that the fourteen-reel version was a butchery at 220 minutes! The truth is that his original cut at thirty-two reels was impossibly long, and even his compromise version of eighteen reels would have lasted 280 minutes, more than four and one-half hours.

Both the reviewers and the public found even the fourteen-reel film much too long. Universal, no doubt, agreed, and so the film's mixed reception caused the shears to come out again. Soon whole episodes were scrapped. One sequence was omitted because it provoked incredulous mirth: at the end of the film, after Mrs. Hughes leaps from the tower, she gives birth to a premature baby. A journalist described the reaction. "A great audience had burst suddenly into howling gusts of laughter that lapped and sucked and whirled about the pit and lofty tiers of the auditorium like water stirred to frenzy in a tank. Without warning, as a hen might lay an egg, the heroine had given birth to a baby. It was outrageous, it was uproarious. Von Stroheim had been seen to rise, white as death, and leave the theater, to disappear God knows where. Broadway hummed with rumors of suicide."[15] Although this scene was cut, stills of it still exist.[16]

How could a husband, asked many of the reviewers, not suspect an impending child? Apparently, Stroheim had included all kinds of hints that the wife was pregnant. He said in an interview, "I had worked and studied and striven on that very thing, introducing little things, suggestions, incidents, motives until I had accumulated enough power and momentum to make the baby the most logical thing in the world. . . . But they cut that all out, every bit of it, and, my God! left in the baby!"[17] According to the interviewer, Stroheim, after he said this, flung up his hands in a helpless gesture and gave a shrug of resignation.

If Stroheim was unhappy, so was the New York Censorship Board, which screened the film on January 8, 1922, and ordered cuts in the pocket mirror scene, the episode when the count pulls on Mrs. Hughes's stocking, five shots of the roulette wheel, half of the scene when the maid starts the fire, and the killing of the black cat that crosses Karamzin's path by the sewer. Censors in other states were even more finicky and condemned a large number of other shots including all those in which men and women were shown brazenly smoking cigarettes! Fortunately, some shots the censors disliked were not cut from the original negative or from the European print and therefore survive.

Universal, understandably anxious to get back its million dollars, tried to entice the public into seeing the film. On January 23, 1922, the New York Censorship Commission took exception to their efforts: "This morning's *Times* contains an ad in which the description of the picture conveys an immoral thought in language that is unmistakable. This advertising appeared early last week, and is one of the main reasons that we demand to review all advertising matter. Unless you can satisfactorily arrange with us that such matter will not appear, we shall have to order that all advertising matter, including that intended for newspapers, shall be submitted to this office, before printing." What bothered them was this statement: "Fascinating in its wickedness, absorbing in its story of Life as it actually is, a wonderful study of WOMEN in all their varied moods of inconsistency, in this great, gigantic, overwhelming and stupendous romance, told in epoch-making scenes." Another line, in a different ad, perhaps also bothered the censors. It mentioned "the most fascinating villain who ever decoyed a pretty woman into a compromising situation." Such was the state of public morality in 1922.

Universal had more cause to worry about laughter than censorship at this point. Although the baby scene was cut, followed shortly after by many more episodes, the general complaint remained: the film was too long. Within ten days, it shrank to about twelve reels, a change considered by many to be an improvement, although not by Stroheim. But exhibitors did not even want a three-hour movie on such a subject, so Universal announced that the picture would be cut to ten reels.[18] This was the version that made the rounds of the United States when *Foolish Wives* received general release in March.

One can only speculate about what Stroheim's original plans were and what he eventually filmed. From certain remaining stills (at the New York Public Library) and from some titles in the film's existing continuity, one can surmise that Karamzin sleeps with one—and probably both—of the "cousins," that he is shown on horseback saluting troops in the main square, that the mentally afflicted counterfeiter's daughter is in the streets with her doll where children point at her and others ward off her "evil eye," that the monk (who later appears in the witch's hut) offers the girl some bread and that she steps back in fear, and that in a scene in a police station questions are raised about counterfeit money.

The original story also had a subplot (prefiguring the one in *Greed* of old Grannis and Miss Baker) dealing with Mr. and Mrs. Judd, described in the original program as "the couple from home." They were intended, no doubt, as a contrast to the envoy and his wife and also to Karamzin and his women. The Judds were entirely removed from Universal's modified print; in a surviving European print, there is only a brief shot of them at the pigeon shoot, one so fragmentary and meaningless that when I reconstructed the print, I removed it entirely.

In one version of the continuity, there existed this title: "We're on our way to the Oceanographic Museum to look at the wonderful fish—they say some of them are almost human." The identity of the "we" is not clear, but possibly it is the Judds. This title is followed by another one: "Old 'Doc' Judd, but they've been saving twenty years for this trip—nice old couple." Probably this was followed by a scene in an aquarium. Earlier, Karamzin has warned Mrs. Hughes that there are "many hungry sharks lying in wait to get hold of one's money." Obviously, Stroheim was developing some kind of parallel between fish and humans, one that would tie in with the ending of the film, in which Karamzin's body floats out to sea to be consumed by an octopus. As in *Blind Husbands,* in which a vulture hovers over von Steuben, horrible creatures devour horrible people.

The plot of *Foolish Wives* was thinned, but the plot of its subsequent history thickened. Its controversial subject matter, its cost, and the resultant publicity attracted audiences, although not enough to make the film very profitable. Patrons throughout the country, and particularly in smaller towns, thought the film not only appalling but, worse yet, not entertaining. After playing throughout the country, *Foolish Wives* was finally laid to rest in the Universal vaults.

Shortly after sound came in, the studios had a degree of success rereleasing *The Big Parade, Ben Hur, The Birth of a Nation,* and *Way Down East* with added sound effects and music. So Universal decided to prepare synchronized versions of its most prestigious productions, beginning with *The Phantom of the Opera.* Editor Ted Kent and title writer Walter Anthony were assigned to "modernize" *Foolish Wives.* They shortened the story, changed the plot line, rearranged sequences, and rewrote most of the titles.

The husband, Andrew Hughes, who had been America's envoy to Monte Carlo, now became Howard Hughes (probably an inside joke on someone's part), an American businessman. This modification removed an aspect of the story that had irritated many American viewers, who considered the portrayal of the envoy to be an arrogant slap in the face of our diplomatic corps.

As a result of this change, all the scenes of the envoy arriving on an American ship, his being greeted by the Prince of Monaco's aide, his review of the troops, and his presentation at court were dropped. Stroheim's plot hung on the fact that the count intentionally makes the acquaintance of the envoy's wife so that he can pass counterfeit money through her respectable fingers. (Even if the fraud were later discovered, the situation would be too embarrassing to prosecute.) This element was entirely spoiled by making the husband just a businessman. Other scenes, such as the pigeon shoot, where the count shows off his marksmanship, were also dropped, as was much of the opening part of the film. A scene that had appeared in the middle of the original, in which Karamzin visits the counterfeiter, was shortened and moved to the beginning. The suicide of the maid, one of the film's more poignant moments, was omitted entirely.

Universal filmed new titles and cut them into the trimmed and rearranged original footage. The adjusted negative now ran 7,655 feet (eight reels). A print was struck off and shown to the studio's executives, who decided that rereleasing the film would not be worth the trouble. The project was abandoned. In 1936, when the Museum of Modern Art in New York asked for a copy of *Foolish Wives,* it was given a print of this altered negative. The Museum had no idea of the severe changes that had been made, and for almost forty years, this was the version shown in the auditorium and released on 16 mm for rental. Later, when other archives in the world wanted prints, they obtained them from the museum. In the 1940s, Stroheim viewed the film at the Museum of Modern Art and almost had apoplexy. As late as 1947, Stroheim believed that Iris Barry, the curator of the Film Department, had "appointed herself as supreme censor"[19] and had reedited his already truncated work.[20]

Thus, *Foolish Wives* was seen only in this form in America and some other countries. Meanwhile, unknown to benighted American viewers, there was another print in Europe, one in which the husband was still an envoy. This print, an Italian version, had been copied by the Cinémathèque Française and the British Film Institute. Eventually, an American film distributor began to rent the BFI's version, and when I saw it I was amazed. The cutting style was entirely different, and so was some of the action.

One thing that misled many film historians over the years was the fact that the two prints were roughly of the same length. How could the European print contain reels of material missing from the American version and yet be no longer? The answer was simple. Whoever edited the Italian print must have been a butcher by former profession. His method was to include as many shots as possible, but only after trimming them at both ends. Thus, an actor no longer approached a chair and sat down but got near the chair and then, in a jump-cut, was shown already seated. A twenty-frame reaction shot became four frames, a three-foot shot became two feet. The result was that Stroheim's meticulous direction and smooth continuity occasionally resembled the pace of Eisenstein's Odessa Steps sequence in *Potemkin*.

I then made copies of each 16 mm print and edited them together into a fuller version to show in my classes at the university. When I mentioned what I had done to friends at the American Film Institute in 1971, they asked me to prepare a "good" version from 35 mm material, which they would then screen at a Stroheim retrospective scheduled for April 1972 in Washington, D.C. Subsequently, the British Film Institute sent over a 35 mm copy, and the Museum of Modern Art provided its original 35 mm print. Together, the two versions added up to about fifteen thousand feet.

Before I originally began on my reconstruction using the 16 mm prints, I thought all I had to do was cut in the missing scenes. It became immediately clear, however, that the two films were not made from the same negative. Most films in the late teens were shot by two cameras at the same time, with the extra negative used as protection or sent to foreign lands to make prints. This European print, though, had been made from alternate takes. Thus, the action was not always the same. For example, in one print, Karamzin wet his eyebrows with his finger; in the other, he sniffed his finger. Also, the action was sometimes blocked out differently, with characters standing in different places.

Some scenes were generally the same in both prints, but others were severely cut. Many of these changes were initiated by censors. The sexier moments had been altered, but in different ways in each country, thereby making it possible to reassemble much of the original action. Stroheim, let us say, filmed an episode that took a dozen shots. The American print might have shots 1, 2, 5, 6, 8, 10. The European one would have shots 1, 2, 4, 7, 10, 11, 12. Of course, one can try to put the shots back in proper order, but there is no way to replace the still missing shots, 3 and 9. Their absence leads to a new problem for the restorer because shots 2 and 4 and 8 and 10 probably will not cut together smoothly, resulting in a jump-cut and/or a continuity error. How could this new version be made to work without the reconstruction seeming as if the "new" editor was incapable of making a matching cut?

The most heavily modified scenes were the opening breakfast episode, the arrival of the counterfeiter at the villa, the sections dealing with the retarded girl, and many moments with the maid. In the re-

The young Stroheim in the only genuine uniform fate allowed him.

Photos from the author's collection.

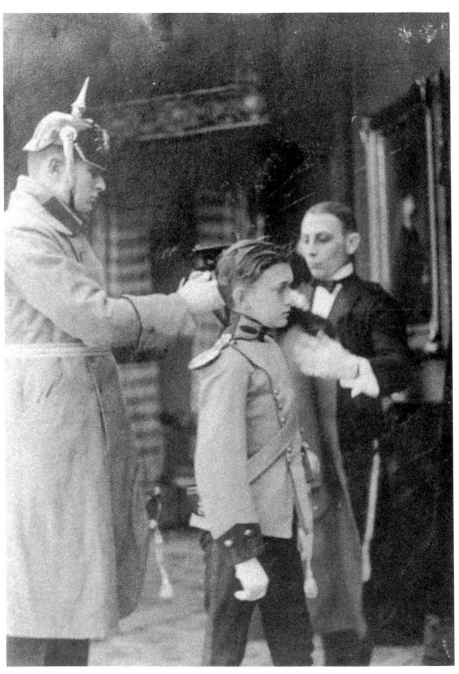

Stroheim as the ever watchful and somewhat obnoxious overseer of the young prince in *Old Heidelberg* (1915).

Stroheim dressed as an elegant gentleman, a vision long recalled on the studio lot.

Left: Scenes from *Old Heidelberg.*
Below: A very young-looking
Stroheim in a small part with
Dorothy Gish and Wallace Reid
as the doomed lovers.

Sets for *His Picture in the Papers* (1916). *Above:* "Keep off this set" says the sign on Stroheim's conception of a steak house restaurant. *Below:* Stroheim's graffiti on walls that would be unseen by the camera.

Margaret (Francelia Billington) leaves a letter addressed to "Erich von Stroheim," later changed to "von Steuben" in *Blind Husbands* (1919).

The "good" man and the "bad" man in *Blind Husbands*.

The Picture You'll Never Forget

THIS IS the *third* monthly advertisement of "BLIND HUSBANDS" in this magazine—published for the reason that we do not want *any* picture-goer to miss seeing this utterly absorbing photodrama. One of the great Trade-papers, whose chief business it is to value plays for the Theatre-owner, says that Von Stroheim's Wonder-play, "BLIND HUS-BANDS" reaches the highwater mark of entertainment. "*It throbs with vitality—and soars with tremendous sweep straight to its climax. Nothing is missing to make this picture a great achievement.*"

Truly, it is the picture you'll never forget.

Carl Laemmle presents

Von Stroheim's Wonder-play

The Universal-Jewel Production de Luxe

Ask your Theatre When you can see it

"Blind Husbands"

Photoplay advertisement for *Blind Husbands*.

Carl Laemmle
offers

The Most Enthralling Picture Drama
that the Art has ever produced

Stroheim's
Wonder-Play

"BLIND
HUSBANDS"

A LOVE-STORY as appealing as the most
beautiful romance in your memory—an
adventure story as gripping as any Serial
thriller—a scenic marvel as wondrous as the
most inspiring travel picture you've ever
known. But most of all, a *human drama*
whose people are real flesh-and-blood—
whose faithful details are an eye-and-mind
delight—whose story holds your heart a
helpless prisoner until the last great moment
comes and brings the glorious surprise that
sends you away in a glow of happiness. See
it without fail—"BLIND HUSBANDS"—
the picture you'll never forget.

UNIVERSAL-JEWEL
PRODUCTION DE LUXE

Photoplay advertisement for Blind Husbands.

Advertisement for *The Devil's Pass Key* (1920).

Above: Von Steuben (Stroheim), kindly Sepp (Gibson Gowland), and inattentive husband (Sam de Grasse) in *Blind Husbands*. *Below:* A cut scene from *Foolish Wives* (1922), shows the phony Count with one of his mistresses. Note the black bed and statue.

Above: One of the last scenes of *Foolish Wives* (1922). The gray-haired man on the right, trying not to show too much of his face, was the unconvincing double for the actor who died. *Below:* Publicity shot of a group of censors on the set of *Foolish Wives*, where these doughty women and blue-nosed men were being tempted to dull their scissors.

Stroheim with monocle, medals, sharp uniform, and mourning band in *Foolish Wives*.

Above: Stroheim working on a scenario. Notice, as usual, the gold bracelet on his right wrist, and the odd wristwatch. *Below:* Arthur Lennig editing *Foolish Wives* at the American Film Institute, April 1972.

Stroheim, the artist-thinker, with cane and wristwatch.

A portrait of the older Stroheim. Despite numerous comments, he had thinning hair but was never bald.

Stroheim in a rare smiling shot.

An autographed photo.

A prophetic shot of Stroheim in front of his "cutting" rooms. Note the misspelling of his name.

construction, one shot from the American print might be followed by one that remained only in the Italian, and that might be followed by an American shot because the Italian one had been abruptly shortened.

There were further complications. The Italian print was heavily damaged by splices within shots and was, in general, rather scratched. Whenever faced with a choice, provided that the action was similar, I stuck to the American version. But this, of course, could not be done when the Italian print contained the only footage that existed. What at times looks like inept editing in the reconstructed print is due to problems in the only available material. What does one do with a four-frame close-up that separates two shots taken from the same camera position? The close-up had been about twenty or thirty frames long, originally; now, at four frames, it lasts on screen for one-fifth of a second and is far too brief to be effective. Yet to omit the close-up would cause an even worse problem, by cutting directly between two similar shots and having the actors leap absurdly from one position on screen to another. In some cases, I had these brief shots double-printed and even triple-printed (that is, individual frames were printed more than once to lengthen the take). The effect of the strangely frozen frames may not be entirely satisfactory, but it is better than inserting a four-frame shot in the middle of a slow scene.

The breakfast episode in which Karamzin joins his "cousins" had been shortened in both prints, in the American one severely. The insertion of many of the missing shots made the episode play much better by retaining the subtle interplay of the count's women, as well as his breakfast manners.

Other nuances that Stroheim had intended had been cut from each of the prints, but not consistently. The retarded daughter's scenes were changed the most because its child-molesting content upset viewers. When the girl first appears at the villa, she crosses herself, thinking she is in church, or perhaps sensing the evil awaiting her. Cut from the American print, that gesture remained in the Italian. Also missing from the American print was the tilt of the camera from her feet to her face as Karamzin surveys his virginal victim. All the American print contained was a close-up (as if printed on canvas) of her face. The tilt-shot had originally been in the American version, for the Kansas State Board of Review had specifically ordered it omitted. Fortunately, this shot remained in the Italian print, so I put it back, followed by the shot of

Karamzin licking his lips, then the close-up of the girl. Unfortunately, both versions cut the shot in which the count touches her (although it had once been in the release print, for the New York State Censorship Board had ordered it removed). In the Italian version, the counterfeiter takes Karamzin's money, kisses it, and, seeing the gleam in the count's eye as he sizes up the simpleminded girl, looks suspiciously at him and intimates that anyone who touched her would be killed—all of which was missing from the American print.

When Karamzin visits the counterfeiter's quarters, he enters the sleeping girl's room and approaches her bed. Then he looks out the window (in the Italian print) to check the possibilities of a later entry. Both prints cut much of this scene in her room, but fortunately, each country considered different things unsavory, so it was possible to put much of the episode back together.

Other scenes missing from the American print that have been restored include one in which Karamzin prevails upon the maid to lend him money. The American print merely shows him receiving it, whereas in the Italian print he refuses the coins she offers and instead asks for and receives all her paper money. The Italian footage also contains nervous looks between the cousins, when they pass the bogus money at the casino; the entire scene in which the count kisses the distraught maid and then surreptitiously wipes off his lips; and certain moments during the storm in the swamp and at the witch's hut. The scene in which the count, with a mirror, watches the woman undressing was trimmed in both prints. Now we can see him put his hand in his pocket, remove something, then look in the little pocket mirror, observe her bare back, and leer. This all had to be reconstructed. Many other additions were not as significant, but missing shots were scrupulously reinserted.

The restored version of the film also uses the original 1922 titles. Some of them had been changed by the New York Censorship Board, but a search through their files provided the original words. For example, "And night—Mysterious!—Fragrant—Bewitching!—Glamorous—Enticing! The Great enchantress of the world!" was the cleansed version of "And night—Voluptuous!—Sensuous!—Erotic!—The Great Procuress of the world!" A humorous article in *Photoplay* provided a parody of this type of title: "Passion—soft—insidual—sexitive—the radiator of the soul."[21]

In reconstructing *Foolish Wives,* I shortened all of the titles so that they remain on the screen more briefly than the originals, because modern audiences who see silent films tend to have a faster reading speed than the general public of 1922. This trimmed footage adds up to many hundreds of feet. As a result, the reconstructed print is the equivalent of eleven reels, about ten to fifteen minutes longer than the general 1922 release.

One could argue that the reconstructed version is not authentic, but neither is the American one or the Italian one. At any rate, the choppiness of the Italian print has been partially alleviated, and the many eliminations from the 1928–30 version have been reinserted, which does bring us, in a sense, closer to what Stroheim had filmed.

I must admit that at the world premiere of the reconstructed print, one of the great lovers of the silent film leaned over to me at the end of the picture and said, "Great job, but I'm glad you didn't find any more." Stroheim's original thirty-two-reel version, or the eighteen, or even the fourteen might have demanded far more patience and *Sitzfleisch* than most mortals possess. Nonetheless, it is a pity that so much is lost, however perverse and rambling and occasionally absurd it might have been.

I only hope that Stroheim would be kind enough to shower a few of the extra apple blossoms from *The Wedding March* upon my head and not some of the effluent that he would have been quite capable of throwing. I assume the Italian editor received much of that, and the editor at Universal a goodly portion, and the innocent Iris Barry a considerable inundation. In any case, I think I am the only Stroheim editor who added rather than cut. Still, I cannot help hearing a muffled voice from on high yelling down, "It's still only the bones, you *Schweinhund!*"

Although the basic ideas of *Foolish Wives* are not difficult, most film critics of the time seemed unwilling or unable to perceive them. *Photoplay* disliked what it saw, and the animus that it revealed in the August 1921 issue took more vicious form the following March: "*Foolish Wives* is an insult to every American. . . . Stroheim has made a film that is unfit for the family to see; that is an insult to American ideals and womanhood. To point a doubtful moral the director has adorned a gruesome, morbid, unhealthy tale. . . . It is a story you could never permit children to see or even adolescents. It is a story that sickens you before you have seen it half told."

Arthur James, the editor of *Moving Picture World,* also disapproved of the film. He referred to Stroheim's "simian effronteries to women [which] will offend all decent members of the sex and his cheap sneering at the supposed bad manners of American marines." He sensed that the film was "a studied and flippant slam at all things American." *Foolish Wives,* he declared, was a "striking example of what not to do in making moving pictures."[22] Nor was the film's reception any better in Britain. *Kinematograph Weekly* said: "A more pointless exhibition of picturized pornography has never been seen on the screen. . . . To present such a studied composite of bestiality and downright suggestiveness to go into the theater under the guise of 'entertainment' is deliberately to pander to the worst elements in film audiences."[23]

This self-righteous and moral tone partially conceals a number of extraordinary fallacies. Stroheim is pulling back the protective curtain of lies and hypocrisy to examine the actual life of the international smart set. Such a life is perhaps not a "good" one (it smells of money, chicanery, intrigue, lust, and murder), but Stroheim's view is not inaccurate. What reviews were reacting to is Stroheim's unwillingness to sentimentalize and sweeten reality. The film is an "insult" only if truth itself is an insult to every American. (That this indeed might be the case provides a delightful irony.)

The assumption that films should be made so that children could see them was not an isolated view, nor was it confined to motion pictures. Indeed, William Dean Howells, the American literary critic of high reputation, said the same thing about novels in 1891. He too felt that art should not bring to light the sordid passions but should filter truth so that young girls could read without blushing. Although literature did not follow Howells, the motion picture, because of its greater immediacy and its middle- and lower-class market, was successfully subjected for over fifty years to a tight moral code. It became Stroheim's burden to come at least two generations before his time in his uncompromising treatment of life.

It must have galled Stroheim to have his film harshly reviewed in *Photoplay,* a magazine devoted to puffery, whitewashed biographies, inane gossip, and infantile publicity releases—and to be told, by a staff of hacks dealing continually with half-truths and living in a city devoted to mammon, that his comparatively tame vision of Monte Carlo was "sickening." In an interview made after the film was released, Stroheim was angry: "'There is one thing I would like to say.' Those thin eyebrows, drawn down, whipped the soft eyes to sudden menace. 'I would like to have you quote me, Erich von Stroheim, as having said on this day of this month of this year this one thing: you Americans are living on babyfood. Since that first showing of *Foolish Wives* I have seemed to walk thru vast crowds of people, their white American faces turned toward me in stern reproof. My ears have rung with their united cry: "it is not fit for children!" Children! Children!'" Stroheim explained that he had "not one thought for children, any more than [did] Hugo, or Voltaire, or Shakespeare, or any writer of intelligence and sincerity."[24] He went on to argue for freedom of the screen, adding that adults should not be governed by what children should see. Despite *Photoplay*'s strictures about the film's content, in August 1922, the magazine ranked *Foolish Wives* among the eight best pictures of the year.

Most of the male critics disapproved of the film on moral grounds; it took a woman, Harriet Underhill of the *New York Tribune,* to appreciate its honesty. She reported that many people said Stroheim "must be a pretty bad lot himself, or he couldn't play the part that way." She, however, liked the film and, at a lunch she had with him, was charmed by the polite and elegant Austrian. When she praised his work, he replied, "You are so kind, but your sympathy is like the handclasp of a friend at the open grave of a loved one." Miss Underhill told Stroheim that the packed theater was by no means an open grave and that she considered the film the best picture she had ever seen. "You are too kind," he averred. "But over there is only the skeleton of my dead child."[25] He regretted the cuts that had reduced his large vision to merely a short glimpse. Stroheim, in the next few years, would witness a lot of skeletons.

If Stroheim's detractors had been less irate, they would have seen that the film was not the wholesale indictment they thought it to be and that some (though not all) of the insults against Americans were to be taken ironically. Stroheim's purpose is clearly to show beneath the pretensions and hypocrisies of modern Europe various proofs of man's irrationality, destructiveness, and lust for financial, social, and sexual goals. That society is not what it pretends to be can be illlustrated not only by the very fact of the First World War but also by the tenacity and enthusiasm with which the belligerents had attempted to annihilate one another. This disaster hovers over the whole film.

The time is 1919, and soldiers and sailors of all nations mill aimlessly about. Cripples pass by in wheelchairs, a young girl moves on crutches, an armless man stands impassively, a witchlike creature hobbles on paralyzed legs, a mindless young girl clutches a doll—these are all eloquent symbols of the best of all possible worlds. In the street, children don helmets and flourish swords, the supreme irony proving that the lesson of the war has not been learned.

The opening of the film in Monte Carlo symbolizes the lusts of the world. It is Vanity Fair:

> Therefore at this fair are all such merchandise sold, as houses, lands, trades, places, honors, preferments, titles, countries, kingdoms, lusts, pleasures, and delights of all sorts, as whores, bawds, wives, husbands, children, masters, servants, lives, blood, bodies, souls, silver, gold, pearls, precious stones, and what not.
>
> And, moreover, at this fair there is at all times to be seen jugglings, cheats, games, plays, fools, apes, knaves, and rogues, and that of every kind.
>
> Here are to be seen, too, and that for nothing, thefts, murders, adulteries, false swearers, and that of a blood-red color.

This description by John Bunyan in *Pilgrim's Progress* (published in 1678) applies equally to the film's Monte Carlo. Like Bunyan, Stroheim chronicles the various evils and hypocrisies of Europe and, by implication, the whole world. Not only did he dwell on man's sins, but he had the courage, or audacity, to offer no grace. Stroheim depicts a hell and intimates, at best, only a limbo. No glimpse of the City of God—the really good life without any ironic overtones—appears. The only moments of true affection are in the ugly maid's jealous love for Karamzin and the counterfeiter's for his afflicted daughter. If there is any love or tenderness between Mr. and Mrs. Hughes, it certainly is not shown in the surviving footage.

Although Stroheim's detailed treatment of Europe's corruption did not raise controversy but seemed rather to confirm what Americans already felt, his criticisms of his adopted land were passionately resented. He was accused in the *Photoplay* review of making "con-

tinual innuendoes as to American ideals; sly little thrusts at our tradition and sentiments." This resentment of his "thrusts" was perhaps
motivated by a passage from a supposed book, *Foolish Wives,* from which
the film ostensibly derives: "To the average American, written or un-
written codes of honor and etiquette are unessential, as, in his tiresome
chase after the dollar, he has no time to cultivate that for which the
European mainly lives. In his battle of wits fought for commercial
superiority, the fatigued body forgets sometimes to react even to the
most primitive and fundamental laws of politeness."

Although it was written by "Erich von Stroheim," the book's
author is a *persona,* a kind of mask of "the man you love to hate," and
is not Stroheim (the director) himself. This passage must not be accepted at face value but ironically; what the book says, the film pa-
tently denies. In the film, the count's behavior clearly demonstrates
that his manners are only a deceptive veneer and that the American
husband, though lacking savoir faire, has more of the "fundamental
laws of politeness" in him than the count. Stroheim is saying, in fact,
that Americans lack "class" but European phonies are even worse. This
intention, an essential part of the picture, has not been superimposed
by the studio in an attempt to placate chauvinistic audiences. The film's
major aim—when shorn of its complexities—is to show that a wife
can be foolish in thinking that her husband, though somewhat of a
clod, is worse than a bogus count. The closing title puts the basic theme
clearly: "And thus it happened that disillusionment came finally to a
foolish wife, who found in her own husband the nobility she had
sought for—in a counterfeit." This does not mean, however, that the
American husband is entirely good. (He is not.) In fact, none of the
characters comes off unscathed. Stroheim does not present "good" or
"bad" people but rather creates genuine personalities faced with complicated situations.

Although the passages from the *Foolish Wives* book have ironic
overtones, there is another statement of equal interest, though not one
discernible to the casual viewer. When the book is opened in the film,
the camera photographs the passage about the unmannered American
and his pursuit of the dollar, but pertinent things are said on the right-
hand page of the book. Although the print is too small for an audience
to read, with the aid of a magnifying glass the following passages can
be deciphered:

Could anything be more full of charm for a young wife than to embark on the ocean of social events under the guidance of an aristocratic husband?

The appearance of his manners, his delicate tact supplemented by a sounding title opens every door, every salon, and every most exclusive circle; no wonder then that the Wall Street heiress, the daughter of Fifth Avenue, or the pecunious widow of the steel magnate, all of them eagerly gravitate towards him.

The best proof of this assertion is the large number of noblemen to be found at London and Paris, at Berlin and Rome, or any other capital of Europe.

Now, of course, this is all tosh, about which Stroheim is being ironic. For within the so-called elegant aristocracy, boorishness and vulgarity flourish. Stroheim is basically a debunker, and only the most obtuse could miss the fact that he takes no class of people at face value but reveals each for what it is. The poor come off no better than the rich, the lower class no better than the upper. He is a moral, not a political, commentator.

The key to understanding the film is to recognize the three roles of Stroheim: as persona, he goads the public, knocking America and praising Europe; as the count, he is an interesting but villainous creature—a seducer, a blackmailer, a fraud, a rapist; and as an artist, he stands between these two opposites—that Europe is all good and that Europe is all bad—and tries to portray life in all its fullness. His use of irony, contrast, complex characterization, and thematic richness triumphs far beyond the puerile simplicities of other American films of the period.

Count Karamzin stands for the aristocracy, or at least for some aspects of it. Superbly played by Stroheim, the count appears to the foolish wife as the height of sophistication and fine breeding. But, as the layers of aristocratic veneer devastatingly peel off, his coarse sensibility reveals itself: he sits elegantly at the breakfast table but unceremoniously dumps food onto his plate; he neglects to stand up when the counterfeiter and his daughter arrive; and he jumps from the burning balcony, leaving the wife to fend for herself. He is not really polite; he only pretends to be. When knocked down by the husband, Karamzin says, "As an officer and a gentleman, I demand an apology." The next title, said by the husband, sums up Karamzin's character: "Officer and gentleman, hell. You're not even a *man!*"

In spite of Karamzin's boorishness and villainy, however, audiences are attracted to him in some perverse fashion, just as they are to Steuben in *Blind Husbands.* Perhaps this is why some unperceptive viewers think that he was meant to be a hero and that Stroheim admires the character he is portraying. To believe this is, of course, a mistake. Though evil fascinates Stroheim, he is essentially a moralist—the cruelest satirists of mankind usually are. Probably no writer in English literature suffered more hostility than Jonathan Swift, and none told more of the truth about mankind.

An astute observer of manners and morals, Stroheim depicts the corruption of aristocratic and pseudoaristocratic society, not necessarily to the advantage of America. If the count and his cousins come off poorly, the Americans do not contrastingly show up as angels. Stroheim's vision is consistently piercing. When Mrs. Hughes, for example, comes home from a boat ride with the count, she casually leaves her clothes around the room and begins to prepare for bed as the husband enters the room wearing a rather dumpy pair of pajamas. This scene of domestic familiarity is devastating in its lack of romantic glamor. When the husband intimates that the count had perhaps been "*too* attentive" to her, Mrs. Hughes replies, "At least these European gentlemen have agreeable manners." This statement is made ironic by the facts: the count is not really a gentleman; his manners are only "put on"; and at this moment she is greasily applying cold cream all over her face. Although this is probably one of the "sly little thrusts" about which *Photoplay* was so disturbed, Stroheim is not really being too harsh. True, he depicts Mrs. Hughes as provincial, sexually naive, and inelegant—essentially a hausfrau with a fur coat—yet she is a pleasant enough woman. Although lacking chic, she is sympathetic, as her reaction to the armless marine indicates. Her good heart is an American trait, as is, perhaps, her dullness. Certainly, in contrast to her, the more polished and worldly cousins appear fascinating until one learns of their parasitic life, their gambling with counterfeit money, and their living in alternating sin with the lecherous count. In conclusion, it can be said that Mrs. Hughes is the heroine, but by no means a perfect one. Her faults are cataloged as faithfully and as scathingly as those of the other characters. No wonder the film was disliked; it dared to disobey the Hollywood rules of conventional life.

Although Stroheim was often criticized by the front office for his meticulous and sometimes absurd attention to details, the success of his films depends on that very quality that doomed his career. He depicts the life of Monte Carlo with authority: the decor, the faces, and even the clutter are invariably authentic. Probably no director has provided greater verisimilitude. Every one of his settings—whether of the streets, or the villa, or interiors such as the cloisterlike chamber of the servant and the romantic, churchlike tower room—has an air of inevitable rightness about it.

Yet this rightness is not a mere recording of fact, a kind of scientific objectivity. To the contrary, Stroheim adds the personal touch of his bizarre and baroque imagination: the frogs, the owl, and the hideous rags of the crippled witch create in the hut an appropriately Calibanish setting for the intended seduction; the tower room's flickering candles, crucifix, odd-shaped door, and brooding darkness suggest a kind of parody of a church. The counterfeiter's house—its squalor, its slanted and shimmering light, its hundreds of statues, its pitiful array of geranium pots—provides a fitting place for the rape of an afflicted girl and the murder of her attacker. And how perceptive was Stroheim to present the dim-witted girl in an equally half-lit room. Stroheim's scenes are more than "real"; they are suggestive and individual, and they well befit the mood or idea he seeks to present. Stroheim is not a dogged slave to facts, a stubborn adherent to mere actuality. He is an artist, and his *Foolish Wives,* though unfortunately mutilated and long neglected, testifies to his unwonted ability.

Stroheim also sees the world as peopled with predators and victims, often reinforced by references to animals. When the count plans to charm and then "con" Mrs. Hughes into giving him money, Stroheim's explanatory title reveals his attitude: "Preparing to stroke [originally, the word was *stalk*] the white doe—Brass buttons were strong magic." Here he is the hunter and Mrs. Hughes the prey. When the heartbroken maid sets fire to the tower room, she does not forget the bird in the cage; after kissing it, she allows it to go free so it will not perish in the flames. Like McTeague in *Greed,* she has a soft side to her. This is an interesting contrast to the earlier scene in which Karamzin shoots helpless pigeons.

The film also contains many of Stroheim's private obsessions. His interest in the maimed is seen in all the wounded sailors and soldiers milling about, and also in a shot of Karamzin and Mrs. Hughes on their visit to the country, as a person on crutches hobbles by in front of the Hotel des Rêves.

The idea that a black cat is bad luck is shown when Karamzin, on the way to see the counterfeiter's daughter, kills a cat that crosses his path (cut from the prints). On her windowsill, the simpleminded girl keeps a geranium, Stroheim's often-present symbol of affordable beauty. When the count sneaks through the window, the pot falls to the floor and awakens the father. Shortly after, when the counterfeiter drags Karamzin's body across the room, a black cat dashes by (a reminder of the cat Karamzin killed earlier and a kind of prefiguring of the cat that flees when Mac kills Trina in *Greed*). Then the counterfeiter stuffs the rapist's body, along with the cat Karamzin had slain, in the sewer.

Stroheim has few opportunities in the existing film to indulge his fascination with the number three and its permutations, but a calendar on the wall at the Hotel des Rêves reveals a twelve, meaning that the scene in the witch's hut occurs on the thirteenth. At one point in the casino, the count rubs the back of a hunchback for good luck.

In one interview after the release of *Foolish Wives,* Stroheim revealed a great deal about his artistic aims and himself:

> I recognized a great desire in the minds of the American people—do you know that Freud's *Interpretation of Dreams* is the most widely circulated book in this country?—for knowledge of life as it is. I tried to give it to them, the thing they wanted. I still maintain they wanted it. My proof? The picture has made its million back in four months; I have been overwhelmed by letters, hundreds of them, literally, begging me in my next production not to swing over the shallow trash of mother love, father love, sister love, brother love. And yet because of my attempt at sincerity I have been condemned, hooted at, reviled; filthy rumors have been circulated about me, not about my characterizations but about me personally, my private self.[26]

In a curious aside, Stroheim then called the journalist's "attention,

savagely, to his various physical peculiarities, his bull neck, head flat"
and remarked that he had no illusions about his appearance but said
that he was "bitterly disappointed" about

> the attitude of the American public in its apparent condemna-
> tion of me personally. They never say "Count Karamzin, the
> beast!" They say, "von Stroheim, the beast!" Why? Do they
> not know that if I, as the count, insulted the American ambas-
> sador, I, as the author and director of the picture, also made the
> American ambassador punch me in the nose? Originally I had
> the American ambassador smoke Bull Durham and roll his
> own. I was told in horrified whispers that I was insulting the
> American. And yet I had put it in simply as a contrast to the
> elongated, perfumed cigarets [sic] of the Russian count, things
> no honest-to-god American he-man would smoke! Bull
> Durham to me is a national trait in America. I see no reason
> why you should be ashamed of it. There is too much shame in
> America.[27]

After making this declaration, Stroheim, according to the interviewer,
"sat for a moment in silence, his round, cropped head bent slightly
forward, his heavy mouth working slowly. When he looked up, his face
was set and hard, the thin incisive eyebrows curved in swooping lines
of decision, his eyes gleaming." Then he added ponderously, showing
his white teeth, "I have been reviled and condemned without mercy
or hearing and beyond any possible knowledge of my accusers; but I
shall go on."[28] This interview certainly shows Stroheim's sincerity, but
he seemed unable to realize that audiences believe what they see on
the screen. After playing a coward, a child-molester, a liar, and a cheat,
he sounds almost surprised that his screen self is confused with the real
individual. He rightly claimed that they were not the same. However,
his performance was just too convincing for a naive public to draw a
distinction. Nor did he realize that throughout the film he had shown
the American wife, the husband, and the marine unfavorably and that
a few concluding moments of dramatic reversal—when the truth comes
out—cannot overcome the audience's irritation and anger engendered
during the screening. Orson Welles would confront a similar problem
in *The Magnificent Ambersons* with the spoiled and selfish main charac-

ter, who is so irritating that his comeuppance in the last few minutes cannot compensate for the audience's constant and hearty dislike for him for the previous hour and a half.

Stroheim did manage to learn something from this experience with *Foolish Wives*—certainly it was not economy or brevity—by finally abandoning "the man you love to hate" image. His later works would have heroes who are morally flawed but not wholly dissolute. They have enough charm and vivacity to be essentially likable. Although "the man you love to hate" disappeared, "the director the studios grew to hate" went on to triumph and to fail.

7

Merry-Go-Round

The history of each Stroheim film is a nightmare, but *Merry-Go-Round* is perhaps the most difficult to discuss, not because of its intellectual complexity but because of its confused authorship. Stroheim's other films—except for *Walking down Broadway*—were cut and mutilated by others, but at least he had done all the writing and filming. *Merry-Go-Round,* however, was not entirely his.

Stroheim conceived the story of *Merry-Go-Round* in the late winter of 1922. Soon after, he consulted with Irving G. Thalberg, the new head of production at Universal. The youthful Thalberg was a sharp businessman who believed in organization, discipline, and the idea that a director was a hired hand, not a law unto himself. In March, Stroheim offered Thalberg a twenty-six-page, single-spaced treatment and was encouraged to turn it into a scenario. By May 1922, after further consultation with Thalberg, Stroheim had completed a detailed shooting script and was paid five thousand dollars for the property. Thalberg, however, made further suggestions and demanded that the scenario be abridged.

Well aware of the excesses of *Foolish Wives,* Thalberg insisted that Stroheim list the length of each shot so that he could get a solid concept of the film's running time. Of the several scripts Stroheim prepared for *Merry-Go-Round,* the one in my possession, of June 20, contains 976 shots (plus additional unnumbered shots and intertitles that almost double that number). One might recall that *The Birth of a Nation,* which lasted almost three hours, had over 1,300 shots (many of them containing the rapid action of chase scenes), whereas Stroheim's more slowly paced project in script form already totaled almost 2,000 shots, besides many longish titles. His script divides into six parts, each of which presumably represented a reel (lasting twelve to fourteen minutes), which would result in a film running about an hour and a half, the length of most contemporary productions. However, the wary Thalberg must have nodded, for in no possible way could this scenario be done in that running time, yet Stroheim received permission to begin.

After extensive sets were built and props amassed—no easy task for a man who wanted to reproduce Vienna—shooting commenced on August 25. The film would be lavish, but, as Universal announced, it was not an "all Star" production; instead, it would rely on what *Moving Picture World* referred to as "an interesting group of players."[1] This statement meant that Stroheim would not use established box-office names but would create—as did Griffith before him—his own "stars."

Soon Stroheim forgot his promise to Thalberg to be reasonable. Brief sequences in the already long scenario began to expand. Again, there were lengthy shooting days that ran late into the evening and often into the morning. Stroheim frequently halted production because some background detail displeased him. After his directorial eye was satisfied, he would begin on his actors and stubbornly demand numerous retakes in his search for perfection. After five weeks or so, Stroheim had shot 271 scenes, totaling eighty-three thousand feet.[2] The film's unrepeated footage ran three to four reels, even though Stroheim had not proceeded more than halfway through the second of the script's six parts. Thalberg realized that the studio was going to get another four- or five-hour film, a commercial impossibility, so, on October 6, he fired the meticulous director. In 1947, Stroheim recalled the situation in a letter to Peter Noble:

When the picture was nearly three-fourths finished, I was discharged by Irving G. Thalberg during the absence of Carl

Laemmle because he did not want to take the responsibility of having me make another film as expensive as *Foolish Wives* had been. I was the first director in the history of Motion Pictures to be taken off during the making of a film and it was a test case. I did not care anything about it from a financial stand-point because two weeks after I was engaged at five times the salary I got previously—by the Goldwyn Company—but natu-rally it broke my heart to see the work circumcised and cas-trated. I asked through my attorneys Universal Company [*sic*] to take my name off the film as author as well as director, but the exhibitors persisted nevertheless in putting my name on the marquees.[3]

Stroheim was by no means "three-fourths" of the way through. In fact, he had shot far less than one-fourth. Thalberg, of course, had been concerned about the expense, but it was the *needless* expense—money wasted on scenes that would have to be cut because of the film's length— that really bothered him.

Stroheim was obviously disappointed that he had been pulled off *Merry-Go-Round,* his loving re-creation of Vienna, especially since he later regarded the script for that film as the best one he ever wrote. Other firms now became interested in Stroheim. Among them was the Goldwyn Company, whose stated aim was that directors should have a free hand. Stroheim hoped that he would be able to make a film in his own way and at his own pace, without being hampered by nagging cries for efficiency. And so he would begin on his long-held dream: *Greed*.

On *Merry-Go-Round,* Stroheim was replaced by the rather medio-cre Rupert Julian, who severely reduced much of Stroheim's already shot footage and, along with a new scriptwriter, Finis Fox, made sig-nificant changes in the story in order to simplify and shorten it. Even under the supposedly more efficient Julian, shooting lasted from the second week of October to the first week of January. According to Julian, the cost sheet, when he took over, stood at $220,000, a not impossible sum considering the fact that most of the sets had been charged to Stroheim. Julian spent an additional $170,000 to complete the picture. This total of $390,000 was a considerable sum for the usually frugal Universal Studio but far less than the million that *Foolish*

Wives had cost and that Stroheim's *Merry-Go-Round* would probably have surpassed.

In the second week of January, Julian began the giant task of putting the film together from his and Stroheim's footage. By the first week of March 1923, he was, according to *Moving Picture World,* "in the last stages of editing. Its 200,000 feet of negative are down to about twenty reels. This will be halved before it is ready for the screen."[4] Indeed, it was. The release version ran 9,178 feet, approximately ten reels, which lasted well over two hours. While the film was being edited, Universal took out a full-page ad in the February 3 issue of *Moving Picture World* and announced it as being directed by "Rupert Julian and Von Stroheim." After Stroheim protested, another full-page advertisement in the March 3 issue identified only Julian as director.

As a result of Stroheim's firing, *Merry-Go-Round* became a work of divided authorship. Because of the change in directors, the responsibility for various episodes (or even for the individual shots within them) cannot always be ascertained. Because Stroheim generally shot in continuity, the first part of the film, though heavily cut, is clearly his and shows his stamp. Julian claimed that he used only about six hundred feet of Stroheim's work. Even if this is so, those six hundred feet, plus Stroheim's very specific shooting script and his sets and costumes—and the fact that some of his scenes were reshot—definitely establish at times the Stroheim vision. Furthermore, Julian retained most of the main actors and technicians—only Wallace Beery, as the villain, was replaced.[5] Apparently, Beery decided to leave the cast—was it out of loyalty or fatigue?—when Stroheim was fired. His part was taken over by George Siegmann, who had played Silas Lynch in *The Birth of a Nation* and the German "heavy" in *Hearts of the World.* Some of the scenes with Siegmann are visually striking and unlike other scenes that we know Julian added, so it seems likely Julian copied Stroheim's footage carefully, or at least followed the explicit directions in Stroheim's shooting script. Wherever changes were made in the scenario—in short, where there were no scenes that Stroheim had photographed or shooting guidelines for Julian to follow—the film invariably suffers, and the actors, settings, camerawork, editing, and pace became pedestrian.

In general, Julian's footage cannot always sustain, though neither can it entirely negate, that peculiar mordant tone, that bitter, cruel, yet imaginatively honest atmosphere that pervades Stroheim's work.

Stroheim's habit of adding too many details may have lengthened scenes excessively, but the results—although not vital—were never boring. This is not the case with Julian. Several of his scenes drag, with no redeeming qualities. The final film is by no means what Stroheim intended; the poignant sense that *Alt Wien* (Old Vienna) has vanished forever, the observations about the breakdown of the social structure, the complexity of the characterizations, and the overtones and reverberations of his vision are weakened, if not altogether absent.

Stroheim's "improvers" tried to sidestep most of the unpleasant insights the Austrian director hoped to impart. They were looking for quick and superficial peeks at life, peeks that would occasionally shock—and, more often than not, cater to the stereotyped romantic needs of the average audience. They succeeded; a review in *Variety* referred to *Merry-Go-Round* as "a whale of a picture."[6]

In short, Stroheim's comprehensive, somewhat soured vision of life was short-circuited by Julian. In the midst of a devastating and even cruel panorama of Vienna—that peculiar juxtaposition of high life and low, of lust and love, of practicality and the dream—Julian gives us picture-postcard views and romantic posturings. He festoons white satin over rotting flesh. As a result, the style of Julian's love scenes—when he is not working from Stroheim's script—is completely opposed to Stroheim's realistic tone. This is not to say that Stroheim would not have had sentimental moments in the film—he had them in some of his other works, and they are present in the script—but their lilac blossoms, Viennese violins, and moonlight would have been offset by certain indications of the baser desires of humanity. Stroheim could see the beauties of love amid the sordid mechanics of courtship, but he never let romanticism appear without intermixing it with more "basic" material. He mocks man's pretensions, not because he does not like those pretensions but because he knows that man cannot maintain them. Like Jonathan Swift, but without his sprightliness, Stroheim cuts through the facade to present a tragic picture of man's unworthiness, of his frequent inability to be good and even, at times, to perceive what good is. He depicts his male protagonists, even when they are in love, as also rejoicing in the fact that they are "racking up" another conquest. These dichotomies he presented with humor—not the guffaw of the groundlings or the nudge in the ribs, but rather the sneer of a man who knew too much to believe entirely in love. This film, then, with its dual directors, provides devastating insights, then controverts them with romantic flummery. As a result, the film's weltanschauung alternates between life as it is (Stroheim's vision) and life as it ought to be (Julian's and Hollywood's vision).

Merry-Go-Round is essentially a love story, but a rather unconventional one, even with Julian's happy ending. It tells of a count, Franz Maximillian von Hohenegg (Norman Kerry), a rake who, posing as a necktie salesman, falls in love with and seduces Agnes (Mary Philbin), "a girl of the people." Affectionate, attractive, and virginal, Agnes is an organ grinder who accompanies the merry-go-round at the Prater, the amusement park of Vienna. She is lusted after by Schani Huber (George Siegmann), the carnival boss who dominates her kindly father, Sylvester (Cesare Gravina), the Punch and Judy man, and who torments and finally tries to rape Agnes. She is also admired by Bartholomew, a sensitive hunchback who is not only a barker but also the gentle keeper of a caged ape. Ultimately, Huber is killed by the ape, the father dies, and Franz goes off to war, returning to marry Agnes. The poor, faithful, and loving hunchback (in the release print) is left with only his ape.

At about the time that Stroheim was taken off the film, he met Gladys Adelina Lewis, a rather free spirit who wrote under the name of Georges Lewys. He told her the story of the film, gave her his scenario, and explained what scenes he would have included (or wanted to include). He then agreed to have her novelize the story. In 1923, the result of this collaboration was printed in a private, "unexpunged," and numbered edition. The title page said that it was "from the Austrian," an inside joke, and it was dedicated "to my friend, Erich von Stroheim, who was the inspiration of this work." In the preface, Lewis says that the story "is of a continental (European) flavour and portrays the life and manners of the city of Vienna prior to and since the war. . . . It is not necessary to blush for the truth nor to apologize for realism; the book must be accepted for what it is worth: not the triumph or failure of virtue or vice, but the frank weighing of values in the scale of social depravity and regeneration. . . . Caution is merely made against any attempt to approach incidents in the story from a too-sensitive (American) viewpoint."[7]

This comment tried to take the onus off the fact that the book might be interpreted as a "dirty" one, although it was intended for that kind of market. Its scenes are by no means pornographic, but they are quite rough for the day, suggesting sexual practices—voyeurism, beatings, degradation—rather unmentionable in Puritan America. In allowing Lewis to use his manuscript, Stroheim probably felt it had no cinematic future and wanted, at least, to see it in some permanent form.

Except for the novel's first five pages (which are unnecessary and foolish), the book follows Stroheim's ideas quite thoroughly and is perhaps the best way to understand what he tried to do in his Viennese films. The book is basically a retelling of the scenario, opening with the same titles and including most of its scenes, as well as explicating more fully Stroheim's obsessions. As a result, the novel is far more impressive than the mutilated film we now have. Indeed, it is a superb examination of the life and times of Vienna and its inhabitants, far better than the novels that Stroheim later wrote himself. However, there was a falling-out between Lewis and Stroheim—threats, lawsuits, recriminations—a skirmish traced in Richard Koszarski's *The Man You Loved to Hate.*

Stroheim's abilities as a scriptwriter are evident in his published scenario for *Greed,* but that work was an adaptation. Only in his meticulously detailed scenario for *Merry-Go-Round,* unmodified by Lewis in her novel, can we see his mind at work on original material. It is a tale of extraordinary vision that deserves to be recounted, for it reveals the basic ideas that would form the background of all Stroheim's imperial films.

The story, Stroheim writes in his scenario, occurs "before, during and after the war." He describes a globe slowly turning, revealing the word "Merry-Go-Round" along its equator. This is followed by Stroheim's hand writing his name on a blackboard. Then come shots of the main cathedral, the Danube, city hall (on top of which is the "man of armor," known later in *The Wedding March* as "the Iron Man"), and a woman abandoning one child on a bridge and then plunging into the waters with her baby. This is followed by shots of the Corpus Christi ceremony during which two crippled beggars ask for money as two Polish Jews approach and all are brushed away by military officers.

After this opening, the scene shifts to Franz, who, resenting being awakened by his valet, throws a pillow at him. (A similar act occurs in the parents' opening bedroom scene in *The Wedding March*.) After Franz's dog jumps on him, the playboy picks up some souvenirs of his previous night, as we see the faces of various girls associated with the mementos. Thus Stroheim demonstrates visually how much of a womanizer the count is.

During shooting, Stroheim added to his scenario an episode—retained in the release print—of the valet carefully preparing his master's bath, even checking the water's temperature. The dog enters the bathroom and jumps into the tub. The valet hurries the dog out just before Franz, unaware of the previous occupant, enters the tub, an instance of Stroheim's wry sense of humor.

Incidentally, sometime in the twenties an editor rearranged the opening of the film. As a result, certain prints of *Merry-Go-Round* (held by at least two European archives—France and Denmark—where I have screened them) begin with Franz at the Prater and then show him getting up the next morning. The original release—there are extant copies of it—opens, as Stroheim intended, with the count waking up, after which he goes to the Prater. Stroheim always felt that we had to know the private man before we see him in public. Perhaps the editors who revised the opening thought the Prater scenes would be a more engaging way to start the story. Such major shifts of material also occurred in the revised but never officially released version of *Foolish Wives*.

In the script, Stroheim crosscuts between Franz's awakening and his smartly dressed fiancée (Gisella) riding her horse. When she returns to the stable, the groom looks slyly at her and they exchange kisses. This sequence is missing from all the prints I have seen, although at least a portion of it was in the original release. The review in *Variety* described Gisella entering the stables, where she draws the groom into a dark corner and, after "letting her affections have full reign," strikes him with her riding crop when he "would likewise express his aroused passion."[8] A still from this scene, of the two lying in the hay, can be found in Deems Taylor's book *A Pictorial History of the Movies*.[9]

Thereafter, the groom and, for the most part, Gisella, disappear in the released version. In the original script, however, the groom played a large role. He represents the lower classes, who, after the collapse of the monarchy, lord it over the former aristocracy in Vienna. (Such a shift in the class structure was earlier demonstrated in Griffith's *The*

Birth of a Nation.) Certainly Stroheim, in his mind's eye, saw himself as part of the aristocracy and felt that the postwar demise of privilege and class was a tragedy.

In the script, the headstrong Gisella will break her engagement with the count and run off with the groom, who, in the Lewys book, treats her horribly, steals her money, becomes a grafting crook in America selling horses to the French government, and grows rich. The scenario omits his American activities—although they might have appeared in an early draft—but somehow he gains enough money to return and buy the count's residence after the war. In the script, Gisella has sunk as low as possible, becoming an alcoholic prostitute who drowns herself under the very bridge the broken and crippled count stands on toward the end of the story. (This is a curious echo of the opening, in which a woman commits suicide with her baby.) Because of the omission of these episodes, Stroheim's intended social observations about the fall of the aristocracy and the rise of the lower classes have been entirely cut from the film.

In Stroheim's script, after the scene with Gisella and the groom, we return to existing footage of the count as his fiancée telephones him. Having finished his bath, Franz dons his mustache-band and converses on the telephone with Gisella; she, attended by her maids, is lying on a couch and smoking a cigar. Certainly this realistic and rather disenchanting view of the courting couple—he with his mustache-band and she with her cigar—was Stroheim's particular province. Lubitsch was not the only director to show intimate and debunking glimpses of upper-class life. Franz lies that he has been busy with military affairs.

Then follows an elaborate scene of the annual event of Holy Thursday, in which the emperor washes the feet of the "oldest and poorest" men, an event intended "to symbolize his great humility."[10] (Needless to say, this is also an example of Stroheim's obsessive interest in feet.) The ceremony is mocked by Vienna's socialists, who proclaim with banners "Long live the Revolution." There is a scuffle: "Comrades. . . . Let us weep at the sight of this farce. . . . They wash their feet up there and down here they kick them." The minister of war asserts, "It is positively a sin not to turn our machine guns on this poisonous vermin." When Franz voices a degree of sympathy for the rebels, he is berated by his fellow officers. This is the first indication that the scenario will deal with the collapse of the aristocracy.

Later, Franz's fellow officers, dressed in civilian clothes, go to a café. When the count arrives alone—his intended date has canceled—the men look in their address books for a replacement. Each book lists a girl named Mitzi, and each man thinks she has slept only with him; in fact, she has been with them all! Finally, this group of fun-lovers goes to the Prater. These scenes were to be crosscut with Gisella at the stables, where she is doing more romancing with the groom.

In the release print, after the count wakes up and speaks with his fiancée, he goes to the court (there is no foot-washing ceremony and no demonstration) and immediately accompanies his friends to the Prater.

According to the script, the count, his pals, and their girls arrive at a Prater shooting gallery, where Franz carefully punctures a number of heart-shaped targets, the kind of symbolism in which Stroheim delighted. Franz wins two dolls—one a girl, the other a soldier. Part of this scene remains in the film, but the dolls appear only briefly, despite their constant symbolic presence in the script.

As the group leaves the shooting gallery, they pass by the fire department (another Stroheim obsession) and approach the merry-go-round. There we meet Schani Huber, the large, unpleasant man who runs the concession, and his "sad and wretched" wife, who sells tickets. We also encounter Agnes Urban, who cranks a grind organ to provide music for the carousel. Franz, according to the script, is "taken by her beauty—but not moving picture love-on-first-sight expression." They exchange meaningful looks, and the jealous Huber warns her not "to make goo-goo eyes at a guy that never done nothin' for you any time." He firmly grabs her arm and demands: "And me, who has done everything for that lazy bum father and puny long dyin' mother of yours. . . . Where does I come in?" Huber's wife, in her ticket booth, gives a long-suffering glance at her lusting husband.

Franz gets rid of his friends by paying for another ride, puts the boxes of dolls on the organ, and tells Agnes that she is beautiful. She replies, "Gee, you flatter like a lieutenant. You look like a swell. Are you?" He responds, "Would you like me better if I were one?" She answers, "No. I don't like soldiers. Father says all they do is get girls into trouble." Franz realizes that his position would scare her off and so claims that he is a necktie salesman. After more flirtation, Franz gives her the soldier doll. Then the count and his friends proceed to the next attraction. Huber, angry, breaks the doll.

The hunchbacked barker, Bartholomew, gives a spiel about "a lady without lower body and without arms." The count cynically speculates that she might have "a husband and eight kids," a remark that one of the count's companions feels is unsympathetic: "Do you believe in anything but yourself?" The count replies, "Not much." Bartholomew then introduces his orangutan, Boniface, who throws nuts at the audience. The always angry Huber picks a fight with Bartholomew, which ends when the hunchback's lady boss enters the fray. The ape escapes and goes to Agnes and helps her grind the organ. Huber notices this and hits the animal. After the Prater closes, Bartholomew and Agnes visit her ailing mother, who lives upstairs in a rather primitive room. Huber tries to kiss Agnes, but she evades him.

In Stroheim's script, this scene concludes the first of the film's six sections, which contains forty pages and 169 shots. Unnumbered, but included in the script, are an additional 170 shots, plus ninety-seven titles and a few inserts (close-ups of letters, for example). In short, this first section, which should have run no more than twelve minutes, would have taken more than half an hour. Furthermore, Stroheim added still more action during the shooting, such as the dog jumping into the bathtub. In Stroheim's original twenty-six-page synopsis, this first part represents slightly more than two pages.

Except perhaps for the foot-washing scene, this first section of the script is by no means padded, and it provides an efficient introduction to the main characters and their interrelationships. But one can easily see that at this rate, Stroheim could never have made a film of his entire script that would last less than four or five hours.

Part two of the script begins as Agnes's mother lies in her bedroom, dying. Bartholomew shows Agnes a lottery ticket, with the drawing scheduled for June 20, 1914. The scene then shifts to Huber's quarters, where he eats big chunks of meat and bread while going over the accounts. He slaps his wife for holding back a few coins. This is crosscut with Sylvester, Agnes's kind and loving father, who cuts a single sausage in equal parts to share with his daughter, while glancing tearfully at his dying wife. During shooting, Stroheim added a humorous but telling contrast by having Huber cut off a large piece of sausage for himself and slice a paper-thin one for his wife.

These scenes of the common man eating are contrasted to a party where Franz and his rich friends are drinking champagne as a gypsy orchestra plays amid flying confetti. This is crosscut with Agnes in her humble quarters, where she makes a mixture of flour and water and pastes together the soldier doll that Huber had broken. She places it next to her on the pillow, handling the doll, as Stroheim writes in the scenario, not as if it were a baby but like "a mature woman" with a lover. Back at the party, Franz playfully stabs his girl doll and its sawdust falls out. His female companion pours champagne on the sawdust and Franz stirs the mixture, but when the woman tries to throw the emptied doll on the floor, he grabs her wrist and puts the doll in his pocket. Stroheim here suggests that Franz is interested in Agnes (he retains the doll) but is hardly head-over-heels in love.

The next morning, while being shaved by his valet, Franz glances at the dilapidated doll, its "body hanging head downwards." He reveals a trace of a smile, then yawns. Meanwhile, Agnes examines her damaged soldier doll and lovingly holds it, while across the room a doctor takes the ailing mother's temperature. Franz shows up at his headquarters and talks with his fellow officers. Later, Bartholomew goes to the lottery office and finds out he has not won. He then buys another ticket with the same numbers.

A title comes up: "And the merry-go-round goes round—and round—and round—." This is followed by shots of Huber and his merry-go-round, Sylvester at his Punch and Judy show, and the mother breathing her last—all examples of the comedy and tragedy of life. Agnes is notified of her mother's imminent death and stops cranking the hand organ; Huber, furious, grabs her. "Let her die," he says. He puts his "dirty white canvas shoe" on top of her foot and forces her to continue. Huber then runs up to the room, grabs Sylvester, who had rushed up to see his wife, and forces him to go on with the puppet show. However, a providential thunderstorm scatters the crowd, allowing the family and Bartholomew to be present at the deathbed. The storm swings open the shutters, and a bird flies into the room. (This scene is in the print.) The mother sees the bird as some angelic and apocalyptic omen and then dies, a touch that was surely Stroheim's, considering his preoccupation with religion and superstition. A dog howls. It is over.

This death scene is followed by a banquet, where Stroheim provides more of his "continental touch," footage that Julian acknowledged using. Franz sits between two women, and when one becomes too flirtatious, the other tries to stab her rival. Franz coolly takes the knife from her—he has been through such jealous scenes before—and nonchalantly throws it over his shoulder. A moment later a large loving cup is carried in and placed on top of the table. Franz excitedly starts pouring bottles of champagne into the bowl and adds pineapple and other ingredients. Here is a familiar Stroheim fruit punch, but one with an extra kick! Out of it eventually come the arms and naked shoulders of a beautiful wench, seductively writhing. Franz, with a silver ladle, starts to fill the glasses. (Today, such an event might seem merely an extravagant invention of Stroheim's, but such orgies did occur, even in proper old New York.)[11] In contrast to this frivolity, Agnes and other family members gather around her dead mother.

Franz is now seen at home, his dog at his side. As his valet helps him into a robe and slippers, he sits down to read Artur Schnitzler's *Reigen,* a play that certainly suggested the content of this film. (It also became the basis of Max Ophuls's 1951 picture, *La Ronde.*) There is a cut to Agnes and then back to Franz, who glances at his dilapidated doll and decides to visit Agnes at the Prater. He arrives in his carriage just as the hearse bearing the mother, accompanied by Agnes and others, pulls away, but he is unaware of its significance. He goes to the merry-go-round and is told by Huber that the girl was kicked out for being "a no good tramp." After a brief scene at the mother's grave, we see Sylvester looking at funeral and doctor's bills, another example of reality. None of the above scenes was included in the release print because at about this point shooting was halted when Thalberg realized that Stroheim, after five weeks, was not far in the script and was even enlarging scenes. From here on, the film only approximates Stroheim's intentions.

The next scene in the script was retained by Julian and is one of the most effective episodes of the released film. After the Prater closes for the night, Huber accosts Agnes while she is sweeping the floor, locks the door behind him, turns off the light, and advances on her. She hides among the now quiet horses of the merry-go-round. Aroused as well as angry, Huber grabs a bridle rope from one of the horses and begins to whip her. This exciting scene either was filmed out of sequence by Stroheim with Beery and later redone by Julian with Siegmann, or was made by Julian shot-for-shot from Stroheim's meticulous scenario. Finally the father, hearing Agnes's screams, enters the room and stabs Huber in the shoulder. The police soon arrive and arrest the father, though Huber has not been badly hurt. Agnes tearfully kisses her father before he is carried off in the police wagon.

In part three of Stroheim's scenario (entirely omitted from the film), Agnes goes to St. Stephen's Cathedral and prays, a scene crosscut with Sylvester being jailed. As Agnes and Bartholomew leave the church, they encounter Franz exiting a clothing store. He is delighted to see her and lets her believe that he—the supposed necktie salesman—is just off from work. Learning that her mother has died, he "looks sympathetically at her—then a thought comes into his mind that after all this might be a very favorable opportunity for him to get the girl, as all her moral holds and ties have ceased to be."[12] Agnes introduces Bartholomew to him. Franz does not "want to lose the girl that Fate had put in his path" and "with a faint trace of a cynical smile," an idea occurs to him; he suggests that he might be able to get her father out of jail. He urges her into a cab, leaving behind the "dumbfounded" Bartholomew. At the same time, his fiancée, Gisella, spies the couple entering the cab and follows them. Franz takes Agnes to Madame Elvira's, a place of assignation, where he pretends that his friend, Elvira's husband, can help dismiss the charges against her father. After serving tea, Elvira (having exchanged some winks with Franz) offers them a room filled with mirrors and nude marble statues that suggest the sexual exploits he has in mind. Elvira leaves them alone, then takes off her shoes and sneaks back to listen at the door. She picks up a book, *Dr. Freud's Psycho Analysis.*

The innocent Agnes has no idea what might be in store for her. After some awkward conversation, Franz, not sure how to begin his seduction, shows how "sensitive" he is by picking up a violin and playing it. (In *Blind Husbands,* von Steuben uses the same tactic to woo the woman.) Elvira, curious about the count's techniques, peeks through the keyhole. When the count finishes playing, he asks Agnes whether she has ever loved anyone. Her naive answer shows that she is a virgin. Finally, he kisses her passionately, after which "a quiver runs through her slender body—her face flushes—the woman in her has just matured." He advances toward her as she retreats, a chair is pushed over, and he leads her to the couch. She is appalled at his behavior. "You are just like Huber and the rest of them," she says, and tearfully adds, "My dream—is gone." When he is about to force his attentions on her, the

E string on the violin snaps by itself. "A great change comes over his face." He becomes tender, tells her he loves her, and "reverently kisses her," as Elvira abandons the keyhole in disappointment.

Portions of this scene play well, and there is a possibility that Stroheim filmed or at least rehearsed the episode. Some of Agnes's expressions recreate the intent of the scenario, but other shots—in which the actress does not emote as well and which seem a little inconsistent with what was written—hint that Julian reduced the sexual electricity. Agnes leaves the room, then reconsiders and returns. In Julian's version, there seems to be a suggestion that Agnes, after resisting Franz's aggressive attack, gives herself to him. (This was not Stroheim's intention.) Afterward, Franz takes her back to the main square and she kisses him good-bye. After all this, according to the scenario, Agnes feels hungry and buys a pair of wieners! The newspaper that the frankfurters are wrapped in contains a photograph of the count with Countess Gisella, and its caption states that the couple are to be married. Agnes, impressed by the count's resemblance to her necktie salesman, keeps the paper to show her suitor. (In the release print, it is Bartholomew who buys the frankfurters and recognizes Franz. Perhaps Stroheim wanted to show that the heroine has appetites of sex and hunger but Julian considered that inappropriate.)

Soon after, in the scenario, there is an elaborate birthday celebration for Gisella. Her father tells Franz that it is all right to "sow your wild oats" but (recalling Franz's earlier political sympathies) advises him never to "flirt with democracy." As the couple dance to the song "When Love Dies," Gisella informs Franz that she is breaking the engagement because she has seen him with Agnes. She adds that she loves another and asserts, "I want to live my life as I see fit to live it." This sophisticated couple continue their dancing and agree to end the relationship and part amicably. After downing a glass of champagne, Franz leaves the house as a street-cleaning wagon passes. Toward dawn, the headstrong Gisella takes her jewels and two suitcases and runs off with the groom, who wears a meticulously described loud, checked outfit. Stroheim liked to depict vulgar, low men in tasteless clothes, and the groom's apparel is similar to that later worn by Marcus in *Greed*.

In the release print, all of the above is omitted. Instead, Franz, definitely in love, mentions this fact to his cronies, who only laugh at his taking such a "girl of the people" seriously. Deciding not to ruin his career or his social standing, Franz becomes pragmatic and marries Gisella, after which she virtually disappears. At the end of the film, we discover that Gisella has conveniently died during the war. Thus, the nuances of this willful woman's decline into prostitution and privation—the topsy-turvy switch of the classes—are totally excised.

In part four of the scenario, Franz's valet delivers two boxes to Agnes, one containing flowers, the other, candies. Bartholomew watches this, saddened by the wealth and attention that his rival can offer. Franz has extricated Sylvester from prison and returns with him to the Prater. Agnes, extremely grateful, shows Franz the newspaper clipping, but he shrugs off his resemblance to the aristocrat. When no one is looking, he kisses her.

Later that night, Agnes slips away from her bedroom to meet the count, and they walk toward the garden:

> A GRASS COVERED PLACE, with lilac bushes all around—one large, heavy-trunk chestnut tree with large white blossoms in full bloom—the background is black except for tiny little lights far off, and the outlines of the Ferris wheel which stands still— above all is an unusually large moon, truly a lover's moon (on location, but black perforated background with lights behind)— the place must be significant for its action through the abundance of blossoms—there is a park bench near a tree—between the black drop and the bench is seen a light shimmering path or walk with a lit street lantern—Agnes and Count enter arm in arm—they stand near the bench and look dreamily toward the tiny lights that signify Vienna. (4:9)

One can easily compare Stroheim's careful evocation of a romantic mood to the unimaginative set that Julian used for this scene: Agnes is seated on a bench (made of tree branches) while Franz stands behind it, both framed by giant tree trunks and a canopy of leaves. The camera stays mostly in long shot, with a few medium shots interspersed, but the characters do not really interact. The two dull figures pose in front of the camera and merely go awkwardly through a series of postures. The result is a corny and artificial scene, bereft of atmosphere, beauty, and lyricism, and lacking the minute gestures and psychological shadings that would have raised it above the prosaic.

According to the scenario, Bartholomew, who has followed the couple, spreads apart the lilac flowers and jealously watches them. A nightingale on a branch full of chestnut blossoms sings its love song as the lovers watch a falling star. This scene fades out, followed by a title: "Why love forswore him in his mother's womb . . . or he should not deal in her soft laws." This title is followed by a shot of Bartholomew lying on his bed, crying. The quotation in the title, unidentified in the script, comes from Shakespeare's *Richard III* and refers to the misshapen title character. Obviously, Stroheim was familiar with Shakespeare's play. The scene then switches from the unhappy Bartholomew back to a long shot of the garden, "with artificial cloud slowly passing over moon—until scene is almost invisible—then fade out completely" (4:11).

By showing Bartholomew back in his room, Stroheim allows the lovers to be alone and unwatched, and it is here that the seduction takes place—certainly not at Madame Elvira's.

The next scene opens as a guilty Agnes enters St. Stephen's Cathedral and goes to the confessional box, where, with tears streaming down her face, she speaks to the father confessor. Meantime, we see a more mundane act in the church—a man with a hot iron blotting up the melted candle wax that has dripped on the rug. The wax, like Agnes's "sin," is removed by the church. This whole sequence was never filmed, but the confession and the wax removal were lovingly resurrected by Stroheim in *The Wedding March*.

After exiting the church, Agnes sees the haberdasher store "Mandlebaum & Rosenstein," a Jewish store not unlike the Stroheim family's enterprise. She is about to enter, but upon the striking of the church clock (fate?), she changes her mind and takes a bus back to the Prater. The scene then shifts to the count at the emperor's quarters as a visit to a hospital is planned for later that day, at 3:30 (again, the threes).

Back at the Prater, Huber is angry at Agnes's father for interfering with his rape, for attacking him with a knife, and—insult of insults—for leaving his economic domain by opening a rival show and becoming a success at playing a clown. Huber watches Sylvester's clowning for a moment, then seems to make up his mind. The scene shifts back to the emperor. A bell rings three times, a sentry yells three times, and an officer salutes three times. At this significant hour, Huber climbs a building at the Prater and cuts the wires of a sign. "Close-up of Agnes in bus—Suddenly she startles, with hand on heart—wide-eyed fear—." She has a presentiment of tragedy. The scene returns to Huber, who cuts more wires, and then shifts back to the agitated Agnes. After several more crosscuts, the sign falls, striking Sylvester. (In Julian's version, Huber pushes a potted tree down on the old man's head and there is no crosscutting with Agnes.) After this "accident," Stroheim planned a series of shots of a police call box, a large switchboard, an ambulance yard, an ambulance driver, and so forth. Finally, after more crosscutting with the bus, Agnes runs down the street and discovers her injured father. After further detailed shots of a doctor and the ambulance, Huber observes the situation and, when the ape approaches, he kicks "Boniface's vitals."

The scene shifts to Sarajevo, as we witness the assassination of the archduke, thereby drawing a parallel between the murderous attacks on two innocent people. We then return to the hospital as a priest, an acolyte, and two nursing sisters attend the dying Sylvester. Outside, the emperor, unaware of the assassination, arrives for an official visit to the hospital and, after some ceremony, walks down the corridor, accompanied by Franz. At Sylvester's bed, the count and Agnes recognize each other. "Close-up of violin filling the whole screen. 'E' string broken—ends coiled—a white kid-gloved hand holding a tiny gilt knife, enters, deliberately cuts the 'A' string—the two ends curl—it quickly dissolves back into her face—" (4:29). This symbolic shot of the gloved hand probably suggests that Franz, by lying to Agnes, has destroyed the "beautiful music" they had created and that the social structure has doomed this love affair between an aristocrat and a commoner.

Agnes faints. In a close-up, Franz "is visibly heartbroken and his expression shows his real heartfelt sorrow and love for Agnes." Although Franz wants to stay and explain, duty calls. He cannot leave the emperor. As the entourage departs, Franz is the last to go. "We keep on grinding for a few feet to show the big empty space in door," a subtle use of filmic space to evoke the emotional situation. A sister pulls the sheet over the dead Sylvester's face, as Agnes weeps by the side of the bed for the loss both of her father and her lover (4:30).

In the release print, the emperor does not visit the hospital. Instead, in a kind of informal inspection tour, Franz enters with his wife, Gisella. Agnes realizes that her necktie salesman is not only a count but also a married man. In an interminable scene, Mary Philbin as Agnes makes a number of sour faces (proving that she was a poor actress unless controlled by Stroheim), while the father, also overacting badly, curses Franz in a series of grimaces.

In part five of the scenario, a subtitle again says: "And the Merry-go-Round goes round—and round—and round—," followed by an iris in on Huber's merry-go-round "just long enough to drive home the motive and title" (5:1).

We see a most unhappy Agnes leave the hospital, as a title then observes: "if our inward griefs were seen written on our brow . . . how many would be pitied . . . who are envied now." The scene then cuts to the emperor receiving news of Sarajevo. A shot of a mourning flag on a tower makes the deed official. Stroheim reveals in his script how sensitively he envisioned the next scene:

> IRIS IN ON AGNES' ROOM—she enters—it is dark, only faint light from the different lanterns comes through the window—she doesn't turn the light on, but goes to bed and sits down—her hands in her lap, utterly apathetic—a beam of light strikes her face just enough to see her outlines—she turns—lays [sic] face downward on pillow—her hands embracing the cushion, and going underneath—she raises her head—her hand has touched something beneath the cushion that drives her thoughts into a certain channel—she half sits up again and extracts the object that she had touched—it is the doll dressed as an officer.
> CLOSE-UP OF DOLL—the nose and the chunk of the cheek that she had once pasted in, have fallen out again
> CLOSE-UP HER FACE—her eyes are wide open—she has no more tears, and with a little sad smile over the funniness of fate, she breaks down on cushion, still clinging to doll—IRIS OUT ON HER. (5:11)

In a parallel scene, Stroheim describes Franz moving around in his study, depressed. He stares at the girl doll, which is "in terribly dilapidated condition, all chewed up by the retriever."

> MED CLOSE-UP OF COUNT, with doll in his hand—he looks casually at uniforms in clothes closet until his look is fastened on certain object—he holds doll in right hand—he changes doll

from right to left—never turning his eyes off object in closet—then with free hand he, still deeply thoughtful, touches subconsciously the gold sword knot, and lets the fringes glide through his fingers—then he caressingly touches the sleeve of his uniform-coat and then in a symbolical way, though unconsciously, puts his left hand holding the doll behind him—turns—walks back to dresser—takes doll from behind him and looking at it for the last time, he puts it on the dresser—thinks for a second—rings the bell—valet enters—count gives order—valet bows and goes to clothes closet—starts to take out civilian clothes. IRIS OUT.

As can be seen in these excerpts from the script, Stroheim was not interested solely in photographing actors merely playing their parts but also in showing the characters' thought processes by means of symbolic objects, settings, parallel actions, and camera placement.

The saddened and lonely Agnes pays a visit to the bench in the garden where they once had their tryst, as the moon comes out from behind a cloud. The script mentions close-ups of chestnut blossoms, lilac blossoms, a nightingale, crickets, and then Agnes's face. Meanwhile, the count arrives at the Prater and, not finding Agnes, goes to the garden, where he tells her how sorry he is. "Trying to be as cold as possible," she accuses him of intending to lead her on a little longer. He protests that he loves her, but she is skeptical. Why would a nobleman marry the likes of her? He explains that the engagement with Gisella has been broken off and that he could "keep" her, "make it nice" for her. She replies in the negative. "I love another. . . . I knew him as a necktie salesman." She gets up to leave, presses a lilac blossom to her lips, and throws it to him. He kisses it. Meanwhile, a loving couple enter and sit at the other end of the bench. More close-ups of lilac and chestnut blossoms are followed by one of a cricket and then an owl. Franz puts the blossom in his wallet, as a cloud passes over the moon.

Back at the Hubers' apartment, Huber's wife tells him that Sylvester has died. "Who the hell asked?" he says and "viciously throws contents of beer glass in her face." Huber then torments the ape, an act he will soon regret. A title states, "All guilt is avenged on earth." Later that night, the ape climbs up the wall and kills Huber. The next morning, the count's valet, Nepomuck, who has become smitten with Mrs. Huber, arrives to give the unhappy lady some flowers. As she awakens, she discovers the body and yells murder. Shortly after, the police arrest her.

The scene then shifts to the sad emperor, as the country declares war. There is an iris-in on a grindstone as a "Brute" sharpens a sword, followed by a miniature globe and "out of the part representing Europe rises a miniature figure of Mars" (5:14). (Stroheim most likely drew his use of this figure from Griffith, who contrasted a sword-wielding Mars to the Prince of Peace in the conclusion of *The Birth of a Nation*.)

Retribution comes not only to Huber but also to the whole Western world, for war has broken out. Troops parade through the city on their way to the front, and Agnes tearfully watches from afar as her count rides away with his regiment. A title saying "the merry-go-round" is followed by the boarding up of the Prater. Then Stroheim depicts the war, not through major battles but more efficiently with five stylized shots—of boots advancing and then running in double time, explosions, dead bodies, and the legs of dead horses. Flame and smoke cover the screen, followed by a title, "And women's souls," which dissolves into: "VIOLIN AGAINST BLACK B.G. [background] smoke here and there curling up—the 'E' string is broken—the 'A' string is cut—the two broken strings are curled around the violin—a leg from the knee down clad in heavy medieval armor, with a steel thorn on the heel, steps with all its might on the violin, crushing it to pieces—DISSOLVE OUT AND INTO WOMAN CRUCIFIED ON SWORD—FADE OUT" (5:16). For a so-called realist, Stroheim was hardly averse to abstract, symbolic images.

After a fade-in on the coffin of the emperor, the script shifts to an artificial limb factory where Agnes works. She stops at a horse-meat store and, after studying the inflated prices, buys a sausage. She passes a garbage heap where people are searching for food. There she meets Mrs. Huber, acquitted of her husband's murder, who is pleased to have found some bones. Agnes induces her to throw the bones away and invites her back to her own pitiable tenement, where the soldier doll with the broken face sits on a little shelf. Mrs. Huber brings along the faded flowers that Nepomuck had given her. Thus Stroheim shows the consequences of the war: poverty, hunger, thwarted love, social disruption, and death.

In the Julian version, almost all of this has been omitted. Franz, about to go off to war, visits Agnes to beg her forgiveness. She turns from him. After he leaves, she stands by a tree in the park and cries. Julian then includes some expensive battle scenes of the type Stroheim had rejected because they were too familiar and of no thematic value. As Stroheim stated in his treatment, he intended to include only a few suggestive shots, "leaving the melee to the imagination."[13]

On Julian's battlefield, Franz meets the severely wounded Sylvester. Evidently, Julian decided not to have the old man die in the hospital, and so provides the absurdity of having Agnes's aged father enrolled in the army! With such decrepit old men, no wonder the Austrians did not do well in the war. The father's injury seems to have stayed with him, too, for on the battlefield he is still swathed in head bandages! At least Julian should have provided him with a different place for a war wound. Maybe a chest injury? With no explanations, it seems as if the ailing man was carted from the hospital directly to the battlefield. The dying Sylvester curses Franz, who in a guilty need for expiation hands him his gun. Agnes's father aims it at Franz's head but succumbs before he can pull the trigger. This business of Franz offering himself to be killed is both ridiculous and completely unnecessary.

As the war drags on (according to the script), Franz's left leg is severely injured. A man crawls in the shell-hole to help him—it is Nepomuck, wounded in the arm. They apply tourniquets to each other.

In the midst of Julian's war scenes, there appears an allegorical shot of the naked god of war spinning a merry-go-round, the sole remnant of Stroheim's intended symbolism about war and fate. Stroheim, however, had planned to end his brief, impressionistic version of war with a different symbolic shot: the "personification of death: he is playing a gilded harp—he walks toward camera—turning back he waves toward someone yet unseen to follow." This shot dissolves to "a monster in the form of a crawling animal representing disease—this animal catches up with Death—Death takes hold of one leg of the animal as if joining hands—they walk toward camera until light is extinguished—FADE OUT" (5:20).

In the morning, stretcher bearers pick up the injured men, while around them burial squads are at work. A title indicating that it is All Soul's Day is followed by Agnes and Mrs. Huber taking wreaths to the cemetery. A horse pulling a cab nibbles at some of the wreaths on the back of the bus that the women are on. The grieving women have to smile at their partially eaten floral offerings. In a new section of the cemetery, Bartholomew is discovered working as a gravedigger and, with conscious irony, the former barker says, "Ladies and gentlemen ...walk right in ... the greatest performance begins just now ...please don't push ... there's a place for everybody" (5:22).

Agnes is surprised to see Bartholomew and embraces him in sisterly fashion. He explains, "I wasn't good enough for anything else" except digging graves. He could not afford to feed Boniface, so he sold the ape to a clinic. Agnes tells him that she is working at an artificial limb factory. "Business is booming. . . . They are going to enlarge the place." Bartholomew notes that his "business is pretty good too." He writes down her address and tells her he has a lottery ticket. The women leave the cemetery.

After the armistice, a ceremony at St. Stephen's Cathedral is attended by women in mourning clothes and a number of cripples. After the priest holds the monstrance and the church bells ring, an organist plays "Silent Night" as snow falls outside (another of Stroheim's Christmas references). Beggars, some of them former soldiers, stand in the snowdrifts as Agnes and Mrs. Huber leave. Mrs. Huber recognizes Nepomuck, who is holding his cap out with his artificial arm. (Stroheim intended to dissolve to a shot of his real hand holding the peppermints he had once offered the lady.) Agnes and Mrs. Huber, when they learn he has no place to stay, invite him to their tenement. Agnes patiently holds back her curiosity but finally asks about Franz and learns that he has fallen. This is followed by an editorial title: "So many great nobles ...things ... administrations ... so many high chieftains ... so many brave nations ... so many proud princes ... and power so splendid ... in a moment ... a twinkling ... all utterly ended" (5:29). We then see a prince who is now a street-cleaner shoveling manure, a count who is watering a street, a baron who is shining the shoes of a Polish Jew in a caftan, and Gisella, who has become a prostitute.

Agnes walks by Franz's former residence and weeps. Shortly after, we see him standing in front of the building—on his artificial leg. The new owner, with his flashy car, is a "coarse, horsy-looking individual in big checked suit, with heavy gold chain over his stomach—horseshoe necktie pin, diamond rings, big cigar—in whom we recognize the former groom and clandestine lover of Comtesse Gisella—he steps into car—car pulls out—a cloud of black and yellow smoke comes from the exhaust, in which the Count becomes almost invisible" (5:30). The building's janitor recognizes Franz and invites him in. The kindly man has saved the count's trunk containing his violin. With its broken strings and its crushed bridge, the damaged instrument reminds us of its earlier symbolic use.

In the sixth and final section of the scenario, Franz goes to the main square, applies for a job, is rejected, and then enters St. Stephen's Cathedral. Renewed in spirit, he exits and passes by the very store where he had pretended to be a necktie salesman.

At Agnes's tenement, a cab pulls up, and the joyful Bartholomew bounds in, saying that he has won the lottery and become rich. He brings food and presents and shows Agnes his money and the pearl-handled pistol he now carries for protection. He gives her a ring. In the street, a grind organ plays "Out There in the Blossoming Garden," which reminds Agnes of her love for Franz. The scene shifts to Franz playing his violin in his tenement, then back to Bartholomew telling Agnes that he loves her. Now, he says, he has enough money to go into partnership at the Prater.

Franz, in a nostalgic mood, visits the Prater, which is in dilapidated condition and boarded up. He goes to his former trysting place in the garden, but the plants are bare, the bench gone—"the whole scene dreary."

Not long after, Mrs. Huber and Nepomuck, who have married, accompany Agnes to the Prater, which is now undergoing reconstruction. The merry-go-round is being repaired and painted. Entering, in a wheelchair, is the former minister of war (Gisella's father), "an imbecile old gentleman" who suffers from "locomotor ataxia" and uses an ear-trumpet. At the sight of the merry-go-round, he happily claps his hands like a child. With him is a stately matron, once the stylish Madame Elvira. The old fellow insists on riding the merry-go-round, and while he gleefully spins around, Elvira and Agnes recognize each other. "How is our mutual friend, Mr. Meier [the phony name the count used]?" Agnes's expression betrays the fact that she now knows Franz's real identity. Elvira, smiling "the vile Maude Georgian smile" (Stroheim often wrote his scripts with specific actors in mind), says, "And have you heard of him since?" Agnes replies that he died during the war. Elvira responds, "He was such a likable fellow, wasn't he?" Soon after,

Elvira and the old man leave, ending a remarkable scene of decline: old age, infirmity, loss of position, and the seeming death of love—all juxtaposed with the carousel suggesting that life goes on.

The workmen who are restoring the Prater carry away the sign that killed Agnes's father, which of course reminds her of the past. Then there is a close-up of hands playing a violin. As blossoms move in the wind, Agnes walks toward the arbor where she last met Franz. There is another close-up of the violin, followed by a shot of the blossoms. As she continues to hear the very tune her necktie salesman had played at Elvira's, Agnes moves toward the merry-go-round and cautiously approaches the white-haired musician. She recognizes Franz, and the nickel-plated steel braces of an artificial limb can be seen beneath his trousers. Two tears trickle down her cheeks. Still unaware of her presence, Franz takes from his wallet the lilac blossom that he has saved. He looks at the tree arbor where he last saw Agnes and sighs deeply. The script says, "she realizes that he is thinking of her—and with a sob" she sinks behind the lilac bush. Franz hears someone crying and pushes the branches apart to find her kneeling on the ground in tears. Realizing that it is Agnes, he kisses her, but she bows her head and draws away. He attributes her reaction to his missing leg, but she indicates that his crippled state is not the reason. She tells him that she thought he died and has since promised herself to Bartholomew, who, hidden in the bushes, is quietly observing this scene. Although she loves her necktie salesman, she does not want to break the hunchback's heart.

When Bartholomew hears this, Stroheim planned to "track up to Bartholomew, until his face fills entire screen (like I did with Dale Fuller in *Foolish Wives*)." The completely crushed man decides to commit suicide, and, after Franz and Agnes exchange their sad farewells, we see "a little puff of smoke" emerge from the lilac bush. Agnes hurries back, fearing Franz has done himself in. Instead, she discovers Bartholomew. She takes hold of his "hand in the grass—amongst the daisies and kisses it, she lets go the hand [and] drops to ground where the pistol lies—she lets the branches glide together again—she stays in kneeling position—and sobs—Count stands with bowed head—bends down lovingly and touches her shoulder. SLOW FADE OUT." The subtitle reads, "Upon such sacrifice . . . The gods themselves throw incense . . ." This is followed by an iris in on the merry-go-round spinning as some of the principals stand nearby, followed by the subtitle "and the merry-go-round—goes round—and round—and round—." And so Stroheim's film would have ended, with the symbolic image of the spinning world as a merry-go-round.

In Julian's version, Agnes is told that Franz is not on the casualty lists but neither has he been found. Loved by Bartholomew, she decides to marry him. One day, while she is grinding the barrel organ outside the amusement park, she thinks she feels the presence of her lover. She looks up and, yes, he is there. All of him! No messy amputation, only a head of white hair. Franz says he is sorry, asks again for forgiveness, and she replies that she had forgiven him even before he left for the war. He explains that because his wife is dead now he and Agnes can marry. Bartholomew sees the couple through a broken window—symbolic of his own shattered dreams. (A good image and, incredibly, Julian's.) He returns to the ape's cage, crying, and holds the animal's paw in his hand, an action that today appears slightly comic. The last shot of the film is set in the arbor bursting with flowers and lush foliage, where Agnes and Franz embrace.

Throughout the film, Julian either omitted or short-circuited almost every reference to the social, political, and moral world that Stroheim was creating. He softened everything: no collapse of society, no privation, no loss of leg, no suicide, and a pretty concluding shot of a happy couple. Thus, the world is no longer a symbolic merry-go-round. Instead, the people in the film merely work on a carousel; it could just as well have been a factory assembly line.

To Stroheim, however, the image of the merry-go-round was significant in many ways. It views Huber's lust, Franz's seductions, Bartholomew's hope for happiness, and even the war itself as a circular chase that gets nowhere. One pays to ride the merry-go-round, and the price may be greater than the fun derived. In short, the world is a swirling mass of humanity, of pitiful pawns spinning on a wheel of fate in which rank, society, even life itself are tossed about by an uncontrollable destiny—the sole hope, love.

Unhappiness, helplessness, and disillusionment haunt Stroheim's scenario, unlike Julian's version. Entirely missing from the released film is Stroheim's depiction of the tensions of prewar Austria, the cries of the rabble for justice and fairness against the nobility. As Jean Renoir does in *La Grande Illusion,* years later, Stroheim here laments the demise of the aristocrats, despite their excesses. The years of Franz Josef might have been decadent, but what follows—the new democracy—is worse. People who were servants, with no touch of class, now become the masters. The lowly groom, basic, elemental, coarse, buys the castle. This view is quite close to that of William Faulkner, who saw the old, gentlemanly South superseded by the grabby and greedy Snopeses. Stroheim in his story treatment, mentioned "the leveling of the classes through the merry-go-round of life," adding that "social and economic conditions are topsy-turvy." Julian leveled it all into merely a love story.

Merry-Go-Round has echoes of Stroheim's earlier works. It employs the Austrian setting of *Blind Husbands,* the exciting atmosphere of Monte Carlo from *Foolish Wives,* and the male rake of both pictures. The film also includes plot elements that Stroheim would develop more fully in *The Wedding March* and *Queen Kelly,* such as the engaged aristocrat who falls in love with a lovely commoner. As in all of Stroheim's films, the background settings support the action faithfully and often comment ironically on what transpires.

In Stroheim's original plan, the role of the count would, of course, have been played by Stroheim. Thalberg, however, was too smart to let the director act in the picture, because he would then be unable to fire him. For a substitute, Stroheim chose Norman Kerry, but this decision was unfortunate. Not only is Kerry mediocre in looks, but he also lacks dynamism. The dash, the sparkle, and the blend of passion and cynicism are simply not there, despite (or because of) the fact that Kerry frequently showed up on the set inebriated. Apparently, not even alcohol could make him lively or likable or lend him panache. Scenes that would have worked if Stroheim had played the lead—the proof of which can be seen in *The Wedding March*—often lack vitality.

A few years later, Stroheim wanted to use Kerry in *The Merry Widow,* but Thalberg—quite rightly—insisted on the more attractive and appealing John Gilbert. Kerry later appeared in *The Phantom of the Opera* (1925), which Julian also directed, and was equally dull—just a stick, not a passionate and dynamic hero. Nor did his screen presence improve. In an early sound film, *Bachelor Apartment* (1931), he has a small role and does poorly in it; ironically, Mae Murray, another Stroheim veteran, was equally bad in the same film. Perhaps Stroheim could have forced Kerry into some engaging vitality, but even in the scenes Stroheim directed, Kerry does not succeed. Stroheim's judgment was not always perfect.

Under Stroheim's direction, the young and pretty Mary Philbin seems quite endearing as Agnes, but under Julian's she often degenerates into broad gestures and inappropriate facial expressions, habits she also reveals in *The Phantom of the Opera*. In fact, her performance in that film embodies the general public's idea of awful silent film acting. Philbin was not devoid of talent, but she needed strong and sympathetic direction. Years later, a fan magazine article related how D.W. Griffith, when seeking a heroine for his newest film, *Drums of Love* (1928), somehow screened *Merry-Go-Round*.[14] To him she appeared "arch, innocent, gay—and breathtakingly beautiful." He exclaimed, "This is the girl I want. Send for her." When she arrived, Griffith saw only a "small, timid person in rather unbecoming clothes, with prim old-fashioned manners." Probably Philbin, knowing Griffith's predilection for waifs, dressed the part. To him, said the article, "she might have been a little country schoolmarm or a small town librarian." But he wanted a gorgeous Spanish beauty, and so he politely sent her away. Then, according to the article, he looked at *Merry-Go-Round* again and realized "that she could change from a scared, repressed schoolgirl to a radiantly beautiful woman, a woman with all a woman's knowledge of love and joy and suffering." And so she won the part. It is revealing that Stroheim and "the Master" saw the same qualities: the innocence and the mature woman rolled into one.

The released version of *Merry-Go-Round* is an uneven work. Some scenes directed by Julian are satisfactory because he had Stroheim's detailed shooting script to work from, but whenever Julian provides scenes independent of Stroheim's script, they fall painfully flat. Julian is no more than a traffic cop, ordering people into and out of camera range. He seems to have no concept of character and only the faintest idea of what a nuance could be. For example, in Sylvester's hospital room, when the father and daughter realize that the necktie salesman is really a count, they just stare; then, in a shot of long duration, they "act." There is no subtle interplay of close-ups between Franz and Agnes when she realizes that her romantic dream is over, that she has been lied to and betrayed. Franz's dilemma of loving her but being married to another is only briefly touched upon.

Julian's reputation took a surge forward after *Merry-Go-Round,* but after *The Phantom of the Opera,* his career faltered. By 1930 it was over.

Stroheim's ambitious script perhaps touched on more autobiographical elements than he ever would have acknowledged. Without getting too Freudian, one may conjecture that Stroheim divided himself into several characters. In the film there is a count pretending to be a salesman in a Jewish store, which is the obverse of the hat salesman who pretended to be a count. Had the youthful Stroheim in Vienna already affected a degree of class beyond that associated with being a mere graduate from a commercial high school? Certainly, from his arrival in America he gave the illusion that he had left a distinguished past. In his dreams he was the fun-loving and wild-living aristocratic count. But Stroheim, in quiet and devastating moments of truth, may have thought of himself also as Bartholomew, the misshapen but sensitive fellow who loses out to his rival because of class, money, and good looks. In reality—or at least in Stroheim's perception of reality—he was the hunchback, doomed by his mercantile background, his rejection by the army, and the fact that he was probably spurned by women because of his relative poverty, size, and looks. Bartholomew might be kind and sensitive and loving, but his deformity dooms him as a sexual being. Bartholomew's alter ego is Boniface, the orangutan, who, like the puppet in the later *Great Gabbo,* can do what his master cannot do. He can pet Agnes, and he can kill Huber. And who knows whether the feeble old man in the wheelchair was an image of Stroheim's father or a fearful projection of himself in his old age? And what about the many uncharitable references to Polish Jews? After the financial and social turmoil of the First World War, some of those Jews did supplant the aristocrats, a situation that Stroheim did not witness but did perceive. (Doesn't Rosenthal in *La Grande Illusion* also mention that the Jews now own a good part of France?)

Certainly, Stroheim's original plan for *Merry-Go-Round* was much too full of incident and, if carried through, it would probably have sometimes dragged a bit. Nevertheless, it was an ambitious undertaking, showing social, moral, and religious aspects as well as some touching romantic scenes that are sensitive without being cloying. Indeed, the script for *Merry-Go-Round* is, in its dramatic situations and their implications, probably the most intelligent and perceptive scenario of the silent era. Julian's film lacks much (but not all) of the irony and bitterness that distinguish a Stroheim work from the typical Holly-wood product. The script is what might have been; the film is, unfortunately, all that remains of an inspired dream. However, Stroheim's vision appears often enough to make the film worth viewing, and these moments are a vivid reminder that in this wild and stubborn Austrian director lay one of the cinema's major talents.

8

Greed

One day prior to 1919, Stroheim's eye fell upon a book called *McTeague: A Story of San Francisco,* by Frank Norris. The subtitle may have attracted him, because he had lived in that area, but it was the content that held his attention. Here was a story that had guts, honesty, and drama, the very qualities he most admired. Although the novel had been filmed in five reels as *Life's Whirlpool* (1916), it is doubtful that he ever saw it at that time.

Norris, born in 1870 in Chicago to a well-off family, studied art in Paris in his teens, and at the age of twenty went to the University of California at Berkeley. During his four years there, he published numerous articles about the purposes of literature. He was deeply influenced by Joseph Le Conte, a professor at Berkeley, who attempted to relate Darwinism to man's spirituality. Le Conte asserted that mankind developed in two stages—animal evolution, controlled by heredity and environment (with physical strength a vital factor), followed by spiritual evolution, in which the "mind" shaped human advancement.

Norris saw these factors at work in a gruesome murder he read about in the newspaper in October 1893. A working-class man who frequently beat his wife and forced her to give him money finally stabbed her to death in a kindergarten where she worked as a janitor. This event provided the stimulus for a novel, which Norris began the next year while taking a writing course at Harvard. In 1897, he revised the earlier parts and completed the book, which was published in

1899 as *McTeague*. Three years later, the young writer died from appendicitis and was buried in Oakland.

Norris's book, steeped in French naturalism (a mode created by Émile Zola in the late 1800s), was a far cry from the belles lettres of contemporary American writers such as Edith Wharton and Henry James. Filled with minute detail, *McTeague* treated the lower classes in a realistic manner and showed that man's nature, despite free will, is determined by genetic and environmental factors. Norris claimed that naturalism was not realism, although the two were often lumped together. The realists, he explained, dealt with common people who did nothing out of the ordinary, whereas "terrible things must happen to the characters of the naturalistic tale. They must be twisted from the ordinary, wrenched out from the quiet, uneventful round of every-day life, and flung into the throes of a vast and terrible drama that works itself out in unleashed passions, in blood, and in sudden death. No teacup tragedies here."[1] Norris's description of naturalism was also an apt description of *McTeague*. His tale takes place in a harsh but familiar world, a grim and unsavory universe of common people beset by ungovernable drives. This treatment was consistent with Stroheim's own mordant views.

Stroheim not only studied *McTeague* but also became familiar with Norris's essays, one of which rang a responsive bell in Stroheim's psyche. In his foreword to the film, he cites a portion of that essay (shown in italics in this quotation from the foreword):

> To make money is not the province of a novelist. If he is the right sort he has other responsibilities, heavy ones. He of all men cannot think only of himself or for himself. And when the last page is written and the ink crusts on the pen-point and the hungry presses go clashing after another writer, the "new Man" and the new fashion of the hour, he will think of the grim long grind of the years of his life that he has put behind him and of his work that he has built up volume by volume, sincere work, telling the truth as he saw it, independent of fashion and the gallery gods, holding to these with gripped hands and shut teeth—he will think of all this then, and he will be able to say: *"I never truckled, I never took off the hat to Fashion and held it out for pennies. By God, I told them the truth.*

*They liked it or they didn't like it. What had that to do with me? I
told them the truth; I knew it for the truth then, and I know it for the
truth now."*[2]

Stroheim admired Norris's respect for truth and his stubborn disregard of what was commercially fashionable. "Where is the man,"
wrote Norris in 1897, "that shall get at the heart of us, the blood and
bones and fiber of us, that shall go a-gunning for stories up and down
our streets and into our houses and parlors and lodging houses and
saloons and dives and along our wharves and into our theaters?"[3] Where
is this man? The man, of course, was Norris. And now the man would
be Stroheim! Self-anointed, he would take upon himself the holy mission: to do in film what Norris had done in literature.

As early as January 1920, Stroheim mentioned to the press his
intention to film the book.[4] However, he postponed this project, made
Foolish Wives, and then embarked on *Merry-Go-Round.* The loss of that
project might have been a disappointment when Thalberg fired him
on October 6, 1922, but Stroheim was not overly heartbroken, because he knew that other studios wanted his services.

The firing of Stroheim was a significant step in the motion picture
industry. It was a harbinger of what would become standard procedure: the director was not a boss but an employee. Those men who had
made their films in their own way, such as D.W. Griffith, Marshall
Neilan, Maurice Tourneur, and Rex Ingram, soon found their careers
aborted. The producer was now in charge.

One exception to this new attitude was the philosophy of Abe
Lehr, a lifelong crony of Samuel Goldwyn since their early days of
cutting gloves in upstate New York. Goldwyn believed that writers
were of vital importance, but his policy of hiring famous authors to
create great screenplays failed. When Goldwyn in March 1922 was
forced out of the firm that bore his name, Lehr had been left in partial
control. He was described as a "kindly, courteous person" but one
who would prove to be "a poor executive."[5] Lehr decided that "each
director will have his own staff and will be given every facility in
putting into his productions his own individuality and personality. He
will have the co-operation of the department heads of the Culver
City studio, but each unit will be separate unto itself. Lehr asserted,
"Great motion pictures cannot be made by the factory system. We

have on our directorial staff men of outstanding accomplishment." He proudly explained his aims: "We are now undertaking the production of an important cycle of pictures on which several million dollars will be spent. We want to make them a noteworthy contribution to the steadily advancing art of the motion picture; we want no one of these pictures to be like another. Our aim will be to make each a distinct entity breathing the spirit of its creator."[6]

Lehr may have been a trifle idealistic, but he believed that Stroheim was capable of a giant box-office success. The Goldwyn company hoped for a subject with continental settings, sophisticated glamor, and perhaps some scandalous—though releasable—scenes of stylish sexual innuendo that would intrigue the public. There was mention of his doing *The Merry Widow*. Stroheim—oh, what a master of sweet-talk he must have been—deftly shifted the executives from this wish for stylishness and somehow convinced them that a film of *McTeague* would be preferable. This project, they were relieved to know, would involve no expensive sets but would be shot mostly on location. How could they err with such a bargain? By February 1923 the press announced that Stroheim, who had "run rather freely to large sets in the past, seems to have reformed—or surrendered—for it is announced that he will not build any sets at all."[7] Instead of the castles, uniforms, and romance of *The Merry Widow*, the company got slums, squalor, murder, and a grim, ironic ending. And so Stroheim embarked "untruckled" on his impossible dream, a cinematic crusade for truth.

Well aware of Stroheim's excesses at Universal and hoping to avoid them, the company's lawyers drew up a unique contract. It severely limited Stroheim in terms of length and subject matter and would pay him thirty thousand dollars for each completed film. The company believed that this financial limit would hold him in check because there would be no economic advantage if he worked longer on a picture. Even if they did not see much box-office potential in a film of *McTeague,* they were willing to indulge this flamboyant artist in the seemingly low-budget project in order to get him to do *The Merry Widow* later.

Stroheim signed the agreement on November 20, 1922—perhaps even with the sincerest intention to be reasonable. He also was pleased to know that he would not be hampered by Thalberg's notions of efficiency and would be allowed to make films his own way. The company hoped to receive in the year-long contract three features (of between forty-five hundred and eighty-five hundred feet each) and naïvely rejoiced in its good luck, not knowing that the gifted Austrian, when in the midst of creation, considered contracts mere words. Like an alcoholic swearing to drink no more, Stroheim could not resist just a nip, and off he went on the most notorious binge in cinema history.

Stroheim devoted his every waking moment to rendering the novel into a highly detailed scenario indicating dialogue, camera placement, color tints, and even camera movement. He paused only to complete the casting. He had most of the principals in mind, but he hesitated about the role of Trina. After reportedly testing "half-a-dozen well-known actresses," he picked Zasu Pitts at almost the last minute.[8]

At first, the studio referred to the film as *Greedy Wives,*[9] which would have been a parallel to *Foolish Wives,* but the realization that there was only one greedy wife prompted the title change in March.[10] Actual shooting began on March 13 and did not end until October 6. No film, except for *Foolish Wives,* had ever had such a long period of constant shooting. Most features were done in a few weeks. Griffith's lengthy and complicated *The Birth of a Nation* took only about three months to complete, and although *Intolerance* had taken much longer, it was an infinitely more complex work spanning four different time periods and involving thousands of costumes and vast sets. The scope of *Greed* was far more modest, but it proved time-consuming because Stroheim gave himself a severe challenge—authenticity. He chose to deal with real places and to shoot the entire film on location in San Francisco and related places—even in the actual buildings Norris had mentioned. He included places such as Polk Street, the bay, the Cliff House, a gold mine, a ferry, a post office, and Death Valley. Whenever possible, he used no sets in the accepted sense. Certain interior settings, however, such as saloons, coffee joints, butcher shops, and wooden shacks, were either actual buildings thoroughly revamped or constructed sets that were so meticulously dressed that they appeared genuine.

Location work appealed strongly to a man who, from the beginning of his career, was obsessed with accuracy. Furthermore, the essence of naturalism was the accumulation of detail, and no one was better at details than Stroheim. However, despite what some critics have said, he was never a slave to reality; he was not a pure documentarian. Instead, even at his most realistic, Stroheim "adjusted" his settings—for he was an artist, not a mere recorder. As Norris wrote, "Fiction is what seems real, not what is real."[11]

Many of Stroheim's commentators seem to suffer from the delusion that he slavishly presented every scene of the book and altered nothing. His detailed script (which has been published and runs over three hundred pages, almost the length of the novel) shows that he did not merely translate *McTeague* into visual terms but rethought it. Stroheim *renders* the book. At times, he substantially adds; occasionally, he subtracts. The film is by no means just a dogged copy of the original.

One of Stroheim's changes involved moving the time frame of the story forward twenty-five years, so that the film opens in 1908 and ends in the year of production, 1923. However, the general impression, because of the costumes and settings, is that it takes place in an earlier period. For example, Mac leaves home in a horse-drawn carriage and drinks in a saloon, not a speakeasy. Except for a couple of long shots of city streets that contain automobiles, there are few references to more modern times.

When, actually, do events occur in the film? In Norris's book, we learn that Mac was a car boy in the gold mine ten years before the novel opens.[12] "Two or three years" after the death of Mac's father, the boy leaves with the dentist, "Painless" Potter. In Stroheim's script, the film opens in 1908, when Mac, a car boy, experiences his father's death; if he joins Potter three years later, that would make the year 1911. The script has Mac helping Potter on Market Street in San Francisco in 1913. Shortly after, Mac opens his own dental parlors. Stroheim originally had a title saying that five years had passed since Mac started his private practice, which would make the year 1918.[13] Mac meets Trina that year; in May 1918, she wins the lottery ticket, and in June they marry. They live happily in their apartment until February 1922, when the letter from the dental board arrives. The severe cutting of the film moves many of these events too close together, making Trina an almost complete miser right away and losing the fact that the couple live in relative harmony for four years.

Norris's novel told the story of a man who, through the efforts of his mother, fulfilled her dream for him to become a success, in this case a dentist. Ill luck and circumstances drive him out of this comfortable niche, and he descends the economic and social ladder. In some ways, unbeknownst to Stroheim, this novel—and his most famous film—prefigured his own life. By fate, luck, and determination, Stroheim became a successful director, dedicated this very film, *Greed*, to his mother, then through circumstances, poor decisions, and bad luck, he also descended the ladder of success. A strong believer in fate, he was often curiously prophetic. However, there can be self-fulfilling prophecies. This dedicated artist, in his holy passion for truth, would not perish in Death Valley but instead would wander unfulfilled in a creative desert for almost a quarter of a century.

The only existing prints of *Greed* are one-fourth of what Stroheim filmed. What a pity he did not spend a few thousand dollars and keep a full version for himself. The missing footage is now irretrievably lost, and all that remains are the shooting script and a few hundred stills. In 1972, Herman G. Weinberg, long an admirer of Stroheim, issued a book of photographs from the film, including many from the deleted sections. These, plus the script, can give us a limited idea of what Stroheim originally filmed.

Frank Norris begins his book with McTeague sitting comfortably in a chair in his dental parlors. On the second page, the novelist provides a brief, two-paragraph summation of Mac's past life as a worker in a gold mine, of his mother's life of drudgery as a mining-camp cook, and of his father, a hardworking fellow who, at payday every two weeks, became "an irresponsible animal, a beast, a brute, crazy with alcohol." Stroheim could easily have arranged his film in the same way. Mac might have walked around the room, glanced at a picture of his father (flashback) and then of his mother (likewise). However, Stroheim never liked flashbacks or juggling time periods, so he decided to start at the beginning. As a result, he attempted not only to handle the novel faithfully but to expand the parts that Norris had not explained fully. He wanted viewers to *experience* firsthand the background, both behavioral and genetic, of his principal character.

The major figure in the book is, of course, McTeague, a heavyset fellow, ponderous, dull, and slow to action. As Norris said, "There was nothing vicious about the man. Altogether he suggested the draft horse, immensely strong, stupid, docile, obedient."[14] Lacking in intelligence, McTeague is more often than not the victim of his own heredity and instinct—the naturalist's secular version of original sin and predestination. The son of a man who dies in delirium tremens, he has blood that is directly tainted. Mac floats unthinkingly through life, becomes a dentist of sorts, and would have finished his life as a good but dull fellow. However, the envy and malice of his best friend, the loss of his job, and the miserliness of his wife shake him out of his niche. He starts to drink, to slip down the ladder of civilization. Although he does not quite become the beast that Norris depicted in another novel, *Vandover and the Brute,* he does become a bum and a murderer. Only when his structured life collapses (Norris was thinking along the same lines as Conrad in *Heart of Darkness*) do the baser instincts, long held back by the strict forms of society, come to the fore. Mac, unlike his smarter friend, Marcus, who consciously makes his own decisions, does not really know what is happening to him.

Stroheim's script shows the young man's life as a miner, his extraordinary brute strength, his kindness to animals, and the love of the hardworking mother for Mac. Much of this material is now heavily cut, but one incident—not in the novel—was retained. It depicts Mac's guileless naïveté in Griffith-like terms as he picks up and kisses an injured bird. Mac compassionately shows it to a fellow worker, who cruelly knocks it out of his hands. In anger, Mac throws the man down a deep gully. Thus, with great efficiency, Stroheim establishes Mac's sensitivity, his strength, and his instinctive way of responding to events. Other scenes, now entirely cut, show the father's drunken rowdiness, his carousing with haggish prostitutes, his collapse from alcoholism, his death struggles, and his funeral. (Did this additional material about the father stem, however transmuted, from Stroheim's own past?)

Stroheim also illustrates the mother's desire for her son to transcend this arduous lower-class life. She tells Mac that she has "great ambitions . . . and great hopes" for his future and that the coming of the dentist was an "intervention of Fate" (58). She clearly loves her boy and tells him she has apprenticed him to Dr. "Painless" Potter, the traveling dentist. The mother, bidding an emotional farewell to her son, gives him a watch and a twenty-dollar gold piece. This lengthy inclusion of the mother's warm relationship to the son seems to do more than explicate the novel. There is an autobiographical resonance here. We may recall that Stroheim dedicated *Greed* to his mother and that Mac's mother is the only unblemished and entirely sympathetic person in the film, the only one not satirized or demeaned or criticized. If we can return to Vienna of 1909, we know that Stroheim's mother was estranged from his father, that the boy—if not in deep

financial or legal trouble, as Stroheim intimated—was at least at logger-
heads with reality and disappointed about his aborted military dream,
which had ended with such humiliation. Certainly he was at that time
going nowhere in terms of a career. Or it might be that his mother—
having faith in her bright but undisciplined son—gave him some of her
last money and sent him to the New World to succeed. Maybe she
could give a spin to the wheel of fate and set him off on a new life.
Maybe he could get a job with one of her relatives in the clothing
business in New York. And so, although sad to see her beloved boy go,
she also hoped that the move would be successful. This emotional
baggage, I believe, was drawn upon in the farewell scene between Mac
and his mother. Furthermore, Stroheim felt that his best qualities—his
sensitive, sentimental, and loving side—came from his mother and that
his "bad" qualities—his lusty urges, his cynicism, his selfishness—stemmed
from his irresponsible father, who had managed to run the family firm
into backruptcy. Thus, in the script, the father is seen stealing the
mother's paycheck and blowing the money on drink and the local
whores. Would not Stroheim's mother, to whom he was closely attached, come to the fore in tracing the background of poor, fate-
driven Mac? I think a case could be made for this interpretation. *Greed*,
the great labor of love and proof of his genius, is his gift to his mother
for her faith. No wonder the dedication.

Mac forlornly packs up his few possessions, among them a concertina
and a little cage containing the bird he has saved. Waving good-bye to
his tearful mother, the young man leaves with the dentist, from whom,
in the next few years, he will learn certain rudimentary dental procedures. Stroheim details some scenes of Potter and Mac at work. At one
point, the strong Mac pulls a patient's tooth out using only his fingers.

Later in Stroheim's explication of what Norris had merely skimmed,
Mac goes to the post office and receives a general delivery letter telling him that his mother died months before, on December 23.
Stroheim's own father died, according to my information, on Dec. 22.
Did Stroheim perhaps think it was Dec. 23? Why else would he include such an extraneous detail—one not in the book at all—in a film
dedicated to his mother? What autobiographical demons was he exor-
cizing here? The letter is dated December 24 (the first instance of
Stroheim's fascination with Christmas Eve). That this is no incidental
detail or mere coincidence can be seen in the script: "His finger goes

up to the date of the letter." Stroheim also stresses the day that Mac receives the letter: "His look falls on a calendar, seen through the grating of the window . . . showing February 12th" (63). This date means that Mac—with the money his mother has willed him—can begin his life anew on the following day, the thirteenth, when he rents his new quarters and first encounters Marcus (63–64).

Norris's brief summary of Mac's past was expanded by Stroheim into approximately thirty pages of script (which in all likelihood would have taken about an hour of screen time). True, he filled in a lot of information on Mac's early life, his environment, and his genetic background. But even this was too fragmentary for Stroheim. He could not allow himself to shift abruptly from the mining camp to Mac sitting comfortably in his dental parlors. Instead, he felt compelled to show McTeague arriving in San Francisco, walking down the street, looking at a building, going to the post office, receiving the news of his mother's death, meeting the landlord, and renting his dental office. Stroheim, in his thoroughness, considered all these details to be essential not only to the characterizations but also to the proper establishment of the plot. This material, however, is not *vital* to the narrative and could easily have been cut (as it almost wholly was in the existing print).

Stroheim's script, in a revealing departure from usual dramatic practice, introduces the principal characters who live in the building— Miss Baker, Marcus Schuler, and Mr. Grannis—*before* Mac encounters them. Thus, all of these people with their separate lives and personal habits become mere pawns brought unknowingly and unconsciously together by fate, which will now mete out their individual destinies.

Among these characters is Mr. Grannis, the elderly proprietor of a dog hospital, whom we first meet as he cuddles some puppies. His employee, Marcus, enters carrying a bottle of chloroform and a gunnysack (66). Here, Stroheim introduces key aspects of his characters by means of animal imagery, as did Griffith. McTeague rescues a bird; Grannis is kind to puppies; Marcus kills animals. Stroheim, by this means, provides far more insight into the characters than does Norris, who merely mentions that Marcus works for Grannis and does not hint of Marcus's nature at this point, except that he is "a bungler in the profession" (13).

Grannis is a gentle, sweet soul who appears in a subplot with Miss Baker. When we first meet her, Stroheim includes one of his private symbols: She carries a potted geranium (68). For years, these two elderly people, who live in the same building, have been too timid to speak with each other. Their relationship, which eventually leads them to marriage, was included in Stroheim's film, although handled rather briefly (for Stroheim). Intended by Norris as a gentle contrast to the overpowering passions that possess the other characters, their story probably appeared to Stroheim as somewhat sentimental and insincere. This is suggested by the fact that, as they embrace for the first time, the script counterpoints a shot of them kissing with the following:

> A street car passes, a garbage wagon goes by in the opposite direction, an Italian organ grinder stands on the sidewalk with two small monkeys that jump up and down while some kids stand watching.
>
> Quick lap dissolve to the monkeys kissing each other. Dissolve back to a close-up of Grannis' left hand held by both of Miss Baker's, while his right hand pats her left. (285)

Stroheim, no doubt, included the crosscutting of the monkeys with Grannis and Baker to reduce the sentimentality and probably to add some mordant humor. Could he also be suggesting that even this sweet and gentle Victorian couple had some Darwinian ancestors in their past, some primitive urges long repressed?

The Grannis-Baker relationship was one of the novel's subplots; the other dealt with Zerkow and Maria. Both of these stories—which paralleled the Mac-Trina relationship—were entirely cut from the final film. Zerkow, a Polish Jew junk-dealer, collects all kinds of things. His main lust is for gold. He believes the wild tales of a crazed woman, Maria, about an immense dinner service of gold. In his greed, he marries her in the hope of finding the plates.

After Stroheim sketches in some of the people who live in the apartment building, he shifts to another part of town and introduces another new character, Trina, who is, we discover, already quite concerned with money. She is pleased at what she earns carving toy animals and selling them to her uncle. Stroheim avoids an explanatory title by having her inform the uncle that she has a date with Marcus and must hurry up to shop (77).

This scene is intercut with one showing Mac entering a pet shop and, after much hesitation (he has visited the place frequently), buying a canary, which he keeps with him in a cage right through to the end of the film. The bird, of course, echoes the one in the mining camp and establishes a thematic image that embodies his positive qualities and, perhaps, suggests his own caged soul. Stroheim then cuts to Trina in a butcher shop. She orders some frankfurters and, carefully studying the scale, quibbles over the slight short weight. The butcher crabbily adds another link to the pile. Thrift is clearly a part of her character, even at this early stage. In these scenes, Stroheim broke completely from the novel: Norris introduced Trina as she entered the dental parlors, but Stroheim had to start earlier, just as he did with Mac, to let us know what kind of person she is before she meets Mac. All this material was cut from the final print.

Trina starts out as an attractive, hardworking, and thrifty young girl and slowly transforms into a complete miser. This descent can be seen not only in her clothing and her environment but even in her facial expressions. In the novel, Norris at one point describes Trina as making a gesture of touching her finger to her lips. Stroheim took this hint and made it a recurrent physical action that indicates her greed. This miserliness could be described by Norris with words; Stroheim chose the gesture—a finger to the lips, the squint of one eye, a slight grimace of the face—and made it a superb, yet economical, way of conveying her mania in a visual manner.

After introducing Trina, Stroheim returns to Zerkow and Maria and illustrates their obsession with gold. The scene then shifts to Marcus's date with Trina, during which we meet her comically grotesque Teutonic family and witness her fall from a swing, resulting in a damaged tooth. And so fate draws these characters together when Marcus takes Trina to Mac's dental office. It has taken Stroheim 67 pages of script, approximately one-fifth of the scenario's length, to bring us to the point where Mac meets Trina on page 104. It took Norris only thirteen pages, one-twenty-fifth of the novel!

When Stroheim introduces Marcus in the script—a scene missing from the print—he reveals how carefully he conceived his characters:

> A man enters ... wearing a very loud black-and-white-striped shirt, college-cut pants from a pepper-and-salt suit and bulldog-tipped tan button shoes. His shirt sleeves are rolled up, his waistcoat open and he has a loud red, white and red [sic] watch

fob with the name "Marcus" in brass letters across it. Also a red bow tie with white dots and stripes, underneath which is a horse-shoe fake diamond necktie pin stuck into his shirt. A brown derby with a black band sits at a cocky angle on the back of his head. He has the stump of a dead cigar, with the belly band still on, in his mouth. (66)

Was there ever such a meticulous description in a Hollywood script?

In adapting Norris's novel, Stroheim made a significant change—one can easily say improvement—by enhancing the bird symbolism. In the novel, Mac simply has a pet canary. Stroheim reinforces its symbolic value by including the wounded bird in the beginning, the long deliberation about whether to buy a canary, and then Mac's wedding gift to Trina—a female canary. Marcus ridicules this gift, and Trina is also disappointed. To her, another bird is a foolish waste of money. To Mac, however, the two birds are now love birds. And the birds coexist well throughout the early parts of the film. They represent the married couple's togetherness and perhaps suggest that they are both trapped in a cage of greed and genetic forces.

When Marcus visits Mac and Trina for his final farewell (after having secretly informed the dental board that Mac does not have a license, as we later find out), Stroheim crosscuts to a cat stalking the birds. He even dissolves between a close-up of the menacing cat and one of Marcus's face. All of this bird-cat interaction was added by Stroheim; there is no mention of it in the novel. Afterward, when the married couple squabble, the birds fight in their cage. Later (in scenes now cut), after Mac kills Trina, the female canary also dies. Throughout the rest of the film, Mac continues to care for the surviving bird and, indeed, his last gesture is to free it, although it dies, as does he.

In the Zerkow-Maria subplot, the junk-dealer spends hours spying on Maria and digging under the floorboards and out in the yard, searching to find the golden plates. Maddened by his greed, he uses a whip to try to force the hiding place out of her. After cutting her throat, he flees and drowns in San Francisco Bay. "Clutched in both his hands," says the novel, "was a sack full of old and rusty pans, tin dishes—fully a hundred of them—tin cans, and iron knives and forks, collected from some dump heap." Trina (aware of Zerkow's folly but not her own) comments, "And all this on account of a set of gold dishes that never existed."(247) The only shots that remain of this important and faithfully filmed subplot are of emaciated hands fondling treasure—an image from Zerkow's crazed mind.

The preceding pages have explained some of the relationships between the novel, the full print, and the released version. From here on, perhaps the best method of explication is to work from the existing print as it unfolds, with occasional references to the book and the script. Even though the two subplots are completely gone (and the tale of Mac and Trina severely cut), the film's message is still clear. Stroheim's exploration into the mind of man has been trimmed, not softened.

Greed begins in a gold mine and ends with coins scattered upon the shifting wastes of Death Valley. What transpires between the documentary-like opening—gold mining as a business—and the hellish torture of Death Valley becomes an indictment of greed and perhaps even of humanity itself.

Stroheim's film recalls the Seven Deadly Sins of medieval drama, and especially the allegorical figure Greed, who brings unhappiness and death to all he infects. In the play *Everyman* (1485), Greed (called Goods) tells Everyman that wealth is not his forever:

> As for a while I was lent thee;
> A season thou hast me in prosperity.
> My [disposition] is man's soul to kill;
> If I save one, a thousand I do spill.

And Everyman comes to the conclusion:

> Ah, Goods, thou hast had long my hearty love;
> I gave thee that which should be the Lord's above.

To underline his message, Stroheim included hallucinatory scenes of treasure, the symbolic image of a giant hand crushing two nude male and female figures, certain shots featuring the gold coins that were (originally) hand-colored, and the predominant symbol of a gilt birdcage.

The main story begins as Mac's friend, Marcus, in the novel a loudmouthed socialist (all political aspects were omitted by Stroheim), arrives with Trina at the dentist's office. He is an excellent example of Stroheim's devastating sense of character. He wears a loud suit, boasts an "Oh You Kid" button in his lapel, chews gum, and is a backslapping, brash, and deliciously crude low-class individual. While Marcus sits in McTeague's office, he first picks his teeth, then his ear, and finally his nose. One contemporary reviewer, Aileen St. John–Brenon, writing in the uppity *Theatre Magazine,* said that Jean Hersholt's performance "is convincing in spite of his unnecessary bits of grossness."[14] Although the reviewer did not approve, Marcus is accurately presented. The horror, of course, is that he is a reflection—although perhaps an exaggerated one—of a large percentage of the filmgoing audience. Marcus is far more lively and sharp than dull-witted Mac, but he lacks the dentist's sensitivity. One could never imagine Marcus carrying a bird, only a grudge.

While waiting to have her teeth fixed, Trina buys a lottery ticket from the crazed Maria (one of the few times we see this person, even though she appeared in countless scenes in Stroheim's untrimmed version). Then, while doing the dental work, Mac feels attracted by Trina's beauty, which sparks in him an ambition to repair her teeth correctly. She becomes a frequent patient for the next two weeks, and McTeague finds her more and more appealing. During one visit, when her pain grows unbearable, he gives her ether.

McTeague hovers over the helpless girl, as lust rises within him. "Iris down on her face; camera pans along her body and stops at waist height for a second. Close up of McTeague looking at her and breathing hard. Back to shot from his angle, in iris; camera continues to pan until it comes close to her feet with her trim ankles" (115). These three shots, if filmed, have been cut, but the rest of the scene was not substantially altered. McTeague struggles against desire and begins again to work, but then pauses; he cannot control what Norris and the title card call the "foul stream of hereditary evil" that flows through his veins. McTeague kisses Trina full on the lips, followed by a shot of the excited bird—his symbolic self, trapped by heredity—hopping around in its cage.

In this scene, Stroheim adds a touch of his own: as Trina lies anesthetized in the chair with white linen wrapped around her hair and chin, she resembles a sleeping nun, which heightens the inappropriateness of this passionate kiss and increases the sense of her violation by his act.[15] (The calendar, by the way, reveals that it is the thirteenth.)

The book explains Mac's actions more fully: "Below the fine fabric of all that was good in him ran the foul stream of hereditary evil, like a sewer. The vices and sins of his father and of his father's father, to the third and fourth and five hundredth generation, tainted him. The evil of an entire race flowed in his veins. Why should it be? He did not desire it. Was he to blame?" (*McTeague*, 29). This passage from Norris was modified slightly in the film: "But below the fine fabric, bred of his mother, ran the foul stream of hereditary evil . . . the taint of generations given through his father" (116).

Stroheim here seems to take pains to attribute Mac's good qualities (sensitivity, kindness, generosity) to the mother and to blame the hereditary evil on the father. Norris, when he used the term father, meant ancestor, man's Darwinian past (thus, humankind), but Stroheim further delineated Mac's genetic past and thus exonerated the mother from sin. Perhaps Stroheim wished to separate his own conflicting tendencies—his baser as well as his more loving sides—and to attribute each to an individual parent.

This "foul stream" is a rather curious phrase, as if the sexual urge itself were foul. Norris seems to reflect Victorian attitudes here, yet the author (like Stroheim) acknowledges the sex drive as a part of life. Although some commentators have felt that Trina is frigid, that is hardly the case. Both in the book and in the film, Trina is a passionate girl; only later does her passion shift from sex to money.

After Trina regains consciousness, McTeague asks her to marry him. Surprised and frightened, she cries out "No," then (in the book and the uncut film) vomits in reaction to nerves and the ether. At this point, Marcus enters the office, and soon he and Trina leave. Her dental work done, she intends to see Mac no more.

Some time later, Marcus and McTeague are seated in the Cliff House, a restaurant near the boardwalk. McTeague is depressed and finally confesses that he is in love with Trina. As he and Marcus discuss their predicament, Marcus indicates that he likes her but not enough to marry her. People can be seen walking in the background along the boardwalk, not only providing visual interest but reinforcing the idea that life goes on, despite the momentous decision being made by the two men. An advertisement with a picture of a jolly monk hangs on the back wall during this scene and functions not only as a symbol of brotherly love but also as an ironic commentary on what is to come.

Marcus is at first annoyed at Mac, but soon he says, "I'll give her up to you, old man." And then he adds, "By damn." (The "By damn" was added by Stroheim.) As a result of this seemingly unselfish decision, all three—Trina, McTeague, and Marcus—become damned.

On the next holiday, July Fourth, Trina's German family—each member festooned with American flags, even on their hats—goes on a picnic with McTeague and Marcus. Norris himself had used these Germans as comic relief, and Stroheim explored their adventures with good low humor, although much of the broad satire has been cut. Poppa marches his family down the railroad tracks like a general heading an army. They go to an amusement park and ride a merry-go-round, a scene expanded by Stroheim, perhaps in memory of his previous film, *Merry-Go-Round*. As they ride the horses, they turn from sunlight into shadow, from silhouettes to full illumination—a good example of Strohcim's interest in active visuals. American flags hang everywhere, as if in their profusion Stroheim were mocking the holiday spirit.

Later, McTeague visits Trina again. "Let's go and sit on the sewer," she says, a line that always provokes merriment in audiences. This title is hardly subtle, and it is neither Stroheim's nor Norris's, but MGM's. The setting symbolizes both artists' view of humanity: we live above an intricate and labyrinthine sewer of instincts. These two naive people—as yet unacquainted with the world's evil and their own—sit on the concrete sewer and gaze out upon a slimy landscape and a dead, sodden rat. This specific setting, however, is Stroheim's addition. In the novel, rather than the sewer, they sit on the railroad tracks "at the edge of a mudbank." McTeague, who has brought his concertina, plays the six mournful airs that he knows. In the released film (but not in the script), Mac asks Trina what she would like to hear. After a moment's thought, she replies "Hearts and Flowers." But McTeague does not know this old war horse and plays, instead, "Nearer My God to Thee." Although the later title writer may have added this, it is not unlikely that Stroheim departed from his script to include the irony of playing "Nearer My God to Thee" in such a setting.

A few minutes later, rain begins to fall, and they run into a railroad shelter. There Mac kisses Trina, much to her fear, while a train (in both the film and the novel) approaches, symbolizing the strength and inevitability of passion. According to Stroheim's script, the train "with its flaming headlights (hand-colored green and red, like the eyes of an evil demon) roars past" (143). On the back wall of the shelter hangs a large advertisement for Pluto mineral water. Later scenes in Marcus's room (now cut) also included a sign for Pluto water, and a bottle of it appears on a nightstand by the marital bed. The presence of the Pluto water is no accident, for the brand name hints that man stands infirmly upon an underworld, a kind of biological and psychological sewer of instinct.

Frightened at Mac's passionate embrace (Trina is, of course, a naive and typically Victorian product), she breaks away. As a title indicates, "mysterious undercurrents . . . were knitting their lives together." She hurriedly tells him to come again next week and dashes off in the rain. He cries out to himself in triumph "I got her. By God! I've got her!" as another powerful train rushes past behind him (143).

In the script, as in the novel (but cut from the film), Stroheim shows Trina returning home, where her mother is baiting a mousetrap with cheese. Trina tearfully explains what happened. In the novel, the mother slams the trap down, but in the script Stroheim reinforces the parallel by having Trina absentmindedly catch her finger in the device, which prefigures her impending entrapment by passion. The script clinches this episode by crosscutting to McTeague sitting in the train and repeating, "I got her, by God!" Later that night, Mac tells Marcus what happened. Then Stroheim's script shifts back to Trina:

> Iris in on Trina's bedroom (camera on perambulator). Trina is in her nightgown, with her wonderful hair down, brushing and brushing it. She stops, looking into space in a preoccupied way. Camera moves up until Trina is in close-up.
>
> Close-up of her. She stares into space, thinking, imagining McTeague in front of her, looking at her sore finger tied up in a white linen rag. She suddenly but decidedly shakes her head and says: "No—No" She almost shivers at the thought. She is very unhappy. Camera slowly moves back and she throws herself on the bed, almost covered by her marvelous hair. Iris out. (146)

Here, Stroheim has taken Norris's several pages of soul-searching and rendered them concisely, poignantly, and, more important, visually.

At Trina's next meeting with Mac, she confesses that she has "acted like a bad girl" (146), meaning that her sexual side, never before broached, has come to the fore. She tells him that she does not love him, but when he ignores her words and embraces her, she responds immediately with, "Oh, I do love you, I do." Her mind has said no, but not her body. Trina might grow to have an appetite for gold, but her appetite for sex is strong, too. Unfortunately, all of the above scenes, except for the embrace at the train shelter, have been cut.

Soon after, the family goes to a vaudeville theater (presumably on Saturday, May 13, because when Trina hands in the lottery ticket on Monday, the check she receives is dated May 15) (162). At the theater, Mac is impressed with a professional rendition of his favorite, "Nearer My God to Thee," played on beer bottles. (In the novel, "Nearer My God to Thee" is played twice, once at the theater and once at the wedding.) After the performance, they return to Mac's place for a late evening snack and are greeted by an excited group. There follows a close-up of a strange-looking man—he reminds one of an undertaker—with an ominous adhesive patch like a bandage on his right cheek. (It covers a boil, which, in cut scenes, had already been established.) He announces that Trina has won five thousand dollars in a lottery. The physical boil of the messenger now becomes a psychic boil for Marcus; he curses McTeague's luck and regrets now that he gave up Trina.

The wedding of Trina and McTeague a month later shows Stroheim's penchant for the grotesque and the bizarre. Among the guests are the very fat harness-maker and his midget wife, the hunchbacked photographer, the bucktoothed niece of Mrs. Sieppe, and the elderly Mr. Grannis and Miss Baker. Mac awaits the wedding music; then, entering the room, he trips over the threshold (to Stroheim, a sign of impending bad luck). As the ceremony proceeds, we see a close-up of Marcus's clenched hands, revealing his jealousy, a shot similar in style to one during Mae Marsh's courtroom appearance in Griffith's *Intolerance*.

Outside the window, in counterpoint to the wedding, Stroheim adds a funeral procession, juxtaposing matrimonial white and funereal black: joy and grief, beginning and ending. This scene was a genuine challenge to the cameraman, for he had to balance the light in the actual room with the brightness of the street exterior. Stroheim then dissolves to a closer shot of the procession "just long enough," says the script, "to make sure that no one in the audience has missed it" (178). The funeral procession includes, briefly, a boy with one leg hobbling along with a crutch following what, no doubt, is a dead parent. The ironic contrast provided by the funeral is solely Stroheim's and is in fact more imaginative and symbolic than what Norris had included: "Outside the noises of the street rose to the windows in muffled undertones; a cable car rumbled past; a newsboy went by chanting the evening papers; from somewhere in the building itself came a persistent noise of sawing" (*McTeague,* 130).

In the script, Stroheim did follow Norris's lead by shifting to a shot of a saw cutting wood. Norris included this detail to show that life goes on, that sounds go on, but in the film it would have been a distraction. It was wisely cut, either by Stroheim or by the editors of the extant print.

The wedding scene shows that Stroheim was a master at editing and by no means a filmmaker who relied only on mise-en-scène for his effects. The actual ceremony is preceded by twenty-seven shots of the room in which the minister, McTeague, and others are waiting. When Trina enters and approaches the minister, the service begins. There follows a total of thirty shots of Trina, the melodeon keyboard, Marcus, the minister, the funeral procession, and members of the family. (In the script, this section contains forty shots.) Even in its trimmed form, the sequence is edited in a far more complex manner than one would expect of such a basically static scene. Compare this, for example, to the stodgy camerawork and sloppy organization of the wedding ceremony at the end of Griffith's *Way Down East* (1920). Stroheim was not only a keen observer of detail but also a master at selecting just those points that make a scene play well and interestingly.

After the ceremony, the wedding gifts are examined. Here, Stroheim departs from the novel and has McTeague present to his wife a birdcage that now contains two canaries, a gesture that reveals his naive and simple heart. Trina is disappointed because the gift is not practical, but she politely smiles. Marcus, who has given her a watch, derisively cleans his ear and sticks his tongue out at what he considers Mac's stupid wedding present. These birds are now associated with the McTeagues and will form a motif that runs throughout the rest of the film.

Then the wedding feast begins. It is not a polite and joyous gathering of poor but simple folk. The Sieppe kids act up and are spanked by their father, while the dinner itself is a sordid *Fresserei* in, which Stroheim ruthlessly satirizes the animality and gluttony and indelicacy of these low-class people. Mr. and Mrs. Sieppe both chew on calves' heads (in the novel, only Mr. Sieppe has one), the hunchback drinks from a glass with his middle finger stuck obscenely out, and the skinny minister delicately nibbles on chicken bones. Stroheim depicts this group of humanity, except for the minister, as eating like pigs. The novel describes the conclusion of the meal: "It was a devastation, a pillage: the table presented the appearance of a battlefield."

At just the opposite philosophical pole, compare the eating scenes of similar or even poorer classes of people in most American movies. Family and friends eat together in a kind of communion, not an orgy of gluttony. To Stroheim, such an event reveals the horror of humanity, its animalistic lust for food. He is not so much a faithful recorder of life as he is an enhancer of it, and more often than not he prefers (unlike most Hollywood directors) to get his flies with vinegar, not honey.

After the feast, the family and guests begin to leave. Stroheim records unflinchingly, though compassionately, Trina's wedding-night fears. Faced with being alone with her husband, Trina runs down the stairs after her mother, who tells her to go back. Her fright at what is to come is evident on her face. Stroheim here includes some deep-focus shots looking up the stairs to the top, similar to a shot of Kane and Gettys on another staircase almost twenty years later in *Citizen Kane*. Stroheim supports Trina's feeling of isolation by showing the girl, dressed in her wedding white, climbing the shabby stairs, a shy and forlorn wisp nervously moving through the dark hallway. Back in the apartment, Trina sees the birdcage in a subjective shot that goes out of focus because of her tears. When McTeague finally lumbers toward her, oblivious of her crisis, she cringes. In close-up, we see she is terrified. And in another close shot, Mac advances toward her and then kisses her. She responds to his kiss as her feet stand on tiptoe in close-up, and the birds in the cage also seem to kiss. Trina is not a frigid woman, and even toward the end of their disintegrating relationship she still feels passion for Mac. Tragically, both Mac and Trina have the potential for a satisfying life together; indeed, there are many scenes, unfortunately cut from the print, that show their happy domesticity. It is only when financial disaster occurs that her incipient miserliness comes obsessively to the fore. Ultimately, only gold coins provide her with sexual pleasure.

The couple settles down to a pleasant married life. They get nice curtains and furniture, and Trina tries to give Mac a semblance of gentility, advising him about table manners and dress, but it is soon apparent that the money is corrupting her. One Sunday, as they return from church at Easter time, a flower seller offers some lilies. This flower, a symbol of both life and death, has its ironic overtones that recall the wedding-funeral combination. Certainly no resurrection can be expected here. Trina (with a curious conniving expression) pretends to McTeague that she does not have any change, although a close-up reveals that her purse is full of coins. This is the first indication in the extant print of her irrational greed's overcoming her better nature. She decides, too, that they will not rent a nice house but will continue to live in the dental parlors to save money.

Stroheim's amazing attention to details can be seen in the way Trina takes care of her hands. In the early parts of the film, she is very careful of them. She puts lotion on them and uses rubber gloves to do the dishes and other household tasks. Much later, when she is carving toy animals, she takes off her gloves, which indicates that she no longer cares about herself. Afterward, when Mac bites her fingers (recall the agony she experienced with the mousetrap), and later, when some of her fingers are mere stumps, the disintegration of her hands, like that of their marriage, becomes glaring.

The money not only begins to affect Trina, but it continues to gnaw at Marcus as well. While Mac is drinking beer and smoking his pipe in a saloon (a sign, "Smile, darn you, smile," hangs on the back wall), Marcus sits at a separate table in the foreground, playing with a coin and growing increasingly more annoyed. This is one of the few scenes in the film where Stroheim eschews cutting and allows a single camera placement to run for a long period (two minutes and fifteen seconds), interrupted only by dialogue titles. This helps the viewer to see the tension build until the envious Marcus can withhold his anger no longer. He accuses McTeague of taking Trina and his money from him. Then he knocks the pipe out of the uncomprehending fellow's mouth and throws a knife at him. By the time the slow-witted McTeague realizes that his pipe is broken—he is never quite aware of the knife—Marcus has left. (In the book and the script, this scene, resulting of course in hard feelings, occurs before the wedding and accounts for Marcus's evident resentment at the ceremony and the fact that he gives a present only to Trina.) What ends the friendship completely (in Stroheim's script) is a friendly wrestling episode at a picnic after the wedding. When Marcus starts to lose the match, he viciously bites McTeague's ear, and Mac responds instinctively, breaking Marcus's arm.

Somewhat later, while Trina is cuddling with Mac—she still feels affection and desire for this giant hulk—Marcus pays them a visit. As they open the door, a cat sneaks in and eyes the birds. (The cat was not in the novel.) Marcus tells them he is going away (Trina is pleased at this news), and, as he bids them his soured farewell, the cat studies the birds. Unknown to the couple and the viewers, Marcus has informed the State Board of Dentistry that McTeague lacks a diploma. As a consequence, an official letter (dated February 10, 1922) arrives, stating that McTeague can no longer practice. As the couple examine the letter, which they received on the thirteenth—the anniversary of his first moving to the dental parlors—the cat crawls through an open window and jumps on the birdcage. Trina wears a light dress; because of cuts in the film, the next scene seems to occur on the same day, but it actually occurs two days later—the calendar reads the fifteenth. The once fresh flowers in the vase are now wilted. Trina, seen now in a dark dress, comes to the conclusion that it was Marcus who brought this disaster upon them, an act that precipitates their doom.

The halt of Mac's professional life—and its income—causes Trina's already parsimonious urges to come to the fore. Desperate that they not dig into their funds, she now dedicates herself to whittling toys for a living and becomes even more compulsive about saving money. In cut scenes, she abandons their apartment, calls in an auctioneer to sell most of their possessions, lies to her husband about the money received, and insists that they move into a cheap back room of the building. A horseshoe is nailed to the door, but there is no good luck. Trina's original five thousand dollars remains untouched and has been invested with her uncle. She continues to practice thrift and adds to a hidden cache of coins she has saved and filched from Mac's pockets. A cup on a dresser next to where she carves the toy animals has the ironic motto "Love the Giver," but Trina is hardly a "giver." (A still of this can be seen in Weinberg's *Greed*.) As their once lower-middle-class existence disappears, they descend into squalor: dirty dishes sit in the washtub; rumpled, soiled sheets remain on the bed; and wood parings lie scattered on the floor. Trina devotes all her hours to whittling the toys and (in scenes cut) will not even leave the house, for she feels she cannot afford the time.

The societal props that held the slow-witted McTeague in his comfortable niche vanish, and soon he falls prey to the instincts that have so long lay dormant. He gets a job in a surgical instrument factory but is fired. He returns home to Trina. Close-ups of his feet on the hallway floor indicate that she hears someone approaching. She quickly hides the coins she has been worshiping and is surprised to see him. She takes his pay envelope, searches his pockets for any stray coin, and orders him out to look for another job. He goes halfway down the stairs and then stops. It might rain, he tells her, and he wants carfare. She assures him it will not rain, but of course it does. His friends invite the thoroughly drenched man into a bar and convince him to have hard liquor.

The wheels of fate and heredity now start in motion. Mac returns home drunk, angry about Trina's being too cheap even to give him a nickel for carfare. As he looks around the sloppy room in disdain, the two birds fight in the cage. She smells his breath and accuses him of drinking. He threatens her and then falls asleep. Trina had felt sorry that he got wet and was terrified when he became abusive, but now her mood changes. In a devastating moment, she makes her familiar gesture of putting a finger to the corner of her mouth and, slyly squinting her eyes, wonders how he paid for the liquor!

Some time later, Mac is drinking in the saloon and runs out of money. He returns to the room and, in a scene that is relatively complete, grabs Trina and bites her fingers to force money out of her. She fearfully gives him some and then asks, "Don't you love me anymore, Mac?" He replies, "Sure I do," and shoves her down on the bed and exits. Much of this episode is done in close-ups and shows that Stroheim could not only extract fine performances but could render them cinematically with great skill. On the back wall, the wedding picture provides an ironic contrast. The sordid and revolting action of Mac biting her fingers should not invite too much pity for Trina, for they are both culpable, perhaps she far more than he, because her wits are not slow.

More thrifty than ever, Trina next forces McTeague to move their lodgings from the back room to the now dead Zerkow's shack. This change is not shown in the existing print, and Zerkow has been completely dropped, so the shift to his squalid quarters loses its dramatic power. To a viewer of the whole work, moving to Zerkow's shack would be seen as the depth of degradation. Mac and Trina are now both untidy and slipping rapidly downward. Their wedding picture is out of its frame and a partial rip separates the two figures. It is a perfect symbol, for Mac has become a sadistic drunk and Trina a masochistic miser.

When Mac was in his dental parlors, he dreamed of having a great golden tooth hanging in front of his shop as a sign of his professional success. Trina, knowing this, bought him one as an engagement present. Mac is now forced to sell the tooth, signaling the death of all his hopes. He gets five dollars for it and gives Trina one of the dollars to get him some decent food. All of this has been cut from the film. She goes to a butcher, not her regular one, but the "Semite Market" (the book makes no mention of the type of market,[19] but Stroheim's script does). Here, she thinks she can get a better deal and picks around in a slop barrel for some three-day-old chops "hardly fit for dogs" and, with a miserly expression, pays fifteen cents for the meat. Her nervous little fingers handle the change. She then returns to the shack and starts to cook the chops. Mac asks for his change and she gives him back twenty-five cents. He looks skeptical. "Do you think I'd . . . cheat you?" she asks in false innocence. He glances around the dirty shack with a cynical expression.

A few minutes later, the dull-witted Mac decides that he has had enough of the marriage, takes his fishing pole, and without a change in facial expression says "So long" to her. She moves up to him, says "Kiss me good-bye," and kisses him on the lips. This moment of affection (or passion) lasts only a second, for the thought now crosses her mind— the finger again rising to her lips—that he could bring back the fish. He growls, "It might save you a nickel." He looks at the chest that contains her money, and then, knowing that he is going to leave forever, he takes the cage with the birds with him. Thinking he plans to sell them, Trina becomes alert, a scheming expression on her face, and ponders whether he could get five dollars for them, or maybe even six. In front of the disreputable shack, he pauses for a moment and then walks away. She is inside, hugging her money.

In the book and the script—but not in the release print—the following events transpire: when Mac does not come back that night, Trina goes out looking for him, wandering the streets, distraught. In the midst of her search, she suddenly thinks of the money she has left hidden in her trunk. Fearful, she rushes back and finds her worst nightmare realized: Mac has broken the lock and stolen the hundreds of dollars she had so carefully saved. In despair, she bangs her head against the floor. A doctor is called in and, while treating her bruise, notices her hands. Because McTeague bit her fingers, the lead paint infected them, and some now have to be amputated. As a result, she can no longer work at carving and painting wooden figures. The original title, similar to what is in the book, says: "One can hold a scrubbing brush with two good fingers and the stumps of two others, even if both joints of the thumb are gone, but it takes considerable practice to get used to it." This was followed by an iris shot of "a hand with two good fingers holding a scrubbing brush, scrubbing the floor" (302). The present print jumps from when Mac leaves the shack to a title that states simply that Trina has become a scrubwoman, omitting all references to her missing fingers. She takes a job working in a kindergarten, where she lives in the back room.

In other cut scenes, Trina examines the chamois bag where she had kept the money that Mac stole and sees only the few new coins she has saved from her meager earnings. She becomes so depressed at not having money to caress and fondle that she draws out all her savings and keeps the 250 twenty-dollar gold coins with her. (Curiously, neither Norris nor Stroheim noticed that interest would have made the amount somewhat larger.) Meanwhile, in more cut scenes, Mac inquires about her whereabouts from her uncle and learns that she has the money. He has squandered what he stole, is hungry, and has no place to sleep. As the existing print shows, he goes to the kindergarten. In the garbage can outside he finds their wedding picture. It has been torn into two pieces, and, because it has no material value, she discarded it. (This is Stroheim's addition to the story—an excellent visual way of revealing their estrangement and Trina's total noninvolvement with anything that is not money.)

Mac walks up to her window and knocks. Trina's greed has become, literally, her passion, for at night she undresses and lies nude in bed, luxuriating among her gleaming golden coins. Her reverie is shattered as she hears Mac's knock at the window. She jumps up from the bed, covers her beloved coins, wraps a sheet and dark blanket around herself, and crosses the room. She resembles a mad Greek heroine, doomed by the vengeful fates. The camera looks down on Mac's face as he peers up at her through the window and asks for money. He says that he would not even treat a dog the way she treats him. But the strange apparition before him holds up her mutilated fingers and says, "Not even if the dog bit you?" She slams the window shut. This scene remains in the film, but without any reference to Trina's missing fingers, its significance is not fully understood by viewers.

In scenes now cut, Mac gets a job as a furniture mover, and one night, he sees his concertina in a store window. Stroheim, for additional irony, switches the date from the novel's "about a week after Christmas"[20] to Christmas Eve, a time that, according to the original title, changes "all griefs and quarrels into love" (314). The shopkeeper says that the concertina costs eleven dollars. Mac protests that it was stolen from him. With only four dollars in his pocket, he grows angry at this loss of his prized possession and goes to Trina. In footage that remains, the enraged McTeague enters the school, which is decorated with wreaths and a Christmas tree. He attacks Trina near a sign saying "Merry Christmas," as a black cat scurries around. The two struggle in and out of shadow, but the gruesome details of the murder occur off camera. Finally, wiping the blood from his fists, McTeague picks up Trina's 250 twenty-dollar gold pieces and moves off into the night. Meanwhile, in front of the building, in darkness broken only by pools of light, two policemen stand talking, upholders of the law unaware of and incapable of stopping the enforcement of an even more ancient law. These policemen were added by Stroheim. Another addition, but cut from the print, shows Mac returning to his lodgings, where he finds one of the birds—his wedding present to Trina—dead. Mac knows that he must flee but is reluctant to abandon the surviving canary. Later the police will track him more easily because not too many fleeing criminals wander around carrying a birdcage.

In other cut scenes, Mac returns to the place of his youth and works again in the mines. Sensing that he might be pursued, he leaves, gets involved with a prospector, and discovers a vein of gold near Death Valley. Again sensing capture, he wanders off, ironically leaving behind this newfound wealth. Life, not gold, is his desire.

Soon after, in scenes that remain, a posse is recruited to find McTeague. Marcus learns of this and offers his services; he wants revenge, as well as the money that he feels is rightfully his. Anxious to settle his vendetta, Marcus breaks away from the sheriff and his men and strikes out alone into Death Valley. Water or no water, Marcus will find McTeague.

Stroheim, in a letter, explained how he handled the concluding scenes of the film:

> When I came to the desert sequences which were laid in Death Valley, the company suggested that I'd take them in Oxnard near Los Angeles where traditionally all desert scenes were and are being taken. But having read the marvelous descriptions of the real Death Valley as Frank Norris had depicted it, I knew that Death Valley did not look like Oxnard and as I had gone as far as I had for the sake of realism, I was not going to conform to the company's desires at this time. I insisted on Death Valley and Death Valley it was. This was in '23 when there were no roads and no hotels as there are today. We were the only white men (41 men—one woman) who had penetrated into the lowest point on earth (below sea level) since the days of the pioneers. We worked in 142 degrees Fahrenheit in the shade and no shade. The results I achieved through the actual heat and the physical strain were worth the trouble I had gone to. It would have been impossible to get anything near it in Oxnard.[21]

Fortunately, much of the last part of the film remains in the existing print. Mac moves laboriously across the vast desert, appalled at Death Valley's depressing landscape and the creatures, such as Gila monsters and rattlesnakes, that inhabit this scalding oven. Here the reality of life is far different from the sentimental image of loving birds in a cage. Overcome with fear, appalled at the immensity of the bleak landscape, beaten down by a combination of fate and circumstance and his own slow-wittedness, he now drops further into relying on sheer instinct.

Desperately, Mac continues across the desert in the hope of eluding his trackers. But Marcus, anxious for the money, soon catches up with Mac and holds him at gunpoint. However, fate once again takes a hand. Mac's mule, having eaten loco weed, runs away. Marcus shoots the animal, but the bullet also pierces the water canteen, and the precious fluid streams onto the dry sand. Both men are now faced with death. Marcus's greed overcomes his sense of self-preservation, and he begins fighting over the gold coins that lie scattered on the ground. Mac struggles with Marcus and kills him, but not before Marcus has slipped handcuffs on them both.

In the book's last words, as the dying Mac finds himself handcuffed to the dead Marcus, he looks at "the half-dead canary chittering feebly in its little gilt prison." Stroheim changes this ending by having Mac crawl over to the birdcage and compassionately release the canary. He kisses it and then tosses it into the air, but like his own gentle nature, which had long ago faded, it dies. The camera cuts from a medium shot to a long shot and then to an extreme long shot of the two men in Death Valley. And there the film ends.

The bird represents McTeague's love, sensitivity, and vulnerability, and, ultimately, man himself—his capabilities, his freedom, his wish for untrammeled flight caught in a cage of heredity, environment, and the actions of other people. The two men, bound to each other and rendered helpless by the handcuffs (like the bars of a cage) smolder and die in the desert amid a useless fortune in golden coins. And McTeague, who in the script comes out of the mines (from the earth, from the womb) will sink into the barren sand of the desert.

One wonders just how chaotic conditions must have been at the Goldwyn Company that no one in charge glanced at the bulky script (particularly after the immense cost and length of *Foolish Wives* and the notorious collapse of *Merry-Go-Round*) without raising some practical questions. Stroheim's introductory scenes alone would have run about an hour before the main story had even started! If length were a problem, certainly this opening section was less essential than the main story, which in itself was a long one. It could have been cut, as indeed it was. In fact, some of the early material of the mother and father was shot last and therefore could have been halted by a vigilant studio.

Although it seems that, indeed, no executive ever looked carefully at the script, at least someone at the Goldwyn Company might have remembered that Stroheim's original contract asked for a film under 8,500 feet. Did no one notice the seemingly endless reels being logged daily, consisting of countless retakes and miles of fresh material—a total of 446,103 feet? A special feature such as *The Birth of a Nation* ran 12,000 feet, far longer than other films. By the time Stroheim finished editing *Greed,* he had forty-two reels of *unrepeated* narrative (about 42,000 feet), a total of almost eight hours at sound speed and more than that at twenty or twenty-two frames per second.

Until Stroheim's dying day, he could see nothing wrong with this length. In defense, he often said that *Gone with the Wind* was a long film and a success at about four hours. What he did not realize was that Selznick's film had the Civil War, the burning of Atlanta, the tensions of Reconstruction, beautiful costumes, lavish settings, hundreds of wounded soldiers, the dramatic birth of a baby, a love triangle, as well as Clark Gable and Vivien Leigh fighting and embracing and separating—all based on one of the most popular books ever written. *Greed,* no doubt, is the better work—just as Beethoven is better than the Beatles—but with scruffy Gibson Gowland and a haggish Zasu Pitts, its hours of unrelenting gloom would hardly attract and hold audiences who went to the movies for entertainment.

In writing about *Greed* in a letter to Peter Noble, Stroheim chose to remember his agreement with Goldwyn quite differently from what the contract actually stated:

> At the time when I began my work the slogan of the Goldwyn Co. was "the author and the play are the thing," and I was given plein pouvoirs to make the picture as the author might have wanted it. But when Goldwyn Co. became M.G.M. . . . (That happened during the time I was cutting the film) The new firm (with Irving G. Thalberg as new general manager) did not give a whoop about what the author or I or the former company had wanted. [Not true. The company had wanted a film no longer than 8,500 feet.] The new slogan was "the *producer* is the thing." L.B. Mayer, the head of the company, made it his business to prove to me that I was only a small employee in a very large pants factory (pants that incidentally had to fit grand-father, father, and child).
>
> Again I had set out with the idea to make the picture in

two parts. Ten or twelve reels each time with time for dinner in between (still a long time before Eugene O'Neill executed this idea). When I got through making the film as written and okayed by Goldwyn. [Stroheim must mean the company, because Goldwyn had already been ousted, but in no way did the company "okay" such a long film.] I found myself with forty-two reels [what an odd remark, as if, somehow, the additional reels merely landed on his doorstep] that necessitated, even if I wanted two parts, to cut half of it out, which I accomplished myself. When I had arrived at twenty-four reels, I could not, to save my soul, cut another foot. But the new company insisted on cutting it down. Unknown to them I sent one print to my friend Rex Ingram who worked at that time in New York and begged him to cut it, if he could. He returned it in eighteen reels having eliminated six reels, having accomplished for me the impossible. He sent me a telegram: "If you cut one more foot, I'll never speak to you again."

I showed the telegram to Mr. Mayer but he told me that he did not give a damn about Rex Ingram or me [Mayer certainly did hate Ingram's surly independence] and that . . . the picture must be cut to ten reels. It was given to a cutter at thirty dollars a week who never had read the book nor the script, and on whose mind was nothing but a hat. That man ruined my work of two years. During these two years I had hocked my house, my car, my life-insurance, to be able to continue to work as I was neither paid during the writing, nor during the cutting of the picture, but I received a certain sum of money [for] the nine months of shooting which would have been the same, had I made the picture in two weeks. [This is true.] I knew *Greed* was my masterpiece and that it would be not only to my advantage but also to that of the company to have built a monument to realism.

The rest of the negative was burned to get the forty-three cents worth of silver out. Only twelve men saw the picture in 42 reels. . . . The picture was comparatively a failure at the box office because the M.G.M. Company did not advertise it and having written it off their books as a total loss, (for Income Tax purposes) did not care to exploit it properly.

According to the company's books, the entire cost was $546,883.18, which, despite the six-month length of production, is a rather high figure considering the nonstar salaries of the actors, the virtual absence of sets, the small crew, and the relatively cheap raw stock. The company probably padded its costs on *Greed* (which was averaged in with the profits of *The Merry Widow*) to prevent Stroheim from receiving his percentage.

Greed has long been considered Stroheim's "great" work, as if, somehow, his other films were of much less merit. Admittedly, the facts that it was based on a famous novel, was a stunning exercise in screen realism, was disastrously cut, and was an effort of high seriousness with no box-office compromises have all had their effect. Undoubtedly, Stroheim made a fine, unflinching examination of lower-class American life and recorded much of its ugliness, brashness, vulgarity, and pathos. Too often, critical histories seem to hint that Stroheim was a one-film man; he was hardly that. His films with European settings are also revelations and perhaps are even more individual because he wrote them himself. All of his works are of considerable interest and show that the artist, not the source material, was responsible for their success.

Stroheim was bucking an already clearly established Hollywood tradition that films ought to be entertaining, provide happy endings, and deal with people who either are rich or end up at least quite comfortable. Stroheim's predilection for honesty in his films set in Europe did not offend too many people because audiences enjoyed peeking behind the boudoir door to see how those classy "furreners" really lived and were intrigued by European lower-class characters because they were picturesque. But when Stroheim pulled back the curtain on lower-middle-class American life in *Greed* and then showed the main characters slipping lower and lower, the unsavory details were too much to bear. Audiences used to the normal confections from the Hollywood Sweet Shoppe were appalled to find on the sugared shelves a dead rodent, degradation, poverty, and ugliness. In the average film, everybody was beautiful or handsome, bathed every day, and lived in a cute house in the country or a swank city apartment. But in *Greed* the two lovers are badly blemished: a neurotic miser and a drunken bum. The audience could not identify with anyone pleasant because there was not anyone pleasant, at least in the existing print. All it could do was watch the wheels of fate grind, in a growing gloom, until Trina is murdered under a Merry Christmas sign and Mac faces certain death from thirst and heat.

A review by Aileen St. John–Brenon in *Theatre Magazine* of February 1925 aptly reflects the so-called enlightened press:

> The persons in the photoplay are not characters, but types— they are well selected, weighed, and competently drilled. But they do not act; they do not come to life. They perform their mission like so many uncouth images of miserliness and repugnant animalism. Gibson Gowland, as McTeague, is striking at first glance, but as the play moves, is only an unusual figure of amazing bulk and equally amazing dullness. Zasu Pitts, the heroine, has nothing in common with the Trina of Frank Norris. She has none of the extreme youth and prettiness of the book.

Of course, when Miss St. John–Brenon says that the performers "do not act," she really means that they do not "emote" in typical silent-screen fashion. The performances throughout the film are superb, with not a dated gesture or an insincere move. And when she says that Gowland is a figure of amazing bulk and dullness and that Trina is not as pretty as she ought to be, she reveals, alas, the dubious values of both Hollywood and its public. But even she had to admit that *Greed* was one of the better pictures. *Variety* took its usual practical approach: "Nothing more morbid and senseless, from a commercial picture standpoint, has been seen on the screen in a long, long time."[22] Yet even *Variety* had to grant the "excellent acting, fine direction and undoubted power of the story." Still, its main criticism remained: "It does not entertain."[23]

Although almost all intelligent people have regretted the severe cutting of the film, the undistinguished reviewer for the *New York Times,* Mordaunt Hall, had a different view. He noted that the people at MGM who "clipped this production as much as they dared . . . are to be congratulated on their efforts, and the only pity is that they did not use the scissors more generously in the beginning."[24] Hall seldom had an insightful moment in his long career—at best, he recounts plots— but in this instance, he is completely obtuse. To cut *more* from the film?

Stroheim may have had a dogged respect for every detail of the book, but he was visually quite astute. He never just set up his camera and ground away. Like Griffith, he had an uncanny instinct for what should appear in long shots, medium shots, and close-ups; but unlike Griffith, who viewed scenes as if through a fourth wall, Stroheim shot from many sides and from differing angles; he also used deep-focus, meaningful foregrounds, and effective camera movement. He is not a *stage* director, but a *film* director.

Stroheim is usually thought of as a grimly serious purveyor of the seamy side of life, but he also had a sense of humor, although many instances of it in *Greed* were cut because of length problems. Stroheim had lots of fun with the Sieppe family: the way the Poppa marches the family, little "Owgooste" peeing in his pants, the twins acting up at the wedding, and their grotesque relatives. Even the usually angry Marcus is shown in humorous situations: he imitates Napoleon, and—in cut scenes—he sits in the bathtub reading while everyone anxiously waits in the hall to use the one bathroom. True, the original film was no barrel of laughs, but the grim tone was relieved at times.

When the film was released, it had, unlike *Foolish Wives,* few censorship problems in terms of sex, but even so the New York Censorship Board ordered the following eliminations on November 25, 1924:

Reel 2: Elim. view of administering ether.
Reel 3: Elim. underlined words from title: "I've got her. *By God,* I've got her."
Reel 4: Elim. title "Damn his soul."
Reel 7: Elim. all scenes of McTeague biting Trina's fingers.
Reel 10: Elim. last view of horse [mule] shown kicking in agony on ground after it had been shot.
The reasons for the above eliminations are that they are "inhuman" and "sacrilegious."

The company complied.

MGM was convinced that such a film as *Greed* could not possibly succeed at the box office, but their decision to cut it down to ten reels, when a twelve-reel length was still a commercial possibility, certainly wounded the overall effect. At ten reels, it was already a "special" film that did not fit into the usual seven- or eight-reel format of features for most theaters. Thus, two more reels would not have been detrimental to its viability as a commercial product. Perhaps the reviews would have been no better and the financial returns no more lucrative, but the additional reels might have opened up the action. They could have filled out the Mac-Trina story and made the couple's decline at least more varied. The fight at the amusement park between Mac and Marcus, the auction of Mac and Trina's possessions, the acquisition and the sale of the gold tooth, Trina's desperate search down the dark streets looking for Mac after he leaves her—would have provided viewers with additional action rather than just a series of grim scenes of the isolated couple. Other cut scenes would have allowed viewers to experience rather than merely observe Mac and Trina in their increasingly squalid living conditions. Thus, the use of varied locations and a closer handling of the couple's decline might have made the film play faster rather than slower.

For Stroheim, *Greed* was a bitter disappointment, for it was his sincere attempt to make a screen masterpiece, a film that would have demonstrated his genius not only to his Hollywood colleagues but to the world. Even though the truncated version at least partially accomplished this, it also stamped him as an impractical artist. The personal and professional wounds of this disaster would never heal, but, rather than learn from the painful experience, he would try again and again to make The Great Film. To him, by definition it had to be a long one; he could not accept the fact that a picture of normal length could also be great.

9

The Merry Widow

When Stroheim was fired from *Merry-Go-Round* in the fall of 1922, the Goldwyn Company was in the process of purchasing the rights to Franz Lehar's *The Merry Widow,* which had proved an extraordinary success since its 1905 premiere in Vienna. With a logic peculiar to Hollywood, the studio seemed to regard the operetta as having the potential of becoming a profitable silent film because of its familiar title and its music, which could be used as a background score, even though the lyrics, of course, would be lost. In early 1923, the studio announced proudly that *The Merry Widow* would be Stroheim's next picture after *Greed.* The Austrian appeared to know more about continental matters than anyone else and seemed to be an ideal choice, with his penchant for detail and obvious expertise at creating a believable milieu. Furthermore, he was a writer as well and could draw upon his European background to flesh out the operetta's flimsy plot.

As a result of the Goldwyn Company's merger with Metro in April 1924, the new firm—now called Metro-Goldwyn-Mayer—inherited the *Merry Widow* property. Despite violent arguments over the severe cutting of *Greed,* Irving Thalberg, now the company's production chief, believed that Stroheim had great talent and that he could, if properly constrained, direct the film, as the Goldwyn Company had previously planned. Stroheim's coffers were exhausted after his two-year stint with *Greed,* and Thalberg suspected that the director might accept this piece of Ruritanian fluff without too much argument.

Stroheim, however, was still obsessed with the tale of an aristocrat falling in love with a commoner and so was not excited by *The Merry Widow's* feeble plot. Thalberg also recognized that the story needed elaboration and so agreed to have Stroheim rewrite it, as long as he kept the waltz and the scene at Maxim's. At the same time, Thalberg recalled Stroheim's impressive but much too long script for *Merry-Go-Round* and vowed not to make the same error again. There would be no lengthy tome this time. Having lived through the nightmares of *Foolish Wives* and *Merry-Go-Round,* he knew that he would have to force Stroheim to bring the film in on schedule, on budget, and at a reasonable length.

The reason that Stroheim agreed to this project at all can be found in an interview Stroheim granted to the German *Film Kurrier.* When he saw how his *Greed* was mutilated, a film he made with his "own heart," he said: "I abandoned all my ideals to create real art pictures and made pictures to order from now on. My film *The Merry Widow* proved that this kind of picture is liked by the public, but I am far from being proud of it and I do not want to be identified at all with so-called box-office attractions. So I have quit realism entirely. . . . When you ask me why I do such pictures I am not ashamed to tell you the true reason: only because I do not want my family to starve."[1]

Stroheim salved his conscience because he had been given a relatively free hand in the writing (with only the slightest assistance from Benjamin Glazer) and managed to transfer some of the romantic aspects of his *Merry-Go-Round* story into the first two-thirds of the new script. Then he hooked on the musical's plot for the last third, but he did so reluctantly. Stroheim was not opposed to filming the waltz, despite what has often been written, but he did not want the story to be bogged down by a giant dancing scene. He wanted the episode to be revelatory of character, not merely an exhibition of fancy footwork.

Stroheim sought to impose his mordant views onto the relatively innocent operetta, but Thalberg did not want such a bleak vision. He simply wished to have Stroheim create a marketable commodity. Stroheim, always in love with tragedy, wanted his hero to be killed in a duel, but this depressing conclusion was vetoed. The film had to cater to the public's desire for happy endings, the kind that MGM knew would make them a profit. Furthermore, the picture should have actors the public wanted to see.

Already not entirely pleased to use even part of *The Merry Widow* story, Stroheim was especially upset about the casting of Mae Murray. She was one of the company's leading stars, but she was also a demanding and somewhat harebrained lady, and—to compound his difficulties—she was a dancer who wanted to demonstrate her skills. She definitely had her own ideas and had grown used to being indulged by her compliant husband, Robert Z. Leonard, who had directed many of her previous films. Stroheim detested "stars" and for good reason. Often, they were more concerned with their effect on audiences than with the requirements of the role. As a result, they would resent Stroheim's frequently honest and thus unflattering portraits of humanity and would deplore any scenes that did not involve them. He was also not sure that such a star as Mae Murray would patiently endure his rigorous and often dictatorial methods. Stroheim anticipated trouble. And there was trouble. The film could not satisfy his obsessions and also be a vehicle for Miss Murray. Even before shooting began, they fought. She had not appreciated *Greed* and years later (in her as-told-to autobiography) called it a "horrible picture. Not a moment of beauty in it; heavy, hopeless and it didn't make a cent at the box office."[2] Thus, Miss Murray's taste and value system.

But if Mae Murray was singularly obtuse about art, she was not uneducated about the box office. She and Thalberg rejected Stroheim's choice of Norman Kerry (who had played the lead in *Merry-Go-Round*) and argued for John Gilbert. In this they were right, for Gilbert was far more lively than the rather wooden Kerry. Stroheim himself wanted to play the part of the hero, Danilo, but the studio rejected this idea for the obvious reason that if Stroheim had a major role, he could not be fired, a problem that Thalberg had faced with *Foolish Wives* and solved with *The Merry-Go-Round*. Gilbert was a perfect choice. He had the looks, the charm, and the wild energy that the part demanded and—far more than Mae Murray—became vital to making the film a success. Indeed, *The Merry Widow* elevated him to stardom.

Stroheim's script provided not only a dashing hero but also a reprehensible villain, Crown Prince Mirko (played by Roy D'Arcy). At

Stroheim's insistence, D'Arcy grotesquely and entertainingly overacted his role so that he was as unpleasant as possible. In fact, he was so hateful that audiences were delighted to see him constantly thwarted, and of course they rejoiced when he was hit over the head with a vase and were pleased with his assassination. Furthermore, Mirko was given a speech habit—not necessarily odd for a silent film because it could be conveyed in titles—of pausing between words all the time and then coming out with an "ah." It was an effective addition to his character.

After Stroheim's contract was signed in late May 1924, he worked in earnest on the new script. After many consultations with Thalberg, a final scenario was approved in October 1924. This version of 477 scenes was substantially filmed, although Stroheim made several modifications during production. For example, the assassination of Mirko is not made by an anonymous "fanatic" but by a crippled doorkeeper whom Mirko earlier had kicked. Other aspects, such as the heroine's friends in the dance group and their interactions, were shot but removed in the editing.

With Thalberg's watchful eye upon him, Stroheim began production on December 1, 1924, and did not conclude until March 9, 1925, many weeks longer than most MGM productions, which, on average, took no more than a month. Stroheim, as was his habit, shot mostly in continuity. He immediately began putting Mae Murray through her paces. Patiently, and then not so patiently, he had to break her of her cutesy gestures and affected mannerisms. He was also compelled to photograph her carefully. Already thirty-nine years old, she was starting to get wrinkles and was inclined to a double chin. Throughout the film, a baby spotlight glows on her face to erase the age marks, a necessity that Stroheim made into an advantage: she is always a glowing luminescence, a vision of brightness. Furthermore, Stroheim had to photograph her so that she was constantly looking up, to avoid the double chin. When, at one point, she has to look down on Danilo when he lies on the ground, wounded, Stroheim solved the problem by having her wear a white scarf under her chin, which he probably relished, because it made her resemble a nun. Only at the end of the film does Stroheim sneak in a profile shot of her, as she looks down on the bed where the convalescent Danilo lies. And there, finally, is the double chin! It was, perhaps, his final revenge for having to work with her.

The waltz scene, which Mae Murray kept anticipating—to her it was The Big Moment of the film—seemed to be constantly postponed by her hateful director. Enraged and disgusted, she impatiently waited while Stroheim agonized over minute details (uniforms, furniture, flowers, drapes, dishes, food) and then spent many nights on the orgies at François's (most of which, unfortunately, were edited out). Finally the waltz scene arrived and with it a gigantic row! Mae Murray wanted to show off her dancing, and Stroheim wanted to keep her scenes within the shape of the film. He would tolerate no such pandering to the audience.

According to Miss Murray's book, Stroheim stated that he "had no desire to do a musical comedy." He obviously still wanted the bones of his *Merry-Go-Round* story to be unsullied by the aging star's indulgent footwork. (He preferred other footwork, particularly that of his invented character, the Baron Sadoja, who has a pronounced foot fetish.) As Mae Murray glared, Stroheim started to tell her *how* to do the dance. Her temper flaring, she called him "a dirty Hun," and soon director, stars, extras, and technicians stormed off the set in various partisan groups. The aroma of this fracas was aired in front-page headlines. The MGM chieftains scurried around and soon the two egos were uneasily calmed and the film completed. The waltz remained.

At the heart of the difficulty, of course, was a basic philosophical dichotomy. Miss Murray wanted something pleasant, lighthearted, and appealing, but Stroheim wanted decadence, debauchery, and perversions. She wanted sunlight and romance; he wanted mud, rain, snow, greed, and lust. Murray's reaction to the Baron Sadoja's foot fetish was sheer revulsion. She did not want that dirty old man rejoicing over his collection of shoes from his previous inamoratas, nor did she want him slobbering over her feet on her wedding night. She had better attractions. The scene in which Sadoja surveys his previous conquests by means of his shoe collection was cut from the film, as well as scenes of the aged baron taking pills and potions to bolster his failing potency for the wedding night before he lingers lustfully over her feet. All we see is that he collapses while pausing at her shoulder on his trip down. Still, the fetish is there. When Thalberg reportedly asked Stroheim about these scenes (which were only hinted at in the shooting script), Stroheim replied that it was a foot fetish. Thalberg is said to have replied, "And you, Von, have a footage fetish!" (That may never have been said, but it should have been.)

The film, as it turned out, was a combination of pretty scenes in the Hollywood manner and less pretty ones in the Stroheim manner. Despite the basic difference in aims between star and director, the picture proved a considerable success at the time and still holds up quite well. One can assume that what most of America liked at the time was the Mae Murray–John Gilbert romantic aura, but what audiences today like are the Stroheim interpolations.

The Merry Widow would not be Stroheim's long-dreamed-of Viennese tragedy, but still it provided far more bite than the typical Ruritanian romance. In fact, it is probably MGM's most sophisticated film, one in which more things are dreamed of, hinted at, and actually shown than were in Louis B. Mayer's homely philosophy. Despite the picture's ultimate success, Stroheim tended to dismiss the film as a mere commercial work. His comments implied that he went about this project with little interest, but this is not the case. The film is a handsome one, beautifully decorated, with elegant set design, wonderful acting moments, subtle details, and impressive lighting—in short, a Stroheim production in the fullest sense of the word. It was not the job of a hack but of a hungry man incapable of restraining his genius.

The film opens with a shot of Castellano, the "city in the sky," a cloud-tinged fairyland dominated by a huge stylized cathedral glowing in a strange kind of haze. This shot, according to the continuity of the script, was intended to be in color. Actually it was a glass shot, and not a very perfect one either. Contrary to legend, Stroheim was not such an extreme realist that he could not resort to some trick shots when he had to. From here on, until the last few minutes, the film leans toward Stroheim's more realistic mode. Overall, the picture is an odd blend of romanticism and realism. At times, scenes are of an almost documentary quality; at other times, the interior settings are stunning designs almost too beautiful to believe.

Although an introductory title assures us that the people are "proud and brave—fearing only God—loyal to their King till death" (not unlike the opening of *The Heart of Humanity*), this East European country is no fanciful land of make-believe. It has appropriately dirty streets, mud puddles, pigs, bedbugs, roaches, and flies. And just as appropriately, there is lechery as well as love and meanness of spirit as well as patriotic zeal. In short, Castellano is a Stroheimian world. Mae Murray and her waltz provide the glitter and the glare, while Stroheim provides his usual soured vision. He was the bug under the Hollywood icing.

As the action begins, the king and queen descend the grand steps of the huge cathedral, followed by the richest man in the country, Baron Sadoja (Tully Marshall), who walks with canes, for he has an advanced case of syphilis, which he must have contracted before devoting himself entirely to feet. Thus, within a few shots, we have moved from a fairyland setting and its king and queen to a syphilitic cripple with *locomotor ataxia*. Stroheim is definitely in charge.

The scene shifts to a small village, one of those smell-ridden places of crumbling walls, peeling paint, and animal and human refuse that is a visual delight on a postcard but an olfactory offense on a warm day. To this village, rather reluctantly, comes Crown Prince Mirko, teeth clenched in a perpetual sneer. His car pulls up in front of a mud puddle. Not far away a sow and its litter snort. Mirko glares through his monocle and hisses out between clenched teeth that the place is a "pig sty"; he takes the town and its smells as a personal affront to his royal nature and says to his adjutant, "I'll remember this," as if the poor man had constructed the village and imported the pigs just to offend his lordly master.

The scene then cuts to another car driving down the picturesque road. It contains the young and dashing Prince Danilo (John Gilbert). He is looking at some dirty pictures his valet has obtained from his barber. What an introduction to a fairy-tale hero! Only Stroheim could conceive of a romantic lead as such a worldly man; Danilo has seemingly slept with half the country's female population and imagined doing so with the other half. He is by no means a clean-cut, all-American fellow in a foreign uniform. Danilo enjoys and accepts life. When his automobile arrives in front of the same mud puddle that so offended Crown Prince Mirko, Danilo steps blithely into it, smiles, says "nice little place," sees the pigs, "nice little pigs," and glances at the local girls, "nice little women." Exaggeration and caricature, yes, but Stroheim is having fun with this property, and so does an audience when the director is allowed his own way.

At the inn, Mirko suspiciously pulls back the bedcovers and sprays the mattress with a little device. He notices something crawling on the wall and has his servant carry out minor extermination. Mirko definitely will not enjoy his state visit to this forsaken part of his kingdom. Danilo sweeps into his room with a far better attitude. (In the script, he takes Crown Prince Mirko's picture, which hangs on the wall, puts it under the bed face down, then places a chamber pot on it.) He lies down on his bed and has a drink, after which his valet furtively sips from it also. A servant girl comes in, and Danilo kisses her passionately, while the valet watches through a keyhole and smirks. Stroheim would put his audience at a keyhole, too, for this film in some ways provides a glimpse of kings and queens and princes not as their public selves but as their private ones. Such an attitude provokes humor—*The Merry Widow* is a funny film—but it also allows us to see the darker side, almost the tragedy. Stroheim could do Lubitsch, but Lubitsch could never quite do Stroheim.

To this "nice little town" comes the decidedly second-rate Manhattan Follies with its star dancer, Sally O'Hara (Mae Murray). Irrepressibly American, pert, alert, and a magna cum laude graduate of the school of hard knocks, she sticks her tongue out at the soldiers ogling her legs as they observe her from the inn. A minute or so later, Danilo goes downstairs, spies the servant girl, and kisses her again, not knowing that Sally has entered and is watching. He assumes what dignity he can and tells her that he speaks English. She is pleased at this news and introduces herself, but she mistakes the prince for a mere colonel. Her manager at this moment is arguing with the innkeeper, because there are no rooms for the troupe. Danilo suggests that his officers double up and tells Sally, "I'll gladly let you use my room." She is delighted at this, then thinks a moment, but does seem to agree.

Mirko is jealous and drinks to the "World's Indoor Champion of Sports." He and Danilo sit down at the supper table on either side of Sally and start to inch their legs toward her. She pulls her feet away, so that the men end up playing footsie with each other. Finally, Danilo figures out the situation and slams his foot down on Mirko's. (Feet are an important aspect of the film, whether as a means of flirtation, an essential element of a dancer, a sexual attraction, or an appendage to be maimed.) In the script, Danilo then kindly gives a dog a bone. Mirko repeats the action, but not before he puts hot pepper on it. In retaliation for this mean action, Sally and Danilo put hot pepper in Mirko's food and wine. (Unfortunately, this scene is not in existing prints, even though it would have provided not only humor but also insight into the characters of the two aristocrats.)

The film then resumes as Danilo dances with Sally and kisses her.

She is offended by his liberties and tearfully says that she had hoped he was different from other men. As the film points out, his desires are not different, but his ability to care is. Thus, Stroheim has shaded in tones of superb gray what other directors would have left crudely in black and white.

Sally is still not aware that she is dancing with a prince. Mirko had earlier promised that he would not reveal Danilo's identity but breaks his word and tells her that Danilo is a prince and "an unscrupulous despoiler of womanhood," one who loves for a day and then rides away. When she tells this to Danilo, he deftly replies, "If I am a prince, he's a crown prince," pointing to Mirko, whose sneer grows even more extreme. "And me," she says gaily, doing a ballet turn, "I'm Pavlowa." (Anna Pavlova—spelled "Pavlowa" in the film's title—was a world-famous ballet dancer of the time.)

The scene now dissolves to the theater in the capital city, where many of the nobility are in attendance. When Sally dances on stage, Baron Sadoja looks through his opera glass at her feet. Mirko stares at her pelvic region, while Danilo concentrates on her face—a wry, witty, and economical way of communicating the gentlemen's various interests in Sally and, of course, also demonstrating the body and skills of Miss Murray. The scene is reminiscent of one of Stroheim's early films, Allan Dwan's *Panthea* (1917), in which three men examine a female performer in a similar manner.

Danilo hurries off to Sally's dressing room, where he inserts a card in an immense bouquet of flowers he has provided. A moment later Mirko enters, so Danilo slips behind a screen. Stroheim then stages a most humorous ballet as Mirko, in his slimy fashion, slinks around the room while Danilo keeps dodging out of sight. Mirko checks the champagne that Danilo has brought and reads Danilo's card: "To my sweet Irish rose." (This is written, by the way, in Stroheim's own handwriting). Mirko rips it up but, being completely unoriginal, repeats the same comment on his own card. Stroheim caps this scene by having Mirko sit on the bed and begin to lie back just as Danilo slips a piece of fly paper onto the pillow. Mirko is not amused, though we are. It is broad humor, perhaps, but quite effective—just the right low note to conclude the elaborate sneaking around the room by both men. This demonstrates once again Stroheim's considerable sense of humor. The scene ends when, at Danilo's request, Mirko leaves.

Meanwhile, the grotesque and fearsome apparition of the dissolute Baron Sadoja arrives backstage with his canes and pockmarked face. He stares lasciviously at Sally's feet. When his invitation to supper is refused by her, she suggests he ask her fellow dancers. He looks at the feet of the other girls, who ironically are fixing their faces, his peccadillo unknown to them. Their black-shoed feet do not entice him, and he looks longingly after Sally as her delicate feet in close-up flutter down the corridor in a curiously tantalizing manner. Stroheim is superb in transforming her two white shoes into a sensuous vision and successfully conveys their perverse fascination for the baron.

Mirko also asks Sally to supper, and when she refuses, he gets quite unpleasant. "Get out of my way, you big bum," she tells him. Returning to her dressing room, she is pleased at the flowers but less so at finding Danilo there. There is an odd and very brief shot of some of her clothing on the floor. After looking at this a moment, she glares at Danilo. (This shot always seemed puzzling. Probably Danilo, when alone in her dressing room, had originally picked up her lingerie and dangled her panties and garter belt, a recurrent Stroheim obsession. Thalberg chose to omit this action because it made the dashing Danilo a little too perverse.)

Finally, Danilo's charm wins out, and Sally agrees to have dinner with him. He takes her to François's, a private place where the aristocrats dabble in sin. A title describes it: "Weeping violins and joyous cymbals—the walls are thick—the carpets muffle sound—and François is discreet." An old doorkeeper, using a crutch and wearing an eye patch, admits them. Danilo takes Sally to his private apartment, which is furnished with numerous religious artifacts—a painting of Christ, a crucifix, a bishop's miter, a holy water pedestal, a couch that resembles a pew, and ornate chairs that belong in a church. Upon the bed are a young, blindfolded, and almost naked girl and boy who play instruments, thus providing soft music without being able to see. During dinner, Sally tells Danilo that she has been out with many men, but when they got fresh, she would run away. "Did you always run away?" he asks. "Always," she replies.

Danilo, not quite believing this, is anxious to seduce her and decides to hurry matters by spilling soup on her dress. As a result, she has to don a robe. A cross hangs from her neck, and other reminders of Christianity are visible on the walls. He holds her hand, then kisses her firmly. (In the script, he begins to force her, and the blindfolded girl musician lifts her blindfold to peek. Sally then kicks with her knees and feet. Danilo pulls back his leg, which he had draped over hers, and brings it back in "a movement of self-protection.") She starts to cry, saying that she thought he was "different" and backs away from him. "Is it because you don't care for me?" he asks, and she answers, "Because I care so much." This is followed by a lovely close-up of her, with her hair backlit. "It's very strange," he says. "I brought you here at the whim of the moment and now I can't let you out of my life. You're so sweet and fine—" This scene is quite close to that between the count and Agnes at Madame Elvira's in *Merry-Go-Round*.

In the meantime, according to the script, the baron is in another room. When he learns that Sally is in the building, he sends her a note, signing it "At your feet." Later, we see the dance girls walking around with napkins tied to their feet, because the baron has bought their shoes and put them in his closet. All of this material was removed from the print—in fact the baron is not at François's at all—and so were all the scenes of the dance-troupe girls cavorting with the men at the club.

In a nearby room, Mirko has been carousing, and now, overcome with jealousy as well as curiosity, he brings along his drunken friends and peers in through the curtains, then pulls them open to expose the couple to his fellow revelers. Danilo is enraged, and Sally finally learns that her dashing partner really is a prince. Danilo tries to convince her that he was going to tell her. Mirko backs out of the room, but he is so annoyed and jealous that when he exits the establishment, he displays his rage by kicking the doorman's crutch out from under him and stomping on him.

Humiliated by the intrusion and saddened by Danilo's lie that he was not a prince, Sally closes the curtains, dresses, and apparently leaves. Danilo goes to the window and looks out on the street, which is covered with white down (because there had been a pillow fight at Mirko's party). This poetic image suggests that the grime of the street can be covered with sheer whiteness. The feathers, however, are swept up, and a sanitation truck, another Stroheim motif, hoses the street.

Danilo sits sadly at the window, a cross visible in the background. Finally, he decides to leave but is surprised to find Sally still in the room. "I just couldn't go," she says. After a shot of the courtyard door being locked, the scene fades. Sally and Danilo become lovers.

At the palace, Danilo tells the king and queen that he loves Sally and wants to marry her. He is told by his cynical father (George Fawcett) that one "can't marry every woman one—" and adds that marriage and love have very little in common. The mother looks sad for a moment and then agrees. Danilo remains adamant, and the king, outraged, threatens to make a beggar of him, a scene reminiscent of the historical confrontation between Franz Josef and Ferdinand.

At her quarters, Sally, wearing a wedding outfit with a white headdress, looks radiant. A choir boy lights the candles in the church. (The wedding, according to the script, is to take place at 3:30.) Baron Sadoja comes to talk with her, but someone is at the door. She thinks it is Danilo, but it is Mirko, who tells her that there will be no marriage.

Back at the palace, Danilo, saying that he cannot give her up, stands by the window, the rain trickling down the panes like tears. His mother tells Danilo that he belongs to the state and admits that she was once in love with a commoner, sadly acknowledging that life, for royalty, is complicated: "What does our own happiness matter?" Stroheim adds dimension to this familiar plot situation by showing the mother saddened about her own life but practical enough to convince her boy to avoid the marriage. Reluctantly, he agrees to write an explanatory letter. Afterward, the queen opens the envelope and, realizing the complications if Sally receives it, burns the note.

The smirking crown prince tells Sally that she must leave the country forever, according to a royal decree. She cries, her face and outfit shimmering in white. He peels off some money "—to compensate you—for—ah—for—ah—" She quite correctly thinks that Danilo had nothing to do with the cash offering, but the circumstances are not reassuring.

With no word from Danilo, Sally is heartbroken, but then she considers the situation and laughs bitterly. The camera dollies back as she rips off her wedding apparel and stamps on it. The choirboy puts out the candles in the church. Stroheim conveys this whole dramatic episode by the careful handling of the actors, the delicate placement of the camera, and the supportive design of the sets, the editing, and the lighting.

The baron now enters and, hovering over the woman like a black raven, offers the saddened girl wealth and power. Over the bed is a gigantic figure of Christ. As the rain on the windowpanes changes to ice, the camera dollies in on Sally's tearful face; snow begins to fall.

This is an apt simile for her frozen dreams, as she agrees to marry Baron Sadoja.

After an exterior shot of a church as the snow falls, the wedding ceremony occurs. A title, "—Wedding night—holy night—," is followed by a shot of Sally in a bedroom. A black-garbed maid (Dale Fuller) with a cane cackles to the bride about her impending bliss. Blossoms are strewn all over the bed.

In a snowy hunting lodge in the mountains, Danilo sits drunk and heartbroken. In a rage he throws a glass at his majesty's picture as his adjutant turns his back so as not to notice this treasonous gesture.

In the meantime, Sally awaits her decrepit bridegroom. That the scenes between these two must have particularly inspired Stroheim is seen not only in the dramatic action, but also in the camera work, the set design, and the careful arrangement of the furniture and props. Entering the bridal chamber, Sadoja approaches Sally and, as he is about to touch her, he falls backward in a stroke, his body lying amid the blossoms. (As mentioned earlier, Stroheim first had filmed the baron looking over his collection of shoes, perhaps trying to excite himself by gazing at all of his previous conquests; he then stares at Sally's feet, kisses them, and collapses.) In the film, when Sadoja's corpse is laid out, the body is placed so that the feet are toward the camera with dark baroque columns placed on either side. Behind is a large window. The camera fades out on this strikingly visual scene. (In the script, the baron does not die right away, but suffers a stroke that paralyzes half his face and all of the rest of his body. After a couple of months—including the Christmas season—one night his bed is found empty. He has crawled out of it and is found dead among Sally's shoes and slippers, a peculiar analog to Cecelia's death in *The Honeymoon*.)

Here ends Stroheim's wholly original work (two-thirds of the film) and now begins the operetta's plot. After a year of seclusion, says a title, Sally, a rich widow, goes to Paris. Meanwhile, at the palace, Mirko gleefully tells Danilo that Sally is the sensation of the city and is known as "The Merry Widow." Mirko smirks about their "sweet Irish rose." Danilo hits him for his remark—a deed audiences love—and the two struggle before being separated. Mirko callously states that he is going to Paris; he is not interested in Sally the dancer but in Sally the heiress. Enraged at this cynical attitude, Danilo gives Mirko a clunk over the head with a vase of flowers.

Danilo also goes to Paris, and at Maxim's confesses to a cigar-smoking woman the tragedy of his love affair. Soon after, the widow sponsors a giant ball and an eager Mirko and a reluctant Danilo attend. Sally is beautifully dressed and festooned with jewels. When Mirko kisses her hand, the camera dissolves away the flesh; only the jewels can be seen. And when he looks at her face, that, too, disappears, with only the necklace and earrings remaining visible. Stroheim renders this complex situation in purely visual terms. (In the ball scene in the original script, a khedive smiles sensuously and envisions Sally wearing tights, an Indian prince imagines her in a harem dress, a French marquis perceives only the jewelry on her head and neck, and an English lord notices her rings and diamond bracelets. Stroheim quite rightly condenses all this and has Mirko do the observing.) (However, stills reveal that the khedive was at the dance and suggest that perhaps some other portions of this episode were filmed.)

Sally tells Mirko that he is most kind, "tonight," but then she sees Danilo. The orchestra starts up the famous "Merry Widow Waltz," which the couple had danced to earlier at the inn, and they now swirl elegantly around on the ballroom floor in the scene on which Stroheim had been so reluctant to dwell. But Sally and Danilo are too proud and too hurt for an immediate reconciliation, despite their contact during the waltz.

Subsequently, Danilo drinks himself into oblivion, and one morning, Sally and Mirko, followed by her entourage, ride on horseback in the Bois de Boulogne and find him passed out on the bridle path. The action occurs in a white hazy fog, a triumph of pictorialism. She gets off her horse and mentions to the groggy Danilo that he has failed in his mission to marry her. Danilo says he has not failed, that he did not even attempt it. Severely piqued, she announces she will marry Mirko. Danilo cannot stand the smirk on Mirko's face and knocks him down, which results in an arrangement for a duel the next morning. That night Sally goes to Maxim's to see Danilo in an attempt to avert the impending fight. A bouquet is on the table, recalling, of course, "my sweet Irish rose." She loves him, but he does not know this and believes that she is concerned only for Mirko.

The next morning, at the dueling grounds, Danilo fires his pistol in the air while Mirko takes careful aim and shoots Danilo in the chest. Sally arrives too late to stop the duel but runs to Danilo and embraces her wounded lover. Here, Stroheim wanted him to die, but MGM would have no tragic ending to its ostensibly happy operetta. In 1955, when Stroheim introduced the film in Brussels at a gala showing, he ordered the houselights in the theater to be turned on when Danilo fell in the duel. "That's where my story ended, but they insisted on the ending you will now see," he announced.[3] Nonetheless, the happy ending that was filmed was in Stroheim's script that Thalberg had approved.

The next shots show the church steps and a funeral in progress. The king has died, and Mirko has become king. As the mourners pass by, Mirko is careful to walk around a puddle in the street. The crippled doorkeeper, whom Mirko had kicked earlier at François's, gets revenge by shooting Mirko, who falls into the puddle, which evokes the one he so abhorred in the opening moments of the film.

The next shot is of a balcony. Apple blossoms are in profusion, prefiguring the blossoms that would later pervade the love scenes in *The Wedding March*. If MGM wanted a happy ending, Stroheim would give them one, but one with enough blossoms to make it almost satirical. To emphasize the artificiality of this happy ending, he shot this sequence in color. Danilo is lying on his sickbed. He asks Sally why she is there, and she answers, "Because—I love you." Suddenly, they learn that Mirko has been assassinated.

At the cathedral, there is a large wedding ceremony. Danilo, who wears the crown, puts the queen's crown on Sally. She is, of course, all in white, almost luminescent. "Well, Sally O'Hara," he says, as they march down the aisle, think of me as "just plain Danilo Petrovich."

The Merry Widow may not be the equal of *Greed* or *The Wedding March*, but it is still an extraordinary film. Its photography, art direction, and use of detail are exemplary, and the story is entertaining. The latter part might drag slightly, the waltz and then the conversation in Maxim's may take a bit too long, but it is still a film that no one else but Stroheim could possibly have conceived and directed.[4]

Thalberg supervised the editing of the film and omitted or trimmed many scenes. Stroheim had photographed the royal parents in their bed, with the mother smoking a pipe—her false teeth in a glass nearby—while the husband wears a mustache-band. In another cut scene, Danilo is being shaved by a maid while a well-dressed, sophisticated woman (a prostitute?) sits in the bed next to him. Also omitted were additional scenes of the baron's foot fetish, wild moments at Mirko's party at François's, and some scenes of seminude dancers at Maxim's. The belief (held by Weinberg and others) that only two thousand feet were trimmed seems unlikely when one considers the original script and the fact that many stills exist from sections that were cut. Yet the essentials remain. Stroheim may have later denigrated *The Merry Widow,* but nonetheless it demonstrates the unique imagination with which he infused everything he ever made. Genius will out.

In a review of *Foolish Wives,* a perceptive observer noted that "Von Stroheim needs a strong leash."[5] The director found that leash in Irving Thalberg, the best producer Stroheim ever had. By riding herd over the director—supervising and changing some of the script, preventing him from overshooting, forcing him to use more appealing actors, insisting on a happy ending, and supervising the editing—he was able to coerce Stroheim into making a giant box-office success. Had Thalberg hired Stroheim to make *The Wedding March,* the film might not have been quite as good as the one Stroheim shot, but neither would it have contributed to the demise of his career. The calm and reasonable, if mercantile, Thalberg was just the man to overcome Stroheim's stubbornness and even his arrogance.

The Merry Widow had taken fourteen weeks to film, and so the bonuses that Stroheim would have earned if he had shot it more quickly were denied him, even though the results certainly warranted the additional shooting days.

Although Stroheim was to receive 25 percent of the profits of this very successful film, the company exercised its creative bookkeeping by blending the costs of *Greed* and *The Merry Widow* together. As a result, Stroheim never realized any additional money. To put it bluntly, he was cheated.

After *The Merry Widow* was edited by Thalberg, a task that was rightfully Stroheim's, the two egos agreed to disagree. On April 14, 1925, the contract for future films between MGM and Stroheim was dissolved. This was probably a mistake on both sides. Admittedly, MGM had become an efficient factory where there was no room for creative and independent directors, and Stroheim could not abide the close supervision. However, the success of *The Merry Widow* seemed to show that Stroheim could be strong at the box office and that, despite his reputation for being difficult, he was worth hiring. Indeed, he was listed as one of the ten best directors of 1925. What other producers, now anxious to hire him, did not know was all the pressures that had been put on Stroheim to keep him in check. Without these pressures, the idealistic and impractical Stroheim would careen into self-destruction, unaware that he was his own worst enemy.

10

The Wedding March

Shortly after the end of shooting on *The Merry Widow,* Stroheim ran across a major figure in Hollywood, Pat Powers, who many years before had been a partner of Carl Laemmle at Universal. As a result of his nasty habit of not letting anyone look at company books, Powers was severed from Universal and became an independent producer, eternally looking for a good "deal." Initially, during the Patent Wars of the early teens, he had made his fortune supplying pirated cameras. By 1928, he again smelled easy money and became a purveyor of sound equipment based on rather dubious patents. At that time, he bamboozled the naive Walt Disney to sign with him on a percentage basis, and it was only later that the cartoonist realized he was getting little money for his popular films and found Powers persisting in his old habit of secret bookkeeping. Walt's brother Roy concluded in late 1929, "That guy's a crook."[1]

Powers may have been a crook, but to Stroheim in 1926, he appeared to be simply a gruff but forthright and clever Irishman who knew his way around Hollywood. Fay Wray described him as being "tall, with a kind of Paddy Irish face, bushy black eyebrows, and an easy, kindly manner." She believed that "he thought his business acumen would guide him to know how to cope with von Stroheim's

Above: The master between his two long-suffering cameramen, William Daniels and Ben Reynolds. *Below*: The valet pours a drink for the Count (Norman Kerry) in *Merry-Go-Round* (1923).

Above: Trina's resemblance to a nun makes Mac's kiss while she is anesthetized even more of a violation in *Greed* (1924). *Below*: Stroheim was intrigued enough to emulate Mac's act.

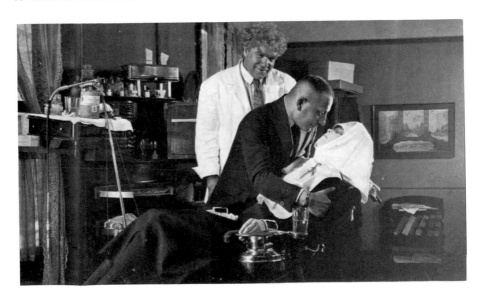

Above: Religious overtones, even in a barroom, when Marcus gives his Trina to Mac in *Greed*. Between the two men, an advertisement with a jolly Monk. Notice Marcus's flashy suit. *Below:* Marcus in his loud trousers and oafish Mac on the bed, with decorations on the wall, including a sign for "Pluto water."

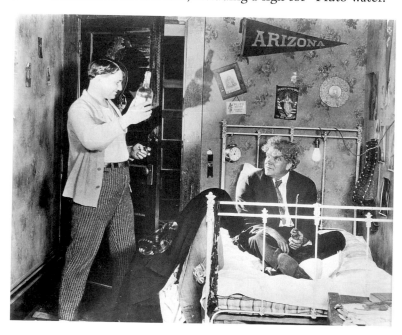

Above: Zerkov dreams of gold. Even a minor detail on a gravestone, virtually unseen by viewers, contains the death date, December 24. *Below*: Adjusted reality in *Greed*. Stroheim's fascination with fate and palmistry is echoed by the "Know Thy Future" sign on the second story. The implied street number of Mac's address is 613.

MAE MURRAY
plays the Widow.

JOHN GILBERT
plays the Prince

ERICH VON STROHEIM'S *Production*

THE MERRY
WIDOW

*Revealing the spice of Viennese life and love,
a subject at which he alone is master*

A SENSATIONAL production from the world-famous stage success. Ravishing Mae Murray and John Gilbert, the Screen's Great Lover, bring a new dash and magic to the gayety, the pathos, the tense, gripping drama of this superb masterpiece. And only a Von Stroheim could re-create, in so masterly a fashion, the swirl and glamor of Vienna's mad night life.

Von Stroheim and Benjamin Glazer made the adaptation and scenario from the famous dramatic operetta by Franz Lehar, Victor Leon and Leo Stein, as produced upon the stage by Henry W. Savage.

*More
stars
than
there
are
in
Heaven*

"The Merry Widow" is a

Metro-Goldwyn-Mayer
Picture

Photoplay advertisement for *The Merry Widow* (1925).

A seduction scene in *The Merry Widow* in the midst of religious artifacts, including a bishop's mitre on the left and paintings and crucifixes on the walls.

With a change of camera position, the bishop's mitre becomes a kind of crown.

A shocked bride (Mae Murray) looks down on Baron Sadoja (Tully Marshall), who has just keeled over from a stroke in anticipation of his wedding joys in *The Merry Widow*. Notice the scattered flowers and the grotesque arrangement of the body.

The Queen, with a band to hold back her double chin, retrieves her false teeth from a glass of water. This scene was not considered entertaining and cut by Irving Thalberg from *The Merry Widow*.

Suffering Christ and Sally in *The Merry Widow*.

Superb set design for *The Merry Widow*, as the bride, dressed in black, nurses her paralyzed husband while a doctor watches. The world, as the window indicates, is now frozen.

Above: One of the understandably censored scenes from *The Merry Widow* shows Danilo (John Gilbert) trying to forget his troubles at Maxim's. *Right:* Stroheim on the *Foolish Wives* set with his new wife, Valerie.

After a night of debauchery, Prince Nicki restores himself with a raw egg in his sherry in part of the opening scene, now cut, from *The Wedding March* (1928).

Stroheim as Prince Nicki with Josef, his "Poopsie."

Above: The girl he loves: Mitzi (Fay Wray), "the sweet maiden," and roguish Prince Nicky in *The Wedding March. Below:* The girl he marries: Cecelia, "the limping heiress," and her reluctant husband being reminded of apple blossoms in *The Honeymoon.*

Prince Nicki enticing Mitzi to come out in the garden and play in *The Wedding March*. The situation may be similar to the balcony scene in *Romeo and Juliet*, but notice that her underwear is on the wash line.

Above: Stroheim's faithful reconstruction of Vienna, including another instance of his fascination with ambulances in *The Wedding March*. *Below:* Nature mourns as Mitzi waits in the rain to see her lover marry another.

extravagances, but it was probably their mutual Catholicism that brought them together."[2] At the time, Powers was courting Peggy Hopkins Joyce, a celebrity known for collecting millionaire admirers and/or sleeping with famous people to further her career. At her prompting, Powers hoped to transform his ambitious lady love into a major actress. If Marion Davies, with Hearst's backing, could win stardom, why couldn't Miss Joyce? And who could better achieve this miracle than Stroheim, the director who obtained a good performance from the rather ungifted Mae Murray? These two no-nonsense men met and convinced each other that they had the deal of their lives!

Soon Peggy was dropped from the project, the femme fatale being replaced now by an *homme fatal*, a superbly convincing Stroheim who dangled before the enthralled Powers a vision of a splendorous Vienna. The canny producer was hooked by Stroheim's charm, despite the director's reputation. He was also shrewd enough to recall the extraordinary box-office success of *The Merry Widow*. What he did not know was the tight control Thalberg had wielded on that production. And so Powers agreed to back Stroheim as director, author, and actor in a project that turned out to be *The Wedding March*. In some ways, it was a rewrite of *Merry-Go-Round*, though without the Prater and the orangutan. Although the script was cowritten with Harry Carr, Stroheim's collaborators seldom ever did anything more than listen and perhaps suggest that a particular section might run too long. Otherwise, it was a pure Stroheim creation in its conception as well as its details. Furthermore, it allowed Stroheim to act the role of his dreams: an aristocratic rake in the doomed prewar Vienna of his youth. It was his greatest wish-fulfillment.

The script for *The Wedding March*, dated April 23, 1926, ran 154 pages. The present print of the film covers the action depicted in the first 67 pages, and of the carefully delineated events in those pages, only about one-half exist in actual footage.

One would think that the well-known facts about the inordinate length of *Foolish Wives, Merry-Go-Round,* and *Greed* would have cautioned Powers or one of his minions to ask some legitimate questions about the scenario's extraordinary size. But, incredibly, no one seemed to worry, and once again Stroheim began on his quixotic dream to make a giant film. And once again, the author-director would witness its virtual destruction.

Elaborate sets were built, among them St. Stephen's Cathedral and the streets adjoining it, various palatial rooms, and an apple orchard in which thousands of blossoms had to be tied onto the trees. Stroheim later explained, "They say I give them sewers—and dead cats! This time I am giving them beauty. Beauty—and apple blossoms! More than they can stand!"[3] In June 1926, Stroheim began shooting; in January 1927, the production was halted.

Not only did Stroheim have a long script, but he also took infinite care about filming every scene in it. A *New York Times* reporter on the set observed that Stroheim had adopted "the maxim that genius is the capacity for taking pains."

> Not only in details of setting and of conception, but in the exact performances of the actors, von Stroheim wants what he wants, all of it, when he wants it.
>
> A scene in *The Wedding March* had been photographed several times, and still the performers failed to register just the expression and exactly the synchronized action which von Stroheim has conceived. The impatient director got up from his chair beside the camera and, with restraint, made a crisp speech: "Everybody may as well understand," he said, "that we are going to get this scene right if we have to take it 24,000 times."[4]

And so it went.

In her memoirs, Fay Wray (who played Mitzi, the female lead) recalled that the first episodes shot were in the wine garden. A scene at the table took until dawn, and Stroheim was so weary he forgot some of his lines. Without pausing, Wray cued him with some improvised lines, and the scene continued smoothly. "He was happily excited about that," and called her "a Pro."[5]

Wray felt that she and Stroheim had a wonderful "rapport." During the scenes of their first meeting in the street, Stroheim acted his flirtatious role and then switched to becoming the imperious director shouting at the crowd. He told them to be surly because they had been waiting so long and were "sick of seeing horses' rosettes." Her description continues:

> How impossible to relate the mood, the enormous capacity

von Stroheim had for every minute detail of the setting, the costuming, the emphasis on symbolism, the richness of understanding about human behaviour, the evident knowledge of old Vienna. *His* Vienna. There was never any sense of having to compete with time. Time was his, he owned it. He used it as it should be used by an artist. He ignored it.[6]

If this sounds as if Wray was fascinated by Stroheim, she was. In her memoirs, she goes on to say that she told him that she loved him. "In a flash, he had me pinned against a corridor wall, his body pressing against mine. He looked and looked into my eyes. I don't think I said a word. I know I didn't push him away even though I wanted to, knowing that I should. Perhaps he heard someone coming. He let me go." Thereafter, every day he would tell her that he had thought of her the night before. Later, he made an assignation with her, but she did not go, and after a while he perhaps decided that it would be best not to have an affair. At Christmastime, Stroheim gave her a box of exotic chocolates and on Christmas Eve invited her to his home, where he and Valerie had a tree with lighted candles on it. Obviously, the real Stroheim was far different from the public persona, for Wray remembered him sixty years later with the warmest admiration.

During the six months that Stroheim spent shooting his immense script—long days as well as late evenings—the cameras consumed approximately two hundred thousand feet of film before the emotionally and financially exhausted producer gave up on the project. Wasn't the canny Powers, after the first few months, aware that Stroheim was making an incredibly long film? One might well ask how any veteran of the movies, even if he never visited the set, could not have known. It is possible that Powers thought the footage comprised numerous retakes rather than different scenes, but someone involved with the production should have warned him about what was happening, that the mad director was back to his old habits. Perhaps, if questions were raised, Stroheim turned on his charm and enthusiastically declared that he was creating a masterpiece and—not to worry—it would be a great success, an even greater one than *The Merry Widow.* In any case, the director was allowed to go on—and on.

When Powers finally stopped production in January 1927, the not-quite-completed film would have run about eight hours. Stroheim screened the immense amount of footage and began the giant job of cutting it down to some manageable length. As usual, Stroheim hoped for a two-part film to be shown on successive evenings or, as an unhappy compromise, in a version of four to five hours, interrupted by a dinner break. His initial cut of the first half ran 25,795 feet (over four hours).[7] During the first half of 1927, Stroheim continued his labors but was unable to condense the film any further.

In the meantime, Powers arranged to have Paramount distribute the picture. During the latter part of 1927 and much of 1928, the studio wrestled with how to release this expensive and lengthy piece of merchandise. Admittedly, there was no satisfactory solution to the problem. The only efficient use of the miles of footage seemed to be to issue the work as Stroheim intended, in two parts. But Paramount knew exhibitors did not want a film any longer than two hours, and emphatically not one that took two nights. The studio executives decided that not many people would want to see a continuation of part one, which to their eyes did not seem that exciting or entrancing in the first place. Indeed, their commercial instincts were right, for when part one was eventually released, it hardly received raves from the public or the critics. (To be fair, its comparative failure could have been the result of the severe cutting.) Although the first part did not seem likely to be a box-office smash, still there would be some people in the audience willing to come back to see what happened in the second part.

Twelve months after editing began, the studio put together a version in January 1928 that, according to a reporter for the *New York Times,* would soon be released. In March 1928, a shortened print was previewed at the Egyptian Theater in Long Beach, California. After the screening, the *Hollywood Filmograph* sensibly noted that Paramount should scrap the single-feature version and allow Stroheim to recut the film back into its original form of two parts. It reasoned that for a small additional investment, the second part could be whipped into shape—a better solution than scrapping all of it. Admittedly, attendance for the second feature would have been small, yet this lavish part had already been completed. What could the studio lose?

Paramount's ultimate decision hardly alleviated the impending financial disaster. After months more of quibbling and indecision, the studio ignored *Filmograph*'s practical suggestion and, in its infinite wisdom, decided to break *The Wedding March* into two separate features, rather than two parts of the same one. The first feature, *The Wedding March,* released in October 1928, was cut to fourteen short reels (totaling about eleven thousand feet), lasting a little over two hours. This was the only footage the American public would ever see. The second feature, called *The Honeymoon,* which continued the story, was severely mutilated and released in eight reels. In order to do this, the first part's story was reprised and condensed into three reels, leaving room for only four and one-half reels (4,588 feet) of new material, one-fifth of Stroheim's first cut. Stroheim claimed—quite rightly, it appears—that this second part was a travesty.

What was going on in the collective mind of Paramount? Surely, no audience who had seen part one would want to see a major repeat of it in *The Honeymoon.* Stroheim supposedly forbade its release in the United States, as his contract allowed, but he could not prevent it from playing in other parts of the world, although the truth of this cannot be verified. In any case, *The Honeymoon* never appeared in America. The truncated version only obtained play dates in Europe and South America. However, one wonders why in these foreign lands where, presumably, *The Wedding March* had already appeared, audiences would be any more content to endure such a repetition. As a result, a financial disaster was made worse.

The sole remaining print of *The Honeymoon,* in the possession of Henri Langlois in France, perished in a fire five days after Stroheim's death in 1957. Langlois, unabashed at the loss, claimed poetically that it "est mort volontairement" [died voluntarily].[8]

In a reminiscence of 1947, Stroheim explained that he "had finished cutting the first part of *The Wedding March* when the rest of the film not even put together correctly was given to 'von' Sternberg to make a separate and independent film of the second part. . . . The cost of the whole film (both parts) was just a little over $900,000. Both Powers as well as Paramount made a good deal of profit whereas yours truly never saw one cent of his 25% of the net profits."[90]

Stroheim is wrong here. There was no way this expensive film, considering its lukewarm reviews, could ever have made a profit, especially as its long-delayed general release occurred while dialogue films were capturing the market. In addition, the nine-hundred-thousand-dollar cost was expended in late 1926, so that by October 1928 when the film began its release, almost two years' worth of interest plus the additional expense of making a sound track (on discs) and printing the color sequence had increased its costs to over a million dollars.

While the film had been in its editing stages, Stroheim confessed that he could not condense his two-part version any further. When Paramount told Stroheim that someone else would have to trim it, he rejected the suggested editors and only relented when Josef von Sternberg's name was mentioned. Stroheim ultimately did not appreciate his efforts and would continue to bear unwarranted resentment against "von" Sternberg, who explained years later that Stroheim had

> asked me personally to take over the assignment, and I did so without any protest on his part. I told him precisely what I would shorten; we were friendly before, during, and afterwards. . . . I showed him the shortened version and he thanked me. Had he objected to anything, I would not only have restored the film to its original length but would have refused to have anything more to do with it. I am explicit about this for it seems to be generally thought that I edited his work without his O.K., which is something I would not have done under any circumstances . . . I had been strongly impressed with his earlier *Greed*. . . . I know nothing about the division of the film into two parts. I never saw the film again and how it was finally shown is unknown to me.[10]

Sternberg is quite believable in his comments. He was by no means the typical studio toady and was arrogant enough about the role of the artist not to interfere, if he had not been asked. Needless to say, it was a thankless task.

Stroheim later explained his situation in regard to his ruined masterpiece:

> From the time I started to write the original story, the scenario, made the preparations, waited for the arrival of uniforms from Vienna, the shooting of the film and the cutting of the first part took exactly 13 months. Had I been less conscientious and . . . had only my financial advantage at heart I

could have made the same amount of money had I delivered any sort of picture within four or six weeks.

Each time I set out with renewed hope that this time I would be able to make a film as I thought it should be made and as I know the public would have wanted to see it, but each time either the Producer or the exhibitors at large objected vehemently. As you know exhibitors have nothing on their mind except to make money on the films which they exhibit. They naturally want to turn over their house at least twice in an evening, which, with a film as long as I wanted it, would have been physically impossible but later on, when the respective company exerted enough pressure on them or when the companies had their own theaters to show their long films, the extremely long pictures were extraordinary successes not necessarily because of their length but because their length permitted the slow development of the characters, either in evolution, or deterioration and demoralization.[11]

True, there were some long films released in the teens and the twenties, but nothing approaching four hours, especially with a story about a long and generally unhappy romantic relationship: no wars, no shipwrecks, no exciting chases, just the exploration of the characters of a few people faced with difficult problems.[12]

When *The Wedding March* was released in October 1928, it was not a great success, despite all the press coverage about its extreme length and the consequent cutting. *Variety* called it "a ponderous slow moving production" and said it was "fair but hardly brilliant program material which the boys have salvaged from a regiment of reels."[13] The review concluded that the film "rates as the most costly and overly studio handled program picture ever made" but did hint that it might have won "fair success" if it had not been so mutilated and been allowed to play for a full evening. The film did not fare too badly in metropolitan areas, but in smaller towns it was considered a clinker. Nor was its financial situation helped by contemporary events. The talkies started to come into vogue during late 1928 and became popular in the beginning of 1929. *The Wedding March*, like all other silent films, quickly lost whatever box-office appeal it had and virtually disappeared. *Variety*'s prediction that the film would lose money proved true.

The long-neglected original 35 mm negative is now only partially intact. However, Stroheim, shortly before his death, was given a release print of the first part, as well as the original music track on discs. He slightly reedited a few scenes, added some sound effects (the sound of horses, guns, and so forth), and left his modified version to Langlois's Cinémathèque Française. It is this version that exists on clandestine 16 mm prints. Interestingly, when Stroheim discussed the film with his sound assistant, he would never say, "The prince does this." Instead, he always referred to that character as "I."[14]

In 1987, Paramount issued the original release version on videotape. Unfortunately, it does not use the superb music track (with orchestra and sound effects) that was supplied with the film, but a new organ score. The difference is immense. The emotional power is significantly weakened. In fact, the original J.S. Zamecnik sound track is one of the best of all the scores from the twenties. The music adheres closely to the story and is devoid of the musical clichés that were prevalent at the time.[15]

Despite its financial failure, *The Wedding March* ranks among Stroheim's best works; it is a complete film and satisfying as an individual entity, even though it is only a fragment. Henri Langlois, speaking at Lincoln Center in September 1965 after the film's first New York showing in over thirty years, likened *The Wedding March* to a torso without its head. However, the film is so extraordinary that one finds it difficult to imagine a second part that would equal it. Indeed, it is possible to think that, like a Greek statue, it is more beautiful and suggestive in its fragmentation than in its original entirety. Just as no imagined pair of arms could conceivably improve the Venus de Milo, neither could any continuation seem likely to add to the drama of *The Wedding March*.

Certainly *The Honeymoon,* as released, is a disappointment. (This opinion comes not from a viewing, which is no longer possible, but from a close study of the release print's continuity.) The shooting script is another matter, though. I am convinced that there would have been no lessening in the second part if it had contained what was shot. The head was as beautiful as the torso, the arms as lovely as the rest of the Venus. Stroheim seemed fully able to sustain the emotional power of the first half.

The Wedding March is an unswerving drama that never loses sight of its theme or lessens its power to move. It captures not only a country and its lifestyle but also the psychological depths of the principal characters. It shows a creativity far more complex and imaginative than that revealed in any of Stroheim's other works. Admittedly, it omits the generalizations about the shift in the social structure—the decline of the aristocracy and the rise of the proletariat—that were such an important element in *Merry-Go-Round*. But it depicts its characters with far greater sensitivity and adds a note of genuine compassion.

Usually, *Greed* has been considered the Stroheim super-masterpiece, but after repeated viewings of all his films and close scrutiny of the scripts, I feel that Stroheim's Viennese film is at least *Greed's* equal. The director's broad vision, his subtle interweaving of comedy and tragedy, his dramatic flair, his intriguing plot, his sense of doom and fate, his delicate handling of actors, his creation of a foreign milieu, his use of symbols, his genuine pathos, and his deft characterizations are simply overwhelming—far in advance of what anyone in the 1920s in America, and perhaps even the world, was doing. This is a mature work in style, in attitude, in philosophy. It has the density of a big nineteenth-century novel coupled with twentieth-century insights. To an uneducated palate, a good dry wine is merely sour. To most viewers, Stroheim may seem the same. The fault, however, lies not in the wine but in the palate.

Stroheim had grown to have a thorough command of the medium. His *Blind Husbands* is crude when compared to *Foolish Wives,* and that film is comparatively crude when compared to *The Wedding March*. His style is not obviously "cinematic." Stroheim is not interested in rhythmic cutting or other experiments—rabid devotees of the Soviet cinema regard him indifferently—but he manages to get *within* a scene and to present a dynamic interplay of subtle actions and reactions. The editing tends to be "invisible." That is, the camera viewpoints are constantly shifting, but they are so inevitably in the right place and so smoothly edited that they do not draw attention to themselves. A film containing 1,560 shots (many of which are close-ups) and 238 subtitles is hardly a stagy one, relying solely on mise-en-scène, and compares favorably, we may recall, with the more than 2,000 shots of *Intolerance.*

Those critics who say that Stroheim's sense of cinema was limited, that he let scenes play mostly in long shots, that he worried more about what was happening in the background than in the foreground action, that he could not see the splendorous forest for the nasty trees (which he garbed in poison ivy), that he was indifferent to involved camerawork, and that he was a poor editor, are proved wrong by *The Wedding March*.

Stroheim also made considerable use of soft focus, possibly following in the footsteps of Griffith in *Broken Blossoms,* and photographed many of the romantic scenes through gauzes. Alas, these shots suffer greatly in modern 16 mm prints—such as the one Stroheim made—by losing even more sharpness.

In essence, *The Wedding March* tells the story of Prince Nicki, a rather charming rake who falls in love with and seduces (not necessarily in that order) Mitzi, a girl of the lower classes, and then leaves her for monetary reasons to marry Cecelia, a crippled heiress.

The film is "dedicated to the true lovers of the world." This opening statement involves the viewer in the first difficulty of interpretation. To the modern audience—an audience that, in Herman G. Weinberg's view, is a "savage" one because it will not admit to sentiment—this dedication might appear ironic. But it is not meant to be viewed ironically. Stroheim is honestly offering his work to the true lovers of the world; however, this does not mean that his characters are motivated only by pure love. In fact, his point may be that there is no such thing as "pure" love, for it is not in the nature of man. He realizes that the aim of every lover is to go to bed with his beloved; what separates the cad from the true admirer are the gentleness, compassion, and understanding that lie beyond this basic fact.

The presence of sexuality prevents *The Wedding March* from being merely a sentimental tale. The implications of the film are that man is a creature full of animal drives, perversions, greed, and hypocrisies and that somehow, by a strange miracle, man does transcend his baseness. Havelock Ellis, in his *Studies in the Psychology of Sex,* explains the problem: "To look upon love as in any special sense a delusion is merely to fall into the trap of a shallow cynicism. Love is only a delusion in so far as the whole of life is a delusion, and if we accept the fact of life it is unphilosophical to refuse to accept the fact of love."[16] This delicate balance is important. Without an awareness of it, viewers tend to see the love story either as a parody, a satirical thrust at romantic love, or as a pure romantic story, with the man and woman as star-crossed lovers. In actuality, the film is a mixture of both.

There is no doubt that Mitzi—the innocent girl—is a true lover. But what about Prince Nicki (played by Stroheim)? His name, Nicholas Ehrart Hans Karl Maria Wildeliebe-Rauffenburg, is obviously symbolic. "Wildeliebe" [wild-loving] Nicki is a playboy who spends most of his time and all of his money in the pursuit of pleasure. And pleasure to Nicki is "Wein, Liebe, und Lieder" [wine, love, and song]. Although he is attracted to Mitzi and eventually falls in love with her, he hardly becomes an innocent child in the process. He retains his worldly view, his cynicism, perhaps even a slight touch of sexual perversion (notice how he slips his overcoat over her, as if Mitzi dressed like an officer— or as himself—is more desirable).

Men of sophistication can fall in love, but they are not fools, nor have they forgotten the ways of the world. It is possible for Nicki to spend the early part of an evening in a brothel and then to visit his beloved. Love, even an overwhelming kind, does not necessarily answer all of one's needs. Nicki may be a lover, but he is an aware one, conscious always of the complexities of his own emotions. He is charmed by Mitzi's naïveté and overwhelmed by her loveliness and dedication, but how long will these qualities last? How can they compete with the money he would get from marrying an heiress? These are not fanciful alternatives. Stroheim has not forgotten his inclinations toward realism in content as well as style.

In Stroheim's earlier films, he had played villains without any redeeming features. He was truly the man audiences loved to hate. The lecherous lieutenant in *Blind Husbands* and the corrupt phony count in *Foolish Wives* evolved into the roguish count of *Merry-Go-Round*, who, with not too many qualms, falls impractically in love with a simple girl, Agnes, and only after he has lost his position and his money will he marry her. Prince Nicki in *The Wedding March* is also a womanizer and even more complex. He too falls in love, but he is realistic enough to know that such an alliance would doom his lifestyle. Prince Nicki faces a serious dilemma, the fact that the heart and the purse are antithetical. Stroheim may have mellowed—who is not humbled by life?— but his all too human Nicki is not transformed by love into a pure hero. Nicki shows that one may keep his sexual curiosity and have a wandering lust as well as a wanderlust, while still being drawn to a creature as loving and sincere as Mitzi. Underneath the cynical facade, Stroheim shows a compassion that is far more honest than that in the numerous saccharine films of the 1920s.

The script of *The Wedding March* introduces the viewer to Vienna with establishing shots of the city: the Danube, St. Stephen's Cathedral, and the Hapsburg throne: "A town of blossoms," says a title. This is followed by close-ups of lilacs, jasmine, violets, and apple trees in bloom. After a statue of Psyche and Amor is crosscut with a loving couple, a title refers to the town's "evil smells—and cynicism—and bold and brazen sin—" followed by a shot of a prostitute and her hunchbacked pimp. Then Stroheim describes shots of statues of Beethoven, Haydn, Mozart, and Schubert, as well as a military band, marching troops, and people waltzing. This opening, quite similar to the beginning of *Merry-Go-Round*'s script, was mostly cut, as *Merry-Go-Round*'s was.

Stroheim next establishes two legends, which he had invented, that become the opposing symbols of the film. At one extreme are the Danube Maids (symbolic of "eternal Spring," "dance," "music," "happiness," and "love"), and in opposition the Iron Man ("the symbol of the spirit of the Dark Ages," "prejudice," "hate," "preposterous prerogatives," "intolerance," and "war"). This "eiserene Mann" [Iron Man] was suggested by a copper figure of a banner-bearer that was perched on top of the 322-foot tower of the Vienna Rathaus [town hall]. According to Stroheim, this metallic figure represents the tragedy that will befall Mitzi. These symbols transform the love affair into a tale of mythological import.

Stroheim's original intent was to follow a shot of the Rauffenburg family crest with a close-up showing a slight crack, which suggests the family's ultimate breakup. A chambermaid and a lackey carry boxes of garbage out of the mansion. The boxes contain dust, dirt, broken glass, perfume bottles, dry flowers, empty champagne bottles, "all suggesting high life and waste." A refuse wagon comes by and picks up this debris. The maid slips the garbageman a bottle of champagne and a roast chicken. Thus, Stroheim's essay on aristocracy begins at the bottom, with their refuse. A letter carrier then arrives and hands the servants a bundle of bills. The Rauffenburgs are in serious debt.

The scene then shifts to a "Gallery of Ancestors," where portraits surround the family crest. The maid asks what the crest's motto means, and a lackey replies, "For the glory of God—the Emperor—the Fatherland and the Family." The maid replies flippantly, "Mostly the family."

The existing print omits all of the above. After a few shots of Vienna, including St. Stephen's Cathedral, it moves right into the family mansion. (When Stroheim restored the print shortly before his death, he inserted a long shot of the mansion, which he borrowed from *Merry-Go-Round*.) Stroheim here introduces Nicki's aristocratic mother and father in their bedroom as they awaken. "Maria Immaculata," as a title calls her, wears a band around her head to alleviate her double chin. She is entirely disgusted with her husband, who, tossing and turning in his bed, is equally repelled by his wife. In shots cut from this version, the father finally gets out of bed, stubs his toe, furiously flings furniture to the floor, and puts collodion on his corn. The maid starts to shave the mother's mustache as the mother lights a cigar. (Similar scenes were also cut from *The Merry Widow*.)

Stroheim then shows the squabbling parents' "love-child," the prince. As Nicki lies in bed, a maid enters and picks up a stocking from the floor, a remnant of the prince's night of illicit love with one of his "girlies." The maid tells him it is Corpus Christi Day. Nicki rubs the sand out of his eyes and endeavors to caress her. But his breath is foul—a true Stroheimian touch—and the woman averts her face. This makes Nicki momentarily unhappy, but he senses the cause of his difficulty and sprays his mouth with an atomizer.

Nicki prepares a concoction of sherry and egg. When an aide arrives, Nicki, irritated at having to get up, chucks eggs at him. We then have a series of short shots of Nicki in the bathtub; getting a massage; being shaved, manicured and pedicured; standing in his silk underwear; and being sprayed with perfume. (Similar content can be seen in the opening of *Merry-Go-Round*.) Nicki's valet hands him his monocle and his elaborate cape. Finally, Nicki asks his servants, "Has anyone of you got any money?" He takes a few bills from the cynically smiling maid and strides out. The contrast between Nicki's spoiled and pampered existence and the fact that he has to borrow money from servants establishes the tone of the film. (All of the foregoing was cut, but the next scenes survive in the print.)

Nicki makes a surprise visit to his parents' quarters, but they know precisely why he is there: he wants money. The father refuses to give him any, saying rather inelegantly, either "blow out your brains" or "marry money." The son then visits his mother, who is smoking her cigar. Nicki kisses her hand, and she cynically asks how much the hand-kiss is going to cost. Finally, she gives him some cash but also advises him to "marry money." Nicki—facing reality—tells her to find him a rich bride, kisses his mother's maids good-bye, and leaves.

All of Vienna is preparing for Corpus Christi Day, the day on which the Body of Christ (as represented by the Host) is carried in a procession through the streets. This religious event forms an ironic background for the ensuing action and shows again Stroheim's preoccupation with the counterpoint of good and evil, God and man, virtue and sin, and—his persistent concern—the sacred and the profane. One might recall that in *Merry-Go-Round* the emperor is seen in the Holy Thursday foot-washing ceremony. Here, in *The Wedding March,* the ceremony of Corpus Christi takes place in front of the church. This rite, considered by many to be "the most colorful and gorgeous spectacle ever seen in old Vienna," according to the memoirs of the emperor's valet, was much "loved" by the aged ruler.[17]

Among the people drawn to this public event at St. Stephen's Cathedral are Mitzi, her father, her scheming mother, and Schani with his immensely fat father. Schani, a low-class person, pushes and shoves his way to the front of the crowd. His father owns a *Weingarten* in Nussdorf, a suburb of Vienna, where Mitzi plays the harp and her father the violin. She is urged by her practical mother to marry Schani, who is a butcher by trade.

As the procession begins, Nicki, in his plumed hat and fancy uniform, arrives on his horse and is stationed next to Mitzi. Attracted by her beauty, he gives her the eye, and she responds. Schani is contemptuous of the officer and gives his opinion by spitting. Mitzi would like some flowers, but Schani will not buy them, complaining that all he smells is the stink of horses. Finally, he relents and, sticking the end of a string of sausages in his mouth, digs into his pockets and buys a little bouquet. Stroheim takes great pains (too many, perhaps) to present Schani as an animal-like creature, lacking all elegance and style. After receiving the flowers, Mitzi puts a sprig in Nicki's boot, and he takes it, smells it, and kisses his hand.

While Mitzi and Nicki exchange glances, the prince's sword is raised vertically in the air, but when Schani interferes, the sword descends—one of Stroheim's sly Freudian touches. Meanwhile, within the cathedral (a nicely ironic locale for calculating a purely mercenary marriage), Nicki's parents observe Cecelia (Zasu Pitts), the daughter of Schweisser, the corn-plaster king. She is rich and therefore would make an ideal wife for Nicki. When Nicki's father notes that the girl limps, the mother replies, "What's a little limp—with twenty millions?"

The ceremony ends, and the emperor emerges from the church, accompanied by the sound of rifles being fired. Startled, Nicki's horse rears and knocks Mitzi down, injuring her. She has been impressed by this charming man perched on a horse—a romantic image of masculinity—and now falls for him both emotionally and literally.

A policeman goes to the call box and orders an ambulance (familiar Stroheim motifs). Soon it arrives and carries the injured girl off to the hospital. Schani, angry at Nicki, starts an argument and is arrested. A title observes that there is no such thing as an accident: "It is Fate—misnamed." Then follows the Corpus Christi ceremony, which Stroheim filmed in two-color Technicolor, footage that still exists.

Afterward, Nicki visits the girl at the hospital, walking through corridors and past white-garbed nuns. Once again, Stroheim recalls what for him is a primal experience—the entrapment of a virginal girl by an experienced man. In Griffith's films, Lillian Gish as the embodiment of virginity was often threatened with rape. Stroheim adapts Griffith's stock device by avoiding the melodrama and having the girl seduced instead. Nicki gives Mitzi a large box of candy; she tells him most gratefully that she has never had such a gift, only once a few pennies' worth of jelly beans. Here, certainly, is a girl who has not been spoiled, and Nicki appreciates the fact. He is attracted by her purity and is eager to alleviate that condition. Her vulnerability and fragility are emphasized by her leg injury, so that, although she soon leaves the hospital, she continues to limp through other scenes. (Cecelia, the girl Nicki is to marry, also limps, but her affliction is permanent.)

Nicki goes out to the *Weingarten* at Nussdorf where Mitzi works. He passes a litter of pigs, putting a handkerchief to his nose, and then enters the garden, where, in close-up, fingers are shown playing a harp. They belong to Mitzi, and Nicki licks his lips. On the music stand beside Mitzi is the title of the selection: "Paradies" [Paradise]. Indeed, Mitzi is an angel and does play the music of paradise. But she is a doomed angel, caught between the grossness of Schani and the rakish intentions of Nicki.

After the performance, Nicki takes Mitzi, who is flattered by the attentions of this suave aristocrat, into a garden under a canopy of apple blossoms. Nearby is a life-sized replica of Christ on the cross. Nicki salutes the crucifix and begins his blandishments, a situation reminiscent of one in *Blind Husbands.* Such a seduction, under the image of Christ, adds a sacrilegious overtone, one that persists in all of Stroheim's works.

The two then stand by the shore of the Danube, and she tells him of the Danube Maids and how they bring love; she also speaks of the Iron Man, who, bringing "sorrow, grief, and death," comes to carry away sinning maidens. This balladlike reference adds immeasurably to the tale of these lovers by providing a tragic aura to her seduction. She, like the Danube Maids, will have love and happiness, but these emotions will vanish and she will suffer the consequences; the Iron Man (reality, pregnancy, materialism, war, lust, death) will attempt to vanquish her and vanquish love. But Nicki tells her to ignore this story, this fear. "You were made for love—Mitzerl."

The name of the *Weingarten* is Zum alten Apfelbaum [At the old apple tree], which suggests the Garden of Eden before the Fall, a garden Christianized by the presence of religious images. Here, Nicki in a sense proves to be the tempter, the serpent amid the cascading apple blossoms, but he is not really evil. Stroheim uses this setting to add complexity to the transpiring events. The bower of trees hints of Eden but is not purely a symbol; it is rather a suggestion of innocence and beauty without a heavy-handed, literal meaning.

Nicki and Mitzi adjourn to another part of the orchard, where she leads him to an abandoned carriage, a kind of fairy coach. In this idyllic setting, he sits down—on a nail, which he carefully removes in one of those comic, realistic touches that puncture the fantasy and sweetness, at least to some extent. She commands him to take her for "a drive through paradise."

This romantic scene is one of the most touching and poignant in the whole oeuvre of Stroheim. Mitzi is in love, but to attribute this feeling to Nicki would be not only sentimental but inaccurate, at least at this point. His motivations are complex. He wants her, of course, but he is not truly in love; she is an affair, a rather refreshing one in contrast to the partners found in the terribly experienced circles in which he travels. Although he does eventually fall in love with her, it is not the same kind of attraction that she feels for him. After all, how can a man with so many mistresses and brothel escapades feel the same pure affection that this young girl experiences? Her love is poignant because it is her first; his because, perhaps, he believes it is his last.

Mitzi's session with Nicki in the carriage comes to an end when Schani's father and her mother call her. She limps back to them and is smacked for dallying with the prince. Nicki walks slowly through the bower of blossoms, holds a sprig in his hand, sniffs it momentarily, and then drops it. This action, superbly observed by Stroheim, the director, is not without meaning. Unfortunately, it has been ignored by those who feel that Nicki is now head-over-heels in love. He is not. He has had an experience, and a delightful one, but he hardly feels what Tristan felt for Isolde. Recall that in *Merry-Go-Round* the count takes a sprig of lilac and carries it with him throughout the war. Nicki is not so daffy. The early film was sentimental; this later version is more realistic.

Later, Schani returns from prison, and the mother tells him that Nicki is "working fast." The angry butcher chops bones, cuts off a piece of raw meat and eats it, then goes after Mitzi. He walks through a puddle where pigs are wallowing to where Mitzi sits in the buggy waiting for Nicki. Schani kisses her, and she spits out his kiss as the two struggle. White doves flutter about in the background. Finally, she hits him on the head with her crutch—a comical moment—and gets away safely.

Meanwhile, Nicki visits a "crooked house on a crooked street"— in the script the house number is 69, the shot was intended to be tinted red, and the brothel was filled with seductive women: oriental, Turkish, French, and so forth. A party is being given by Schweisser, the corn-plaster king, and Nicki's father is present. He is a familiar sight there, and although the girls all want Nicki to stay, he refuses, telling them, "Tonight I crave apple blossoms." With kisses all around, Nicki leaves. His father and Schweisser (whose German name means someone who sweats a lot) get more and more drunk.

After bribing the watchdog with links of sausage—a brilliantly grotesque and humorous action—Nicki stealthily approaches Mitzi's house and whistles. She appears at the window, a pair of underdrawers visible on the washline in a portion of the screen. After a moment, she shyly removes the drawers from the line. Nicki takes a nearby ladder, climbs to the window, and looks in at her bed. She makes him turn his head. He says that he is sorry to be late, explaining that he was "on duty." They descend the ladder into the garden. (The scene seems a bit like a satirical version of the balcony scene in *Romeo and Juliet*.)

The couple goes to the fairy coach. A nightingale sings, an owl hoots, and the two kiss. The scene fades out and changes to the party, where Schweisser is putting a corn-plaster on Nicki's father's toe. Too drunk to properly moisten the plaster, they pour champagne on the foot. Then they discuss the possible wedding of Cecelia and Nicki. The irony of a marriage being arranged by two drunken fathers lying on the floor of a brothel and haggling over the amount of one father's "commission" is certainly mordant enough, but it is compounded by crosscutting to the tryst of Nicki and Mitzi. Finally, the price is settled: Nicki's father will receive one million kronen.

In the meantime, Nicki has had his way with Mitzi and symbolically brushes apple blossoms from her lap. Tearfully, she envisions the Iron Man stalking her as the wind blows in the garden. Nicki tries to comfort the girl as the giant figure of the Iron Man moves across the screen in double exposure. In a scene cut from the print, Schani wakes and sees the two from his window. He grabs a knife and runs into the garden to attack Nicki, who wards him off with his sword and wounds Schani in the arm. Schani switches the knife to his other hand and is wounded again. Then they wrestle, a fracas crosscut with barking dogs, shying horses, and squealing pigs.

The next morning Schweisser, still slightly drunk, returns to his house and tells his daughter that she will soon be married. Cecelia, dressed all in white and holding a dove in Griffith fashion, is a lovely embodiment of innocence, the sacrificial offering to a father's desire to marry into the nobility and to the nobility's need for money. No wonder that a crucifix appears on the wall behind Cecelia. Christ was not the only martyr.

Cecelia cannot quite understand the situation and asks how the prince could be in love with her. Her father replies succinctly, "You have twenty millions." He adds that love will come in time. She looks at her foot (a close-up) and says, "A limping princess," and cries. With most directors, the father would appear as merely a stock villain, but Stroheim makes both the father and the daughter human and not just instruments of the plot. Schweisser does love his daughter and looks forward to the prestige the marriage can bring him and her. The scene is played with great delicacy, a tribute to Stroheim's sure touch.

At the palace, Nicki is informed by his parents of the impending marriage to Cecelia. He asks whether it ever occurred to them that he might be in love. The father replies, "You idiot!" The mother adds that marriage is one thing and love another (a response reminiscent of *The Merry Widow*). The father says, "I command!" to Nicki, and the mother speaks of the girl's money. Nicki complains that the selected fiancée "limps on both legs."

Meanwhile, Mitzi goes to church and prays to the Madonna and Child. In the background a woman holding a baby passes by, an intimation that Mitzi, if not pregnant, is at least no longer a virgin. Mitzi confesses to a priest, her face soft and exquisite behind the screen of the confessional. Stroheim cuts away to a hunchbacked church worker removing dripped wax from the carpet with a hot iron and paper. The wax is like frozen tears, and the world is full of weeping. The shots also imply that life goes on, despite everything. The priest in the confessional looks sad but not surprised; he has heard this story countless times and can say no more than "Peace be with you." (This whole scene is directly from the *Merry-Go-Round* script.)

Cecelia, in her quarters, looks in a mirror, turns her huge diamond engagement ring around to make it look like a wedding ring, then moves her foot. These actions show that she knows she is not beautiful, that she would like to be married, and that she is aware of the drawback of her lameness.

These scenes with Mitzi and Cecelia show how sensitive Stroheim was as an artist. The feelings of violated innocence and infinite sadness are conveyed movingly but without sentimentality through the direction of the acting and the handling of the camera. Such scenes, far more than worries over details of uniforms, are what distinguish his work from that of the many lesser figures of his time.

A title says at this point that nature mourned and that it rained and rained. Schani is in the slaughterhouse holding onto a pig when Mitzi comes by. Still grasping the pig (Schani is a mental as well as a physical butcher), he shows Mitzi a newspaper item about the upcoming wedding of Nicki and Cecelia. He again offers himself—not everybody would be so "broadminded," he says—but she refuses. He lets go of the pig and attacks her. "I hate you," she says, and adds, "I love him—I always will!" Schani's fat father, who can barely get through the doorway, stops the assault, but Schani vows to kill Nicki.

On the day of the wedding, the rains are heavy. During the ceremony the hands playing the organ turn into skeletal fingers, a grotesque and rather baroque way of suggesting the death of love and—in the light of the second part of the film—the further tragedy that is to come. The young bride, oblivious of Nicki's attachment, slowly limps down the aisle and says, "I love these apple blossoms." "So do I," he replies.

Outside, Mitzi waits in the rain. Schani is also there, with a gun in his pocket, ready to shoot Nicki. To save him, Mitzi promises to marry Schani. The bride and groom march by, with only the slightest glance from Nicki to his beloved. Schani hoists Mitzi onto his shoulders, the rain pouring down on her face, so that, in Schani's words, she can say "Ta-ta" to her lover for the last time. As Cecelia gets into the carriage, she asks who was that "sweet girl and that awful-looking man." Nicki says he does not know. The bride then says that the flowers will always remind her of the wedding, and Nicki replies, "Yes, always." A shot of the Iron Man fills the screen—"bringing sorrow, grief, and death," as an earlier title said—and so the film ends.

The Wedding March is in many ways Stroheim's greatest work; it is also his most personal film in almost every way. It was written by Stroheim and acted by him, and it touches upon many of his strongest obsessions. Mitzi and Cecelia are his most sensitively and sympathetically portrayed women. When Cecelia limps down the aisle and speaks about apple blossoms and when Mitzi waits in the rain with the reprehensible Schani, Stroheim reaches emotional heights he never quite achieved in his earlier films. He also gives human dimension to his own role, but he has not sentimentalized it. He portrays a sophisticated man who has been touched by love, and although he will not act on the emotion (that is, marry for love), he can feel it.

Stroheim has captured in this film what he has not achieved in others: genuine emotion and empathy. Audiences feel for the characters, particularly Mitzi, and few can be unaffected at the end of the film when she looks after the departing carriage with the rain pouring down on her saddened face.

The film's opening title, "Vienna—Anno Domini 1914," is not without its ironies and implications. This is indeed Vienna, the over-ripe capital city of an empire that is shortly to crumble, but it is also the year of God, and God is absent or certainly silent in this pitiful tale of greed and lust and love.

Many critics betray a kind of unconscious chauvinism when they praise Stroheim for showing the corruption of the old world, as if somehow the new had none. These critics seriously misinterpret Stroheim's *weltanschauung*. He chooses the decadence of Vienna for its exotic qualities, its style, and its splendor; it is not that Vienna is so extraordinarily decadent, though (what big city is not?), but rather that the city is an example of man's institutionalized, organized folly. To a moralist like Stroheim, every city is Vanity Fair, and he could easily have done the same for New York, although America's class structure is not so strikingly defined. After all, isn't *Greed* as strong an indictment of American life as any of Stroheim's other films are of life in Europe? Aren't the low-class friends of McTeague similar to Schani's family, and isn't Schani really Marcus Schuler with an Austrian accent? Stroheim is no debunker of the upper class only, as some leftist critics have tried to make him. He is beyond such simplicity; each segment of society receives its due.

Like all moralists, Stroheim is fascinated by man's evil and corruption. Sodom and Gomorrah are well-known cities because of their sins, far better known than more virtuous places of the Holy Land. Stroheim feels genuinely the sins and corruptions of the world; but, unlike most moralists, he is honest enough to acknowledge his own predilections toward sin. For this reason, he is never self-righteous—and this is perhaps his main strength as a commentator upon mankind. Ruthlessly, he examines the sensual and financial and social lusts of man. His depiction, however, does not reek entirely of tragedy. To him, life is a macabre comedy; it is this quality that preserves his work from being soft and sentimental or unremittingly grim.

Unfortunately, film critics betray that they are working with a young art and all too often reveal a partisanship that does injustice not only to themselves but also to the works they wish to defend. Faults are granted even to Shakespeare, but somehow to criticize a movie master is to invoke a fanatic's ire. *The Wedding March* is not a perfect work. At certain times Stroheim overstresses characterization to the point of caricature. For example, Schani spits too much; Stroheim does not have to continue to telegraph to his audience that Schani is not a delicate person. The apple blossom shots are perhaps also excessive, and certainly the frequent cutting to a nightingale brings the scene almost to the point of parody. Such a grotesque image as having the hands that play the organ during the wedding change to skeletal bones is effective once, but on repetition it loses much of its power. Some of these complaints might be due to the editing of the film by other hands. But these are matters of discretion. Although Stroheim's work may not be perfect, it is superb.

When *The Wedding March* was shown at the third New York Film Festival in 1965, Bosley Crowther proved himself singularly obtuse by calling the film "disappointing" and saying that "it is the sort of thing that should go no farther than the auditorium of the Museum of Modern Art."[18] Despite Crowther, the film was again exhibited at Lincoln Center on April 23, 1970. (I was present on both occasions and can testify to the fact that the film received tumultuous applause.)

The Wedding March is a film, to paraphrase one of the picture's titles, whose ruination must have made the gods weep. The word *genius* has often been used in terms of the cinema, but it would not be misapplied here. Stroheim was more than a grimy realist or a fabricator of continental sin who doggedly recorded miles upon miles of footage. Unlike Griffith, whose career faltered in the 1920s because he was repeating himself and not making full use of the cinematic language he had developed, Stroheim was growing. That his potential was never allowed to develop fully is an almost unspeakable tragedy.

11

The Honeymoon

The Honeymoon is a difficult film to assess for the simple reason
that the sole remaining print was destroyed in 1957. *The Devil's Pass
Key* suffered a similar fate, but this loss is the greater tragedy, for it was
a portion of one of Stroheim's greatest works. Fortunately, we can
draw upon written and photographic material to convey at least some
of its substance and effect. *The Wedding March* establishes the plot and
also acquaints us with the faces and personalities of the principal characters. Furthermore, we have a carefully delineated scenario as well as
a cutting continuity that describes every shot in terms of its length and
the camera's placement (long shot, medium shot, or close-up). In addition, there are a good number of stills to provide us with the look of
the scenes. These aids are by no means an adequate substitute for the
lost footage, but they can help show what Stroheim had intended. As a
result, the film may be gone, but it is not entirely lost.

Although *The Wedding March* was severely cut, its second part, *The
Honeymoon,* sustained even more drastic excision. In terms of the scenario, the second section of the film ran longer than the first, consum-
ing 87 pages of the 154–page script. Despite Stroheim's later assertion
that he did not finish putting the second part "together correctly," he

had taken its approximately 30,000 feet of unrepeated material and made a rough cut and, according to Herman G. Weinberg (not, I am afraid, an always reliable source in such matters), reduced it to 22,484 feet,[1] a little over four hours at sound speed. Even Stroheim acknowledged that the second part was too long, and he may have compressed it to between 15,000 and 20,000 feet (running about three hours). When he found himself incapable of trimming it further, the studio brought less gentle hands to bear. After much wrangling and, finally, wholesale butchery, all that remained of this footage was about 4,500 feet, approximately fifty minutes.

The story of *The Honeymoon* has hitherto been summarized in only a few paragraphs by other writers. Drawing upon the original scenario and the cutting continuity, I shall attempt to convey not only its content but, in some ways, its artistry.

At the conclusion of *The Wedding March,* Mitzi promised to marry Schani so that he would not kill her beloved Nicki at his wedding with Cecelia. The second part of the script begins with the title, "— Of all tales 'tis the saddest," adding that it is "more sad—because it makes us smile!—" The following scene shows an extremely unhappy Mitzi being measured for her wedding dress by a shriveled, hunchbacked seamstress, while Schani, in turn, is being measured by an extraordinarily skinny tailor. Shortly after, the families of the couple celebrate by opening some bottles of wine and toasting one another. Schani's vigorous slap on Mitzi's back causes her to drop her wine glass on the floor and break it. This is the first of many bad omens.

This episode, as well as one in which Nicki and Cecelia arrive at a train station in the mountains, is crossed out in the script. Part two, therefore, would probably have begun, as did the released *Honeymoon,* with a long shot of the mountains as Nicki's marriage coach races along. Suddenly a wheel falls off, the coach lurches to a halt, and Nicki falls almost on top of Cecelia in the "same position as he did with Mitzi so often." Nicki gets out and looks at the carriage. There is a dissolve to the fairy coach in Mitzi's apple orchard with apple blossoms all around it. Although Cecelia is shaken, she is not hurt. An old man on crutches looks at the broken carriage and the distraught characters, saying that it hints of bad luck to come.

The couple arrives at the castle, and servants greet them, nudging each other discreetly at Cecelia's limp. As the bride crosses the threshold, she slips and falls, another omen. (Recall that Mac in *Greed* trips on the threshold during his wedding.) Three old women servants, recalling the Fates, exclaim separately, "Grief," "Sickness," and "Death." Cecelia and Nicki climb the stairs and pass by a suit of armor, which reminds him of the Iron Man. In the script, this arrival required twenty-one shots and titles. All that remained in the release print were five shots of Nicki and Cecelia entering, lasting for one minute.

The script next calls for a scene (omitted from the film) in the cathedral, where skeletal fingers pull the celestial voice stop on the organ and play the wedding march. The unhappy Mitzi and the pleased Schani stand at the altar. As the ceremony proceeds, Mitzi faints and the hands stop playing the organ. The furious Schani—now aware that she will not marry him—swears to kill Nicki.

Cecelia and Nicki are in a room at the castle. He is bored and unhappy, and Cecelia tearfully acknowledges that she knows he married her for her money, adding that he also has to put up with her limp. She says rather desperately that she may not compare to his "gay and giddy" ladies, but she will do "anything." She wants just "one little bit" of his love. He pours her some champagne and grows slightly interested in his virgin bride. She tells him to make her drunk, asks for a cigarette, and gamely puffs on it. Suddenly she feels ill, and he laughingly reminds her that she said she would do anything. She stamps her foot, "I can—too." She takes another drink, then another cigarette. She seems appealing in her adoration and giddiness, and he says, "Let's go to bed!" "He looks rather sensuously and appraisingly at her—Cecelia becomes aware of Nicki's expression—she bows her head in modesty and then starts to giggle." After a moment, he "looks wonderingly at his little amorous wife—makes her face him and suddenly kisses her grossly on her mouth—she closes her eyes in ecstasy and trembles violently."

Nicki carries her up the stairway past suits of armor. He places her on the bed, and she covers her face with her hands, then peeks through her fingers at him. Looking "devilishly" at her, he starts to take her stockings off. Suddenly she grows fearful and, as if to distract him, points out the bridal bouquet of apple blossoms. He looks "wide-eyed" at the flowers and is reminded of Mitzi. "He slowly turns—looks at her—she looks at him lovingly—he looks away—CAMERA

MOVES BACK—Nicki sighs a bit—rises slowly—absent-mindedly looks at his wrist watch—then back to Cecelia AS CAMERA MOVES BACK."

Here Stroheim uses the moving camera for symbolic reasons to indicate Nicki's psychological withdrawal from her. Nicki cannot forget his loved one. Over the bridal bouquet appears superimposed the face of Mitzi. He feigns a yawn. Cecelia is "indescribably disappointed" as he coldly pats her head and prepares to depart. She embraces him, but he shakes his head, "smiling ironically," and leaves her. She looks at her taffeta sheets and cushions and beautiful honeymoon nightgown on the bed. The disappointed bride smiles bitterly, and tears come into her eyes. She suddenly grabs the nightgown, crumples it up and, in a tremendous fury, throws it into the corner and collapses onto the bed, sobbing. (These scenes between Nicki and Cecelia were included in *The Honeymoon*.) There is then a cross-cut to Schweisser and Nicki's father as he receives money for agreeing to the marriage.

The next morning Nicki decides to climb the mountain. Cecelia is crestfallen that he is leaving her. As he departs with the hunting party, she wishes him good luck. Nicki, almost gruff and with squinting eyes, hisses, "It's an ill omen to wish a hunter luck." She tearfully replies that she always seems to say or do the wrong thing. As he leaves, she climbs the staircase; she bumps into a suit of armor and slides down it, then collapses "into a little heap."

Schani arrives at the village by train, intending to kill Nicki, who has ruined his life because of Mitzi's refusal to marry him. He hires an idiot boy to lead him to the castle. Meanwhile, Cecelia, praying at the castle's chapel, seems to have a premonition. (In *Blind Husbands,* the heroine at the end of the film also has a premonition about her husband being in danger in the mountains.) Schani, somewhat drunk, begins his climb. Nicki, too, has been climbing and reaches the hut at the top of the mountain, where he is greeted by a comely peasant girl who points to a sign above the door: "On the Alps there is no sin." They laugh. (A similar sign appeared in *Blind Husbands.*)

Toward dusk, another train pulls into the station, its headlights "like two glaring eyes of a demon" (as in *Greed*). Mitzi gets off, finds that Schani has already arrived, and starts off to warn Nicki. Meanwhile, the equally worried Cecelia begins to climb to the hut. Mitzi arrives at the gatekeeper's place and learns that Nicki has gone up the mountain and that Schani, too, has recently passed by. When she asks for directions, the idiot offers his services; he looks lustfully at her.

At the top of the mountain, Schani sees Nicki playing a zither in front of the hut. He takes out his pistol, but, being drunk, he staggers, falls part way down the mountainside, and injures his head. Cecelia arrives with her entourage, overjoyed that the zither music means Nicki is still safe. Meanwhile, Mitzi, still climbing, pauses before a shrine to pray. The idiot is about to attack her when the lantern glare shows him the Madonna on the wayside shrine. His lust is momentarily thwarted but not eliminated.

At the hut, Cecelia is resting. She explains to Nicki that she would have died down in the valley worrying about him. He smiles sarcastically, saying that there is no danger, and pours her and himself some rum. Cecelia asks whether she can do anything for him. He looks astonished at her but does not reply. Finally, she limps over to the piano and offers to play. What would he like to hear? After a moment he asks whether she knows a piece called "Paradise." She does not, but if he would play the melody, maybe she could follow him. Pleased, and looking adoringly at Nicki, Cecelia begins to accompany him. The image dissolves to Mitzi's hands strumming her harp and to Mitzi's face, then back again to Nicki. Cecelia looks at him closely. "How lovely she must be—if you love her." He is perplexed. "Your eyes betrayed you," she says. He denies it, but she continues. "'Paradise' brought you wonderful memories of someone."

Nicki laughs, "but sheepishly," and says, "We better go to bed." She looks wonderingly at him as he leads her to the room. She stretches her arms out to him, but again he ignores her overture, politely bids her goodnight, and leaves. She sadly goes to sleep.

A lightning and hail storm whips up, and in this cosmic turmoil the idiot can restrain himself no longer and attacks Mitzi, but the frightened girl escapes his clutches. At the same time, Schani regains consciousness and again starts to climb. Stroheim crosscuts between Schani and Mitzi, then shows Cecelia awaken screaming from a nightmare. Nicki hurries in from his room and tries to comfort the terrified bride. Even Nicki starts to catch her fear. She cries out, "It's coming nearer." Intercut with her remarks, Schani and Mitzi encounter each other in the storm. She asks Schani whether he has killed Nicki, and he hisses, "No," but adds that he will.

Cecelia and Nicki become terrified when they see the front door of the lodge shake back and forth. Suddenly, from the darkness, Mitzi appears, soaking wet and scratched. She enters and slams the door shut as Nicki stares at this apparition. She gasps one word, "Schani," then sways and falls to the floor in a faint. He carries her to the couch, where she awakens and starts to sob uncontrollably. Cecelia stares at her. The image dissolves to the scene in front of the cathedral at the wedding in *The Wedding March*. Cecelia suddenly recognizes Mitzi and turns to the window, where she sees Schani's face appear in a flash of lightning. She throws herself on Nicki as Schani's gun fires. "Did you get hurt, Nicki?" she asks, and then her hand goes to her spine. Blood soaks through her back. Schani's face again appears at the window, then disappears. Several hunters awake and enter the room as Nicki explains what has happened. They rush out in pursuit.

Later, an extremely tall priest, a nun, and a doctor arrive. Nicki enters to comfort his wounded bride. He tells her not to be afraid. "I am so young," she says. "I don't want to die yet." Nicki is touched and tries to calm her. The priest and the acolytes enter for the last rites. "Don't leave me, Nicki," she says. "I love you so." They all kneel.

The doctor explains to Nicki that he is going to improvise a temporary spine brace. If Cecelia can lie quietly without the slightest movement, she will live perhaps "fifty years." She asks the doctor about the numbness in her legs. The doctor smiles as if this were a joke and cautions her about not moving. She understands now. She will be paralyzed. "Fifty years?" she asks. Two tears trickle down her cheeks.

Later, Mitzi, who is leaving, asks to see Cecelia. The wounded girl extends her hand, and Mitzi takes it. Cecelia observes Mitzi's convulsive sobs and asks, "Do you love him very much?" Still looking at the sobbing Mitzi, she says, "I love him, too!" then adds sadly, "but he loves you!" The injured girl asks, "Could you die for him gladly?" She studies Mitzi's face carefully and says, "I too." They look deeply and compassionately into each other's eyes.

Mitzi leaves, and, at a rock ledge, she accidentally meets Nicki standing with the priest. The two lovers look at each other, while Nicki's eyes fill with tears. Mitzi says, "Be kind to her," and bends closer to him, "*Very* kind." As she sadly departs, he stands there, a lonesome figure looking after the sobbing girl now running down the trail.

At night, the pendulum of the wall clock swings as it strikes eleven. Cecelia looks at the clock. While the doctor gives her medicine, Nicki stands close by. She asks him to play his violin for her. After some persuasion, the nun and Nicki go to the next room where he picks up his violin, and the nun sits at the harmonium. Cecelia asks that he play "Paradise." Nicki returns and looks at her, dumbfounded, but he "cannot hold her look, his eyes falter, he turns and exits." He plays for a bit and then stops, his eyes full of tears. Returning to her room, he bids her good night. She says, "Turn out the light," and continues, "Close the door." Cecelia indicates that she wants him to kiss her on the lips. He closes his eyes and does so, as she puts her arms around him.

> She lets go of Nicki—her hands playfully slide from his head to his shoulder and from his shoulder down his arms until they have found his hands—she is holding his hands—as if she would believe this is the last time she could hold Nicki's hands—her eyes bore themselves into Nicki's—the nun has lit the little night lamp and turns out the kerosene lamp, which leaves a weird lighting effect. . . . Cecelia turns and watches Nicki as long as she can see him with tremendously pathetic expression as if she would believe this to be the last time she would see Nicki. . . . She gazes wide-eyed into space.

In the next room Nicki breaks down, sobbing. "To lie there," he says to the consoling nun, "fifty years—until she is an old woman—" He pauses, looking at the nun, "and I an old man!" Cecelia overhears this. In the corner of the room, where a cross hangs, there appears a dim halo with rays emanating from where Christ's head would be. She takes this as a sign. "God have mercy on my soul," she says, "but I love him more than my life. Forgive me—Amen." She makes the sign of the cross, then starts to unstrap herself. The camera moves toward the cross, which slowly fills the entire screen—the light becoming more and more brilliant, and then fading out.

The nun enters the room, sees the bed empty, and finds Cecelia dead. Nicki "very tenderly takes Cecelia's body and lifts her from the floor into his arms." He places her on the bed, then takes a bunch of edelweiss and puts it between her folded hands. A title, "Upon such sacrifice the Gods themselves throw incense," concludes the sequence.

Mitzi returns to her family and informs them of what happened. Her furious mother blames everything on Mitzi and orders the "strumpet" and her father to get out.

The scene then shifts to the Rauffenberg mansion, with its main entrance draped in black. As Nicki stares at the glowing embers in the fireplace, his parents squabble. The mother smokes a cigar, and the father drinks a whisky and soda and endures a sneezing fit as he huddles before the fireplace. The mother says, "You are getting very old," and the father replies, "and of course—*you*—are getting *younger!*" He adds, "Pretty soon you'll have to shave twice a day." She kicks him in the shins. (This semicomic interlude is intended to set off the drama that has just preceded it, as well as to contrast with Nicki's quiet sorrow.)

Completely unmoved by Cecelia's fate, Nicki's parents rejoice in their good fortune. The mother says, "Your matrimonial venture was a *huge* success!" Nicki is astonished at her insensitivity. The parents cannot understand his sudden feeling for Cecelia, since the marriage had been a mere financial arrangement. When they question him about the money, he replies that he has not "examined the *loot* yet, mother dear." The family crest, Nicki notes, is now "plastered with gold." He adds, "In fact—cornplastered with gold!" Nicki studies the family motto and repeats, "Pro Gloria Deum—Patria—Et Familia" (in three separate titles). A forester enters and announces that Schani has been killed. Nicki and his parents glance at each other.

In the release print of *The Honeymoon,* the material from the tearful scene between Mitzi and Cecelia to the end of the film was butchered down to only three minutes. There are shots of Cecelia's casket, announcements that Mitzi has joined a convent and that Schani has been killed, and the concluding scene (much shortened) shows the family discussing its financial success.

Part three of Stroheim's script (only a portion of which was filmed) now begins. Mitzi wanders into the wine garden by herself and watches men saw down the apple tree, which falls and crushes the "fairy coach." Only the crucifix remains. Mitzi looks at the Adam and Eve statues, then leaves with her father. The Garden of Paradise is now ruined. Meanwhile Nicki, his parents, and Schweisser accompany Cecelia's casket to the cemetery.

"June passed—long weary summer days—then July dragged on to its close—" Nicki returns to the deserted wine garden, where a solitary waiter greets him. Looking at the spot where Mitzi used to play the harp, Nicki sees a dirtied sheet of music for "Paradise" lying on the ground. He picks it up and puts it in his pocket. He remarks that all the blossoms have gone. When he finds out that Mitzi and her father have left, he is shocked. He walks to the garden door, but it is locked: the way to Paradise is barred. Standing on a bench, he looks over the wall. In a shot framed with weeping willow branches, he sees the shattered buggy and the bare tree stump. The waiter asks him whether he has lost anything, then watches Nicki leave and scratches his behind.

Nicki gets Mitzi's address from the police and is horrified at the tenement. He learns from her father, who is living in great squalor, that Mitzi has entered a nunnery. Nicki arrives there and over the opposition of the mother superior insists on seeing Mitzi. He glances at a painting of Mary Magdalen. When Mitzi enters, he pleads with her to leave and declares his love. He also explains that Cecelia has died. He tells her, "We will follow spring around the world" and that he wants to see her framed in apple blossoms. Although she admits that she loves him, she says that she wants to find peace for herself. The mother superior leads her away.

In the next scene, Nicki arrives drunk at Madame Rosa's brothel. He decides not to go in, but some brother officers see him and insist that he enter. The scene switches to the Royal Palace, where the emperor signs the war decree. The Iron Man in double exposure walks toward the emperor and his ministers.

Back at Madame Rosa's, a big party is going on. The men pour champagne into a bathtub and then a young girl dressed in white is thrown into the bubbling drink, a scene reminiscent of one in *Merry-Go-Round*. The Iron Man in double-exposure enters. War has been declared, announce the newspapers. Although he does not have to, Nicki decides to go to war.

Men march, drums play, horses' hooves clatter over cobblestones, and tractors and mortars roll, followed by the title, "And even now—smiling carelessly—these young aristocrats—sons of a thousand years of forgotten knighthood—ride gaily away—to expiate their sins and frivolities—at a rendezvous—with a Grim Bride!—" Nicki prances his horse in front of St. Stephen's. "His Wedding March!" The scene then cuts to a convent church, where a young nun in white robes is led toward the altar. It is Mitzi. The organ is played by beautiful hands and the title "Her Wedding March!" appears. The church bells ring. Finis. This section of Mitzi taking her vows is crossed out in the script, so that the film would conclude with Nicki riding off to war, thus allowing the audience to believe that there may be a happy ending for the couple. At the bottom of the script was typed, "Powers Manor, Flintridge, Friday, April 23, 1926."

Appended to this saga was an undated fourth part. None of this section was filmed, perhaps wisely, although Stroheim might not have been happy about the omission. Most likely it was removed because it would have taken too long. There are no penciled scene numbers on it, indicating that it was not planned very thoroughly. Although Schani dies in *The Honeymoon*, he obviously is still alive in this version. In any case, here is a brief summary of this section, which has been hitherto unmentioned in print.

It opens at the convent of "The Bleeding Heart," set amid mountain crags near the Serbian border. As a consequence of the war, law and order have broken down, and a roving band of ruffians decides to attack the convent. Among them is a man dressed in a dilapidated uniform like Nicki's. It is Schani, whose intentions are clear: drink the wine and rape the better-looking nuns. Schani and the hunchbacked leader of the brigands inspect the women. Schani is surprised to see Mitzi and tells her that they came damn close to marrying once and now he is going to get closer still. The hunchback also takes a liking to her, which leads to a knife fight at the foot of the altar with the ruffians gathered around in a circle (an uncanny parallel to Luis Buñuel's 1961 *Viridiana*). In the meantime, the mother superior climbs down a cable from the tower and rides away on horseback to the headquarters of the troops! Nicki is told by the colonel to "ride like Hell and mop it up."

Back at the convent an orgy is raging. The ruffians force the nuns to drink wine, while Schani pulls Mitzi onto his lap. "You was always a good looker!—but now!—with this Nun's dress—you sure got me goin'—" These scenes are intercut with Nicki and his men riding to the rescue. Schani takes off his boots as he looks with an insinuating smile toward Mitzi. At this point Nicki and the dragoons enter and fight with the brigands. Grabbing a crucifix from the wall, Mitzi hits Schani. He twists it out of her hands, and, as he begins to attack her, she faints. Nicki breaks into the room, and the two adversaries confront each other. Schani throws himself at Nicki, who shoots him, the bullet penetrating Schani's forehead. Nicki discovers that the unconscious nun is Mitzi. Title: "—and again—there is no accident!—it is *Fate*—misnamed—"

Fade in on the convent garden, with an apple tree in bloom. Nicki is bandaged, and Mitzi is still in novice robes. After some discussion, they kiss. Fade out. Fade in on the now-restored convent chapel. The two are married. A battle draws near, and Nicki tells Mitzi that he has made out his will to her. "Our Wedding March," he says, as the guns fire. "Nobody can say—we didn't have a—lot—of music—" he adds, whimsically. She breaks off a sprig of her apple blossom bouquet, which he puts in his pocket, and he rides away with his troops. From the top of the tower, she watches him disappear into the distance, followed by images of guns booming. Final fade-out.

Admittedly, this section does round off the story, but a good part of it seems melodramatic and far weaker and less sensitive than the preceding parts. Its moral chaos will reappear in the African sequences of Stroheim's next work, *Queen Kelly.*

Stroheim was obviously a novelist at heart, an artist who wanted such full characterizations, such intricate plotting, and such effective symbolism that no one evening could possibly encompass his vision. To have the living, breathing drama he had filmed reduced to its mere bones seems a blasphemy. But every art form has its limitations; in film, it is length. For a film such as the uncut *The Wedding March,* with its close and sensitive examination of a small group of characters, only present-day television with its miniseries could allow it to be possible.

Because the material had already been filmed, *The Honeymoon* should have been released in its full-length form, because that would have entailed little further cost. The folly—if folly it was—had already been committed. But, alas, that was not to be. One thinks of the weathered, broken, and transported frieze of the Parthenon. What a fragmented remnant of a timeless vision!

One can easily criticize Stroheim for his insane dream to make lengthy films, but with the *Merry-Go-Round* script and this one of *The Wedding March,* his intransigence can at least be understood, if not quite forgiven. Stroheim's visions were simply too grand for the puny medium he worked in.

Stroheim would essay this imperial world once more in *Queen Kelly*, but the real energy and inspiration of *The Wedding March* would not return. In a sense, his passion had been expended and would only lamely be reprised in the later work. *The Wedding March* was his last great effort.

To those people who think that Stroheim had no heart, no idealism, no sensitivity, one can only reply, "*The Wedding March*." If he did not achieve genuine tragedy in this work, then no one has in the long history of film.

12

Queen Kelly

Although Stroheim's artistic connection to *The Wedding March* had virtually terminated by August 1927, he was not a free agent. He remained under contract to his angry producer, Pat Powers, to make another picture, with an option for two more. In no way did Powers want to use Stroheim again, but he would not allow him to work for any other "of the half dozen companies who are seeking his services as director, writer, or actor," said *Hollywood Filmograph.*[1] A generally smart operator, Powers could not understand how he had been so hoodwinked by the extravagant and irresponsible director. Feeling betrayed and facing miles of film that could not possibly become a single feature, he refused to release Stroheim from his commitment.

While idle but still legally constrained, Stroheim worked unofficially on a script of *The Tempest,* which dealt with the Russian aristocrats being brought down by equally arrogant revolutionaries. Lewis Milestone planned to direct this vehicle, starring John Barrymore, for United Artists. Eventually, it was directed by Sam Taylor, and its story credit was given to C. Gardiner Sullivan. This tale of a "poor dragoon and a proud princess in the last long calm before the red tempest of terror," as an opening title puts it, has many Stroheimian elements. A nasty officer (Ulrich Haupt, in a sneering portrayal that has many of Mirko's mannerisms in *The Merry Widow*) puts out his cigarette on the back of a soldier's neck. After the revolution, the soldier retaliates by burning the officer with a cigar! George Fawcett, who played Nicki's father in *The Wedding March,* is a Russian general. The aristocratic heroine (Camilla Horn) is perversely bitchy and, in one scene, whips the Barrymore character. There are other touches reminiscent of Stroheim, besides the hateful acts of the villain, which remind one of his Hun portrayals: in one scene, when the heroine is bathing naked, her clothing is taken away; in another episode, the hero passes by a nude statue and salutes it.

Although Barrymore acts his role with his usual skill and panache, he is much too classy to be wholly believable as a peasant. The film is otherwise well done, but it lacks the directorial touches that would have made it memorable. The collapse of the old regime and the victory of an unsavory proletariat was a theme close to that of *Merry-Go-Round* and *The Wedding March* and would certainly have intrigued Stroheim if he had been allowed to direct *The Tempest.*

While Stroheim was embroiled with the problems of editing *The Wedding March* and squabbling with Powers, another confident Irishman, Joseph P. Kennedy, now entered his life. A relative novice in the movies, Kennedy had become entranced with Gloria Swanson, the famous star who left Paramount in 1926 to become an independent producer for United Artists. Considering himself incapable of bad judgment, Kennedy began to arrange her life both personally and financially. Besides bedding Gloria, he convinced her to form Gloria Productions, which he and his associates would manage. He claimed that under his brilliant guidance they would earn a great deal of money. His overwhelming desire was to make an "important" film, not only for her but for himself, because he wanted to be known as the world's greatest producer. For his initial project, he needed a good script and a gifted director. The undoubted skills of the presently unemployed Stroheim appeared to meet his needs. As Swanson wrote in her autobiography, Kennedy "was anxious to enter the temple of art in the company of an acknowledged genius."[2] And soon, like Powers, he succumbed to the seductive Stroheim.

Swanson had recently made *The Love of Sunya* (1927), which did fairly well at the box office, and then had embarked on *Sadie Thompson* (1928), which Kennedy assured her would fail. In fact, it proved to be a great financial success, the first instance of Kennedy's poor but consistent judgment. Raoul Walsh not only starred in *Sadie Thompson* but directed it as well, and his strong guidance gave new life to Swanson's career. Kennedy now hoped that Stroheim could enhance it further by making a success like *The Merry Widow.* Swanson, however, had her reservations. She asked Kennedy whether Stroheim, with his "growing reputation for being an undisciplined spendthrift, a hopeless egotist, and a temperamental perfectionist," was a good choice. Kennedy assured her, "I can handle him."[3]

At Swanson's first meeting with Stroheim, she found him "gracious and charming but at the same time aloof and conceited." Whenever Stroheim made "a lofty observation, Joe would look at me and smile broadly enough to show his teeth, like a dog who had run up out of the garden and presented me with a choice bone he had uncovered, as if to say, What do you think of that?"[4]

Stroheim then began to tell his story, called *The Swamp,* which traced the life of Patricia Kelly, a convent girl, who is wooed by a prince and then called to Africa by her aunt and put in charge of a brothel named The Swamp. At the end, she returns to marry the prince. Swanson felt that Stroheim knew Kennedy would warm to this tale of an Irish-Catholic girl. The story seemed satisfactory, and by March 1928 Swanson was reading a massive completed script.

However, Stroheim was still contracted to Powers. Finally, Powers and Kennedy had a talk, and by the end of April, the trade papers declared that Stroheim would return to direction with a Swanson vehicle. The director confidently informed the press that there would be no delays or squabbling and that the film would not take long to shoot. These were familiar words. When United Artists announced that it would soon release *The Swamp,* exhibitors disapproved of this unappealing title and urged a change. Although Stroheim firmly disagreed, he finally relented and the title was altered to *Queen Kelly.* The press was told that Stroheim would need eight weeks to work out the continuity and two weeks more "to prepare and cast" the film. Stroheim described it as "a sort of beautiful love tale," one which "will command as great attention as *The Wedding March* will when it is finally released." *The Hollywood Filmograph* concluded:

> the much talked of ban on the famous director's either wielding a megaphone, acting or writing for the screen, has been lifted and don't be surprised at all if when von Stroheim fin-

ishes the Gloria Swanson picture, that he will sign to make
three pictures for one of the largest producing firms now making pictures on the West Coast; when seen by Ye Editor Erich
von Stroheim was elated with the outlook for his future and
thanked *Hollywood Filmograph* for the hearty co-operation and
support that we had tendered him and his fight for his rights
in the P.A. Powers matter.[5]

Everything looked rosy as Stroheim began the project that would help
doom his career.

Through the summer of 1928, Stroheim worked on the script and
made a revised shooting schedule of twelve weeks for a 510-scene
film. By August 4, the press was informed that "the transformation of
the impish little Irish girl into 'Queen Kelly,' mercenary woman of
the world," would grant Swanson "a range of characterization un-
equalled in any previous picture."[6] Walter Byron, a young English
actor, was hired to play the prince. Production was to begin on November 1.

   During the summer and fall, the film industry began to revise its
views on talking pictures. Earlier, in May, the *Hollywood Filmograph*
opined that "it is extremely unlikely that the spoken [film] will ever
entirely—or even to a great extent—replace the silent drama." This
opinion soon changed. In July, Warner Bros. released its first all-talking
picture, *The Lights of New York,* and then in September, the mostly
talking *The Singing Fool,* with Al Jolson. Both were extraordinary successes. In September and October, Paramount, Fox, First National, and
MGM released other synchronized (but not dialogue) films. Certain
Hollywood chieftains, such as Joseph Schenck of United Artists, sagely
declared in September that talking pictures would not survive and that
"audiences will continue to patronize silent pictures."[7] The always
shrewd Mary Pickford knew better, though, and announced that her
next film would be in sound. Most of the other studio bosses shared
her opinion and began constructing stages for the production of talking pictures. On October 12, *The Wedding March* finally appeared, accompanied by a music track on discs. The next week, Universal and
Warner Bros. released two all-dialogue pictures, and the next week
two more. (There was usually a several-month wait between the

completion of a film and its release, meaning that these films were made during the summer of 1928.)

In an article written during July or August 1928, director Paul Sloane declared that "the scramble for sound-proofing goes wildly on" and Hollywood stars are frantically trying "to stem the tide of disaster by studying the use of their voices." He said, "The panic is on! *Hysteria Talkerfilmus* is upon us!"[8] But no panic seemed to affect the great Kennedy or Swanson. In the fall of 1928, Fox shot *In Old Arizona* (released in January 1929), and MGM made *The Broadway Melody* (released in February). Even though A budget productions by the other studios were being conceived as talking pictures in late 1928, Kennedy, Swanson, and Stroheim, who should have known that talkies were the coming mode, were getting their script ready and preparing the sets for an expensive silent effort!

Stroheim was to begin filming on November 1, but the sets were not quite finished, so he shot some of the country scenes (which later were reshot after Paul Ivano took over as cameraman). Thus, at its start, the film was already one week behind schedule. In 1971, Swanson, who threw nothing out, left papers concerning this film to the Eastman House, where Richard Koszarski examined them. In an appendix to his book *The Man You Loved to Hate*, he reproduced Stroheim's daily shooting schedule.

Normal shooting days for most Hollywood productions ran from 8 or 9 A.M. to 5 P.M., but Stroheim quickly changed that. He began a six-day-a-week regimen with filming beginning at 8 A.M., then later, 9 A.M., and running until late at night and often far into the morning. Of the first forty-two shooting days, twenty lasted until after midnight. On December 18, Stroheim concluded at 5 A.M.; on December 19, at 5:55 A.M.;, on December 20, at 2:20 A.M.;, and on December 21, at 5:30 A.M. These records of the actual shooting times prove that an article in *Film Weekly*, dated December 31, 1928, was probably no exaggeration: "Extras are swooning daily on the set from overwork, and that work goes on all night and continues through the day without a break."

Swanson, in her autobiography, wrote that Stroheim "was so painstaking and slow" that scenes that would have been "wrapped up in an hour" with other directors "might take Von Stroheim all day, fondling and dawdling over the tiniest minutiae."[9] There were squabbles with the actors, with the cameramen, and with other technicians, as well as countless delays over sets, costumes, and props. Nerves no doubt became even more frayed as fewer and fewer pages of the script were being completed each day. Admittedly, Stroheim's demands may have seemed unreasonable, and no doubt some were, but the film truly is a handsome-looking one.

Stroheim shot the film roughly in sequence and by Christmas had completed the opening European section; this took forty-three shooting days, plus two additional days later. On January 2, when work began on the African section, the film—despite the long hours—was one month behind schedule. On January 6, Swanson held a story conference concerning the length of the film, and Stroheim reluctantly dropped an expensive and long section from the script. Work continued, but in the second week of January, Swanson held another meeting to discuss how sound could be added to certain episodes, because the popularity of talking pictures was growing rapidly. On January 20, a Sunday, she spent the day screening the rushes of the brothel scenes, in which a revolting crowd of low-lifes hover around the newly married Kelly; her groom, a degenerate old wreck (Tully Marshall), shakily approaches her, but she threatens to kill herself with a pair of scissors if he touches her. On Monday morning at 9 o'clock, Swanson, Stroheim, and the crew began the seventeenth day of filming this African section. As the hours proceeded, two shots were made, then Stroheim began on a medium close-up of the groom dribbling tobacco juice on Swanson's hand. The star was disgusted by the action, saw nothing entertaining in it for the public, and realized that they were progressing more slowly than ever. By 7 o'clock that night, three hundred feet had been exposed, but Stroheim would not deem any take acceptable. Suddenly the nerves of the wearied and worried Swanson broke. She telephoned Kennedy in Miami, and he called Stroheim and fired him. This costly decision did not affect Kennedy directly, for Swanson was to find out that the only money lost was her own!

Although the project had been one month off schedule, the January 6 script revision took up most of the slack, and when Stroheim was fired he was not more than two or three weeks behind, and possibly four or five weeks from completion. Stroheim later said that four hundred thousand dollars had been spent and that another four hundred thousand dollars would have completed the film. Swanson often stated that she had lost eight hundred thousand dollars on it. Whatever the figures, the production was temporarily halted. No one ever thought it would be abandoned.[10]

A number of factors were responsible for the halt. (1) It was clear that talkies were the coming mode and that sound, in some fashion, would have to be added to the picture. (2) Stroheim was stressing certain aspects of the script that would prove censorable or at least unpleasant. (3) Stroheim was taking more time than he should; if the film had adhered to normal working hours, it would have taken almost double the number of shooting days. (4) The wearied Swanson, solely in charge of the production, cracked under the pressure. (5) She had had conversations with director Edmund Goulding, who seemed to have sensible ideas about talkies, and who convinced her to get on the profitable bandwagon of dialogue films.

The film called *Queen Kelly* that Swanson eventually released—it includes only the European section—appears to be one of Stroheim's weakest efforts. Separated from the African footage, which would have added thematic strength and visual contrast, it becomes a rather trite love story only partially redeemed by handsome sets and beautiful photography. Unfortunately, it has a slow pace, the result of creating a feature-length film out of what had been just a portion. Stroheim himself, upon seeing the film years later, complained that it dragged because more shots were used than he had intended.

> In order to get a satisfactory laughing scene from one of the actors, I made him laugh several times in several different ways in succession, so as to be able to select the best one for the finished print. Now, in Gloria's version, we have every one of that actor's successive laugh sequences all following each other, in order to "pad out" the picture. Many times, when I intended only to show a flash of a scene on the screen, this version runs the whole scenes right through to the bitter end. This makes the film appear to drag, and for that reason the present version is a bitter disappointment.[11]

Stroheim is right, to some extent. Swanson perhaps used one face, then cut to another, and then went back to the first face, thus stretching out the scene. But this was not the major problem. The major problem was that Stroheim filmed more episodes than were necessary. If he complained that too many scenes were used, one could well ask why he had filmed them all in the first place. Here lies Stroheim's basic problem. Although the European section was intended only as a preface to the African footage, he had already photographed enough action to make a feature-length picture. One must conclude that Stroheim had not cured himself of his propensity for filming in extenso and was well on his way to another multihour epic.

Some criticism could also be leveled against Stroheim's producers, who knew that he had a fatal tendency toward long films and yet, somehow, approved gigantic shooting scripts. Everyone in power who read these scripts (did anyone really *read* them?) must have been carried away by Stroheim's imagination and his detail, because no one had the strength or foresight to trim the excess before shooting began. Kennedy could be forgiven, as a novice, but not Swanson.

Years later, Stroheim, with his selective memory, chose to attribute *Queen Kelly*'s demise to the introduction of sound, as if somehow the magic of talking pictures had suddenly appeared in the midst of shooting, and the film was halted solely for that reason, not because of any fault of his own. He said that "scandal-mongers . . . searched diligently for any other possible reason for the sudden end of the film, and hearing nothing from Gloria nor from me, they invented internal strife, stories of 'difficulties on the set,' and so on, all of which were lies."[12]

Queen Kelly was the last of Stroheim's imperial films and, in terms of the European section, the least interesting. The wit and irony and humor have weakened. For once, the characterizations are not vivid enough. Although Walter Byron, as the prince, is handsome, he lacks the dash of John Gilbert in *The Merry Widow* and has none of the sardonic persona that enlivens Nicki in *The Wedding March*. And Swanson's heroine is not as vivacious as Mae Murray or as lovely and sensitive as Fay Wray. In short, Stroheim is going through the motions. In his other imperial films there is depth, not only in the characters but also in how they are seen in a historical-social context. As a result, one regrets the severe editing they endured. But *Queen Kelly* offers merely a pretty girl and a handsome prince, with no milieu in which to place them. The film lacks depth and passion, and no one wishes the film were any longer. Perhaps in the African section Stroheim would have become more inspired, but unfortunately, most of that was not shot. Of the few scenes included in a "restored" print now available, the photography, the lighting, and the faces seem more engaging than the subject matter itself.

As the film now stands, it concentrates on the prince. Only during the African scenes would Swanson's character, now on center stage, have been placed in the limelight. Even so, the film, if completed, would not have been the star vehicle that Swanson's fans would have relished. With the African section missing, the film is wholly out of balance and, as a result, unsatisfying.

Queen Kelly opens with Queen Regina the Fifth (Seena Owen) lying in her bed. Although she is naked, nothing is censorable because vital parts are hidden and a white cat is draped across her bosom. On the table are the memoirs of Casanova and the tales of Boccaccio; close by, a crucifix rests on a Bible. Stroheim's fascination with juxtaposing the sacred and the profane never left him.

The character of this decadent queen is described not by titles but by the visuals. An ashtray full of cigarettes and various kinds of cigars reveals that she likes variety in the bedroom. She spends her time making love, drinking champagne, and taking veronal (a barbiturate). This, then, is the queen, the mad queen, the diseased flower of a decadent society, who, as a title concludes, knows "no law but her own desires." (She is similar to Gisella in *Merry-Go-Round,* who wildly rides her horses, toys with a groom, smokes cigars, and is a liberated soul who falls into prostitution when her aristocratic standing collapses.) The queen's affections are centered on a prince of a distant line, "Wild Wolfram," a young and handsome rake whom she plans to marry. The humor of the "Wolf" is intended, and the other part of his name, Falsenheim, is likewise not to be ignored. Although this is a kind of fairy tale about a beautiful queen and a handsome prince, it is hardly one geared for children.

Wolfram, returning with a bevy of girls from an all-night party, falls drunkenly off his horse at the entrance of the palace. There is a superb shot of him walking across a highly polished black and white marble floor, climbing the graceful shining steps of the grand staircase, and collapsing between his footmen. The scene ends as the prince is carried up the stairs, the contrast of elegant architecture and inelegant behavior remarkably clear.

In his bed, the prince drunkenly sleeps. Behind him is a statue of a man and a woman in an embrace (Rodin's *The Kiss*), and around his bedroom stand other statues of nudes. The irate queen visits him and hovers over his bed as Wolfram tries to focus on her. Stroheim provides a quick shot of her white cat hissing at Wolfram's dogs, which (like the birds and the cat in *Greed*) suggests the relationship of the humans. Annoyed at him, the queen says she will make an important announcement the next day and therefore orders him to drill on the Kambach Road with his regiment so that he will keep out of trouble and be "in condition" for her.

But Wolfram is one of those men who find trouble and delight wherever they go. On the road he meets a number of maidens from a convent, among them the pretty and vivacious Patricia Kelly (Gloria Swanson).[13] As Wolfram, on horseback, stops to observe her, a calamity befalls the young girl: her underpants fall down. Seeing them around her ankles, Wolfram begins to laugh, but when she realizes why he is amused, she kicks them off in a rage and throws them at him. He catches the missile, but before he puts it in his saddlebag, he sniffs her underpants. As he brings them to his nose, a portion of this censorable shot has been spliced out, as evidenced by a slight jump in the action. The nuns are shocked, as are the other girls, and they begin retreating to the convent. But Wolfram, not easily deterred, rides alongside Kelly. Finally, in answer to her pleas, he orders his troops "eyes right" and throws back her underwear. At this moment, a farmer's wagon comes by loaded with new-mown hay, hay that seems to cry out for use as nature's own couch. A shot of the top of the wagon reveals the bare, stocky legs of a peasant girl. Wolfram and Kelly each take a sprig of the hay, and he promises to see her again. As they recede in the distance, a roadside cross broods over the bucolic scene.

That night at the convent, when Kelly is questioned about her conduct, the girl asks the mother superior what she would have done if *her* pants had fallen down. This question provokes snickers among the sisters and then punishment for Kelly. She is ordered to refrain from supper and to pray. In a superb scene, she moves from a statue of Christ to one of the Virgin and Child, where she says, "Forgive me," but adds, "Please let me see him again." Candles flicker in the foreground, the wax drips slowly, and her face, bathed in candlelight, looks beatific. She is full of adoration, not of God but of Love. (This is the scene used in *Sunset Boulevard* when Swanson shows William Holden a film clip from her past.)

That evening, during a state dinner at the palace, the queen announces that Wolfram will not marry her later in August but instead on the very next day. He drops the saltcellar in surprise. At this bad omen, he throws salt over his left shoulder—a bit of superstition typical of Stroheim.

Later that evening, another officer taunts Wolfram that he has smelled new-mown hay for the last time. On a screen that divides the room are numerous photographs of previous conquests, and a crucifix lies next to a nude statue on the bureau. Wolfram examines the little bundle of hay (which he and Kelly had shared on the road) and, disagreeing with his friend's prophecy, decides to heed Hamlet's advice and get himself to a nunnery.

Climbing a ladder, he and his brother officer enter the convent through a bathroom window and are faced with a series of doors. Stymied only for a moment, Wolfram starts a fire, which sets off an alarm. When the girls run out of their rooms, he spies Kelly, picks up the fainting girl, and carries her down a ladder framed by a tree in blossom. (This blossoming tree is reminiscent of the orchard in the love scene in *The Wedding March*.) As Wolfram leaves the gate of the convent, the sign, "Magdalenen Kloster," is visible. The name of Magdalen, the fallen woman who became pure, functions, of course, ironically. The prince takes Kelly away in his car—the only evidence of the twentieth century in the film.

At the palace, the prince's footmen close the drapes; they know what is coming. Wolfram quickly gets rid of his officer friend and wakes the girl from her swoon. As in a fairy tale, she finds herself in a palatial room containing exotic foods and a charming prince, if not exactly a Prince Charming. When she asks where she is, he tells her how he removed her from the convent (a long scene of recapitulation, which Stroheim, one hopes, would have condensed). Overcoming her fear and marveling at his audacity—Kelly has spirit—she sits at a table before the fireplace and sips the champagne given to her. Naively, she wrinkles her nose at its effervescence. On a plate next to the champagne lie oysters on the half shell. (They can be seen clearly in a still photograph of the scene.) Stroheim, no doubt, recalled Casanova's theory that oysters are an aphrodisiac. The drink quickly affects Kelly's mind just as the fireplace affects her body. She starts to take off her coat—it is his officer's coat—but stops when she realizes that she is in her nightdress. She crosses the room to search for her day clothes (which he has hidden); her backside wriggles high in the air as she hangs over the back of the couch seeking her outfit.

A few seconds later, as she stands in front of a three-sided mirror, the sight of her pretty face and her lovely body draped in his coat appeals strongly to the prince. Is there a sexual aberration hinted at here, or does her male attire merely add piquancy to her beauty? He pins some orchids on her lapel (the orchid is frequently likened to a woman's sex organ) and, with a sudden wave of desire, embraces her. His hand is seen in the mirror going around her shoulder, the reflection adding a less romantic aspect of voyeurism to the scene.

Then they proceed to the balustrade. Flowers grow profusely in stone vases, and a full moon shines in the dark sky. It is the classic setting for transforming the prince from a mere rake into a full-fledged lover, one who at least temporarily succumbs to the spell he was weaving for another. He embraces Kelly and carries her to his bedroom.

Meanwhile, Queen Regina has finished her bath. Donning a seductive black gown trimmed with white fur and carrying her cat, she investigates the prince's apartment. Hearing his voice, she goes out on the balustrade and looks through the gauze curtain of the French door. Her face is photographed in a close-up, the crossweave of the curtain like a matte before her face. Furious, she enters, grabs a whip from the wall, and starts after the couple. First, she hits Wolfram and, when he restrains her, she asks indignantly how he dare raise his hand against his queen. She then turns to Kelly, who retreats to the door. When the young girl hears that Wolfram is to be married the next day, the camera looks down upon her to emphasize her pitiful state. Jealous and enraged, the queen pursues her down the hall, whipping her insanely and no doubt getting a certain pleasure out of it. In despair, Kelly jumps into the castle moat.

Here, in Swanson's released and modified print, Stroheim's intentions end. The subsequent footage of the prince in prison and of the queen has been given new captions. The queen agrees to release him with the proviso that if he does not marry Kelly within the day he will have to marry the queen. Overjoyed, he leaves his cell and its pitiful geranium and rushes to the convent. In the retitled version, and in new footage, he finds Kelly's dead body. He then takes out his sword and stabs himself, as the camera backs away and the film ends.

In the original script, Kelly is saved from the water of the castle moat by a policeman and is returned to the convent. A telegram from Dar es Salaam says that her aunt has had a stroke. The prince, imprisoned for a six-month term, plays his violin, serenading Kelly's nightgown hanging on his cell wall.

Kelly arrives in Africa and is taken to a low-class brothel on Poto-Poto Street. The place is full of characters who could easily have come from Polk Street in *Greed*. The aunt, rendered deaf and dumb by her stroke, writes a note to inform Kelly that she is broke and that the girl should marry a rich planter, Jan Vryheid (Tully Marshall). This degenerate man hobbles around on crutches (like Baron Sadoja in *The Merry Widow*, also played by Marshall). The last rites are given to the aunt by a bevy of priests while the wedding proceeds, officiated by a black priest. A piece of mosquito netting is used for a veil, and someone gives Kelly an artificial orchid (contrasting, of course, with the fresh orchid in the European sequence). This combination wedding-funeral recalls a similar juxtaposition in *Greed*. Just as the wedding concludes, the aunt dies. Jan orders Kelly to prepare for bed and joins the revelers downstairs to celebrate. He invites the crowd up to their room, but Kelly takes a pair of scissors and threatens to kill herself. She will do anything but sleep with him. (It is at this point that filming ended.) When Jan introduces her to the mob as the brothel's new madam, Kelly grabs his crutch and chases them all out of her room, then stops to ponder a cigarette and a glass of whiskey she has been given. Here would have come a ten-minute intermission.

Eight months later, the brothel has been given class. Kelly is a sexy creature with a police dog, orchids, and whips, seemingly a parody of Queen Regina. A cruiser arrives in the harbor, carrying the prince, a fact that she has learned from a newspaper. She goes to the pier to welcome him, but realizes what she has become. She burns a letter he has sent her. The prince sidesteps the official ball and goes immediately to Poto-Poto. Kelly is depressed and contemplates suicide, but instead she goes downstairs and flirts with sailors from the ship. Jan, who has not slept with her, suddenly demands his marital rights. Hysterical, she offers herself to the mob, who rush Jan. He fires his gun at them and is killed. As the crowd fights over Kelly, a huge Oriental runs upstairs after her. The prince arrives, struggles with him, and is knocked out. She takes poison, but the prince revives, knocks out the attacker, and retrieves the girl, who explains that she has kept herself clean for him. A doctor arrives with a stomach pump and the prince goes to pray; his prayers are answered. Not only does Kelly live, but also a telegram announces the death of Queen Regina. Kelly thinks the prince will now leave her, but he says she is coming with him. Back in Europe, they are married. She concludes with almost the same line that Prince Danilo uttered in *The Merry Widow*: "Majesty—me foot! Just plain Queen Kelly." This dramatic action at the end of the film is quite close to the lurid melodrama of the third part of *The Wedding March*, when Schani attacks Mitzi and Nicki comes to the rescue.

There is no doubt that Stroheim is repeating himself in this film, taking parts of *Greed, The Merry Widow,* and *The Wedding March,* and making a pastiche out of them. The social context, missing from the European section, enters in the African one. Undoubtedly Stroheim wanted to contrast Europe and Africa. In his mind, Africa became a moral Death Valley. One could easily repeat McTeague's line, "God, what a country," for in this Africa there is no control, no civilization, no grace, no style. Everything is low. It is the underside of the world, figuratively as well as literally. These contrasts are leveled by sex—despite class, it is at the bottom of everything—and rather nasty sex, at that.

The story seems an odd tale for Gloria Swanson to want to appear in, all pretty dream touched with nightmare in the European section and almost all nightmare in the African section. Could the unlikely happy ending have satisfied a mass audience?

In retrospect, Swanson's decision to stop production was a disaster both for Stroheim and for her. She could have cut out the raunchiest scenes, threatened Stroheim with professional suicide if he did not shape up (would he have listened?), and shortened but completed the African section in a few more weeks, probably after some retakes. If Stroheim refused to do them, she could have hired someone else. The film might have been in release by spring 1929 and would have recouped at least some of its cost because of the box-office strength of Swanson and Stroheim. Furthermore, the publicity value about "ruining" another masterpiece would have helped attract attention. The sets were there, the costumes had been made, the cast was under contract, and time was of the very essence. Alternatively, Swanson could have quickly released just the first part (as she later did), perhaps making a part-talkie of it by adding dialogue. Even just a music track and a theme song sung by her would have made this silent film a marketable product during the late spring or the summer. In fact, there were still some silent pictures released toward the end of 1929, such as Greta Garbo's *The Kiss* (November 1929). When Swanson irrationally had Kennedy fire Stroheim, she perhaps felt that Edmund Goulding would pick up the pieces and finish the film in a hurry, as Rupert Julian had done with *Merry-Go-Round*.

Instead of that, with the departure of Stroheim, the project lost all momentum, for his was the venture's only controlling brain. Panicked, Swanson sought advice from all kinds of experts. Everyone had a different opinion. She hired Benjamin Glazer, who had worked on *The Merry Widow;* he concocted a script about a former convent girl in love with a prince, who discards her to marry the queen. Although the prime minister and the police commissioner try to hush up the affair, she sings at the wedding and makes their relationship known. An orchestra conductor is in love with her and has faith in her voice and her future career. Finally, she leaves both men and goes to Paris to pursue a career.[14] This elaborate plot drew on some of the existing footage but did not exactly please Swanson. And rightly so. It is awful. Furthermore, it would have required a lot more filming and, thus, expense.

When production was stopped, Edmund Goulding—eager to make his name as a director—convinced Swanson that it would be easier to create a new film, a talking one, than to spend time on the old picture. In three weeks, he wrote a scenario. Production began almost immediately, and after eighteen days of shooting, *The Trespasser* was in the can. Copyrighted in July, it was released in October 1929 and ran 8,223 feet.

Swanson then returned to rescuing *Queen Kelly.* Of the 206,304 feet of negative shot, 129,835 were considered acceptable. She hired other scriptwriters, obtained a new director (Richard Boleslawsky), and began shooting in December 1929. Within a few days they had twelve minutes of usable material, but Swanson grew discouraged. More script doctors were called in.

Let us examine the existing film and see what might have been done, if it had been transformed into a talkie. The opening sequence of the losing of the drawers could have been "saved" by a couple of close-ups of Swanson and the prince speaking. The scene in the church, where Kelly is punished, could have been "rescued" by a talking head of the nun. The banquet episode would have needed only unsynchronized sound effects of dishes and voices and could have been enlivened with two smirking waiters in the kitchen providing exposition. The rescue scene during the fire would have been satisfactory with some agitato music; the private midnight repast could have been reshot with dialogue at no great cost; the action of the queen spying on the couple and then beating the girl does not need dialogue; the despairing queen could have died off camera from a drug overdose; and the prince could have announced that he would not be the king without the woman he loved. Two weeks of additional shooting might have saved the footage. If Swanson could make a whole talking feature in a few weeks, why couldn't she have doctored *Queen Kelly* in the same period of time? A smart woman with knowledgeable friends, she could easily have turned a total loss into at least a partial success. Certainly Thalberg would have rescued the film. Unfortunately, those around Swanson had their own interests rather than hers at heart.

Instead of finishing with *Queen Kelly,* Swanson turned her attention to another new project, *What a Widow,* released in September 1930. During this time, revised and "improved" versions of the *Queen Kelly* script were bouncing around her office. Toward the end of 1931, she finally decided against any radical revisions and issued the film in a form very much like the original. She omitted the African sequences but kept almost the entire European section. All she did was change some of the concluding titles and tack on a short new ending, shot on November 24, 1931.

In early 1932, the film was ready and submitted to United Artists for release—three years too late to be marketable. The distributor rejected it as an inferior product. As a result, *Queen Kelly* failed to get any commercial showings in the United States, although it did play in an art house in Paris in late 1932, and perhaps in a few other places in Europe. Basically, the project was a total loss. The temper flare-up of January 21, 1929, came close to bankrupting Swanson—her stardom

ended almost completely in 1934—and helped ruin Stroheim's reputation. The industry concluded that the man was simply impossible.

In *Queen Kelly,* Stroheim once again proves himself a meticulous
observer of detail and a marvelous stylist, but also an artist who could
not subjugate the part to the whole. He was incapable of fading out on
his hero at the palace and fading in on a long shot of the convent and
then dissolving to an interior shot of him looking for the girl. Instead,
he chose to show the hero entering, walking down the corridor, glancing at each of the closed doors, and deciding to start a small fire to
smoke her out. This was followed by numerous shots of the smoke-
filled corridors. Then, after the girl is found, Stroheim showed many of
these things again as the hero escapes with her. In practical terms, he
needed only to have his hero start the fire and peer through the smoky
corridors until the girl came out, fainting. The hero could then have
picked her up, as the scene faded out. The next scene could have opened
with the girl already in the palace. Nothing in terms of characterization would have been lost, and a week's shooting would have been
avoided.

In September 1985 a "restored" version of *Queen Kelly* played in
New York and was later released on videotape. The ending that Swanson
had provided in 1931 has been removed, and the African footage as
well as a few stills have been added. Although one is grateful for a
chance to see the African footage, this restored version, now clearly a
fragment, is even less satisfactory than the earlier one.

If the film had been completed, its artistic success would still be
doubtful. The tale of an innocent girl immersed in a sordid African
setting was hampered by several problems. At thirty-one, Swanson was
a little too old to play the part of a convent girl. She could not quite
hide her age, nor could her acting obscure the fact that she was too
worldly and sophisticated for the part. The youth and innocence of a
Fay Wray seemed beyond her. The scenes in Africa, when she becomes
the proprietress of the house of ill repute, would have been more credible. But one wonders if audiences would have enjoyed seeing their
beloved Swanson thrust amid the sordid grotesqueries of Stroheim's
imagination.

What coursed through Stroheim's mind after he was fired? Obviously, he had not learned any lessons from his previous experiences. As
he saw it, the fault lay, as usual, in others, not himself. Naively, he

assumed that this disaster would quickly be forgotten. But in the motion picture world, dedicated to profit and entertainment, it was not forgotten. Such an impossible spendthrift as Stroheim seemed to have become anathema. He was virtually finished.

13

The Descent

The collapse of *Queen Kelly* in January 1929 was more than just another unhappy event in Stroheim's directing career. It heralded its end. Like the main character in *Blind Husbands,* he had fallen from the pinnacle, not to death, but to a life of continued disappointment. As if the superstitious man had broken a mirror, the next seven years would bring only bad luck—domestic problems, professional humiliation, and growing poverty.

At first, the failure of the *Queen Kelly* project seemed only a minor setback to Stroheim. However, as the months drew on, he began to realize that no producer was interested in his directorial skills. Needing money, he reluctantly turned to acting as a temporary solution. Who could have guessed that he would sustain himself in this profession for the rest of his life? What roles might he play? His reputation as the "man you love to hate" was only momentarily softened by the lead part in *The Wedding March.* Now, with his unhandsome looks and his age (forty-four), his opportunities as a rake were limited.

But there was another role as well, one that drew on aspects of the real or perceived-to-be-real Stroheim. His stormy reputation as an impossible madman prompted screenwriters to fashion stories that capitalized on that "legend." These scripts—at least in most of his American films—usually concern an extremely talented egomaniac (a stage performer, movie director, scientist, writer, or military officer) who also is jealous, vindictive, and almost always cruel—particularly to his women. Each of these films has Stroheim's character repeat the same primal arc: he would soar high, bask in the sun for a moment, and then be dashed to the depths.

Stroheim's first sound film, *The Great Gabbo,* was also the first to employ this format. Although he knew that a return to acting in other directors' films would not enhance his Hollywood career, Stroheim reluctantly accepted this role of a mad ventriloquist. *The Great Gabbo* (released in September 1929) was an independent production made for Sono-Art, a poverty-row firm, and directed by James Cruze (once a major figure but by this time on the decline). For status-oriented Hollywood, an involvement with such a production suggested that a performer or director was on the way down. Still, the facts that Stroheim was allowed to rewrite much of the script and that he would be in almost every scene—except for the musical numbers starring Cruze's wife, Betty Compson—convinced him that this leading role would not be too detrimental to his reputation.

Static and stagy like most early sound films, *The Great Gabbo* betrays little inventiveness and shows few of its actors to advantage. In fact, its budget was so low that occasional line-flubs were allowed to pass. The story and the dialogue are generally pedestrian in terms of dramatic values and audience appeal, but the film proves interesting because it not only exploits aspects of the Stroheim persona but also contains remarkably insightful autobiographical elements. At times, Stroheim seems to be encapsulating and objectifying certain confessions that he could have related on a psychiatrist's couch. Gabbo is egotistical, stubborn, and mean, yet he also reveals a vulnerable and sensitive side through his dummy. Furthermore, the picture also contains a number of his private obsessions.

As the film opens, Gabbo (smoking incessantly) is playing solitaire in a shabby room. When his female companion, Mary (Betty Compson), gives him flowers in remembrance of their being together for two years, he replies nastily that flowers are for dead people. A moment later, when she throws his hat on the bed, he jumps up in fear and rage, claiming that such actions bring "bad luck." She then speaks words of wisdom that apply not only to Gabbo but to the man playing the part: "Oh, hats on the bed, and black cats, and spilling the salt, and walking under ladders—you make your own bad luck!" Gabbo bitterly complains that he is performing in Paterson, New Jersey, instead of the big time. Mary replies, sensibly, that he should call his agent, but again the response is typical of Stroheim himself: "Why should I call him? Let him call me! They should be glad to get an act like mine. They can't get Gabbos every day." Then he angrily states that the coffee is cold, and when she says that the last time he complained it was too hot, he rages back (shades of the director), "If I want anything done right, I have to do it myself!"

Following this, Gabbo goes on stage to perform his ventriloquist act. His dummy, Otto, talks back to him, criticizes him, and, according to Mary, reveals Gabbo's kind and rational side, the side she loves. The wonder of the act is that Gabbo can talk, smoke, eat, and drink while the dummy sings. This is so palpably impossible that the film is weakened, particularly when Otto's voice does not have Stroheim's accent. (This, incidentally, was a time when it was technically impossible to dub in a voice-over for the dummy.) At any rate, all that Gabbo's mistress, functioning as his assistant, has to do in his act is to bring out a glass of water on a tray. When she comes out late, Gabbo glares at her and makes a sarcastic remark. A moment later, she drops the tray, thus damaging the effect of his performance.

Afterward, Gabbo fumes, "Of all the stupid, bungling idiots I have ever seen in my life, she is the worst." A stagehand hears this and says, "Somebody ought to knock that guy's block off," which clearly indicates that Gabbo is not intended to be a sympathetic character. However, despite the stagehand's comment and the scriptwriter's intentions, Gabbo does not seem—in this instance—to be unreasonable in expecting the woman, after two years, to carry out a glass of water on cue and without accident.

As a result of this gaffe, Gabbo and the lady have an altercation, and she decides to leave. Gabbo does not want her to go, but he will not admit it and pigheadedly tells her to get out, cruelly adding that she is nothing without him. Although fed up with his nastiness, she leaves reluctantly, declaring that she only likes Otto, the kind side of Gabbo. A moment later, he looks out the door as she departs, but he remains too proud to call her back. When Otto declares that she will not return, Gabbo arrogantly replies, "I need no one!" In a sense he does not, for two years later he has made "the big time" and stars in a Broadway review. But he misses her.

A star he may be, but he is still impossible. Gabbo pulls up in his chauffeur-driven Rolls Royce, enters a famous restaurant with Otto, and has a meal of squab and truffles, followed by a cup of coffee (which Otto criticizes to the waiter). His former girlfriend sees him, and her male companion notes that Gabbo is a man completely satisfied with himself: "Of all the egotistical fools I have ever seen, he is the worst." Mary replies, "You must admit, he is great," and refers to him as a "poor soul." Gabbo sees his former lover from across the room and has the waiter invite her to his table, where they converse. Afterward, he sends giant bouquets of flowers to her dressing room (an interesting variation on his earlier comment that flowers are only for the dead). Her companion (we find out later that he is her husband) is resentful and sums up Gabbo as a "swell-headed nut, kissing your hand, bowing down, clicking his heels and all that imported baloney," an attitude not unlike that of the husband in *Foolish Wives*.

Later, in his dressing room, Gabbo—in an uncharacteristically good mood because he thinks Mary will return to him—speaks to his valet quite kindly (and mostly in German), asking whether he has a sweetheart and giving him some money to go out that night. A moment later, after the valet commits some minor infraction, Gabbo's kind side completely disappears, and he becomes extremely cruel to the fellow and fires him. He then goes on stage, dressed in a white uniform with a ton of medals on it, and performs his act.

Afterward, Gabbo, having overheard his former girlfriend's remark that "there is a sweet side to him," is convinced that they will now reunite; as a result, he once again becomes haughty and arrogant and says to Otto: "Of course, why would she want to stick with him when she has a chance to come back with Gabbo?" He telephones the restaurant and asks for a private dining room with flowers and candles, adding that "everything must be the very best." He then orders hors d'oeuvres, squab cooked in coconut, hearts of palm tree salad à la vinaigrette, and Veuve Cliquot, "very dry" and "very cold." This is not the first, nor will it be the last, of Stroheim's elaborate cinema menus.

But all is not as Gabbo wishes. He learns that, although his former girlfriend feels some affection for him, she has a husband whom she loves. Gabbo is heartbroken, then enraged, and finally goes berserk. He punches Otto, then pulls the dummy close to himself, comes out late for the finale, and disrupts the show with his shouting. The producer fires him (an event recalling the termination of many of Stroheim's films) and, out in the street with Otto under his arm, Gabbo stands by the marquee while workmen take down the letters of his name. As he carefully avoids walking under the ladder, the film ends.

Obviously, *The Great Gabbo* capitalizes on the general perception of Stroheim as an outrageous person. It also allows the actor to indulge himself by adjusting his monocle, smoking, smirking, raging, and parading around in immaculate uniforms bestrewn with medals. The film shows that Stroheim is not only aware of himself but, indeed, can satirize himself. However, what might have been a somewhat private joke perhaps had fateful consequences. It objectified on-screen Hollywood's negative view of him, an odd kind of résumé for someone seeking employment.

Variety's review of *The Great Gabbo* acknowledged Stroheim's "dominant screen personality." It also referred to his voice as "one of the strongest threads compelling audience concentration and carrying the interest" over the stage-show interludes.[1] Other critics generally considered the film acceptable, but it was by no means a great box-office success. Despite Stroheim's good notices, there were no calls for the services of the great Erich von Stroheim for some time.

Stroheim may not have been acting or directing, but he was writing. On September 4, 1929—about the time that *The Great Gabbo* went into release—he signed a contract with MGM for fifteen thousand dollars to write an original story. A few months later, his rather grim project—called *Wild Blood*—was rejected, and Stroheim received only five thousand dollars. Its concept seems to suggest that he had not forgotten Griffith's 1914 film, *The Escape,* which dealt with a somewhat degenerate family and the malign influences of environment. Stroheim's story concerns five young people and their varying backgrounds. Some, tainted by the "wild blood" they have inherited—like poor McTeague—hang around a place called "The Devil's Garden." A botched abortion, prostitution, disease, *locomotor ataxia,* and other Stroheim obsessions add to the naturalistic tone. This story was hardly suffused with the wholesome types that Louis B. Mayer liked and would not have been pleasant entertainment. Ignoring what audiences wanted, Stroheim was still grimly determined to show the unsavory sides of life. Later he would resubmit this 262–page manuscript to MGM in July 1941; once again it was returned as not commercial material.

Throughout Stroheim's career, he was always working on one project or another. During the teens he had submitted a number of scripts, and even in the midst of his own directing career, he was hatching other plots. As early as November 1925,[2] there had been an announcement that Stroheim would act in and direct a film based on George Barr McCutcheon's *East of the Setting Sun,* which dealt with European royalty. Nothing came of this, but in 1929 he returned to the adaptation, which he submitted to MGM. According to a studio reader's synopsis:

> There are two kingdoms in the Balkans. One is ruled by the hated despot, Queen Draga, and her dissolute son, Prince Vladimir. The other kingdom is ruled by a kindly king, Nikita, whose one love is his daughter, Princess Milena. The marriage would be expedient for both countries, but the daughter rebels against the match. Not long after, the queen's penchant for killing her subjects results in a revolution and her subsequent death during a state visit by Milena. She cannot escape back to her own country. Her only recourse is to arrange a marriage with Jimmy, an American who has come to the country to open a Ford agency. He doesn't know that she is a princess but marries her to help her out. Meantime, Vladimir, disguised in woman's clothes, has crossed the border with his mistress. Vladimir is furious with Nikita and Milena, for he wants the princess's body, dowry and kingdom. However, he is stymied by the in-name-only marriage. Jimmy now goes to the King who is deeply appreciative and the princess and the American have some tender moments. Meantime, the revolution has been put down, and Vladimir, now King, demands the princess. He stabs Nikita and escapes but waylays the princess and the American on a mountain road. Vladimir half-strips the American, has him tied to a tree, and whips him and tops his villainy by breaking a bees' nest, hoping that they will sting the victim to death. Vladimir grabs the princess and takes her further up the mountain to an inn called "the sign of the Devil," marked by an iron figure of Satan holding a trident. He locks her in her room and starts to drink champagne.
>
> "Sunbeam," a "darky" employed by Jimmy, contacts U.S.

Marines stationed nearby and tells them that Jimmy, who had once been a marine, has been attacked. The men rush up the road and free the American. The wounded Jimmy is sent back to the ship and the marines storm the inn and overcome Vladimir's henchmen. Vladimir, who is about to rape the girl, escapes by leaping out the window. Jimmy, who has quickly recovered, returns and leaves the inn in one of the cars with Milena. She feels blood dripping on her and looks up to see Vladimir impaled on the devil's trident. The story ends as the two now marry in a big ceremony in the presence of the happy King Nikita who has recovered from his wounds.

The reader's report concluded that the project was an "amusing satire against royalty that is so characteristic of Von Stroheim. The temperamental scenes between Milena [and] her father are delightful; and the vulgarity of Queen Draga is stressed, also the dissolute, loathsome nature of her son, Vladimir. It is a sort of fairy-tale thing, but don't we like them." The reader suggested that Norma Shearer would be "particularly lovely in such a part."[3]

What a lively romp this could have been—a mixture of *The Merry Widow* and *Queen Kelly*—with Vladimir surely a man you could love to hate. The original project of 1925–1926, Stroheim later observed, "never went into production as the last moment Joe Schenck [head of United Artists] had misgivings of letting me play a part in a picture which I directed myself." In 1929, when Stroheim sent the story to MGM, he suggested the use of Walter Pidgeon as Jimmy, George Fawcett as Nikita, Josephine Crowell as the Queen, and—of course—himself as "black Vladimir." MGM was not interested, perhaps feeling that its melodramatic happenings and air of mythical unreality were better suited to the silent film than to the talkies.

Meanwhile, over at Warner Bros., Darryl F. Zanuck, chief of production, decided to redo *Three Faces East*. This stage play, set during the First World War, had previously been filmed in 1926 with Jedda Goudal as the female spy and Clive Brook as Valdar, the German agent. Directed by Rupert Julian (who had completed Stroheim's *Merry-Go-Round*), the film had received mediocre reviews. "It is supposed to be a melodrama, but to any one who has worked in the Secret Service of any country it is a farce," said the *New York Times*.[4] Zanuck, who evidently felt that the original story still had box-office potential, thought Stroheim perfect for the part of the German spy. Later, in 1940, Warner Bros. would resurrect the property again, with Boris Karloff playing Stroheim's role, and title it *British Intelligence*.

After a stormy gestation, *Three Faces East* was released in September 1930. Years later, Stroheim wrote about this experience: "After I had read the scenario I made some vital suggestions to Darryl Zanuck himself who liked them very much and begged me to write them out in scenario form. They pertained mostly to my own scenes." Zanuck, who had been a writer, could see that Stroheim gave depth to his characterization. But Roy Del Ruth, the film's thirty-five-year-old director, became furious that Stroheim had gone over his head. According to Stroheim, Del Ruth

> never forgave me. As some of these scenes included [Constance] Bennett, she too was incensed over the fact that another actor had had the audacity to change some of her action and dialogue. What Del Ruth and Bennett forgot was that I was not only an actor but had written . . . all the stories of my own films and others and that I was a director also and that I did not look at that scenario only from an actor's standpoint but that I had the faculty of visualizing the finished film from reading the scenario.
>
> It is that same striving for perfection which caused me after that experience several other frictions with producers in whose pictures I worked as an actor when I, as a writer and director of many years experience, insisted on some changes in the script. Those that have listened to me, never had to regret it. Those that have not, are most likely sore because they did not. It is my past and present activity in all three fields which makes me more critical in reading a scenario and I have no ambition to work at this stage of the game just to make money (I could be a multi-millionaire if I had wanted to do that) but besides my financial remuneration I desire to make films worthy of making. Sometimes we have to bite into the bitter apple and make something of which we do not approve because even writer-director-actors have to eat . . . at least once a day.
>
> Stories about my changing the script and the dialogue

before I accept a scenario were many times told and retold and written about by disgruntled scenarists and dialogue-writers who had come to believe that every word that they had written was a diamond set in platinum. Real artists such as Jimmy Cruze and particularly Jean Renoir, the maker of the *Grand Illusion,* not only accepted willingly and gladly my suggestions but asked for them. Small minds like the director above mentioned have never and never will make anything important because in order to do so you have to have an open and flexible mind and not believe that one knows everything.[5]

It is an ironic fact that after *Three Faces East* the "small" mind of Roy Del Ruth directed an additional fifty-two films, his last effort in 1960, shortly before he died. He also, as Stroheim predicted, never really made "anything important." However, it must have been difficult for a man like Stroheim, who agonized over every detail and movement, to work with an efficient, successful, and not-untalented hack who efficiently turned out six films in 1930.

Even before shooting began on *Three Faces East,* Del Ruth obtained his revenge. Stroheim related the agony:

When I first reported for the picture, I rode out in my car with ten uniforms. All the way out I kept saying to myself, "Erich, don't lose your temper, whatever you do. Erich, keep your mouth shut." I went to the hotel where Del Ruth had a whole floor, and I asked him most politely where I should dress. He said to me, "Dress in your car, where else?" So I went to my car. I tell you that very few men, women, and children in Beverly Hills missed seeing me in B.V.D.'s that day, climbing in and out of uniforms, putting my body in and my head out of that damned car. I swore continually, I ripped my trousers, I bumped my head.

I said to myself: "You are getting paid and it's money you're in great need of. Don't let me hear another word out of you." So, despite these embarrassments, I went through with the picture. That is called a comeback. To me it is a go-back, a fall-back, and a back-flip. I tell you my luck has been just too damned bad.[6]

Three Faces East opens during a large military ceremony as Stroheim, dressed in a black uniform, walks painfully forward, using two canes, to receive a medal for bravery from the Belgian government. The scene then shifts to a town just captured by the Germans, who interrogate a French nurse (Constance Bennett). This attractive woman is actually a German spy, and she is sent to England, where she becomes a houseguest of the first lord of the admiralty. There, she encounters the butler (Stroheim), also a German agent. These two spies seek to learn when American troops will sail across the ocean, so that German submarines can sink their ships.

Upon first seeing the attractive woman, the butler tells the maids to make an unused bedroom ready. In a detailed list that surely Stroheim created, he orders them to "Draw the drapes, open the windows, sweep the floor, vacuum the carpet—in both rooms, of course—dust the furniture and I mean *dusted,* fresh linen on the bed, scrub the tub, fresh towels and rugs in the bath." He then descends to the conservatory, where he cuts some prize roses and takes them to the freshened room. He lifts up the carpet and, seeing dirt under it, glares at the maid. He then opens the guest's luggage, removes the bullets from her handgun, and inspects her lingerie. While the maids peer through the keyhole, he holds up her slip and jiggles her briefs as if they were occupied.

Later, when Bennett goes up to her room, she is surprised to find that her belongings have been laid out neatly. Stroheim then brings up a hot-water bottle, wraps it carefully in a white cloth, and puts it in the bed. He lights a fire, moves an easy chair closer to the fireplace, carries over a small table, and finally places a lamp on it. She asks whether there are three windows that face the east (the sign of recognition, therefore, the film's title), after which they finally acknowledge each other as German spies. Smitten with her, he remarks, "You are too beautiful." She wants to meet the head spy, but Stroheim replies, "He's a machine. He is the personification of duty above everything. He is without conscience, without heart, without soul."

Later in the film, the heroine slips down to the study, opens the safe, and reads about the troop movements. She is almost caught, and there is much lurking around as the plot creaks on. She supplies Stroheim with the information, and he sneaks out of the house to a hidden transmitter, where he radios the submarines as to the location of the ships. Then the plot becomes even more heavy-handed, when the viewer's belief that Stroheim is an enemy agent is contradicted by a scene at British Intelligence, which states that Stroheim is really a British agent; meanwhile, the girl explains to the young man of the house that she, in fact, is a British agent. The plot finally untwists itself, and we find out that she actually is a British agent but Stroheim is a German one, and the information about the ships was intentionally false. When Stroheim hurries to his secret radio to amend the message, he is shot.

The film is marred by the mutual antipathy that existed between Bennett and Stroheim. Although the story indicates some degree of sexual attraction by him and some discreet flirtation by her, Bennett seems aloof, cold, and unfriendly, and he gives little evidence of liking her—a failing that Del Ruth was unable to overcome. Furthermore, Bennett, usually a lively actress, is awkward and unbelievable in this film, a failure that must have stemmed from the offscreen conflicts. As Curtiss noted: "After a scene in which the unwelcome actor was called upon to kiss her, Miss Bennett shouted to her maid to bring her mouthwash at once. Not to be outdone, von Stroheim, after the next kissing scene with Miss Bennett, ordered his dresser to rush up to him with a bottle of Listerine."[7]

Although such behavior seems like an exaggeration, Constance Bennett was an argumentative and self-centered actress who, according to her sister Joan's autobiography, was noted for her "arrogance and emotional outbursts, ruthless business deals, and bullying to get what she wanted"; she also was "capable of the most extreme selfishness." She had a "natural tendency for high tension, and when she rankled she never kept it a secret."[8] Incidentally, by this time she was having an affair with Gloria Swanson's husband, the marquis (Henri Falaise), whom she would later marry, and perhaps already held a grudge not only against Gloria but also Stroheim even before *Three Faces East* began.

The film as a whole is often awkward, poorly acted, and stiff. Such an old-fashioned melodrama has to be done with verve and speed. This version lacks both. When Stroheim is on-screen, the film gains some life, but otherwise it resembles a poor theatrical production—wooden, stagy, and dull. However, someone at *Variety* liked Stroheim's performance: "The role is pie for von Stroheim. . . . That guy is a figure in the American picture business. With the way they are throwing

money into talkers nowadays, it's a wonder he isn't once more directing. He couldn't possibly burn up more than some of the others are
doing."[9]

If Warner Bros.—one of the few major studios that had not hitherto employed Stroheim—ever entertained the idea of using him as a
director, the impulse must have been squelched by the tense atmosphere on the set. Obviously, Stroheim was considered the source of
the trouble, for Del Ruth continued to direct films for the company,
whereas Warners found no further use for Stroheim, even as an actor.

Around this time, after many rejections by other producers,
Stroheim had an opportunity to return to Universal. Carl Laemmle
Jr., who was now the head of the studio, wanted to make more prestigious films than Universal's usual fare of westerns and B pictures. *Merry-
Go-Round,* which had been a success in 1923, seemed a good property
to remake as a talkie. Stroheim was paid ten thousand dollars, and
Georges Lewys received an equal sum, for the talking rights; in June
1930 the press learned that Stroheim was to direct. But economic
reality took over. Universal's expensive *King of Jazz,* released in the
spring, proved in the following months to be a major loss. Furthermore, the Depression was beginning to affect the studio. In 1930, with
a gross of slightly more than $25 million, Universal had lost over $2.5
million, the worst deficit in its history. Costs were being cut throughout the studio in a desperate attempt to remain solvent. Suddenly a
production of *Merry-Go-Round,* with its high budget, seemed unwise.
However there was a less expensive project: *Blind Husbands.* The original film had been of standard length, and the remake's production
costs, Universal reasoned, would remain modest.

On July 27, 1930, Stroheim was paid five thousand dollars for the
rights to *Blind Husbands* and began to work on a sound version. The
previous decade had honed his gifts as a scenarist, and he looked forward to improving his earlier film. Even though Stroheim may have
grown more astute, he had also become incapable of introducing any
character without providing interesting, but not germane, background
information. Scenes that in the original were short and to the point
now became enriched but, alas, cluttered with physical as well as psychological details. On December 15, he submitted a monstrous 618–
page continuity.[10] Although this first draft, consisting of hundreds of
scenes, would have proved impossibly long, it also revealed a more

sophisticated cinematic style and a more mature handling of characterizations. He clearly was trying to create a novel-like texture.

In Stroheim's revisions, Lieutenant von Steuben was no longer an officer but now an aristocrat, Hans Carl Maria Baron von Truenfels. The elevation to the nobility was warranted by the fact that Stroheim, who was to play the part, was now too old to be a mere junior officer and that he enjoyed being an aristocrat. Stroheim's scenario was more than a revamping of the silent film. It attempted not only to make use of spoken dialogue but also to employ sound imaginatively. For example, a pair of newlyweds, because the hotel does not have a honeymoon suite, must share a small bed in an upstairs room. Meantime, in her quarters below, the frustrated Mrs. Armstrong observes that, once again, her inattentive husband has fallen asleep. Hearing a rhythmic squeaking noise above, she looks up to see the chandelier swinging back and forth. After the bawdy implications of this become apparent, Stroheim intended to cut upstairs to show the husband moving back and forth in a rocking chair!

In the original version, Stroheim efficiently introduced three Americans in the piazza. The revision adds further details. One man, named Prindle (a name earlier used in *His Picture in the Papers*), sells zippers. The second, Jeremiah Smith, sells bedsprings, and the third, Hancock, sells sanitary tissues. The sexual implications of their professions are clear. But these details, although amusing, are unnecessary and indicate that Stroheim was encumbering his narrative with non-essentials.

In the new scenario, Stroheim offers a revealing bit of dialogue in which the baron says, "I'm in love—like a silly little school boy!" Margaret replies (almost tenderly), "That's what I really think you are! Just a *bad* little boy—who really wants to play grown-up!" The baron answers (dreamily), "Every man is a little boy at heart." In this exchange, perhaps Stroheim exposed a hidden part of his own character. This softer side of the sexual predator is not evident in the original film. Stroheim also revised his attitude toward the rogue's fate. At the conclusion of all drafts of the remake, the officer does not die but descends from the mountain safely. Obviously, Stroheim's guilt feelings about his first wife must have waned; furthermore, America's attitude toward sin had changed in the previous decade. Stroheim realized that the original drastic conclusion was too strong for a "villain" who did not really deserve death just because he wanted to sleep with Mrs. Armstrong. In Stroheim's first draft of the remake, however, there is a death—but it is Sepp who dies in a fall. In the final script, Sepp does not die but remains to bid farewell—as he does in the silent version—to Dr. and Mrs. Armstrong.

In all the remake's various versions, Stroheim gives the film a provocative ending. The frustrated officer, his sexual longings thwarted by Mrs. Armstrong's virtue, leaves the village, but his experience certainly has not converted him to morality. He rides away, but only after taking a long and searching look at a fourteen-year-old girl. In later drafts, because of the studio's fear of censorship, the girl who receives this lecherous glance grows to be sixteen and then, finally, is just described as being "young."

Stroheim's new continuity was, of course, much too lengthy, and he was advised to shorten it. By March 14, 1931, the 618 pages shrank to 258 pages, running well over four hundred scenes. On April 4, it took final form at 158 pages. After each revision, this scenario grew both shorter and, in many ways, less interesting. However, the executives were pleased that Stroheim was trimming the giant work. On the other hand, knowing Stroheim's past history, they harbored fears that he might restore during production the hundreds of scenes that he had reluctantly cut. When endless lists of props, costumes, medals, and specific details about the sets started pouring in, the film no longer seemed the modest venture it had first appeared. However, the studio could not have lost money in a worthier cause.

Universal hesitated. As receipts continued to wane during the summer of 1931, the studio's finances grew desperate. Despite Stroheim's protestations that he would stay on budget, Carl Laemmle Jr., recalling *Foolish Wives* and the more recent *Wedding March* debacle, was fearful of letting Stroheim act in the film, because he could never be fired if he became impossible as director. Laemmle asked the exhibitors whether they would be interested in the film without Stroheim as its star. They would not.

The decisive moment supposedly occurred when Stroheim—with production about to begin—announced that he wanted the sound of church bells in his opening scenes. When told he could use a recording, he had a royal tantrum and broke his cane in fury. He demanded that bells be brought to Lake Arrowhead, along with a sound truck, because, he claimed, bells sounded different over water. An employee ran into the main office and recounted the problem. Suddenly the Laemmles (Poppa and Junior) and their executives envisioned the troubles to come and immediately abandoned the project. They had enough worries trying to stay out of bankruptcy without daily squabbles with Stroheim.[11]

In 1947, Stroheim recalled these events rather differently. He said that the "story, script, and preparations were finished on the first of July and I was supposed to begin production on the tenth of September." When his mother grew ill, Stroheim and his wife and son went to Austria, his first return to his native land. Besides seeing his mother and his brother, he purchased furniture, costumes, and other props for his film, for which, he bitterly noted, he was never reimbursed. On his return to America, Stroheim said, he reported at the studio on September 10, the date production was to begin, and was told that the project had been canceled.[12] Stroheim, however, did not state the cause of the cancellation. The fact that the film would not have box-office appeal without Stroheim acting in it, plus his general imperious attitude, doomed the project.

Undeterred, Stroheim began writing another script, *Her Highness,* which takes place in a small garrison town on the Austro-Russian border. (Was Stroheim recalling the script of *Hotel Imperial,* which he had planned to direct for Paramount around the time of *The Wedding March?*) In this story, the local barber's daughter has "airs" that cause her to be called "Her Highness." She is in love with the dashing Lieutenant von Ebenstein, who does not want to marry her. She hides the fact that she is carrying his child and accepts the marriage offer of an elderly baron. Their life together becomes awful, and when she tells her husband that she still loves the lieutenant, the father of her child, the decrepit old man dies of sheer rage. Now a rich and merry widow, she soon marries Prince Dubrovsky, colonel of the regiment, a handsome, dignified man of middle age, who had earlier admired her in the village. She is now a great lady, the envy of all who had snubbed her. She feels affection for her new husband, but her heart is still Ebenstein's. When war breaks out, she learns that the lieutenant is being sent to certain death. She rides after him, reveals that the child is his, then returns to bid her husband farewell as he too goes off to war, after which she faithfully prays for her mate's safe return.

Stroheim submitted this story to MGM in June 1931. Samuel Marx, the studio's scenario editor, replied that "Paul Bern's verdict . . . was similar to mine . . . that . . . the ending was a distinct weakness. That about makes it unanimous."[13] Understandably, Stroheim did not want to copy *The Merry Widow* too closely and therefore had complicated the story by having the heroine marry a kind and decent man but still be in love with the dashing lieutenant. The result was an unhappy ending and, in some ways, a not-too-admirable heroine. Perhaps Stroheim could have changed his story and made it more palatable by having her merely be tempted to marry the kindly prince. She could then reject her comfortable life for the lively lieutenant, who would come to a great awakening and marry her. Commercial, yes. Phony, perhaps. But probably salable! Stroheim, however, remained adamant.

All was not lost, however. Stroheim conferred with his attorney, I.B. Kornblum, who was a fledgling composer, and with another man who wrote lyrics, and soon *Her Highness* became an operetta! Stroheim hired some musicians to perform the work in the presence of Winfield Sheehan of Fox Studios. Sheehan's wife, Maria Jeritza, a fellow Austrian, had been an important prima donna at the Metropolitan Opera since 1926, and she approved of this musical effort. Jeritza's enthusiasm, the pseudo-Viennese music, and Stroheim's sweet-talk and passionate explanations worked. Sheehan bit for twenty-five thousand dollars.

A clipping from the *L.A. Examiner* of October 8, 1932, announced that Lillian Harvey and Henri Garat, who had appeared in the English-language version of the world-famous German film *Congress Dances,* would star in a musical, directed by Stroheim. This dream, however, soon collapsed. Later, the studio, overburdened with debt, tried to sell its expensive property to affluent MGM. Fox received this curt reply: "I am sorry but the producers here did not seem sufficiently interested."[14] And that was the end of *Her Highness*—with or without music.

When Stroheim was writing the original *Her Highness* script in the summer of 1931, he had been unemployed for about a year, ever since shooting *Three Faces East.* Fortunately, RKO made him an offer, and after scrutinizing the script, he accepted. *Friends and Lovers* (released in November 1931) was directed by Victor Schertzinger and starred Adolphe Menjou, Laurence Olivier, and Lili Damita. According to Olivier, during rehearsals Stroheim agonized over the best means of giving himself a sinister image. He tried wearing a black patch over one eye and a monocle in the other, while fretting about which eye to use for the monocle. The director took one look at this strange apparition, thought it too much, and Stroheim had to relinquish the patch.[15] Despite Stroheim's intense performance and the presence of important actors, in Olivier's words, "the film died the death of a dog." The box-office failure caused RKO to lose $260,000.[16]

Friends and Lovers was based on a novel by Maurice de Kobra called *The Sphinx Has Spoken*. The book's hero is forced into debt by a cardsharp called Nogales, whose accomplice, his femme fatale wife, threatens the hero's friendship with his best pal. The novel concludes with her becoming a cocaine addict, a just reward for her evildoing. The film changes the characters and much of the plot. The cardsharp was transformed into Colonel Sangrito and the wife into someone worth fighting for. However, part of the film's failure stems from the heroine's characterization. In the beginning she is a mere lure who sleeps with a moneyed man as part of an extortion plot, but shortly afterward, her character becomes a "good" person, truly in love. This was a difficult transformation for audiences of the time.

The beautiful and charming Alva (Lili Damita) and a rich army captain (Adolphe Menjou) have spent the evening as lovers. When they return to the apartment, they encounter her husband, Colonel Sangrito (Stroheim). Bestrewn with medals ("I, too, served in an army"), the colonel is an aristocratic collector of rare porcelains. When he asks the couple about their night at the opera, they are trapped into agreeing it was *Aïda,* but he corrects them by saying it was *La Bohème.* He sarcastically warns Alva, "Be careful, my precious. These army officers are dangerous," and suggests that she retire: "*La Bohème* is so wearing."

After she leaves the room, Sangrito tells the captain that the opera was actually *Tannhäuser* and indicates that he knows how they spent the evening. When the captain offers to give satisfaction in a duel, Sangrito displays his pistols, indicates that he is an excellent shot, and suggests that, because collecting porcelain is so expensive, he would prefer five thousand pounds. The officer says, "To think of a woman like Alva being married to such a man!" Sangrito sadly agrees. "Deplorable! Sometimes I wonder myself how she can bear it." He provides the officer with a checkbook from the man's bank and a pen; he even gives him a pillow, and rests a hand kindly on his shoulder as the check is made out. (This scene of the colonel urbanely forcing his victim to write the check bothered the New York censor, who felt it was an "incitement to crime" and that it tended "to corrupt morals.") The officer then leaves for his desert outpost, and Sangrito reminds his smitten wife, "You wouldn't really desert me, would you? You're not ungrateful."

Some time later, the colonel tells his wife, "Imagine my forgetting—a letter for you—from your Captain Roberts." She eagerly takes it and notices the ripped envelope. "But of course I opened it. I'm a romantic. I love to read other people's letters. Everybody does. Only they won't admit it so honestly. But I must not detain you. You must be eager to read those lonely, lovely words of *passion*." He draws out this last word, then pauses. "He doesn't write well, your Captain. See what he says about me? He says Sangrito is a monstrous blackguard. That's very bad, is it not? To think, of all the names he could have called Sangrito, he must write that. To me, it lacks imagination. He also complains that he longs for a letter from you. You must write to him, my precious." At this point he provides his wife a pen and paper.

Sangrito grows tired of his despairing wife, who seems to have fallen genuinely in love with Roberts. Pacing around in his high boots, Sangrito says that he has been too kind to her. "Now, you will do as I tell you." She answers that she is through forever. He becomes enraged at her remark. "You think you can talk like that to me?" When he threatens her, she replies, "My life is finished anyway," and hints at suicide. He remarks, "That would be too easy. You can't escape that way." He takes his whip and starts to beat her. A male servant, who has witnessed this exchange, grabs a dueling pistol and kills him. After this, the film concerns itself with solving the problem of who gets the woman, Roberts or his fellow officer and best friend (Olivier). Without Stroheim, the subsequent action in the film is far less engaging.

Stroheim provides a well-honed performance as Sangrito, redolent of sarcasm, irony, and class. He is a villain, but an urbane one. Furthermore, his scenes show that he had considerable input in terms of "business" and even set decoration. Stroheim invests his role with the usual details: the medals, the swords on the walls, the pistols, the monocle, and his cigarette ashes nonchalantly flipped on the floor.

Some moments in the film, when Stroheim is not even present, seem to show his influence. When Alva finishes taking a shower, she sits down and raises a leg high in the air so her maid can take a towel and dry it. The scene then shifts to an outpost in India, where this image is repeated in a rather suggestive pinup picture on a barracks wall. Another sexual moment (probably suggested by Stroheim's persistent interest in lingerie) occurs when a general, known for his racy stories, tells a joke about Madame Tussaud's waxworks: a reporter asks a laundress who works there whether the queens and duchesses wear anything under their velvet robes. She replies, "No, sir, as a matter of fact, they do not. But I'd rather you didn't mention it because nobody knows it except me and a few Australian soldiers!"

It was during this time that Stroheim met Wallace Smith, the co-author of the screenplay and the dialogue writer. A former newspaperman, Smith had written *The Delightful Rogue,* a 1929 film that reviewers and the public thought awful but which was suffused with wit and cynical wisdom; it also had a very sophisticated, intricate script that concerned itself with the conventions and mechanics of melodrama. Some of Stroheim's dialogue in *Friends and Lovers,* such as his discussion of the captain's writing style and his use of the word "blackguard," recalls that of *The Delightful Rogue.* This type of witty observation was quite close to Stroheim's own sensibility as well, and some later films in which Stroheim had a free hand would reveal a similar tone. That Smith and Stroheim were simpatico can be seen in the fact that the two soon worked together. In fact, Stroheim had so impressed Smith that when the writer made a scenario out of a Dick Grace aviation story, he conceived the role of a mad movie director for Stroheim.

The resulting film, *The Lost Squadron,* deals with three disillusioned First World War aviators who, after the war, end up working as stunt pilots in Hollywood. Starring Richard Dix, Robert Armstrong, and Joel McCrea, *The Lost Squadron* (released in March 1932) was directed by George Archainbaud for RKO. The film began production in the middle of October, originally under director Paul Sloane, but when he went on an alcoholic binge, it was postponed a few weeks. Archainbaud then took over direction, and by late December the film was completed.

The Lost Squadron begins on November 11, 1918, when the American aviators reluctantly have their last dogfight a few minutes before the cessation of hostilities. The excitement, fun, and camaraderie they have experienced during the war soon end. On their return to America, one has lost all his money, the other his job, and the third his girlfriend, who has proved "weak" and "ambitious." The ensuing years are not kind to these brave young men. Finally, two of the aviators become hobos and hitch a ride on a freight train to Hollywood, where they encounter their stunt-flying pal at the grand opening of Artur von Furst's new aviation film. Later, their friend explains that von Furst (Stroheim) is "a terrible fathead. No on-the-level producer would give him a job." Von Furst has married the career-oriented former girlfriend of the third flier. "They say he beats the behoosus out of her and I wouldn't put it past him."

Von Furst is cruel, dictatorial, selfish, and insanely jealous. He tells his camera crew, "Listen you—be sure and keep them [the airplanes] in the cameras. We might catch a nice crackup." One of von Furst's scenes includes a detail no doubt contributed by Stroheim: a line of six megaphones of increasing size. At another point, the director, exasperated at another foul-up, furiously hands his cane to one of his aides, who already holds an armful of them.

Von Furst barks out orders during a rehearsal of a First World War battle scene full of soldiers, damaged houses, and swooping airplanes. He screams commandingly, "Those men supposed to be wounded— act like wounded! And those supposed to be dead—act like dead! And don't *mooove!*" It is a simply marvelous moment: absurdly funny, yet probably not far from Stroheim's own directorial methods. The character tells one actor, "Remember, you're being shot—not serenaded! For once in your life try and give me a little expression. Don't stand here like a stuffed cow." He then explains that the pilot is "going to swoop his plane to you as close as possible. I hope he doesn't knock your head off. If he does, there's one consolation: you'll never miss it!"

At times, *The Lost Squadron* is extremely amusing. In the midst of a complicated war scene, everyone seems to be scrambling around and von Furst again falls into a rage. Removing his natty overcoat in a tantrum, he screams out, "Fools, idiots, nitwits! Attention!" He glares around him. "I am speaking now. I don't want to hear another sound." At this point, a machine gun goes off, making him even more angry. "This is a war picture—not a musical comedy," he yells. "Haven't you

any brains? This is supposed to be WAR, DEATH, HELL, DESTRUCTION—
not a Sunday school picnic! I am making this picture for the theater,
not the ashcan!" And now von Furst says what Stroheim himself must
have said thousands of times during his career: "Now we're going to
retake it and we're going to retake it until you do what I tell you!"
After this tirade, he indignantly puts his coat back on and buttons it up.
A moment later, he again loses his temper, and once more the coat
comes off.

Von Furst becomes extremely jealous when he sees his wife (Mary
Astor) talking to one of the aviators (Richard Dix, the former boyfriend). A few moments later, he twists her wrist and leads her into the
next setup, saying sarcastically, "This is a scene of love and Miss Marsh
has been rehearsing to get into the proper mood, of course."

Von Furst tells the cameraman, "If he crashes, keep on grinding."
When he is told, "There's no crash in the script," the director replies,
"Of course not. Just in case, you never can tell." In fact, he has a pretty
good idea that something will happen, because he has spread acid on
the wires that control the plane in order to kill the boyfriend.

At the end of the film, after the plane crashes and the pilot is killed,
the other pilots capture von Furst (who yells "Hilfe! Hilfe!" meaning
"help" in German). Trying to escape, he runs to a stairway, but they
shoot him and he falls. Stroheim later claimed to have broken some
ribs falling down those stairs. Although he perhaps performs the rather
gentle first portion of the action, the second shot of the long fall down
the stairway is done by a stuntman who is scrupulous enough not to
show his face. When the police come, the men prop up the dead von
Furst in a chair and pretend to talk to him. Later one flier sacrifices
himself by taking the body up in an airplane and purposely crashing it.

In his role as the fictional director, Stroheim is simply delightful,
but when the plot requires him to be a villain, he once again becomes
simply the "man you love to hate." Certainly, he is the controlling
presence in the film. After his character dies, so does the film; it just
lumbers along until the end. Stroheim's contributions can be felt in his
dialogue and in the brilliant attention to details. He ensured that the
war scenes appeared authentic and were replete with gritty details, and
he even managed to get an ambulance in the film. Little touches, such
as the megaphones and the business with the overcoat, the canes, and
the fancy sword he flourishes, give flavor to an otherwise stock villain

part. These additions indicate once again that Stroheim had a splendid, if sardonic, sense of humor. Offscreen, however, Stroheim's sense of humor became sorely tested as his professional life continued to founder.

However, there was some hope. In 1931, Stroheim had begun negotiations to direct a film for Fox called *Walking down Broadway*. He worked on a script, and when production was about to begin, the film had to be put on hold so that Stroheim could appear in *The Lost Squadron*. After he again became available, studio politics caused the project to be canceled.

Meanwhile, MGM, eager to find a new vehicle for its most famous star, Greta Garbo, decided to film a rather avant-garde play by Luigi Pirandello, which eventually became *As You Desire Me* (1932). Reportedly, Garbo demanded that Stroheim be cast as the nasty novelist with whom her screen character is living. Such a request by the usually taciturn Garbo might seem odd, but Garbo had previously expressed interest in Stroheim's work. In early 1929, in one of her few interviews, she told a reporter, "I would like to do something unusual, something that has not been done. . . . I don't see anything in silly love-making. I would like to do something all the other people are not doing. If I could get von Stroheim! Isn't he fine?"[17] Fortunately for Mayer and Thalberg—and perhaps for Garbo, herself—she did not demand him as a director. What a dilemma that would have been for Mayer: his most famous actress teamed with the unspeakable Stroheim! Nevertheless, MGM put aside its resentment of Stroheim and employed him as an actor for the new Garbo film. Seven years after he marched out of the studio, Stroheim was back.

In *As You Desire Me* (1932), directed by George Fitzmaurice, Garbo plays an amnesiac, a dissolute entertainer who drinks too much champagne and, although living with a count (Stroheim), also flirts and probably sleeps with other men. The count is a famous novelist, albeit a decidedly unpleasant one, who exploits the woman's weaknesses. Accompanied by his trademark monocle and cigarette (on which he constantly puffs), the count is possessive, sarcastic, and somewhat sadistic. Stroheim gives this unsympathetic role a certain panache. He flicks his lighted cigarette onto the carpeted floor, picks up a partially full champagne glass and indifferently flings out its contents, then pours himself a fresh drink, which he tosses down in pure Stroheimian fashion. He exercises his power by roughly kissing Garbo. Furious when she plans to leave him, he shoots at her, but she escapes.

Soon after, she is brought to a rich estate where she is believed to be the owner's wife, who disappeared during a climactic event of the war. Is the Garbo character really the long-lost wife shocked into amnesia, or is she just pretending to be the missing woman? The husband (Melvyn Douglas) thinks she is genuine, but just as she is being accepted by everyone, the count arrives and—wanting her back—tries to ruin her new life by claiming she is an impostor. He fails, although we are never sure whether the Garbo character is the real wife or not.

Garbo offers one of her best performances in *As You Desire Me,* but Owen Moore is most unconvincing as the friend who discovers the amnesiac and believes she is the missing wife. Even the usually urbane Douglas appears uncomfortable in his role as the credulous husband. Stroheim's early scenes seem to have the stamp of his directorial authority, but his later moments are more perfunctory. Years later, Douglas noted that he had looked forward to meeting and working with the famous Stroheim but found him "rude and common." He concluded, "I was very surprised that a man who had shown such gifts had no subtlety, no savoir faire, and was what is called today a square."[18] Admittedly, Stroheim was severely depressed at this time, but one wonders whether Douglas is being fair here. After all, Douglas was a New York sophisticate and a political liberal and leagues away from Stroheim's background, real or invented.

Hedda Hopper, who was in the cast, offered a different perspective. She remembered that Stroheim had caused many delays by not being able to remember his lines. Garbo never complained and, on the occasions when Stroheim was ill, she herself would claim an indisposition, thus covering for him. "On the last day of the picture, he surprised everybody by serving vintage champagne. It may have been his way of apologizing to the star, who never showed a bit of annoyance at the many hours' delay his actions had caused her."[19]

Perhaps because of the film's ambiguity about Garbo's character, its critical reception was mixed. What were not mixed were the reactions to Stroheim's performance. Mordaunt Hall of the *New York Times* referred to Stroheim's "blundering antics and curious grimacing. . . . He is too eager to appear ruthless and his violent kissing of . . . [Garbo] recalls the old time embracing by John Gilbert."[20] *Variety* was equally harsh: "Von Stroheim fails signally to make himself the man you love to hate by revealing an accent of blended Yorkville [a German section of New York City] and Ninth Avenue. A heavy with a comic dialect is pretty hard to take."[21] Stroheim's accent was never cultured German (like Conrad Veidt's) and is studded with what sounds like midwestern "r"s, but it is by no means "comic," despite *Variety's* claim.

At one point during the filming, Garbo (as usual) took off her shoes—besides the fact that she preferred wearing slippers, she also did not want to increase her five-foot-seven-inch height—and Stroheim, the foot fetishist, noted to her, "I don't think they're as ugly as everyone says." Garbo found this observation amusing and quoted it herself.[22]

The harsh views of Stroheim's performance in a film that was by no means a great success did not help his reputation as leading player. Although he had won his greatest success at MGM for *The Merry Widow* as a director—and had earned for the company a great deal of money—the studio chose to forget him and would never again call upon his services as an actor. The irony of the situation could hardly have escaped him.

14

Walking down Broadway

Stroheim's well-publicized difficulties with *The Wedding March* and *Queen Kelly* and the revocation of his agreement with Universal for a sound version of *Blind Husbands* had damaged his reputation as a director almost irrevocably. In the Hollywood film industry, a director is considered only as good as his last film, and Stroheim was rapidly fading. Although hardly forgotten, he was remembered as "difficult," talented but profligate. Furthermore, with the coming of sound, numerous silent film directors were dropped, and a revolution in style, technique, and subject matter took place.

The Fox Studio—which in 1930 had been wrested away from William Fox, its founder—was in corporate difficulties. In 1931, with a gross of almost $39 million, the hitherto profitable company lost $5.5 million. The year 1932 would be even worse, with a gross of about $30 million and an astounding loss of almost $17 million.

In charge of production at the foundering studio was Winfield Sheehan, another Irishman, who respected Stroheim's talents and was convinced by the persuasive Austrian that he could once again direct a marketable and profitable film. In the summer of 1931, Sheehan agreed to let Stroheim develop a property called *Walking down Broadway*. Wary of the difficult artist, Sheehan had the legal staff draw up a contract on

September 2, 1931, which stated that Stroheim was to limit himself to eighty-five hundred feet (about ninety-five minutes), that he would draw one thousand dollars per week but not in excess of seventeen weeks, and that he would be paid thirty thousand dollars upon the film's completion. Either party could terminate the contract. Stroheim was to be assigned a business manager, and the director could not spend any money without permission. In addition, Stroheim was not to appear in the film. Sheehan, in short, tied Stroheim's expensive hands rather tightly.

Walking down Broadway was based on an unproduced play by Dawn Powell, a New York novelist who often examined the problems of small-town Americans who leave their provincial precincts for the big city, as Powell had left her own unhappy Ohio past. On the surface, the project might seem uncongenial to a man who had rendered the Alps, Paris, Monte Carlo, and Vienna, but life in New York City in a lower-middle-class milieu was close to Stroheim's own experience and not that different from the world of *Greed*. Furthermore, *Walking down Broadway* dealt with a subject that he had covered before: innocents abroad, not in this case Americans in Europe but small-town people thrown into the cauldron of the city. He was keenly interested in taking average Americans and giving them the neuroses that would enrich their characters on the screen.

Although well regarded in her time, Dawn Powell (1897–1965) was never a popular novelist—someone once remarked that all her books were first editions—but a major article by Gore Vidal in the *New York Review of Books* (November 5, 1987) helped bring her renewed recognition. By 1989, five of her novels had been reissued; in 1994, a volume containing two of her novels and several short stories appeared; and in late 1998, a biography of her was published. Powell once wrote: "My novels are based on the fantastic designs made by real human beings earnestly laboring to maladjust themselves to fate. My characters are not slaves to an author's propaganda. I give them their heads. They furnish their own nooses."[1] How remarkably close this is to Frank Norris!

A clearheaded observer of humankind, Powell had no agenda. She was not of the "left" (so popular and fashionable in the thirties), nor can she be adopted by the feminists as a crusader, for both her men and her women have flaws. The editor of a recent collection of her writings, Tim Page, describes her as "a worldly, determinedly clear-sighted, deeply skeptical romantic—but a romantic all the same. Love and joy, however transitory they may prove, both *exist* (Powell had seen them plain) and are well worth fighting for, at virtually any cost this side of self-delusion."[2] Obviously, Powell and Stroheim were kindred spirits. They both saw reality, admitted that love—even if transitory—could exist within it, and had no agenda but to tell the truth.

Fox paid $7,500 for the play, and Powell noted in her diary on September 11, 1931, how delighted she was to receive a check for $6,509.70.[3] Later, in 1942, this dedicated artist, feeling suicidal, observed ruefully in her diary that "my fate was offered me in 1936," when she was offered a three-year contract at $1,250, $1,500, and $1,750 a week and that "on rejecting it I must pay forever for not being commercially opportunistic" (198). These could well have been Stroheim's words. In 1953, Powell reread her old play and remarked in her diary that she was "astonished how good it is. Expert, touching, simple and true" (325).

Stroheim worked on the script of *Walking down Broadway* in the late summer and early fall of 1931; a collaborator, Leonard Spigelgass, helped write the dialogue. During this time, Stroheim was offered the tailor-made role of von Furst in RKO's *The Lost Squadron*. Fox gave him permission to suspend his contract on October 7, after which shooting on *The Lost Squadron* began. At its conclusion, Stroheim went back on salary at Fox on December 31.

Suddenly, elemental forces at Fox Studios began to clash. Sheehan was sent away to Europe for a few months in February 1932, and Sol M. Wurtzel, who believed that films were mere products, began an economy drive by canceling contracts, among them Stroheim's. The studio owned the story, for which they had paid seventy-five hundred dollars, and now they had various hacks shape and reshape the Stroheim-Spigelgass script.

Discouraged, Stroheim went to MGM, where he acted opposite Greta Garbo in *As You Desire Me*. Then in June 1932, Sheehan, who had returned to the Fox lot, rehired him. According to *Variety*, Stroheim was now reducing his nine-hundred-page script to a manageable size.[4] Two more versions were made, and by July it was down to ninety-eight pages and was expected to take five weeks to film.[5] Production of *Walking down Broadway* began in mid-August.[6]

Stroheim managed to return to the long shooting sessions that had so distinguished *Queen Kelly*. He worked six days a week and well into the evenings. After forty-eight days, the film was finished at a cost of around $300,000. In comparison, MGM's *As You Desire Me* (1932), which had a famous cast including the very expensive Garbo and other relatively well paid actors, cost $469,000 after only forty-two days of shooting.[7]

Stroheim completed *Walking down Broadway* on time (he claimed later that he was "three days under schedule").[8] The facts that the film was made in such a brief period and that it was "$100,000 below the $357,000 budget" (in Hollywood, budget figures always seem to vary) were so remarkable that they merited a mention in *Variety* on October 11. The trade paper noted two weeks later that Stroheim's "only indulgence" was the concluding fire scene, which was supposed to cost $5,000 and ended at $7,000.[9] Although the film did not have a blockbuster budget, it was certainly more expensive than a typical programmer and showed that the studio, specifically Sheehan, was willing to invest quite a bit of money in Stroheim's meticulous methods of direction. In fact, most of the budget was spent on sets and endless shooting, with only a minute portion devoted to wages for its virtually unknown actors.

After Stroheim completed production in mid-October, the studio seemed pleased, and it announced in *Variety* that he would next direct a film called *His Highness*.[10] The last part of Stroheim's directorial salary for *Walking down Broadway* was paid on November 5, 1932. Publicity began to go out, synopses were printed, pressbooks were made up, and even the stills for the production were sent to the New York Public Library, where they were received on November 21. Stroheim must have felt that the curse had been lifted. After all, he came in with a film of commercial length, on schedule, and without any major fights or even tantrums. He hoped that the mad-movie-director legend had been dashed. But then the euphoria ended, and Stroheim's fate caught up with him.

In early November, the completed film was screened. Stroheim later said, "It was not the usual Fox output, to say the least, because I had some quite unusual characters (not unusual in real life but for Fox pictures)." Suddenly the sexual obsessions, neuroses, and other grim aspects of the film were noticed by the Fox executives and in particular by Sol Wurtzel—in Stroheim's words, "a low-brow if there ever was one."[11] Stroheim's opinion might seem harsh, but Budd Schulberg, in his book *Moving Pictures,* corroborated it by describing Wurtzel as "a prototype of what outsiders thought a Hollywood producer should be. A burly cloak-and-suiter who had never read a book and who had his scenarios synopsized for him by more literate assistants. Sol was known in Hollywood as The Keeper of the B's, the penny-pinching minor mogul who ran the old Fox studio . . . that specialized in oaters and mellers."[12] Wurtzel was a person who felt he had "all the answers," and when he encountered the young Schulberg, he shared his unique wisdom: "If you got a good story, stick to it. The public loves to see the same goddamn story over and over again. They feel comfortable with it. To hell with unhappy endings, offbeat material. I hear these directors bitching about what they really wanna make. Fuck 'em. What they wanna make, maybe five thousand highbrows in the whole country will pay their four bits t' see. I don't give a shit about art. It's a business—and anybody who doesn't think so oughta get out of it!"[13]

Wurtzel took an immediate dislike to *Walking down Broadway* and regarded it as unworthy of Fox. Stroheim explained, "My story went over the head of Wurtzel and my realistic characters were not to his liking (because he believes that all other people are morons like himself)."[14] Wurtzel may have been genuinely appalled by the film's content (as much as he could comprehend), but more likely, he saw the film as a means to undermine his rival, Sheehan, by making it an example of the "high-falutin'" taste that was bankrupting the studio. Sheehan, trying to hang onto his job in a rapidly failing company, buckled under and agreed to have the film reshot. Suddenly lies began to emanate from the studio, and the legend of the impossible Stroheim was dredged up to denigrate the director. The November 15 issue of *Variety* quoted a studio spokesman saying that Stroheim "completed" the film in twenty-one reels and agreed to reduce it to twelve, but that with a new director, Al Werker, it would be brought down to about nine. This tale about its length was a complete lie; the film was of normal length, but the canard was believed because of Stroheim's reputation. Perhaps Stroheim's original film was unpleasant or shocking at certain points, and perhaps some editorial supervision was needed. Offensive scenes undoubtedly could have been rewritten, and perhaps a few lines of dialogue excised or rephrased. What occurred, however, was not an exercise of cool logic but a passionate vendetta against Stroheim or Sheehan. One wonders what Stroheim could have done to engender such hate. This would be no minor bandaging of wounds, but wholesale slaughter.

The decision to reshoot the film was made *before* a preview that occurred sometime in late November, so one can conclude that the preview was a mere formality. *Variety,* on November 22, stated that the studio

> decided to remake about 50% of the picture. . . . Impossible story plus miscasting of Zasu Pitts and Boots Mallory are the reasons. Raoul Walsh will handle the retake. In spite of Miss Pitts' ability, audience refused to accept her in a strongly emotional role. Figured it must be comedy since she's always cast for humorous bits. She will probably be replaced by some other actress not so definitely identified with comedy parts. James Dunn and Terrance Ray, other two members of the cast, gave poor performances with the direction rather than their ability blamed for the result. Boots Mallory in her initial screen effort failed utterly to impress.[15]

This summation of the studio's reaction was clearly a hatchet job, knocking *every* aspect of the film: the story, the direction, and all of the actors. Only the photography went unscathed.

Itching hands grasped at the finished reels. One of the hacks assigned to rework the script a few months later in February 1933 now divided the film into "new" scenes and "old" scenes and reshaped almost the whole story.

Five weeks of additional shooting finally finished the picture. James Wong Howe, the cameraman, remembered Raoul Walsh doing some of the work—probably the Coney Island scenes—but most of the retakes were photographed by other cameramen and directed by Alfred Werker and Edwin Burke. (The *New York Times* erroneously cited Alan Crosland.)[16] Copyrighted and then released in May as *Hello Sister!* with no director credited—no one wanted to be associated with the resultant mess—the film was considered a stupid little trifle and quickly forgotten.

Variety gave an unfavorable review to the fifty-five-minute film (a very short length for such an expensive project):

As screen entertainment, the picture has little to recommend it. Direction and dialog are particularly feeble.

Best item lands when a smart-aleck friend of Dunn's stages a fight with a tough young lady (Minna Gombell). It's a realistic battle. [This scene was Stroheim's.]

Von Stroheim, who directed, is not included in credits on film, press sheet or advertising. Picture does not list any other director since its remake.[17]

Although Stroheim's original film may have been a bit raw and gritty for mass taste, it would have engendered critical interest, and even some notoriety, if for no other reason than Stroheim's wild reputation. There was merchandising value to his name, especially just following his bravura performance in *The Lost Squadron*. The free publicity might have drawn people to see it just because it was infamous or controversial. When the studio decided to junk Stroheim's version and spend additional money for five weeks of extra shooting, it ruined whatever appeal the film might have had. Perhaps one can countenance a producer's tampering with a property for commercial reasons, but the changes in *Walking down Broadway* transformed a probable modest success into a complete flop. It was a bad decision for the studio and absolutely the last blow for Stroheim. In fact, it was the end of his career as a director.

Richard Koszarski and William K. Everson examined the changes in the film in an excellent article in *Film Comment* (May–June 1975). Through a close study of the stills, they demonstrate that only a few scenes are Stroheim's and that the effects on the audience he sought to achieve were almost completely ruined by the meddling. As Stroheim explained, "When people were supposed to laugh they cried, and when they should have cried, they laughed."[18]

Let us try to piece together what Stroheim's original film was like. Below the title *Walking down Broadway* was written on the original script: "An Inconsequential Story concerning small people, along THE GREAT WHITE WAY."

On Broadway on a Saturday night the crane-mounted camera, like fate itself, swoops down on a few mortals below: Peggy (Boots Mallory), Millie (Zasu Pitts), Jimmy (James Dunn), and Mac (Terrance

Ray). In the background in the existing film are signs advertising "Hot Nuts" and "Pleasure beds." Peggy is, as the script says, an "Irish-type, freshly pretty, and a little embarrassed and shy." Her friend, Millie, is a frustrated and rather lonely woman whose main thrills are going to funerals and caring for her pet turtle, Lady Godiva. In the original play, Millie was just an average woman, but Stroheim transformed her into a humorous and pitiful creature—not good-looking, sexually obsessed but unfulfilled, and desperately longing for companionship. Millie, complex and certainly neurotic, has inveigled Peggy to go out and perhaps meet some men. The two fellows they encounter are almost complete opposites of each other in personality. Jimmy—a boy from the country—is nice and sincere, whereas Mac is crude, selfish, and manipulative. One thinks here of the McTeague-Marcus, Danilo-Mirko, and Nicki-Schani contrasts. Mac, described in the script as a "smart-aleck," looks at the sweet, innocent Peggy "lecherously" as the "camera pans down along her body until it strikes her hips." Jimmy, in contrast, looks at her face. This device of delineating male characters by the way they look at women can be seen as far back as *Panthea* and most prominently in *The Merry Widow.*

Stroheim was trying to achieve some social realism, to depict common people with a deeper psychological background than they are usually given in films. These characters may appear as everyday types, but governing their behavior is the instinctive sex drive, a drive that creates love, lust, and jealousy. Stroheim has not forgotten his interest in naturalism.

The boys introduce themselves: when Mac says he is Clark Gable, Millie announces that she is Garbo and avers that Peggy is Gloria Swanson. Mac says, "Well—if it ain't Gloria—I didn't know you with your clothes on." (Was Stroheim taking an opportunity to needle his *Queen Kelly* star and former employer?) An ambulance goes by, and Millie says she loves ambulances. "I'm just a *fool* about accidents." Later, she says, "Oh, I'm just a *fool* about funerals!" Ultimately, she will also announce, "I'm just a *fool* about fate." (All of her interests, of course, were shared by Stroheim himself.)

Jimmy and Peggy immediately like each other, and Millie too is drawn to Jimmy, but Mac makes an immediate move on Peggy and shunts Millie onto the none-too-happy Jimmy. They go to a speakeasy. In the script, when a radio broadcasts the voice of the U.S. prohibition commissioner, the waiter turns the dial in a bit of heavy-handed irony. Mac pulls out some pornographic postcards. (Dirty pictures are also in *The Merry Widow* and, even earlier, in *The Social Secretary*.) "My barber got 'em from Paris," he says, but Jimmy has him put them away. When the girls go to the ladies' room, we overhear another feminine voice in the lavatory say, "So—I went to my doctor—and was back to work on Monday." This casual but realistic reference to abortion prefigures Peggy's future situation. This might seem like some of Stroheim's realism, but allusions to abortion occur in Powell's play as well.

After Peggy and Millie rejoin the boys, Peggy describes her life in New York: "Say! When you've been as lonesome as *me*—with nobody to talk to—but a deaf landlady an' that old club-footed foreman down at the shop—an' you gotta hang on a strap in the subway—an' be pushed around an' stepped on—then work an' work for a couple of measly dollars—washin' an' ironin' an' darning—night after night—*never* goin' anywhere—*never* havin' any *fun*—watchin' the *other* girls with their *fellows* laughin' an' dancin' an' joy-ridin'—! When you been through all that for *seven long* months—you got no pride *left*!" When Mac goes to the washroom, he buys a hot diamond ring with money borrowed from Jimmy. (All of the above has been cut.)

Later, the four go dancing and, on the way home, are surprised to find that they live in buildings almost opposite each other (the boys at number 10, leaving no doubt that the girls are at number 13). Powell originally placed the setting in a boarding house in the West Nineties, but Stroheim shifted the locale to Forty-seventh Street and Ninth Avenue, two blocks south from where he had lived in 1917. Peggy refuses to go to the boys' rooms, but Millie persuades her to invite them to their building. Millie scurries across a board over a sewer excavation and manages to fall in. "Once in my life I'm having a little fun—an' I gotta fall in the sewer," she says unhappily. (Although Stroheim considered Zasu Pitts a great tragedienne, in this film he also makes use of her comic potential.) In a scene later cut from the film, a fellow with a Jewish accent hands Millie a business card and says she can sue. At the sound of a yelp, they spot an injured dog and Jimmy picks it up (compare McTeague's compassion for his birds). Millie says that she has iodine, a salve, and some Pluto water for it. (Pluto water had appeared throughout *Greed*.) When she goes upstairs to shower, Jimmy dresses the dog's wounds and decides to keep the animal. Mac dislikes the creature, complaining that they have enough fleas already. Mac would have thrown the dog in the garbage. (One thinks here of Marcus at the dog hospital, where he kills puppies and disposes of them in the refuse.) Jimmy decides to call the dog "Pick Up," but Peggy suggests "Lonesome," thus clarifying the characters' situations: their relationship is a pickup but also the result of lonesome people coming together.

Mac complains that he is hungry, so Jimmy volunteers to get some hamburgers. Millie asks for a large dill pickle ("I'm just a *fool* about dill pickles"), an allusion to her sexual frustration. After Jimmy leaves, Mac makes a pass at Peggy, who resists by saying she is a "good girl." At this point, Mona (Minna Gombell), a part-time model and an occasional prostitute, enters. Mac recognizes her from a deodorant advertisement that he keeps over his bed. She mentions that she also did ads for Black Raven corn-plasters and for fallen arches. Her modeling jobs echo *The Wedding March's* Schweisser [one who sweats], who was in the corn-plaster business. As an ailment, fallen arches are usually highlighted as comic, but they also suggest lameness, which fascinated Stroheim.

Mona invites the group to her apartment, while Peggy, repelling a kiss from Mac, retreats upstairs. Mac shows Mona the risqué photos he procured from his barber. Shortly after, he gives her the diamond ring for her favors. Millie enters and finds Jimmy busy in the kitchen. She ecstatically takes a giant pickle from Jimmy and is disappointed to hear that he plans to take food to Peggy in her top-floor room. He and Peggy find out that they are both new to the city, and he explains that he works for the People's Bank. He compliments her on her room and sympathizes that she has no window. She tells him that she does in fact have the greatest window in the world. She pulls out the little kitchen table and puts a chair on it; together they climb up and open the skylight. With their feet on the chair, their heads and shoulders are at roof level. A cat crosses the roof. They kiss to the accompaniment of "boat whistles, auto horns, other noises, bell of street-car, elevated train thunders past" (script). The lesson from Frank Norris that life goes on even in significant moments was not lost on Stroheim, and here, as in *Greed,* the thundering train represents the force of human passion. When Millie enters and sees them, she is shocked and disappointed. She mumbles, "Jimmy!" "He does not hear her. Tears rush to Millie's eyes—her lips quiver—her hands fly to her mouth! From outside comes *sound of shrieking siren and ambulance gong—then elevated train thunders past.* Slowly she turns away—with head bowed—heart-broken—she exits. The sound of an ambulance and the rumble of an elevated train accompany her exit. Jimmy spends the night with Peggy and at day-break exits as a street-cleaning truck [similar to the one in *The Merry Widow*] goes by."[19]

On the stairs, Mona says, "Fast work, hayseed," but Peggy replies, "We love each other." Mona says that the only thing that counts is what you get out of the guys. She flashes the diamond ring she obtained from Mac, who enters the hallway and pretends to leave, but then sneaks upstairs into Peggy's room. "So you're a 'good' girl—are you?" he asks. "Well—we'll see just how good you are!" Mac grabs Peggy and is about to rape her, but Mona interferes. Mona and Mac have a roaring fight, kicking and punching each other, in the hall and down the stairs. Mac returns home with some scratches and a black eye and asks Jimmy whether he made the "grade."

The next morning, according to the script, Jimmy takes a shower, "scrubbing vigorously." The scene then shifts to the girls' building, where Mona, in her pajamas with towels on her arm, bangs on the bathroom door. Finally Peggy comes out, "fresh-sweet-clean." Mona grimly says, "You've been in there long enough to wash your ears," a suggestive line indicating that Peggy has taken a long time showering to cleanse herself of the night's passion, leaving only warmth and love.[20] Peggy sees Millie sitting on her bed, pathetically holding Jimmy's hat and weeping. Poor Millie admits she's funny-looking but adds that she has a heart. (Stroheim can be quite compassionate at times.)

A month or so later, at the seed-packing company where Peggy and Millie work, the clubfooted, "nasty" foreman and his cross-eyed assistants watch as Peggy suddenly faints.[21] When she goes to the cashier's window, festooned with a sign wishing "Peace on Earth, Good Will to Men," she is wished a "Merry Christmas" and told that she is fired. Millie, ever helpful, advises Peggy that a good dose of Pluto water will make her feel better. Peggy suspects that she might be pregnant and goes to the medical building, in front of which a number of afflicted people hobble about. She enters a doctor's waiting room—a still includes four people with crutches—and then, after receiving the news of her impending motherhood, calls Jimmy and tells him to meet her. In the street during a heavy rainfall, she informs him that she is pregnant. He is delighted and kisses her passionately, as six men with sand-wich boards advertising wedding rings on the installment plan walk past them.

Jimmy goes to the bank president and with an impassioned speech convinces the boss to transfer him to the bond department and give him a raise. Jimmy returns to his room, where Mac—having learned that a lottery ticket they shared has won—inveigles the ticket from Jimmy. Mac sneers about the wedding, making intimations about Peggy's virtue, and as a result the men fight.

Jimmy hurries off to the marriage bureau, where Peggy has been waiting—the date is December 24 and the clock in one shot reads 3:33. They just miss each other and he rushes to her place, where Millie, burning with jealousy, says that she and Peggy have had lots of lovers. She tells Jimmy that Peggy only took up with him because Mac had left with Mona. Jimmy throws her to the floor and rushes away, as Millie calls hysterically after him. In the street, Jimmy encounters Peggy and angrily tells her that she has played him for a sucker. When she seems bewildered, he asks whether Mac went to her room on the night they met. She says yes and Jimmy, without giving her time to explain, hurries off down the street as a truck passes, advertising balo-ney and playing Christmas carols.

Peggy is heartbroken, and Mona decides to intervene. She goes to Jimmy's place, where she and Mac have an altercation. Then Millie arrives and admits to Jimmy that she lied, but Jimmy refuses to believe her.

Millie returns to the apartment house, stuffs rags under the doors, and turns on the gas. Meanwhile, Jimmy and Mac are seen talking in the street. A fellow approaches and tells Mac that he does not need to get the winning ticket after all, because the lottery turned out to be a fraud. Jimmy realizes that Mac cheated him and decides that he had probably lied about Peggy, too. Just then, an explosion occurs. Fire trucks arrive, and an injured Millie is brought out of the building. Believing Peggy to be inside, Jimmy tries to rescue her, but the ceiling collapses on him and he is carried out, bleeding.

We see that Peggy is in fact at Grand Central Terminal, all set to return to her hometown, but she reads a newspaper report of the explosion and hurries to the hospital. She meets Jimmy and together they visit Millie, who confesses that she loves Jimmy, that she lied about Peggy, and that she tried to commit suicide. The bandages under her chin and over her forehead strongly suggest a nun's wimple. As "Silent Night" plays on the organ of a neighboring church, Peggy and Jimmy exchange gifts. Millie smiles feebly at their happiness and then, crying "Jesus," she dies.

At Eastertime, another religious holiday, Jimmy, with a mourning band, and Peggy are seen walking down Broadway, where they encounter the now married Mac and Mona pushing a baby buggy. A thin stream of liquid trickles out of the buggy, and when Peggy looks in she sees no baby at all but some broken bottles of bootleg liquor. Peggy and Jimmy then look in the window of Betty's Baby Shoppe as the camera pulls back to lose them among all the other people walking down Broadway.

Although Stroheim had worked from Powell's play, by the time of filming he had almost entirely transformed it into a Stroheim creation. The film contains a host of his obsessions: fire engines, lottery tickets, prostitutes, geraniums, dirty postcards, animals, street-cleaning machines, sewers, hospitals, deathbed scenes, hunchbacks, cripples, abortions, attempted rape, and Christmas. The script mixed tragedy, romance, and comedy, and is a considerable improvement over *Queen Kelly*. It shows (as *Greed* had) that he could deal effectively with the American working-class milieu and did not always need Europe as his backdrop. *Walking down Broadway* by no means repeats its predecessors, although it does draw on elements that always seemed to engage him. He could shape the same ingredients into various delicacies.

Stroheim demonstrates his philosophy in the film's imagery: the virginal whiteness of Peggy's room, the religious details, and especially the scene in which they stand on the chair to look out at the stars. If not quite the opposite of the "Let's go sit on the sewer" moment in *Greed,* this scene does reveal that there is a potential for beauty even in proletarian life. Peggy has decorated her squalid room so that it looks pretty, and it even has a view of the heavens; and there is a place on the roof where her geraniums can grow. The film also demonstrates Stroheim's modern morality. He sees nothing wrong with Jimmy and Peggy sleeping together because they do so out of love, but he frowns on crass relationships where there is no emotion, just lust—though he often takes great pleasure in depicting such scenes. Stroheim is sympathetic toward people like Millie, who are eager for sex and companionship, capable of sincere love, but receive nothing.

As usual, Stroheim paid close attention to the look of the film, in terms of such details as furniture, pictures, posters, and advertisements. For a so-called silent director, he was well aware of the dramatic use of sound and included many aural effects in his scenario. He was also fortunate to have a young but excellent photographer, James Wong Howe, who in an interview recounted his experiences. "I was scared when I was assigned to the picture. But we got along fine. We had respect for each other."[22]

Howe recalled that in a dime-a-dance scene Stroheim asked for "a dancing camera." When Howe said he did not know what he meant, Stroheim explained that he wanted "a camera I can move around the floor with," so Howe mounted the camera on a sturdy light stand and wheeled it around to follow the dancing couple. At the end of the film, Millie—severely burned in the fire—was placed "under a canopy in a hospital. We put electric bulbs under it and it created a great effect."[23] Howe also spoke about Stroheim's methods of getting his actors to perform. He especially remembered one very curious incident:

> One day Von Stroheim was directing Terry Ray [who played Mac], and he wanted a certain expression from him, something hysterical, and he couldn't get it. He worked for hours trying. Finally Von Stroheim called the propman over and said, "Do you have a very strong piece of thread about twelve feet long?" The prop man brought him a spool of thread and Von Stroheim took Terry Ray behind some scenery and said, "Take down your pants." Terry did, and Von Stroheim tied the string onto the end of his penis and brought the string down through his pants leg. Now he put Terry in front of the camera and said, "Action." When he wanted the particular expression, he jerked the string![24]

This was not quite method acting, but it was Stroheim's method!

The release print of *Walking down Broadway* retained many of Stroheim's expensive street scenes and the fire episodes but changed most of the story. Millie's characterization is almost completely ruined. Instead of having her attempt suicide by turning on the gas, the new version attributes the explosion to a drunken tenant who collects dynamite. However, it does retain in the reshot footage a telling detail—undoubtedly Stroheim's concept—of Millie burning an area of her slip, suggestive of her pubic area, with a hot iron when she hears about Jimmy and Peggy. The realistic scene at the marriage bureau is Stroheim's. So is the episode in which Jimmy convinces the banker to give him a raise. Jimmy's melodramatic rescue of Peggy from the fire was added, but Millie's death was eliminated.

The existing film is almost a complete travesty, and one of the most frustrating of all Stroheim's works because of its ruination. What a pity that the studio did not at least retain a print of the original cut. One wonders what could have provoked such malevolence in Wurtzel. Some of Stroheim's past producers ruined his films out of necessity—in order to create a salable product by shortening them—but in this case the Fox company seemed to take delight in trashing almost his entire work and, as a consequence, they lost even more money for themselves. Perhaps Stroheim's dedication, assertiveness, and undoubted skills struck a raw nerve in Wurtzel, who may have resented the seeming Austrian aristocrat and wanted to give Stroheim his comeuppance, showing him that he was no better than Wurtzel.

Some of the appeal of Dawn Powell's play must have been that it, in some ways, echoes the director's own biography. After all, he had lived in a similar New York City boarding house, had fallen in love there, had impregnated Mae Jones, and had married her. He had also spoken to Laemmle as convincingly as Jimmy speaks to the bank president. Shrewdly, Stroheim places his more cynical and lecherous side in Mac, reserving his kinder, more sentimental, and more loving side for Jimmy. Because of these personal elements, it must have been painful for Stroheim to see this particular work eviscerated.

As a consequence of the disaster of *Walking down Broadway,* Stroheim's other projects with Fox disintegrated. According to *Variety* on November 29, Stroheim was slated to direct a film called *Her Highness Commands* (unrelated to Stroheim's similarly titled script), a UFA picture bought by Fox to remake. A week later, *Variety* said that the film would now be directed by William Dieterle. Then, in its December 13 issue, there was a mention of Stroheim "dickering with Goldwyn" to direct the first Anna Sten picture. Nothing happened with that project either. Nor would it with any other.

Her Highness Commands finally came out as *Adorable,* released in May 1933. This operetta, written in part by Billy Wilder, is about a dashing officer (Henri Garat) who is elevated by a royal woman (Janet Gaynor) from a lieutenant to a prince. According to *Variety* it was "well done in many respects—and in many respects, overdone." The reviewer noted that fairy-tale musical comedies had become too familiar and that Henri Garat, who had starred in the French version, would have "no sock according to American standards."[25] *Variety* was right. It was his only American film. One wonders what Stroheim might have done with this project. Would he have given this expensive but sugar-coated tale enough bite to make it a hit, which it was not? Would it then have raised him to the first rank of directors and brought the same commercial and artistic renown as *The Merry Widow*?

It was not only Millie who was "just a fool about fate." In early November 1932, Stroheim was a contented man—or at least as contented as a man like him could be. He had completed a film on time and on budget. Now all kinds of new projects were waiting. But then fate stepped in. One month later, by Christmas, his dreams of a rewarding future had dissolved into a nightmare more hideous than even his own fertile mind could have created. One can only imagine his sardonic and cynical smile as he sat during a time of carols and wreaths, thinking about the fractured and bare bones of what would be his last child.

15

The Depths

Beset by financial worries and seemingly banished from directing, Stroheim grew more depressed and more desperate. Director Rouben Mamoulian related to me a strange story about Stroheim at this period. "It's a tale in which I don't particularly shine," he said, "and which I am not proud of, but I'll explain."[1] In early 1933, when Mamoulian was casting *The Song of Songs,* he needed a continental type and thought Stroheim would be ideal. He respected Stroheim very much and was anxious to meet him. However, he was a little reluctant to offer such a great talent a mere acting role.

Stroheim came for the interview and, after a few minutes, became chatty, relating some graphic stories about his sexual exploits. Although Mamoulian did not consider himself a puritan by any means, he disliked this kind of talk and was terribly disappointed that the director he so respected would mention such things. In fact, the conversation was so distasteful that Mamoulian decided not to use Stroheim. Feeling that he could not say "No" to such a man, Mamoulian said he would let him know. A few days later, Stroheim inquired about his decision. Mamoulian, uncomfortable about what to do, had an assistant tell Stroheim he would have to make a screen test. This, Mamoulian thought, would be such an insult that Stroheim would refuse. But he showed up for the test, which another man directed. Mamoulian cast Lionel Atwill in the part.

Years later, in 1955, when Mamoulian came to Paris with the

musical *Oklahoma!* Stroheim arrived at the theater. Mamoulian asked him whether he would mind going backstage, because many in the cast would like to meet him. Stroheim complied and later invited Mamoulian to Maxim's, where he mentioned his rejection for *The Song of Songs.* Stroheim confessed that he had been frightfully nervous and, out of sheer panic, had switched the subject to sex. The light dawned on Mamoulian, and he was sorry that he had not understood how desperate Stroheim's situation had been.

Although Stroheim was unemployed, he continued to write, and in early 1933 he put the finishing touches on *Poto Poto,* a script that included some elements from the African section of *Queen Kelly.* He submitted this to MGM, in the form of a dialogue continuity; on April 10, a synopsis prepared by a studio reader was sent to the studio's story editor. This hitherto unpublished document shows how long, complicated, and peculiar one of Stroheim's story ideas could be:

> Mademoiselle Soukoff, a product of the war, known as "Roulette Masha," "The Siren," "The Sweetheart of Seven Seas," a supposed Russian princess, is plying her trade on the palatial ocean liner, *Prince of Wales,* bound from Port Said to Zanzibar on the Red Sea. Her method of conquest is the roulette wheel—if she loses, she gives herself to the winner, and if she wins, she receives the money. Aboard the boat, she meets . . . Henry Smith, an American businessman. After dancing, they adjourn to her rooms where the American wins. The American's wife creates a scene when she learns of her husband's being with the notorious woman and calls for the Captain who arrives at the stateroom with the 1st officer. Mrs. Smith demands that the woman be put off at the next port. . . . The next morning the Captain tells Masha to leave at . . . Mombasa-Milindi, which will be reached in an hour.
>
> She is put off at this out-of-the-way place. At the hotel she meets Mme Celestine, the owner, and Octave, her husband, uncouth and tawdry people. Dining in her room that evening she recognizes the waiter as Atkins, a cockney who had served her in her travels.
>
> Later she goes down to the bar where she is greeted by "Poto Jan"—a Mr. Vrenen, a landowner and trader who has

been in Africa twenty-five years. He has arrived at the hotel for a "bust" and is surrounded by all the "girls" of the place—"Fifi," "Senna," the Siamese twins, Sonya, a mixed group of all nationalities—when Masha comes on the scene. She rebukes his advances and returns to her room where he, in a rage at his first refusal by a woman, rushes after her, breaks down the door and starts to lash her with a whip he always carries. Her cold reaction sobers him and, begging forgiveness, he offers marriage. She offers to play roulette—if red wins she will receive money and if black wins she will marry him. The black wins, so they go down to the bar to order a preacher. A wedding feast is prepared—a Negro missionary arrives and performs the ceremony and a vulgar celebration follows.

Next morning Masha and "Poto Jan" leave in his Rolls Royce—bound for his home. They leave the car and travel by boat, the trip awakening her to her husband's wealth for they pass truckloads of ivory bearing his name. On the boat she meets a friend, Capt. Robert Cavendish, who is bound for his station. The meeting causes jealousy on her husband's part. On trail four days, they arrive at his plantation in the swamps.

Their first evening at home, with Bibi, his Swahili housekeeper, jealously hovering near, is interrupted by the incident of "Poto Jan" being bitten by the Glossina Tse Tse fly. In a frenzy he calls . . . for Dr. Krontz . . . an ex-German Army doctor. The doctor explains the effects of the bite to Masha—the fevers, the sleeping sickness and the hopeless end. He sends for Sister Celia, a nurse, arranges for Poto Jan's care, and leaves.

A few weeks later Jan is in delirium with natives outside performing the protective "Devil Dance." Bibi, the beautiful Swahili housekeeper, tries to put the magic medicine—a live goat's tail—in Poto Jan's hand but Masha interferes.

Four months later Masha, suggesting their going to Europe for medical aide, hears of Poto's distrust of her. She promises to stay and he, in thankfulness, plans a new home for her.

Eight months later, the villa is ready. Masha has contracted malaria and the doctor is nursing them both. Poto Jan suspects both the wife and doctor and refuses to take his medicine. From this frenzy of distrust, he goes to the other extreme and presents her with a priceless strand of black pearls . . . to add to the jewel collection he has given her. He is still able to take care of his business and leaves for one of his posts, being sure the doctor leaves at the same time.

After their leaving a storm blows up, a plane is seen overhead, the motor missing, the aviator takes to parachute and lands in the swamp. Masha with black boys rescues him and learns that it is Captain Tim Hawks who had left Bolling Field on a 'round-the-world flight. A broken ankle is the only mishap to the Marine Corps flyer, who also contracts an affair of the heart—falling in love with Masha. She, also, is attracted, and for the first time since her arrival dons an evening gown. While they are having after-dinner coffee, Jan is silently wheeled into the room by Bibi. After introductions Jan leaves irritably upset. Another incident with medicine and Jan, against his will power, fearing to leave them alone, falls asleep. Masha wheels him to his room and undresses him, leaving Bibi as guard.

Overcome by love, Masha stays in the bungalow with the Captain. Bibi, spying, awakens Jan . . . and the two watch shadows of the Captain and Masha through the windows. In early morning Masha returns and sees Jan in his room watching her. She confesses her love. Later, prepared to leave with the Captain, she meets Jan in the living room and gives him the jewels but finds herself a prisoner.

The Captain, ready to leave, is told by Jan that he is to stay another day. Bibi comes to the Captain that night and says Masha is waiting in her room—she leads him to a tree where he is to climb to Masha's room. He finds . . . he is a prisoner. Jan, after a fight in which he shoots the Captain in the shoulder, orders the two tied and, together with black boys, carries them to a boat where they row in crocodile-infested waters to a swamp where they are tied to a tree—the storm waters rising so that their planned death will be by crocodiles devouring them.

Bibi, in Masha's room, parading in Masha's clothes and jewels, is surprised by Jan's return—he lashes her in a frenzy of disapproval and is overcome by sleep. Bibi, in anger, calls the doctor and tells him what has happened.

The Cross, the maiden, and the half-wit rapist. *The Honeymoon*.

Prince Nicki returning to the abandoned wine garden where he had first wooed Mitzi in *The Honeymoon* (1928). The sign says "For sale," and the woman who accosts him is similarly available.

Prince Nicki in his mountain outfit talking to his beloved Mitzi (Fay Wray) in *The Honeymoon*.

In *Queen Kelly,* the prince (Walter Byron) looks lovingly at the convent girl (Gloria Swanson).

His career in ruins, Stroheim turned to acting with *The Great Gabbo.* Hollywood perceived more than one dummy in this scene.

Above: A scene from *Friends and Lovers* (1931). *Below:* Stroheim playing mad director Von Furst in *The Lost Squadron* (1932). Notice the six megaphones, his white gloves, and his cane.

Above: The "blackguard" Sangrito possessing his "beloved" (Lili Damita) in *Friends and Lovers*. *Below:* Garbo being kissed in *As You Desire Me.*

In *Walking Down Broadway,*
the lovers gaze at the sky as
Millie (Zasu Pitts) mourns
the loss of her Jimmy.

Having betrayed his duty for love
of a woman, this super-spy
injects himself with poison and
plays the piano until he dies in
Marthe Richard.

The lecherous, but not unkind, captain contemplates a new conquest in *The Fugitive Road* (1934).

Stroheim with hair in *L'Affaire Lafarge* (1937) and *Scotland Yard* (1945).

The Kommandant with the neck brace in *La Grande Illusion* (1937).

The Chinese general in *Les Pirates du Rail* (1938).

Above: Stroheim with cane and his confederates, Peter Lorre and Vera Zorina, in *I Was an Adventuress* (1940). *Below:* Denise Vernac and Stroheim as they finish a matinee of *Arsenic and Old Lace.*

In one of the few good moments from *The North Star:* Stroheim as the Colonel wittily derides his assistant (Martin Kosleck).

The once "unfit" soldier now promoted to General Rommel in *Five Graves to Cairo* (1943).

Stroheim was a screen presence even from the back. *Five Graves to Cairo.*

Above: In another of his mad doctor roles, with glasses perched on his forehead, in *The Lady and the Monster* (1944) with Richard Arlen and Vera Hruba Ralston. *Below:* As the "God-damned butler," Stroheim eyes William Holden, the new lover, in *Sunset Boulevard* (1949).

An echo of his former directing days: the last poignant scene of *Sunset Boulevard*.

Among the happy faces of William Holden, Gloria Swanson, and Nancy Olson, the "has-been" Stroheim glowers.

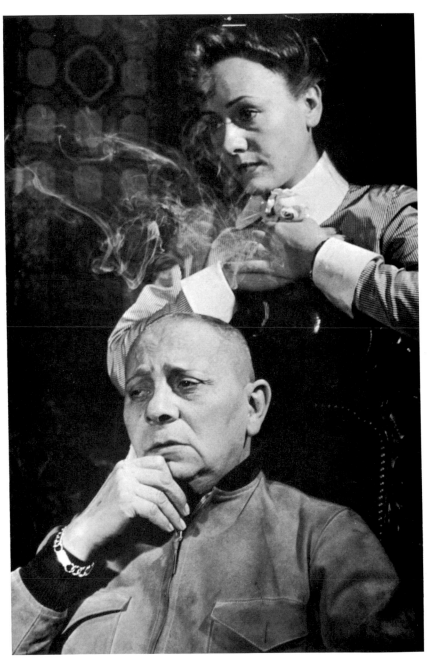

Stroheim and his long-time companion Denise Vernac.

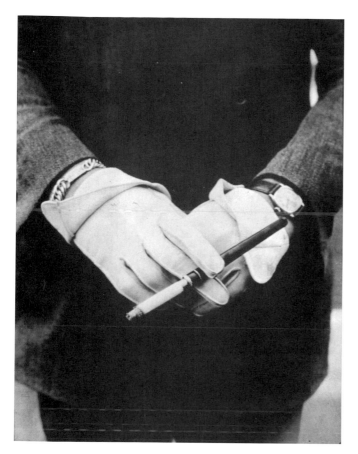

Elegance, including the golden bracelet from his wife, Valerie, which he always wore.

Two months before Stroheim's death, he received the French Lion of Honor—his one true medal—and is congratulated by French director Rene Clair.

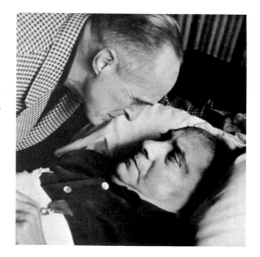

Sweetheart!.

Just a couple of roses --- to let you know I haven't forgotten!.

all my wishes for you go with them!

The rest --- (just a kiss) I'll bring to-night!.

I love you!!!

Erich

x x x x x
x x x x x
x x x x
x x x x
x x x x
x x x x x

An undated letter from Stroheim to wife Valerie.

The doctor arouses Capt. Cavendish and, with 50 men and equipment, they start out in the storm to rescue Masha and the Captain. After fighting the elements and swamps, they arrive at Jan's villa and the doctor tries to find out through Jan where the two are. Bibi starts to tell them and is shot by Jan. The doctor forces Jan to tell and together they start out—blacks, soldiers and officers for the rescue.

The boats arrive just as a giant python is crushing the two tied to the tree—as vultures are hovering near and as crocodiles are snapping at their feet. Returning, the doctor finds that Jan is dead in the boat.

The doctor, with British army surgeon, Raleigh, work over Masha and the Captain—unavailingly. Krontz, a psychologist, recognizes that he must reach their unconscious minds—as they think they are already dead, they are offering no fight. He carries out a plan, despite the feeling of the others that he has lost his mind. He orders Raleigh to prepare hot sealing wax—he tells Cavendish to get blank cartridges and for the buglers and drummers to come to the sick room. At a given signal a bedlam of noise is let loose—the two doctors drop hot sealing wax directly over the heart of Masha and the Captain—and when their eyelids flutter the two are turned to face each other—Krontz then tells them that they are alive—that Jan is dead—and that they must fight. Their work is accomplished—the two, unless complications arise, will live.[2]

Another studio reader offered the following analysis of this tale:

Atmosphere is handled with excellent effect and is the chief value here. The leading character has qualities and some "business" that sell on the screen; but in the higher melodramatics he is too fiendish to be believed. The woman does not ring true at any point and does not win sympathy either as a siren or a regenerate. It is the "villain's" story all through, and he has enough color and strength to be worthy, perhaps, of rehandling. Occasional scenes are extremely good, and all features of "locale" are vivid and picturesque. Dialogue is spotty—some clever, some ponderous.[3]

As was typical for Stroheim, this film story had enough incidents to make a five-hour film, unless it was condensed considerably. From *Queen Kelly* (original title, *The Swamp*), he had brought back Jan, the planter, as well as other plot elements. The story also reveals that Stroheim had a great feeling for atmosphere and for odd but memorable characters. At the same time, the whole concept is childish, grotesquely melodramatic, and in some ways, repellent. Masha, the female lead, is so morally dubious that she would have enraged American censors and displeased the average filmgoer. Furthermore, such unlikely elements as parachutists, giant pythons, and voodoolike rituals are the stuff of a Saturday matinee serial, not a serious, high-budget feature. Much modified and much condensed, with someone like Marlene Dietrich as the star, it might have been made but seems unlikely to have been a success. A somewhat similar story, *Red Dust* (1932), had succeeded with Clark Gable and Jean Harlow as the leads, but that film had warmth and humor, without all the grotesqueries. Wise heads prevailed at MGM, and Stroheim's script was rejected. Nor was any other studio tempted.

It was during this period that the full extent of the *Walking down Broadway* fiasco became evident with the release of *Hello Sister!*, which was a critical and financial disaster and seemed to prove that Stroheim was an uncontrollable fanatic. His name may have been off the credits, but it was still scandalously on everyone's lips. In Hollywood—an extremely trendy community always acutely conscious of status—he had become a kind of pariah. The prevailing attitude was that one should stay clear of people on the way down, for their bad luck might be catching. Stroheim was not on the way down. He was now at the bottom.

The period from November 1932 through 1935 had to be the worst years of Stroheim's life. Not only were there no directing opportunities, but, even more disturbing, there was not even an acting job at a major studio. At home, life was no better. Under all this stress, his marriage was faltering; he began drinking heavily, and at times he felt suicidal. Then fate added another nightmarish experience. On September 2, 1933, his wife, Valerie, went to a beauty shop for a dry shampoo. The solution put on by the beautician suddenly ignited, and Valerie was enveloped in flames. She was rushed to Our Lady of Angels Hospital (Stroheim must have loved the Catholic symbolism), where she

stayed for several weeks, her husband at her side. Although Valerie recovered, she was seriously disfigured. Not long after, Stroheim's son
Josef came down with what was thought to be infantile paralysis. In
December 1934, Stroheim's second wife, Mae Jones, sued him for
nonsupport of Erich Junior, their eighteen-year-old son. Stroheim,
for a change, was not exaggerating about his poverty. He even had to
pawn some of his belongings to make ends meet. News of his plight
reached John Considine, a hard-drinking Irishman who was one of
the producers at MGM. He sent out notes asking for contributions.
Myrna Loy in her autobiography said that she had kept Considine's
interoffice memo as a "warning" of how successful people could
plummet:

Dear Myrna,

Mr. and Mrs. Erich Von Stroheim are in dire want and several
of their old friends on the lot have suggested that we make up
a Christmas Fund to at least help them out of their immediate
difficulties.
   If you feel inclined to join in this much needed collection,
will you please give John Farrow your check for $25.00 or
more and make same payable to Reverend John O'Donnell,
who has done more than anyone else to help the Von Stroheims
through their very serious troubles. Father O'Donnell will give
Von a list of our names, together with the check, as I am sure
that Von would be much happier about the matter if he knew
the names of those who thought of him at this time.

John[4]

Ultimately, Stroheim received a leather wallet containing $850. He
was grateful but so humiliated that he threatened to commit suicide
on Christmas Eve, a day he had always associated with disaster. Talked
out of his decision, he vowed that he would pay back the money given
him (which he eventually did).
   Much later, in 1950, when Valerie was trying to get some support
money from Stroheim, she wrote a letter to her husband in France.
Hurt and resentful—he had tried to hide a considerable sum from her
in the previous year—she summarized her life with him:

The way you speak and write you'd think in my whole life, all I ever thought of was my own welfare.

Just to refresh your memory!

When you were unemployed—you had obligations to your Ex-Wife [which continued for 21 years] in which time I worked, managed to economize in order to meet her demands, and then because of your lack of funds you were brought into court to explain the situation, and in future years, you were made by law, to settle back payments, etc.

Do you remember—

The days when I worked with you on the sets, because you were told by Pat Powers and L. B. Mayer they would let you direct or give you a job, *only* if I would be with you at all times? [She was considered to be the only person who could calm his rages and convince him to be reasonable.] Of course, *I* did not receive a salary for my services from the studios or from you, nor did *I* receive a chauffeur's fee for driving you to and from the studio as far back as 1918—nor did *I* receive a stenographer's salary for taking dictation.

I figured all I could do to help you and your career was no more than a real woman with common sense would do—to see her husband progress.

You *must* remember—when you were unemployed for more than five years and head over heels in debt, and we did not know what to do next, I continued under the most trying circumstances, with burned hands to do the housework, cook over a hot stove, and when you finally got a job, drove the car which had a canvas top, which had holes in it, and leaked in the rainy weather, so that it was necessary . . . to drive along with an umbrella over our heads, with the point of the umbrella sticking through the hole in the top of the car to keep the rain off of us as we drove along.

The time also came when I pawned my jewelry I had—and was ready to melt the 2 gold bracelets you gave me to be able to get money for food. Then—when friends heard of our predicament and they offered us money—to help us out—we accepted their charity—which was headlined all over the world—So—when you speak of diamond bracelets, etc. You'd think my life with you was a bed of roses, gifts of diamond bracelets every morning and two on holidays.[5]

Although some of the stories about Stroheim's life during the early thirties might appear exaggerated, this private letter confirms the grim facts.

With time on his hands, Stroheim began a number of writing projects. One of them dealt with gypsy life. When no studio seemed interested in the subject—he had hoped it would be a good vehicle for Goldwyn's Anna Sten—he transformed it into a novel called *Paprika,* published in February 1935. The sensitivity, broad social vision, and close observation of character that so enhance Stroheim's screenplays of *Merry-Go-Round* and *The Wedding March* are totally absent here, replaced by embarrassingly foolish incidents that essentially go nowhere. The book is so full of sensational and overblown scenes and so packed with detail as to be basically unreadable.

Paprika is a gypsy girl who loves a boy named Janesi, but almost from her infancy, she spends her time tormenting him. What she wants is not his submissive and kind love, but a brutal one. This perverse woman dooms their relationship by her willfulness. Eventually, after hundreds of pages of unhappiness and frustration, the two are killed and, in their dying moments, she finally admits that she loves him. Her exasperating behavior echoes Stroheim's own tendency toward willfulness and his habit of transforming potential successes into failures. When *Paprika* was submitted to MGM, the studio reader aptly summed it up: "A trashy story, written for sensationalism only. Long and Dull."[6]

Desperate for money throughout 1934, Stroheim agreed to appear in *Crimson Romance* (released on September 26, 1934) for Mascot, a small company noted for its cheap "quickies." Stroheim knew full well that by going to such a firm he was giving ample proof he was a "has-been." As Stroheim said years later, "I stooped as low as one can possibly stoop."[7] He would be joined by another once-famous star, Ben Lyon.

Reverting to the old stereotype, Stroheim again played a German officer—in this case an aviator—in a film that, despite its low budget, had good production values. It employed spectacular stock footage of airplanes from *Hell's Angels* (1930) and conveniently reused some cockpit shots of Ben Lyon, who had appeared in that picture. Mascot also filmed on some standing sets at Universal, which were rented for a day or so. The film had effective lighting and even a fairly credible, if unusual, plot echoing the pacifistic sentiments of the time. In short, the result may have been inexpensive, but it did not look it. In fact, with the stock footage and some imagination, it ended up with 481 shots, an ambitious number for a "cheap" film. As *Variety* noted, "By indie standards *Crimson Romance* is a pretentious production."[8]

During the early years of the First World War, Bob (Ben Lyon) and his German friend Hugo are test pilots for a factory in America. When Hugo is fired because of his German ancestry, Bob quits in protest, but no one else will hire the team because of anti-Teuton prejudice. Hugo decides to return to his homeland, and Lyon impetuously accompanies his buddy. It is now 1916 and they both join the German air force, more out of a desire to fly than for nationalistic reasons. They are assigned to a German airfield commanded by Captain Walters (Stroheim), also a flyer. We first see him as he strides into view in full uniform, carrying a cane and wearing a monocle and a black armband of mourning. He regards the two recruits, who are covered with mud because of a slight accident, with disapproval. "Obviously," he says, "you are not German." The fellow answers, "No, sir—American." The captain replies, "A rather dirty American, what?" He is answered with the snappy rejoinder, "Clothes don't make the man." According to the script, the captain's "eyes glint at this remark; He rubs his nose as he restrains his anger" and replies, "We do not tolerate filth in the flying corps." This line is crossed out in the final script and omitted from the film, probably for being too strong. The captain, pointing to his armband, mentions that his best friend was killed by Americans flying in the French Lafayette Escadrille.

Later, during the first dogfight of the film, Bob discovers that the machine gun of an enemy plane is jammed, and so he refuses to fire on it. The captain sees this from his plane and, swearing, downs the helpless opponent. At a later inquiry, he accuses Bob of cowardice, and when the American explains that it seemed unsporting to shoot an unarmed man, the ruthless captain denies that the enemy's guns had jammed and adds that he is happy he made the kill.

Earlier, when Bob and Hugo have an accident while riding along the road, they meet an attractive female ambulance driver. (Incidentally, Stroheim met Valerie, his wife, when she drove an ambulance in

Hearts of the World.) Bob, always a ladies' man, comes on strong with the girl in comparison to the shy German. The girl likes Bob, despite his brashness, and they spend many hours together. As a result, he misses his next air battle. The captain is furious but decides not to court-martial Bob for desertion; he needs all the men he can get.

The plot thickens when America enters the war and Bob must choose between being shot as a deserter or fighting for Germany. The captain orders Hugo to escort the American to his plane and sarcastically remarks, "An amazing finish to a devoted friendship!" Hugo then engages in a sham fistfight with Bob, who knocks his friend down and escapes in an airplane as the German smiles and fires his gun into the air. The captain doubts that the fight was genuine and is convinced that the escape was planned. Meanwhile, Bob lands his German plane in Allied territory and immediately falls under suspicion. To prove himself not a spy, he leads the American squadron to the German munitions depot. In the ensuing dogfight, Hugo saves his friend, who is about to be shot down, by crashing his plane into the captain's. After the war ends, Bob and the ambulance driver visit the dead Hugo's mother in America in a scene full of pacifist statements.

In *Crimson Romance,* Stroheim puffs his cigarettes steadily, seems to enjoy making a few sarcastic remarks, and—never abandoning his obsession with numbers—refers to the fact that only thirteen planes out of fifteen have returned. He is gallant with the woman ambulance driver and, at one point, even sends a glass of beer to Bob. The cordial and polite side of the real Stroheim comes out here occasionally, but otherwise the plot does not allow him to do much, except once again to be the man you love to hate, another ruthless Hun. *Variety* felt that in his "minor role as a captain with a sadistic love of death . . . he did the best acting job in the film," although cattily adding that he is "considerably fatter these days." Stroheim, years later, said, "What the story was about I could not tell to save my soul and I cared less. For the first time in my career I just acted like an automaton to bring home the shekels (and very few at that)."[9] Stroheim was being a bit harsh with himself. It is a good performance and shows that he could not just walk through the part, no matter how limited it was.

Still, Stroheim remembered the period bitterly: "That abortion," he declared, "was followed by another one." The new abortion was called *The Fugitive Road,* made for an independent firm called Invincible Pictures. In 1947, Stroheim wrote to Peter Noble, "I hope you are correct in your cast sheets of the two above masterpieces because with the exception of Ben Lyon and Vera Engels I don't remember any other one of the actors."[10]

Stroheim almost totally forgot *The Fugitive Road,* but despite its small budget, it is a reasonably enjoyable work. In fact, many scenes reveal that he had materially rewritten the script. For a change, Stroheim is not playing the stock villain but in some ways is reprising his Prince Nicki role from *The Wedding March.* Polite, gallant, bored, and somewhat lecherous, he is capable under his gruff exterior of making some gentlemanly gestures. Indeed, it is an interesting study for his Rauffenstein character in *La Grande Illusion* and indicates that Stroheim, more than Renoir, created Rauffenstein.

The film opens on the Austrian border, where a sign identifies Stroheim's character as Captain Oswald von Traunsee (which makes use of Stroheim's actual middle name). The commandant has been banished to command this remote and useless post to keep him out of Vienna. Apparently, he had had too much of an eye for the ladies, particularly the attractive wife of the minister of war. The film's introduction of von Traunsee first shows a pair of boots lying on a couch. The camera pans across the sleeping body to show a detective magazine covering his face. An orderly enters the room to wake the captain and, after a moment's hesitation, carefully moves a heavy object out of reach so he will not be hit with it. The awakened von Traunsee glances at where the missing object was and, with nothing to throw, complains about his useless role as a functionary at this border post, his main task merely to stamp passports.

Von Traunsee goes to a mirror to put on his helmet and bawls out his orderly for handing him the helmet with the chin straps twisted. Then he calls for his gloves and goes outside to inspect the troops. He is furious at their slovenliness. In unsubtitled German, he says, "Lieutenant, I take it as a personal insult. That is impertinence. They look like drunken tailor apprentices, not like Austrian soldiers. The whole outfit, no day off on Sunday, and this tramp, solitary confinement on water and bread!"

A lieutenant who is about to go on furlough back to Vienna playfully taunts the captain by asking him (in German) whether he should call on Fräulein Mimi. Von Traunsee tells him to shut up and speak

English. (They switch languages so that the others will not understand their conversation and so that American audiences will.) The lieutenant refers to the captain's reputation as a lady-killer and says teasingly that in a few hours he will be in the beautiful city of Vienna "and I'll be thinking of you all the time." The captain thanks him and cheerfully adds: "And I hope you break your neck!" The lieutenant torments him, saying that he will send him "photographs of all the pretty girls I meet." Von Traunsee replies, "Well, that will be some relief—better than looking at that!" as the film cuts to a fat peasant woman leaning over to pick up something. As the script says, "her large unshapely legs are exposed." Von Traunsee bitterly remarks, "Of all the hope-forsaken holes in the entire Universe, this is it. It's never been so easy for me to keep the Ten Commandments in all my life!"

When a man in a car crashes through the border gate, von Traunsee pulls out his pistol and shoots a tire. The driver is an American but without a valid passport. Von Traunsee recognizes him as Riker (Leslie Fenton), a gangster whose "wanted" picture he saw in the detective magazine he had been reading. Nonetheless, he politely allows the man to join him in a smoke, whereupon Riker brazenly lights his cigarette with the flame that von Traunsee is using for himself. When the gangster reveals that he had been in the army's Rainbow Division and was wounded at the Somme, the captain replies, "So we have met before." As they discuss the battle, Riker insolently sits on the captain's desk. Even so, the captain generously gives him several cigarettes before having him locked up.

A young and innocent woman, a Russian with a Hungarian passport, hopes to sail to America to join her brother but has been stopped at the border. Von Traunsee hears from his assistant that there is a woman waiting. "Old?" the captain asks. "No, young." "Pretty?" "Very pretty." He goes to the door and glances at the attractive girl. He then combs his hair, throws his daily uniform in his orderly's face, and selects his more impressive dress outfit. The orderly sprays him with cologne.

Looking and smelling better, the captain invites the woman to his quarters and explains that her passport is a forgery. Without a proper passport, she cannot cross the border and thus will miss her boat to America. Von Traunsee decides she is fair game, and the orderly, familiar with the captain's standard procedure for seduction, plays a waltz on the phonograph—the same waltz used in *The Wedding March*. The captain takes off the woman's shawl, admires her face, and tells her that Vienna is the "home of beautiful women" and that there she would be "appreciated." He kisses her hand and is keen to bed this sweet girl. His lecherous mood is broken when he is called away to examine an ambulance containing a comatose man, accompanied by his doctor, who is being rushed for an emergency operation. The captain, skeptical, looks in the ambulance—ah, Stroheim and his ambulances!—and sees the man's face swathed in bandages, reminiscent of Stroheim's wife's injured face. Observing several cigarette stubs on the floor (reading detective magazines has paid off), he orders the patient to be carried into the building and commands that the bandages be removed. Hidden in them are diamonds.

Meanwhile, the American gangster has been speaking with the girl, who intends to join her brother in America. He knows that the brother, a fellow criminal, was killed six months earlier and feels sorry for her. He enters the captain's quarters—a nice dinner has been set, with flowers on the table—and tells the captain to leave her alone. "Under that uniform, in spite of that glass eye [meaning the captain's monocle], you're a human being and a good egg." Let the "frightened kid" go, he says. The captain replies, "Not tonight—maybe tomorrow or the day after—but not tonight." The American replies, "Listen, flap ears. Get this through your square head. She's going with me tonight whether you like it or not." Despite the American's arrogant attitude, the captain retains a gentlemanly sense of humor: "You know, I should get angry with you."

After the American leaves, the girl enters the room where the captain hopes to seduce her. "Don't be frightened," he says. "I want you to enjoy this little dinner." The orderly—used to this routine— pours champagne, but the captain notes that she does not join him in the drink. "I want you to be happy," he says, to "wash away this sordid, filthy place from memory." And, rather poignantly, he tells her to imagine "that I am younger again and you're my companion."

This tête-à-tête with the girl is interrupted by the American, who has taken the captain's gun and threatens to kill him if he does not allow the girl to escape. He explains that he intends to marry her so that she will have an American passport. Von Traunsee is forced at gunpoint to order a car, and they proceed to the burgomaster for the ceremony. The captain tells Riker that he must be insane and that the institution of marriage is equally so. After the two are wed, the American gives the captain back his gun. The captain then reveals that it is empty, a fact that he had known all along. Riker says, "I am your prisoner," well aware of the troops outside. The captain generously replies, "You underestimate me. You don't think I would take you away on your wedding night!" Riker, however, is too much of a gentleman to take advantage of his bridegroom's privileges. The captain has trouble understanding this reluctance to bed the pretty girl, particularly after having married her. "You are more insane than I thought you were.... Don't throw away precious moments." The captain then orders Riker to spend the night with his new wife and tells him that the house "will be surrounded by my soldiers to protect you from intruders." (What a polite way to tell him that he cannot escape!) The American confesses to the girl that he is wanted by the police, but she says she loves him anyhow and will wait for him. He returns her passionate kiss, and they go upstairs for their wedding night.

The next day, at the railroad station, von Traunsee bids the couple farewell with a gallant salute. As the train departs, he observes a shapely leg on a girl at the station, puts his monocle back on, takes another look, adjusts his coat, and moves toward her as the film ends. (This final moment is reminiscent of how Stroheim's sound remake of *Blind Husbands* would have ended.)

Stroheim as von Traunsee appears quite human in this film. He is lecherous, assertive, and bossy, yet also gentlemanly and almost good-humored. Dressed in his uniform complete with all the medals, his monocle glistening, and almost continuously smoking a cigarette, he cuts quite a figure of authority. He would have liked to bed the girl—it would be a diverting way to spend the night at this God-forsaken outpost—but he is not a cad, merely an opportunist.

Throughout the film, Stroheim's interests are well in evidence: the ambulance, the stretcher-bearers, the waltz music, the champagne, the cologne, and the carefully set table with flowers. The dialogue, too, shows that Stroheim had rewritten at least his own lines to his liking. In fact, to this date there was no film, except perhaps *The Wedding March,* that shows more what the offscreen Stroheim may have been like, or what he would have liked to be in real life. Perhaps Stroheim had trouble remembering this film because at the time of its production—it took only a few days to shoot—he was near the depths of his despair.

Except for *Crimson Romance* and *The Fugitive Road,* which totaled no more than a few weeks' work, Stroheim remained unemployed throughout 1934. There was no money, he was being sued for nonsupport of Erich Junior, and his career was in ruins. While waiting for something good to happen or, indeed, anything at all to happen, he started another scenario, called *Blind Love,* and after several months' work, he submitted it to MGM. One of the readers in the studio's story department made a six-thousand-word summary of it on May 18, 1935. Unfortunately for Stroheim, his scenario was rejected. Although the project may have had no commercial appeal, it is revelatory of his mind at this time.

In a small Illinois town, an Irish undertaker and a Jewish junk dealer live next to each other, with a spite fence between them. Although they fight in public, the Jew has saved the Irishman from foreclosure and the Irishman has used his political influence to prevent the town from closing down the junk business. Although the two widowers are complete opposites, they have an odd affection for each other, perhaps because each has an afflicted child: Bennie, a skinny hunchback, and Erin, who is blind. The children have been friends for years. The boy plays the piano and the violin and teaches the girl to sing, and they perform in a little Catholic church and also at a synagogue. This pair of misfits changes to a trio when banker Breckenridge's son becomes their friend. Chris is a handy fellow who fixes up an old Victrola, from which they learn opera. They seem to have an idyllic youth, romping in the fields, riding around on a tandem bicycle, and playing music. Bennie worries that if Erin ever gains her sight, she will reject his ugliness and fall for the handsome, healthy Chris.

An audition for singers comes to town, and when Bennie's old tin lizzie fails, Chris takes Erin in the family Packard. Bennie has to ride in the Irishman's hearse. Although the audition goes well at first, Erin nervously breaks down in sobs. However, she is reassured by one of the singers that she has a fine voice.

Not long after, Chris decides to become a cadet and leaves town to learn to be an airplane pilot. As he and the blind girl part at the railroad station, they embrace. "Their two bodies strain towards each other, and the woman in Erin comes alive. It is only for a second, but in that second each knows they are meant for each other."

Erin's father dies from a cut he receives while embalming a body, but before his death he entrusts his daughter to Bennie's father. In the meantime, Chris has written to Erin telling her of his love in a letter that Bennie reluctantly reads to her. Distressed about the situation, Bennie shrewdly mentions that she will always be a burden to Chris and that she should pursue her singing career. His arguments win, and with her father's insurance money, Erin and Bennie get third-class passage on a ship to Italy, where she can study voice.

When they arrive in Naples, a pickpocket steals their money; Erin is compelled to sing in the streets, accompanied by Bennie on the violin. On another tandem bicycle, they pedal to Rome, where they share modest quarters with other music students. Bennie knows they cannot subsist on street singing. His instincts and his background in the junk business come to the fore, and soon he is doing quite well picking up discarded items in the streets. He pretends to Erin that he has a job with a music publisher. At night, he works on composing an opera. The two live together as brother and sister, although Bennie has hopes of romance.

Finally, Bennie's business becomes so successful that he can afford to pay for Erin's lessons. The female singing teacher believes that Erin has a great voice. Meanwhile, Chris, now working with airplanes, is disturbed that he no longer receives letters from her, even though he writes regularly. In fact, she has been writing to him, but Ben has intercepted both sets of letters. Finally, Chris sends Erin a cable, and from that she learns of Bennie's duplicity. Furious, Erin tells Bennie that she hates him and orders him to leave the apartment and return to the junk heap from whence he came. Erin moves in with another girl, and when she informs the singing teacher that she can no longer afford lessons, she is taken on for free.

Bennie remains heartbroken and even gives up composing. Erin earns a meager living by singing in the opera chorus. Shortly after, when she receives money from the sale of her father's undertaking establishment, she goes to an eye specialist. After Bennie notices her absence from the chorus, he learns of her operation. Finally, the bandages come off, but the procedure proves a failure. Bennie goes to the hospital and tells Erin that he will stay with her and will again be her eyes. Now content, he works feverishly at his opera. After a while, not only is his opera accepted, but Erin is chosen to sing the major role.

Bennie's opera, set in the Holy Land during the lifetime of Jesus, concerns a blind girl and the unattractive crippled man who loves her. As Jesus passes by, she touches the Master's garment. But the hoped-for miracle does not occur. She remains blind.

Chris, performing a Lindbergh-like flight, is scheduled to land in Rome on the very day of the opera's premiere. Erin finds out about this dramatic event and is relieved when he arrives safely. That night, Chris is escorted by officials to the opera house, where he is astounded to find his friends' names in the program. Erin senses that Chris is close by, and during the scene when she touches Christ's garment, suddenly she cries out that she has gained her sight! There is tumult in the theater, and as the curtain is rung down, Chris and Erin embrace. The cries for the composer are unheard, for Bennie has returned to his little shack at the junk heap to join his mongrel dog.

What a odd plot for a film. One can see that, commercially, a story that concentrates on a sightless girl and a skinny hunchback would prove unpleasant to general audiences seeking handsome stars and familiar romance. But for us, Stroheim offers here a most revealing exercise in self-perception, as he probes some psychological depths within him and objectifies them in his main characters. The two male leads are Bennie, the Jew with the same name as Stroheim's father, and Chris, the Christian with good looks, money, and a sense of adventure. Bennie, the hunchback, wrests beauty out of music, and Chris lives the life of an adventurous hero. Without trying to be too facile, one can perhaps decipher the hidden codes. For Bennie, read Erich; for the junk business, substitute the parental hat business; for the Catholic girl, substitute Valerie; and for the opera, substitute the kinds of motion pictures he tried to make. From certain statements that Stroheim made to the press about his physical "ugliness," one can see that he, in a sense, secretly considered himself Bennie, the hunchback, whereas in his dreams he was like Chris, the Christian hero. And when one recalls the psychological state that Stroheim was in at the time he wrote the script—broke and suicidal—we can appreciate the long-dreamed-of moment when Bennie wins success as a composer, which is dashed almost immediately, a situation not much different from Stroheim's rise and fall, from a world-famous director to an out-of-work failure.

Although this story of physically afflicted people seems unusual for a film, a surprisingly similar concept appeared in a 1917 Thomas

Ince production called *Princess of the Dark*. In that picture, a blind girl plays in a secret cavern with her hunchbacked friend (John Gilbert), whom she considers her Prince Charming. The son of a rich mine owner is attracted to the girl and funds a successful operation. Her dream is shattered when she sees the hunchback's appearance. Later, the girl and the rich man visit the cave, where they discover that the hunchback has killed himself, just as Bartholomew did in the script of *Merry-Go-Round*. Quite possibly, Stroheim had seen this Triangle release—after all, it was the product of the studio where he had been working—and found in it some of the roots for his own screenplay.

Stroheim did not give up, and eight years later, in the fall of 1943, he again submitted this story to MGM. A reader on January 6, 1944, reported that there were two manuscripts, Stroheim's original and also an adaptation dated June 8, 1935, by Vicki Baum (author of *Grand Hotel*). The adaptation, said the reader, "makes Ben upstanding and handsome (still Jewish)—a proper hero. His rival now is a vain operatic star, Valdoso. Erin believes she loves the singer, but when her sight is restored her eyes are doubly opened—for she sees Valdoso's worthlessness and chooses Ben. In this version, the starring opera is composed not by Ben but by the opera's conductor."[11] This adaptation, though it made the hero more appealing, proved no more promising than Stroheim's original. Both were again rejected.

On January 13, 1935, Stroheim read in a newspaper about a murder committed in Vienna. Just as Frank Norris had been inspired by a news item, Stroheim found in the article the seed of a dramatic story. A few days later, he contacted Wallace Smith, who had written the screenplay of *Lost Squadron*, and they agreed to work together. Eventually, their hazy verbal agreement had to be settled in an arbitration court to determine who owned the rights to the screenplay and the original idea.

This collaboration led first to a screen treatment and then to a novel, *The Happy Alienist*, which was solely copyrighted and published in 1936 by Smith. Although not as wild as *Poto Poto*, the work contains several grotesque aspects. It deals with a Viennese professor specializing in psychoanalysis. The premise is a rather peculiar one. The professor, an astute observer of the mind who wins the Nobel Prize, lives a simple, forgetful life and seems almost wholly inept. He is cared for and loved by his female Russian assistant. This dignified, famous, and rich professor—as far as we know, still a virgin—spends his private hours conversing with a wax mannequin (as does the doctor in MGM's 1935 film *Mad Love*). Ultimately, he gets involved with an impecunious but charming count and his mistress, a baroness, and marries the woman. The count is basically the conniving rogue of *Foolish Wives,* even to "a precisely limned scar that looked like a saber-cut which ran from his forehead down to his right eyebrow."[12]

The ineffectual professor—in love with the idea of the baroness rather than her lovely, perfumed body—never sleeps with his bride and spends his honeymoon in the Tyrol (evoking *Blind Husbands*), where the count and the baroness, in the professor's absence, make good use of their time. Newspaper articles hint of the scandal of the count playing around in the mountains with the professor's wife (gossip that recalls the plots of *The Social Secretary* and *The Devil's Pass Key*). Eventually, the professor—who reveals his thoughts only to his wax dummies—adds three new and very lifelike figures to his mannequin collection: the count, the baroness, and the Russian assistant. Somewhat later, he shoots these figures in a jealous rage, calls the police to tell them that he has committed murder, and is eventually taken off to an asylum. The moral or point of all this extravagant action is elusive, at best. Smith's novel indicates that the world of literature did not suffer a loss when the writer specialized in screen-writing.

The novel, although ridiculous, is full of Stroheimian details (the Prater, Viennese life, wine gardens, mountain climbing, a count out of *Foolish Wives,* and a baroness out of *Merry-Go-Round*). The story is hardly convincing. Such a learned professor could not be an expert on Freudian matters and at the same time be so shy or confused about sexual consummation without at least acknowledging, if only to himself, his problem. Furthermore, the tale is unsavory, with the count and the new wife constantly cuckolding the poor schmo—dark deeds that are not amusing or erotic or much of anything. The entire concept of the great professor carrying on conversations with mannequins seems far-fetched, to say the least.

For reasons difficult to discern, this story was eventually converted into a musical! One of the characters was named "Vera Huber," and the police inspector was named "Schnorrheim" (Stroheim had previously used the name Huber in *Blind Husbands* and *Merry-Go-Round. Schnorrheim* is a play on the German-Yiddish word *Schnorrer,* which denotes a beggar who makes pretensions to respectability: a kind of sponger or freeloader).[13] How such a weird story, coupled with disparate scenes taking place in a pawnshop and at the Prater, could have been developed into a musical entertainment is most puzzling. However, a production was mounted, and after an out-of-town try-out in November 1935, it opened on Broadway on December 5 as *May Wine,* with lyrics by Oscar Hammerstein II and music by Sigmund Romberg. Walter Slezak played the professor, but unfortunately in his autobiography he mentions nothing about his part or the nature of the show. However, it had a successful run of 213 performances and closed on June 6, 1936. With a divided authorship and with a major lyricist-composer team involved, the financial results for Stroheim could not have been significant.

In March 1935, MGM hired Stroheim as a "technical advisor" on *Anna Karenina* (released August 1935). How did Stroheim again end up at the very studio that had ruined *Greed?* Irving Thalberg, who had his artistic side, certainly respected Stroheim's talents, if not his stubbornness and extravagance. It would be nice to think that he had heard of Stroheim's financial troubles and was willing to help him out and that maybe his conscience bothered him for having deprived Stroheim of *The Merry Widow* profits. If so, such a gesture would have been a rarity. More likely, the all-powerful Garbo, who starred in *Anna Karenina,* was aware of his current status and recommended hiring him for his knowledge of military matters and the officer class.

In any case, the ice was broken and Stroheim went on the MGM payroll. When he did not create a fuss and actually tried to be helpful with his numerous dramatic and technical suggestions, he was engaged in March 1935 on a long-term basis as a staff writer at $150 a week. This was a far cry from the $30,000 per picture he had received as a director, but in terms of salaries of Hollywood writers in the mid 1930s, it was not bad. A 1938 survey analyzing salaries of the 228 writers at three studios (Twentieth Century–Fox, Warners, and Columbia) revealed that about 41 percent of the writers earned less than $250 a week.[14] Although Stroheim was not drawing $1,000, as was Scott Fitzgerald, he was fortunate to be employed at all. At the studio, he spent his time reshaping some scenarios and fleshing out others by adding deft touches (usually of a sexual nature). "I stuck my chin out," he wrote later, "and went to work in a little caboose (6 x 8 feet) in what we writers called the 'crib-joints.'"[15]

While working at MGM, one Saturday Stroheim suddenly received a telephone call from New York engaging him to act in a film that was to start shooting the following Monday morning. He would later refer to this picture, sarcastically, as the "pièce de resistance." As Stroheim recalled, "I had to take a plane and, as I had no idea of what I was to wear, I had to take a wardrobe trunk as excess baggage on the plane for which the company still owes me 260 dollars. This film was made in 8 days. I worked day and night and I met myself at the gate coming in and going out."[16]

The result of the rush across the country was *The Crime of Dr. Crespi* (released by Republic Pictures in September 1935). Arguably the nadir of Stroheim's American work in the thirties, this low-budget quickie was based very loosely on Edgar Allan (misspelled in the titles as Allen) Poe's short story "The Premature Burial." It also may have been influenced by Universal's Poe-suggested film *The Raven,* made a few months earlier. *Crespi's* writer and director, John Auer, also imitates some shots from Carl Dreyer's *Vampyr* (trees seen from within a coffin as it is carried, and other odd camera angles). Otherwise, the film is thoroughly awful on its own. Stroheim bitterly summed up *The Crime of Dr. Crespi* as "the crime of Republic, the author of the screenplay and the director!"[17]

Stroheim plays a mad doctor for the first, but not the last, time. The script provides little in terms of motivation or effective dialogue, but the actor enhances the meagerly conceived role with much "business." He puffs his cigarette, blows the smoke out in several different ways, flicks his ash, pats and smooths his hair, and drinks his brandy in the usual Stroheim manner: head forward, glass to lips, then head thrown backward, as if the liquor must not be savored but tossed down. On Crespi's desk is the skeleton of something about one foot tall. It might be a baby, or possibly a small monkey. He taps its skull at one point.

The story of *Crespi* expands the Stroheim screen persona: here is a bitter and vindictive doctor who loved a woman, but she ignored him and married a medical rival who went on to win international renown. Some time later, the rival suffers a serious auto accident and (in a scene that definitely recalls *The Raven*), a doctor declares, "Dr. Crespi is one of very few men, perhaps the only man, who can save him."

The patient's wife, aware of Crespi's antipathy, asks, "Isn't there some-one else we can get?" When the answer is negative, she reluctantly goes to Crespi and asks for his help, adding, "Why cannot you forgive and forget?" He fumes and declares, "He made love to you right un-der my own eyes." She replies, "Steven never knew you cared for me in that way." After she leaves, Crespi opens a file containing clippings of the husband winning an award in Paris and a picture of the couple's wedding. Crespi's sardonic voice is heard behind the image, saying, "My dear friend, my very dear friend." He starts to bang his pencil against the desk. After a few minutes, he snaps the pencil; he has made up his mind.

At the conclusion of the operation, which is a brilliant success, Crespi returns to his office at a few minutes before six and fills out a death certificate, stating the time as 6:15. He then returns to his patient and administers a seemingly lethal drug. He consoles the widow and, afterward, has a wonderful scene telling the corpse about the funeral and recalling that carnations were his favorite flower. Actually, the doctor has administered a drug that induces a deathlike condition, and he rejoices that his rival will wake up eight feet down and attempt to scratch and crawl to escape his grave. When Crespi's assistant (played by Dwight Frye, who was also Dr. Frankenstein's helper at Universal) unwisely mentions the time discrepancy on the death certificate, Crespi ties him up and then goes to the funeral. He smirks during the funeral rites.

Returning to the hospital, Crespi—in a stupid turn of the plot—releases his assistant, who scurries away to tell another doctor of Crespi's deed. After the buried man is dug up, the "corpse" awakens at the hospital and confronts Crespi. In the presence of the wife and two doctors, Crespi pulls out a gun, saying, "It's all finished. I'm through, the great Dr. Crespi," and kills himself. These lines about being "through" have a grim autobiographical resonance for the actor who has found himself "buried alive" in such a film.

Although *The Crime of Dr. Crespi* has a few good sardonic and sarcastic moments, it is generally wooden and pedestrian. Sometimes Stroheim underacts, almost shyly reading his lines, and in a few places he is perhaps overly strident. It is not a comfortable performance. No doubt he felt awkward in such a ridiculous role, and he also must have regretted that in such a low-budget film he had no time to hone his portrayal because many scenes were done in one take. For a meticulous craftsman such as Stroheim, the film must have been sheer hell.

"After this artistic endeavor," wrote the sarcastic Stroheim years later, "things went from bad to worse. In order to support my family during this crisis in their lives and mine, I accepted the offer from MGM [he forgot that he was already engaged there] to work for them as a 'hack-writer' at the salary of $150 a week after I had received there $3,000 per week rain or shine."[18]

Back at MGM in June 1935, Stroheim was assigned to improve a script called *Dolly,* which ultimately became *Suzy* (released in July 1936), directed by George Fitzmaurice. The script is a hopeless hodgepodge, starting off in one direction, then sashaying in another. There are a few scenes that perhaps show the Stroheim influence. The film features a charming rake (Cary Grant), a famous aviator during the war, who marries the devoted Suzy (Jean Harlow) but is too fun-loving to be faithful. At one point, he happily leads a goat into a bistro. He spends his last night before going to the front carousing with a couple of girls instead of bidding farewell to his loving wife. In a surprise visit to the railroad station, his father (who has brought along the wife) meets his son first, takes away two little doll trophies that the lad has won while carousing, then allows Suzy to see him. (Is this an echo of the doll trophies from *Merry-Go-Round?*)

Later, in a hospital where the husband lies slightly wounded, there is a catered meal full of such Stroheim items as champagne, marrons, and beluga caviar. There is also mention of a famous hotel in Monte Carlo being turned into a place for convalescent soldiers (an echo of *Foolish Wives*). In another scene, the wife visits the husband in the hospital and discovers him with another woman (a reversal of the sickbed scene in *Merry-Go-Round*). One trouble with the film is that Cary Grant, like many of Stroheim's rakes, is so thoroughly likable as an impulsive rogue that—after his death—Suzy's impending marriage to the caring and somewhat dull Franchot Tone is not as happy an ending as it should have been.

Stroheim's next task as a screenwriter was to work on *The Witch of Timbuktu* in October 1935, which was released in July 1936 as *The Devil Doll*. Although it has been long ignored by writers on Stroheim as an inconsequential effort, the film does, in fact, suggest his influence. The credits say that the film was suggested by a novel, that it was based on a story by Tod Browning, and that the script was written by Garret Fort *(Dracula),* Guy Endore *(Mad Love),* Stroheim, and Tod Browning.

Actually, Browning had been inspired by a novel by Abraham Merritt, called *Burn Witch, Burn!* which dealt with a woman of supernatural powers who has a doll shop and animates the dolls to kill. Apparently, Browning added voodoo to the original story and called it *The Witch of Timbuktu.* Meanwhile, the British Board of Censors, which had had enough of American horror films (particularly *Mad Love* and *The Raven,* both 1935), decided to ban this type of film. MGM was forewarned of this decision and so, to forestall censorship, dropped all references to Africa and voodoo rites and instead gave the film a science fiction background. This switch took away the supernatural elements and weakened its horrific overtones.

A man (Lionel Barrymore), who has been falsely imprisoned for seventeen years on Devil's Island, escapes with a mad scientist (Henry B. Walthall), who previously worked on reducing living creatures to miniature size. During his absence, the scientist's companion—a semimad woman who hobbles around on a crutch—has obtained a simple-minded girl as a servant. She refers to her as a "moron," explaining that she came from a "Berlin slum" and "is an inbred peasant half-wit." Upon the scientist's return, the girl is used in their experiment and is reduced to a miniature. With the girl's brain now "corrected" to do only what she is commanded, the other escapee—after the mad scientist dies—utilizes her to get revenge on the three bankers who falsely imprisoned him.

Wanted by the police, the escapee disguises himself as an old lady (as did Lon Chaney in Browning's *The Unholy Three*) and visits his blind mother. On the windowsill is a geranium. His daughter slaves away in a laundry and hates her father for having ruined his family. The girl bitterly explains, "It hasn't been pleasant . . . to be pointed at, singled out, despised" as a child. "It does something to you when you are very young—it grows up with you. It got so that I hated to go to school, hated even to leave the house." (Is Stroheim being autobiographical here?) In her apartment, she has a rosary that her father once gave her.

The escapee, in his feminine disguise, becomes a toy seller. On a ruse, he lures one of the bankers to his shop and reduces him to an Apache toy. Afterward, he sells the miniature servant girl as a Christmas gift and commands her to steal some jewelry. Then, he has her stab the second banker with a poisoned stiletto. Most film plots would have the villainous banker die, but in this case the man is "hideously paralyzed." Gloatingly, the toy seller sums up his condition as, "a brilliant mind imprisoned in a useless body." Still during Stroheim's favorite season, the Apache is hung on a Christmas tree as an ornament and later climbs down to carry out his murderous mission. Just as he is about to stab the third banker, the terrified man confesses, thus clearing the former prisoner's name. Afterward, the father, posing as a close friend, bids farewell to his daughter, who regrets that she has hated her father for so long. He goes off, presumably to commit suicide.

Although there are certainly some Stroheimian echoes in *The Devil Doll,* one must not forget that Browning himself was no mean creator of grotesque incidents. Nonetheless, the lady on the crutch, the geranium, the rosary, the blind mother, and the Christmas season suggest Stroheim's input.

Late in 1935, Stroheim submitted to MGM the first part of his shooting script of *Merry-Go-Round,* which he had used at Universal. A studio reader made a synopsis,[19] but there was no opinion attached to it. In any case, nothing came of this project.

While at MGM, Stroheim spent considerable time working on an original screenplay called *General Hospital,* which he hoped to direct. The studio was not interested in reviving his directorial career, nor was it interested in the script. Later, Stroheim stated that in 1937 someone at MGM heard about his success in France and "was supposed to have said, 'That son of a bitch has been working here on a story for half a year—where the hell is it?' They dug it out of the slime and usual shit and read it (those who could read)....As the whole damned thing was *so* ready for shooting, they started production immediately. [They] ... reversed the cast—having Virginia Bruce play the *wife* instead of the nurse and Franchot Tone the doctor, in place of Clark Gable. Anyway, when the thing was finished, they found out that they had made a big mistake. It turned out to be an 'A' picture."[20]

The film, renamed *Between Two Women,* was directed by George B. Seitz and released in the summer of 1937. Although the script had the potential of being an A production, *Variety* felt the film was "somewhere between Class A and B" and too reminiscent of another hospital picture, *Men in White* (1934).[21] Maureen O'Sullivan, who played the nurse, was far younger and prettier and gentler than Stroheim's choice, Virginia Bruce, and there is no doubt that Gable would have been better than Franchot Tone, who seems far too upper-class and sophisticated to be a dedicated doctor unconcerned about a moneyed existence.

Seitz was an efficient and prolific director but by no means one who understood the subtleties of Stroheim's original story. Although Stroheim's detailed script was shortened and many of its quirky details ignored, the story itself had so many complicated situations that Seitz, who kept individual scenes moving at a good pace, barely managed to hold the film to eighty-seven minutes. Had Stroheim been allowed to direct, surely disaster would have followed, because he would have devoted much more time to enhancing the characterizations and embroidering the details. Even if he had only stuck to the script, it still would have run well over two hours.

Stroheim's script contains a number of his obsessions. For example, in just the first section, there is a cleric blowing out a candle at a death and a convalescent patient confined to a wheelchair. One of the nurses playfully throws a movie magazine at the doctor, who examines the picture on the cover: "First molar artificial—reconstructed cartilage—receding gums show general acidity—a slight tending to thyroid. Otherwise, a very nice-looking guy." The superintendent of nurses is described: "Her iron-gray hair is in severe fashion. On her left breast she wears the bar of the Purple Heart, the American War Cross, and the Croix de Guerre." An ambulance appears, as does a hook and ladder truck of the fire department. A Catholic priest gives the ritual of Extreme Unction. An ailing man needs his arm amputated, and soon after, the hospital's chapel clock strikes. All of these atmospheric touches are within only the first twenty-two pages of the script.

The setting of the story had been suggested by Stroheim's experiences in 1933 at a hospital where his wife was recovering from severe facial burns. This disaster provided him with enough details to flesh out his story of a good doctor who, ignoring the love of an unhappily married nurse, gets enmeshed with a rich society woman and eventually marries her. The bride resents the countless hours he spends at the hospital as well as their less affluent lifestyle (the husband insists on living on his salary). Instead, she wants to party. (Could this have been echoed in Stroheim's own life when his wife, Valerie, who had grown used to a reasonably good lifestyle, became understandably unhappy with their now straitened circumstances?)

In opposition to the good doctor at the hospital, there is another doctor—a rich, spoiled, indifferent, and incompetent wastrel who is fond of performing amputations even when patients do not need them. This man, who cares nothing about his patients and who drinks on the job, begins to woo the good doctor's discontented wife. When the nurse's husband, a hopeless drunk and a wife beater, is hurt in an accident, the good doctor has been inveigled by his wife to go to a party, and the incompetent doctor performs an unnecessary amputation. The patient dies. Although the bad doctor is described in the film as "a pathological case" and loses his license, he still seems quite appealing to the spoiled wife, and she runs off with him. A train wreck ensues and causes the rich wife to be facially disfigured. Finally, after the wife heals, she wants her husband to open a private office on 333 Park Lane (note Stroheim's obsession with threes). He refuses, the couple plan to divorce, and thus the doctor and the nurse will be free to marry.

The original script was not just autobiographical in terms of the facial disfigurement. Stroheim's marriage to Valerie had long been failing. Obsessed with his own career—to him, filmmaking was a mission, not merely a livelihood (sentiments he shared with the doctor in the film)—he certainly neglected Valerie and his son, and after a while, their relationship must have suffered. Beset with financial and professional worries and given to bouts of drinking and depression, Stroheim's marriage began to resemble that of Mac and Trina. The relationship was already drawing to an end when Valerie (like the wife in the film) suffered the disfiguring accident, and so, out of loyalty and guilt, Stroheim stayed on for a while.

Although the bare bones of Stroheim's story remain in the film, many details that would have enriched it are gone, resulting in a relatively unimaginative soap opera. However, certain of Stroheim's peculiar interests were retained: the head nurse still has the military honors, a priest gives the last rites, and (as the marriage collapses) one of the payments for the diamond ring is made on December 24! There also is a loose parallel to *The Wedding March* in that the doctor is torn between two women. The switch comes from the fact that this man (unlike Nicki) does not want the money of the rich girl and marries her, despite her wealth, which he proudly and idealistically refuses to use.

The audience watches with frustration as he marries the spoiled woman and then foolishly stays with her. Although the two quickly grow apart, he feels obligated to her, despite the fact that he is becoming increasingly fond of the nurse. This doctor, however, is not a "lech" but unbelievably honorable, and he suffers silently. In the film, the doctor decides to leave his wife, but when she has the accident he feels guilty about abandoning her and so pretends that he still loves her. However, when he discovers that her face is not permanently scarred and that she wants him to abandon his career as a doctor, he finally has the courage to leave her.

Between Two Women, because of its many changes in plot and switches in tone, did not please Stroheim and certainly did not please a public who had to endure a basically unhappy love story studded with amputations and accidents and thwarted desires. As *Variety* said, it was a "stereotype yarn" that ran "too long," boasted "no dramatic wallop," and at best was "a workmanlike job."[22]

In 1936, before MGM decided to film *Between Two Women,* the depressed Stroheim continued to labor at his writer's desk. In July 1936, he was assigned to work on a sequel to the successful *Arsene Lupin* (1932), which would logically, but unimaginatively, be called *Arsene Lupin Returns* (released January 1938). If he had any influence on this script, it was obliterated by other screenwriters. A robbery could have taken place at Christmastime, someone could have been maimed, someone could have gone to a specific opera, and room numbers could have included threes. But no such touches are present. Perhaps the only Stroheim contribution is that Melvyn Douglas (as the reformed Arsene Lupin) has decided to become an honest gentleman farmer, but one who has chosen an odd retirement: the raising of pigs, rather than the far more seemly race horses or polo ponies. At one point, baby pigs are chased, caught, and handed back and forth among the characters, but the scene, which could have been delightful and funny, is generally witless. Stroheim might also have suggested the casting of wizened Tully Marshall as a jewel "fence"; otherwise, his input cannot be detected.

Several months later, in September 1936, Stroheim worked for two weeks on *The Emperor's Candlesticks* (released in June 1937), which George Fitzmaurice directed. The film begins in Vienna, moves to a compartment on a train, and depicts a few other locales. Except for a maid called Mitzi and the name Huber in an address book, both of which could be coincidences, Stroheim's influence is virtually absent: not a cripple or a crucifix or a suggestion of Christmas in the snow scenes can be found. There is, however, a scene in which spies in adjoining hotel rooms try to convince each other that they have retired for the night. The man sits on the bed and pushes the squeaky bed springs, while the woman in her room does the same. This is slightly reminiscent of a scene in the sound film script for *Blind Husbands,* where regular squeaking suggests that the honeymoon couple are making love, though in reality the husband is simply moving back and forth in a rocking chair.

Stroheim dutifully showed up every day in his cubbyhole at MGM, adding bits of dash to pedestrian scripts. Although his labors allowed him to pay the rent, they could hardly have been enjoyable or even slightly fulfilling. In his pessimistic but realistic fashion, he saw ahead of him a mountain of other people's scripts, not the pinnacle of his own dreams.

16

𝔄 Star in France

While Stroheim was slaving away in MGM's script department in late 1936, having not acted for a major studio for over four years, he received an offer from France to play the typical evil German officer in a film about spies in the First World War called *Marthe Richard*. Taking a leave of absence from MGM in late November 1936 and bidding farewell to his family (with whom he would never live again), he embarked for the continent and thus began a whole new life. As Stroheim later explained: "One cannot imagine what I went through in the making of this first picture in a strange country, the language of which I did not speak, and completely alone."[1]

Stroheim was not exaggerating. Raymond Bernard, the director of *Marthe Richard,* was absolutely flabbergasted when he realized that Stroheim "ne savait pas un mot de français" [did not know a word of French].[2] Stroheim himself later explained:

> My comparative success in this, the first of my French films, was almost entirely due to the kindness of director Bernard and all the others with whom I had to work. Strangely enough, my psychiste in Hollywood had predicted that not only would I work in the one film for which I had been signed, but that I

would be engaged for a second film before the first one was finished, and would continue to go on from one film to another, remaining in France for three years. Naturally, at that time, I could hardly believe her, especially since my engagement on *Marthe Richard* was for four weeks only. But the facts bore her out. I left Hollywood on November 26th, 1936, and quitted Paris on November 26th, 1939, having made twenty-four films [actually, seventeen] in three years, almost exactly as she had foretold.[3]

Marthe Richard, released in Paris in April 1937, featured Stroheim—although he got fifth billing in the credits—in a role reminiscent of the super spy in *Three Faces East.* In September 1914, at the beginning of the First World War, Von Ludow (Stroheim) and his troops break into a French house and order the parents to be shot. They stand in front of a firing squad, and in a close medium shot, Von Ludow gestures with his sword, shots ring out, and then he casually lights a cigarette.

Later, in Spain, we see Von Ludow, now chief of the German spy service, talking with the dancer Mata Hari in her quarters. Stroheim, wearing a civilian outfit (white pants and a suit jacket), is seated and holds in his white-gloved hands a cane, the handle touching his shoulder. He is smoking. They discuss a spy who has switched to working for the French. They decide to kill him the next day. "Here?" he asks. She replies, "Why not, darling?" This casual decision to commit murder is followed by her passionate line, "Embrasse-moi." He continues to draw on his cigarette and, in fact, blows smoke in her face. She tells him lustfully to get rid of the cigarette and complains that he does not love her anymore. "Me?" he asks, then rather coolly and sarcastically adds, "Madly!" As she kisses him, he nonchalantly flicks his cigarette ashes.

Meanwhile, Marthe Richard, the daughter of the executed parents, arrives in Paris and goes to the intelligence unit, where she faints from hunger. When she recovers, she explains that she wants to avenge their deaths. After a lengthy discussion—with the acknowledgment that she must be willing to sacrifice everything for the cause—she decides to become a secret agent.

Back in Spain, Von Ludow enters Mata Hari's room as shots ring out. He is wearing black formal attire, sports a straw hat and cane, and is puffing his usual cigarette. Two men enter from side doors and carry away the body of the French agent.

In France, the girl is shown pictures of the two main German spies in Spain. She chooses to pursue Von Ludow, who is described as "a gentleman without scruples, esthetic, pianist—dangerous. He was wounded twice, in Belgium and at the Marne. At the beginning of the war he was captain in an Uhlan regiment."

The scene then shifts to a Spanish nightclub. Mata Hari is dancing, as Von Ludow unhappily scrutinizes the clientele. "Always the same women in this place!" He also complains, "The music is terrible. Give me Wagner anytime." When Marthe enters the room, he adjusts his monocle and remarks, "Nice body" [Joli corps]. He dances with her and lies that he loves Paris, loves France, and hates war. When she joins him at the table, he looks at her and says, "Do you know whom you look like? Isolde." Mata Hari observes the two and, jealous, pretends to hurt her leg in the dance. (Was this leg injury a Stroheim addition to the script?) He goes to her dressing room, where he discovers that she has faked her accident. Repelled by her manipulation of him, he slaps her and declares, "You disgust me!" [Tu me dégoutes] and leaves.

In the following days, Von Ludow and the French girl become close, and he starts to fall in love with her. At one point, they are shooting at a target, a black figure with a heart, in a scene that echoes the shooting gallery in *Merry-Go-Round*. Suddenly, she turns the gun on him, and for a moment he is uneasy. Shortly after, in a scene that seems quite Stroheimian, Marthe goes to a church and meets her contact, a priest. Von Ludow, suspicious, enters the church and strolls closer, trying to hear what she says in the confessional booth, a situation reminiscent of the confession scenes in *Merry-Go-Round* and *The Wedding March*. Meanwhile, Von Ludow lights some candles and, when they leave, he and Marthe put their hands in the Holy Water and cross themselves—another contrast between the sacred and the profane: confessional truth and patriotic lying.

Afterward, there is quite a curious moment. With martial horns playing on a phonograph, Von Ludow sits on a horse saddle at his dinner table and bounces up and down on it while eating! This scene, which Stroheim had insisted on adding, is not quite funny—because of the seriousness of the film and of the spy chief's character—but it verges on the grotesque, another instance of Stroheim's strange sense of humor. It may, indeed, have been a sly reference to Kaiser Wilhelm's habit of dealing with official documents while seated on a saddle that had been mounted on top of an elevated stool![4]

As the plot grinds on, Marthe's spying results in the successful bombardment of German submarines, during which she witnesses the death of her fiancé. She returns to Von Ludow's quarters, where he is seated at the piano. He has obtained a diamond for her and expects that she will become his wife. As she enters the room, she says that she has betrayed him. "Yes," she exclaims to the surprised man, "I have my victory. My little victory." She tells him that he has "been fooled by a young girl who did not give you anything—who will never give you anything. I hate you. The day I held you at the end of my gun, my finger was trembling, I thought I could not help myself. And I laughed— I hate you. You are lost. I see that you do not believe me yet. [In German:] You have lost everything. I hate you to death." Earlier, she had pretended that she did not know German.

Von Ludow, shocked and hurt, realizes that he has betrayed his country. "So now you speak German. Supposing I kill you?" She replies, "Kill me—you will render me a service. I have nothing left." She then tells him that he earlier had killed her parents. He says, "You are free." She replies, "No, I do not want your leniency. Avenge yourself. It's part of the game." He says, "I had believed [with a bitter laugh] it was the Great Adventure." He pauses. "You were nothing— a little spy like all the others. That is all." He leaves the piano, and, with a hypodermic, gives himself poison. "I am doing this for myself!" he says and tells her to go away. She answers "No!" and he replies, "Oh, never mind then." She watches as he sits down and plays the piano until his fingers pause and he dies. It is a dramatic scene and in some curious way a moving one. Von Ludow violated the rules of spying by falling in love with Marthe, and one feels more sympathy for him than for her. In fact, her personal loss and her patriotic motives do not quite redeem her betrayal of him.

Stroheim provides a good performance. Although he may have moved from Hollywood across a vast ocean to Paris, he was still playing the same kind of role as he did in America—except this time in very halting French. He had been hired to act the nasty Hun, but he moved beyond that one-dimensional role and tried to make his character a bit more human. However, his inclinations were not quite at the service of the plot. The seemingly gratuitous shooting of the parents and the mistreatment of Mata Hari are Hunnish deeds that cannot be forgiven or forgotten, yet he genuinely loves Marthe and is devastated by her betrayal. In the final scene at the piano, Stroheim lends his role some tragic overtones. Even the hard-nosed *Variety* considered the suicide "most moving."[5]

When the film finally played in New York in 1944, in the midst of the Second World War, the *New York Times* stated that Stroheim "is still the best Prussian the screen has yet discovered . . . and is the last word in arrogance."[6]

A decisive moment occurred for Stroheim during the making of *Marthe Richard*. He had been shown great respect and had taken pleasure in his leading role, so he did not look forward to returning to a writer's cubbyhole at MGM. The French producer of *Marthe Richard* wanted Stroheim to leave immediately for America without appearing in any other French films because he had paid his passage both ways and did not want anyone else to hire the actor more cheaply. Fate now took a hand, and Stroheim, for a change, made the right decision.

Jean Renoir in his memoirs said that he had tried "for three years" to find backers for *La Grande Illusion*.[7] He had been offering his project as an adventure film about an "escape" rather than as a serious work with a message. "Later," Renoir explained, "the real theme, which was that of human relations, was understood and accepted."[8] When Renoir finally found people to finance the film, they were fearful from the start that the story would have little commercial appeal. However, the project would have had one major French player, Louis Jouvet, to portray the role of the prison commandant, Rauffenstein. When Jouvet dropped out of the production because of prior commitments,[9] the part was offered to Stroheim, who accepted. Renoir's backers rejoiced, feeling that Stroheim's name could prove helpful in the world market. It was for this commercial reason that he was hired.

Although Renoir and the writer, Charles Spaak, had worked on their script for a long time, many significant changes would soon be made. "Most" of these changes, Renoir acknowledged in his memoirs, "were due to the arrival of a heavy-weight in the scales—Erich von Stroheim." The often-repeated account is that Stroheim was only concerned with his own role. But there was more involved than this.

As Renoir wrote, "There are instances of stylization in *La Grande Illusion* despite its strictly realistic appearance, which takes us into the realm of fantasy, and these breaks into illusion I owe largely to Stroheim. I am profoundly grateful to him."[10]

In an essay printed with the published script of *La Grande Illusion,* Stroheim said that he "had been sent a first, hasty draft of the script which I had read and—being incorrigible—I began making a few hesitant suggestions." He was delighted that Renoir "was incapable of taking offense at what more narrow-minded souls would have considered crimes of impertinence. I could talk to him as openly as to a brother, without hedging." Stroheim recalled that Renoir listened to his ideas "with an enthusiasm that brought tears to my eyes. He had given me a pleasure which I had forgotten for some years."[11]

Stroheim suggested combining the part of the prison commandant with the role of the German aviator (which he had already portrayed in *The Crimson Romance*). This not only made his part more substantial, giving it an added grandeur, but also strengthened the script line by adding structure to an otherwise rather sprawling story. Here was a war hero so seriously injured that he could no longer fly but who continued to do his duty by serving as a commandant in a prison. Stroheim also tried to improve the dialogue—specifically, his—and many of his offerings were enthusiastically accepted by Renoir. But the easygoing Frenchman soon encountered the dictatorial side of the ex-director. Stroheim "behaved intolerably," said Renoir, and demanded many additional scenes.

> We had an argument about the opening scene in the German living-quarters. He refused to understand why I had not brought some prostitutes of an obviously Viennese type in the scene. I was shattered. My intense admiration for the great man put me in an impossible position. It was partly because of my enthusiasm for his work that I was in the film-business at all. *Greed* was for me the banner of my profession. And now here he was, my idol, acting in my film, and instead of the figure of truth that I had looked for I found a being steeped in childish clichés. I was well aware that those same clichés, in his hands, became strokes of genius. Bad taste is often a source of inspiration to the greatest artists.[12]

The argument raged about the wild parties in the barracks (the kind of scene that Stroheim had contributed to Griffith's *Hearts of the World*). Such goings-on were sheer fantasy, and Renoir was ultimately so upset by Stroheim's insistence that he burst into tears. Both men were affected by this effusive moment and, shortly after, "Stroheim promised that henceforth he would follow my instructions with a slavish docility. And he kept his word."[13]

Stroheim recalled that Renoir was "incredibly patient. Without ever raising his voice, he asks over and over again until he gets what he wants. His politeness toward everyone he works with was a source of endless amazement to me, especially as I personally cannot say three words in succession without swearing in whatever language I am using."[14]

Stroheim contented himself with the changes he had made in his own role and in a few other portions of the script. What he fashioned for himself became fantasy fulfilled; here he played the aristocrat, the officer, the sensitive man recalling a better past, a man suffused with weltschmerz. As in *Merry-Go-Round* and *The Wedding March,* the World War in *La Grande Illusion* brought the end of a whole lifestyle forever. And, interestingly enough, not only did the role fulfill Stroheim's wildest dreams; it also seemed to satisfy the public's dreams as well. It is with this image that the man as an actor is best remembered.

There seems to be some contention about Stroheim's uniform in the film. One may be sure that Stroheim wanted it to be as elegant and elaborate as possible. Renoir claims that Stroheim "took liberties" with it and that it is "authentic, but with a flamboyance quite unsuited to the commander of a POW camp in the First War."[15] The facts probably are that Stroheim created the uniform and persuaded Renoir to accept it for dramatic purposes.

The film begins in a French barracks. (Renoir originally wanted a lavish party at a chateau, but the producer considered that too expensive). Renoir filmed much of the opening scene in a single shot (lasting seventy seconds), as the camera moves from a phonograph to close shots of the men, to longer views, then back to some closer details. It was Renoir's method not to break up space through editing, as Stroheim was wont to do, but to let a scene play without interruption. (Incidentally, when *Grande Illusion* first opened in America in 1938, this introductory scene and many others were cut.)

The French then discuss some aerial photographs that prove unclear. The aristocratic Captain Boeldieu (Pierre Fresnay), the more proletarian Maréchal (Jean Gabin), and some others decide to fly over the controversial area once more.

The film now switches to the German barracks. For economy reasons, and dramatic ones as well, the same barracks set was redressed for the German locale. This was a good point, Renoir noted, in that it showed that both sides were working under the same basic conditions. The scene in the German barracks is also handled in a long take. Dressed in his aviator's flight jacket, Rauffenstein (Stroheim) strides into the room, cigarette in mouth. He downs a drink, puts his finger in his ear to relieve the pressure, announces that he has shot down a plane, and says, "If they are officers, invite them over for lunch." He orders music (on the phonograph), tosses down another drink, and tells a comrade to "concoct one of your famous fruit punches for us to celebrate the downing of my second plane." He provides the complete recipe: three bottles of Moselle wine, two of Rhine wine, one bottle of champagne, a small bottle of Martel, some pineapple, three lemons, and sugar. The camera then shows some photographs pinned on the wall of the women of the time, and the scene fades out. All of this occurs in one sixty-second take.

Then there is a fade-in on Rauffenstein (with a black mourning band on his arm) as he greets his adversaries and, with appropriate heel clicking and bows, introduces himself to Captain Boeldieu. The perfect host, he explains that he is honored to have French guests; he politely pulls out chairs for them and then sits down. He mentions that he knew a Count Boeldieu in Berlin and Boeldieu replies that the man was his cousin. These two haughty, aristocratic, monocled men with their ever-present white gloves are both career officers, know the same people, and, in short, have the same background. They even briefly converse in English (the shared language of the upper classes). The two are actually closer to each other than to their respective countrymen. At the same time, Maréchal (a common man who has joined the air force) and a German discover that they both worked at the same restaurant in France. Class distinctions are more important than national barriers, despite patriotism. A French laborer has more in common with a German laborer than with the aristocratic class of his own nation. Ultimately, the film's message is that the ancien régime did not end with the French Revolution but with the First World War. As

Renoir said in a preface to the published script, "In certain ways the world war was still a war of formal people, of educated people—I would almost dare say, a gentleman's war."[16] The bloody four-year conflict smashed that social order. Renoir's views were no different from those of Kaiser Wilhelm, who disapprovingly noted to the American ambassador during the early years of the war that the French "were not like the French of '70, but that their officers, instead of being nobles, came from no one knew where."[17]

We follow the French prisoners until, after several escape attempts, they are eventually quartered in a seemingly impregnable fortress. The camera begins on a large cross in the back of a chapel, descends past a picture of the kaiser to a white bed, then passes a geranium, a bottle of wine in a silver champagne bucket, a picture of a sturdily built woman, a sword hilt, guns, and riding crops; it finally stops on an orderly blowing open the fingers of a white glove. Offscreen, Rauffenstein's voice is heard: "Open the window, it stinks here! One could vomit." The orderly announces that there are only two pairs of white gloves left. The camera then pans slightly and backs up to reveal the arm of Rauffenstein with a cup of coffee. In German, he observes, "If you call this liquid manure coffee, it's okay with me." What an introduction, this long take of seventy seconds! It is pure Stroheim in content and pure Renoir in style. (Stroheim would have shown all these details in separate shots.) Acknowledging that the ersatz coffee will "at least warm my cold guts," Rauffenstein is told that new prisoners have arrived, so he sprays himself with cologne before greeting them.

Rauffenstein is delighted to see Boeldieu and shakes his hand, although Boeldieu at first awkwardly holds back. Stroheim then examines the lengthy record of their escape attempts. Such details as Maréchal's disguising himself as a woman may be Stroheim's additions to the script. "Droll," says Rauffenstein, his face twitching slightly, as Maréchal remarks that a German soldier had taken an interest in him. Rauffenstein gives the new arrivals a tour of the fortress. Later, during a room inspection, Rauffenstein asks Boeldieu, on his word of honor, whether his belongings should be searched. Boeldieu asks why the word of Maréchal or Rosenthal would not also be accepted. "It is as good as ours," he says. Rauffenstein replies, "Perhaps."

Later, in Rauffenstein's quarters, these two aristocrats discuss the state of the world. They both have manners, class, money, and position, but their interests are limited, relating almost solely to their military backgrounds and their upper-class status. Certainly, they are not artists or intellectuals; they seem to prefer a picture of a good horse to an artwork. They both have a dim view of the future, and their passing, Rauffenstein articulates, will be a pity. Yet Boeldieu later will sacrifice his life to allow his countrymen to escape, and Rauffenstein will have to shoot his "brother" for the sake of his duty. After the death of Boeldieu, Rauffenstein cuts the geranium, the only flower in the fortress. As Renoir writes, "The relationship between Rauffenstein and Boeldieu ... was simply a love story," not in a sexual sense, but a loving friendship."[18]

Failures have no fathers; success has hundreds. Eugene Lourie, the set designer, in a self-serving article, avers that he was responsible for placing Rauffenstein's living quarters in the chapel under a large crucifix.[19] Stroheim, he says, was delighted with the idea, and when asked what props were needed, he submitted three typewritten pages: "six pairs of white gloves, a collection of riding crops, five photographs in silver frames of heavyset blonde Wagnerian singers, the book *Casanova's Memoirs,* and more." Then Lourie claims that he (Lourie) wanted to add "a little speck of color amid the gray stone surroundings." An interesting concept for a black-and-white film! Lourie said that he asked Renoir if he could add a geranium. *Merde.* It is more likely, because geraniums and crosses had long been Stroheimian obsessions, that he suggested these details himself and that the French designer later appropriated them as his own contributions. In fact, Charles Spaak, the screenplay's coauthor, wrote in 1946 that he did not approve of some of Stroheim's changes and referred specifically to the cutting of the geranium, which he regarded as sentimental, a "very bad" [très mauvaise] scene.[20]

With little doubt, we can conclude that all of Stroheim's scenes reveal his input: the snow falling outside the window as the geranium is cut (reminiscent of the rain turning to snow in *The Merry Widow*), for example. Renoir, in his easygoing Gallic manner, generally adopted Stroheim's ideas in other scenes as well, including one involving feet. That Maréchal's feet in an early prison scene are washed by another man seems more than coincidental. Later, during the escape, Rosenthal hurts his ankle and uses a stick as a crutch. Although this seems like a Stroheim addition, it was part of the original script. However, Stroheim's

fascination with the Christmas season may have affected the important romantic scene at the farmhouse that takes place on Christmas
Eve. In the original script, which lacked the warmth of the film, the
farm woman encounters the men asleep in the hay in the barn and,
sex starved, sleeps with them both! In general, the Spaak script was
much too political and unsubtle and gained dimension only because
of Renoir, Stroheim, and budgetary limitations. How delicate is the
process that produces great art.

Although the faithful admirers of either Renoir or Stroheim might
be appalled at this idea, perhaps the two men would have made a
wonderful codirection team, with Stroheim ballasting Renoir's somewhat light approach, and Renoir humanizing and lightening Stroheim's
heavy-handedness—in short, a mixture of a croissant and peasant bread,
a soufflé and a hard-boiled egg, a delicate sauce and a hardy sausage.
But except for *La Grande Illusion,* this was not to be.

Soon after Stroheim was engaged for the film, Renoir hurried off
to Hoch Koenigsberg, where he began shooting. Meanwhile, Stroheim,
as he recalled in a letter,

> searched for something visual and pictorial that would get over
> the fact that I had a broken spine and for that reason in the
> second part of the film became commandant of a prison. Walk-
> ing on crutches or with a cane or even with two canes or
> being pushed in a roller chair was not what I wanted because
> it gives an impression of senility. Suddenly (after the nth shot
> of good "Black and White") I got the idea to wear a leather-
> and-steel brace for my neck and chin. That would do the trick.
> The trouble was that I arrived late Saturday afternoon in Colmar
> and I was supposed to come on the set on Sunday morning
> just to look around and get acquainted. I had the intention of
> appearing before Renoir in full uniform to make a good im-
> pression upon him and so in order to have him see me on
> Sunday completely dressed with all the details I had to find
> that brace somewhere in Colmar by hook and crook.
>
> After half a dozen attempts in the wrong direction I came
> to a very German maker of orthopedic braces and told him
> what I wanted. He immediately asked me to undress, to take
> my corporeal measurements. I explained to him that I wanted

this brace to stick slightly into the standing collar of my tunic but he insisted that that would not do me any good. "Venn somepody hass a proken spine he musst haff der truss der vay I make dem." I explained that I really did not have a broken spine but— He would not let me finish. "Venn you tont haff a proken spine . . . denn vat you vant dis for? You musst be crazzy." I told him that I was only an actor and that I was just making believe I had a broken spine. "Oh . . . ein schauspieler! . . . Mama! Come in here!..(he turned and called his wife) "Das ist ein schauspieler! . . ." "Freut mich sehr . . . sie kennen zu lernen."

I felt that I was deceiving the man so I added that I am a *motion-picture* actor and not a stage-actor. "Oh . . . ein Kinema-actor . . . oh also Mama . . . ein Kintop actor." "Vy tont you vant the prace like it shoot pe?"

I told him that naturally I would not want to have a cumbersome, heavy and hot leather-and-steel brace down to my hips as in any case . . . it would not be seen.

"Also dann must you go to somepody else! Vell ich make only der *real* ding. Pesides I musst haff the prescription from a doctor."

At this time I took out my traveling-flask filled with "Black and White" and as if I had not heard his objections I handed him the flask which made the round several times. I felt in my not broken spine that I was going to have some trouble with that man.

"We better start working on it because I guess it'll take some time even to do that upper part of the brace . . . and I've got to have it by tomorrow morning by six o'clock."

"Vatt? morgen Frueh?"

"Yes . . . tomorrow morning—at six I have to leave for Hoch Koenigsberg!"

"Vy you musst pe appsolutely der craziest mann in der world . . . a prace like that I tont make under *four veeks!*" (My whole engagement was for four weeks!)

By now I felt that it would be better if I would speak German to him although I had not spoken my mother language for 28 years but I did the best I could after a few more nips of "Black and White." I explained to him that the whole motion-picture-going public would be indebted to him if he would make an exception and make for me this little piece of leather seamed in a shiny frame of tin to simulate the steel so I could begin my work tomorrow morning. I even went so far as to lie in telling him that I would insist on having his name as the maker of the orthopedic brace on the screen. That got him!

"Das vould pe shoen . . . hein vatt Mama? . . . Mein name und . . . tont forget die adresse! Dass vill pe goot reklame . . . vass Mama? Also let's see—" he took his tape-measure and started to take measurements all the way down my back around my waist and under my arms. Again I told him I only wanted it from the neck up.

"Put that vill not pe goot!"

It took me another half hour to convince that son of a bitch that I only wanted a piece of leather shaped to my chin and neck with framing. I did most of the work. We nearly came to a fist-fight. It was four o'clock in the morning when my secretary and I left his shop. I finally had what I wanted. I paid him royally and he begged me to write to him and send him a photo with that famous brace on my neck. When I came to the hotel I tried the brace with my uniform tunic, the collar of which was a real German hand-embroidered cuirassier collar which was pretty tight to begin with . . . but the goddamned thing would not close anymore with the brace on. Between four and six my secretary, the bellhop and the night clerk and I tried to stretch the collar. First I wetted it and then we stretched it on each side—as much as we could— nailing it to a board with very fine nails.

When I arrived at the fortress of Hoch Koenigsberg I had everything on but the kitchen stove. Renoir was so pleased with my conception of the commandant "von Rauffenstein" that in front of all the people he embraced and kissed me in his jovial effusive way. But immediately after this ceremony I went into the *can* and took the neck brace off. What I went through when we took the scenes—nobody will ever know . . . but what don't we do for "art's sake?"[21]

What makes the scene that Stroheim describes so memorable is the idea that Stroheim, for once, had encountered his mirror image, a brace maker who steadfastly refused to "fake it," who was determined to be thoroughly accurate—a "realist." However, it is doubtful that Stroheim saw any connection between the stubbornness of this particular "son of a bitch!" and himself.

When *La Grande Illusion* opened in Paris in June 1937, the reception was mixed. There was no doubt that it was a work of high quality, but its subject matter offended militarists, who felt its message pacifistic or at least too humanitarian (there are no villains). It also offended liberals because of its fond treatment of the aristocracy, its references to the Jews, and its complex treatment of the common man. Certain sections were removed or shortened—particularly those featuring Dalio, the Jew—and in France its 114 minutes were reduced by approximately 10. When the film opened in New York in September 1938, the cut print ran 8,977 feet. After the war, Renoir managed to buy the rights to the film and eventually restored the missing ten minutes. With new titles by Herman G. Weinberg, it reappeared in America in 1959 at its complete 10,109 feet. That is the version now known.

Despite the controversy over *La Grande Illusion* when it was released in 1937, it was a considerable box-office success. "The funniest part of it all," noted Stroheim, "is that Spaak got credit for many things he never even thought of."[22]

Suddenly the Austrian actor was a "star." No longer would he play a major part and yet find himself billed fifth in the credits, as in *Marthe Richard*. Although he still would be typecast in the same kinds of roles he had received in America, his name was considered such a draw at the box office that he was not totally relegated to Prussian parts but was given the opportunity to play many different types of characters as well.

Although unable to direct, Stroheim unleashed some of his creativity, depending on the director and producer, by changing and adding to the scripts he was handed. He invariably shaped the look and action of his own scenes and sometimes, if not hampered by a stubborn director or a minuscule budget, added other scenes as well. It was this intrusive personality that made his performances memorable and ensured his continuing success on the screen.

With his renewed fame, but in this case still playing his familiar "officer" role, Stroheim was hired to appear in a British production of *Mademoiselle Docteur,* based on an actual female spy of the First World War. This espionage drama was previously made in France under the same title in 1936 (released in Paris in April 1937) and starred Dita Parlo, Pierre Fresnay, and Louis Jouvet as the German secret agent. Directed by G.W. Pabst, this version loosely followed the plot of a 1934 American film, *Stamboul Quest,* starring Myrna Loy and George Brent as the lovers and Lionel Atwill as the German intelligence chief. The English version of *Mademoiselle Docteur* (aka *Under Secret Orders*) employed a different director, a British crew, and, except for Dita Parlo, a different cast: John Loder replaced Fresnay and Stroheim portrayed the chief German agent.

Mademoiselle Docteur is a reprise not only of *Stamboul Quest* but also of *Marthe Richard* and, to some extent, *Three Faces East.* Spies, double agents, love, betrayal, and death run rampant through this story of a German woman who gives up her budding medical career to become a spy.

In March 1937, shooting began in England. Three days into the film, Edmond T. Greville, the director, came down with the flu. Because Stroheim was being paid by the day, the producer was anxious to continue shooting and arranged for another director to make some scenes with Stroheim. As Greville remembered, "Erich wouldn't hear of it, saying that he would not appear in front of a camera until I was back on my feet. [When asked again,] Stroheim blew his top. He jumped onto a table in the studio commissary and, announcing that he would show the producer 'the only argument he could understand,' dropped his pants and exposed his posterior! No one could recall anything so scandalous ever happening in a London film studio."[23]

Stroheim's remarkable act probably stemmed from his longtime battles with producers, from his painful memory of having been replaced by another director on *Merry-Go-Round,* and from his recollection of the loyalty of his crew and actors when he was about to be fired from *The Merry Widow.* Stroheim remained firm, and a few days later Greville returned.

. The film begins before the First World War as secret plans of the channel defenses are surreptitiously transmitted from London to a German lieutenant in Paris. When his fiancée, Dita Parlo, a medical student in Germany, hears that her future husband is in that beautiful French city, she impetuously asks for a week's leave just before her final exams and visits him. Unfortunately for the German spy, he is being closely watched by an assortment of British secret agents and by an unscrupulous double agent. When the lieutenant obtains the plans, he slips them into the girl's pocketbook and tells her to take them to Hotel Europe in Munich. The leading British agent, who has followed him, commands his men that under no condition should they commit violence.

Later, while waiting for her at this hotel, the German lieutenant telephones the German secret service. We see a close-up of a hand, wearing a heavy gold bracelet and toying with a letter opener in the shape of a miniature sword. The next shot reveals Stroheim in his colonel's uniform and wearing a monocle. Just as the lieutenant in his hotel room is about to relate information, he hears a noise. Some agents have entered the room—there is much confusion—and the British agent shoots the German and escapes. The double agent is arrested.

After the murder, the colonel visits the jailed agent. Wearing a resplendent uniform, he makes quite a sight with his officer's hat, white gloves, and sword, as well as a mourning band on one arm. The prisoner, even though he did not do the shooting, has been understandably anxious. There is a row of cigarette stubs on a table (indicating his nervousness), which the colonel pushes off one by one as he begins to question the agent. Smoking a cigarette in wonderful Stroheimian puffs and then flipping the finished cigarette to the floor, he threatens the agent with death, using his hand with a flourish to pantomime the noose around the neck and the hangman's knot. Shortly after this gesture, the agent confesses that the girl possesses the secret document as well as good looks, which he describes with an enthusiastic whistle.

Earlier, when the girl entered her lover's hotel room in the hopes of greeting him, she finds her fiancé's dead body on the floor and the room full of agents and police, her life and her hopes ruined. So when the colonel later visits her to retrieve the plans, she is disheartened and quietly hands them over. "Please accept my most sincere regrets," he says, bending down to kiss her hand. A spray of flowers, which he has presumably brought, falls to the floor, surely a Stroheim touch. Anxious to learn who killed her lover, she listens to the colonel's request that she fulfill her duty to the fatherland and become a spy. By doing so, she might find the murderer and satisfy her desire for revenge. With her future happiness seemingly doomed because of her fiancé's death, she agrees and becomes the notorious "Mademoiselle Docteur."

Time passes, the First World War breaks out, and we soon see posters of her face with the caption "wanted for espionage" in England, in Italy, and then in France. Although an effective spy, she is not a vindictive one. There is an air of sadness, the same resigned quality that Parlo had in *La Grande Illusion*. At one point she says regretfully that her intended career was to be a doctor and to save lives and not, because of her spying, to end them.

The location now shifts to Salonika where we see a supposed native: Stroheim in fez and white suit, with a pencil mustache, a patch over his right eye (where before there had been a monocle), a dotted tie set off against a striped shirt, and a sash wound around his waist. This remarkable apparition—he looks like a moralist's idea of an Eastern pimp—is waiting to be contacted by the female spy.

Posing as a Swedish baroness doing charitable work, the female agent becomes friends with the British officer (John Loder) who earlier had been in charge of trailing her fiancé in Paris. He has in his possession more vital war plans. Although he has fallen in love with her and she is responding, again duty calls. She makes contacts with her secret agent, the disguised colonel. Once more invoking duty, he commands her to get the plans. She, in love with the British officer, resists. At this point, the colonel reveals that the man she now loves was involved in the death of her fiancé. She does not quite believe this and pleads to be told the truth. He then admits, quite honestly, that he does not really know.

Upon her return to the officer's quarters, she and the British officer have a long conversation in which he confesses that years before he was responsible, in a way, for the death of a German agent. He reveals no more. We must remember that he had advised his associate not to use any violence and, therefore, is not entirely responsible for the agent's panicky shot. The female spy now faces a serious dilemma. She loves someone who is the enemy and who was, to some extent, accountable for her fiancé's death, and she must now choose between betraying him or her country.

An anonymous letter arrives saying that the baroness is a spy. Although incredulous at first, the British officer realizes that the woman he loves is the famous mademoiselle. Both she and the other agent are arrested by the British. The film concludes as both of them, in silhouette (photographed from the back against the brightness of dawn), await execution. A blindfold is placed on her, but the man, with a shake of his head, refuses. And so the spies die, not for personal gain, but for duty. Needless to say, this depressing conclusion differed considerably from the original source, *Stamboul Quest*. In that film, there was a false execution and—in true American fashion—a happy ending.

Throughout the film, Stroheim, speaking slowly, tries to invest his superficially defined character with as much drama as he can, though his dialogue is unimaginative, consisting only of reiterated comments about duty to fatherland. Ultimately, Stroheim is far more memorable in the role than Lionel Atwill was in *Stamboul Quest*. Probably, had Stroheim had his way, the script would have paid more attention to the girl's dilemma and to the colonel's growing admiration and affection for her. Thus, all three would have been torn between duty and honor: the British officer who has to arrest his loved one, the girl who loves her enemy, and the colonel who sends someone he likes to certain death. But this was not to be.

Greville, in his memoirs, recalled his problems with his stars. Both Parlo and Stroheim were eager to outshine and outsmart each other. At one point, she did a convincing "little girl act" for Greville to get what she wanted, whereas Stroheim's method was to present always a fait accompli. When production began, the director arrived at the studio, assuming that Stroheim would be wearing a regular German uniform. He was astounded to find Stroheim "wearing an immense white cape, a white dolman, a white officer's cap, and white gloves." Dita took one look at this, cried "treason," and left in a rage for her dressing room. She would not return unless Stroheim switched to a regular uniform.

Greville tried to satisfy the egos of both Parlo and Stroheim. He went to Stroheim's room and told him that his uniform was "wonderful" but then reminded him that he should not forget that the colonel is in mourning. "I was making rather Machiavellian use of his own contribution," because Stroheim had earlier insisted on his usual mourning band. Greville explained that because the film took place during the war, Stroheim should wear combat dress. "That would look more martial." Stroheim was not buying this and began "bawling me out, albeit in a friendly manner, for playing into Dita's hands." Greville realized that Stroheim would be hard to convince and resorted to a ruse.

> "I'm going to add a scene," I told him. "You'll be seen preparing for the ball, putting on your magnificent uniform, parading in front of a mirror, hoping to seduce Mlle Docteur. Then the air raid siren will be heard. Brutally brought back to earth, the lover will become a warrior again. You'll take off your fine uniform and put on your combat dress, like a great soldier."
>
> Erich looked at me for a while. "You bastard," he said. "You win."[24]

Stroheim, in 1947, did not mention his rivalry with Parlo or the arguments over the costumes. He merely referred to the project as a "sad experience." It "had to be made on a shoestring" and the "director's hands were tied behind his back and in spite of our sincere endeavors . . . it was love's labors lost." When he finally saw the film in Hollywood in 1944, he said, "I crawled out beneath the chairs on all fours." He felt it "was one of the most colossal stupendous super-duper stinkeroos that was ever made." This judgment is a bit hard. He had appeared in worse!

Stroheim's sour attitude toward the film perhaps came from the fact that the director did not include details that would have made the characterizations more meaningful. Greville noted that Stroheim had a "blithe disregard for the constraints of both screenplay and budget." After one scene in which Greville had the colonel dry the tears of Mlle Docteur with his handkerchief, Stroheim suggested the addition of four or five scenes in which he would be seen "gazing with longing at that handkerchief in the trenches, during a shelling," then "lovingly washing it in his washbowl and ironing it" and finally carefully tucking it away in his knapsack to have it close to him during his leave in Germany![25] This motif of treasuring keepsakes runs throughout Stroheim's work: recall the lilacs in *Merry-Go-Round,* the apple blossoms in *The Wedding March,* and the sprig of hay in *Queen Kelly,* for example.

Greville correctly concluded that Stroheim was incapable of "taking shortcuts in filmmaking."

Any breaking up of an action for synthetic purposes was incomprehensible to him. As in a basic filmmaking class, I explained to him that, in order to show a character going up a flight of stairs, there is no need to show him climbing each single step. You can show him at the bottom of the stairs, cut to another shot, then come back to him as he reaches the top. Erich didn't agree; he felt the actor should be followed step by step. I objected that according to his method, no screen narrative could last less than several hours. "That's exactly what I mean," Erich replied. "It's impossible to give life to a character in a hundred minutes or so. That's why my productions sometimes take several days to screen. Hollywood never forgave me for it!"

The first scene he acted for me showed him reaching the top of the stairs in a house in Salonika. When it was over, he asked, "When do we shoot the scene where they see me entering the house?" I tried to explain that, logically, the fact of being inside a house, even on the top floor, is proof enough that one has entered the house at some point. He threw up his arms and said dejectedly: "I believe you, because you are the director and one must always believe the director blindly no matter what. . . . But I'm not convinced!"[26]

Greville mistakenly felt that Stroheim knew little of the art and technique of film editing. In fact, Stroheim's use of editing in *Greed* or *The Wedding March* is extraordinarily subtle and sophisticated, but he was somehow psychologically incapable of cutting from one dramatic point to another without including material that was meaningful but not really necessary. Stroheim felt compelled to show the entrance to the house, which Greville omitted; for the same reason, the dramatic scenes within the house, which Greville would cover in an efficient manner, Stroheim would have expanded and made psychologically true and emotionally stirring—so much so that they might have had to be trimmed. Greville was a good hack, Stroheim an undisciplined genius.

For his next film, *L'Affaire Lafarge,* Stroheim had a part that was so ill-defined and unessential that one feels he was hired as an afterthought merely to bolster the credits. Stroheim claimed he never saw the film, but he remembered, "I had the chance to wear a wig, rough clothes, a wide–open shirt, leather apron, and wooden sabots which was quite an agreeable change from the usual tight fitting uniform and because the character I played was vastly different from the ones I am usually in for."[27]

L'Affaire Lafarge was based on an actual event in France in 1840 when a woman was accused of poisoning her husband. As the film opens, a man is dying upstairs in his bedroom. Everyone is naturally concerned. Stroheim (wearing a wig with hair longer than usual, and with a few curls in the front) plays a character who enters the downstairs dining room in a dark suit, sits down at the table, and crosses himself. Shortly after, when the master of the house dies, this mystery man slips into the bedroom and sits by the corpse. He twiddles his thumbs for a few seconds, then rummages through the dead man's clothes and retrieves a key. He goes over to a desk, opens it, removes a few documents, and pockets them. He then puts back the key, arranges the hands of the corpse, crosses himself, and prays. The irony of this man praying piously after he has stolen something is somewhat amusing and pure Stroheim. Unfortunately for the story, the theft of the documents does not affect the characters' motivations or even the plot.

In another scene, Stroheim smokes a pipe, and later, in a blacksmith scene (the one he remembered), he wears a kind of eye shade, leather cuffs, and an open-necked shirt; he also does some genuine laughing. During the trial of the woman accused of poisoning her husband, the Stroheim character is dressed quite peculiarly and looks like a monk with his all-black outfit and hood! He lies in his testimony, but whatever he says is basically irrelevant to the story. In fact, all of his scenes are extraneous, as if the director said, "Well, Stroheim's in the film; let's at least give him something to do." And Stroheim, knowing this, at least tried to enhance his part by wearing outlandish outfits.

Stroheim's next venture, *L'Alibi* [The alibi], directed by Pierre Chenal, was far more pleasing. In it, he plays a blindfolded mind reader who, during his nightclub act, identifies various patrons. He is told by one of his friends that an American, Gordon, is seated at a table. When Gordon realizes the mind reader's identity, he hurriedly leaves with his mistress. Soon after, the mind reader follows him in his car and shoots him, then goes to one of the nightclub girls and gives her money to provide him with an alibi for the night. The police interrogate him.

During his next performance, the blindfolded man identifies an American who he predicts will be arrested for income tax evasion and another customer, a German, who he claims (speaking German) is married but whose partner at the table is not his wife. He then identifies the police inspector (Louis Jouvet). Later, he sits at the relentless inspector's table and, speaking to him in English, declares: "I was married once. I loved my wife more than anyone, more than I will love anyone. I guess that is funny to you." He explains that Gordon had run off with his wife. These comments, including the little touch of autobiography about loving his wife, were most likely added by Stroheim.

There are many additional touches to Stroheim's performance. He appears not only in an outlandish mind-reading outfit but also strides about with straw hat, white gloves, and cane. In one scene, he carefully combs his extremely short hair and walks around in a black robe and hood, similar to what he wore in the trial scenes of *L'Affaire Lafarge.* In another part of the film, he wears a narrow white strip of material, with a hole in the middle for his head, that covers his black, monklike outfit front and back, like an apron. Elsewhere, he drinks coffee while sitting in a bubbly hot tub close by his oriental female assistant. Other moments show him carefully adjusting his costume in front of a mirror. In short, he did everything he could to make his scenes distinctive.

When he is taken to police headquarters, the mind reader brings along a dictionary and, after searching in it to find the appropriate word ("désolé"), declares his feelings about Gordon's death: "Je suis désolé." It is not a vital contribution to the plot, but it makes his feigned sadness even more sarcastic and certainly amusing. At the end of the film, a male friend telephones to tell him that the girl has been tricked into saying that his alibi is a fake. In English, the mind reader says, "I guess that's the finish," and thanks the friend, adding, "You've been swell." Shortly after, the police enter his dressing room. He is dead, and on his round makeup mirror he has written gallantly in white grease paint: "Bien Joué [Well played], compliments."

In a letter to Peter Noble, Stroheim discussed making this film:

> After reading the script, I made suggestions as to changes and additions, particularly concerning my part and my scenes[,] which were not readily accepted by the writer. The play had

been written with no one in particular in mind for the role for which they had selected me and therefore was like a medium-sized ready-made suit to fit any French actor playing that sort of character, but not me. First of all because I am not French, and my accent and my deliberate delivery has stamped me automatically as a man of foreign birth or ancestry, in our case at least as an Alsatian. Second: I am not the type that talks much—not even in my own language—and I have played mostly characters who expressed themselves laconically and frugally. So, I wanted that aforesaid ready-made suit altered to my size.

My great trouble was and is in working in a story and script written by someone else than myself that I suffer through the lack of imagination shown by most of the scenarists who, turning out scenarios by the dozens, are easily satisfied with a thin situation and a thick layer of dialogue whereas I *see* scenes in which the characters express themselves pictorially instead of verbally. And, after all, we are supposed to make motion-pictures, which means pictures in motion and not photographed stage plays or photostatic copies of books. Which in a way explains also the fact that I get along very well with directors, who, whenever possible, accept my suggestions and are generally greatful [*sic*] for them. Anyway, I got what I wanted and my association with Pierre Chenal was the most pleasant one and I am sure he felt the same way as he entrusted me twice after that part.

In this film I met the great French actor Jouvet and believe it or not I shook in my pants and even a not too sensitive sound detector could have indicated the rattling of my knee-joints. We had to work together in a scene, he the commissaire, I, the suspected murderer. Short and snappy incisive questions . . . and just as short and staccato answers. It was one of the nicest scenes I ever had to play. . . . Later Jouvet told me that he too suffered "trac." [Nerves] I am still hoping that I shall have another opportunity to play with Jouvet again before I shove off. Apart from my personal liking for him I know the audience likes to witness scenes of two clashing characters of equally strong personality.[28]

When *L'Alibi* opened in New York in April 1939, *Variety* noted Stroheim's "excellent acting" and mentioned that there were "several spicy episodes." It also observed that the "reappearance in the film of Von Stroheim actually saves innumerable sags in script and action. He dominates every scene and overcomes several unpalatable episodes and implausible moments." The reviewer added, "Production carries the Hays seal, Ripley or not." He believed that the censors had cut out the spicier moments but had to leave some in for the film to make sense.[29] Perhaps the scene in the hot tub with the oriental woman close by was one of them.

In 1938, Stroheim found himself playing a Chinese general in director Christian-Jaque's *Les Pirates du Rail,* an ambitious film with striking visuals and lots of Soviet-style montage. It concerns the constant battles in China between uniformed troops and nonmilitary factions. After many Chinese are killed, the tide of warfare shifts, and several Caucasians are held as hostages. The beautiful wife of one hostage enters the headquarters of the governor to plead for mercy. She approaches the uniformed leader sitting quietly at his desk, then screams as he falls forward, dead. Troops enter the room, lift up the body, open a large window, and dump it outside. Then, through a distant doorway in the palace, an officer enters and comes closer to the camera. It is Stroheim, with a sword, a mourning band, binoculars hanging from a strap around his neck, a gun in its holster, a leather case at his back, a military wristwatch, a whip, and his usual array of medals! He announces, with a gallant bow, that he is the *new* governor. He is all politeness. He sits down at the desk and accidentally puts his hand (seen in close-up) in a pool of blood left from the dead man's head, then dries his hand on the desk blotter. He explains to the woman that he is not an "excellency" or a "mandarin" and that such oriental formality is over. He tells her that he graduated from West Point and says in English that he prefers "straight-from-the-shoulder talk and whiskey." He asks, "Would you like to have a highball?" She declines, so he drinks alone from his pocket flask. In the ensuing conversation with the woman, he intimates through his remarks and facial expressions that he is interested in her.

Meanwhile, the combat continues, and soon the new governor's side loses. Later, at a formal dinner, he wears an all-white uniform with epaulettes, medals, and tons of braid. After a few toasts by the rival warlord, Stroheim's character coolly excuses himself, gets up from the table, and walks down the corridor. A moment later we hear shots. He has been killed.

Stroheim later confessed in a letter that he "made a great mistake in regards to 'dressing' that part. . . . Dressing a character correctly is 75% of the success." He explained that "Chinese officers always have been and are sloppily dressed." Stroheim claimed that he was afraid the public would blame him for an ill-fitting uniform and so made one that was "smart," and he had "every goddamned thing hanging on me including the kitchen stove." He added that "with my very good make-up" he should have worn "nothing but an ill-fitting uniform," which "would have been more authentic."[30] Stroheim did not exaggerate about his apparel. In his final scene at the formal dinner, he looks like an admiral and a general and a hotel doorman all rolled into one.

Stroheim's eyes were made up to look oriental, and he carries off his role well, even though he only has a few minutes of screen time. This film was another instance of his being used for box-office appeal rather than for dramatic necessity. Still, what actor would not have taken some pleasure in the distinctive and dramatic introductory scene that he, no doubt, conceived for himself?

By 1938, Stroheim had become a star in France and was offered top billing in a mystery drama called *Les Disparus de Saint-Agil* [Missing from St. Agil], also known as *Boys School*. At last he had a chance to play someone who was not a spy or an officer. The director, Christian-Jaque, recalled in a memoir his adventures with the actor. He wanted Stroheim to play the role of a professor of English in a boys' boarding school. Stroheim agreed but demanded twenty-four hours to think about his costume. The next day he declared that he had found his character and announced triumphantly that he would wear a white chasuble with a large black cross in front and another one in back. The director was seized with panic at this peculiar outfit and, trying to hide his concern, explained that one would hardly encounter a monk thus attired teaching English in a secular institution. Moreover, the director had not envisioned a personage so solemn in a film that was to be nothing more than an entertainment.

Stroheim was very reluctant to abandon his idea. He grew more and more excited. Suddenly he could no longer find the right words in French and switched to English. After a barrage of more words and a flurry of hand gestures, the director called in a secretary-interpreter. At a pause in the argument, the director suggested that the professor could wear two pairs of glasses, one on his nose, the other on his forehead, and that sometimes he might use both simultaneously. He also mentioned that the professor should have a full head of hair. Stroheim, immediately envisioning the theatrical "business" he could create by moving the glasses back and forth on a thatch of hair, rejoiced at this intriguing possibility. He renounced the chasuble.[31]

Considering Stroheim's interest in religion, we can well understand his first choice of costume, however inappropriate it might have been for the film. But he was by no means wrong in giving serious thought to his appearance. After all, it was his close attention to such matters that gave his screen persona the panache that made and sustained him as a star.

In his role as the professor, Stroheim is a quiet, gentle man, and, according to one of the other characters, not possessed of "a very pleasant face." On occasion, however, he is given to losing his temper. Clearly a foreigner to his colleagues, he keeps to himself. In all the outdoor scenes of the film, he wears a scarf wrapped tightly around his neck, almost like Rauffenstein's brace in *La Grande Illusion*. His head is not closely shaved, as it is in most of his other films. Instead, he has a somewhat longish brush-cut. He also seems to have ear trouble and sports a small ball of cotton in his right ear. In some scenes, as the director had promised, Stroheim busies himself with putting one pair of glasses down, moving the other pair up, and even wearing both of them at the same time. On his desk, he has a picture of a woman and a child, actually Valerie and his son Josef. The photograph is never explained but creates the impression of a mysterious but sad past for this lonely man. Although every day he asks whether a letter has come, he never receives one.

The plot concerns the kidnaping of one of the boys and the disappearance of two more. When the mystery is solved, the boys initiate the professor into their secret society. They allow him to make their sign of brotherhood: both hands put to the head like giant ears and wiggled. The film ends with this gesture: the lonely man has now become one of the boys. In this episode, and elsewhere, the film reveals a seldom-seen aspect of the Stroheim persona—vulnerable, gentle, and, indeed, humane. Although Stroheim did as much as he could to make his role memorable, he had by no means a leading part. In fact, there are no leads. The story concentrates on a number of adult characters, as well as the boys.

Les Disparus de Saint-Agil premiered on May 14, 1938, in Paris. *Variety's* reviewer thought the film's "unique subject and names [meaning Stroheim and Michel Simon] will sell it" in France. "Story is a bit thick for the Yanks but it might go."[32]

Stroheim was then offered the role of a colonel in a film called *Ultimatum,* directed by Robert Wiene (who had made *The Cabinet of Dr. Caligari,* 1920). Although Stroheim got second billing—first went to Dita Parlo—he felt that it would be a bad picture, "because the story was lousy" and "had to be made on a small margin." Despite his doubts, he agreed to participate. "Even actors have to eat (at least once a day) and as I had a great many debts in Hollywood to be paid on account of my wife's accident and my inactivity over quite a period, I had to accept now pictures which in themselves were not good but offered at least the 'Ham' a chance to play various characters—even sympathetic ones—in different costumes and make-ups, and which satisfied his craving to show his versatility."[33]

Stroheim was unnecessarily harsh in his appraisal of *Ultimatum,* for it provides him with a rather good part as the gentlemanly, gallant, and polite officer who heads the Serbian Secret Service. In some ways, his role here is an echo of the one in *The Fugitive Road,* as well as a reprise of his Rauffenstein characterization. To make this performance memorable, Stroheim decided to give himself a far more serious disability than the broken spine of *La Grande Illusion.* As he later commented, "I was so tired already of playing those stinko-parts in stinko films that I could not stand it any more so I wrote myself into a roller chair and I took that one at least sitting down."[34] Indeed, he rides around in a black wheelchair and carries with him a pair of black crutches.

The film begins with some inept and irrelevant travelogue-type footage of livestock and singing peasants along the Austro-Serbian border, showing the summertime fun and games of July 1914. This is followed by scenes of Stanko, an officer in the Serbian Secret Service, cavorting around his apartment with his new bride (Dita Parlo), who has relinquished her Austrian citizenship for love of her husband and has become a Serbian national. About to bed his bride, Stanko is called to headquarters, where he explains to another officer that "the All Powerful is asking for me." After a big buildup as the camera moves through rooms and hallways, and with a grand and imposing flourish of background music, the colonel (Stroheim) enters in a wheelchair, with a mourning band on his arm. A few minutes later, he announces that Franz-Ferdinand has just been assassinated and that war seems imminent.

The colonel orders Stanko on a secret mission, cautioning him not to inform his bride of this action. He is to cross the Danube into Austria to pick up useful information. Stanko and his wife were once close friends with Burgstaller, who pretends to be a journalist but is actually a captain in the Austrian secret service. When Burgstaller arrives in Serbia, he telephones Stanko's wife, and they meet. She tells her old friend that she deeply loves her husband and recalls the good times they formerly had in Austria. "Do you remember our last evening in the Prater? We were so happy. We had a little drink, I think. We were like children, Stanko and me."

The plot is complicated by an innocent letter, which she hands to Burgstaller to deliver. To the spying eyes of an agent, this letter appears suspicious and is believed by the Serbians to contain secret information. Stanko attempts to cross the border and is apprehended by Burgstaller, but when he recognizes his old friend, he allows him to escape, a plot device similar to one in *The Crimson Romance*. The Austrian troops trap Stanko, and in trying to escape once more, he is shot in the leg. Eventually Stanko is fatally wounded during another escape attempt.

In the midst of these happenings, there are some gallant and polite exchanges between the colonel and Stanko's wife as he investigates the suspicious letter. He chooses to believe her. Afterward, a telephone conversation brings a tragic look to the colonel's face. With great effort, he struggles to stand up from his wheelchair by using his crutches and announces that war has been declared. At the end of the film, the Stroheim character says to Burgstaller, "Now we are enemies, Captain. But I think we may still shake hands, as man to man."

In *Ultimatum,* the spy services on both sides still play a gentleman's game, which, of course, after the war breaks out, will no longer be the case. Although Stroheim did not think much of the film, he seems to have made a few contributions besides his physical disability, such as references to the Prater, comments about how lovely Vienna was, and Stanko's leg injury.

During production, in July 1938, a disturbing event occurred. Stroheim noted that there is a theatrical superstition about using the word "cord" without that person buying drinks for everybody. On the set late at night, Stroheim's secretary innocently uttered this word, but nothing could be done because all bars were closed at that hour. The always superstitious Stroheim feared the worst and recalled, "Everybody felt worried about it, as it is an ill omen." Stroheim had a right to feel uneasy. The next morning the director, Wiene, was found dead. Robert Siodmak completed the picture.[35]

Variety, reviewing this film's Paris premiere on November 19, 1938, considered it "a rehash of an outmoded theme." The reviewer praised the cast, for the little that they had to do, and observed that "Stroheim continues to play the perpetual role in which French directors have cast him. . . . His broken accent is fast losing its dramatic value for French consumption."[36] This comment about Stroheim was a bit unfair. He could hardly be blamed for the weakness of the film and, in fact, offers its only interesting characterization.

In September 1939, a print of *Ultimatum* arrived in New York, but it did not open until the following February. When Stroheim was in New York City in 1942, he saw a revival of the film in a "flea-pit" on Forty-second Street. "All seats 5 cents. Even there I blushed."[37]

Stroheim concluded 1938 with one more film, *Gibraltar,* directed by the talented Russian émigré Fedor Ozep. In this story, Stroheim once again heads an international spy ring. *Variety's* Paris review of January 27, 1939, said:

> Vivianne Romance, as a Spanish dancer, is Stroheim's aide and mistress of Roger Duchesne as a young British officer, who's spending more time and money on the dancer than he possesses. As a result he's persuaded by the dancer to steal a secret British code for Von Stroheim in order to pay his debts. He's discovered, degraded and imprisoned. An escapee sees him join Von Stroheim's band, but when he discovers it is sinking British ships he turns the dope over to his former commander.
>
> Von Stroheim kills the dancer, thinking she's the giveaway,

and Duchesne kills Von Stroheim in escaping. . . . Miss Romance and von Stroheim walk away with the honors.[38]

Stroheim later wrote that this film had the "American tempo,"
although this quality no doubt stemmed from Ozep's Russian school
of montage, as could be seen in his earlier works. Stroheim, at least in
retrospect, was happy.

> Again I wrote my own part and dialogue and even though it
> sounds like bragging, the producer told me, afterwards, that he
> did not regret letting me do what I wanted. It was a pleasure
> to work with Vivian Romance who is about the sexiest of all
> the "it-girls," and who found there a part tailored for her. Vain
> as ever I insisted on doing the fall down a steep stairway my-
> self, even though they had a double ready, haircut, white mess-
> jacket and everything, and after doing it half a dozen times I
> found I had three broken ribs one of them sticking through
> my flesh. But the company had been smart and they had re-
> served this scene for the last one.
>   Everybody in the film industry—(what there was of it)—
> expected fire works with two supposedly over-temperamen-
> tal individuals like Vivian and myself and everybody worried
> with and for the poor producer to have such a vivacious team
> on his hands and around his neck . . . and on his checkbook
> vouchers. We fooled them all. There was never a loud word and
> the producer became and still is a friend of mine. I am burning
> numerous candles that I may again make a picture for him.[39]

Gibraltar was very successful and played for quite some time in America,
under the title It Happened in Gibraltar. That Stroheim had a strong
input into the content may be indicated by the New York Times mention of the film's "blunt salacity."[40]

Stroheim continued to get sporadic acting jobs and otherwise lived
the life of a bachelor. Lonely and a bit nostalgic, he wrote a letter to Valerie
in October 1938, remembering their eighteenth wedding anniversary:

> To my Darling Sweetheart—
> Count them—they are 18! So—I didn't forget the 16th of

October. But I had no money worth while sending you—
The present will come—soon. (I hope.)

So much love and so many kisses that I couldn't possibly
put it into words—

So—just *all* the love that a man *can* have for a woman I
have for you and lay it in front of your feet—[41]

Was this reference to feet merely an expression or is it more meaningful, as in Baron Sadoja's note in *The Merry Widow*, which the foot
fetishist signed, "At your feet."?

Stroheim next played a small part in *Derrière la façade* [Behind the
facade], known in America as *32 Rue de Montmartre* (and later, in 1952,
as *A Girl in Every Room*). This "fast moving, well directed murder drama"
was released in Paris in April 1939.[42] As the *New York Times* said when
the film appeared in America, the authors used the *Grand Hotel* technique by drawing "a dozen or so pungent vignettes" of tenants in a
building.[43] Indeed, the film is packed with interesting people and spar-
kling dialogue.

A landlady is found murdered, and the police visit each of the rooms
in their attempt to find the killer. In one segment, the police speak with
a woman who discusses her "business." As she says, "It is a business, and
yet it is not a business." She explains in lines that Stroheim could well
have contributed: "A man is not always happy at home. Sometimes he
needs a little distraction. Or else he is alone, a bachelor. Then they make
use of one of these 'salons.' They cater to the rarer sides of life."

Alas, these words were found offensive by the New York censors
and were omitted from American prints. Later, in a night club scene, a
woman provides a piece of remarkable philosophy: "One thing I know
is that you can never make someone happy without making someone
else unhappy."

Stroheim said that he accepted the bit part of a cardplayer

because everybody else in the picture (and we had some big
names) played bits. They only picked on me, not because I was
the man to fit the part, but because my name completed the
list on the billboard.

At that time, I was in swing because the exhibitors demanded me. I was "box-office" as they say.

The producers did not cherish the idea on account of my salary and so they chased me through my work from early morning until late at night to get as quick as possible rid of the main expense. This did not help the director, neither me nor the film. I was told during the occupation the picture was shown in France with my episode completely eliminated as per request of the Nazis. Personally I have never seen the film.[44]

Although *Derrière la façade* had a whole raft of famous French actors and was fast-moving and amusing, Stroheim's section is flat and not engaging. He is shown playing poker with an attractive female confederate and another man. After a few hands, there is an altercation between the two men and ultimately a rough-and-tumble fight. Stroheim pitches his opponent to the floor, and the angry man throws something that bloodies Stroheim's cheek. At this moment, the police enter and survey the disordered room. Stroheim explains that they have been having a boxing match! After the police leave, the three people resume their cardplaying. This episode was hardly one of the best in the film and proves Stroheim's contention that the part was not tailored for him at all but was merely a means to use his name for the box office. Except for the fight, he does nothing more than sit at a cardtable and smoke a cigarette. He makes no interesting remarks, movements, or even gestures and is not in any way a "character."[45]

Stroheim's next film, *Rappel immédiat* [Immediate call], released in Paris in July 1939, was slightly more challenging. At least he had something to do, even though *Variety* called the film "an unconvincing mixture of comedy and drama" that was "further damaged" by the casting of Stroheim as a mysterious American diplomat. "The film is due for limited success here [in France], with little chance elsewhere."

Capt. Stanley Wells (Von Stroheim), who dashes about the European capitals with highly important diplomatic assignments, has a capricious American actress-wife, Helen Wells (Mireille Balin), of French origin, who keeps that secret for professional reasons. Tired of living in a mysterious, international milieu with a husband who is secretive and who sacrifices her for his work, she ultimately falls for an actor.

To cast Stroheim as a Yankee diplomat shows a total lack of comprehension of the American character. Stroheim just bristles all over with his German origin, physically and mentally.[46]

In fact, the reviewer found the whole premise of the film unconvincing. He could not see how "the young, alluring wife" could ever have "loved the older, severe, heavy Von Stroheim." Perhaps the relationship was unbelievable on film, but in real life such an event would soon occur.

Shortly after making *Rappel immédiat,* Stroheim met Denise Vernac, who would become his companion-lover. Denise had played an extra in *Derrière la façade,* but in nightclub scenes in which he did not appear. If he had met her then, he said, "I might have picked on her already."[47] Stroheim certainly proved the idea, expressed by a character in *Derrière la façade*, "that you can never make someone happy without making someone else unhappy." For many years during this relationship, Stroheim would secretly write his wife, Valerie, telling her how much he loved her and would always love her, yet he firmly remained with Denise. Anita Loos tells how the two got together, a story that Denise herself later affirmed. "She had come to Von's hotel to interview him for some theatrical publication when, early in the interview, Von interrupted to pose a question of his own—in effect, to ask the young lady whether she enjoyed being made love to, phrased in those old Elizabethan terms which are still written on fences. The young journalist, after a moment of shock, replied 'Mais oui, Monsieur.' 'Then' asked Von, 'what are we waiting for.'"[48]

They did not wait and, in fact, stayed together for the next eighteen years, as Denise shared the vagaries of Stroheim's precarious career. This beautiful and talented woman certainly was not drawn by his good looks and riches but instead by a heart almost completely hidden under a formidable facade.

Stroheim's marriage to Valerie had disintegrated in the early thirties. At that time, he was doing a considerable amount of drinking, his career was in ruins, and there was no money. He could hardly have been easy to live with. All these problems were compounded by the burns she had sustained on her face. Could he leave her after such a terrible accident? Did he still love her? Did she still love him, or couldn't she tolerate his presence anymore?

Perhaps when he went to France, the a separation was a godsend for them both. Understandably, he was lonely, living in a country whose language he did not know, with no close friends. He surely thought often of his wife and child. He even included a photo of them in *Les Disparus de Saint-Agil*. From his meager income, he continued to send money to Valerie. The reason that Stroheim never divorced her, according to Anita Loos, was that "underneath Von's bombast was a pathetically masculine lack of courage."[49] Perhaps. And perhaps not. His effusive notes on birthdays and anniversaries and at Christmas and Easter suggest that he continued to love his wife, or that, while writing, he became emotional because, at heart, he felt guilty that he did not love her. Who knows? And probably even Stroheim didn't know. But what we do know is that he continued to live happily with Denise for the rest of his life. However, in his will—signed in 1943, while he was living with Denise—he left all his property to his son Josef and made no provision for Denise.

Stroheim next acted in Edmond T. Greville's *Cinq jours d'angoisse* [Five days of fear], which was later, in Stroheim's word, "rebaptized" *Menaces*. It was another *Grand Hotel* story that dealt with the problems of various refugees living in a hotel for foreigners in Paris during the dramatic days between September 26 and 30, 1938, when the world was on the brink of war. The temporary peace signed by Hitler and Chamberlain in Munich soon proved to be a mistake, and the script of this topical film was constantly changed to keep up with contemporary events. Production began in the early part of 1939, but the film's release was delayed by a studio fire and by several more attempts to update the story. When war broke out in September 1939, there were more revisions. Finally the film was released on January 27, 1940, but its theme was by then hopelessly out of date. Its patriotic sentiments were received with derision, and it was "booed at the premiere by a French audience," according to *Variety*.[50]

Stroheim's belief in superstition was again confirmed when, around two in the morning on the set of *Menaces,* his "same fool secretary" once again uttered the word "cord" during the last scene of the picture, and again it was too late to buy drinks. Later that night, four men were burned to death in the laboratory, along with several negatives, including that of the just-completed film. Nobody at the laboratory had known of the uttered word, so, Stroheim explained, it could not have been "auto-suggestion." He summed it up as "unexplainable" but believed the word had caused the tragedy, just as he believed that whenever someone whistles in a dressing room at the theater "invariably the show closes." Fortunately, there was a work-print in the studio, and after considerable trouble, a dupe negative was made, which, Stroheim said, "accounted for the indistinct photography." The *Variety* reviewer did not mention the problem and kindly described the photography as "average."

Stroheim played Hoffman, "a mutilated refugee Austrian professor, a vet of the last war. A Francophile, and on the verge of becoming a French citizen, he suddenly finds himself an enemy of the country he loves, loses his job and commits suicide in a moment of despair."[51]

The director wanted Stroheim to play this character, but initially Stroheim would sign a contract only if he could play "a legless man." As Greville recalled in his memoirs,

> I thought he was joking, but he explained that playing a legless person had always been his dream as an actor. He then elaborated: "I would like to be a legless man who lives on the seventh floor of a walkup building. My only companions would be the neighborhood kids; they'd carry me downstairs and back up again. They'd borrow the concierge's baby carriage (there's always a baby carriage stored under the stairs in French apartment buildings!) to wheel me about. They'd put the top up or down, depending on the weather." I couldn't help smiling. Erich got angry: "You new-generation directors—you're all the same! You don't understand anything about human problems!"
>
> I felt it would be useless to argue. I took my leave . . . and came back two days later. Erich was sticking to his amputee fantasy. This time he went even further: "One day, we see the kids in school. The teacher explains the principle of the hoist. So they set up a pulley at the top of the stairs and hoist me up and down." I went to great lengths trying to explain to him

that his idea, although a stroke of genius, had no place in my story. He started sulking, and once again we parted rather coldly.

My third, fourth, and fifth attempts were equally fruitless. On my sixth visit, he even added a dramatic twist to the pulley business: "One day, the rope gets stuck. I'm left suspended between two floors. Just imagine, a legless man suspended in space! Isn't that novel?" This time I couldn't resist bursting into laughter, with the result that Erich almost kicked me out. "Well, since you don't understand anything, I won't play in your damn movie!"

For a whole week I played dead. It was risky, since I needed him to complete my casting and I was committed to the producers. Negotiations had to be resumed, and I started visiting him every day again. It was quite by chance, reading an interview with Erich in an old newspaper, that I hit upon a solution.

The article told about Stroheim's ... wife suffering severe burns in an accident at her hairdresser; a whole portion of her face had been disfigured and Erich was devastated. The next day I came to see him and, after the customary two or three scotches, I presented him with the following offer: "You won't be legless but you'll have serious face burns sustained during the 1914–1918 war. You'll wear a mask on the disfigured portion of your face—the other half will be normal. You'll have your peace face and your war face, so to speak. And this black half-mask will look fantastic on you."

Erich embraced me: "Wonderful," he cried, then added, to my terror, "With one condition." I thought he still wanted to be legless, but fortunately he did not. "With one condition: I'll disclose the monstrous wound under my mask at least once in the film. It will symbolize the horrors of war."

I agreed, and drank another scotch to my victory.[52]

One might suspect that Greville is exaggerating; but there are many such stories, and there are enough grotesque scenes in Stroheim's films to indicate that he did, indeed, think along such odd lines. Although he somewhat restrained his acting roles in the films he directed himself, when he was acting in other people's films, from *His Picture in the Papers* onward, he strove to be as outlandish as possible.

Stroheim obviously had a strong influence on his scenes in *Menaces*. As the gentle and melancholy Austrian refugee, the barking, commandeering Stroheim is entirely absent. Although he looks sinister and grotesque with half his face covered by a black cloth mask, the other hotel residents seem to accept his affliction nonchalantly, as do the local children. This kindly man uses his medical knowledge to help some children's wounded dog (similar to a scene in *Walking down Broadway*). He also has a sensitive moment when he picks up a woman's perfumed handkerchief and speaks about his past in a soft and sad voice, his face revealing a man on the verge of tears. Later, staring up at the sky, the mutilated veteran predicts that war will come and the heavens will be full of planes showering flames and death on humanity. Toward the end of the film, in thorough despair, he is speaking to a woman and starts to take off the mask, followed by a quick cut to her as she screams and quickly averts her eyes. Shortly after, he shoots himself. It is only then, in a discreet long shot, that we see his disfigured face.

Stroheim reveals an interesting range in his scenes, despite the kind of mask that evokes the villain of a Republic serial. *Variety*, perhaps sharing the French audience's displeasure with the film, summed Stroheim up in two words: "Performance passable."[53] Although the film may have been maligned because of its sentiments, its striking visuals partially redeemed it.

Stroheim soon had another opportunity to play someone other than an officer or a spy. *Pièges* [Snares] premiered in Paris in January 1940, and as *Personal Column* it opened in New York the following February. It is a murder mystery about women who disappear after answering newspaper ads for "lonely" girls. A "taxi dancer" friend of one victim goes to the police, who ask her to act as a decoy. The brave girl agrees to help.

Scripted and directed by Robert Siodmak, *Pièges* is an episodic work that centers on the various people the heroine meets. (At its premiere in Paris, according to *Variety*, the film was 115 minutes long, but French reference works list it as 99 minutes, which probably means that shortly after its initial showing, sections were removed.) The girl's adventures begin when she answers her first ad. Protected by a watching policeman, she ventures down a dark street for a meeting. A mysterious apparition, garbed in black hat and overcoat (Stroheim), looms before her. Despite the menacing approach, all he does is to make an appointment with her for a later time.

When she goes to his house, he greets her wearing a black frock coat adorned with medals. Except for those medals and the usual white gloves, Stroheim presents a new persona here. With a dark mustache and medium-length white hair, he speaks in soft, humble tones. We learn, via his maid, that he is a *grand couturier* who has grown harmlessly insane. The maid explains that he "was a king in those days: Paris, London, New York. The parties, the millions he spent. Competitors conspired to ruin him." He wants the girl to model his dresses and begins to speak to an imaginary audience. After this peculiar encounter, the girl signals the policeman outside. The enraged couturier accuses her of being a spy and forces her upstairs so he can show off his collection of dresses and wax mannequins. Asserting that his competitors will never steal his designs, he goes completely insane, sets them afire, and presumably dies with them. In the street, standing by a fire alarm box (surely a Stroheim addition), is her police guard. The girl escapes to continue her investigation.

The rest of this French film noir, depicting a romance with Maurice Chevalier and his false imprisonment, suggests that Stroheim probably made additional contributions, although some might be coincidental. When the Chevalier character orders Heidsieck Monopole, the heroine changes the order to Moet et Chandon, Brut Imperial—one of those specific details Stroheim relished. There is an amusing reference to "Seven Siberian Dwarfs"; a lustful, fetishistic butler who provides a nightdress for the girl he wants to sleep with because he abhors pajamas; and a specific menu order of caviar, chicken aspic, Russian salad, and strawberries. Stroheim said later that "it was a pleasure to work with Siodmak," which probably means that some of his suggestions were taken. In the original film, there were several references to sexual aberrations. Even the shortened American version retained some of the spicy dialogue, but it was not fully translated into subtitles. Stroheim regretted that he never had a scene with Chevalier, whom he met only afterward.[54]

Years later, in 1947, Boris Karloff played Stroheim's part in a Hollywood remake of *Pièges* called *Lured*. In a strange coincidence, in 1942 Karloff's role in the stage play *Arsenic and Old Lace* was taken over by Stroheim.

Suddenly, the fates seemed to tire of tormenting Stroheim and appeared to smile once more. Demofilm signed him to act in, write, and direct a film based on his original story *La Dame blanche*. Stroheim's imagination slipped into high gear, and once again he was designing costumes, planning sets, and working out a scenario. In the midst of this frenetic activity, he was told that the company had decided to shoot a story called *Golden Fleece*. Although Stroheim had agreed to make his own story, he listened to the producer's tale, full of coincidences, and "to show my willingness to do anything to get along," tried to improve it. "After much quibbling," Stroheim quit trying to rewrite an impossible scenario and returned to working on *La Dame blanche*. For his Viennese heroine, he wanted "the traditional blue-eyed blonde" but found that behind his back they had hired "a little Italian girl." When he demanded that the company make some preliminary preparations (such as costumes and plans for sets), it demanded that he finish the scenario first, which he knew would take several more months. "All this embittered me to such an extent that I asked for my release—as otherwise I would have been tied up for approximately a year. The company called for arbitrage and in spite of the fact that Jean Renoir acted as my attorney, I *lost* and was as per judgment to repay all the salary I had received in advance while writing. As I had been writing for about four months, it amounted to quite a lot and of course I was unable to repay that immediately. The story reverted to me and I am still the proud possessor of the same."[55] Stroheim said that he was "terribly glad" that he did not make the film for that company because he knew "it would have ended disastrously." "If I have another chance to direct," he noted ruefully to Peter Noble, "I want to be god-damned sure that I will be able to carry my plans out to the very end alone, and not be hampered by incompetent would-know-it-alls, who just want to have a finger in someone else's pie. The few things I have done were good or bad and I was solely responsible. Maybe someday I'll find an understanding Angel who would stake me to one of my own stories. Meanwhile I carry on."[56] Stroheim was undoubtedly right in wanting no interference as an artist; but apparently he saw no irony in the fact that he was constantly adding to other people's scripts yet would brook no interference with his own!

The cancellation of *La Dame blanche* was a serious disappointment, for Stroheim had devoted considerable effort to his meticulous script and its production design. In fact, he had made countless pencil draw-ings of uniforms, helmets, insignia, and faces (indicating hairstyles, glasses, collars, etc.) and had even sketched out a foot-washing scene. Forty-nine of these drawings were reproduced in 1959 in an Italian book, *Von Stroheim* (Edizioni di Bianco e Nero).

Because he "could not afford to be a picker," Stroheim agreed in 1939 to appear in *La Révolte des vivants* (original title, *Le Monde tremblera*) and played the part of Emile Lasser. A few years later, Stroheim could not remember the story ("I am surely better off for it") and recalled laughing with the other actors during "the making of the scenes and between them." He admitted that clowning was not in his character but explained that it was what one could call "humor of the gallows." He confessed that "I did not give a shit—yes, you read correctly—about the story or my part." He did it for "the dough and I had a hell of a time getting it." Stroheim concluded with: "Never saw the picture."[57]

In his next effort, *Tempête* (the title on the print I have seen), also known as *Tempête sur Paris* and released in New York as *Thunder over Paris* (in June 1940), Stroheim played the tricky boss of several dishon-est enterprises, who is also known as the "merchant of mirages." In his dubious business schemes, the character assumes various disguises to evade the police. Stroheim was proud to say that, after "invigorating arguments" with the writer of the screenplay, he "certainly had the chance to show my versatility."[58] He happily masqueraded as a Negro, a woman, and a French senator. He claimed he never saw the picture, and perhaps he never did; in any case, his portrayal of a woman was not in the final release print.

As the film opens, Stroheim in blackface, impersonating a Negro and wearing a loud shirt and a garish tie, darts into his office in New York City. He is the entrepreneur of Carter's Hair Straightener, which he has been selling to gullible blacks in Harlem. Smoking a cigarette and sporting a cane, he moves jauntily around the room. Informed by a henchman that his scam is about to be discovered and he will be arrested, the con man removes his makeup, carefully combs his almost nonexistent hair, and hurriedly flies to Paris, where he visits his daughter, who is married to a police official.

The rest of the plot involves the con man with a tricky and oily blackmailer (Marcel Dalio). In the course of dealings with this fellow, the con man threatens and almost strangles him. When the police official realizes that his father-in-law is the arch crook and is about to arrest him, the con man says that he will have to settle some matters and then, upon his honor, will give himself up. He visits the blackmailer, who is about to flee with some incriminating photographs involving the daughter, and after the con man slaps the blackmailer hard in the face, there is a knockabout fight and the con man is shot. Although severely wounded, he grabs the blackmailer and drags him behind a curtain—as in *Greed*—where he kills him. Then he throws an oil lamp, which starts a fire that consumes the photographs. Dying, he telephones the police to say that he can't give himself up and calls his daughter to bid her adieu before being consumed by the flames.

Stroheim recalled that he "had some good scenes with Dalio and nearly burned to death being so exhausted at the end of the sequence in which I was supposed to die in flames that I practically fell asleep on the floor while the flames set my clothes on fire." Stroheim survived "thanks to one of the pompiers that stood by who thought that the joke had gone far enough."[59]

The plot of *Tempête* is rather involved and rather foolish but at the same time curiously personal. Stroheim in this role was able to be jolly (even impish), sarcastic, furious, and violent. He is also gentle and sensitive with his beloved daughter. In addition, the film provided Stroheim with some heroic and tragic final moments. Perhaps there is no film that shows the various sides of the living and breathing Stroheim better than this one.

Variety, however, was not impressed. It acknowledged that *Tempête* was "the most recent attempt to build up ... Stroheim into a local b.o. favorite, but, like more modest previous attempts falls wide of the mark." The reviewer complained that Stroheim made "no new contribution and gives another repeat performance, with the same deliberate, studied gestures and grimaces of old."[60] To the contrary, there were a number of innovations in Stroheim's performance. Perhaps the reviewer had had a bad bottle of wine that night. Or perhaps he was angry at all Teutons, for the Nazis had just invaded France.

Because Stroheim had not yet paid back all the money he owed Demofilm for the *La Dame blanche* fiasco, the company began another opus, *L'Enfer du jeu,* known later as *Macao,* and agreed to wipe out the debt in exchange for his services for a specific two-week period. But delays occurred, and by the time this expensive and important production was ready, the two weeks had passed, and they had to start paying him. Although there may have been ill feeling, none of this is in evidence in the completed film, directed by Jean Delannoy. Indeed, it is one of Stroheim's major prewar performances and indicates that he had a strong hand in the production. When the Nazis occupied France in 1940, they had such an aversion to Stroheim because of his Hun roles that they ordered his part cut and replaced him with a French actor (Pierre Renoir). In fact, Stroheim was banned from French screens throughout the occupation. A print of the original version with Stroheim was smuggled into Great Britain, where it was reedited, dubbed, and retitled as *Gambling Hell*. After the war, Stroheim's footage was reinserted in the French version.

The shooting of the film took place in Nice, where, Stroheim noted, Denise and he had "a great deal of fun" and, along with his fellow actors, "enjoyed the merry life of the Riviera." Some scenes in the film took place on a boat, supposedly in China. When they were shooting these scenes, the boat set was built on a scaffolding in a swamp, and "billions of frogs croaked so that it was impossible to work." Finally, they had to dynamite them. The frogs that were not killed would be shocked into silence for a half hour or so before chorusing again. Although the company was short of money and many of the most important scenes had to be omitted for budgetary reasons, the film still makes a good effect. Its only weakness is the ending. Apparently, there was not enough money to engage Stroheim, the leading lady, and the crew for the final death scenes, which, as a result, are left to the viewer's imagination. Jean Delannoy, Stroheim concluded, did "pretty well considering what he had to work with."[61]

The film takes place in the midst of military turmoil in contemporary China as Japanese planes bomb the area. Stroheim plays Krall, the down-on-his-luck captain of a boat, who is shown talking with a Chinese military official. The man tells Krall that he has heard Krall has been a gunrunner and gambler. Krall comments dryly, "No smoke without fire." In the midst of their negotiating about the price of munitions that Krall will supply, the official offers him milk. Krall takes out his pocket flask and drinks his own scotch.

Outside, as troops and equipment roll by, a stylish dancer by the name of Mirielle (Mirielle Balin) has foolishly left the boundaries of the international territory. While she adjusts her makeup, the reflections from her pocket mirror appear to be signals, and she is taken for a spy. As she is about to be executed, Krall intervenes and gallantly saves her life. He offers to take her to Macao. On the way to the boat, they walk past a firing squad—visual proof of the fate she has just escaped. On board his ship, Krall escorts her to nicely furnished quarters. "The cabin of the princess!" he announces. A vase contains a bouquet of orchids. She asks, "For me alone?" and he answers, "Of course," and then reveals that his cabin adjoins hers.

Krall tells his first mate that he will soon have money to double the wages of his unpaid, disgruntled, and motley crew. Afterward, when his scruffy servant serves him a drink, Krall asks irritably, "Where are the white gloves?" The servant grudgingly dons an absolutely filthy pair and pours the drink. Later, Krall goes into a storage area on the boat and retrieves a fashionable Parisian dress for the dancer. He apparently collects such items. "Do you collect women, too?" she asks, and he replies, "Of course." He kisses her hands and moves up her arm a bit. He locks the outer cabin door, helps her with the dress, and takes the key out of the door to his adjoining cabin. Then, instead of making the inevitable pass that she fears and the audience anticipates, he puts the key in *her* side of the lock. When she tries the door, he has locked it on *his* side with another key and can be seen sitting in a chair, drinking and smoking, with his feet propped up in the air.

The film then introduces a Japanese underworld leader (Sessue Hayakawa) who runs a gambling den and deals with illegal munitions. He has on his desk a photograph of his Eurasian daughter, presumably from a liaison with a French woman. The daughter has met a young Frenchman aboard a ship coming from Europe, and upon her arrival she is embraced by her doting father. She is, of course, unaware that he is a gangster. The young Frenchman later goes to the gambling casino, where he wins a great deal of money. The father has the Frenchman waylaid. His money is stolen, and he is thrown in the river, where Krall's crew spots him. They interrupt Krall while he is speaking with Mireille. He offhandedly suggests that the crew throw the half-drowned fellow back in the river, but she intervenes. Krall examines the rescued man and, recognizing him from his past, says, affectionately, "You son of a bitch!"

Later, Krall goes to the gangster, but he will not give him the munitions unless Krall has cash. Meanwhile, Krall has given Mireille some money to gamble with, and she has done quite well, but then he joins her and takes over. Soon, he is broke and covers his debt with a worthless check. The gangster has Mireille escorted to his quarters and wants to sleep with her, but she refuses.

Back on the boat, Krall is depressed. He is now wearing a dark naval jacket, as opposed to his all-white uniforms. He tells Mireille if he does not supply the arms, he will be killed, and if he is not killed, the bad check will get him three years in jail. She says that she will help him, for Krall is the first man who has not asked her for anything, despite the fact that he saved her life and has her at his mercy. When she leaves, he picks up her slip and wiggles it.

Mireille returns to the gangster, who burns the check, but when she does not seem cooperative, he starts to rape her. She throws pepper in his eyes and escapes. As the temporarily blinded father staggers about, his daughter sees him and realizes that he is the criminal boss who had tried to have her boyfriend killed.

When Mireille returns to Krall and tells him that the check was destroyed, Krall, thinking she has slept with the criminal, slaps her. After she explains, he begs her forgiveness. Now she uses the French familiar *tu* rather than the more formal *vous,* and they become lovers.

There are further plot complications: at one point, the gangster's daughter is kidnaped and put on Krall's boat. Meanwhile, the gangster's henchmen arrange to have the boat bombed. When he realizes that his daughter is on the ship and that she will be killed, the gangster shoots himself. Unbeknownst to him, however, the daughter has been allowed to leave the ship with her lover. As the film ends, bombs land on the boat, killing Krall and Mireille. Thus perish the two caring but ruthless father figures, the two auslanders—one from Japan, who loves his daughter, and the other from Austria, who loves a woman young enough to be his daughter.

Stroheim's role of Captain Krall was the lead, and he rose to the occasion with a performance carefully honed and full of personal touches. He was given the opportunity—more likely he gave it to himself by rewriting his part—to create a more complex individual, one who maintains his grace under pressure. He is gallant, caring, sensitive, vulnerable, and sad and conveys these effects with consummate skill. As in *Tempête,* Stroheim enriched the part by drawing on the various sides of his personality. He is not the man you love to hate but seemingly the man himself.

Jean Delannoy, the director, created a visually striking film; he made many scenes of Macao look quite authentic by the clever use of Nice's waterfront and nearby locations. The near perfect illusion was enhanced further by the hiring of many Orientals as extras to provide local color. The camera work is often fluid, and the compositions are complex and beautiful, with much use made of foreground. Furthermore, the director, like Jean Renoir before him, listened to Stroheim's suggestions. As a result, Stroheim's scenes, in particular, have his individual stamp. He was allowed not only to create his own costume, but also to invent or, in some instances, modify the dialogue and physical details. The drinking of scotch, the orchids in the vase, the choice of a dress, the dirty gloves of the waiter, the locked cabin doors, the brief scenes at the roulette wheel, the earthy "son of a bitch" line, and the gallantry of the romantic scenes show his strong influence. Stroheim also made his character somewhat poignant. As a result, the film appears more tragic than perhaps its original plot was intended to be. Certainly Stroheim had no reason to be ashamed of *L'Enfer du jeu*.

The year 1939 was a tense one, and time seemed to be running out for the uneasy peace of Europe. Stroheim would make a brief appearance in another film, called *Paris–New York* (1939), in which a large number of important French actors played minute parts on board the *Normandie* during its last voyage before the Second World War began. "The work," Stroheim said, "was quite pleasant but absolutely inconsequential." A surviving photograph shows Stroheim aboard ship with the New York City skyline in the background. The *Normandie,* with Stroheim and Denise still aboard, then returned to France on August 23. When the film was finally shown in Paris on May 1, 1940, Stroheim had been replaced in his part by another actor.

Stroheim claimed that after the war began on September 1, 1939, he offered his services to the minister of war because he felt indebted to the French people for his "second rise to popularity." Perhaps his age of fifty-four or his Austrian background might have been a factor or perhaps this sudden surge of patriotism may have been another of his exaggerations, but in any case, his endeavors proved, as he said, "fruitless." Although the French were worried about another bloody war with Germany, they felt secure behind their impregnable Maginot

Line. Despite the declaration of war, life and industry and even some filmmaking, after a momentary halt, continued during this period called "the phony war."

Back in America, Darryl Zanuck, the head of Twentieth Century–Fox, was impressed by Stroheim's performance in *La Grande Illusion,* which was then playing throughout the country. Zanuck had also seen a French picture called *J'Étais une Adventurière,* which he wanted to remake, and decided that Stroheim would be perfect for a part in the American version. Stroheim was contacted, but the actor had mixed feelings. The thought of returning to America, the scene of his former triumphs and failures, did not appeal to him. Stroheim later explained that because "I did not want to go, I made my conditions so high that I did not expect them to accept. But to my great surprise and chagrin they did."[62]

Stroheim and Denise traveled to Lisbon in late November 1939, and on the stationery of the Hotel Aviz the emotional and sentimental side of him came out as he penned a letter to Valerie. At the top of the page he wrote: "I am flying tomorrow morning at 8 A.M. across the Atlantic." Aware of the fact that the plane might be shot down, Stroheim was understandably concerned.

> I hope this letter is useless—and that I shall arrive at the same time (or even before)—but—as one never knows—I write these lines to you and Josef—in case—anything happens to me.
>
> From the day I met you—I never loved anyone else but you—when Josef was born—you and our son!—So help me God—Amen.
>
> If anything should happen to me—I want you sweethearts to know that if I have time to think of you and Josef—!!!
>
> Let us hope that all will go well on the transatlantic flight! and that we shall soon be reunited for *ever*!
>
> My love to you both—!! God bless you—and think of me kindly. All my earthly goods are yours.[63]

Fortunately, the flight was without incident. Stroheim and Denise arrived in New York on November 25, 1939, and went directly on to Hollywood. And so Stroheim's life entered another phase.

17

America Again

Stroheim's return to Hollywood was not as a victor, but as a loser. The fame, notoriety, and respect that he had enjoyed in France were not to be encountered in a town where he was almost forgotten and that regarded him as a quaint relic from the heady silent days.

The emotional strain of the flight, the trip across the country, and his arrival in Hollywood was compounded when he met with Valerie and Josef, who was by now sixteen years old. The meeting was perhaps cordial, maybe even more than cordial, but also awkward. There was still a mutual warmth, but not enough to cause the family to reunite. The marriage was over—at least practically, if not legally. Although Stroheim would continue to express his love for Valerie in letters, he remained with Denise. In the following years, when he was away from Hollywood on tour, he would faithfully send Valerie anniversary gifts, flowers at Easter, and presents at Christmas. He also renewed his personal relationship with Josef and saw him whenever he could. To an outsider, Stroheim's behavior would probably seem hypocritical or insincere, but it was more complex than that. Although the couple may have loved each other, either Valerie or Stroheim saw that the relationship could no longer work. Denise must have had some difficult times with this complicated and gifted man, and yet they stayed together until death did them part.

Stroheim and Denise soon found quarters in Hollywood, and Stroheim began studying the script of the odd, caper-like film, *I Was an Adventuress,* in which he had been given a role. It was scheduled to be a rather lavish production directed by Gregory Ratoff.

Stroheim, remembering that Zanuck, a writer himself, had liked his additions to *Three Faces East,* immediately began making changes and additions. As a result, Stroheim's part grew larger and became redolent of his time-honored obsessions. The character that he plays was not very interesting in the French film on which the new project was based. Stroheim gave the role further dimension and vitally improved the original. He and Peter Lorre portray two swindlers who, in one case, switch paste jewels for genuine ones. Stroheim plays a "colonel"; Lorre his helper, Paolo; and Vera Zorina (in real life a ballerina), a "countess." When the colonel has an argument with her, he says, "Please don't try to overawe me with that countess stuff, will you? Have a heart. After all, it was I who invented it." From a man who once masqueraded as a count, it is a curiously autobiographical statement. She admits, "You invented me." Stroheim also adds the little details that always enrich his work. When he notices she has chipped her nail, he extracts a manicure kit from his pocket and adds polish to the missing area.

Later in the film, the colonel examines the biography of a new victim he intends to swindle. He notices that the man was born on September 22 (Stroheim's own birthday) and says, "Astrologically speaking, he is a Virgo." He then adds with a curious smile, "They're very fine and clever people."

When the countess falls in love, she escapes the clutches of the two crooks and marries the hero, who has no idea of her criminal past. Without their classy feminine confederate, the colonel and Paolo's con games fail. In dire financial need, the colonel orders Paolo to discover her whereabouts and then waits at an outdoor café. When his accomplice returns, the colonel remarks, "You've tramped all over Paris and found no trace of her." When Paolo asks how he knew, the colonel replies, "Your feet. Those ugly Italian peasant feet. They tell the story. You see, I studied hands and feet. I can read them like you could read a book, if you could read." He lectures the abashed fellow about his expert knowledge of feet. "For instance," he says as a close-up of a girl's feet appears, "those are just a woman's feet, but I tell you she is a *vendeuse* in one of the department stores. Stood on her feet all day, but she isn't tired now. She is going to meet her sweetheart." The colonel notes another passerby. "The woman with the bunions; she has given up hope of meeting anybody." He then points out an American tourist who has a "big corn on the left little toe." The camera then watches a man's polished shoes as they pass by and stop in a *pissoir,* surely another touch of Stroheim's unflinching sense of humor. All of this material was absent from the original.

The colonel treats Paolo, who is an habitual pickpocket, in a condescending fashion. Clearly the brains of the pair, the colonel indulges Paolo's petty thieving ways. What he wants is a big haul of jewels from the house guests of the feminine confederate, who has now married and gone straight. After the jewels are taken, the men plan to meet aboard ship to escape. Paolo—out of loyalty to the girl—secretly returns the loot, and when handing the now empty case over to the colonel at the ship's rail, he "accidentally" drops it into the ocean.

Stroheim, cool, collected, and aristocratic, and Lorre, whining, compulsive, and somewhat simpleminded, interact beautifully and are infinitely more interesting than their counterparts in the French film. The two could well have become as successful a team as Lorre and Sydney Greenstreet would later.

Although Stroheim's character is a rogue, he is almost likable in his villainy, and he embellishes his role by tossing down drinks, adjusting his monocle, kissing hands, clicking heels, and occasionally smirking. Much more comfortable as an actor than he used to be and working under pleasant conditions—obviously the director, Gregory Ratoff, was taking his suggestions—Stroheim clearly enjoyed his role and delivers one of his most entertaining performances.

Stroheim's influence can be felt even in scenes in which he does not appear. For example, when the hero and the heroine are in a room at an inn, a cross looms on a wall in the background. Later in the film, when a man signs a hotel register, the third name up is "Franz von Starheim" from Vienna. Also, though one would not think that Stroheim would have influence on an automobile chase, the car passes a large Madonna by the wayside.

After *I Was an Adventuress* finished shooting around February 1940 (it was released in May), Stroheim and Denise prepared to fly back to France. After a considerable wait, they eventually were booked on a June 18 flight, but the Germans entered Paris on June 14 and were well in control by June 17. The couple's return became impossible. Indeed, Zanuck's offer may have saved Stroheim's life, for he, considering his Hun roles and his Jewish heritage, would have been prime fodder for the Nazi camps.

Now in America for the duration, Stroheim looked for further work. And history repeated itself. Once again he was relegated to being the bad German—not the Hun this time, but the Nazi. After a wait of several months, he was cast as a Gestapo agent in *So Ends Our Night* (released on January 27, 1941). This serious film about European refugees was based on an Erich Maria Remarque novel and was well directed by John Cromwell, with brilliant photography by William Daniels (who had worked on *Blind Husbands, The Devil's Pass Key, Foolish Wives, Merry-Go-Round, Greed,* and *The Merry Widow*).

Stroheim lends an air of class to his portrayal of Brenner, the Nazi officer. He is polite and elegant and first appears in the film wearing white gloves. He congratulates Steiner (Fredric March) on his escape from the high-voltage wires and machine guns of Germany to Austria, where he has just been arrested for not having a passport and thus is subject to deportation. Lighting his usual cigarette, Stroheim as the Gestapo agent offers Steiner a passport if he will betray the people who helped him escape. Steiner refuses and, after his release from the Austrian prison, sneaks across the border to see his ailing wife. After this brief visit, he flees once more.

Later, when he learns that his wife (Frances Dee) is on her deathbed, Steiner returns to Germany, where he is captured and again interrogated by Brenner. Steiner promises that, if he is allowed to see his dying wife, he will reveal the names of his fellow conspirators. Brenner believes his offer and accompanies him to the hospital, where the escapee shares his wife's final moments. Brenner says, "You have certainly taken unfair advantage of my kindness. You kept me waiting here over three hours." This line seems quite inconsiderate and cruel, because Stroheim had elsewhere tried to humanize his role by being more than a mere brute, a kind of gentlemanly Rauffenstein. This interpretation was somewhat antithetical to the script, which created only a reprehensible Nazi. As the pair descend a high, glassed-in stairway overlooking a busy street, Steiner realizes that his destiny is either to betray his comrades or spend the rest of his life in prison, so he leaps through the window to his death, taking the Gestapo officer Stroheim with him. Even allowing for the political sentiments of the time, it is a shocking and somewhat unwarranted ending. The Stroheim character does not seem to deserve this fate.

There is one episode that may suggest Stroheim's influence, a scene in a shooting gallery in the Prater in Vienna, which is quite reminiscent of a similar one in *Merry-Go-Round*.

So Ends Our Night may have been an important film and certainly was a serious one, but it gave Stroheim barely five minutes of screen time and suggested that once more he would spend the war years playing a Nazi villain. This was not a pleasant prospect, but it was better than no work at all. Yet even that work eluded him. After *I Was an Adventuress,* he was inactive for almost a year, except for the few days' work in *So Ends Our Night*. Stroheim came to the conclusion that he was being blacklisted. Lesser actors from Europe were finding jobs, but he was not.

In January 1941, a black comedy—one of the first—became an instant success on Broadway. Called *Arsenic and Old Lace,* it featured a crazed villain (played originally by Boris Karloff). The play was so popular that other stage companies were formed, and Stroheim was hired to play the role in Chicago. First, however, there was a tryout in Baltimore. Stroheim had never before appeared on the professional stage; understandably, he was nervous. Richard Maney, the company's press agent, described Stroheim's debut.

> At the end of the first act on the opening night, von Stroheim announced that he was taking the next train back to California. After thirty years' success on the screen, he said, he didn't propose to submit to such abuse in his first stage role. "What abuse?" we all asked. "I was hissed all through the first act," he raged. "Why didn't someone put a stop to it?"
>
> In the nick of time a stage-hand named the culprit. The hisses came from a leaky off-stage radiator. This monster muffled, von Stroheim went on to Chicago, head high.[1]

On the way to Chicago, Stroheim appeared for a week's run in

New York City in late March 1941.[2] Stroheim cared for the money but not the exhausting schedule or the role. He disliked being dressed shabbily in a suit two sizes too large, and he reluctantly had to shed some of his "Prussian" mannerisms. The constant repetition did not satisfy his creative side, either, but the part occupied him for a year or so. It was grueling work as he appeared in Chicago, Philadelphia, and numerous other cities.

Stroheim recalled a visit from D. W. Griffith in his shabby dressing room in Philadelphia. "I was just getting a rub down after the last act when the door opened and D. W. entered. He kissed me on both cheeks. I have received quite a few honors in my life, but that kiss of the master was the highest honor that could be bestowed on me."[3]

On September 16, 1941, Stroheim, touring Connecticut at the time, revealed the softer side of his nature in a letter to congratulate his son Josef on his eighteenth birthday.

Dear Poopsie,

I hope that this letter will arrive in time—that is precisely on the 18th and that it will reach you in good health (except for your poor feet). I received your letters and you have no idea how they made me happy. I am so glad about your advancement and I hope you'll keep up your interest in your work—particularly now that you are in the Publicity Dept. I know I just feel that you will make good because you are bright and unspoiled. Just don't associate with punk kids who might get you into trouble. Keep up your interest in photography and continue to be a good mixer. That was one of my many shortcomings. I couldn't mix and make friends.

Now my "sweetheart baby"—(you'll always be that to me)—I wish for . . . your birthday all those things that only a father and a mother can wish for their only son. Health above all! Then happiness and success in business and life in general. My prayers will follow you where you will be.

I have sent for a little present in a package 1st class mail—Special Delivery and I trust it will reach you in time. I thought it might please you. It is a seal with your Crest which you can emboss on your letterheads either in the center at the head of the paper or on the left upper corner as well as on the rear-flap of the envelopes. I am also enclosing a *small* money-order but it comes from my very heart. I hope I'll be able to send you soon some more.

We opened last night and as you can see from the criticisms it went over all right. . . . I hope I'll see you in the near future and can kiss and hug you in reality instead of only in my mind. Have a good time but be careful. Now I have to go run to rehearsal. All my love and 1,0000 xxxxx.

Your Dad[4]

A few weeks later, in October, he addressed Valerie as "My Sweetheart!" and sent her twenty-one roses and a crest ring for their anniversary as a "*small* token of my *undying* love."

On December 7, 1941, the Japanese attacked Pearl Harbor, and World War II officially began for America. There was panic on the West Coast, with fears that the Japanese would invade California. Valerie wired Stroheim, who was in Pittsburgh still touring with *Arsenic and Old Lace,* that their boy was now in the military. The worried father and husband immediately sent a letter to Josef in which he shows his concern about his wife and son, although he acknowledges that they might laugh at his advice. Meticulous as always, he provides lists of things to do and items to keep in the event of an attack. He may not have been directing films, but he would be technical director of the Stroheim family's survival! The letter is so revelatory of his mind that it deserves to be printed in toto:

Dearest Poopsie!

This sounds ridiculous, I guess, now—that you are a real soldier—and at war-time at that! But if you should become a General—to *me* you will always only be "my poopsie"—and I would like to scratch your head back as I used to do so often when you were a baby and then even when you were quite grown-up—

I hope that all the little things I taught you in regards to being a soldier will come in handy and plus the things you learned at Military School you should be able to get along nicely.

Always stay as you are—nice—kind—good natured—but *on duty*—*strict*—and if necessary *hard! Obedient* to your superiors—as you want your subordinates to be to you. I know you are brave—you even were that as a little kid when I made you climb between two burning buckets in the garage on N. Oxford Ave. You are an excellent shot and with constant practice you'll be sharpshooter. Naturally when you are going to get the new "Garand(?)" semi-automatic rifle—it's going to be a bit tougher—because it has a tremendous recoil. Please write to me whether this outfit you are in—is the replacement of the "Calif. National Guard" the so-called "Home Defense" or "State Defense" or is it actually a USA outfit—as mother wired me. If so—I have up to now never heard of an "Evacuation Corps." Please describe to me the correct status and its functions—uniform—arms—whether mechanized or what. Please write at once to Detroit where I am going to be for Xmas. I can hardly wait to hear everything about it.

Be careful—don't fool around with loaded guns or, *better* said, don't let others fool around you. I know you have enough skill and experience in that line—to do anything like that. Don't let tough guys get you down and don't drink whiskey—ever—except when you are cold or sick.

Where are you going to drill? What about gas-masks? I have my two in a trunk in N.Y. Do you think you can buy some for mother and you? What about masks for the family? I think you ought to have buckets of *sand* outside in front and rear also in the house for incendiary bombs—also a garden hose constantly attached with a *spray* attachment (as you might have read or heard the Inc. Bombs must *not* be watered with a stream but only with a spray!)

Have flashlights with extra batteries ready. Also your old satchel which I used . . . in France with all the necessary things in it. A thermos quart with drinking water, two lemons, 12 cubes of sugar, Hershey bars (without nuts) lemondrops, cigarettes, matches (plenty), first aid kit (small), rubber bands for tourniquets, cleanex, zweiback, chopped beef, a small "sterno" heater and small pot (aluminum), rubber gloves, rubber goggles and two towels to be soaked in carbonate of soda (over your

nose and mouth) in case you can't get gas masks. Your loaded
revolver and rifle with cartridges two flashlights (with blue
and red slates) extra batteries, loaded camera (if possible), the
portable radio I sent you (have batteries (b) replaced for new
ones) so you don't get stuck.
Show mother again how to use revolver and rifle.

When you get your uniform have Hatzfeld fix it up so
you don't look like Mountain Guide—comfortable—but
snappy. Be smart in addressing your officers—salute smartly,
don't forget the "sir"! I just can't help giving you all this
bunk (I can hear you and your mother laugh) but believe
me, poopsie, I have been through it—I know! Use your good
sense and your inventiveness God gave you and don't hesitate to speak up if you have something to say (ask first for
permission to speak).

I hope you can drive—ride or drive—as your poor feet
won't be much good for hiking. Stick *always* to your post!
God be with you. God bless you! . . . He'll watch out for you!
I am praying every day for you and your welfare. I guess I am
too old (56) to do any real service—anyway at present I'll try
and make money as long as God lets me. Write me at once
everything! All my love to mother and you! Be good and careful! See that mother is not alone in the house if you are out
drilling at night.

Love to all! Your loving

Daddy[5]

Stroheim's fears, along with America's, about a possible Japanese attack
soon faded.

Arsenic and Old Lace continued to prosper as it traveled from city
to city. Sitting in hotel rooms, Stroheim thought frequently of Valerie.
In April, while in Toledo, Ohio, he wrote to her on her birthday:

Again one year has passed—with a great deal of trouble and
work—but no matter how much time passes—and no matter
how many thousands of miles on land or sea we are apart—
know this!:
You are always uppermost in my mind—*always!*

You are my first thought when I get up! you are my last thought when I lay me down to sleep!

Again I wish you a most happy birthday and beg you to accept my *little* physical proof of my *great* love for you. May God bless you—and protect you—I pray for that!

If God is with me—I may take over for Boris Karloff in New York—for the rest of the "run of the play" on B'way! (Till Jan. 1st, when our present tour is at an end on June 1.)

I wish I were there to kiss your blue eyes—and your lips and your fingers with my beautiful nails.

Think of me as much as I think of you and we shall be together again!

I love you!

I love you!

I love you!

Please wire me to Cleveland whether you received my present and when.

With 10000000 kisses

By the summer of 1942, Stroheim had returned to the Fulton Theater in New York, where he replaced Karloff, who had gone back to Hollywood. The traveling was now over, but he still had nightly performances as well as Wednesday and Saturday matinees. The brief biographical note in the Fulton Theater's play program, which he himself wrote, claimed that he had "served as second lieutenant in the Austrian army. . . . He joined the First Cavalry, then enlisted in the Mexican Army under President Francisco Madero. After working as railroad section foreman, magazine salesman, deputy sheriff, life saver and riding master he finally drifted into motion pictures as an extra." The program also mentioned *Blind Husbands, Foolish Wives, Merry-Go-Round, The Merry Widow,* and *Greed* (but not *The Devil's Pass Key*).

That the above was not compounded by a press agent was confirmed in an interview in which the fifty-seven-year-old actor declared that he was hopeful of being accepted by the U.S. Army, explaining that he had been an Austrian cavalry officer and had served in the Mexican army![6] This fib was for the public, but what of his personal life? Never one to forget a holiday or an anniversary, Stroheim wrote Valerie:

Even though I am far away—I'm with you in Spirit—always—but particularly to-day—Oct 16th—a red-letter day——!

Twenty-two years ago—we were married—it seems like a few years ago only—but when I look at Josef's picture a soldier—I realize—that it was not yesterday.

In these twenty-two years many things have happened. I realized some of my ambitions—I failed in many attempts—we have had wars—and peace, joy, and bitterness—happiness and tragedy—but my love for you has *never* changed!

Only you have not believed! I love you just as dearly—as I loved you when we stood side by side at the Altar at the old St. Brendan's church—

That I want to impress on you today—our anniversary—

I love you! I love you! I love you! Accept this little gift from me and carry it in your purse—so that at least when you use it—you may think of me a moment!

I shall be with you all day and night! Particularly at 6pm which is 3 o'clock in Los Angeles.

All my love and sincerest wishes for many many more anniversaries.[7]

At Christmastime in 1942, Stroheim sent his wife, whom he always addressed as "Vally," a "bracelet as a small token of my unending love for you." He explained:

It is only gold—the time of diamonds and sapphires has passed for me—I guess—but it comes from *my very heart*—and I believe it'll match the brooch. Unfortunately they were unable to engrave anything—they haven't got the men to do it. Perhaps after Xmas we can have it done out there.

Merry Xmas. Health and happiness!
See you soon—I hope!
All my love!

Erich

In another letter, written at about the same time, he discussed additional jewelry he was sending. Because the pins had sharp points, he implored her to send him immediately two pennies to ward off bad luck. The sentimental and perhaps guilt-ridden man added: "I wish I were in Los Angeles to wish you a merry Xmas personally and from lip to lip—as conditions are I am happy to know that you are comparatively well and that I am still able to support you. May God grant that I can keep up to do so! I am thinking of you and Josef and your loved ones and I trust you'll be thinking of me." He wrote that he was having "two performances—one at 8:30—and one at midnight—so I won't be able to celebrate myself. But I will have *one* drink at midnight which will be 9 o'clock in LA. If you will take one with Josef at *that* time—our minds and hearts will meet. I kiss you now and then—in *never-ending* love."[8]

Here one can see that certain sentimental details in his films—the lilacs in *Merry-Go-Round* and the apple blossoms in *The Wedding March,* for example—were not just "Hollywood" but part of his nature. One wonders, too, whether Denise was aware of these emotional excesses on paper and whether in his day-to-day life he ever indicated that his loyalties were divided. Undoubtedly, Denise also received Christmas presents. Did those packages too contain little notes? Perhaps, like the complex Prince Nicki in *The Wedding March,* Stroheim could function on two levels simultaneously.

Suddenly, Stroheim's career took another unexpected turn. Billy Wilder made him an offer. Yes, he would play a German officer, but not one who was a monstrous Nazi or a mere captain or colonel; he was to be the highly respected General Rommel. Bidding a not too reluctant farewell to *Arsenic and Old Lace,* Stroheim ventured back to California for *Five Graves to Cairo* (1943).

Billy Wilder and his writing partner, Charles Brackett, had been rummaging among old Paramount properties and decided to dust off *Hotel Imperial,* a 1927 Pola Negri vehicle (directed by Mauritz Stiller) that dealt with Russian troops taking possession of an enemy town during the First World War. Ironically, Stroheim himself once had been slated to direct and perhaps to act in it, if *The Wedding March* had been completed efficiently. Paramount had intended *Hotel Imperial* to be a great picture, but it proved a disappointment critically and financially. The *New York Times* noted that George Siegmann as the Russian general "hardly lives up to expectations."[9] Clearly, the role needed Stroheim to give it the proper embellishments, and years later, in *Five Graves to Cairo,* the role of the German general *would* live up to expectations.

Despite Paramount's disappointment with *Hotel Imperial,* the studio remained fond of this property and began to remake it in the early 1930s with Marlene Dietrich. She worked on it for a few days and then quit. Soon, a second start was made with Margaret Sullavan, but she broke an arm on the set, and production was again halted. Several years later, it was finally shot with a new cast and was released in May 1939 to very unenthusiastic reviews.

But Wilder and Brackett felt the story still had potential. They transposed the setting from an Austrian town overwhelmed by Russian troops to a North African village captured by the Germans during Rommel's 1942 African campaign. The film became so up-to-date that its final shooting script, dated December 17, 1942, contained a scene of Rommel's defeat, which had occurred that November. The picture was shipped to New York in early April 1943 and was released the next month.

Wilder recalled the day Stroheim first arrived on the set:

I was shooting exteriors with the tanks in the desert near Yuma. I came back to my office and they said, "Mr. Stroheim has arrived—he's upstairs in the wardrobe department." So I just rushed upstairs, clicked my heels, introduced myself, and there's that joke—which is true—where I said, "This is a very big moment in my life . . . that I should now be directing the great Stroheim." And he just didn't say anything. Then I said, "Your problem, I guess, was that you were ten years ahead of your time." And he looked at me and he said, "Twenty."[10]

After Wilder had first contacted Stroheim, the actor began making contributions to the script and started constructing his characterization of Rommel. The great lover of detail examined news photos, then chose the specific type of camera to carry (Rommel used a Leica) and insisted that it contain film. He meticulously planned what he would wear and convinced Paramount to let him design his own outfits. Photos showed that Rommel wore casual and loose-fitting uniforms. "We are changing that in the picture," Stroheim said in an interview. "I will wear a uniform as a uniform is supposed to be worn, but otherwise I will not be a lovely creature."[11] Stroheim ultimately felt that he was more what Rommel should have been than the actual Rommel himself.

As the film opens, a British soldier (Franchot Tone) enters a partially destroyed hotel in a small desert town in North Africa shortly before the victorious Germans enter. His life at stake, he pretends to be a clubfooted waiter who had been killed the night before in a bombing raid. Later, we learn that the waiter had been a German spy. (There was no clubfoot in *Hotel Imperial,* so it is quite likely that Stroheim, with his foot injury obsession, suggested this detail.)

We first see a shot of Rommel from the rear and from above, as if viewed from a balcony, as he strides back and forth in the hotel, wielding a curiously shaped three-foot whisk, which he flicks repeatedly to shoo away the flies. (The script calls it a "fly-swisher.") He is dictating a message to the Fuehrer: "Nothing can save the Eighth British army from a colossal catastrophe. They say the Red Sea once opened by special arrangement with *Moses* [he drenches the word with sarcasm]. A similar mishap will not occur this time." So far, all we have seen is the back of Stroheim's neck, damp with sweat. Only at the end of the speech does he turn, so that we can see his face. What a striking and dramatic introduction to a fascinating performance! Years later, Wilder described the power of Stroheim's personality. "Standing with his stiff fat neck in the foreground, he could express more than almost any actor with his face."[12]

Next Rommel orders cognac and tosses it down in the usual Stroheim fashion. For the next day, he orders "strong black coffee" (Stroheim always seems concerned about the condition of his coffee). Hearing this, the disguised British waiter decides to enter Rommel's room the next morning and shoot him, but the maid (Anne Baxter) goes instead. Rommel, lying in bed, is annoyed when he sees her and not the waiter. He dislikes encountering women in the morning. When she hands him the breakfast tray, he observes, "Your hands are neat. Why isn't the spoon?" and wipes sand off it. He then commands her, "Two steps back." When she mentions that she has a young brother in a German prison camp, he concludes, "You're suggesting some kind of bargain."

Rommel then has an interesting speech that shows an awareness of theatrical conventions, such as Stroheim had revealed in *Friends and Lovers,* in which one character sees another in terms of a stage play. "This is a familiar scene, reminiscent of bad melodrama. Although usually it is not the brother for whose life the heroine comes to plead;

it is the lover. The time is midnight. Place: the tent of the conquering general. Blushingly, the lady makes her proposal and gallantly the general grants her wish. Later, the lady very stupidly takes poison. In one Italian opera the two even go so far as to sing a duet." With a curious glance, Rommel concludes, "There will be no duet today." He calls in his adjutant and announces to the girl that requests for a prison release must be made to the commander or through the Red Cross or the Quakers. And it must all be done in triplicate. "Everything must be in triplicate. We can use paper in Germany—a great deal of paper." This need for paper is of course left unexplained, although the statement suggests that bathroom tissue was in short supply! The reviewer for *Variety* enjoyed this breakfast scene, calling it "a masterpiece of sarcasm" and concluded that throughout the film Stroheim did "a capital job."[13]

Later, Rommel invites the British officers to lunch (as in *La Grande Illusion*) and gives them a lecture on tactics and preparation. He moves the saltcellars and pepper shakers around the tablecloth and answers many of the officers' questions, but not the big one—Where does he get his supplies? At the end of the luncheon, Rommel accidentally spills the salt and tosses some over his shoulder for good luck. He adds a sarcastic observation about the dessert: "Rice pudding in Egypt. One never knows whether it's raisins or flies."

Rommel gives orders to the waiter, who is being sent on to Cairo, about his future arrival there at Shepherd's Hotel. He will want "a lukewarm bath drawn in the royal suite" and in the evening a "command performance at the opera—*Aïda*—in German, omitting the second act, which is too long and not too good." Thus does Stroheim embellish his dialogue with minute details. Lesser mortals would have merely ordered a room and a bath at a hotel. Not Stroheim. The bath was to be "lukewarm," the suite "royal," and the opera a specific one, along with a criticism.

The adjutant, who has promised to help the girl's brother in exchange for sexual favors, discovers the body of the real waiter in the cellar and is killed. When the dead adjutant is found, an investigation occurs, and Stroheim as Rommel, unlike what we know of the real Rommel, uses the fly whisk on the maid like a whip, to get the truth. When it appears that she killed the soldier, he says, "To prove to you that we are not merely the Huns you think we are, you will be tried according to your own French law—the Code Napoleon. There will be a court martial." This dialogue is reminiscent of that in *La Grande Illusion* when Rauffenstein tells the prisoners they will be governed by French rules.

Stroheim presents an uncanny impersonation of Rommel, except that he is more military and more strict than the actual general. He either flicks the fly whisk or smokes a cigarette, and he definitely commands every scene he is in. One wonders if Rommel ever saw this film. He perhaps would have enjoyed it, all except where the character hits the girl with the whip. This is a fallback to the Terrible Hun roles of Stroheim's early career, and it is a question whether Wilder originally wanted the episode or whether Stroheim added this bit of unpleasant business. In any case, it prevents Rommel from appearing too likable, a necessity for wartime propaganda. After all, Rommel was an important enemy general. Even with the whipping scene, he still appeared too gentlemanly and gallant for some rabidly patriotic critics, who would have preferred a thoroughly monstrous Nazi. (Incidentally, a year later, in 1944, the Gestapo discovered that Rommel was associated with the plot to assassinate Hitler, and the general—to save his family—was compelled to commit suicide.)

The film was released to enthusiastic audiences, and Stroheim once more was a major star. His picture appeared large in the ads, and the letters of his name were the same size as those for Tone and Baxter.

On April 14, 1943, Stroheim wrote a birthday note to his wife. "As Life begins only at forty—you are to-day only six years old—to prove that there will be forty six roses in a vase." Furthermore, "to prove my never dying love," he sent her "a small token which I hope you will like—it matches your other jewelry—somewhat." He added that, if he was not working, "I'll be out to see you." He sent his wishes for "continued health" to her dear Mother and other "members of your family." He concluded with "I love you from the *very* depth of my heart."

Stroheim was still striving to return to directing and hatched a new scheme. The *Hollywood Reporter* of May 3, 1943, described the situation:

Deal is on between Pola Negri and Mexican moneyed interests for the actress to go south-of-the-border to appear in a film version of Erich von Stroheim's novel, *Paprika*.

Set-up would also include the services of von Stroheim to direct the picture in English and Spanish versions.

Actually, this plan sounded quite promising, but nothing came of it.

From the featured role in *Five Graves to Cairo,* with lots of dialogue and screen time, Stroheim slipped backward and exchanged his general's outfit for that of a colonel and became a nasty Nazi in his next film, *The North Star.*

The decidedly left-leaning Lillian Hellman, who had profited mightily by depicting capitalistic greed in *The Little Foxes,* decided that she could both salve her own political conscience and make even more money by praising Russia for Sam Goldwyn. The result was a pretentious and expensive propaganda effort called *The North Star,* released in October 1943. The film is so slanted, one-dimensional, and simpleminded that it stands out as an unmitigated embarrassment, even among the ridiculous propaganda films of the time. Unrelieved by wit or humor and pompously self-righteous, it is so extreme that it is often unintentionally funny, despite the visual skills of Lewis Milestone, who had directed *All Quiet on the Western Front* (1930). There is nothing worse than failed pretentiousness.

Stalinist Russia is depicted as nirvana, packed full of kindly old grandfathers, cherubic children, sensitive teenagers untroubled by raging hormones, and musically inclined peasants who, at the drop of a shovel, break into heartfelt song. There is not a gulag to be seen. All is blissful.

After starting out with badly acted domestic scenes of Russian peasants speaking with flat American accents, the film slips into what looks and sounds like a musical. After the Nazi invasion, there is a parade of atrocities, as well as an overabundance of pompous speeches. The turgid film, striving to create some drama, concludes with a guerrilla-good-guys versus Nazi-bad-guys shoot-out.

Hellman's eagerness to show German *Schrecklichkheit* [dreadfulness] and the sterling qualities of the Russians allows little common sense to intrude. Toward the beginning of the film, as our peasants happily journey down a country road, out of the horizon comes a droning sound. Eden will now be blasted by the Devil's minions: a swarm of Nazi airplanes. Their strategic mission for the day, apparently, is to bomb farmland. Having blown up struggling crops, rampant weeds, pebbles, and mounds of earth, the planes then concentrate on another prime military target, some horse-drawn carts slowly wending their way along a dirt road. With such strategic bombing, no wonder the Germans lost the war!

After the victorious Germans enter the village, break an arm and a leg of the mayor's wife, and otherwise spread good cheer, the story really runs amok as it envisions the Germans as vampires, draining the blood from defenseless children to make up for their dwindling plasma supplies. The children are bled white, stagger, and die. Although the Nazis were hardly kind, such outrageous scenes approach the absurd.

Amid the poor acting, tepid dialogue, and gross sentimentality, a few moments have life, and those involve Stroheim in the role of a German military surgeon. The Normanoff Rockwellovitch glow mercifully fades, and Stroheim, with his vast energy, shifts the film to reality. Suddenly we witness a genuine human being (intelligent, sensitive, sarcastic, nostalgic, sad, wearied), not the ogre "Hun" that Hellman had intended. Surely, Stroheim added his own lines here. They are specific, not general; witty, not gassy; vivid, not vapid.

Dressed as an army colonel and wearing a Red Cross armband, Stroheim, as Dr. von Harden, is riding in the back of an open staff car and smoking a cigarette, which he holds in his black-gloved hand. He plans to set up a field hospital to tend the wounded. "I don't want doctors," he declares. "I need surgeons." Puffing merrily away, he proceeds to denigrate the abilities of the colleague sitting next to him, whom he sarcastically addresses as "Doctor" Richter.

The insulted Richter, played by the diminutive Martin Kosleck, says, "The colonel has forgotten me. I am a surgeon."

Von Harden considers this declaration and, reveling in the sheer pleasure of making a rejoinder, notes witheringly, "A surgeon is a man who can operate, Doctor Richter. I have not forgotten." Enjoying himself mightily, the colonel continues to bait his companion. "Doctor Richter, where did you take your medical training?"

Richter replies, "Freiberg. I have told the colonel many times before." The colonel snorts.

"That was a good school!" Richter says, "I must beg the colonel's pardon. With respect to the colonel's superior rank and reputation, I must beg the colonel's pardon and say—"

The much-addressed colonel smiles witheringly and then interjects: "Do not beg my pardon so often, Doctor Richter. Good manners do not make a good surgeon."

Richter notes that the colonel "studied at the University of Leipzig." Von Harden replies, "In the great days—I was a pupil of Friedenthal—his most famous pupil."

"Friedenthal—a Jew?"

"Yes, Friedenthal, the Jew!"

"The colonel did not mind his being a Jew?"

"Mind? I never thought about it in those days."

"It must be pleasant to be so sure of oneself. I should like to think I was so good as the colonel thinks he is."

The colonel laughs. "The day you think you're as good as I am, Doctor Richter, I will know that you're suffering from delusions of grandeur and I shall commit you to an asylum. Trust me, Doctor Richter." He concludes by patting Richter's leg condescendingly.

The vitality of this less-than-two-minute scene far outweighs the uninspired gloom of the previous hour.

Later on, children are led into the hospital, where their blood will be drained. The village doctor (Walter Huston) enters and, with hardly a moment's hesitation, tries to stab the German soldier who is receiving the transfusion. He is stopped, and Richter is upset. The colonel tells him, "Do not be so nervous, Doctor Richter. We are well guarded in this room from the feeble attacks of an old man." The colonel then explains to the elderly doctor, "I realize this is difficult for you to understand, but our plasma supply was insufficient so we had to take blood for our wounded where we could get it and where the donor is easiest to control." When a weakened child staggers toward the old man, the colonel allows him to carry the child away. The colonel then addresses Richter, who is surprised that the colonel has not had the old doctor arrested. "If you wish to be a warrior, Richter, you must take chances with your life. Doctor Kurin is a famous man of science; he is not a man who kills, and therefore no danger to us."

Eventually, after more histrionics, the old doctor, armed with resolve and a gun, returns to the hospital. The colonel tells him, "I do not like incompetent doctors. I do not like much of what I have done for the past nine years."

"You do not like bleeding children to their death?"

"The boy died?"

"You knew he would die!"

"They took too much blood! I am sorry for that."

"Yes, I believe you when you tell me you're sorry."

This exchange between intelligent, somewhat sensitive people who in the midst of war are regretting an awful situation provides a rare moment of dramatic truth amid the rabid propaganda.

The colonel adds, "I'm sorry for many things, Doctor Kurin, most sorry it isn't the world we used to know." Here, there are shades of Rauffenstein from *La Grande Illusion,* but this nostalgic mood is punctured by Kurin, who delivers an odd speech that eradicates the compassionate tone of the previous lines and instead voices Hellman's venom, which seems to put down every German.

> I have heard about men like you—civilized men who are sorry. This kind [indicating Richter] is nothing—they will go when their bosses go, but men like you, who have contempt for men like him . . . to me you are the real filth—men who do the work of fascists while they pretend to themselves that they are better than the beasts for whom they work—men who do murder while they laugh at those who order them to do it! It is men like you who have sold their people to men like him. [At this point Kurin rather nonchalantly shoots Dr. Richter in the back!] You see, Dr. von Harden, you are wrong about many things. . . . I *am* a man who kills!

He then shoots the colonel in the stomach.

The *New York Times* praised Hellman for writing this speech, which, it claimed, "lifts the film to a thrilling peak." However, its patriotic fervor seems now—and possibly did then to sober eyes—rather pompous and preachy. The *Times* rationalized this serious drawback with the statement that the film "has so much in it that is moving and triumphant that its sometime departures from reality may be generally overlooked."[14] In fact, the script works against itself; even *Variety* noted that "in parts it is seemingly a too-obviously contrived narrative detailing the virtues of the Soviet regime."[15]

Overall, Stroheim's surgeon seems to be the only intelligent, sensitive, and reasonable person in the film. He acknowledges the bravery of the Russians, regrets the war, and consistently looks with disdain on weak bureaucrats like Richter. Furthermore, he regrets that the trans-fusion caused the child to die. He is hardly as guilty as the others. Like Rauffenstein, who treated Boeldieu with respect in *La Grande Illusion,* he regards the Russian doctor as a comrade and an equal. Ironically, such gentlemanliness brings about his own death. The makers of the film seem to have missed this essential point and intolerantly imply that all German doctors should be shot in the stomach. This murder is shocking, as if Boeldieu had vengefully fired his gun at Rauffenstein while on his deathbed.

Not all the blame for this mishmash can be placed on Hellman. In fact, when she saw a rough cut, she started to cry. Goldwyn angrily ordered her to shut up. "Don't tell me when to cry," she replied. A terrible shouting match ensued, and she told the fuming Goldwyn that he had allowed Milestone to turn her script into "a piece of junk." She screamed: "It will be a huge flop, which it deserves to be."[16] Among other things, she was incensed that the Nazi atrocities that she had only suggested had been spelled out. After this contretemps, she bought out her contract with Goldwyn, and their association ended. Later, in her memoirs, she said that the film "could have been a good picture instead of the big-time, sentimental, badly directed, badly acted mess it turned out to be." Years after, when Hellman went to Moscow, she recalled that the Russians had considered the film "a great joke!"[17]

Proud of what he thought was a magnificent patriotic effort, Goldwyn, with his famous logic, later declared, "I don't care if this picture doesn't make a dime just so long as every man, woman, and child in America sees it."[18] When Goldwyn showed it at a special screening in Hollywood, many people walked out during the preview, and those who remained occasionally laughed at the goings-on. Goldwyn ignored this reception and the next day told one of his em-ployees at the studio that it was a great film. The man replied, "I saw it, Mr. Goldwyn. I went to the preview." Without missing a beat, Goldwyn snapped, "It can be fixed."[19] It couldn't be.

As Stroheim later recalled, "The film caused a great deal of con-troversy, the rightists clamoring that Goldwyn had made out and out communist propaganda, while the communists shouted that it was falsified . . . etc. etc."[20] Stroheim also noted, "My part was so small and I only came on about two reels from the end [Stroheim exaggerates a bit here] so that in Paris, when the picture was shown after the war with my name all over the front of the theater, a great many people believed that it had been a mistake in advertising and that I was not in the picture at all. (Some of them are supposed to have left before I came on.)"[21]

The North Star proved a considerable embarrassment after the war, when relations with Soviet Russia disintegrated. In May 1957, the film was revised by cutting footage and adding narration. The result was a less politically suspect film called *Armored Attack,* which no longer took place in kindly Russia but in an "Eastern country." A narrator explains, "The communist leaders wanted no peace. . . . From the ruins of one armored empire rose another, greater threat to the world—the Red menace." The concluding words of the reissue magically transformed the rebellious and victorious Russians into "Hungarian freedom fighters" and cautioned the viewers that "every person and every nation must beware of the menace of Communism."[22]

After Stroheim appeared in *The North Star* in 1943, the market for monstrous Nazi officers waned. He had faced a similar situation after World War I when Hun roles ceased, but then he had turned to directing. In 1944, he had no recourse but to revert to the type of roles he had played in the early thirties: egotistical villains. Seemingly blacklisted by the major studios—there were many films in which he *could* have appeared—his only recourse was Republic. As Stroheim explained in a letter,

> Now came a period in which I had to take anything that was offered me because as I have said once or twice before even actors have to eat two or three times a week. I guess it is unnecessary to explain that the problem of a free-lance actor is quite different from the one of a long-term contract-actor attached to a studio. I wish I could forget these monstrosities that I had to make myself part of but my duty as the chronicler forces me to mention them. I am turning the light out as I am writing.[23]

Curt Siodmak's novel, *Donovan's Brain,* was purchased by Republic Pictures and filmed as *The Lady and the Monster* (released in March 1944). Its engaging story, which since has been twice remade, deals with a scientist who removes a brain from a man and keeps it alive in a large glass jar. After a while, through telepathy, the brain starts to take control over the doctor's assistant.

The film starred Stroheim, Richard Arlen, and Vera Hruba Ralston, the inamorata and future wife of Herbert J. Yates, the president of Republic Pictures. Her narrow, ferret face and mediocre acting talents were hardly assets. Capably directed by George Sherman and carefully scrutinized by Yates, *The Lady and the Monster* had good production values and contained 623 shots, far more than the usual Republic "cheapie" offering. Yet, despite Yates's hopes, it was a typical B picture.

A narrator tells us that the film takes place in the desert at a "fantastic place called the Castle." A scientist by the name of Franz Mueller, played by Stroheim with a severe limp, is dedicated to the study of the brain. The doctor is drawn to his female aide (Ralston) and betrays some jealousy when he discovers she is about to accompany his assistant (Arlen) to a party, which Mueller had refused to attend. "You ought to know by now," Mueller explains with heavy irony, "how I love society. No, those things are not for me. Besides, I have some work to do." He has bought an ailing monkey from an organ-grinder and tells her, "It won't live through the night." "Then why did you buy it?" she asks. A second later, she seems to understand. "Yes, Janice," he says, "another experiment."

His goal is to keep a brain alive even after the death of the body. "What do I know about the brain itself? Nothing. Can it think? Remember after its body is dead? Could it be made to feel? To hear, perhaps? To express itself in some way, to control the living?" His dream is to give immortality to the mind of a great man. He then starts the operation on the monkey, saying sarcastically, "No experiment could possibly be successful without my two loyal assistants, provided your interest in science still comes before dinner parties." The experiment succeeds for a short while, but then the brain dies.

When an airplane crashes nearby, Mueller and his assistant hurry to the wreck and take an injured man back to the castle, where he dies. The man proves to be Donovan, a rich and powerful executive. Mueller sees his opportunity and removes the brain. The assistant questions the legality of this, but the doctor replies, "When you try to solve the mysteries of nature, it doesn't matter whether you experiment with guinea pigs or human beings." Mueller orders "strong, black coffee," as Stroheim's character did in *Five Graves to Cairo,* and smokes a cigarette after the operation.

Later, after the inquest, the girl decides to leave with the assistant and explains that Dr. Mueller "couldn't feel love. It's his sense of possession." Thus, Stroheim is once again cast as the jealous egotist, a role defined in *The Great Gabbo.* Stroheim tries, as usual, to give his character some theatrical "business." In later scenes, even though it is night, he adorns himself with a black eyeshade and at other times pushes his glasses up on his forehead.

The film soon leaves Mueller and follows the assistant as he falls under the influence of Donovan's brain. At the end of the picture, the jealous housekeeper (an otherwise unimportant character but useful in concluding the film) shoots Mueller, and the brain is smashed. The narrator explains that the doctor's death was "well deserved. He tried to distort an experiment of science into a diabolical plot to further his own personal gain."

Although *The Lady and the Monster* is not a masterpiece of the genre, it is reasonably engaging. Stroheim, excellent in all of his scenes, tries hard to make his role memorable, but when the focus shifts to Arlen (who is relatively dull), the plot merely grinds on. More time should have been spent on Stroheim. He later remarked, "The book was very interesting. The film—the less said the better."[24]

The owner of Republic pictures, still not giving up on the career of his beloved, Vera Hruba Ralston, placed her name above the title in *Storm over Lisbon* (released in September 1944). She again costarred with Richard Arlen and Stroheim. Once more playing a spy, Stroheim is the owner of a Portuguese café–gambling den, where he is anxious to obtain secret information that Arlen has brought with him from the Far East in order to sell it to the Japanese government.

Despite the fact that the film paid careful attention to detail and contains impressive sets, numerous extras, lavish production numbers (in which Ralston "dances"), and many imprisonments and escapes, its almost one and one-half hours of running time seem interminable. The lighting of Ralston's close-ups is carefully done, but not even the expert camerawork of John Alton can transform her face into beauty, and absolutely nothing can be done to alter the wooden delivery of her few lines of dialogue. What is even worse, Stroheim enacts his familiar role of spy without his usual unique embellishments, as if director George Sherman purposely prevented him from stealing any scenes from Ralston. In her case, the theft would have been an improvement.

Republic seemed pleased with Stroheim and cast him more advantageously—without the curse of Ralston's presence—in a more modest, but better work, *The Great Flamarion* (released in February 1945). Directed by Anthony Mann, it begins with a shot of the dying Flamarion (Stroheim), over which we hear his voice explain what brought him to this point. He had been a famous vaudeville performer who in his stage act expertly shoots bullets at light bulbs behind a constantly moving human.

The scheming but attractive heroine is married to a drunk (Dan Duryea), who plays the man in front of the light bulbs. She wants to rid herself of her husband and pretends to love Flamarion, but he no longer wants to get involved with women. He has been hurt badly once before. Finally, he does fall in love, and she soon inveigles him into "accidentally" killing her husband. After the death and the inquest, she convinces Flamarion that they must part for three months to avoid suspicion. She tells him that she will stay with her mother and that there should be no contact. He gives her most of his money, and they agree to meet later at a certain hotel. Finally, the date comes for their reunion. Eagerly, he engages the bridal suite and awaits her arrival. Flamarion gives an elaborate order to the bellboy: "Tomorrow morning I want six dozen roses—various colors—long stems. I want some gladiolas for this vase and a little basket with mixed flowers—six gardenias for her pillow—a standing order for corsage—three orchids every morning with our breakfast." Later, he arranges vases of flowers around the room. After many calls to the desk and hours spent in the lobby, he discovers that she never went to see her mother—there is no such address.

He then desperately searches the breadth of America for her. He loses at roulette (shades of *Foolish Wives*), sells his wonderful set of pistols, and grows more and more down-at-the-heels. Finally, he learns that she ran off with a handsome guy from a bicycle act, and he traces her to Mexico City, where he overhears that she is now cheating on the bicycle fellow. Finally, Flamarion encounters her. She pretends to be glad to see this pathetic sight and then, seeing how furious he is, promises to give him back the money. While talking to him, she grabs a gun and then speaks the truth: "You poor sucker! How could anyone love you? That fat bull neck—those squinty eyes! You're old! You're ugly! Even the touch of you made me sick! I hate you and I've always hated you!" (One wonders how Stroheim felt about these lines; of course, self-critical as he always was, perhaps he even added them himself!) Enraged at this disclosure, Flamarion says, "That was your curtain speech, Connie," and menacingly moves toward her. Although she shoots him several times, the wounded man manages to kill her and then climbs the catwalk over the stage, from which he plummets to the theater floor. It is from that position that he tells the whole story in flashback. A similar flashback structure was used the year before in *Double Indemnity* (1944) by Billy Wilder, who felt that his brother, Willy (the "dull son of a bitch"), who produced *The Great Flamarion,* had copied it.[25]

Stroheim never liked the idea of using a flashback structure. In this case, he felt the producer was trying to transform "a small picture with a short purse and a still shorter schedule" into something "more important by making it upside down. All my advices were for nothing. The end was the beginning and that was the beginning of the end. Again and again I say that the people at large are not interested in a story when they know from the beginning that one of the principal actors is dead."[26] With his linear mind, Stroheim could not accept this method of storytelling; he disapproved of *Citizen Kane* for the same reason. He could not understand that an audience might be curious to know *how* an event occurred. He may later have had similar reservations about the structure of *Sunset Boulevard,* although there is no record of his mentioning it.

The Great Flamarion is by no means a great film, although it has a certain expressionistic quality, not only in its settings and lighting, but in its story of a relatively good man and superb performer being ruined by a woman. Stroheim once again invests his role with considerable business. As usual, he belts his whiskey down, wears white gloves, sports a cane, and adorns himself in tight-fitting suit jackets. He wears a monocle onstage, but not off. Several times during the film Stroheim provides a bit of humor by patting down and arranging the hair on his almost completely shaven head. He gives his death scene a degree of poignancy and shows again what a fine actor he had become.

Stroheim next appeared in yet another Republic effort, *Scotland*

Yard Investigator (released in September 1945) and received second billing under C. Aubrey Smith. Stroheim plays Hoffmeyer, an obsessed art collector, who by illegal means has amassed a great number of master-pieces. "To know that I'm the secret owner of a collection which even kings or maharajahs could not buy—that is the only satisfaction I get out of life! And I won't rest until I have the Mona Lisa." He cleverly bilks the British Museum, whose director (Smith) has been storing the *Mona Lisa* for the French during the war, and steals the painting. When Hoffmeyer examines it at his home, he discovers that it is a clever fake and concludes that an antique dealer has absconded with the original. Hoffmeyer visits the museum director and returns the fake painting to the shocked official, who exclaims, "You stole it!" Hoffmeyer replies, "Stole is a rather a harsh word—let us say, acquired." When the direc-tor states that "all those amazing stories about you are true," Hoffmeyer agrees, "There have been stories—there certainly have." The other man replies, "But this time you've overreached yourself." These lines could apply not only to Hoffmeyer's career but to Stroheim's as well.

Throughout his quest to hang the painting in his personal gallery, Hoffmeyer, flourishing a sword cane, dispatches a number of people, including a sleazy London antiques dealer. Finally, he is able to gloat over his most famous acquisition, but not for long. He is shot by the wife of the antique dealer. The ardent collector gives one more admir-ing look at the *Mona Lisa,* approaches the painting, and is about to destroy it with his sword cane when he falls to the floor. His death evokes no pleasure or sadness in the viewer; it just happens.

Once more Stroheim is supposed to be a somewhat charming arch villain who is crooked but polite. The film, however, did not seem to inspire him at all. Besides giving himself a moderate wig of gray hair, he otherwise avoids his usual theatrical tricks and obsessions. He wears normal clothing (a business suit), adds no afflictions or peculiar habits, and for about the first time in his work even refrained from his primary acting resource—smoking. Admittedly, Stroheim's role is not very challenging, but usually he would invest even insignificant parts with some panache. Although this role is a major one, he seems to have had no input into the script at all, and his work therefore is competent rather than inspired. Hoffmeyer *could* have worn an elaborate dressing gown, combed his hair in an antique mirror, fed a pet tarantula, lit up a cigarette in a long holder, and opened a bottle of champagne to toast his acquisition. But that was not to be. The actor often disparaged his Republic films—certainly *Scotland Yard Investigator* is the weakest of the group—but the studio did provide him with work, allowing him not only to survive but to save some much needed dollars.

When the Second World War in Europe ended in May 1945, Stroheim looked forward to returning to France, where he hoped he was still regarded as a master. Hollywood was too painful for him, a town that constantly reminded him of his former glory. As a has-been, he could only play small parts in major productions or leads in poverty-row quickies. He waited impatiently for the French film industry to return to normal production and make him an offer. Meanwhile, he was asked to appear in another low-budget Hollywood picture. Not only did he need the money, but he also knew that American dollars would have extraordinary value when changed into French francs. And, after all, as he said in a letter to Peter Noble, "What's one more stinko to one's credit?"[27]

The "stinko" was *The Mask of Diijon* (released in January 1946). Although a low-budget PRC release and shot (according to Stroheim) in ten days, it was well directed by Lew Landers (formerly Louis Friedlander, who had directed Karloff and Lugosi in *The Raven,* 1935). Stroheim, in another vaudevillian role, plays a magician who is no longer successful.

As the film opens, we seem to be in a French town square, where a man (Edward Van Sloan) gloats as he releases a guillotine's blade onto the neck of a writhing blonde woman. We soon find out that we are in a shop and that the beheading is an illusion being demonstrated to a magician (Stroheim) and his wife. The salesman says to his customer, "Less than a year ago you were one of the top magicians in vaudeville—a headliner. Why did you quit? Of course, I know it's no business of mine, but with my new illusion added to your old routine you could get bookings just like that!" The Great Diijon answers disparagingly, "I'm no longer interested in gags, tricks, and illusions." His wife, embarrassed and disappointed, says that she has trying to put them "on their feet again." Diijon responds, as Stroheim himself must have so many times, "I can stand on my own feet! I need no help from you or anyone else!" One of Diijon's acquaintances concludes, "He's a stubborn egomaniac." This dialogue is quite reminiscent of *The Great Gabbo* and, of course, of Stroheim's real life.

Again we have the Stroheim persona of an extremely gifted performer down on his luck because of his egomania, stubbornness, and suspicion. Although his wife is fed up with being treated "like dirt," she convinces an old friend to arrange to get Diijon a spot in a night club. When his illusion of suspending a girl in the air fails, Diijon blames his wife's friend. Could we say that Diijon can no longer cut the mustard?

Meanwhile, Diijon devotes his time to the occult. He wants to go beyond mere tricks to command mystic powers. In time-honored film parlance, it is his mad dream: to venture beyond God's domain! He will soon prove his ability. While Diijon is in a diner, a holdup occurs and Diijon plays with his lighter, flashing reflections into the crook's eyes. Amazed that his hypnotism works, he goes out into the street to check his new powers and successfully commands a newsstand operator to give him papers. Now convinced of his mastery, he orders an acquaintance to write a suicide note and then kill himself, which the man does.

Diijon grows suspicious of his wife, and, believing that she is unfaithful (not true at this point), he decides to have her shoot the supposed lover during a performance at the nightclub. Although he succeeds in influencing her, she mistakenly loads the gun with blanks. After his plot is discovered, the police pursue Diijon. (Their description of him notes that he is five feet ten inches tall, but five feet six inches would have been more accurate.) To avoid being caught, Diijon returns to the magician's shop and unknowingly crawls into the guillotine, where a cat plays with the cord and causes the blade to descend and behead him. (Was the cat a Stroheim addition?)

This plot is no better or worse than those of many minor horror pictures of the time, but *The Mask of Diijon* does offer more production value in its sets and more artistry in its lighting than many of its ilk. In addition, the film has more close-ups than the usual cheap production. As Diijon, Stroheim is quite comfortable as an actor and provides a good performance. He employs his usual shtick of puffing on his cigarette and flicking the ashes with no concern for where they fall. He lets some sardonic smiles cross his usually sober face and comes out with a few sarcastic lines about his wife and others. *Variety* felt that his role, "incredible from the first, is aided by the von Stroheim sour countenance."[28] Incidentally, Denise appears in a small part, playing someone else's wife.

In general, the film seems to have followed its script closely, without being unduly complicated by Stroheim's contributions. One wonders what Stroheim (with his interest in amputations) must have thought of the beheading.

After *The Mask Of Diijon,* Stroheim and Denise decided to return to France. Normal passenger service had not yet started, so they booked passage on a nondescript French freighter. Herman G. Weinberg described Stroheim at a shipboard party: "Turkey leg in one hand, bumper of Scotch in the other, he grimly regarded a snarled coil of rope on the deck, a flagrant violation of one of the cardinal rules of the sea. 'Just look at that,' he said. 'That would never happen on a German boat. Well, if you don't hear from me anymore, you'll know why.'"[29]

As the ship steamed out of New York harbor, ahead lay his second adopted country, France.

18

The Last Years

When Stroheim arrived in France on December 5, 1945, he hoped that his career of playing major roles in significant films would resume. But many changes had occurred during the war years. Because American pictures had been banned by the Nazis, and those made by the Fuehrer's minions had not been popular during the occupation, the French industry itself actually did quite well. But after the war ended, American films again flooded the theaters and French production declined. Furthermore, the type of film that Stroheim could have appeared in waned. No one wanted to see spy stories from the First World War, and certainly no one in France wanted to be reminded of the Second World War, with its quick defeat by the Germans and its embarrassing collaboration. There also had been a sociological change. The old-world elegance and formality of behavior that Stroheim could portray so brilliantly had vanished. In addition, of course, was the fact that he was now close to sixty years old, which made romantic or even lecherous roles somewhat unlikely.

While still in America, Stroheim had received from France a six-page synopsis of a film, *La Foire aux chimères,* which he felt had "great potentialities." It was about "a terribly burned man falling in love with a blind girl because she does not see how ugly he is."[1] He commits forgery out of love for her, but when she regains her sight, she runs off with another man. Because the film resembled quite closely

Stroheim's script for *Blind Love,* he understandably became vitally interested in how the story was handled.

Although production was supposed to begin immediately after Stroheim's return to France, there was a wait of many months. When Pierre Chenal, the director, who had been out of the country, finally returned to Paris, he scrutinized the prepared scenario. According to Stroheim, Chenal "throws it in the ashcan and starts to write from scratch."[2] After even more waiting, Stroheim started "to receive the script piece-meal." The results of this frantic activity were, according to Stroheim, awful. What Chenal finally gave him "had no resemblance with what I read in Hollywood on the strength of which I accepted. Sessions—arguments—pleadings—agreements—forgotten the next day. Disagreements lasting for ever."[3] Stroheim clearly recalled all the quibbling but forgot to mention that ultimately at least some of his contributions were incorporated into the scenario.

The film opens in the offices of an engraving company where Frank (an interesting name, considering that the story deals with counterfeit francs) is the boss. Played by Stroheim, Frank has a face heavily scarred on one side—as it was in *Menaces* but this time completely uncovered—and again it evokes Valerie's terrible accident. To examine the banknotes, he wears a pair of glasses to which is appended a set of magnifying lenses—a curious contraption, to say the least.

For lunch, he goes to a restaurant where he finds a fly in his soup—surely a Stroheim addition—and when he complains, other people in the restaurant mimic him. One of the diners, imitating the double spectacle device, leans forward over his plate and pretends to look for a wayward fly.

It is Frank's birthday, and later that night the lonely man goes to a carnival, similar to the Prater of *Merry-Go-Round.* At an outdoor table, he orders champagne and invites two young women to join him. They happily sit at his table, but when they see his disfigured face, they abruptly leave. He stops at a gaming concession, which has a large numbered wheel; when the number thirteen comes up, he wins a girl doll as a prize, as did the count in the earlier film. Sadly, he leaves his table, sits down on a bench, and tenderly holds the girl doll. Then from out of the misty background and the whirling lights of the carnival, a long-haired blond woman, dressed in white, approaches, leading a horned white goat! They speak, and he learns that she is blind, having lost her sight in a fall from a trapeze. Her job at the circus is in a knife-throwing act, in some ways similar to the pistol-shooting routine in *The Great Flamarion*. Because she cannot see, she is unafraid of the knives, and, of course, she is not repelled by the scarred man's appearance.

When Frank returns home that night, his housekeeper has a birthday cake for him. He thinks it is his fortieth birthday, but the woman reminds him that it is his fiftieth. He remarks that his life ended ten years before. The next night, he returns to the carnival, purchases a little bouquet of violets, and buys out the house so that he can witness the woman's act privately; it is called "The Devil and the Angel." A man, Roberto, dressed as the devil (with horns), throws knives at the woman, dressed as an angel with big white wings, who is perched high up in the tent. The knives slice off first one wing and then the other. Shortly after, the woman stands against a board with her arms outstretched in a crucifixion-like position, as the man throws knives that surround her body and her head. This episode—and, indeed, much of the film—shows Stroheim's strong influence: the blind girl and the ugly man, the angel and the devil, the angelic vision accompanied by a goat, and some of the carnival atmosphere.

Frank later marries this fairy princess who wears only white, and they live in a beautiful building with white walls and a long white staircase. They seem to be happy; at one point he buys her an expensive fur, also white. Apparently, he has been financing his new life with counterfeit money. All is well until she goes for an operation. Frank visits her in the hospital room (lit with light coming through venetian blinds) and a moment later, he goes into an adjoining room, where he kneels down and prays for her. When we next see his wife, she is dressed in black. Although she has regained her sight, she hides this fact from him and now, knowing his appearance, treats him coolly. One day, she returns to the carnival, where she responds to Roberto's kiss. Intertwined with these events is a plot concerning the counterfeit money, various crooks, and the police. Finally, Frank has a confrontation with his wife. Knowing now that she no longer loves him, he kills one of the crooks, calls the police, throws the counterfeit money all around the room, sets the place on fire, and, when the police arrive, retreats to the balcony and falls to his death.

As Stroheim later noted, "Chenal did not like the subject to start with and it showed." Stroheim believed that the revised scenario changed the characters and the whole milieu and thus spoiled what could have been a poetic tragedy. Understandably, Stroheim was disappointed, because he was sympathetic to its theme and wanted it to be carried out sensitively. Furthermore, he was hoping, as usual, to appear in some kind of masterpiece rather than this muddled, if sincere, effort.

Although the film has its gentle moments and good production values, Stroheim lamented that in trying to make a "showy" film, the director transformed the characters, who were intended to be "shabby everyday creatures" (like, we assume, those in his scripts for *Blind Love* and *Walking down Broadway*), into "fictitious characters overdressed and overfed, living a phony life. Everything in the best tradition of A films. But no heart—no soul!" He complained that there were no moments of "intimacy" and that "most of the love scenes [were] played in the entrance hall and on the stairway." As a result, Stroheim felt that "all the poetry" was taken out of the film. His criticism is correct. Its most serious failing was the girl's characterization. Her sudden coolness toward her husband, when she is able to see him, is handled matter-of-factly, and nowhere does she seem to feel at all guilty about the change in her emotions. Thus, there is an inconsistency between her angelic initial presentation and her subsequent rather selfish and carnal actions.

This sad story of unhappy people was pumped up with Hollywood gloss (fancy sets, elaborately lit close-ups, and unnecessary prettiness) and, despite Stroheim's excellent acting, was neither as convincing nor as moving as it could have been. He imposed great discipline on himself by completely repressing his usual persona and avoided, except for the glasses, most of his usual routines: no white gloves, no cane, no elegant clothes, no flamboyant gestures, and no cigarette smoking. He was just an average man in a rumpled suit seeking some happiness in a world that had disfigured him.

When *La Foire aux chimères* opened in Paris in October 1946, *Variety* found it "well photographed and ably directed" but added that it was "depressing without comedy relief." The reviewer acknowledged, however, that Stroheim gave "a fine performance." Later, when the film was released in America, the *New York Times* unkindly and unjustifiably called it "a rusty Gothic tin can."[4]

Stroheim next appeared in "another nightmare," *Ne meurt pas comme ça* [That's not the way to die]. Directed by Jean Boyer, the film was hurried out in six days. Stroheim plays a celebrated movie director by the name of Eric von Berg, and Denise has the main feminine part. Stroheim again provided a caricature of a movie director, with gold bracelet, long cigarette holder, and exaggerated mannerisms. In a film studio, von Berg rehearses a scene where a character is to be killed. The victim falls to the floor, and the director begins to shout and curse: "That's not the way to die!" He orders the "dead" man to get up so that he can show him how to do it properly. But the man does not get up because he really is dead, a situation borrowed from an American film, *The Death Kiss* (1933). *Ne meurt pas comme ça* was released before *La Foire aux chimères,* and after a screening of it, Stroheim and Denise left the theater "ashamed to show our faces." Oddly enough, Stroheim recalled, "the criticisms—and that is the funny part—were not bad at all" and added that it made "a pile of money." Because, according to Stroheim, Denise's face was on the poster and they spelled her name right, he claimed to be reasonably content, but he privately referred to this venture as "On meurt comme ça."[5]

In 1946, Stroheim worked on a screenplay based on August Strindberg's drama *The Dance of Death.* Stroheim was also to star as a martinet captain who commands a prison and is, in turn, enmeshed in an extraordinarily unhappy marriage. Denise was to appear in the leading role of his shrewish wife. Whenever possible, he seemed to find a part for her.

Although plans for the film proceeded, again came difficulties. The producers did not like his script. In an interview at the British Film Institute in 1954, Stroheim explained that the play deals with a couple married for twenty-five years whom we never see as young people. We only hear about their past through their comments: "But that is theater. Why did he [Strindberg] make it that way? Because of the limitations of the theater, and because he was crazy and because he produced it—he ended in an insane asylum. [At this point, he knocked three times on wood, an action that achieved laughter in his listeners.] And because his producer said 'we can only have one set.' Now you can't make a picture that way."[6]

As in *Greed,* Stroheim wanted to show the background of the couple before the play began. He managed to insert one early scene of the main characters at a ball and also opened up the action to show the captain parading his troops and barking out orders. In another sequence, when a prisoner attempts to escape in a rowboat, the captain sets off fireworks to reveal him and then calls out his name—Boeldieu (the name of the Pierre Fresnay character in *La Grande Illusion*). When the escapee refuses to halt, the captain, like Rauffenstein, is compelled to kill him.

Other parts of the scenario, which would have fleshed out the drama and made it *cinema* instead of a mere photographed stage play, were either not shot or eventually cut. Admittedly, Stroheim wanted to film most of the play (which would have run too long), but severe alterations were made in his scenario. The ninety-minute release print was too short to do justice to the material and was sufficiently disappointing that it was not even released in America. As William K. Everson noted, "The film is really just the first half [of the play], with certain elements (and the climax) transferred to it from the second half."[7] Eventually, the disputes about the scenario resulted in a lawsuit, and the credits finally read that the "screen adaptation" was made by Stroheim and Michel Arnand.

The big production that Stroheim had been promised ended up having a very small budget. To save money, the film was shot in Italy. When he and Denise arrived in Rome, almost nothing had been done and there was not even any film stock. Stroheim, the great stickler for accuracy, was appalled to learn that the troops he would command had the wrong hats, the wrong uniforms, and the wrong rifles (the rifles, he noted witheringly, were from 1866!). He tried to correct these errors by modifying the uniforms and by purchasing more appropriate hats at the Vatican. Even worse, the bayonets the producer found did not fit the rifles, so Stroheim personally tied them on with wire. One of his few satisfactions was the outfit he created for himself as the captain. He made quite an appearance in his black tunic, trimmed with various orders, and his enormous black cape. But making the film was not a happy experience. Once more, his hope to be involved in a great picture, even if only as scenarist and actor, were dashed by the producer's financial and artistic limitations.

For about two years after returning to France, Stroheim and Denise stayed in an old hotel at the edge of the Fontainebleau forest. Later, in 1947, they moved to Maurepas, the property of Denise. "This house," wrote Thomas Quinn Curtiss, "on the outskirts of a tiny hamlet, lies in the heart of the Corot country and he seemed content here, especially during the summer months when he would write at a table in a lovely rose garden basking in the sunshine."[8] Anita Loos, a frequent visitor on her trips abroad, described Stroheim and Denise's home: "The interior was always dimly lighted and it had an atmosphere of such heavy-footed *gemuetlichkeit* that one felt it belonged in the Black Forest of Germany. The dun-colored, pockmarked plaster walls were hung with sabers and guns arranged in patterns, together with some German officers' tunics, and over the huge fireplace of the living room was a collection of enormous beer steins."[9]

Here, no more than forty minutes from Paris, Stroheim spent the last years of his life. Indefatigable, he was constantly working on screenplays and on a novel, *The Fires of St. John*. However, writing unsold scenarios and novels that are not best-sellers is not lucrative, and so Stroheim continued to accept most of the acting jobs offered to him, although not, at times, without regret.

In *Le Signal rouge* (1948), directed by Ernst Neubach, Stroheim portrayed the absentminded and kindly Doctor Berthold, who is first seen, along with his wife and child, riding in a railroad compartment. Suddenly, there is a train crash. His wife is killed, and his son's legs are injured. Later, in a touching scene back at his house, he goes to the bedroom (with all its feminine touches), looks at her photograph, and, in tears, falls on their bed. Subsequently, he tells the surprised maid that hereafter he will sleep on the sofa and that the bedroom should be closed.

The doctor has arranged for assistance with his crippled son; he is surprised to find that the new doctor is a woman (Denise Vernac). The distraught man is tormented by the train accident and begins to hear voices. In one of his trances, he puts fireworks on the railroad tracks, an act that causes consternation but no accidents. Appalled at his inexplicable behavior, he decides to go to a sanitarium. There, during the holidays, the female doctor brings him a small Christmas tree. She also brings his son, who has now progressed to walking on crutches. Meanwhile, she is being wooed by a local rake, a "lady-killer," with whom she goes to bed. The doctor leaves the sanitarium because he misses her and brings with him a bouquet of flowers, only to find the two in an embrace. He drops the bouquet. The woman is touched by the doctor's kindness and decides not to get further involved with the rake.

When a serious derailment occurs, the doctor is considered the prime suspect. The disturbed man menaces the woman, but she escapes through a window. Despite this, she still hopes to save him. In the meantime, the police discover that the rake is the culprit, but the doctor believes that he himself has committed the deed. Still hearing voices, he returns to the tracks and, as we see the headlights of the train approach, throws himself in front of the speeding locomotive.

Although no masterpiece, the film has several dramatic and poignant moments. It shows Stroheim in a tragic light, a mild and sensitive man emotionally disabled by his wife's death and yet attracted by another woman's comradeship. Denise capably creates a believable human being: she is a professional who treats the injured boy with sympathy and the bereft doctor with loyalty and warmth, but she is also a vulnerable woman unable to resist the sexual blandishments of the other man.

Undoubtedly, Stroheim convinced the director to include the wife's funeral cortege as it passes by the town square. The scene begins with the ringing of church bells (how Stroheim loved public ceremonies accompanied by the sound of bells!) and allows the husband, dressed in black, to follow the coffin down the street, while a military band in the background plays solemn music. The saddened man looks upward at some of the religious statues as he passes by the church. Other Stroheim embellishments include keeping the wife's room as a kind of shrine, setting a scene during Christmastime, wearing his glasses perched on his forehead, and his dealing with the bouquet of flowers. For a change, Stroheim's character has a specific cause for wearing a mourning band.

In the concluding scenes, which reveal the doctor in a semimad state, Stroheim convincingly portrays the man's distraught side, but without overacted eye-rolling or other conventional tricks. Furthermore, he suppresses all of his aristocratic bearing and instead is merely an ordinary man haunted by his wife's death.

Meanwhile, back in America, Billy Wilder was working on a script about a famous silent movie actress (eventually played by Gloria Swanson), which he would call *Sunset Boulevard* (1950). He decided

that Stroheim's presence would add immeasurably to the baroque atmosphere of his new film. But Stroheim was not interested. Although
he was to be Max von Mayerling, one of the three greatest silent film
directors of Hollywood, the role was not heroic or grand. This was
no Rauffenstein or Rommel but a has-been, a man no longer important, someone similar enough to himself to be unsettling to
Stroheim's ego. Furthermore, he was afraid—and correctly so—that
this was the way he would be remembered. But when Wilder made
the offer extremely lucrative, Stroheim agreed to play what he called
the "God-damned butler." Shooting began on April 11, 1949, and
principal photography concluded on June 18, although a few scenes
were added later. According to Gloria Swanson, the film was shot
mostly in continuity.[10]

To be back in Hollywood was bad enough, but to play a servant to
a woman whom he had once directed and to accompany her onto the
Paramount lot where she visited the still active C.B. DeMille must
have been galling. Here was a lesser talent still making films, still a
success, still a foremost director, and here was Stroheim playing a butler. He may also have felt foolish during the car scenes on the Paramount lot, for Stroheim could not drive and had to fake turning the
steering wheel while the automobile was towed.

The film told of an struggling screenwriter, Joe Gillis (William
Holden), who by happenstance encounters Norma Desmond
(Swanson), a faded movie star of the silent period who lives in a mansion with her butler, Max (Stroheim). When Gillis remarks to her,
"You used to be big," she replies, "I *am* big—it's the pictures that got
small." Anxious to make a comeback, she engages Gillis to help her
with a gigantic and ridiculous scenario she has been working on for
years. As Gillis reads her script, Max moves a lamp closer, a solicitous
gesture that Stroheim had used twenty years earlier in *Three Faces East*.

Later in the film, when Gillis is moved to a bedroom in the main
house, Max says, "It was the room of the husband—the husbands, I
should say. Madame has been married three times." Here Stroheim,
who had in his films played the lover, is now in a sense the cuckold,
one of Norma's husbands who will soon be replaced by the young and
vigorous Gillis.

Stroheim hoped to revise the script and insert his personality as
much as possible into the film. He wanted his character to be more

than just a devoted servant and protector, to be someone active, not passive. Wilder, however, was no Renoir, and he resisted many of Stroheim's ideas. In Swanson's memoirs, she noted that DeMille "took direction like a pro," but that Stroheim "kept adding things and suggesting things and asking if scenes might not be reshot—very much in his grand old manner of perfectionism regardless of schedule or cost." Wilder, she noted, "always listened patiently to his suggestions, and took some, but more often he would say that he really didn't see how this or that change would improve the scene or further the story, and therefore he thought we should leave it alone."[11] In short, Wilder was shrewd enough to avoid Stroheim's tendency to wander into the kind of details and pieces of business that had resulted in Stroheim's own films being of such inordinate length.

Stroheim wanted to give himself a severe limp, but Wilder did not think audiences wished to see Max clumping around throughout the film. Stroheim also had to forgo his incessant cigarette smoking— butlers cannot smoke—but he did include his perennial white gloves, which he wears even when playing the organ!

Although the strong-willed Wilder kept Stroheim in check, there are many aspects of the film that reveal Stroheim's influence either directly or indirectly. At one point, Max wheels in a cart containing champagne and caviar, pure Stroheimian fare. When Norma Desmond thinks of employing the screenwriter, she asks under "what sign of the zodiac" he was born. Gillis's birthdate of December 21 is about as close to Christmas as possible. When the roof leaks over the garage, it is during "the last week of December," another reference to the Christmas season. It was definitely Stroheim's idea that Max be the one writing fan letters to Norma Desmond, and it was his suggestion to include the footage from *Queen Kelly* that shows Swanson praying in the church with flickering candles in the foreground.

At the New Year's Party, while Gillis reluctantly dances with Norma, he jokingly says, "Come midnight, how about blindfolding the orchestra and smashing champagne glasses over Max's head?" an oblique reference to the wild party scenes in *The Merry Widow* and *The Wedding March*. Gillis soon leaves the house and attends a different party, where he is introduced by a friend as "Joe Gillis, the well known screen writer, geranium smuggler . . .," so Stroheim once again inserted a geranium into a film. Perhaps the dead monkey—certainly a bizarre touch—also stems from him, because such an animal had appeared in *Merry-Go-Round* and also in *The Lady and the Monster.*

The monkey could be a coincidence, but the references to feet are definitely Stroheim's little additions. In Stroheim's first scene, the butler tells Gillis to "wipe your feet." After Norma attempts suicide, Gillis rushes back to the house, enters her room, and then symbolically removes her shoes, after which they become lovers. At another point, Max says, "There was a maharajah who came all the way from India to beg one of her silk stockings. Later he strangled himself with it." Stroheim had another suggestion, one similar to a scene in *Three Faces East,* but it was rejected. He wanted, as the butler, to "be shown washing out Norma Desmond's lingerie and experiencing an erotically fetishistic thrill as he dallies with her brassiere and stockings."[12] There is perhaps one other instance of Stroheim's imagination at work. Waiting by the car on the studio lot, he points toward one of the buildings and tells Gillis, "I had the upstairs . . . I remember my walls were covered with black patent leather." This image is a far cry from the 6 x 8 cubicle he encountered when he became a writer in 1935 at MGM.

Stroheim's character certainly is a unique figure in the film: foreign, odd-looking, strangely accented—as run-down and shattered and remote as Norma and her house. Stroheim was not ungrateful for the butler role—he could use the money—but he was unhappy that the part gave him little to do. One searches for a moment that is his, as doer rather than reactor. It is not there. His reluctance to appear in the film was right, in a sense. It was unrewarding—good for the picture, but not good for him. He was used more for himself, as an icon of old Hollywood, than for his abilities or even his persona, although what he does is superb. Especially memorable are the film's final moments. Max grasps the leg of one of the tripods holding the newsreel cameras and barks out his orders. It is Stroheim supreme, and so is his faint, sad expression, his pause, and the gentle lump in his throat as Norma blissfully and radiantly descends the staircase into madness. *Variety* certainly appreciated his performance, declaring that he "delivers with excellent restraint."[13]

Sunset Boulevard—romantic, nostalgic, cynical, and hard-biting—is probably Wilder's best serious film. Swanson plays her scenes broadly, with lots of panache, and appears intentionally more corny than her real silent film acting, which was usually well modulated. The film proved to be a great success and brought the almost forgotten Swanson back into the limelight, where she stayed, to some extent, until the end of her life.

Every time Stroheim returned to Hollywood, memories of his former fame tormented him. More and more of his contemporaries were dead or forgotten—or both. He was as unique, grotesque, and antique as the car he had tried to drive in *Sunset Boulevard*. More than ever uneasy about being a has-been, he longed to return to France, where he was still regarded as an important man and as an actor who did not just play a caricature of his former self.

After *Sunset Boulevard* was completed, Paramount sent the film to New York and submitted its 11,002 feet for censorship on September 26, 1949. Meanwhile, various preview audiences on the West Coast found the opening scene, which took place in a morgue where bodies discuss how they died, absolutely hilarious. After much thought, Wilder cut the introductory scene and shortened the film to 10,119 feet. A few more changes were then made, and the modified script, dated January 24, 1950, was sent to the New York censor.

In April 1950, Wilder finally showed the shortened version at a theater on the Paramount lot to a number of prominent Hollywood figures. Wilder recalled, "Word was out that this was a stunner, you see. After the picture ended, there were violent reactions—from excitement to pure horror."[14] Louis B. Mayer was mightily offended. "You bastard," Mayer said to Wilder. "You have disgraced the industry that made you and fed you." Shaking his fist at the director, Mayer added, "You should be tarred and feathered and run out of Hollywood." Wilder replied with a "Fuck you."[15] This is one scene that Stroheim would probably have enjoyed witnessing. Actually, Mayer's reaction was unwarranted. The film is by no means anti-Hollywood and in fact depicts various aspects of the industry with unprecedented honesty and sympathy. Wilder never could understand Mayer's violent reaction and later correctly claimed, "I don't say anything derogatory about pictures."[16]

On May 26, 1950, the final 110-minute version of *Sunset Boulevard,* running 9,912 feet, was sent to New York. There the film languished in the vaults for a few more months—Paramount may have had some misgivings or perhaps was waiting for the close of the summer season. Finally, it opened at the Radio City Music Hall on August

11. Not only was it a great critical and box-office success, but the almost forgotten Stroheim once again surged forward in the popular press, and a new generation became familiar with the legend. He and Swanson were both again famous, but fame does not always equal employment. She starred in only one other film, a poor one, and Stroheim, his services not wanted, never appeared in another American picture.

A few years later, in the mid-1950s, Gloria Swanson, who possessed a fine singing voice, decided that *Sunset Boulevard* would make a good musical. She had a score composed and changed significant portions of the plot to give it a happy ending. She tried to interest Stroheim, who she did not know was in failing health, to appear in the show. "These days," she wrote him, "not much is required of actors in the way of singing."[17] Ill health or not, Stroheim would not have cared to play a singing "God-damned butler." Ultimately, Swanson's hope of a musical was dashed by Paramount's refusal to give permission. However, her business instincts were not wrong, because *Sunset Boulevard* did eventually become a musical reality in the 1990s, with a score by Andrew Lloyd Webber and the original unhappy ending. Later, the expensive show was brought to New York, where it closed in 1997 without, incidentally, making a profit. During its various runs, royalties were paid to Paramount, who owned the property, but not to Wilder. "I know those power people at Paramount, as well as in the other studios," Wilder said in a letter to Webber. "They have their pockets made of rubber—so they can steal soup."[18]

When Stroheim was paid his original salary for *Sunset Boulevard,* he had to share a portion of it with his wife. Because of some retakes, he received an additional eighteen thousand dollars, which he had sent to France and converted into francs. His attempt to hide this money from the woman to whom he had been sending affectionate notes on anniversaries, birthdays, and holidays is perhaps difficult to reconcile. In any case, Valerie found out about the money. "Because you wanted $18,000 salary to be called expenses is really fantastic, but, who were you trying to double-cross?" she wrote bitterly on March 22, 1950. She admonished him like a naughty boy, "After all these years and at your age—when it was so simple to do things the right way. Less trouble and expense for you—less trouble and expense for me." She cautioned him, "I think I told you once, don't try to put it over me, because sooner or later I find out about it, and then it's too bad."

Furious at him, she said that she was coming to Paris to live. "I hope you have sense enough to be there when I arrive, so that I do not have to send out the reserves to find you and explain why." She suggested to him that he better put his "affairs in order" or she would have to hire lawyers there to protect her rights. She reminded him that they file income tax returns together and that he has to give her an accurate accounting of his earnings, "according to our contract." Furthermore, she informed him, he would have to send her money in order to pay the additional federal and state taxes on his "expenses."

Rather sarcastically, she concluded:

> As you e n d your letters
> &   "   " say in   "   "
>   Love
>   Valerie

Stroheim responded lamely that he had a reserve fund for her in France and that the expenses were for costumes and housing. On April 7, 1950, Valerie replied that both costumes and housing had been supplied by the studio. As to the taxes, she wrote, "I'm going to dump the whole thing in your lap" and declared that she would not "be held responsible for the so-called complicated deals of my husband." Stroheim had suggested that perhaps her intended trip to Paris was the result of spring fever, but she replied sharply that although many people going to Europe that year might have it, she was "going to France on business—you really could call it 'monkey business.'" She reminded him that in his next picture he better not consider his wages again as expenses. Apparently, a kind of peace was made between the two, but whether there were further effusive notes for holidays and other significant dates cannot be ascertained.

After completing *Sunset Boulevard* in 1949, Stroheim returned to France, where he soon appeared in *Le Portrait d'un assassin* (released on January 3, 1950). The picture seemed important because of its all-star cast—Maria Montez, Arletty, Pierre Brasseur, Jules Berry, and Marcel Dalio—but its script and direction were relatively mediocre. The main attraction for Stroheim was that once more he could play a severely handicapped person.

The story takes place in a carnival setting. Maria Montez plays a neurotic impresario who loves only men who risk their lives for her by doing dangerous stunts. If they fail, she places their photos in her private hall of fame. As *Variety* phrased it, "Von Stroheim is one of her ex-lovers who lived through his fall, and is a hulk held together by braces, whimpering for affection. . . . Von Stroheim comes off best as the battered remains of a once-great artist. . . . This is the pic Orson Welles was to have supervised, but which he walked out on. It could have used his help."[19]

Indeed, one wonders how Welles would have shaped the story and what he might have done with this marvelous cast. And how fantastic is the idea of Welles and Stroheim working together—two impossible genius-exiles! The result of this blend, or perhaps clash, of egos might have resulted in a great film or perhaps a disaster, but, if nothing else, would have provided a vast storehouse of anecdotes.

More than a year after production had ended, *Sunset Boulevard* found its way to screens in America and Europe, which prompted new world-wide interest in Stroheim. After all, he had not appeared in a significant American film since *Five Graves to Cairo*. The British *Daily Express* sought out this genius of the silent screen and interviewed him. He bluntly spoke about his professional situation:

> I do not kid myself. I look at facts straight. In America I am outmoded. I have had my day. I am the perennial spy, the barking German officer, the Gestapo man. All that stuff is finished now. It is hopelessly old hat. [He examined his plight.] So, if I go back to the States what could I do? You know when I was there in the old prosperous days I would never pass one of those chaps selling shoe laces and pencils on the street corner without dropping a one-dollar bill onto his tray. Why? I figured he might be a big movie producer the following week. Well, if I go back now, it is me who will be selling shoe-laces on the corner. Poor old von Stroheim the has-been.[20]

Stroheim was asked whether he would return to America to take advantage of *Sunset Boulevard*'s success. He replied, "You think it is smart for me to go back on the chance of getting a few more butler roles?"[21] One can certainly sense his bitterness about playing Max, which, in his mind, he coupled with his previous remark, "Poor old von Stroheim the has-been." His first real film role had been as a valet in *Old Heidelberg,* and so he had come full circle in his American career as a butler in *Sunset Boulevard.*

"Mine is a very special trade," Stroheim explained. Other people can ply their trade all over the world, "but me, I have just four places where I can direct—Hollywood, Paris, London, Rome." He then added, "Hollywood is out. London is practically out, and the others are seemingly impossible."

So Stroheim stayed in France, always hoping for another directing opportunity, and feeding himself and Denise by acting. In the remaining years, he would appear in eight more films.

Despite many disappointments, Stroheim continued to keep his sense of humor. In a brief snippet in a newspaper column under something called "Department of Unexpected Honesty," Stroheim was quoted as saying, "I went to have my hair cut the other day and asked the barber if I should take off my scarf. He said, 'Yes, but it was all right if I kept my hat on.'"[22]

In 1952, when Robert Flaherty died, Stroheim recorded for the BBC an obituary that was broadcast on September 2. Speaking of Flaherty's last film, *The Louisiana Story,* Stroheim said that it has "a refreshing absence of all Hollywoodian bunk . . . no 'boy-meets-girl' stuff . . . and no marines landed anywhere." (This marines comment is an odd one because Stroheim had the marines arrive in some of his own scripts!) He recounted his first meeting with Flaherty, described his appearance in immense detail, and concluded, "I am sure he too felt like meeting an old comrade in arms . . . on no man's land . . . having battled against the same enemy—producers and financiers. He too had felt the hurt the Hollywood bosses had caused him in heart and mind. We stood there and looked into each other's eyes, searching, sounding and finding. We knew each other without ever having met before. We were of the same breed, the fighting kind, fighting for what we wanted to achieve." In a sense, Stroheim was revealing more about himself here than about Flaherty.[23]

There were no calls from America for Stroheim, although Wilder could have used him as the German commandant in *Stalag 17* (1953). Perhaps he felt that Stroheim was too old or would add to the role overtones that he did not want. Instead, he used Otto Preminger, another director who occasionally acted. *Stalag 17* would later be transmuted into the perennial TV favorite *Hogan's Heroes* with Werner Klemperer. Ironically, all of the actors playing these imposing Nazi *Kommandants* were Jewish!

Of Stroheim's last films, probably the most interesting is *Alraune* (1952), his first picture made in Germany and in his native language. Directed by Arthur Maria Rabenalt, it harks back to the 1920s in its morbid subject matter and in its stylized visuals (the sets were by Robert Herlth, who had designed many famous German films, among them *Der Letzte Mann* in 1924). In fact, *Alraune* was a remake of a 1930 German film (directed by Richard Oswald) that in turn had been a remake of a 1928 German silent picture (directed by Henrik Galeen). Based on a controversial novel that dealt with artificial insemination, the film is visually lush and suffused with Germanic romanticism, but its subject matter is rather unsavory. In a sense, it is a horror film. There are no physical shocks, but there is a pervasive poetic gloom. It distinctly echoes the Hollywood "mad scientist" genre, but with a difference. We have not a dedicated yet flawed protagonist, but rather a cynical, perhaps perverse professor, who, like Dr. Pretorious in *Bride of Frankenstein* (1935), has been booted out of the university because of his repellent ideas and practices. Although the scenario follows previous versions of the story, this one contains several scenes that suggest that Stroheim had considerable input. The dialogue was originally in German, but copies available in America offer only a dubbed version with another actor providing Stroheim's voice. As a result, we miss his wonderful inflections and nuances. Apparently, Stroheim's original contract stated that if a version was dubbed in English, he would record his own voice. Unfortunately, the contract did not specify a fee, and when Stroheim asked for too much, a substitute was hired.

Alraune begins with a romantic image of a young man on a white horse stopping by a wall and noticing a white-garbed girl climbing up a building. We find out later that he, Frank, is a medical student paying a visit to his uncle (Stroheim). The butler declares that the uncle, who is a professor, has been summoned away. In answer to Frank's query, the servant declares that there is no woman in the house. The scene now shifts to the professor entering a convent, where he speaks to the head nun. With her wide hat and starched white bodice setting off a large black cross, she informs the professor that his daughter, Alraune, has escaped. (She had been locked in a cell as a punishment for having "obscene literature" under her bed.) At this information, the uncle makes the minutest of smirks—an interesting touch and typical of Stroheim.

Frank tells two friends—Ralph, a painter, and Gerald, a count—about the mysterious woman in white. They go to investigate. Each wanders around the property separately, and each beholds her and becomes bewitched by her beauty. When the men reunite, none of them will mention having encountered the apparition. Not long after, one of the students discovers Ralph's sketch of the woman and recognizes her. Then each guiltily admits to having seen her and having jealously guarded his secret. As the film progresses, we observe that anyone who gets emotionally involved with the mysterious woman dies, as if she carries a curse. As the opening titles say, she is like the mythical flower of the mandrake root that grows at the foot of the gallows.

Later, Frank goes to his uncle and requests more money for his schooling. He is refused and is also told that Alraune is the professor's daughter and his sole heir. During this conversation, Alraune comes downstairs and, while gazing at Frank, sensuously bites into an apple. After he leaves, she asks the professor about her mother, and he informs her that the woman died in childbirth. He concludes their talk by adding, "Next time you steal unusual books from my library, hide them a little better."

One scene opens with a wealthy older princess, a former accomplice of the professor in his unethical and illegal schemes. Smoking a large black cigar, the princess tells Frank that his uncle hates him and will not pay for his medical degree because he himself had been dismissed from the college. She gives Frank money to go to Paris, saying, "You'll be safer there." She wants him away from Alraune and intends to induce him to marry her own daughter.

Frank visits the professor again and, smitten with Alraune, wants to take her with him to Paris. The professor tells the eager fellow some startling news about the girl: he has created her! The professor shows him a picture of the mother. "I made a long search for a woman like her in the slums of Hamburg." The princess—"only a waitress in a cheap bar for sailors" before she married the prince—helped him find this low person (obviously a prostitute).

Pointing to a skull on the table, the professor explains that the father was "arrested in 1888 for a double murder" and makes a gesture of a man being hanged, the same gesture Stroheim had used in *Mademoiselle Docteur.* "Immediately before his death, we made a little deal— the price was only a cheap bottle of brandy. After that, I gave him the opportunity of becoming a father. Anonymously, of course. The result of that experiment was Alraune." Then, he describes his ghastly plan. "She's also living proof of my theories on heredity. She already shows symptoms of having inherited all the evil characteristics of her parents."

Appalled at this information, Frank wants to know why he used the "scum of all humanity," and asks, "What right did you have to do it?" The reply is pure Stroheim: "Well, I suppose that criminal characteristics are far easier to discover than good ones." He pauses, "And also it's more interesting. Good people are so uninteresting." When Frank accuses him of creating "a crime against nature," he replies, "And you have fallen in love with this crime against nature!"

There is a strange air of fate that hangs over the action. In the course of the film, each of the young men attracted to her—in fact, in love with her—dies, except for Frank. Alraune confesses later that it seems as if she must have willed them away.

In the background of one shot, as love is being discussed, there is a frieze of several nude female dancers (reminiscent of a similar group in *Queen Kelly*). Alraune complains that she cannot feel her heart at all, and that she has "no tears," but then she begins to cry. She expresses her love for Frank. Not long after, in a dramatic moment, the professor explains to the girl about her origins. "You have been nothing but a means to an end," he declares, "the result of my experiments, the living proof of my theories—my Creation!" This news is, of course, shocking to the girl, but when the professor—smitten now himself— wants her to escape to Paris with him as—we assume—his mistress, she hurries to Frank. The professor's mad dream is ruined, and he shoots the girl in Frank's arms. The last image shows the professor in silhouette (as in *Mademoiselle Docteur*) walking toward the noose of a gallows.

Despite its fascinating topic, *Alraune* has numerous flaws, particularly in its sense of period. It is supposed to be set in 1905 or so, but the costuming varies from the mid 1800s to 1950, especially in the hairstyle and dresses of Hildegarde Neff, who plays Alraune. She is extremely attractive, but not very convincing as a young convent girl—we assume at least under seventeen years of age—who needs a governess. (Incidentally, the equally good-looking governess is played by Denise Vernac.) Alraune's character, at least in terms of the action and dialogue, should be a mixture of youth and innocence intermixed with lust and selfishness. In short, she is both hot and cold, good and evil. Like the Golem, she was intended to be an unholy experiment—a being without a heart and not wholly human—yet she transcends her almost diabolical conception and ultimately indicates her humanity by shedding tears. The actress—both beautiful and gorgeously photographed—assumes languorous poses and exudes seductiveness, but she is basically wooden and does not bring off the destructive aspects. Is her death a tragedy or a kindness? Did she deserve her fate because of her origin, or has she overcome her background through the healing and transcendent power of love? The answers are not clear.

The somewhat muddled script was the result of altercations between Stroheim and the director. William K. Everson reported that Stroheim would arrive on the set

> every morning with a fresh script and the explanation that he'd rewritten everything, and then demand that they shoot it *his* way that day. At first Rabenalt [the director] fought him, but then decided to humor him. It was shot *both* ways— Stroheim's way and the way Rabenalt originally intended. Presumably little of the Stroheim-inspired footage was used. At least I hope it wasn't, for the story of *Alraune* depends for its effectiveness on a convincing femme fatale and on a almost wholly diabolical professor. Because of Hildegarde Neff's limitations as a actress and the restraints imposed on Stroheim, the film lacks a dynamic center that would have made it compelling. It is distinguished only by Stroheim's performance.[24]

Although Stroheim's performance is credible, it is not inspired. He does what he has to do well, and except for the cigarette smoking, he

eschews many of his usual mannerisms. His character, although the leading one and given much serious dialogue, is curiously passive and underacted. He watches events rather than controlling them—that is, until the end, where he becomes possessive of Alraune. The shift from watching his experiment blossom to being interested in her himself— from curiosity to a kind of incest—is not properly developed and so seems more of a surprise than an inevitability, thus weakening the film's concluding moments. This dimension might have enriched the meaning of both Alraune's death and his own. Instead, we are left with melodrama and some rather sick lechery without attaining the script's potential of poetic tragedy.

The reviewer for *Variety,* when the film showed in Vienna on November 11, 1952, did not appreciate some of the sarcastic and cynical overtones of Stroheim's role, which was summed up as "comic malevolence."[25] Although not an entire success, *Alraune* at least had pretensions far above the low fare of some of Stroheim's French and American films.

In 1953 Stroheim appeared in *Minuit Quai de Bercy,* directed by Christian Stengel, and then joined hands again with his old acquaintance Edmond T. Greville, who decided to take his actors on location to Provence where he shot *L'Envers du paradis.* It is a handsome film, but a curious one.

Although no masterpiece, *L'Envers du paradis* comes close to achieving a kind of poetic tragedy. It relates the story of a young girl—she looks about sixteen or seventeen—who has been ill. She has fallen in love with a writer of crime novels. When she accidentally finds out that she is dying, she makes an assignation with the man she loves and plans to kill herself afterward with a pistol. The man's jealous mistress discovers the intended meeting, has an argument with her lover, and is accidentally shot and killed. The man claims that he caused her death, but the girl, because she loves him and will be dead shortly, adjusts the evidence to incriminate herself. Her older friend, O'Hara, a former sea captain, attempts to save the couple by asserting that he is the murderer. All of this plotting seems to take a long time.

The film's only interesting character is O'Hara. Played by Stroheim, who is now rather portly, he makes quite a sight with a captain's jacket worn open over a striped sailor's jersey. O'Hara, whose parents were

Prussian and Irish, drinks heavily and is an unhappy man. The only light in his life is the young girl, from whom he asks a photograph. He has in his rooms a kind of shrine that contains photos of a woman in a wedding dress and some children. Who they are, we never learn. Presumably, the girl's photograph will join them. These shelves of photos give O'Hara another dimension, in the same manner as Stroheim's frequent use of a mourning band in other films, to indicate a sadness over the loss of loved ones. He brings in flowers and puts them in a vase on the shelf among the pictures, like an offering. (Surely, this was Stroheim's contribution to the script.)

Later, there is a remarkable scene when O'Hara staggers up the staircase and pauses to swig some more from a bottle. At the top of the stairs, on a kind of balcony that overlooks a large room, is the wheel of a ship. He dons a captain's hat and proceeds to steer, while shouting out orders to an invisible crew! It's an odd moment, to say the least. On another occasion, we see him scrubbing on a washboard a shirt identical to the one he is wearing, while singing a kind of tuneless mess of German and perhaps Latin words. In a different scene, O'Hara lies on his bed with his dog and holds a sword, which he continues to brandish as he descends the stairs to answer the door.

Further along in the film, O'Hara goes to church and enters the confessional booth to ask the priest to pray not for himself but for the girl. When the girl tells him she wants to have a private place to meet her loved one, O'Hara allows her to use his rooms, although he carefully removes the pictures from his shrine.

Although Stroheim's name appears first in the credits, he has only a minor role. Denise Vernac is mentioned third, but her part is almost nonexistent. Playing a sort of bohemian, she wears some outlandish costumes, wields an unique kind of cane, and at one point is shown showering behind an opaque glass door.

L'Envers du paradis, even though it has a lot of characters and some beautiful shots of the village and the countryside, is not very interesting. The characters are ill-defined, particularly the writer, who is nothing more than a handsome face. The death of the beautiful young girl—almost too young to be having an affair—was intended to be sad, if not tragic, but the director was unable to convey his intentions. Stroheim, however, does contribute a distinct and engaging characterization.

Stroheim's next film, *Alerte au sud,* was a French-Italian produc-

tion, shot in color and directed by Jean Devaivre. It was certainly no masterpiece, but it did allow Stroheim to play a German general who refuses to call off the war! *Variety*'s review of the film's Paris premiere on February 2, 1954, granted that "Von Stroheim manages to get some malice and depth into his silly role as the half-crazy professional soldier."[26]

In January 1954, Britain's National Film Theater began a series of screenings of Stroheim's films and invited him to London. After reading what the press had to say about him and his work, he said, "The morons! Not a word about the films, not an intelligent word. It's all the old stuff about The Bullet-headed Prussian again. I'm not a Prussian, I'm Austrian. It's like calling an Englishman Irish. And my head isn't bullet-shaped. I've seen bullets."[27]

Stroheim had expected a serious examination of his films and not the foolishness that he encountered. Reluctantly showing up at his first London press conference in twelve years, he was already resentful and angry. He tried to contain himself and endured being asked if he had taught Americans how to make love and if he believed in beating women offscreen as well as on. By this time, he was boiling and began to resemble his imperious and raging screen persona. The *London Daily Herald* of January 6, 1954, stated that Stroheim was "on the edge of an insult the whole time." Denise Vernac, seeing that the press conference was not going well, tried to smooth over matters, but Stroheim ordered her to be quiet: "Let me finish my sentence. I'm talking." He explained that he took the kinds of roles he played because "I am homely. It would never have done to show German officers as handsome."

Another newspaper said that he began to discuss *Greed,* claiming that "it was a wonderful film until they started to cut it about." Then, sensing a derisive reaction to his claim that it was wonderful, "he shot to his feet, pointed at a Continental reporter and growled, 'I don't like grimaces behind my back!'"[28] The bewildered reporter stuttered that he was a great admirer.

While Stroheim grumbled, Denise, sensing that he was making a terrible impression, interjected every few minutes remarks such as "He's really very timid" and "He's so charming," and then, "He's sweet." The British reporters did not seem to share her views. If the press did not dislike him before, they certainly did afterward: one photograph the next day contained the withering caption, "And Here Girls, Is the Man Your Mother Loved To Hate."

During the press conference, Stroheim looked around for an ashtray to stub out his cigarette. Someone held out his arm and said that if Stroheim were really the man of his films he would put out the butt in his hand. Stroheim surveyed him coldly and said, "If you were a woman I would."

Karel Reisz summed up Stroheim's remarks: "Questioned on his methods of direction, Stroheim was not very revealing; or, perhaps, revealing by omission. What seems to have interested him most, at any rate in retrospect, was the construction of sets and design of uniforms. Authenticity of detail was a passion with him which has not weakened: he talks at length and with love of the buttons and lapels of a uniform, immensely enjoying his expertise. Any attempts to bring back the conversation to mundane subjects like camerawork or editing are firmly side-tracked. 'I hate technique,' he said."[29] Stroheim hardly hated technique, at least not in the days when he was directing, but his years of acting in other people's films had perhaps shifted his emphasis solely to set decoration and costume—matters he could control.

At the conclusion of the press conference, as Stroheim began to leave, he "murmured with a charming smile to the Continental reporter, 'My vile, vile temper.'" As he exited, he blew a female reporter a kiss, saying, "I make good my temper."[30]

The photographers gathered around. When he was asked to put in his monocle, he said he did not have one. Then, someone said, "fake it with a coin." He bristled that he did not "fake" things and told the photographers, "not so politely, what they could do."[31] Finally, after much pleading by the press and Denise's urging him to cooperate, he reconciled himself to the realities of publicity by inserting a half crown into his right eye. Naturally, this was the picture to be published.[32]

Stroheim's conduct may not have been quite politic, but he was acutely aware that he was now, in his old age, being indulged as a relic and felt (to some extent correctly, particularly in the popular mind) that he and his work were perhaps being mocked. Defensiveness breeds aggression, sensitivity breeds paranoia, and both act as self-fulfilling prophecies.

Not long after, Art Buchwald, of the Paris *Herald Tribune,* spoke with Stroheim about the visit to England and his forthcoming trip to Brazil for another retrospective. When asked about his renewed fame, Stroheim responded, "I'm sixty-eight years old and they probably think it's time for my funeral. I guess they want to do me some honor before I shove off." Stroheim also discussed his present employment situation and seemed to contradict his previous statements when he said that he had hoped to get some additional work in Hollywood after *Sunset Boulevard,* "but I waited around for two and half years and nothing happened." Actually, he had waited only a short time. "The only place I've been able to find work is in France. I've been in four pictures here, all junk."[33]

Buchwald asked him if he were sour on Hollywood:

It would be difficult for me to say I'm sour on Hollywood because if someone offered me a job now I'd go back in a minute. There are some people back there I'm a little sour about, but that isn't the same thing. There is one fellow in particular whom I love, but if God loves him more I would not stand in the way.

So you won't go back to Hollywood unless you have a job? [asked Buchwald.]

No, why should I? If you lost your job on a newspaper it would make you very unhappy to hang around a newspaper waiting for something to happen.[34]

Buchwald then mentioned that Stroheim had been having trouble with his American passport because he had been out of the country for so long. His dilemma, Stroheim explained, was that he could not make a living there, so he had to live in France. "I've been a citizen of the United States since 1909 [wrong], I served in the American Army for three years.[!] I would never want to lose my citizenship."[35]

Buchwald mentioned that Stroheim had once made a lot of money. "Everybody thinks I did. I was the cheapest of the cheap. When Ernst Lubitsch was making $150,000 a picture I was making $30,000. I was really working for art's sake."[36] True. Too true.

Stroheim described the novel he was writing, *The Fires of St. John.*[37] It would be a long book, he explained. "I believe in the origin of things. I have to explain everything." This statement reveals both the strengths and the weaknesses of the man, the ability to create works of beauty, integrity, and genius that are also commercial impossibilities like *Greed, Merry-Go-Round,* and *The Wedding March.*

Stroheim said to Buchwald that he had received offers to make films (were there really any?) and explained that he had turned them all down. "You have to show that you can do it quicker and cheaper than anybody else. Making pictures is tough, but under those conditions I would prefer to starve to death. Maybe I'll find a rich coffee planter in Brazil who will back me in a film, somebody who doesn't know what picture-making is all about."[38] Shortly after, Stroheim went to Brazil for the film festival, but no coffee planter appeared.

In 1954, a Technicolor film called *Napoléon*—"written, conceived, and directed by Sacha Guitry," said a title—was made with an all-star cast. Attempting to cover all of Napoleon's life, the picture was, of necessity, episodic and, despite its subject matter, without interest. Most of the scenes were photographed in long shot, with the camera used merely as a recording device, not an interpreter. Abel Gance's 1927 *Napoléon* had more imagination in a single minute than did the whole of Guitry's pedestrian effort. In one sequence, Stroheim, as an imposing Beethoven with wild hair and fierce expression, is seated at a piano imperiously thundering away at the keyboard. He appears in just five shots and has no dialogue at all. Sacha Guitry perhaps felt that the brusque genius of Beethoven could only be portrayed by a modern equal.

On April 12, 1955, Paris saw the release of another French film, *Série noire,* an imitation of an American crime thriller, which despite being packed with gun battles, fistfights, and car chases, remains dull. There are several scenes in the film in which the characters speak in awe about a criminal mastermind. After this intriguing introduction, which creates some curiosity and suspense, the arch villain finally appears. It is Zavaroff, played by Stroheim. Wearing a dressing gown and an ascot, looking a bit heavy, and toying with his cigarette, he addresses the criminals in his usual assertive fashion. Although Stroheim won third billing in the credits, proving again that producers often used him for his name's box-office value, he appears in only two scenes, neither of which lasts more than a few minutes. His part probably took only one or two days to shoot, but as usual, he dominates his screen time. Stroheim accepted his part strictly for the money, and

Variety said that he "brings his talent to a lesser role" in a film that was "amateurish and too draggy."[39]

After *Série noire* came a 1955 TV pilot that went nowhere, *L'Homme aux cent visages,* and one more film appearance, in *La Madone des sleepings,* which also provided Denise with a small part. These efforts, too, were of little or no consequence. The last film, however, at least allowed Stroheim to invest his character with some imaginative ideas. Once again, he has an elaborate set of glasses extended onto another pair, so that the device stands out almost a foot from his face. When he takes this apparatus off, he dons a more normal pair of glasses but usually has them pushed up high on his forehead. Besides this quirk, the only thing that could possibly have interested Stroheim was his masquerading as a psychiatrist. He removes a picture of Sigmund Freud from a book, forges the famous doctor's name, and then, as a doctor of the mind, he listens to the confessions of a rich lady. At one point, we see a close-up as he sketches the outline of a naked woman on his notepad and adds breasts and a navel. He gets to know his patient and her whereabouts so that he can go to a stockholders' meeting in order to engineer a swindle.

Stroheim's few moments in this rambling and complicated grab-bag of cowboy scenes, Western saloons, shootings, and parachute jumps usually shows him seated. When he walks, he appears to move stiffly and cautiously, as if in some discomfort. Was it age, or was his back already bothering him? Although Stroheim often was killed in his films, it seems rather prescient that in *Série noire* and in *Sleepings,* in which he is shot, he falls to the floor with his eyes open. In each case, someone pushes his lids closed, as if rehearsing the actual death, which was soon to come.

At the age of seventy, Stroheim had slowed down, his advanced age now limiting the kinds of roles he could play, but he still attended theater and film openings and frequented Maxim's and other restaurants. In his spare time, of which there was increasingly more, he continued to write scripts, make attempts at an autobiography, and otherwise keep busy. He resuscitated his screen story of *Poto Poto,* which had been rejected by MGM in 1935, and transformed it into a novel, which would be published in 1956.[40] Like *Paprika* before it, the book was both "overwritten and unreadable," as Anita Loos correctly noted.

Despite her misgivings about its literary merits, she asked Stroheim to sign her copy, and he wrote:"For Anita who is such a wonderful friend that she bought this copy. With all my love, Erich."[41]

In 1955, Stroheim was invited to Brussels, where on November 28, at the Palais des Beaux-Arts, he improvised a speech introducing *The Merry Widow.* He explained that the audience was going to see a 16 mm copy and fretted that it would not have the proper musical accompaniment. He added these disarming words: "Naturally, I like drama ... tragedy.... But the producers do not like it.... They like only what brings money, and, in my youth, I hated money, although today . .. [laughter and applause] ...Therefore, I never wanted to direct stories for infantiles like that ... [laughter]."[42]

Stroheim described his difficulties with the cutting of *Greed* and then mentioned his arguments with Mae Murray during the making of *The Merry Widow.* He again apologized that the audience was seeing a 16 mm print and concluded:"I don't have the sound or the color or the Cinerama.... I have nothing. And so I have made all the possible excuses that I could think of. All the good things in this film were made by me. The things that are no good in it were made by others."[43]

Eerily, Stroheim's fictional fascination with spinal problems now became his own reality. In the summer of 1956, he began to suffer severe pain in his back. It was cancer. Soon, he was unable to mount the stairs, and by late autumn he was confined to his bed. Finally, he lay paralyzed. In March 1957, he was carried down to his drawing room, where—surrounded by his swords, uniforms, crucifixes, and phallic bookends—he was visited by a delegation and awarded the French Legion of Honor. For much of his life he had bestowed medals on himself, but finally fiction and fact merged, and fate granted him the genuine article. Barely able to voice his appreciation, he gamely offered a pathetic salute.

Soon the pain grew worse and he was heavily sedated, though still at times lucid. His close friend, Thomas Quinn Curtiss, reported that one day Stroheim remarked, "This isn't the worst. The worst is that they stole twenty-five years of my life."[44]

As he lay there, nursed by Denise, his mind no doubt wandered over his past: his starving years in America, his good luck in getting into the movies, and his sudden success. Did he ever regret the actions that labeled him a notorious spendthrift and an uncompromising realist in an industry devoted to profit and illusion? Fate gave him another chance with *The Merry Widow,* and grudgingly he used stars, stayed on budget, and included a happy ending. Once again, he found himself renowned, the author and director of a critical and box-office success. Did second thoughts haunt him for abusing this good will and causing *The Wedding March* to be a financial fiasco? The jury might still be out on where the burden of blame lies for *Queen Kelly,* but how did he regard the bad luck of *Walking down Broadway?* A thinking man, a reflective man, he must have mulled over these events. He was not the only person to have lived and died with dreams unfulfilled. It is the lot of most of humanity. The tragedy came from the fact that the dream came to him, he embraced it, he tasted it, and then perversely allowed it to vanish.

Did this great believer in fate ever realize that he himself had shaped his destiny, wresting defeat out of the hands of victory? Unable to move, humiliated by the indignities of a sickbed, did he in his last feverish moments again grasp the megaphone and once more see his visions made flesh? The hours passed, the anguish and the pain ebbed, and then it was over, the slow and inexorable fade to black.

On May 12, 1957, the mortal man merged forever into the immortal Erich von Stroheim.

Filmography

The following list contains all the films in which Stroheim functioned as director, as assistant director, and as actor. His script and novel writing has been covered in the text. The films appear in the order in which they were shot. The dates, generally from the *Film Daily Yearbook,* are those of the films' first releases. Where there was a significant interval between production and release, the fact has been noted. Further information can be found in the American Film Institute catalogs, which provide copyright dates, credits, and sometimes varying footages and release dates. Usually, these discrepencies are not of much importance. Silent films were measured in reels (each reel supposedly about one thousand feet). Such measurements were imprecise: Some reels contained hundreds of feet less and others slightly more. In some cases I have included footage counts as measured by the New York State Censorship Board, for they are almost always accurate.

For Stroheim's American films, I have mentioned the producing firm, but for his European films, because there was no significant studio system, I cite only the country of origin. For the French films, one can consult *L'Histoire du Française Cinema,* a multivolume work that provides stills and release dates. Because the French films sometimes remained unissued for many months—in several cases at least half a year—I have adhered to the order in which Stroheim listed them in his letters to Peter Noble. The specific release dates come from official French premieres as noted by *Variety.* (The absence of *The Birth of a Nation* is explained in the text.) The name of the director follows the length of the film, and Stroheim's role in the production appears at the end of each entry.

Captain Macklin. Apr. 1915. Majestic. 4 reels (lost). John B. O'Brien. Extra.

Ghosts. June 1915. Majestic. 5 reels. George Nichols. Bit part, assistant director.

The Failure. Ma 1915. Reliance. 4 reels (lost). Christy Cabanne. Bit part.

Old Heidelberg. Nov. 1915. Fine Arts. 5 reels. John Emerson. Supporting player, assistant director.

A Bold Impersonation. Aug. 1915. Fine Arts. 2 reels (lost). Fred Kelsey. Extra.

Farewell to Thee. Aug. 1915. 1 reel (lost). Major player.

His Picture in the Papers. Feb. 1916. Fine Arts. 5 reels. John Emerson. Supporting player, assistant director.

Macbeth. June 1916. Reliance. 8 reels (lost). John Emerson. Assistant director.

Intolerance. Sept. 1916. Wark. 13 reels. D. W. Griffith. Stroheim may have assisted slightly and appeared in a bit part, but he is not a pharisee, as frequently credited, and certainly is not discernible in existing prints.

The Social Secretary. Sept. 1916. Fine Arts. 5 reels. John Emerson. Supporting role, assistant director.

Less Than the Dust. Nov. 1916. Pickford Corp. 7 reels. John Emerson. Assistant director.

Panthea. Jan. 1917. Norma Talmadge Film Corp. 5 reels (lost). Allan Dwan. Supporting player, assistant director.

In Again, Out Again. Apr. 1917. Fairbanks Corp. 5 reels. John Emerson. Location assistant.

Wild and Woolly. June 1917. Fairbanks Corp. 5 reels. John Emerson. Location assistant in the few scenes shot in New York.

Sylvia of the Secret Service. Nov. 1917 (completed in June). Astra Corp.

5 reels (lost). George Fitzmaurice. Supporting player, assistant director.

For France. Sept. 1917. Vitagraph. 5 reels (lost). Wesley Ruggles. Bit part.

Reaching for the Moon. Nov. 1917. Fairbanks Corp. 5 reels. John Emerson. Bit part, assistant director.

Draft 258. Nov. 1917. Metro. 7 reels (lost). Christie Cabanne. Bit part.

The Unbeliever. Feb. 1918 (probably shot in Sept. or Oct. 1917). Thomas A. Edison, Inc. 7 reels. Alan Crosland. Supporting player.

Hearts of the World. Mar. 1918. Griffith. 13 reels. D. W. Griffith. Supporting player, technical director, military adviser.

The Hun Within. Sept. 1918 (finished by May). Paramount. 5 reels (lost). Chet Withey. Small part.

The Heart of Humanity. Jan. 1919. Universal. 8 reels. Allen Holubar. Major role.

Blind Husbands. Dec. 1919. Universal. 8 reels (present prints are from the shorter 1924 release). Director, major role.

The Devil's Pass Key. Aug. 1920 (reviewed in Apr. 1920 but not released until Aug. 1920). Universal. 7 reels (lost). Director.

Foolish Wives. Jan. 1922 (shot between July 1920 and June 1921). Universal. Originally 32 reels, cut to 18, then to 14, at 14,120 feet, for the New York premiere; trimmed to 10 reels for its general release. The second negative (used in Europe) was cut to about 7 reels. In 1929–1930, the first negative was also cut by Universal to 7 reels. In 1972, I combined the two versions, restored original titles, and trimmed the length of most titles, so that in terms of images the film runs about 11 reels. Director.

Merry-Go-Round. Sept. 1923 (completed in June). Universal. 10 reels (9,178 feet). Rupert Julian. Stroheim shot during Aug.–Oct. 1922 (probably no more than 600 feet from Stroheim's scenes remain). Director.

Greed. Dec. 1924. MGM. Original 42 reels cut by Stroheim to 24 reels, but released in 10 reels. When finally submitted for censorship to NYS on Nov. 20, 1924, it ran 9,850 feet. AFI lists its length at 10,067 feet. Director.

The Merry Widow. Aug. 1925. MGM. 10,027 feet (AFI). Director.

The Wedding March. Oct. 1928. Paramount. Its 30-some reels finally cut to 13 reels when submitted for censorship to NYS on July 13, 1928. On Oct 2, 1928, with sound synchronization, it was roughly figured at about 12,000 feet. On Nov. 5, 1928, the actual footage ran 10,037. When other prints were submitted for censorship on Jan. 4, 1929, its length was considered roughly 11 reels but issued on 12 reels. AFI mentions it as 10,721 feet and the silent version at 10,659 feet. Director, major role.

The Honeymoon. 1928. Paramount. This continuation of *The Wedding March* was not released in America and contained only 4 reels of new material (lost). Director, major role.

Queen Kelly. 1928–1929. Not released in the USA but received some distribution in 1932 in Europe. This contained only the European footage and a tacked-on ending. In the mid-1980s the film was "restored" by adding the African footage as well as a few stills to round out the story. Director.

The Great Gabbo. Sept. 1929. Sono-Art. When submitted for censorship to NYS on Sept. 6, 1929, it ran 9,033 feet on 11 reels. AFI lists its release on Sept. 12, 1929, at 8,049 feet. On Jan. 4, 1935, its reissue was in 8 reels at 7,600 feet. James Cruze. Major role.

Three Faces East. Sept. 1930. Warners. Roy del Ruth. Major role.

Friends and Lovers. Nov. 1931. RKO. Victor Schertzinger. Major role.

The Lost Squadron. Mar. 1932. RKO. George Archainbaud. Major role.

As You Desire Me. June 1932. MGM. George Fitzmaurice. Major role.

Walking down Broadway. 1932 (released as *Hello Sister* in April 1933). Fox. Only a few minutes of Stroheim's footage remains. Director.

Crimson Romance. Sept. 1934. Mascot. 8 reels, 6,583 feet. David Howard. Major role.

The Fugitive Road. Nov. 1934. Invincible. 6,137 feet. Frank Strayer. Major role.

The Crime of Dr. Crespi. Oct. 1935. Republic. 5,629 feet. John Auer. Major role.

Marthe Richard. 1937. France. 7,457 feet. NYS license applied for Jan. 1940. Raymond Bernard. Major role.

La Grande Illusion. 1937. France. When submitted for censorhip to NYS Aug. 12, 1938, it ran 8,977 feet. When Renoir restored the film, it was released in 1959 at 10,109 feet. Jean Renoir. Major role.

L'Alibi. 1937. France. Pierre Chenal. Major role.

Mademoiselle Docteur (aka *Under Secret Orders*). 1937. Great Britain. Edmond T. Greville. Major role.

L'Affaire Lafarge. 1937. France. Pierre Chenal. Supporting role.

Les Pirates du Rail. 1938. France. Christian-Jaque. Supporting role.

Les Disparus de Saint-Agil (aka *Missing from St. Agil* and *Boys' School*). May 1938. Christian-Jaque. Supporting role.

Ultimatum. Nov. 1938. France. Robert Wiene. Supporting role.

Gibraltar. Jan. 1939. France. Fedor Ozep. Major role.

The following eight French films were shot in 1939, although the release dates in some instances are much later.

Derrière la façade (aka *32 Rue Montmatre* and later *A Girl in Every Room*). Apr. 1939. France. Georges Lacombe and Yves Mirande. Supporting role.

Rappel immèdiat. July 1939. France. Leon Mathot. Supporting role.

Menaces (originally called *Cinq Jours d'angoisse*). Jan. 1940. France. Edmond T. Greville. Major role.

Pièges (aka *Personal Column* and *Snares*). Jan. 1940. France. 8,401 feet; released in America in 1941 and cut to 7,997 feet. Robert Siodmak. Supporting role.

Le Monde tremblera (aka *La Revolte des vivants*). 1939. France. Richard Pottier. Supporting role.

Tempête (aka *Thunder over Paris*). May 1940. France. Bernard Deschamps. Major role.

Macao, l'enfer du jeu (aka *Gambling Hell*). 1939. France. Jean Delannoy. Major role.

Paris–New York. May 1940, shot in Aug. 1939. France. Yves Mirande. Stroheim's small part was cut and replaced by Apr. 30, 1940.

I Was an Adventuress. 1940. Twentieth Century–Fox. Gregory Ratoff. Major role.

So Ends Our Night. Jan. 1941. United Artists. John Cromwell. Supporting role.

Five Graves to Cairo. May 1943. Paramount. 8,699 feet. Billy Wilder. Major role.

The North Star. Oct. 1943. Goldwyn. 9,521 feet. Lewis Milestone. Revised in May 1957 and rereleased as *Armored Attack* with cut footage and additional narration to deflate its pro-Russian slant. Supporting role.

The Lady and the Monster. Mar. 1944. Republic. 7,728 feet. Submitted Feb 1944. Reissued in 1950 in about 6,000 feet as *Tiger Man* with 138 shots removed. Major role.

Storm over Lisbon. Sept. 1944. Republic. 7,691 feet. George Sherman. Rereleased in 1950 as *Inside the Underworld*. Major role.

The Great Flamarion. Feb. 1945). Republic. 7,016 feet. Anthony Mann. Major role.

Scotland Yard Investigator. Oct. 1945. Republic. 6,095 feet. George Blair. Major role.

The Mask of Diijon. Feb. 1946. Producer's Releasing Corporation. Lew Landers. Major role.

La Foire aux chimères. 1946. France. Pierre Chenal. Major role.

On ne meurt pas comme ça. 1946. France. Jean Boyer. Major role.

La Danse de mort. 1947. France, Italy. Marcel Cravenne. Wrote screenplay, major role.

Le Signal rouge. 1948. France, Germany. Ernst Neubach. Major role.

Portrait d'un assasin. 1949. France. Roland Bernard.

Sunset Boulevard. 1949, released 1950. Paramount. 9,912 feet. Billy Wilder. Submitted for censorship to NYS on Sept. 26, 1949 at 11,002 feet. This version was not released. The director recut it in Hollywood and shortened it to 10,119 feet. Then a few more changes were made and the modified script (dated Jan. 24, 1950) was sent to NYS. On May 26, 1950, the print of 9,912 feet on 12 reels was submitted to NYS and then released. Supporting role.

Alraune. 1952. Germany. 8,193 feet. Arthur Rabenalt. Arrived in NYS Oct. 1954. Major role.

Minuit quai de Bercy. 1953. France. Christian Stengel. Supporting role.

L'Envers du paradis. 1953. France. Edmond T. Greville. Supporting role.

Alerte au sud. 1953. France. Jean Devaivre. Supporting role.

Napoléon. 1954. France. Sacha Guitry. Small part.

Sérié noire. 1955. France. Pierre Foucaud. Supporting role.

La Madone des sleepings. June 1955. France. Henri Diamant-Berger. Supporting role.

L'Homme aux cent visages. 1956. France. Robert Spafford.

Notes

1. Beginnings

1. Thomas, *Thalberg, Life and Legend,* 50.

2. Curtiss, *Von Stroheim,* 146.

3. Ibid., 324.

4. *Picture Play Magazine,* Nov. 1919, 61.

5. *Motion Picture Classic,* Jan. 1920.

6. Goldwyn, *Behind the Screen* , 201.

7. Curtiss, *Von Stroheim,* xvi.

8. Curtiss was a charming, courteous man who wrote his highly readable biography of Stroheim as a labor of love. But, like many journalists, he was not averse to fudging facts, inventing dialogue exchanges forty years after the event, putting people in places where they never were, providing details that are wholly inaccurate, ignoring logic, and otherwise failing to do even basic research. The book does, however, contain information that Stroheim undoubtedly told Curtiss about his beginning years in America. Because there are no other sources for that period of Stroheim's life, I have on occasion drawn upon Curtiss when certain incidents seemed plausible; in all of those cases I have mentioned their derivation.

9. Emil Feldmar, "Témoignages sur l'homme," *Études Cinématographiques,* nos. 48–50 (1966): 101.

10. Curtiss, *Von Stroheim,* 8; Feldmar, "Témoignages," 101.

11. Curtiss, *Von Stroheim,* 8.

12. Liptzin, *Schnitzler,* 274.

13. May, *Habsburg Monarchy,* 162–63.

14. Josef von Sternberg, *Film Fan Monthly,* Sept. 1968.

15. Interview with Joseph Henabery, at his home in Tarzana, Calif., March 26, 1975.

16. Letters from Erich von Stroheim to Valerie and to Josef von Stroheim, Brownlow Collection.

17. Curtiss, *Von Stroheim,* 5–8.

18. Ibid., 10–12.

19. *Picture Play Magazine,* Nov. 1919.

20. *Photoplay,* Dec. 1919.

21. Erich von Stroheim to Josef von Stroheim, Sept. 16, 1941, Brownlow Collection.

22. Crankshaw, *Fall of the House of Habsburg,* 287.

23. This and all other information about Stroheim's military career was obtained from the Osterreiches Staatsarchiv and the Kriegsarchiv in Vienna, May 1980.

24. Bob Bergut, "Interview with E.v. S.," *Études Cinématographiques,* nos. 48–50 (1966): 119.

25. Kriegsarchiv.

26. Lewys, *Merry-Go-Round,* 178.

27. Ibid., 180–81.

28. *New York Times,* May 13, 1957.

29. Robert Payne, *The Life and Death of Adolf Hitler* (New York: Praeger, 1973), 102

30. Feldmar, "Témoinages," 102.

31. Stroheim's declaration of nobility was not without some precedent, as a prewar book on Austria explains: "The cabdriver or waiter knows that there is no surer means of extracting a good tip from the ordinary citizen than to address him as 'Count,' and the shopkeeper never forgets to prefix the particle 'von'—the indication of noble rank—to the names of his humblest customers. Servants constantly address very middle-class masters and mistresses as 'Your Grace,' and kiss their hands, in word and act, morning and evening. Snobbishness sometimes amounting to servility runs through the middle classes, whose chief ambition seems to be to resemble the nobility, if not the aristocracy." Steed, *Hapsburg Monarchy,* 133–34.

32. *New York Times,* May 13, 1957.

33. *Photoplay,* Dec. 1919.

34. *Motion Picture Classic,* Jan. 1920.

35. *New York Herald Tribune,* Jan. 26, 1954.

36. Photographic copy of muster rolls from Hanns G. Flebbe, State of New York Division of Military and Naval Affairs, to author, April 4, 1978.

37. Curtiss, *Von Stroheim,* 25.

38. *Film History* 2 (1988): 283–95.

39. In dreaming up this whopper, Stroheim may have filtered in the plot of the first film in which he appeared as an extra, *Captain Macklin* (1915). Macklin, dismissed from West Point, sets sail to fight in Honduras. Through the American vice consul, he meets a general who makes him a captain in the revolutionary army. Although his strict discipline is unpopular, he quickly makes the troops top-notch. Stroheim apparently liked the idea of a foreigner becoming an officer and training and then leading troops south of the border. (For the plot, see *Moving Picture World,* Apr. 24, 1915.)

40. *Picture Play Magazine,* Nov. 1919.

41. Complaint, Margaret von Stroheim vs. Erich O. H. Stroheim, Superior Court of the County of Alameda, May 28, 1914. Richard Koszarski gives a slightly fuller account of this in *Man You Loved to Hate,* 12.

2. Ascent

1. Curtiss, *Von Stroheim,* 31–32.

2. Ibid., 33.

3. Erich von Stroheim, "Letter to Peter Noble." (In response to Peter Noble, who was writing an appreciative book about Stroheim's life and work called *Hollywood Scapegoat,* Stroheim, in 1947-48, sent him about 60 pages of single-spaced typescript, plus hand-written additions describing his work in films. Copies of these are in the Museum of Moden Art Library. The paging of this manuscript is helter-skelter, so that an interested researcher will have to look for material under film titles. Hereafter, these will be listed as "Letters.")

4. Ibid. Whenever Stroheim claimed to have done a stunt, he often proved inept, because he usually claimed that he broke his ribs. For example, see *The Lost Squadron* (1932) and *Gibraltar* (1938).

5. *New York World,* Sept. 16, 1916.

6. Stroheim, BBC broadcast. Quoted in Noble, *Hollywood Scapegoat,* 26.

7. For example, Bitzer (or his editors) said that in returning to the United States from England in 1917, he stopped by the *New York Times* and "chatted with Bosley Crowther, the movie editor" *(Billy Bitzer).* Crowther at this time was twelve years old. He did not join the newspaper until 1928 and did not review films until the late 1930s. Stroheim as "assistant director" is in the same league.

8. In 1967–68 I was doing a considerable amount of research in the Griffith papers at the Museum of Modern Art. There I met Ann Pinchot, Lillian Gish's cowriter. We shared several screenings, had lunch at the museum, and talked over many matters. She assured me, and this was confirmed when I had my own interviews with Miss Gish, that the lady was sincere but wholly vague on factual matters and that she recalled almost nothing from this period. For example, when I asked Miss Gish about the film she made with Griffith, *The Greatest Question* (1919), she had no idea where it was photographed (East Coast or West) and, in fact, had forgotten she had made it at all. Indeed, whatever is in the Gish book dealing with this time period stems almost wholly from Miss Pinchot's reading of the Griffith papers and other books and not from Miss Gish.

9. Henabery, *Autobiography,* 87.

10. *Variety,* Sept. 8, 1916.

11. Slide, *Griffith Actresses,* 132.

12. Henabery, *Autobiography,* 87.

13. Ibid., 88.

14. Ibid., 94.

15. Article dated Mar. 29, *Motion Picture News,* Apr. 10, 1915.

16. Letters.

17. Ibid.
18. *Variety,* Aug. 27, 1915.
19. *Motion Picture News,* Apr. 3, 1915.
20. Ibid., Mar. 27, 1915.
21. *Motion Picture Classic,* Jan. 1920.
22. Robert M. Yost Jr., "Gosh, How They Hate Him," *Photoplay,* Dec. 1919.
23. *Motion Picture News,* Apr. 17, 1915.
24. Ibid., May 8, 1915.
25. *Moving Picture World,* May 29, 1915.
26. *Variety,* June 18, 1915.
27. *Motion Picture News,* May 1, 1915.
28. *Variety,* Oct. 8, 1915.
29. *New York Times,* Aug. 27, 1928, sec. 7, p. 8.
30. "Erich von Stroheim and the Miracle," *Motion Picture Classic,* 1919.
31. Yost, "Gosh, How They Hate Him."
32. Herndon, *Pickford and Fairbanks,* 110.
33. Curtiss, *Von Stroheim,* 89.
34. Erich Junior seems to have inherited some of his father's wit. In 1933, the lad was asked the whereabouts of his monocle, to which he replied: "I put it back on my watch." *New York Times,* Oct. 29, 1968. Later, he was connected to the movie industry in minor ways and appeared, looking much like his father, in an acting role in *Two Weeks in Another Town* (1962). He died of cancer on Oct. 26, 1968.
35. Curtiss, *Von Stroheim,* 89.
36. Letters.
37. *Variety,* Feb. 4, 1916.
38. *Picture-Play Magazine,* Nov. 1919.
39. *New York Dramatic Mirror,* Oct. 23, 1915.
40. Ibid., Nov. 27, 1915.
41. Herndon, *Pickford and Fairbanks,* 112.
42. *Triangle,* Jan. 22, 1916.
43. *Christian Science Monitor,* Jan. 22, 1916.
44. Unidentified clipping, about Mar. 24, 1916, Billy Rose Theatre Collection (hereafter Threatre Collection).
45. *Los Angeles Times,* Feb. 20, 1916.
46. *Moving Picture World,* Mar. 18, 1916.
47. Ibid., June 24, 1916.
48. *Variety,* June 9, 1916.
49. *Moving Picture World,* Mar. 11, 1916.
50. *Motion Picture News,* Mar. 25, 1916.
51. Unidentified clipping, around Mar. 24, 1916, Theatre Collection.
52. *Variety,* June 9, 1916.
53. *New York Times,* June 11, 1916.
54. *Variety,* Oct. 6, 1916.

55. *Motion Picture News*, Mar. 25, 1916.

56. Ibid., Apr. 1, 1916.

57. This is the photo that appears on page 42 of Richard Griffith and Arthur Mayer, *The Movies*.

58. There was an employee of the Fine Arts Company who was known as Baron Erik von Ritzau. He was important enough that when his wife, the baroness, had a baby, the birth was noted in *Moving Picture World*, Feb. 26, 1916.

59. *Variety*, Sept. 8, 1916.

60. Curtiss, *Von Stroheim*, 68.

61. *Variety*, Apr. 7, 1916.

62. Griffith was not the only director to have trouble depicting the Crucifixion. The usually astute C.B. DeMille, in *The King of Kings* (1927), bowed to the pressure of the Anti-Defamation League and had to "exculpate the Jews of guilt for the death of Jesus" and put "the responsibility on Caiaphas, the high priest." *New York Times*, Jan. 6, 1928.

63. Noble, *Hollywood Scapegoat*, 26.

64. *Triangle*, June 3, 1916.

65. Ibid., June 10, 1916.

66. Ibid., Aug. 26, 1916.

67. *New York Dramatic Mirror*, Sept. 9, 1916.

68. Over sixty years later, Loos summed up the plot of this film quite erroneously, saying that the mother hires an unattractive girl so that her son would not be tempted. Loos recalled that the boy marries the girl and only "on the first night of the honeymoon" does the groom remove "his bride's horn-rimmed spectacles, unleashing the full blast of her dazzling beauty." Loos, *Talmadge Girls*, 25. Such errors are often rife in reminiscences made by people so many years later.

69. Ibid., 22.

70. *New York Times*, June 27, 1920.

71. Herndon, *Pickford and Fairbanks*, 154.

72. *Triangle*, Oct. 14, 1916.

73. Bogdanovich, *Allan Dwan*, 43.

74. *New York Mirror*, Jan. 20, 1917.

75. *Photoplay*, Apr. 1917.

76. Letters.

77. According to Peter Noble, Stroheim claimed that he played a tiny role in a dream sequence. *Hollywood Scapegoat*, 22. Koszarski was more specific and said that he appeared heavily disguised as a vegetable! *Man You Loved to Hate*, 24. There are no dream sequences in *Reaching for the Moon*.

78. Balshofer and Miller, *One Reel a Week*, 132.

79. *Moving Picture World*, Sept. 29, 1917.

80. Loos, *Talmadge Girls*, 44.

81. Koszarski, *Man You Loved to Hate*, 25.

82. *Variety*, Feb. 15, 1918.

83. Ibid.

84. Gish, *Movies, Mr. Griffith, and Me,* 174.

85. Curtiss, *Von Stroheim,* 89.

86. Karl Brown, interview by the author at Brown's home, Mar. 25, 1975.

87. *Exhibitor's Trade Review,* Feb. 9, 1918.

88. Ibid., Aug. 14, 1918.

89. *Variety,* Aug. 30, 1918.

90. W.F. Willis, "Reader's Report," MGM, in author's possession.

91. Unidentified clipping about Stroheim appearing as Rommel, ca. 1943, Theatre Collection.

92. "Erich von Stroheim and the Miracle," *Motion Picture Classic,* Jan. 1920, 35.

93. *Variety,* Jan. 10, 1919.

94. Unidentified clipping (see note 91 above).

95. *New York Times,* Dec. 22, 1918.

96. *Ohio State Journal,* May 28, 1919.

97. Mordaunt Hall, "Persistent von Stroheim Conquered Film Magnate," *New York Times,* Dec. 1924.

98. Goldwyn, *Behind the Screen,* 198.

99. Drinkwater, *Carl Laemmle,* 197.

100. *Exhibitor's Trade Review,* May 22, 1920.

3. The Artist

1. Cooper, *Dark Lady of the Silents,* 99.

2. Loos, *A Girl Like I,* 125.

3. Richard Watts Jr., *Film Culture,* Apr. 1958, 5–6.

4. Erich von Stroheim, *Film Weekly,* Apr. 1935.

5. Renoir, *My Life and My Films,* 65.

6. *New York Times,* June 27, 1920.

7. *Hollywood Filmograph,* Apr. 7, 1928.

8. Richard Watts Jr., "Erich von Stroheim as a Realist," *New York Tribune,* ca. 1928.

9. *New York Times,* July 5, 1923, sec. 6, p. 2.

10. *Variety,* June 5, 1914.

11. *New York Dramatic Mirror,* June 10, 1914.

12. *Motion Picture News,* May 8, 1915.

13. *Shadowland,* Sept. 1920.

14. Jacobs, *Rise of the American Film,* 350.

15. Bazin, *What is Cinema?* 1: 135.

16. Unidentified clipping, 1920, Theatre Collection.

17. Higham, *Hollywood Cameramen,* 59.

18. *Motion Picture News,* May 8, 1915.

19. Stroheim, interview at the British Film Institute, 1954, transcript at BFI, London (hereafter, BFI interview).

20. Higham, *Hollywood Cameramen*, 60–61.

21. Ibid., 67.

22. Fay Wray, interview by Roy Kinnard, Aug. 21, 1988, *Films in Review*, Apr. 1990, 265 (hereafter Fay Wray interview.)

23. Ibid.

24. *Motion Picture Classic*, Jan. 1920.

25. Higham, *Hollywood Cameramen*, 60.

26. Dorothy Bay, *Motion Picture Classic*, Dec. 1927.

27. Ibid.

28. "Erich von Stroheim," *Theatre Magazine*, 1927.

29. L'Estrange Fawcett, in *Films: Facts and Forecasts* (Geoffrey Bles, 1927), quoted in Noble, *Hollywood Scapegoat*, 30.

30. BFI interview.

31. John Houseman, "Hollywood Faces the Fifties," *Harper's*, Apr. 1950.

32. Fay Wray interview.

33. *Motion Picture Classic*, Feb. 1917.

34. Zolotow, *Billy Wilder in Hollywood*, 109.

35. Stroheim to Valerie, undated, Brownlow Collection.

36. *Cheiro's Complete Palmistry*, 286.

37. *Motion Picture Classic*, Jan. 1920.

38. Stroheim, *Greed* script.

39. Ibid., 121–22.

40. In shot 77A of the *Merry-Go-Round* script.

41. Ibid., shots 641 and 642.

42. Orson Welles, interview by Juan Rubio, reprinted in Sarris, *Interviews with Film Directors*, 530–31.

43. Von Sternberg, *Film Fan Monthly*, Sept. 1968.

4. Blind Husbands

1. *Dramatic Mirror*, Apr. 29, 1919, 650.

2. Ibid., May 20, 1919, 817.

3. *Motion Picture World*, Sept. 27, 1919

4. The continuity can be viewed on microfilm at the American Film Institute in Los Angeles, Ca.

5. *Picture-Play Magazine*, Nov. 1919.

6. *Northside News* (no city listed), Dec. 15, 1919.

7. *Motion Picture News*, Dec. 27, 1919.

8. Jane Dixon, "Ugh! The Most Hated Man in the World!" New York City *Evening Telegram*, Dec. 11, 1919.

9. *Dramatic Mirror*, Dec. 18, 1919.

10. Ibid., Jan 15, 1920.

11. Dixon, "Ugh! The Most Hated Man in the World!"

12. *Toledo (Ohio) Times*, Dec. 12, 1919.

13. *Chicago Tribune,* Nov. 24, 1919.

14. *Photo-Play Journal,* Jan. 1920.

15. *Photoplay,* Jan. 1920.

16. *Picture-Play Magazine,* Nov. 1919.

17. Herman Weinberg includes a still of this scene in his book, *Stroheim,* 10.

18. *Bioscope,* June 17, 1920.

19. Letters.

5. *The Devil's Pass Key*

1. On September 6, 1919, *Moving Picture World* referred to the new project as *Clothes of Treachery.* On September 20, it became *Clothes and Treachery,* and later in the same issue, the title was given as *His Great Success.* By October 4, it was *The Charge Account* and, on the next page, *The Woman in the Plot.* By January 24, 1920, it finally became *The Devil's Pass Key.* For further information on Mahra de Meyer, and for much more detailed background on this film, see Koszarski, *Man You Loved to Hate,* 46–70.

2. Although "Passkey" is usually printed as one word (by Weinberg, Noble, and others), the title in studio advertisements, lobby cards, and initial reviews employs two words.

3. At least Herman G. Weinberg thought so, although his estimates are often hearsay. Weinberg, *Stroheim,* 21. See also Koszarski, *Man You Loved to Hate,* 51.

4. *Variety,* Apr. 30, 1920.

5. *Moving Picture World,* Apr. 24, 1920, 350.

6. Ibid.

7. *Variety,* Aug. 20, 1920.

8. Ibid.

9. *New York Times,* Aug. 9, 1920.

10. Ibid. *Variety,* Aug. 20, 1920.

11. *Variety,* Aug. 20, 1920.

12. Ibid.

6. *Foolish Wives*

1. *Moving Picture World,* Jan. 22, 1922.

2. *Dramatic Mirror,* June 19, 1920.

3. *Photoplay,* Oct. 1920.

4. *Dramatic Mirror,* July 24, 1920.

5. Letters.

6. *Photoplay,* Aug. 1921.

7. *Motion Picture Classic,* Apr. 1922.

8. *Variety,* Jan. 20, 1922.

9. *Photoplay,* Feb. 1922.

10. *Exhibitor's Trade Review,* Jan 7, 1922.

11. *Moving Picture World,* Dec. 17, 1921.

12. *New York Times,* Jan. 12, 1922.

13. *Variety,* Jan. 20, 1922.

14. Letters.

15. Willis Goldbeck, "Von Stroheim, Man and Superman," *Motion Picture Classic,* Sept. 1922.

16. A photograph of the premature baby can be seen in Weinberg, *Stroheim,* 67.

17. Goldbeck, "Man and Superman."

18. *Exhibitor's Trade Review,* Jan. 28, 1922.

19. Letters.

20. Although Herman G. Weinberg cites my reconstructed print as the longest version, he remained under the misapprehension that Iris Barry, "who was in a censorial position prior to becoming curator of the Museum of Modern Art Film Library, made plot and character changes in the film." I tried to explain to Herman more than once that Universal had made the modifications, but he preferred his own version of the facts.

21. *Photoplay,* May 1922.

22. Arthur James, *Moving Picture World,* Jan. 21, 1922.

23. *Kinematograph Weekly* 67 (Sept. 28, 1922): 76.

24. Goldbeck, "Man and Superman."

25. Harriet Underhill, *New York Tribune,* Jan. 22, 1922.

26. Goldbeck, "Man and Superman."

27. Ibid.

28. Ibid.

7. *Merry-Go-Round*

1. *Moving Picture World,* Sept. 2, 1922.

2. Sherwood, *The Best Moving Pictures of 1922–23,* 85–92.

3. Letters.

4. *Moving Picture World,* Mar. 10, 1923.

5. Ibid., Sept. 2, 1922.

6. *Variety,* July 4, 1923.

7. Lewys, *Merry-Go-Round.*

8. *Variety,* July 4, 1923.

9. Taylor, *Pictorial History of the Movies,* 135.

10. This ceremony is vividly described by the emperor's valet, in Eugen Ketterl, *The Emperor Francis Joseph I: An Intimate Study,* 133–34.

11. James Hunecker recorded a fictional account of one of these New York parties in his slightly racy and privately printed novel *Painted Veils* (1920).

12. Stroheim's script for *Merry-Go-Round,* 3:5 (hereafter cited parenthetically in the text).

13. Stroheim's original treatment for *Merry-Go-Round,* 20.

14. Frances Gilmore, "The World Is Her Convent," *Motion Picture Classic,* Apr. 1928.

8. *Greed*

1. "Zola as a Romantic Writer," June 27, 1896, in Norris, *Novels and Essays,* 1107.

2. "The True Reward of the Novelist," Oct. 1901, in Norris, *Novels and Essays,* 1151.

3. "An Opening for Novelists," *Wave,* May 22, 1897, in Norris, *Novels and Essays,* 1113.

4. *New York Times,* Jan. 25, 1920.

5. Crowther, *Lion's Share,* 71.

6. "Goldwyn Installs Unit System," *Moving Picture World,* Jan. 27, 1923.

7. *New York Times,* Feb. 11, 1923.

8. *Moving Picture World,* Mar. 24, 1923.

9. Ibid., Mar. 3, 1923.

10. Ibid., Mar. 24, 1923.

11. "Fiction Is Selection," Sept. 11, 1897, in Norris, *Novels and Essays,* 1115.

12. Norris, *McTeague,* 6.

13. Script for *Greed,* 65 (hereafter cited parenthetically in the text).

14. *Theatre Magazine,* Feb. 1925.

15. When our correspondence began in 1965, Stroheim authority Herman G. Weinberg reacted violently to my comments about this image in an early book of mine. In a July 17, 1971, letter, he returned to this subject and was again indignant about my comment that Trina was intended to look like a nun. "By what authority do you say this? It's all in your own mind. In almost half a century of reading analyses of *Greed* I never came across any interpretation of that scene like yours." My observation about the use of the number thirteen in the film also bothered Weinberg. "Maybe it's there, but it has no meaning. Maybe it was the 13th that day. *Any* day in *Greed* could have been the mystical '13th'.... But there are no calendars with the 13th in *Foolish Wives* or the other films. Which? Where?" Despite my "errors" (forgivable I guess in a young whippersnapper that I then was), Herman and I stayed close through the years, but I could never convince him of my view.

In fact, Stroheim throughout *Greed* employs the number three whenever he can: (1) The street number of Mac's dental parlor is 613 and the number of Frenna's saloon is 603. (2) When the Sieppes move the day after Trina's marriage, the father has numbered his packing crates and pictures. Two of the most prominent in the scene have a number three on them. (3) Mac gets his big golden tooth on the 30th, with the large calendar number visible on the wall. (4) Other, more significant references to three are mentioned in the text in discussion of various parts of the film.

16. Norris, *McTeague,* 262.

17. Ibid., 283.

18. Letters.

19. *Variety,* Aug. 20, 1924.

20. Ibid., Dec. 31, 1924.

21. *New York Times,* Dec. 5, 1924.

9. *The Merry Widow*

1. Quoted in Jacobs, *Rise of the American Film,* 351.

2. Jane Ardmore, *The Self-Enchanted: Mae Murray, Image of an Era,* 143.

3. *Film Culture,* Apr. 1958, 5.

4. One must also keep in mind that this film was shot at approximately sound speed—around 22 frames per second (fps)—and should *not* be shown at 16 or 18 fps. There are some so-called silent-film purists and purveyors of video tapes who mistakenly think that all silent films were shot at slow speeds. Admittedly, *The Birth of a Nation* and *Intolerance* play best around 18 fps—Griffith and his Fine Arts studio cameramen tended to crank more slowly—but other studios shot at faster speeds, and by 1920 even Griffith was shooting much closer to 24 fps. For proof of this, see the leaders on some films that state the speed, and for confirmation, check the time schedules in major theaters. For example, the first showings of *The Birth of a Nation,* under Griffith's supervision, ran at approximately 20 fps. His *Orphans of the Storm* took exactly two hours when it opened in New York, and that equals 24 fps exactly, even though at times it appears too fast at that speed.

5. *Motion Picture Classic,* Apr. 1922.

10. *The Wedding March*

1. Bob Thomas, *Walt Disney: An American Original,* 93.

2. Fay Wray, *On the Other Hand,* 64-65.

3. *New York Times,* Jan. 8, 1928.

4. Wray, *On the Other Hand,* 67.

5. Ibid., 68, 70.

6. Ibid., 72.

7. Weinberg, *Wedding March,* 3.

8. David Robinson, "Stroheim's Lost Masterpiece," *Times* (London), Jan. 24, 1975.

9. Letters.

10. Herman G. Weinberg, *Josef von Sternberg,* 35.

11. Letters.

12. In the decades since *The Wedding March,* only a few films have even approached this length: *Gone with the Wind* (222 minutes), *Ben Hur* (212 minutes), *Lawrence of Arabia* (216 minutes), and Cleopatra (243 minutes)—all of them epics.

13. *Variety,* Oct. 17, 1928.

14. Renee Lichtig, "En travaillant avec Stroheim," *Cahiers du Cinéma* (Paris), no. 37, 1954.

15. The Viennese waltz playing in the background, "My Paradise," was com-

posed by J.S. Zamecnik and first appeared in a musical called *Alabama Moon*. It was recorded by Prince's Band in New York City on a Columbia record (A-6153) in April 1920. Sheet music, with Fay Wray's picture on the cover, was released along with the film (both in my possession).

16. Havelock Ellis, *Studies in the Psychology of Sex*, 3:139.

17. Ketterl, *Francis Josef I*, 134–36.

18. *New York Times*, Sept 13, 1965.

11. *The Honeymoon*

1. Weinberg, *Wedding March*, 3.

12. *Queen Kelly*

1. *Hollywood Filmograph*, Mar. 31, 1928.

2. Swanson, *Swanson on Swanson*, 346.

3. Ibid., 347.

4. Ibid., 345, 346.

5. *Hollywood Filmograph*, June 9, 1928.

6. Ibid., Aug. 4, 1928.

7. Ibid., Sept. 8, 1928.

8. *Theatre Magazine*, Oct. 1928, 26.

9. Swanson, *Swanson on Swanson*, 369.

10. Herman G. Weinberg wrote in *Stroheim* that "ten reels of the approximately 30 planned were actually shot" (210). There is no way that Kennedy or Swanson would have agreed to a "planned" thirty reels. They would not want a film longer than twelve reels—and even that was an extreme length—for the simple reason that such a long film would be a commercial impossibility. The fact is that the early section of the film, running in its present length (about eight reels), should have been less than one-third of the whole film and ought to have run no more than three or four reels. This portion, said the critic Lotte Eisner, in defense of the director, "Stroheim considered as simply a sketch of a prologue." Eight reels of "sketch"?

11. Letters.

12. Ibid.

13. Although some reference works refer to "Kitty" Kelly, perhaps as does Koszarski, the titles in the film call her "Patricia Kelly."

14. "Papers of Benjamin Glazer," Special Collections, UCLA, script dated Mar. 9, 1929.

13. The Descent

1. *Variety*, Sept. 18, 1929.

2. According to an unidentified clipping, Theatre Collection.

3. Reader's Report, dated Oct. 7, 1929, in author's possession.

4. *New York Times,* Feb. 16, 1926.

5. Letters.

6. This was told to Wilson Mizner, quoted by Curtiss, 266–267.

7. Curtiss, *Von Stroheim,* 265.

8. Bennett and Kibbee, *Bennett Playbill,* 324, 206.

9. *Variety,* Sept. 17, 1930.

10. This and other information about the scripts comes from Universal's files, which I examined at the studio in 1969.

11. Koszarksi, *Man You Loved to Hate,* 236–37.

12. Letters.

13. Samuel Marx to Stroheim, July 9, 1931, in author's possession.

14. Samuel Marx to John Zinn, Fox Film Corporation, June 13, 1934, in author's possession.

15. Anthony Holden, *Laurence Olivier* (New York: Atheneum, 1988), 68.

16. *New York Times,* Mar. 24 , 1929.

17. Curtis, *Von Stroheim,* 284.

18. Hedda Hopper, *From under My Hat,* 213.

19. *New York Times,* June 3, 1932.

20. *Variety,* June 7, 1932.

21. Barry Paris, *Garbo,* 275.

14. *Walking down Broadway*

1. Page, *Dawn Powell at Her Best,* x.

2. Ibid.

3. Powell, *Diaries, 1931-1965,* 35.

4. *Variety,* June 28, 1932.

5. Ibid., July 5, 1932.

6. The script has the following credits: "Story and continuity by Erich von Stroheim. Based upon the play by Dawn Powell. Dialogue by Erich von Stroheim, Leonard Spigelgass, and Geraldine Nomis."

7. Paris, *Garbo,* 572.

8. Letters.

9. *Variety,* Oct. 25, 1932.

10. Ibid., Oct. 11, 1932.

11. Letters.

12. Budd Schulberg, *Moving Pictures,* 449.

13. Ibid., 450.

14. Letters.

15. *Variety,* Nov. 29, 1932.

16. *New York Times,* May 6, 1933.

17. *Variety,* May 9, 1933.

18. Letters.

19. *Walking down Broadway* script, scene 174.

20. Ibid., scene 213.

21. Ibid., scene 234.

22. James Wong Howe, quoted in Higham, *Hollywood Cameramen*, 85.

23. Ibid., 86.

24. James Wong Howe, in Mike Steen, *Hollywood Speaks: An Oral History*, 221.

25. *Variety*, May 23, 1933.

15. The Depths

1. Rouben Mamoulian, interview by the author, at Mamoulian's home, Aug. 1979.

2. Charlotte Woods, "Reader's Report," Apr. 10, 1933, in author's possession.

3. Jessie Burns, "Reader's Report," May 9, 1933, in author's possession.

4. Myrna Loy, *Being and Becoming*, 93.

5. Valerie Stroheim to Erich von Stroheim, Apr. 7, 1950, Brownlow Collection.

6. Lucille Sullivan, "Reader's Report," Feb. 23, 1935, in author's possession.

7. Letters.

8. *Variety*, Oct. 23, 1934.

9. Letters.

10. Ibid.

11. Lillian Culver, "Reader's Report," Jan 6, 1944, in author's possession.

12. Wallace Smith, *The Happy Alienist: A Viennese Caprice*, 25.

13. Tom Dardis, *Sometime in the Sun*.

14. I learned this word from *Animal Crackers*, where Groucho sings about Captain Spaulding, the African explorer, and rhymes *explorer* with *Schnorrer*.

15. Letters.

16. Ibid.

17. Ibid.

18. Ibid.

19. Reader's report, Dec. 4, 1935, in author's possession.

20. Letters.

21. *Variety*, Aug. 18, 1937.

22. Ibid.

16. A Star in France

1. Letters.

2. Raymond Bernard, "Stroheim," *Études Cinématographiques*, nos. 48–50 (1966): 105.

3. Letters.

4. James W. Gerard, *My Four Years in Germany*, 52.

5. *Variety*, May 12, 1937.

6. *New York Times*, Nov. 9, 1944.

7. Renoir, *My Life and My Films*, 142.

8. Ibid., 82.

9. *Variety*, Feb. 24, 1937.

10. Renoir, *My Life and My Films*, 153, 161.

11. Renoir, *Grand Illusion*, 9.

12. Renoir, *My Life and My Films*, 166.

13. Ibid., 166–67.

14. Renoir, *Grand Illusion*, 10.

15. Renoir, *My Life and My Films*, 160.

16. Renoir, *Grand Illusion*, 8.

17. Gerard, *My Four Years in Germany*, 340.

18. Renoir, *My Life and My Films*, 90.

19. *American Film*, Jan.–Feb. 1985.

20. Charles Spaak, "Stroheim," *Études Cinématographiques* (1946).

21. Letters.

22. Ibid.

23. Edmond T. Greville, "The Lady Spy and the Legless Man," trans. Jean-Pierre Coursodon, *Film Comment*, Jan.-Feb. 1998, 58.

24. Greville, "The Lady Spy," 58.

25. Ibid.

26. Ibid.

27. Letters.

28. Ibid.

29. *Variety*, Apr. 26, 1939.

30. Letters.

31. Christian-Jaque, *Études Cinématographiques* (Stroheim issue), nos. 48–50 (1966): 109.

32. *Variety*, June 1, 1938.

33. Letters.

34. Ibid.

35. Ibid.

36. *Variety*, Nov. 30, 1938.

37. Letters.

38. *Variety*, Feb. 8, 1939.

39. Letters.

40. *New York Times*, Nov. 16, 1943.

41. Oct. 1938, Brownlow Collection.

42. *Variety*, May 10, 1939.

43. *New York Times*, Sept. 28, 1944.

44. Letters.

45. Ibid.

46. *Variety*, July 19, 1939.

47. Letters.

48. Loos, *A Girl Like I*, 127–28.

49. Ibid.

50. *Variety*, Feb. 14, 1940.

51. Ibid.

52. Greville, "The Lady Spy," 59–60.
53. *Variety,* Feb. 14, 1940.
54. Letters.
55. Ibid.
56. Ibid.
57. Ibid.
58. Ibid.
59. Ibid.
60. *Variety,* May 15, 1940.
61. Letters.
62. Ibid.
63. Brownlow Collection.

17. America Again

1. Richard Maney, *Fanfare: The Confessions of a Press Agent,* 307.
2. *New York Times,* Mar. 25, 1941.
3. BBC broadcast, Dec. 30, 1948.
4. Letter of Josef, Sept. 16, 1941, Brownlow Collection.
5. Letter to Valerie, Oct, 1941, Brownlow Collection.
6. "Old Arsenic Star Has Good Story," unidentified clipping, ca. Nov. 1942.
7. Brownlow Collection.
8. Ibid.
9. *New York Times,* Jan. 3, 1927.
10. Lally, *Wilder Times,* 122.
11. Unidentified clipping, Theatre Collection.
12. Lally, *Wilder Times,* 122.
13. *Variety,* May 5, 1943
14. *New York Times,* Nov. 5, 1943.
15. *Variety,* May 5, 1943.
16. Berg, *Goldwyn,* 356.
17. Lillian Hellman, *An Unfinished Woman* (Boston: Little, Brown, 1969), 125.
18. Berg, *Goldwyn,* 377.
19. Marx, *Goldwyn,* 195.
20. Letters.
21. Ibid.
22. "Film Script," New York State Public Library.
23. Letters.
24. Ibid.
25. Lally, *Wilder Times,* 141.
26. Letters.
27. Ibid.
28. *Variety,* Jan. 30, 1946.
29. Henry G. Weinberg, "Coffee, Brandy, and Cigars, XXX," *Film Culture,* Apr. 1958, 22.

18. The Last Years

1. Letters.

2. Ibid.

3. Ibid.

4. *New York Times,* Dec. 3, 1949.

5. Letters.

6. BFI interview, 1954.

7. William K. Everson, "Program Notes," The Theodore Huff Memorial Society, Nov. 21, 1981, New York.

8. Curtis, "The Last Years," *Film Culture,* Apr. 1958, 3.

9. Loos, *A Girl Like I,* 127.

10. Zolotow, *Billy Wilder in Hollywood,* 161.

11. Swanson, *Swanson on Swanson,* 482–83.

12. Zolotow, *Wilder in Hollywood,* 169.

13. *Variety,* Apr. 15, 1950.

14. Lally, *Wilder Times,* 202.

15. Zolotow, *Wilder in Hollywood,* 168.

16. Lally, *Wilder Times,* 202.

17. George Perry, *Sunset Boulevard: From Movie to Musical,* 78.

18. Lally, *Wilder Times,* 421.

19. *Variety,* Jan. 18, 1950.

20. *Daily Express,* Oct. 9, 1950.

21. Ibid.

22. Clipping found in British Film Institute, London, marked *S. Pictorial,* 12/4/[an indecipherable digit, and then a 3—quite possibly 1953].

23. Flaherty's biographer, Arthur Calder-Marshall, described this broadcast in which Stroheim, "with a sob in his voice" remembered the meeting "of the two masters for the first time in the flesh, though they had known and admired one another for years. It couldn't have happened any way but this, if they had ever met. Which they didn't." In *The Innocent Eye,* 134. This smug remark indicates that Stroheim made the whole thing up. I doubt this. Stroheim's vivid description of Flaherty is amazingly specific for a nonmeeting. I would guess that the two became acquainted in New York City either in 1942 or just prior to Stroheim's departure for France in late 1945.

24. "Erich von Stroheim," *Films in Review,* Aug.–Sept. 1957, 313.

25. *Variety,* Dec. 10, 1952.

26. Ibid., Feb. 17, 1954.

27. Karel Reisz, *Sight and Sound,* Apr.–June 1954.

28. The *Daily Herald* (London)'s version of the scene was slightly different: "Suddenly his head shot round, he pointed wildly into the crowd. 'Take that sarcastic smirk off your face!'" Jan. 6, 1954.

29. Reisz, *Sight and Sound,* Apr.-June 1954.

30. Unidentified clipping in the files of the British Film Institute, London.

31. *Daily Herald* (London), Jan. 6, 1954.

32. The British Press does not seem to be consistent in its reporting. According to the *Birmingham Post,* Jan. 6, 1954, when Stroheim was asked to pose, he replied, "I don't wear a monocle." And when he was asked to pretend, he replied, "I am not a pretender." The reader can make his or her choice.

33. *Herald Tribune* (Paris), New York Edition, Jan. 26, 1954.

34. Ibid.

35. Ibid.

36. Ibid.

37. Stroheim's mention of *The Fires of St. John* [Les Feux de la St. Jean] seems a bit puzzling. It had been published in 1951, yet Stroheim claimed when speaking with Buchwald that he was still working on it. Perhaps this would be part two. Later, in 1967, a two-volume set was published in Paris by Inter-presse.

38. *Herald Tribune* (Paris), New York Edition, Jan. 26, 1954.

39. *Variety,* Apr. 27, 1955.

40. Stroheim, *Poto Poto* (Paris: Editions de la Fontaine, 1956).

41. Loos, *A Girl Like I,* 127.

42. "The Merry Widow," *Film Culture,* no. 18, Apr. 1958.

43. Ibid.

44. Curtiss, *Von Stroheim,* 334.

Selected Bibliography

I am listing only the works that directly pertain to this biography. My own collection of well over a thousand books, which I began to acquire in the late 1940s, has been, of course, useful in learning the medium and its methods, but I see no reason to waste the reader's time or mine by compiling an impressive bibliography. Needless to say, I have consulted hundreds of books by stars, directors, gossip columnists, press agents—most of which are unindexed—and in those works now blessed with indexes I have had to do the double duty of looking under *S* for Stroheim as well as *V* for von Stroheim! Furthermore, I have done extensive reading into the Austrian-Hungarian Empire, its social and military history as well as biographies and letters of some of its principal artists such as Gustav Mahler, Richard Strauss, Artur Schnitzler (including his plays), and others to acquaint myself with the *zeitgeist*. Such background material has been useful for me but not necessarily pertinent for the reader. Except for books that I make a direct reference to, they remain unlisted. As I said in the preface, the most essential information can be drawn primarily from the films and scripts and from the most accurate information provided by contemporary sources.

UNPUBLISHED SOURCES

Manuscript Collections

Academy of Motion Picture Sciences, Los Angeles
Aitken Collection, State Historical Society, Madison, Wisconsin
Austrian Library, Vienna
Herman G. Weinberg Collection, New York Public Library, New York
Jewish History Museum, Vienna
Kriegsarchiv, Vienna

Letters from Erich von Stroheim to Valerie and to Josef von Stroheim, personal collection of Kevin Brownlow (Brownlow Collection)

Letters from Stroheim to Peter Noble, Film Library, Museum of Modern Art, New York

Billy Rose Theatre Collection, New York Public Library, New York

Motion Picture Collection, Univ. of California, Los Angeles

Motion Picture Copyright Section, Library of Congress, Washington, D.C.

Osterreiches Staatsarchiv, Vienna

Press books, photos, and Robinson Locke Collection, New York Public Library, New York

Script Collection of the New York Censorship Board, New York State Archives, New York.

Vienna City Directories (1880–1920), Vienna Public Library

Unpublished Scripts

Most of the following scripts (dialogue only and footage length) can be found at the New York State Archives, NYS Motion Picture Division, License Application case files. What I choose to call the New York Censorship Board can be found here also.

L'Alibi

Alraune

Between Two Women (in author's possession)

Blind Husbands (in author's possession)

The Crime of Dr. Crespi

Crimson Romance

Derrière la façade

The Devil Doll

The Devil's Pass Key

L'Enfer du jeu

Five Graves to Cairo

Foolish Wives (in author's possession)

Friends and Lovers

The Fugitive Road

The Great Flamarion

The Great Gabbo

The Honeymoon (in author's possession)

The Lady and the Monster

The Lost Squadron

Marthe Richard

The Mask of Diijon

Menaces

Merry-Go-Round (The author provided a treatment and the scenario to the Special Collections section of the Library of New York University at Albany, Albany, New York.)

Merry Widow (in author's possession)

The North Star

Les Pirates du Rail

Scotland Yard Investigator

So Ends Our Night

Sunset Boulevard

Ultimatum

Walking down Broadway (in author's possession)

Wedding March (in author's possession)

BOOKS

American Film Institute. Catalog of Motion Pictures Produced in the United States: Feature Films, 1911–1920. Ed. Patricia King Hanson. Berkeley: Univ. of California Press, 1997.

American Film Institute. Catalog of Motion Pictures Produced in the United States: Feature Films, 1921–1930. Ed. Kenneth W. Munden. Berkeley: Univ. of California Press, 1988.

Ardmore, Jane. *The Self-Enchanted: Mae Murray, Image of an Era.* New York: McGraw-Hill, 1959.

Balshofer, Fred, and Arthur Miller. *One Reel a Week.* Berkeley: Univ. of California Press, 1967.

Bazin, André. *What Is Cinema?* Ed. Hugh Gray. Berkeley: Univ. of California Press, 1974.

Bennet, Joan, and Lois Kibbee. *The Bennett Playbill.* New York: Holt, Rinehart, and Winston, 1970.

Berg, A. Scott. *Goldwyn: A Biography.* New York: Knopf, 1989.

Bessy, Maurice, and Raymond Chirat, eds. *L'Histoire du Cinéma*

Française: Encyclopédie des Films, 1929-1934. Paris: Pygmalion, 1995.

———. *L'Histoire du Cinéma Française: Encyclopédie des Films, 1935-1939.* Paris: Pygmalion, 1995.

———. *L'Histoire du Cinéma Française: Encyclopédie des Films, 1940-1950.* Paris: Pygmalion, 1994.

Bessy, Maurice, Raymond Chirat, and André Bernard, eds. *L'Histoire du Cinéma Française: Encyclopédie des Films, 1951-1955.* Paris: Pygmalion, 1995.

———. *L'Histoire du Cinéma Française: Encyclopédie des Films, 1956-1960.* 1996.

Bitzer, G.W. *Billy Bitzer: His Story.* New York: Farrar, Straus, Giroux, 1973.

Bogdanovitch, Peter. *Allan Dwan: The Last Pioneer.* New York: Praeger, 1971.

Brown, Karl. *Adventures with D. W. Griffith.* New York: Farrar, Straus, Giroux, 1973.

Brownlow, Kevin. *Behind the Mask of Innocence.* Berkeley: Univ. of California Press, 1990.

Calder-Marshall, Arthur. *The Innocent Eye.* New York: Harcourt, Brace, and World, 1963.

Cheiro's Complete Palmistry. Ed. Robert M. Ockene. New Hyde Park, N.Y.: University Books, 1968.

Cooper, Miriam. *Dark Lady of the Silents.* New York: Bobbs-Merrill, 1973.

Crankshaw, Edward. *The Fall of the House of Hapsburg.* New York: Viking Press, 1963.

Crowther, Bosley. *Hollywood Rajah: The Life and Times of Louis B. Mayer.* New York: Dell, 1960.

———. *The Lion's Share.* New York: Dutton, 1957.

Curtiss, Thomas Quinn. *Von Stroheim.* New York: Farrar, Straus, and Giroux, 1971.

Dardis, Tom. *Some Time in the Sun.* New York: Scribner's, 1976.

Drinkwater, John. *Life and Adventures of Carl Laemmle.* London: William Heineman, 1931.

Eames, John Douglas. *The MGM Story: The Complete History of Fifty Roaring Years.* New York: Crown, 1975.

Ellis, Havelock. *Studies in the Psychology of Sex.* New York: Random House, 1936.

Erich von Stroheim. Roma: Edizioni di Bianco e Nero., 1959.

Everson, William K. *American Silent Film.* New York: Oxford Univ. Press, 1978.

———. *Huff Notes.*

———. *New School Notes.*

Finler, Joel. *Stroheim.* Berkeley: Univ. of California Press, 1968.

Fountain, Leatrice Gilbert. *Dark Star.* New York: St. Martin's Press, 1985.

Franklin, Joe. *Classics of the Silent Screen: A Pictorial Treasury.* New York: Citadel, 1959.

Fulton, Albert R. *Motion Pictures: The Development of an Art.* Norman: Univ. of Oklahoma Press, 1980.

Gerard, James W. *My Four Years in Germany.* New York: George H. Doran, 1917.

Gish, Lillian. *The Movies, Mr. Griffith, and Me.* Englewood Cliffs, N.J.: Prentice-Hall, 1969.

Goldwyn, Samuel. *Behind the Screen.* New York: George Doran, 1923.

Griffith, Richard, and Arthur Mayer. *The Movies.* New York: Simon and Schuster, 1970.

Hamer, Sam Hield. *The Dolomites.* New York: John Lane, 1910.

Hellman, Lillian. *An Unfinished Woman.* Boston: Little, Brown, 1969.

Henabery, Joseph. *Before, in, and after Hollywood: The Autobiography of Joseph Henabery.* Ed. Anthony Slide. Lanham, Md.: Scarecrow Press, 1997.

Herndon, Booton. *Mary Pickford and Douglas Fairbanks.* New York: Norton, 1977.

Higham, Charles. *Hollywood Cameramen.* London: Thames and Hudson, 1970.

Hirschorn, Clive. *The Universal Story.* New York: Crown, 1983.

Holden, Anthony. *Laurence Olivier.* New York: Atheneum, 1988.

Hopper, Hedda. *From Under My Hat.* Garden City, N.Y.: Doubleday, 1952.

Hunecker, James. *Painted Veil.* New York: Boni and Liveright, 1920.

Jacobs, Lewis. *The Rise of the American Film.* New York: Teachers College Press, 1968.

Katz, Ephraim. *The Film Encyclopedia.* New York: Thomas Y. Crowell, 1979.

Ketterl, Eugen. *The Emperor Francis Joseph I: An Intimate Study, by His Valet du Chambre, Eugen Ketterl.* London: Skeffinton and Son, 1929.

Koszarski, Richard. *The Man You Loved to Hate.* New York: Oxford Univ. Press, 1983.

Lally, Kevin. *Wilder Times.* New York: Henry Holt, 1996.

Lennig, Arthur. *Classics of the Film.* Madison: Wisconsin Film Society, 1965.

————. *The Silent Voice.* Albany, N.Y.: Snyder Press, 1969.

Lewys, Georges [Gladys Lewis]. *Merry-Go-Round.* Los Angeles: Citizen's Print Shop, 1923.

Liptzin, Solomon. *Arthur Schnitzler.* New York: Prentice-Hall, 1932.

Loos, Anita. *A Girl Like I.* New York: Viking Press, 1966.

————. *The Talmadge Girls: A Memoir.* New York: Viking Press, 1978.

Loy, Myrna. *Being and Becoming.* New York: Knopf, 1987.

Madsen, Axel. *Gloria and Joe.* New York: Berkley Books, 1998.

Marx, Arthur. *Goldwyn: The Man behind the Myth.* London: Bodley Head, 1976.

Marx, Samuel. *Mayer and Thalberg: The Make-Believe Saints.* New York: Random House, 1975.

May, Arthur J. *The Hapsburg Monarchy, 1867-1914.* Cambridge, Mass: Harvard Univ. Press, 1951.

Mordden, Ethan. *The Hollywood Studios: House Style in the Golden Age of the Movies.* New York: Simon and Schuster, 1988.

Mosley, Leonard. *Zanuck: The Rise and Fall of Hollywood's Last Tycoon.* London: Panther, 1984.

Noble, Peter. *Hollywood Scapegoat.* London: Fortune Press, 1950.

Norris, Frank. *McTeague: A Story of San Francisco.* New York: Holt, Rinehart, Winston, 1950.

————. *Novels and Essays.* New York: Literary Classics of the United States, 1986.

Paris, Barry. *Garbo.* New York: Knopf, 1994.

Payne, Robert. *The Life and Death of Adolf Hitler.* New York: Praeger, 1973.

Perry, George. *Sunset Boulevard: From Movie to Musical.* New York: Henry Holt, 1993.

Powell, Dawn. *Dawn Powell at Her Best.* Ed. Tim Page. South Royalton, Vt.: Steerforth Press, 1994.

———. *The Diaries of Dawn Powell, 1931-1965.* Ed. Tim Page. South Royalton, Vt.: Steerforth Press, 1995.

Pratt, George. *Spellbound in Darkness.* Greenwich, Conn.: New York Graphics Society, 1973.

Renoir, Jean. *Grand Illusion: A Film by Jean Renoir.* New York: Simon and Schuster, 1968.

———. *My Life and My Films.* New York: Da Capo Press, 1974.

Sarris, Andrew. *Interviews with Film Directors.* New York: Avon Books, 1967.

Schatz, Thomas. *The Genius of the System: Hollywood Filmmaking in the Studio Era.* New York: Pantheon, 1988.

Schickel, Richard. *D. W. Griffith: An American Life.* New York: Simon and Schuster, 1984.

Schnitzler, Arthur. *Plays and Stories.* Ed. Egon Schwartz. New York: Continuum, 1982.

Schulberg, Budd. *Moving Pictures: Memories of a Hollywood Prince.* New York: Stein and Day, 1981.

Sherwood, Robert E. *The Best Moving Pictures of 1922-1923.* Boston: Small and Maynard, 1923.

Sitney, P. Adams. *Film Culture Reader.* New York: Praeger, 1970.

Slide, Anthony. *The Griffith Actresses.* South Brunswick: A.S. Barnes, 1973.

Smith, Wallace. *The Happy Alienist: A Viennese Caprice.* New York: Harridon Smith and Robert Haas, 1936.

Steen, Mike. *Hollywood Speaks: An Oral History.* New York: Putnam, 1974.

Steed, Henry Wickham. *The Hapsburg Monarchy.* 3d ed. London: Constable, 1914.

Stroheim, Erich von. *Greed, a Film by Erich von Stroheim.* Ed. Joel Finler. New York: Simon and Schuster, 1976.

Swanson, Gloria. *Swanson on Swanson.* New York: Random House, 1980.

Taylor, Deems. *A Pictorial History of the Movies.* New York: Simon and Schuster, 1950.

Thomas, Bob. *Thalberg, Life and Legend.* New York: Garland, 1969.

———. *Walt Disney: An American Original.* New York: Simon and Schuster, 1976.

Weinberg, Herman G. *The Complete* Greed. New York: Arno, 1972.

———. *Josef von Sternberg.* New York: Dutton, 1967.

———. *The Complete* The Wedding March. Boston: Little Brown, 1974.

————. *Josef von Sternberg.* New York: Dutton, 1967.

————. *Stroheim: A Pictorial Record of His Nine Films.* New York: Dover, 1975.

Wray, Fay. *On the Other Hand.* New York: St. Martin's Press, 1989.

Zolotov, Maurice. *Billy Wilder in Hollywood.* New York: G.P. Putnam, 1977.

Index